PRINCE VON BÜLOW

MEMOIRS

1849-1897

LONDON & NEW YORK

PUTNAM

FÜRST VON BÜLOW DENKWÜRDIGKEITEN, VIERTER BAND
First published in Germany April 23, 1931

PRINCE VON BÜLOW *MEMOIRS* 1849-1897
First published in England October 1932
Reprinted October 1932

Translated from the German by
GEOFFREY DUNLOP

AND

F. A. VOIGT

PRINTED IN GREAT BRITAIN.
CHISWICK PRESS : CHARLES WHITTINGHAM AND GRIGGS (PRINTERS), LTD.
BRUNSWICK PARK ROAD, LONDON, N.11.

CONTENTS

CHAPTER I

PAGE

Frankfort—My Parents' Home—Frankfort Diplomats—The Minister, von Bismarck-Schönhausen—Governesses and Tutors —My Father's Educational Principles I

CHAPTER II

Rumpenheim—Queen Alexandra of England and the Empress Maria Feodorovna of Russia as Children—My Father's Educational Ideal—Bible and Select Hymns—Homer and Goethe —At the Frankfort Gymnasium—The Jews in Frankfort— The Rothschild Family 17

CHAPTER III

Hamburg and Klein-Flottbek—Birthplace in the Flottbeker Chaussee—Relatives and Friends of my Youth—My First Sea Journey—Alcohol 28

CHAPTER IV

My Grandmother in Plön—My Grand-Uncle Wolf Baudissin— The Schleswig-Holstein Question—My Father Leaves the Service of the Danish Government (1862)—He is called to Mecklenburg-Strelitz as Chief Minister (1863) . . . 41

CHAPTER V

Mecklenburg—Country, People and Constitution—Neu Strelitz— Grand Duke Frederick William—The " Gymnasium Carolinum "—Virgil or Vergil ?—First Acquaintance with Berlin (1863)—Journey to South Germany—Summer at Doberan— Düppel and Alsen—Neu and Alt-Strelitz—My Contemporary

PAGE

*Ewald Wohlfahrt—Neu Brandenburg—Fritz Reuter—
Walking Tour on Rügen with the Hereditary Grand Duke
Adolf Frederick* (1864) 55

CHAPTER VI

The Pädagogium at Halle (1865 to 1867)—*Life at the Päda-
gogium—Professor Daniel and his Influence—Elocution—
Fellow Pupils—The People of Halle—Politics in Halle—
Democracy and Liberalism—Officials and Academic Circles
Nearly all Against Bismarck—My Confirmation in Halle*
(18.3.1866) 72

CHAPTER VII

The War of 1866—*Appreciation of Bismarck's Policy—Bismarck
and Edwin Manteuffel—Prussian Representatives Abroad* . 85

CHAPTER VIII

*The Battle of Königgrätz—General von Steinmetz—My Father
is Appointed Mecklenburg-Schwerin Minister in Berlin—
Cholera in Halle—A Walking Tour Across the Harz* (*Autumn*
1866)—*A Visit to my Uncle Baudissin in Dresden—Matriculation Examination* (*Autumn,* 1867)—*Puppel—Dulce est
desipere in loco* 99

CHAPTER IX

University of Lausanne (1867)—*Vevey—Donna è mobile—
Leipzig University—Professor William Roscher—Reading
Matter : Influence of the Novel on Knowledge of Life and
Human Nature—Walking Tour through Switzerland—Removal to Berlin University—Professor Rudolf Gneist—Death
of my Little Sister Bertha—Cure in Bad Oeynhausen* (*June,*
1870)—*The Political Situation, the Ems Dispatch* . . 116

CHAPTER X

*France's Declaration of War—Resolve to Join the Army as a
Volunteer—Enlistment in the Royal Hussar Regiment at Bonn
—Lehmop—Rhine Journey to Cologne—Impressions made by
Victorious Battles at Home* 136

CHAPTER XI

Bismarck's Policy in 1870—Austria-Hungary, Italy, England, and Russia—Bavaria's Attitude in July, 1870—Objections of the Bavarian Second Chamber, the Patriotic Attitude of the Upper Chamber—Complete Unity of the Nation—Bismarck's Circular Letter to the Prussian Embassies—Neutrality of Austria-Hungary—Holstein's Mission to Florence . . 154

CHAPTER XII

The Battle of Sedan—Napoleon III sends Prince Jérome to Italy—France's Resistance under Gambetta—Comparison with the German Collapse of 1918—Belgium : Bismarck's Publication of the French Offers made to him at the Expense of Belgium in the " Times "—Effect of the Publication on Public Opinion in Europe and especially in England—Bethmann-Hollweg Forty-four Years Later—Berlin in October, 1870—My First Meeting with Holstein—The Bismarck Family . 172

CHAPTER XIII

Back to Bonn—The Front—Bivouac at Metz—First Letters Home—Reconnoitring and Patrol Work—Major Lentze—Promoted Corporal (15.11.1870)—Advance on Compiègne—1870 and 1918 186

CHAPTER XIV

General von Goeben's Army Orders—27.11.1870—Letters from the Front—December Days, 1870—Rouen—Camp at Camon—The Battle near Hallue (23.12.1870)—Christmas at Altonville 197

CHAPTER XV

On Patrol—Battle of Sapignies (2.1.1871)—Lieutenant Count Max Pourtalès—The Battle of Bapaume (3.1.1871)—General von Goeben—Patrol Service Before St. Quentin . . 214

CHAPTER XVI

Comrades of the Squadron : Guido Nimptsch, Dietrich Loë, Scharffenberg, Pemberton-Ground, Borcke, Beissel von Gymnich, Dietrich Metternich—Sharpened Intelligence Service—Battle of St. Quentin (19.1.1871)—East Prussian Fusilier Regiment No. 33—Lieutenant von Deines, Lieutenant Mossner, Captain Rudolphi 227

CHAPTER XVII

Armistice of the 31.1.1871—Outbreak of Smallpox—Drill as in Peace Time—Preliminary Peace—Lieutenant of the King's Hussars Regiment (8.3.1871)—The Regiment Marches to Amiens—The Crown Prince Inspects the Parade (13.3.1871) —Town Major of Amiens—Field Letters from Amiens . 243

CHAPTER XVIII

Amore Sacro and amore Profano—Ride to Camon—The 8th Army Corps under Orders to March Back—Colonel Baron von Loë—The King's Hussars March through the Eifel to Treves —We enter Bonn (6.7.1871)—Back Home at Klein-Flottbek (20.7.1871) 256

CHAPTER XIX

Lieutenant at Bonn—Preparations for the Law Examination at Greifswald—Prince Franz Arenberg—Chaplain Hartmann —Overwork and Fainting Fit—Professor Wilhelm Studemund—Professor Ernst Immanuel Bekker—Beginning of the " Kulturkampf "—Law Examination at Greifswald (March, 1872)—Pasewalk—Decision to Enter the Diplomatic Service —Leave Taking of the Regiment—At Home in Klein-Flottbek —From Klein-Flottbek to Metz 271

CHAPTER XX

The Imperial Landgericht at Metz—Rudolf Baron von Seckendorff—Public Prosecutor Ittenbach—Junior Judge, Magdeburg—A Speech Before the Metz Jury—The German Theatre

at Metz—A Visit to the Parents of Arenberg at Marche-les-
Dames—Work in the District Council—Cure at Heiden and
Reichenhall—My Father Appointed Secretary of State in the
Foreign Office—I Become Attaché in the Foreign Office—My
Father's Advice in the Art of Diplomacy .   .   .   287

CHAPTER XXI

Work in the Foreign Office (1873-74)—Count Paul Hatzfeldt
—His Hints on Dealings with S.D.—Lothar Bucher—
Wilhelmstrasse 76—Evening Receptions in Bismarck's House
—Anti-Bismarckian Tendencies in German Society—Unpoli-
tical Nature of the Germans   301

CHAPTER XXII

Berlin Social Life in the Winter of 1873-4—The Salons :
Countess Perponcher, Frau von Prillwitz, Mimi Schleinitz,
Countess Louise Benkendorf, Cornelia Richter-Meyerbeer—
Chief Chamberlain : Count Wilhelm Redern—The Diplo-
matic Corps—Die Bonbonnière—Weimar and Potsdam—
Summer on the Pfingstberg and in Potsdam .   .   .   314

CHAPTER XXIII

Attaché in Rome—Tour of Southern France and Italy—Arrival
at Rome (15.10.1875)—Minister von Keudell—Journey to
Sicily—Gregorovius—Mommsen—Roman Society—Pius IX
and the Kingdom of Italy—Church and State in Italy .   .   330

CHAPTER XXIV

The Emperor's Birthday in the Palazzo Caffarelli—Albano—
Walks in Rome and Rides in the Campagna—The Crown
Prince and Princess—First Meeting with Countess Marie
Dönhoff—The Crown Prince's Journey to Naples .   .   342

CHAPTER XXV

My Colleagues in the Embassy—Professor Karl Hillebrand—
Berlin in May, 1875—Soirée in the House Ministry—My

Father on the Political Situation—At Varzin—Visit to the Country—To Ischl via Vienna—Idyll on the Shore of the St. Wolfgang Lake—Salzburg—Lothar Bucher and Life's Problems 353

CHAPTER XXVI

Diplomatic Examination—Transfer to St. Petersburg (1875)— Journey to St. Petersburg—Count Alvensleben—General von Werder—The Rasvod—Tsar Alexander II—The Tsarevitch —Andrássy—Balkan Reform Programme—St. Petersburg Society—Slav Women, Russian Girls—Russian Literature . 369

CHAPTER XXVII

Ambassador Prince Henry VII of Reuss—Ambassador von Schweinitz—The Radowitz Mission—Alexander II— Tsaritsa Maria Alexandrovna—Catharine Dolgoruki—Duke George of Mecklenburg-Strelitz—Tsar Paul and the Knout— Farewell Visit to Gortchakov (1876) 382

CHAPTER XXVIII

Return to Berlin—My Father on the Foreign Situation—Transfer to Vienna—Ambassador Count Otto Stolberg-Wernigerode— Official Vienna, Baron von Schmerling, Prince Richard Metternich, Count Hübner—The Political Feeling towards Germany—Bismarck and the Austro-German Liberals— Count Gyula Andrássy—Revolts in Salonika—Meeting of the Tsar Alexander II with Emperor Francis Joseph in Reichstadt (5.7.1876)—Turkish Atrocities in Bulgaria . . . 393

CHAPTER XXIX

Social Life in Vienna—Folk Garden and Prater. Cures in Montreux and San Remo—Transfer to Athens as chargé d'affaires—Christmas in Corfu—Paxos—Taking over the Business of Office in Athens 406

CHAPTER XXX

The Near-Eastern Crisis (1876-1877)—King George of Greece —The Diplomatic Corps in Athens—The Princess of Wales' Visit to Athens—The English Squadron—Death of the Austrian Minister, Baron von Münch—The Russians March into Rumania—Trip to Olympia—Excavations—Professor Ernst Curtius—The Grecian Monarchs at Tatoi 418

CHAPTER XXXI

Peace of San Stefano (March, 1878)—Summons to the Secretariat of the Berlin Congress—Athens in retrospect—Berlin in June, 1878—Attempts on Emperor William I—Hödel and Nobiling —Dissolution of the Reichstag and new Elections—The Socialist Law—My Father on the Berlin Congress—Dangerous Inflammation of the Throat—The First Session of the Congress 433

CHAPTER XXXII

Bismarck and Gortchakov—Signing of the Berlin Agreement (13.7.1878)—Shuvalov and Gortchakov—Privy Councillor von Holstein—An Engagement in the House of Bismarck— Biarritz, Dr. Adhéma—Books read 450

CHAPTER XXXIII

Transfer to Paris—I take up my Duties—The Ambassador Prince Chlodwig Hohenlohe—Paris Society—Gambetta : His Attitude to the " Revanche" idea and to Social Questions— General Galliffet—Waldeck-Rousseau, Scheurer-Kestner . 466

CHAPTER XXXIV

Marshal MacMahon—His Resignation (29.1.1879)—Jules Grévy—Bismarck's Attitude towards France—The Three Jules—M. de Freycinet—The Staff of the German Embassy— Thielmann, Philip Eulenburg—Friedrich Vitzthum, Nicolaus Wallwitz—The Babylon on the Seine?—A Dream . . 481

CHAPTER XXXV

The German colony in Paris—Count Guido Henckel-Donners-marck—The Païva-Henckel Palace and its guests—" Count " Kessler—Cure in Ems (July 1879)—Emperor Wilhelm I—Empress Augusta—Return to Paris—The clerical constitution in France—Jules Ferry and Paul Bert—Disquieting news of my Father's health—Journey to Berlin 497

CHAPTER XXXVI

Preparation for the alliance with Austria-Hungary—Bismarck in Vienna—Opposition of the Kaiser Wilhelm I—My father on the alliance with Austria—Signature by Wilhelm I (15.10. 1879) : My father's request to resign—Bismarck visits him—Death of my Father in Frankfurt-a.-M. (20.10.1879)—Kaiser Wilhelm's sympathy—Funeral in Berlin—The winter in Paris—At the Hohenlohe's 509

CHAPTER XXXVII

France's former reigning families—The houses of Bonaparte and Orléans—The Duke of Aumale—Espionage—The Corps Dip-lomatique—Monsignore Czaki—The Prince of Wales in Paris 523

CHAPTER XXXVIII

Advancement to the First Secretaryship—Chargé d'affaires—Alfonso XI in Paris—Princess Monia Urusov—Dr. Lands-berg—Visit to Rome—Pietro Blaserna and Marco Minghetti—Naples, Cape Miseno—Journey to Tunis—Dr. Gustav Nachtigal—Algiers—Dr. Julius Fröbel 533

CHAPTER XXXIX

Visit of Herbert Bismarck to Paris—Invited by Herbert Bismarck to London—The Ambassador Count Münster—Mr. Gladstone—Marriage of Adolf von Bülow in Nienstedten (1.7.1884)—Transfer to St. Petersburg—At Prince Bismarck's in Varzin 548

CHAPTER XL

St. Petersburg (July 1884)—Taking over—Death of Gort-chakov and Skobelev—Imperial Secretary Polovtsov—Herr von Giers—Meeting of the Emperors at Skierniewice, prepara-tion for the Interview with Bismarck in Berlin—Journey to Skierniewice—Emperor William I, Tsar Alexander III, and the Emperor Francis Joseph—Warsaw—The Consul-General von Rechenberg—Count Fersen—Count Dmitri Tolstoi—Pobiedonoztsev—Countess Kleinmichl—Madame Durnov—General Tcherevin 566

CHAPTER XLI

Afghanistan, the Anglo-Russian conflict—Prince Bismarck's seven-tieth birthday—In Bismarck's home (1.4.1885)—Conversa-tion with Herbert Bismarck—Bulgaria and Prince Alexander Battenberg—Summer 1885 in St. Petersburg—Annulment of Countess Marie Dönhoff's marriage by the Papal Chair—Marriage in Vienna (9.1.1886) 581

CHAPTER XLII

Salzburg—Visit to Marco Minghetti in Rome—In Berlin—An evening at the Bismarck's—Dinner with the Crown Princess —Visit of the Crown Prince to Frau von Bülow—Her recep-tion by the Empress Augusta—Conversation with Emperor Wilhelm I—Reception in St. Petersburg—Court, society, and diplomacy—The Russian Foreign Ministry : Vlangaly, Lambs-dorff—Revolution in Sofia—Bismarck's attitude towards the Bulgarian question and " Battenbergeries "—Berlin in spring 1887—Luncheon with the Crown Princes—Engagement of Princess Victoria to Alexander von Battenberg ; Bismarck's opposition 594

CHAPTER XLIII

Visit to my mother in Seelisberg—With General Loë and General Count Waldersee in Axenstein—Reichstag dissolution and Septennat—Grave danger of war (1887)—The domestic situation and Russia—The Grand Duke Vladimir—The Re-Insurance Treaty 608

CHAPTER XLIV

Operation on the Crown Prince—Death of Emperor Wilhelm (9.3.1888)—Mourning in St. Petersburg—Frau von Bülow in Berlin with the Empress Frederick and Queen Victoria of England—The Queen on Bismarck—The evening at Bismarck's—Minister in Bucharest—King Carol—Rumanian politicians, Peter Carp and Bratianu—Death of the Emperor Frederick (15.6.1888)—The Mission of the Imperial Minister in Bucharest 615

CHAPTER XLV

Nieuport in the summer season 1889—Franz Arenberg—First signs of Bismarck's approaching fall—In Berlin—Conversation with the chief of the Imperial Chancellery, Rottenburg—Dinner with Count Wilhelm Pourtalès, Herbert Bismarck, and Hugo Lerchenfeld—Return to Bucharest—King Carol on Bismarck—My letter to Philip Eulenburg of 2nd March 1890 —Bismarck's dismissal (20th March, 1890)—Denunciation of the Re-Insurance Treaty with Russia—The Franco-Russian Alliance—German public opinion after Bismarck's resignation 626

CHAPTER XLVI

King Carol on Prince Bismarck's dismissal—Betrothal festivities in the Rumanian Royal House—My appointment to the Ambassadorship in Rome—Farewell audience with King Carol—Last meeting with my mother in Berlin 641

CHAPTER XLVII

Taking over the Embassy in Rome—Situation in Italy—Crispi, Blanc—The German Colony—Kaiser's birthday, 1894—William II visits King Humbert in Venice . . . 652

CHAPTER XLVIII

Journey to Sicily—Prince Paolo Camporeale—Altavilla—Donna Laura Minghetti—Malvida von Meysenbug—The Abyssinian adventure—Crispi's fall—Marchese Rudini . . . 662

CHAPTER XLIX

William II's visit to Southern Italy—Ascent of Vesuvius—
Meeting with Cardinal Sanfelice, Archbishop of Naples—The
Papal diplomacy—Cardinals and prelates—The Russo-Ger-
man Re-Insurance Treaty and Prince Bismarck—The Cretan
question—Marschall's successor—Conferences with Philip
Eulenburg in Meran and Venice—Correspondence with Berlin
—Uncertainty and insecurity before the final decision . . 673

INDEX 687

LIST OF ILLUSTRATIONS

FACING
PAGE

I. BERNARD VON BÜLOW . . . *Frontispiece*

II. BERNHARD ERNST VON BÜLOW 22

III. SENATOR MARTIN JOHANN JENISCH AND SUSANNE VON
WARNSTEDT 32

IV. LUISE VICTORINE VON BÜLOW 52

V. HENRY VII, PRINCE OF REUSS, AND RICHARD, PRINCE
VON METTERNICH 156

VI. LÉON GAMBETTA 176

VII. IMPERIAL CHANCELLOR PRINCE OTTO VON BISMARCK-
SCHÖNHAUSEN 206

VIII. THE BIRTHPLACE OF PRINCE BÜLOW IN KLEIN-FLOTT-
BEK 284

IX. PRINCE ALEXANDER MIKHAILOVITCH GORTCHAKOV . 320

X. ATTACHÉ BERNARD VON BÜLOW 336

XI. OPPERT-BLOWITZ 452

XII. BENJAMIN DISRAELI 456

XIII. EMPEROR WILLIAM I AND THE GRAND-DUCHESS
ALEXANDRINE VON MECKLENBURG-SCHWERIN, AT
EMS 504

XIV. DONNA LAURA MINGHETTI 532

XV. COUNTESS MARIE DÖNHOFF 592

XVI. FRANCESCO CRISPI 674

NOTE

The Publishers desire to state that Prince von Bülow's *Memoirs* are presented solely as an historical document. They do not in any way associate themselves with the views or the criticisms expressed by Prince von Bülow as regards either persons or events.

EARLY YEARS AND DIPLOMATIC
SERVICE, 1849-1897

THE MEMOIRS OF
PRINCE VON BÜLOW

CHAPTER I

Frankfort—My Parents' Home—Frankfort Diplomats—The Minister, von Bismarck-Schönhausen—Governesses and Tutors—My Father's Educational Principles.

> " *Wie an dem Tag, der dich der Welt verliehen,*
> *Die Sonne stand zum Grusse der Planeten,*
> *Bist alsobald und fort und fort gediehen*
> *Nach dem Gesetz, wonach du angetreten.*
> *So musst du sein, dir kannst du nicht entfliehen,*
> *So sagten schon Sibyllen, so Propheten:*
> *Und keine Zeit und keine Macht zerstückelt*
> *Geprägte Form, die lebend sich entwickelt.*" [1]

GOETHE put these verses at the head of his Orphic poems. He remarked that these few lines were not only full of meaning, but that the very sequence of the ideas contained in them was such that once their true sense was perceived it would assist the mind in making its profoundest reflections. Schiller makes his Wallenstein say:

> " *Des Menschen Taten und Gedanken, wisst,*
> *Sind nicht wie Meeres blind bewegte Wellen.*
> *Sie sind notwendig wie des Baumes Frucht,*
> *Sie kann der Zufall gaukelnd nicht verwandeln.*
> *Hab ich des Menschen Kern erst untersucht,*
> *So weiss ich auch sein Wollen und sein Handeln.*" [2]

[1] Just as the Sun, on the day that gave thee to the World, accepted the greeting of the planets, so didst thou grow and flourish forthwith according to the law of thy initiation. So thou must be, thou canst not flee from thyself. So it was said by Sibyls and by Prophets: and no Time and no Power will destroy the form once fashioned that, living must mature by its own destiny.

[2] Know that the deeds and thoughts of mankind are not like the waves of the sea blindly moving. They are inevitable like the tree's fruit. Playful chance cannot change them. Once I have searched the innermost man, then all his wishes and actions are known to me.

On the other hand, Sallust, whose gardens occupied the top of the Pincio where stands to-day the Villa Malta (in which I am dictating these lines) wrote in the second chapter of his *Bellum Jugurthinum*: "*Animus incorruptus, æternus rector humani generis, agit, atque habet cuncta, neque ipse habetur.*" Who was right? The two greatest German poets or Gaius Sallustius Crispus, one of the most penetrating historians of all time? Is man able to shape his own destiny? Or does his individuality, with which a greater Power has stamped him, carry him, willy nilly, here or there, like a leaf driven by the wind? Is there an antinomy in these things, one of those contradictions in which reason, applying its unconditional demands to a conditional world, involves itself? Every sincerely written autobiography should help us to determine this question.

I, having passed the age of the Psalmist and having now begun to dictate my Memoirs, wish the following to be taken for granted:

Whoever looks back upon a long and eventful life knows that memoirs are valuable only if they are sincere and inwardly true, only if the author relates what really took place, describing it just as he saw it happen. Goethe said once that whoever has a piece of paper in front of him and a pen in his hand may set to work with confidence. If he will tell the truth about his experiences and feelings he may write a good, and indeed a useful, book. I do not introduce myself to the reader with the words of Jean Jacques Rousseau on my lips, who holding his *Confessions* in his hand, wanted to say to Almighty God as he rose again at the sound of the last trumpet: "*Voilà ce que j'ai fait, ce que j'ai pensé, ce que je fus. Rassemble autour de moi l'innombrable foule de mes semblables; qu'ils écoutent mes confessions, qu'ils rougissent de mes indignités, qu'ils gémissent de mes misères. Que chacun d'eux découvre à son tour son cœur au pied de ton trone avec la même sincerité, et puis qu'un seul te dise, s'il l'ose: je fus meilleur que cet homme là.*" I shall be content with that utterance of Terence's which met with the approval of Saint Augustine: "*Homo sum; humani nil a me alienum puto.*"

I consider it a piece of good fortune that I received my earliest impressions at Frankfort. When Johannes Miquel, who later on became Minister of Finance, took office in 1880 as Lord Mayor of Frankfort, the Empress Augusta said to him in her meditative and yet charmingly witty manner: "Frankfort is neither North Germany nor South Germany, Frankfort is simply Frankfort."

The fact that I grew up in the city where north German and south German characteristics meet, a city that joins the South to the North, has put me on guard from my childhood even, against

all narrow particularism, making it easier for me to assimilate the
spirit in which the sturdy Ernst Moritz Arndt, who when I was
a child was still alive, had written in 1813: " It shall be one
Germany for all!"   In the Prussian Diet, decades later, on the
thirteenth of January, 1902, I expressed my political creed in this
spirit and in the following words: " I never will adjust this country's
policy to satisfy one particular standpoint. I will no more promote
a Protestant or a Catholic party-policy than a Liberal or Conservative
party-policy. For me, as Premier and Chancellor, there exists
neither Catholic nor Protestant, neither Conservative nor Liberal
Prussia or Germany; before my eyes there stands only the one
indivisible nation, indivisible in all its material as in all its ideal
respects." [1]

There was hardly a town in Germany better suited than Frankfort to impress on the mind of a growing boy the unity, the grandeur,
but also the tragedy of German history. The venerable Cathedral,
Gothic and dark, towers above the oppressive narrowness of the
streets and low houses, over gables and chimneys above the whole
sea of Frankfort roofs. Here the Emperors of the Holy Roman
Empire were elected and crowned. Here Bernard of Clairvaux
preached the Crusade before Conrad III, and the first of the
Hohenstaufen emperors carried the Cistercian Abbot in his arms
out of the jostling crowd. Not far from the cathedral I could visit
the three-gabled " Römer," mount the broad stone steps and stand
in the Imperial apartments.

By the side of my tutor Lohr, a sturdy Hessian, who later did
good work as General Superintendent of the Province of Hessen-
Nassau, I contemplated the more than life-size portraits of the
German emperors. I stood respectfully looking up at the great
Charlemagne, who gave Frankfort its name. The Song of Roland,
so my teacher told me, glorified this first German Emperor as
dreaded by the foes of the Reich, but beloved of the German
people. Twelve Paladins had stood around him as the twelve
Apostles had stood round Christ. History relates that East and
West bowed down before him, the Church placed him among her
Saints, he was both creator and architect of his epoch, and the
founder of medieval culture. The worthy Lohr, a fiery patriot,
impressed on me also those sad verses addressed twenty years
before by Pfizer, the Swabian poet, to the first German Emperor, in
the presence of the two slender mountain peaks that rise from the

---

1 Prince Bülow's *Speeches*, large edition, issued by Johannes Penzler and Otto
Hoertsch, vol. i, p. 260.   Prince Bülow's *Speeches*, small edition, issued by Wilhelm
von Massow, vol. ii, p. 99.

Swabian landscape, the renowned Hohenzollern and Hohenstaufen:

> " *Kaiser Karl, von dem sie sagen,*
> *Dass noch oft Dein Banner rauscht,*
> *Wenn du fliegst im Wolkenwagen*
> *Und Dein Volk dem Siegsruf lauscht,*
> *Wo bist Du ? Den Ruf zum Siege*
> *Freilich hört kein Deutscher mehr;*
> *Und der Glaube ward zur Lüge,*
> *Harrt umsonst der Wiederkehr.*" [1]

Lohr told me of the Saxon Emperors, of the Emperor Henry
the Fowler, summoned to the German Imperial throne from his
Fowler's life in the Harz mountains; of his son, the great Emperor
Otto, who subdued the Slavonic tribes between the Elbe and the
Oder, and compelled both Poles and Bohemians to recognize
German suzerainty: Otto, the victor in the mighty battle with the
Hungarians on the Lechfeld near Augsburg. He also spoke of
his fantastic grandson, Otto III, who, tired of life although hardly
22 years old, died in the castle of Paterno, near Rome. He spoke
of the Salic emperor, Henry III, under whom the Holy Roman
Empire rose to the pinnacle of its might, who won Lorraine
and laid the foundations of Austria, together with those of the
Eastern Marches, who deposed three Italian Popes and installed
four German Popes one after the other, but, alas, died at the early
age of 39. We were even more fond of standing before the pictures
of the Hohenstaufens and most of all before that of the Emperor
Barbarossa. And when Dr. Lohr told me about Barbarossa, who
had taken the splendour of the German realm under the earth
with him but would, in his own time, bring it back again, a great
longing overcame me—a longing that the ravens would at last
cease to fly round the Kyffhäuser, the Emperor emerge from his
subterranean castle, and with him all the splendours of the Reich.
I can well remember the Hapsburg Emperors did not impress
me nearly so much. Indeed, only two of them caught my fancy,
the Emperor Rudolf, because of Schiller's fine poem about the
festive coronation banquet in the ancient hall at Aachen, and the
gloomy Charles V. It is true that the latter's refusal to accept our
beloved Dr. Martin Luther displeased me, but none the less I

---

[1] Emperor Charles, of whom they tell that still men hear the rustle of thy banners,
when thou fliest in thy chariot clouds and thy people hearken to the cry of victory.
Where art thou? No German Heeds that cry any more. Faith becomes falsehood
and awaits thy return in vain.

rejoiced to think that the sun never set on his kingdom. The Leopolds and the Ferdinands, the Francises and the Josephs with their pendulous lower lips seemed dull to me.

My parents lived in the Neue Mainzer Strasse. The Prussian Minister, Herr von Bismarck-Schönhausen, lived near by in the Gallusgasse. He was not very popular in Frankfort diplomatic circles. Prussia was not fashionable either in the German Father-land or in the wide world. The weak attitude of the Prussian Goverment in the conflict over the Electorate of Hessen had badly shaken Prussia's prestige. Everybody was laughing over the dappled horse of Bronzell, the only victim of an outpost engagement between Prussian and Austro-Bavarian troops. The Prussian Premier, Manteuffel, seemed like a petty bureaucrat compared with his antagonist, the haughty aristocratic Prince Felix Schwarzen-berg, the last great Austrian statesman of the old school, while Frederick William IV seemed a feeble idealist and dreamer in comparison to the Emperor Francis Joseph, younger by 33 years, and in all the prestige of the victory of Novara, whose armies had " Father " Radetzky as their chief, and whose dynasty had worn the German Imperial crown for 600 years.

Those who came into closer contact with the Minister, von Bismarck, found that he had wit and temperament. But he rarely associated with anyone except the Oldenburg Minister, Herr von Eisendecher, and my father, who represented the Duchies of Holstein and Lauenburg as Danish Minister to the Federal Diet. He had been accredited to the Diet in 1851, almost at the same time as Herr von Bismarck. His relations with Bismarck soon became cordial and friendly and remained so until my father's death nearly 30 years later. I may have been seven or eight years old when for the first time I consciously saw Bismarck before me. We met him, my father and I, on the Bockenheimer Landstrasse. My father was holding my hand. Bismarck asked: " Is he your eldest son ? " My father said " Yes," and asked his Prussian colleague what he thought of me. The latter answered with a smile: " The boy looks ambitious." My father replied: " I am sorry to hear it. I agree with the good Moravians who sing: " God deliver us from all unrighteous greatness." Bismarck reflected for a moment and then he said: " The good Moravians are right. What shall it profit a man if he gain the whole world and lose his own soul ? "

Between my mother and Frau von Bismarck there was a cordial friendship that nothing could disturb. It lasted for 40 years until they died in the same year, 1894. They resembled each other in the faithful fulfilment of their domestic duties and in their unbounded love for their husbands and children.   They were both of cheerful temperament, natural, and free from shyness.   They were above all united by a deep, sincere Evangelical piety.   Frau von Bismarck was brought up in the " Revivalist " circles of her Pomeranian home.   The home of my mother's parents, the Rückers and of her grandparents, the Jenischs in Hamburg, was pietistic.   She had been educated in the spirit of rigorous piety and of untiring care for the poor and sick, in the spirit of Johann Hinrich Wichern, the founder of the " Rauhe Haus," and of the unforgettable Amalie Sieveking.   I still possess a picture of Christ that Frau von Bismarck gave me in 1857, when I was eight years old.   It depicts the Saviour upon the Cross with the Crown of Thorns on his head and underneath it are the verses:

" O Lamm Gottes, unschuldig
Am Stamm des Kreuzes geschlachtet,
Allzeit erfunden geduldig
Wiewohl du warest verachtet.

All Sünd hast du getragen,
Sonst müssten wir verzagen:
Erbarm Dich unser, O Jesu!
Gib uns Frieden, O Jesu!" [1]

The picture is still hanging over my bed.

In my father's house Herr von Bismarck made the acquaintance of Prince Alexander Mikhailovitch Gortchakov, whom later he was to meet more often.   Prince Gortchakov was then Russian Minister in Stuttgart, and at the same time the Tsar's representative in the Frankfort Diet.   My father asked Gortchakov whether he had made the acquaintance of Bismarck, the new Prussian Minister. When Gortchakov said he had not, my father asked him to dine with us one evening—on which Bismarck also was expected. Gortchakov, he said, would meet a very interesting man.   Gortchakov accepted, and when he came, found Bismarck at his most brilliant.   Gortchakov himself said very little.   When Bismarck left after dinner to go on to a soirée at another house, my father inquired of the Russian: " *N'est-ce pas, qu'il a de l'esprit ?* " Gortchakov answered: " *Il en a même trop.*"

---

[1] O innocent Lamb of God, slain on the cross;
Found ever patient although Thou wast scorned.
All sin Thou hast borne, or else we should despair:
Have mercy on us, O Jesu!
Give us Peace, O Jesu!

I remember with grateful emotion how kindly and wisely my father brought me up. He did his best to check in me in time those dangerous inclinations which slumber in the soul of every child. I began to keep a little diary on the first page of which I inscribed the motto: "*Non impero sed imperam.*" My father gently caught me by the lobe of the ear and asked me: "What does that nonsense mean?" Very embarrassed, I gave him to understand that I hoped to be fit to command in years to come. My father answered: "You must learn to obey, before you can command. And even when you have learned to obey, the important question still remains whether you have the capacity to lead. And in any case, get your grammar straight first. It isn't '*imperam*,' but '*imperabo*.'"

One hot day when I was going to Wiesbaden with my father I fell half asleep in the train. In the same compartment was a somewhat affected and very sentimental lady. As she pointed to me, I heard her whisper: "What a pretty boy. The very personification of sleep in all its loveliness." We arrived at Wiesbaden to see the Greek crypt on the Neroberg where a Russian Grand Duchess lay buried, the first wife of the Duke Adolf of Nassau. I said to my father that I had quite understood what the kind lady said about me. "You have completely misunderstood," said my father, who here again proved himself a born educator. "She said that you looked like a monkey, and I replied that looks didn't matter at all, but only industry and conduct."

My father nearly always had me with him when he went for his daily walk, and on these occasions—though without repressing my childish spirits—took every chance of giving me some instruction. I can still see the Mainz high road where we used to walk. Once we halted before a small meadow upon which an officer was exercising his horse. To accustom the horse to the sound of firing, he fired his pistol at intervals of five minutes. My father noticed that as the moment for the detonation approached, I displayed a certain nervousness, and jumped when the shot was actually fired. He said to me sharply: "Don't be nervous. People who are nervous achieve nothing." "*Keep up your nerves, Sir.*"[1] I have never forgotten his admonition. In more than one critical situation, during stormy debates in Parliament, in more than one solemn audience with William II, at the moment of great decisions, and during difficult passages in my own private life, I have recalled the words of my father: "Keep up your nerves, Sir."

My father soon allowed me to accompany him when he went

[1] English in the original.

out walking with friends. I still recollect many walks with Herr von Bismarck beyond the gates of the old imperial city. Although still very young, I was perfectly well able to follow, but not, of course, in every detail, the drift of their conversations, which often turned on the events of 1848. Both Ministers agreed that the political incapacity of the Germans had seldom been so crassly demonstrated as it was in the Frankfort Paulskirche. My father, as his habit was, expressed this opinion with moderation, with an undertone of compassion and even respect, for the idealism of the leading figures of that time. Bismarck, on the other hand, could hardly give sufficiently strong expression to his sardonic mockery and condemnation of the theorising book-wisdom, the unpractical doctrinaire spirit, the banal narrow-mindedness, and Philistinism of the men of 1848. I remember very well his describing Heinrich von Gagern, who was held in high esteem by many in those days, as an empty windbag and (*horribile dictu*) a political idiot. The only man of '48 for whom he had a good word was Robert Blum, who had at least had the pluck to allow himself to be shot in the Viennese Brigittenau.

Looking backwards, I will not deny that Bismarck's judgment upon the men of 1848 was not altogether just, that it was too severe. The intentions of these people were lofty, and a great deal of their programme was good. It is true that their abilities were by no means on a level with their intentions. But as Schopenhauer says, though good will may be the essence of morals, it counts for nothing at all in art, whose success depends solely on ability. Politics have only the vaguest connection with morality. Nor are they a science, but an art. The leading spirits of the Paulskirche failed because they under-rated material power. They did not admit that he who governs, who wishes to be a leader of men, must hold in his hands an instrument of power, which will serve him in his *ultima ratio*. This had been perceived by the Prussian Minister to the Federal Diet, that man who in the eighteen fifties walked between the Janus Tor and the Allerheiligentor beside my father. Nor had he forgotten this truth when in 1862 he took the helm in Berlin.

Another saying of their envoy to the Federal Diet, von Bismarck, comes back to me. He was saying to my father that Prussia would have to achieve some kind of tie between her eastern and western provinces. My father insisted on the respect due to German sovereigns, and contested this on moral and legal grounds. Bismarck replied, with a shrug: "Frederick the Great stole Silesia, and is nevertheless one of the greatest men of all times."

It is true that this was a definite contradiction of what he had said when he spoke of the Moravians. But where is the man without inner contradiction and antithesis? I venture to assert that the greatest men are those who have the worst conflicts to surmount.

Herr von Bismarck was not the only colleague with whom my father went for walks. We often met the Austrian Minister, The " Präsidial " Minister, as he was called in those days. Count Bernard von Rechberg und Rothenlöwen was externally very different from Herr von Bismarck. He was of small stature, almost dainty, and clean shaven, whereas the bushy moustache was characteristic of the Prussian envoy. Rechberg also wore spectacles; it would be impossible to imagine Bismarck in spectacles. Rechberg in no way resembled " the bold knight, the merchants' and wanderers' terror " of Uhland's poem. He looked like a scholar, but came of a family that belonged to the immediate nobility and had a seat in the Swabian Ducal Diets. Although Rechberg had a reputation for being both fiery and proud, and although Bismarck himself was not exactly a gentle lamb, both men got on quite well together. In any case Bismarck was on better terms with Rechberg than with his predecessor, the highly cultured Prokesch-Osten who was of a more liberal persuasion. Rechberg lived on until 1899, when he died at the age of 93. He lived to witness the death of his great Frankfort colleague and many varied thoughts must have passed through his mind when he heard of the event.

The Bavarian envoy to the Federal Diet, Herr von der Pfordten, was a worthy person, but more of a professor than a diplomat. He was father of the so-called " Trias Idea," that is to say, a triple sovereignty over Germany. Austria, Prussia, and, at the head of the central and small states, Bavaria, were to exercise joint control. In this way Bavaria would hold the scales. It was one of the many abortive ideas born in Germany before 1866, during the period of the Federal Diet, ideas that again and again revealed the melancholy fact that German intellectuals too often lack realism and therefore political sense. The central states would, at best, have submitted voluntarily to Austria, but unwillingly to Prussia, and only under strong pressure. In no circumstances would they have submitted to Bavaria, for to Bavaria they felt themselves fully equal, if not superior.

Frau von der Pfordten was a good comfortable lady, remarkably stout, and therefore slow in her movements. Many years later she was run over and killed while crossing the railway line at

Weesen in Switzerland. Of the Pfordten sons who went to the Frankfort Gymnasium at the same time as myself, the oldest, Max, got into debt and was placed with the firm of the great Parisian Banker, Moritz Hirsch, who was known as " Turk Hirsch " and lived in a sumptuous mansion in the Champs Elysées. His father, who had amassed a modest fortune by his intelligence and economy in his Bavarian household at Fürth, once visited his son in Paris, but when the latter proudly introduced him to young Max von der Pfordten and other cavaliers who had entered his service, the old man said with good-humoured mockery: " Why, Moritz, I did not know you dealt in cast-offs! "

The second of the Pfordten sons, Kurt, became Bavarian Minister at Berne and later poisoned himself under the stress of a very difficult position. The third, Hermann, did well. He wrote musical essays as a university professor at Munich, and, if I remember rightly, also composed a patriotic tragedy. Although Bismarck after the victory of 1866, was wise and considerate in his treatment both of Pfordten himself and of Bavaria, old Pfordten still remained his opponent. After my father's death in 1879, Pfordten wrote to me that the decease of his old Frankfort colleague grieved him, and he personally expressed his heartfelt sympathy with those who were left behind. But he never ceased to deplore the fact that my father had accepted the new Empire. Pfordten belonged to the category of Beust, Dalwigk, Platen, those Ministers of the German central States over whom the wheel of history passed. He was less skilful and gifted than these three, but had greater integrity.

I have already said that both Bismarck and his wife and my own parents were on the most friendly terms with the Oldenburg envoy, Herr von Eisendecher, and his intelligent wife, who came from Bremen. Herr von Eisendecher had two amiable daughters, both of whom were married to Pomeranians, the elder, Gustava, to a Wartez, Herr von Köller, the younger, Christa, to a Count Eickstedt. Christa, who always remained a good friend of mine, was especially intimate with the Bismarck family. She was one of those who stood at the deathbed of the great Prince, of whom it was, however, characteristic, that in spite of the intimacy uniting Christa with the Bismarck family, he would not allow her brother, Karl von Eisendecher, the envoy at Karlsruhe, ever again to enter his house after he, influenced as the Prince believed by the Grand Duke Frederick of Baden, had failed, in March 1890 to display sufficient firmness when informing the Emperor William II of the point of view of his chief, the Prince and Chancellor. When William II paid his last visit to Prince Bismarck in 1897 he brought Herr von

Eisendecher along with him in his suite. As soon as Prince Bismarck heard of this he let the Emperor know that he would not tolerate Herr von Eisendecher in his house and, during the whole visit, the latter had to wait in the special train.

When Herr von Bismarck left Frankfort in 1859 my father was the only one of his colleagues who went to the station to bid him farewell. Bismarck gave my father a powerful handshake, and said good-bye with the words: " The men of the new era are doing their utmost to have me sidetracked by sending me to the banks of the Neva. Who knows how long I shall stay in the service."

Amongst the non-German diplomats in Frankfort the French Minister Tallenay was a quaint character. At the time at which these memoirs begin he was already retired, but had kept on his Frankfort residence. He himself admitted that he was seventy or eighty years old, but it was believed that he was over ninety. With his vividly dyed hair and his turned-up moustache he still looked quite enterprising. He had entered the diplomatic service under the *Directoire* and had been present at Marenco and the Battle of the Pyramids as attaché and Secretary of Legation. He had successively served the First Republic, Napoleon I, the Restoration, the July Monarchy, the Second Republic, and Napoleon III, but found all this perfectly correct. " *Je ne sers pas les différents gouvernements qui se succèdent, je sers la France qui reste.*" His real name was M. Marquis, but he changed it for the more euphonious name of his birthplace, Tallenay. First he called himself M. Marquis de Tallenay, and then the Marquis de Tallenay. He frequented our house a good deal and delighted us children with his funny stories. The First Secretary of the French Legation in Frankfort, M. Gustave Rothan, was the son of a protestant pastor in Alsace, and displayed an exaggerated chauvinism. Later he published a series of books on the Franco-Prussian relations from 1862 to 1870; they were well written although full of the same chauvinist spirit. In Frankfort he was cut dead by the Russians and also by others because, in 1855, when he was a member of the French Legation in Berlin, he had organized the theft by which a confidential letter of the Emperor Nicholas I, to King Frederick William IV, got into the hands of the French. In this letter the Tsar informed his brother-in-law that the Malakov Bastion could only be held a little while longer. This letter, when brought to the knowledge of General Pélissier, decided the fall of Sebastopol and the end of the Crimean War.

A great beau and a breaker of hearts was the Spanish Minister, Rancis y Villanuova, of whom it was rumoured that he had been the first of Queen Isabel of Spain's many lovers. Perhaps it was to do penance for his sins that Rancis retired to a Spanish cloister towards the end of his life, like Charles V. He paid me a visit in Metz in the spring of 1873 where I was working in the District Präsidium. I showed him the battlefields of Gravelotte and Mars la Tour which elicited his cries of astonished admiration for the heroism of the Prussian Guard.

The Dutch envoy Herr von Scherff held a position similar to my father's. In the Federal Diet he represented the Grand Duchy of Luxemburg and that part of the Duchy of Limburg, which, although an integral part of the Kingdom of the Netherlands, belonged to the German Federation. Herr von Scherff's daughter, Pauline, who was called " Paulinche " in Frankfort, was honoured for many years with his simple, honest friendship, by our good old Emperor William I. She died an old maid, but the autumn of her life was enriched by the sunshine of the old gentleman's sympathy, and the many little attentions which he never failed to show her, with all his sincere and exquisite tact. The only son of the Scherff family entered the Prussian service and became an excellent staff officer. He broke new ground as a writer on military affairs, publishing valuable studies of strategy and tactics.

The Mecklenburg envoy to the Federal Diet at Frankfort was a cousin of my father's, Bernhard Vollrath von Bülow. He was the only son of the Mecklenburg Master of the Horse, Vollrath von Bülow, whose sterling qualities, his true attachment to the Grand Ducal family, and pre-eminent horsemanship, won him universal respect in Mecklenburg throughout the first half of the nineteenth century. The son did not inherit the robust constitution of his father. He died, a consumptive in Mentone at the age of scarcely forty-four. His widow, Paula, acted as Mistress of Ceremonies to the court of Schwerin, and was equally well-known and liked in those of Berlin, Vienna, and St. Petersburg. She was a daughter of Count Francis de Paula von Linden (who was for many years Württemberg envoy in Vienna and Berlin) and of a Baroness von Hügel. A Swabian pun, in the days of the Federal Diet, ran as follows: " Upon the hill (Hügel) there is a lime tree (Linde) and before the lime tree there is a watchman (Wächter)." [1] The three families, Hügel, Linden, and Wächter had secured many a fat emolument and therefore exercised strong political influence. My aunt Paula was very beautiful. When she was a young countess in Vienna she had turned the Archduke Max's head. He wanted to marry her at all costs and his mother, the Archduchess Sophie, had

---

[1] *Auf einem Hügel steht eine Linde, und vor der Linde, ein Wächter.*

some difficulty in preventing the match. Perhaps the poor Arch-duke, had he married the intelligent and sensible Paula Linden, would not have embarked on the Mexican adventure in which he perished so miserably. Under the title *Bygone Days* Paula Bülow Linden published a slender volume in which unpretentiously and graciously she relates many charming and some interesting happen-ings in her eighty-eight years of life, from 1833 to 1920. She was broad-minded, although she had always lived at Court and when she was eighty was still conducting a lively correspondence with Ernst Häckel, the philosopher Carneri, Paul Lindau, Joseph Kainz, Cesar Flaischlen, Count Paul Hoensbroech, Wolzogen and many others. Towards the end of her days she inclined towards Socialist ideas and worked with eager zeal on a plan for the collective state education of children, a plan which had been suggested to her by her visit to the Moscow Foundling Home in 1874.

Other Austrians who, later on, filled important positions in their own country, were on very friendly terms with my family. The Secretary of Legation, Braun, subsequently became Baron von Braun, and chief Cabinet Secretary to the Emperor Francis Joseph, whom he advised for many years in all the internal questions of the Monarchy, a position which made great demands on the skill and industry, above all, on the patience of both adviser and advised. The Austrian military attaché Captain Friedrich Beck was a Badener from Freiburg in Breisgau, and had served in the Imperial army since 1846. In 1867 he became head of the Emperor's Military Chancellery, in 1874 Adjutant-General, and in 1888 Chief of the General Staff, where he remained until 1906. He lived until 1920 when he reached the age of ninety. He, who had fought at Novara under Radetzky, lived to see the collapse and the end of the House of Hapsburg.

The first secretary of the Austrian mission was an old Councillor of Legation, who, like the Marquis de Tallenay, had ennobled his surname. His family name was Dumreicher but under the name of Oesterreicher he had been raised to the status of Baron by the Dual Monarchy. In the Austrian diplomatic service of the old days, that is to say before the fateful year 1866, the heads of the more important missions were usually drawn from the nobility. But, unfortunately, since among the scions of the nobility the number of persons of high ancestry did not correspond with their fitness for the service, the aristocratic chiefs were supplied with middle-class councillors by whom the real professional work was done. This Baron Dumreicher von Oesterreicher was a clever official of the latter class. Under the title of *Album d'un Diplomate*,

he wrote a book in French, charmingly bound, giving many hints
still useful to diplomats. Now it is forgotten and out of print.
The first chapter deals with the theme " *Du Calme*," and begins
with the words " *Un diplomate doit avoir un tempérament calme.*"
In a subsequent chapter the author declares: " *On aime à attribuer
une certaine fougue au génie et à se l'imaginer comme dispensé d'être
patient. Mais le vraie génie ne manque jamais de patience; il attend
toujours que les choses soient arrivées à maturité et il ne précipite rien par
une impatiente impétuosité. C'est pour cela qu'un proverbe dit: La
patience, c'est le génie.*" Concerning common-sense he wrote: " *La
diplomatie est le bon sens appliqué aux affaires du grand monde,*" and
of tact: " *Le tact est la faculté de faire spontanément ce qui est convenable.*" At the head of the chapter on intelligence there is a
statement which is unquestionably right and never sufficiently
taken to heart: " *Un diplomate ne saurait avoir trop d'intelligence.*"
If the leaders of our diplomacy in the disastrous summer of 1914
had acted in accordance with the golden words and counsels of the
departed Dumreicher they would not have led the German people
into the most fearful catastrophe that our Fatherland has suffered
since the visitation of the Thirty Years' War.

In later years life again brought me into contact with the two
Secretaries of Legation, who served under my father in the Danish
Legation to the Federal Diet. One of them, H. von Bille, became
Danish Minister in London. I often met him there and in other
places. The other, Herr von Wind, was Danish Minister in St.
Petersburg when I went there for the first time in 1875: and
Danish Minister in Berlin when I became Chancellor in 1900.
Bille and Wind stayed in our house in Frankfort where they re-
ceived a most cordial welcome from my father. My relations with
the two distinguished diplomats always remained friendly.

The Secretary of our Chancellery in Frankfort was named
Kräuter and no little herb [1] in the kitchen garden could have been
more modest than he. He was a friend of the Secretary of the
Prussian Chancellery, Kelchner, who often spoke to him of his
chief, the Ambassador von Bismarck-Schönhausen, whom he called
a " rash character." Kelchner in my presence once characterized
his ambassador as follows: " He is a man who is capable of anything. If he does not wish to be present at a sitting of the Federal
Diet and no better excuse occurs to him he will have his carriage
harnessed, drive along the Mainz high road, from there into the
first convenient field and, together with his coachman, remove a
wheel. Then he sends the man to the Eschenheimer Gasse with

[1] A pun on the word " Kraut " or herb.

orders to inform the bureau of the Federal Diet that owing to a carriage accident he cannot attend the sitting. And he can get away with it! Yes. That's what I call a rash character."

Kelchner had accompanied his great chief from Frankfort to St. Petersburg and from there to Berlin where I found him again, not so greatly altered, when I became Secretary of State nearly forty years later. A frequent visitor on the Frankfort Promenade was Prince Emil of Hessen-Darmstadt, a relic of the times of the Rhenish Confederation. When, at the Battle of Leipzig, he led his Hessian division to the attack, Napoleon shouted: "*En avant, Roi de Prusse*" by way of encouragement. The Corsican Emperor had thought of making the Hessian Prince, who was his zealous supporter, King of Prussia in the event of victory over the Allies.

Very few inhabitants of Frankfort in the 'fifties suspected that there lived in the town two men whose names would be remembered for generations with respect. The Prussian envoy to the Federal Diet, Otto von Bismarck-Schönhausen and the philosopher, Arthur Schopenhauer. Our amiable family physician, Dr. Stiebel, who was greatly loved by us when we were children, sometimes told us about them both. This Schopenhauer, he said, was a strange sort of customer. Nobody knew what he believed in. On his table stood a small Buddha to which, so it would seem, he addressed his prayers. The great philosopher lived on the Schöne Aussicht where we often went for our walks. Once when we encountered a very ill-humoured looking gentleman there, walking hunched up with his hands crossed behind his back, my tutor said to me: "That is Herr Schopenhauer, the crazy philosopher about whom Dr. Stiebel told us."

In Lohr, my tutor, I had a warm-hearted patriot as mentor. His successor Hopf, was also a Hessian but of another kind. From him I was to learn how far German political stubbornness can go. He came from the circle of the Marburg literary historian Vilmar, who was one of the mainstays of the ultra reactionary and rigidly orthodox Hassenpflug system in the Electorate of Hessen. Among the small German dynasties there was hardly one more iniquitous than the Elector of Hessen's, which had covered itself with shame by the sale of Hessian people to England. The Landgrave Frederick II, sent 12,000 wretched Hessians to fight for the British against North America, receiving in exchange 21,276,778 talers, which he used to build the magnificent castle of Wilhelmshöhe. His successors, so it seemed, wished to demonstrate how far a loyal German population could be oppressed without being driven to open revolt.

There is a delightful poem by Chamisso said to have been founded on an actual event. One evening the Elector was strolling through the streets of Kassel his " Residenz." He heard the voice of an old woman at an open window, raised in supplication for the long life of her gracious sovereign. With some surprise, the Elector asked the woman what on earth made her put up such a prayer. She told him that the grandfather of the reigning Elector had taken from her the best of her eight cows, for which she had cursed him. His son, and successor, had taken two cows from her, for which she had also cursed him, and bitterly:

> " *Dann kamen höchst Sie selbst an das Reich*
> *Und nahmen vier der Kühe mir gleich.*
> *Kommt dero Sohn noch erst dazu,*
> *Nimmt der gewiss mir die letzte Kuh.*
> *Lass unsern gnädigen Herrn, o Herr,*
> *Recht lange leben, ich bitte dich sehr!*
> *Die Not lehrt beten.*" [1]

The title of the poem is " The Widow's Prayer." The scandalous private life of the Electors was on a level with their insane methods of government. Nevertheless they found supporters who followed them through thick and thin, and even remained true to them after their fall when, in 1866, an end was put to this disgraceful state of affairs and the Electorate of Hessen was incorporated in Prussia. My teacher Hopf was one of those singular people who supported the old regime. For many years he edited a newspaper which, after the inclusion of Hessen in the Prussian monarchy, stood for Hessian particularism. He lost his ecclesiastical living on this account, but grew all the more stubborn. When I had become Prussian Minister Hopf not infrequently attacked me in his newspaper because I had not remained faithful to the principles of Vilmar and Julius Stahl which had once prevailed in my parents' home at Frankfort. When I laid down my office in 1909 he wrote an article (a copy of which he sent me) expressing the hope that I would now return to the principles and views of the fifties; if I did so my fall would prove to have been all to the good. I was not angry with the pig-headed Hopf, for he, as a true disciple of Vilmar, had awakened my understanding for German legend, for our mighty national epics, and above all for the Saga of the Nibelungs.

[1] Then your Highness's self succeeded to the realm and at once took four of the cows from me. If your son succeeds you, he will be sure to take my last cow. So let our gracious master, O Lord, live long! O Lord, I beg! Need makes us pray!

CHAPTER II

Rumpenheim—Queen Alexandra of England and the Empress Maria Feodorovna of Russia as Children—My Father's Educational Ideal—Bible and Select Hymns—Homer and Goethe—At the Frankfort Gymnasium—The Jews in Frankfort—The Rothschild Family.

NOT far removed from Frankfort is the Hessian castle of Rumpenheim. There, about 70 years ago, ruled the Landgrave William of Hessen who had been in the service of Denmark, where he had risen to the rank of a Danish infantry general. He was the nephew of the Landgrave Karl, who died in 1836 and had played a certain part in the history of Denmark. In my library are his reflections which, printed for private circulation under the title of *Mémoires de mon Temps*, are now long since forgotten and out of print. They are a slender volume and, according to the custom of the time, written in French. They contain some not uninteresting revelations about the tragedy of the adventurer Struensee. Landgrave William was married to Princess Louise Charlotte of Denmark, a sister of the Danish King Christian VIII. His daughter Louise was the consort of Prince Christian of Holstein-Glücksburg, who, by virtue of the London Protocol of 8th May, 1852, was chosen as successor to the childless King Frederick VII.

My parents frequently visited Rumpenheim, and I was sometimes allowed to accompany them. I used then to play with the pretty daughters of Prince Christian. The elder, Alexandra, the future consort of King Edward VII, of England, was a beautiful slim girl. She retained her wonderful waist and her light airy, swinging gait to an advanced age. Later on, when I had the honour of meeting her, she teased me with having cuffed and even scratched her when we played tops, hoops and "rooms to let." Truthfulness compelled me to reply that I also had the honour of having been treated somewhat ungently now and again by the delightful Princess herself. The Princess Dagmar, who later became Maria Feodorovna, Empress of Russia, was more spirited and also more intelligent than her sister Alexandra (who was, three years older) but self-willed. Prince Christian of Glücksburg

who became King George of Greece, was between the two in age.
He was intended for the Danish navy. A year before he ascended
the throne of Greece he came with his father to Frankfort, where
both of them wished to visit Rumpenheim. Prince Christian
proposed a drive to my father round the parks of Frankfort. I was
taken along. When my father wished to take the front seat of
our carriage opposite the future kings of Denmark and Greece,
Prince Christian protested: " My son is still a child. He will sit
facing us with your boy."

I can also well remember a visit which Queen Caroline Amelia
of Denmark, the widow of King Christian VIII, and daughter of
Duke Frederick Christian of Augustenburg paid to my mother.
My father was not at home and, when she was leaving, my mother
asked me to offer my arm to the Queen and accompany her to
her carriage. I made a little bow and escorted her Majesty to
the waiting carriage. She kissed my forehead and said: " You
have done it very nicely. You will certainly become a Danish
Grand Chamberlain one of these days." I related this little episode
of my childhood many years later to the Empress Augusta Victoria,
who was a niece of Queen Caroline Amelia, when I was cruising
off Eckernförde with her and William II, on the yacht " Iduna."
" The dreams of childhood," I remarked, " are seldom fulfilled.
I have never become a Danish Grand Chamberlain. And, taking
everything into consideration, even including the anxieties which
His Majesty gives me now and then, I would rather go walking
in Berlin along the Unter den Linden than along the Langelinie
in Copenhagen." The Kaiser laughed heartily.

One of the reasons why these visits to Rumpenheim delighted
me was that the drive took us through very pretty country. The
Maine, Frankfort's beautiful river, is not woven about with legend
like the Rhine, nor has so much blood flown into the waters, nor
has it played so great a part in history; but its quiet and peaceful
appearance endears it to all who, like me, have lived on its pleasant
banks. I scarcely know any spot more calculated to develop a
feeling for landscape, a sense of beauty, and love of nature than
the surroundings of Frankfort. The Taunus with its gentle slopes
and rounded hill tops is all the more attractive by being too remote
for frequent visits and therefore always reveals fresh beauties.
I have, since then, got to know the Tirol and the Carpathians, the
Italian and the Greek mountains, and above all the Swiss Alps,
but no peak had appealed to my imagination like the Feldberg
with the Brundhildenstein, the steep Altkönig, whose summit is
surrounded by a wall of stone which is said to have been built by

the Germans of old. How fresh were the leafy woods of the Taunus, how magnificent the view from above over the broad plain which spreads out at the foot of the Taunus to the numerous flourishing hamlets and the blue distant heights. We often resorted to a little forest near the town, the Frankfurter Wäldchen, where the Prussian envoy von Bismarck-Schönhausen was fond of strolling with his wife and three children. From there we would go up to the hunting lodge and wander on to the mill. One beautiful Easter Sunday my father and we boys walked as far as the stone where Goethe is said to have composed the " Easter Walk," the stone where Faust rests after having wandered across country with his amanuensis Wagner, where he sees the calm world spread out at his feet in the rays of the evening sun, and loses himself in dreams and soaring reverie:

> " *Wenn über uns, im blauen Raum verloren,*
> *Ihr schmetternd Lied die Lerche singt,*
> *Wenn über schroffen Fichtenhöhn*
> *Der Adler ausgebreitet schwebt*
> *Und über Flächen, über Seen*
> *Der Kranich nach der Heimat strebt.*" [1]

My father steeped himself in Goethe. This was not so common then as it is to-day. In those days Goethe's influence on the nation was not as great as Schiller's. The centenary of Goethe's birth in August, 1849, was hardly celebrated at all. My father's love of Goethe was so intense that he once told me he was sorry he had christened me Bernhard after his grandfather, and wished he had given me the name of Wolfgang.

Until I was twelve my education was entrusted to my Hessian tutors. Before then I had been in the care of English and French governesses, to whom I owe my command of French and English, a command that considerably eased my later diplomatic work. Among the many misunderstood utterances of Prince Bismarck there is his alleged observation that waiters are the only people who have any use for languages. If this is really what Bismarck said, it was, of course a whim. What probably happened was that

---

[1] When over us lost in blue space,
The lark sings his throbbing song;
When over steep fir-clad heights
The eagle hovers with outspread wings
And the crane makes for home
Over the levels and the lakes.

he did not care about accepting any youthful, aspiring diplomat who happened to turn up and that when he was informed that the youth was, after all, good at languages, Bismarck replied: " A fine talent for a head waiter." It was only a form of declining his services. As a matter of fact, Prince Bismarck expected his diplomats to speak and write French fluently and, better still, French and English. I do not think he would have entrusted decisive and fateful negotiations with French generals and diplomats to a man like Matthias Erzberger, who did not understand, and still less speak, a word of French.

In any case I am grateful even to-day to the Englishwomen and Frenchwomen who gave me my knowledge of both languages during my childhood when foreign languages are best and most easily learnt. My English governess, Miss P., was a tall, fine figure of a woman. She had superb teeth and eyes that looked stern even when she was in a tender mood. Miss P. was fond of closing her admonitions with the words: " Mr. Bernhard, behave like a gentleman, otherwise I cannot love you." My French governess, Mlle. T., was small, graceful, vivacious, and little bit coquettish. Mlle. twittered: " *Mon petit Bernhard chéri, soyez bien gentil avec votre bobonne qui vous aime tant.*" I liked both Miss P. and Mlle. T. very much. My father spoke excellent French. My mother was more familiar with English, which in those days was spoken a great deal in the homes of Hamburg patricians. A branch of the Rücker family had gone to England in the 18th century, had become completely Anglicized there, but nevertheless kept up connections with the old home and the Hamburg relatives.

I received my first dancing lessons in Frankfort. Amongst the girls with whom I danced was Fräulein N., whose mother was considered the greatest beauty of Frankfort society. It was whispered that the Austrian envoy, Count Frederick von Thun-Hohenstein, had courted her. He was succeeded in her favour by an elegant Prussian officer of hussars, Baron Max Schreckenstein, so it was said. Malicious tongues murmured that her elder daughter resembled Count Thun, the younger Baron von Schreckenstein. Sensible people agreed with the Emperor Justinian and good Herr N.: " *Pater est quem nuptiæ demonstrant.*" My favourite dancer was Fräulein von X., whose father belonged to the Federal Military Commission. When the dancing lessons finished with the end of winter and I mournfully said good-bye to my dancing partners, she ran after me, and embraced and kissed me, with tears in her eyes. This was the first time in my life that a lady was kind enough to indicate spontaneously that she liked me. I never

saw Fräulein von X. again.   She did not die for love, but married a
stalwart general, to whom she presented seven children.

It is to my father that I chiefly owe my intellectual training.
He laid the foundations of my education.   I look upon the Bible
and Homer as these foundations.   My father called to mind the
words addressed by St. Paul to his righteous son in spirit, Timothy,
to whom he wrote that all scripture given by God served for teaching,
for punishment, for improvement, and for chastisement in righteous-
ness.   Nor had my father forgotten what Goethe wrote ten years
before his death to his friend I. S. Zauger: " Never cease to examine
yourself in the diamond shield of the Greeks, so that you may ever
perceive your faults and virtues clearly."   When I was still a child
I reverently contemplated the beautiful line-drawings with which
John Flaxman illustrated the Odyssey and the Iliad.   I was only
ten years old when I read them both, and received a foretaste of
the calm grandeur and the noble simplicity of the classical world.
Thus I was brought up to understand the Homeric spirit, and I
became Homerically inclined at an early age.   But this did not
signify any neglect of the Holy Scriptures.   We read the Bible
every day, and when I first went to school I had already read the
whole of the Old Testament, and, of course, the New as well.
I knew about fifty select hymns by heart, those magnificent hymns
that are the priceless treasure of the Evangelical Church.   I could
recite many of them even to-day.   Before we went to sleep we used
to recite the old Low German children's prayer about the fourteen
angels:

" *Abends, wenn ik slapen gah,*
Viertein Engel bi mi stahn.
Twei tau min Haupten,
Twei tau min Feutten,
Twei tau mine Rechten,
Twei tau mine Linken,
Twei, di mi taudecken,
Twei, di mi upwecken,
Twei, di mi wiest
Int himmlisch Paradies
Un min Vadding un Mudding ok." [1]

I think Goethe is right when he says (I don't know whether to
Eckermann or to another friend) that whoever reads the Bible with

[1] In the evenings when I go to sleep, fourteen angels stand by my side: Two at
my head, two at my feet, two by my right, two by my left, two to cover me up,
two to wake me up, two to show me the way into the heavenly paradise, and my
father and mother too.

care and insight needs hardly any other reading matter. But it is true that my father did not take this remark of Goethe's literally. I myself read Goethe's *Götz von Berlichingen* and many of his poems when I was a child. I read Schiller most of all. Once when I lay in bed with severe influenza, my father, to comfort me, gave me *The Maid of Orleans* to read. It aroused such enthusiasm in me that when I read the eleventh scene of the fifth act, where Joan's soul soars free from her prison on the wings of warlike song, I burst into tears. My father said I ought not to be so impressionable, but added, smiling: " *Non sine diis animosus infans.*" I understood this even then, and it must have flattered my vanity, seeing that I still remember it.

The first play I saw in the theatre was Shakespeare's *Midsummer Night's Dream*. The comic scenes of this immortal creation of the great dramatist, the jokes of Snout and Bottom, of Starveling and Quince, of Snug and Flute, made me laugh so boisterously that the audience shouted that the little boy making such a noise ought to be turned out of the theatre at once. This, too, brought a justified admonition to exercise greater self-control.

The Schiller festival in the year 1859 was perhaps the first time since 1848 that German national sentiment expressed itself with a mighty impulse. In the evening my parents went for a drive round the illuminated city, taking me with them. On many of the houses there were illuminated patriotic inscriptions, especially quotations from the " Maid of Orleans " and " William Tell : " Worthless is the nation that does not gladly sacrifice its all for honour's sake," " Cling to your Fatherland, your cherished Fatherland, for it is the strong root of your strength," and, above all, the admonition of the dying Attinghausen: " Unite, unite, unite, unite! " There is no admonition the Germans need more, even to-day, than this call to unity. No people has suffered more than the German for 2,000 years from division and faction, from self-seeking particularism in all its forms, from party spirit and the narrow-mindedness of party egoism.

I shall not say good-bye to my early childhood without recalling the hour when death and pain confronted me for the first time. I was five years old. My parents had gone to Wiesbaden, where they had been invited by the Duke of Nassau. I was playing with my brothers, who were one, two, and three years younger than I, Adolf, Alfred and Waldemar, in our nursery. On a table in the middle of the room was a large jug of boiling water which a servant-girl had carelessly put there. The youngest of us, Waldemar, tugged at the tablecloth in childish ignorance. The jug was

BERNHARD ERNST VON BÜLOW, STATE SECRETARY OF THE FOREIGN OFFICE,
FATHER OF PRINCE BÜLOW

upset, and the water scalded the poor boy, who was only two years old. His pitiful screaming still sounds in my ears, I still see before me the dismay and the pain of my parents when they returned from Wiesbaden a few hours later.

The dear little boy died in terrible torment two days after. In his agony, with his dry lips, he kissed the crucifix that hung next to his bed. It was put into the coffin with him when he was buried in the beautiful cemetery. As long as we lived in Frankfort we visited his grave once a week, and, whenever we stood before the little mound, we were convinced that up above us in Heaven our little brother was playing in flowery fields.

Three months after his death my father came into the room with the news that the Emperor Nicholas of Russia had died on 2nd March, 1855. It was a great shock to my father, for he regarded the Tsar Nikholai Pavlovitch as the stronghold of the royalist and conservative order in the world. My father was not the only one to hold this view. King Frederick William IV sobbed loudly as he embraced the Russian aide-de-camp, who had brought the sad news of the Emperor's death to his palace in Berlin. The Prussian envoy to the Frankfort Federal Diet, Herr von Bismarck-Schönhausen, had given his eldest son Herbert, who was born on 28th December, 1849, the second name of Nicholas in honour of the Russian Emperor. My father was, probably in consequence of his friendly relations with Gortchakov, in the good books of the Emperor Nicholas who, during a journey through Frankfort, had received him and decorated him personally with the " Grand Cross of the Order of St. Anne." The deaths of my poor brother and of the mightiest Tsar who had occupied the Russian throne since Peter the Great are the big events in the earliest year I can most clearly remember.

I have never forgotten two solemn services in the Cathedral of Frankfort, for they taught me the transitory nature of mankind and the uncertainty of all aspirations and projects. In March, 1856, prayers of thankfulness were offered in the Cathedral because a son had been born to the Emperor Napoleon III and his consort, Eugénie Montijo, after three years of marriage. In August, 1858, a Te Deum was held for the first-born son of the Emperor Francis Joseph, who received the name Rudolf, in remembrance of the Emperor Rudolf, the founder of the Hapsburg monarchy. I was present at both celebrations. My French governess, who accompanied me to the celebration for the Prince Imperial, wept with emotion and enthusiasm. The French ambassador, who bore the historic name of Salignac-Fénélon, beamed.

Even more impressive than the prayers for the future Emperor of the French was the great part taken by the general public in the festivities in honour of the Crown Prince Rudolf. Austria was very popular in Frankfort. The Prince Imperial was fated to die under the knives and assegais of the Zulus, while the heir to the Austrian, Hungarian, Bohemian, Lombardian, Venetian, Dalmatian, Croatian, Slavonian, Galician, Lodomerian, Illyrian, and several other thrones was destined to perish as the victim of unhappy loves. There can be no permanent alliance with the powers of Fate; disaster comes soon. This truth is not merely a poetic turn in Schiller's " Glocke." It is proved by history itself.

In Autumn, 1861, my brother Adolf and I, who always had our lessons together, were sent to the Frankfort Gymnasium. We were put into the Second Form on the first day. I proudly laid the beautiful satchel, which my parents had presented for the great occasion, on my desk. The letters B.B. (Bernhard Bülow) were stamped on it in letters of gold. The boy sitting next to me also had a new satchel, with the letters H.B. His name was Hugo Bethmann. He emigrated to Paris a generation later, and became a naturalized Frenchman. With that lack of national pride which, alas, only too often mars the German character, he turned Gallic chauvinist. His son fought against us in the World War.

Soon after I had gone into the Upper Fourth at the Frankfort Gymnasium, I got my first experience of the impermanence of all human dignities. Every week we had to do an " Unseen," and we were ranged in order of merit in the class according to the result. I came third in the first " unseen," and was as proud as a peacock. But in the second, eight days later, I came a cropper, and dropped to 17th or 18th place. " *O jerum, jerum jerum, o quæ mutatio rerum.*" I never, in later life, remember having experienced so great a disappointment, or feeling such bitter vexation. Later reverses in my career left me more indifferent. This shows how sensitive and self-conscious the soul of childhood is, and with what consideration it should be treated. The satirist Juvenal spoke wisely when he said: " *Maxima debetur puero reverentia.*"

So as not to get home too soon after school, I did not go direct through the narrow and tortuous alleys of the old town, but walked along the Maine and through the " Schöne Aussicht." I gazed sadly upon the yellow-brown waters of the Maine and the glittering white and stately row of houses of the " Aussicht," upon the venerable old bridge (now, alas, pulled down) with the statue of

Charlemagne and the " Gickel," a golden cock, the emblem of Frankfort.

If the deceased Arthur Schopenhauer, who lived on the " Schöne Aussicht " had seen me, he would have offered his congratulations on my timely recognition of the transitory nature of worldly things, and on the attainment of tranquil disillusionment as to the ways of mankind and the world.

When, at last, after many hesitations, I got home and reported my misfortune to my father, he reproached me for being so crest-fallen. " A good boy ought not to give way so easily. *Tu ne cede malis, sed contra audentior ito.*" He told me to keep my wits about me at the next examination. I would then be able to wipe off the old score. At Christmas I received a good report: Class Two. When I gave it to my father he said: " I would have preferred Class One." Not without pique, I told him that my fellow pupils had either received a Third or a Fourth, or even a Fifth. I asked him: " What would you have said if I had done no better than they?" My father replied: " I would have made a tailor of you." This, too, was not quite in harmony with the ideas of the good Moravians.

It was characteristic of the Germany in the period of the Frankfort Federal Diet that many of my school comrades had visited Vienna or Paris, but that none knew Berlin.

The headmaster of the Frankfort Gymnasium bore a famous name. He was called Tycho Mommsen, and was the younger brother, by about two years, of the historian and classical scholar, Theodor Mommsen. He taught the ancient languages with pedantic severity, but with the excellent result that he created a solid foundation for the future of his pupils. Its advantages became apparent later on in life. Tycho Mommsen, without rivalling his greater brother, made a certain reputation by translating Pindar, by his treatise on the Satires of Horace, and his fine essay on the art of translating into German from other modern languages.

The Frankfort Gymnasium was undenominational. My Catholic fellow-pupils received lessons from Professor Johannes Jansen, who became one of the most fervent champions of the ultramontane tendency when, ten years later, the unhappy struggle between church and state blazed up. His biography of Count Frederick Leopold Stolberg, and above all his *History of the German People Since the Middle Ages* " are executed in the same spirit that fills the monumental work of his pupil Ludwig von Pastor's *History of the Papacy.*

Of my masters at the Frankfort Gymnasium I hold Dr. Theodor

Creizenach, who taught history, in especially grateful memory. He promoted my interest in German history, and thereby my understanding of German national sentiment, thus continuing what Dr. Lohr had begun. Dr. Creizenach was a Jew. Once during an interval between classes, a couple of ill-bred boys drew an ugly caricature of the master on the blackboard, which was intended to show up his Jewish characteristics. My brother and I resented this piece of ill-manners. There was a scuffle in which we were surprised by our master as soon as the interval between classes was over. Of course, we did not sneak on the boys who had done it, but nevertheless Dr. Creizenach appeared to have an inkling of what had happened. He shook my hand and said: " You are a good boy."

The Jews in Frankfort formed an important and clearly marked business and social class. The " Judengasse," where the Jews were compelled to live apart until the end of the eighteenth century, still exists almost unaltered. At nights and on Sundays the gates used to close on the Jewish quarters. I have often been through the " Judengasse." As many as a hundred persons would be living in one tumbledown dwelling. The gables of the black houses slanted crazily. I can well remember old Baron Mayer Anselm Rothschild. My father sometimes went for a walk with him. The kind old man used to tell queer little stories about his childhood when he and his parents were locked up at nights in the " Juden-gasse." One day as he asked to be let in just as they were going to lock the gates, the sentry, seizing him by the ear, said to him in good Frankfort dialect : " Little Jew-boy, I'll let you in just once more."

Mayer Anselm Rothschild had given proof of his humorous good nature in the crazy days of 1848. When an excited mob assembled before his house he appeared on the balcony and made a little speech to the people: " Good friends, you want to divide up everybody's property. There are about 40,000,000 Germans. I possess just about the same number of guilders. We shall begin the division by my presenting every one of you with his share of one guilder." The crowd withdrew laughing.

The Rothschild family were proud of the special position they held among the Frankfort Jewry. When the candidature of Baron Emil Erlanger to the Frankfort Club was being discussed, my father frankly sponsored the election of this intelligent man who was to achieve wealth and position in Paris, where I met him again. Baron Mayer Carl von Rothschild, later a member of the Prussian Upper Chamber and son of old Mayer Anselm, protested keenly against the election of von Erlanger, and finally said to my father: "*Je ne vous comprends pas. En somme, Erlanger n'est qu'un misérable Juif.*" He distinguished between the Grand Jewry, which included specially the House of Rothschild, and the Little Jewry, to which he relegated all other Jews. Many of these have amassed fortunes abroad, notably in Brussels and Paris.

We stayed in the town house of Baron Willy Rothschild in Frankfort. His widow, Mathilde, lived until the World War, when she was over ninety. She was on friendly terms with the Empress Frederick and with my mother-in-law Donna Laura Minghetti, who had often visited them both in the beautiful villa of Grüneburg, near Frankfort. The Emperor William II greatly respected the Baroness Mathilde, who was noted for her charity and her exceptional musical gifts. The garden of the Rothschild house, where there was a pavilion with a view over the Park, has remained one of my pleasant memories. There were yellow plum trees in this garden. We liked the fruit even better than the view. Even now that I am an old man, I never eat yellow plums without thinking of Frankfort. In the doorposts of the Rothschilds' house there were little tablets of ivory, inscribed with Hebrew characters. Our parents explained to us as children that these were the Ten Commandments. That the Jews should have the Ten Commandments before their eyes is very laudable—and yet, would that God would take away the Mosaic bandages that blindfold their eyes and let them see the clear light of the Gospel! The Rothschilds' house in the Neuer Mainzer Strasse was later acquired by the Duke of Nassau and is, I believe, now owned by a bank.

CHAPTER III

Hamburg and Klein-Flottbek—Birthplace in the Flottbeker Chaussee—Relatives and Friends of my Youth—My First Sea Journey—Alcohol.

WE spent the summer at Flottbek on the Elbe in the country house of Frau Emelia Rücker, my grandmother on my mother's side. The Rücker family came from Schweinfurt, the old and picturesquely situated Imperial town, amongst the vine-clad hills in the heart of the Franconian wine district. Its name has nothing to do with that useful but much-abused bristly animal, the pig (Schwein). Schweinfurt is said to signify Sueven or Schwabenfurt, the Ford of the Swabians, just as Frankfurt is the Ford of the Franks. When I was Chancellor a Schweinfurt citizen sent me a picture of a tombstone in the chief parish church. It represented my ancestor, the Mayor Harthold Rücker, kneeling in prayer before Jesus Christ. The inscription of the memorial executed in sandstone read: " *Anno Domini* 1337 *in crastino beati Matthei apostoli abiit Bartholdus Ruecker scultetus in Swinfurt, cujus anima requiescat in pace. Amen.*"

Beside the kneeling Mayor was the coat of arms—a virgin—borne by the Rücker family both in its German and English branches. During the Thirty Years War, when Schweinfurt, despite its status as an Imperial city, was alternately looted by the Swedes and the Emperor's troops, the Rücker fanily went and settled in Hamburg, where they and their descendants became useful senators and citizens.

The journey from Frankfort to Hamburg and Flottbek was not as simple then as it is now. Scarcely ten minutes after the beginning of the journey a long stop had to be made at Bockenheim. For Bockenheim belonged to the Elector of Hessen, and although it was but a suburb of Frankfort, the Elector wished to have his sovereignty recognized in the " newest Hessian town." In Cassel there was a much longer stop. Between Minden and Göttingen there was no connection by rail at all. We had to travel by road. The night was passed at Hanover, where we arrived at about nine in the evening, if we had left Frankfort in good time—and the

journey could not be resumed until next day. By this means the
State of Hanover wished to force travellers to patronise the inns
of its capital overnight. Most of the travellers preferred to spend
the night in the station waiting-room. I can still see that waiting-
room. Its benches were covered with red plush, and I remember
how the travellers grumbled about the enforced break in their
journey and vainly tried to sleep amongst their hand-luggage.
Many a complaint fell from their lips about blind King George of
Hanover and his mysticism, his absolutism, and his conviction that
he did everything by the grace of God.

Early in the morning we travelled through the Lüneburg
Heath. To-day it is the goal of many tourists, and artists live there
to make a special study of it. It has become the fashion. Not to
find it beautiful is to confess a lack of taste and æsthetic appreciation.
Sixty years ago it was quite different. The Lüneburg Heath was
in bad repute. It was a stock joke that when God had finished the
Creation, as He said " Behold it, it is good," he kept His thumb
over the Lüneburg Heath to hide it. The Rhinelanders were said
to have a prayer: " I thank thee O Lord that I do not dwell in
Siberia or on Lüneburg Heath." A French traveller, with French
impetuosity, had mistaken the little blackish sheep of the heath,
the so-called " Heidschnucken," for human beings, and had told
of a " *peuple sauvage* " who inhabited the heath and struck fear
into the hearts of all travellers. It was considered a sign of progress
when, in the 'fifties, a much-read stylist described Lüneburg Heath
as " half boring and half enthralling," for even August Platen had
begun his romantic Oedipus with the melodius words :

> " *Das ist die schöne Lüneburger Ebene,*
> *Wohin des Rufs Trompete mich von fern gelockt.*" [1]

Finally we travellers reached the town of Harburg, which had
begun to consider itself a flourishing rival to Hamburg, since
Hanover was actively promoting its development with docks and
steamships. Harburg was as favoured by Hanover as Altona by
Denmark and Bockenheim by Hessen. In Harburg we took the
steam-packet, and great was our pleasure when finally the metropolis
of the Lower Elbe, with its numerous slender towers, its masts,
its animated life and activity on land and water, was in front of us.
Hamburg made a great, an almost overwhelming impression, even
upon people coming from Frankfort. Old Matthäus Merian aptly

---

[1] That is the beautiful Lüneburg Heath, whither the trumpet of renown called
me from far.

described the difference between the two towns when he said:
" At Frankfort on the Main, when all is flourishing and peaceful,
there's a big crowd of people on market days, but in Hamburg it's
always market day."

In Frankfort the clever banker, speculating in French, Austrian
and Spanish securities, predominated; in Hamburg the honourable
merchant whose life was spent between his offices in the main
streets and his warehouses on the canal banks. The Hamburg
ships, from whose masts fluttered the Hamburg flag with the silver
three-towered castle on a red background, carried his wares to all
parts of the world. Hamburg was a city of world trade.

To us children Hamburg seemed more splendid than Frankfort,
not only because of its harbours and its shipping, but also as a
town. The Jungfernstieg was after all more beautiful than even
the Zeil, and when in the evenings a thousand lights in the patrician's
houses were mirrored in the waters of the blue Alster, we thought
of the well-known anecdote which the Hamburger is fond of
telling when he wants to impress a " Buten-Minschen," that is to
say an outsider or stranger. Once when a German Prince, so the
story goes, saw the brightly illuminated houses of the Inner Alster,
he assumed that the free Hansa town of Hamburg was lit up in
honour of his arrival. So he sent his Chamberlain to the Mayor to
thank him for his kind attention. The Mayor replied smiling that
the Alster was lit up in this way every evening, not for foreign
potentates, but for the pleasure of Hamburg's citizens.

The Hamburgers have since olden times, and, as it seems to
me, with good reason, had a high conception of the beauty and
the charms of their city.

> " Befördrer vieler Lustbarkeiten,
> Du angenehmer Alsterfluss!
> Du mehrest Hamburgs Seltenheiten
> Und ihren fröhlichen Genuss.
> Dir schallen zur Ehre,
> Du spielende Flut,
> Die singende Chöre,
> Der jauchzende Mut!
> Der Elbe Schiffahrt macht uns reicher;
> Die Alster lehrt gesellig sein!
> Durch jene füllen sich die Speicher,
> Auf dieser schmeckt der fremde Wein.
> In treibenden Nachen
> Schifft Eintracht und Lust,

Und Freiheit und Lachen
Erleichtern die Brust." [1]

Thus, back in the eighteenth century, honest Frederick von Hagedorn, sang the renown and praise of his native city, and since then the civic pride of the free, proud Hamburg citizens has not diminished.

The Hamburg that I viewed as a child was the Hamburg of before 1866, or 1870, and before the incorporation in the Zollverein which took place in 1888. In those days a smart coach drawn by four white horses took the owners of the Elbe villas at Blakenese, Nienstedten and Flottbek, to the " city," to Hamburg, between ten and eleven in the morning. This coach was called the " White Lady," the " *Dame Blanche*," in memory of the then popular opera by Boieldieu. In Old Hamburg the shipowner took first place, economically and socially. Industry did not develop on the banks of the Elbe until much later, and its representatives were only very gradually received into the body of Hamburg patricians. The chiefs of the business firms and the import and export houses, who were closely connected with the shipowners, were accustomed to appear on 'change at two in the afternoon, wearing frock coats, black ties, and high, glossy shining top-hats.

The top-hat was the particular symbol of the honourable business man and of complete and prosperous respectability. All the employees, including the confidential clerks had to appear in stiff black English hats. The tall grey hat was only worn by the Senators and the Syndics. This was the tradition. Whatever was traditional in old Hamburg usually came from England. In the " City " of London Hamburg was known as " the London suburb." In the first half of the nineteenth century Hamburg and Bremen felt the same kind of reverence for London and England, as Frankfort and the banks of the Rhine had for Paris and French civilization. Hamburgers who were patricians in grand style, Jenisch, Godeffroy, Rücker, Schröder, Amsinck, had to have a town house on the Esplanade, on the Jungfernstieg or on the Grosse Bleichen, a country house on the Elbe, and an estate in Holstein or Mecklenburg.

My grandmother Rücker was the oldest daughter of Senator

[1] Promoter of many pleasures, pleasant Alster river! Thou augmentest Hamburg's rarities and its merry enjoyments. Singing choirs and exultant emotions resound in honour of thy playful waters!

The shipping on the Elbe makes us richer, the Alster teaches us good fellowship! The Elbe fills our warehouses, and in the Alster we enjoy the foreign wine. Unity and delight travel in the hurrying boat, and freedom and laughter lighten the heart.

Martin Johann Jenisch, whose family was looked upon as the first in Hamburg. This family had also come from south Germany. Before the Reformation it had flourished in Augsburg, the home of the Fuggers and the Welsers, but had left the town for the sake of the Faith during the troubles of the Reformation, and had migrated to Hamburg. It had given the city on the Elbe many an excellent Senator, Syndic and Burgomaster under the old constitution, which the "Travelling Frenchman" called the happiest compromise hitherto found between aristocracy and democracy. Martin Johann Jenisch had won a goodly fortune by shipowning as well as by big banking deals with the Crown of Denmark. But with the pride of the good old Hamburger, he had declined the title of Count which the Danish government offered to him.

In the evil days of the French occupation when Hamburg was called a "*bonne ville de l'Empire Français*," he was appointed "*Sénateur de l'Empire*" by Napoleon. But this did not prevent his standing up to the French in energetic defence of his native city's rights. His oldest son, Martin Jenisch, became a Senator like his father and in this capacity worked as a leader of the Extreme Right. He was a friend of General Leopold von Gerlach in Berlin and of the whole Mecklenburg nobility. He owned a fine city mansion on the Grosse Bleichen, with a good picture gallery where I received my first artistic education. After the victorious Franco-German war the Hamburg Senate gave our old Emperor William I a banquet in this house, when after the Franco-Prussian War he first visited Hamburg as German Emperor.

A good hour away from Hamburg Senator Martin Jenisch owned a park that was often visited by strangers, "Jenisch Park," at Teufelsbrück, on the Elbe. It consisted of the park proper, the Elbe park, and the Spring Park. In the main park there was a fine palm-house and an even finer orchid house, where this flower, which was then still a rarity in Germany, was cultivated in the most wonderful varieties. When Senator Jenisch inspected his orchids, holding a golden lorgnette in his left hand, his right hand resting on a bamboo with a gold knob, he presented such a picture of comfort and complacency as I have seldom seen since then in this world where, as people often say, the number of dissatisfied considerably exceeds the number of satisfied. He owned two estates in Holstein and the domain of Kalö on a Baltic bay in Jutland.

But death put an early end to his good fortune. He died in the prime of life when he was about fifty. He made my mother's younger brother, Alfred Rücker, sole heir to all his property.

SENATOR MARTIN JOHANN JENISCH (GREAT-GRANDFATHER), AND SUSANNE VON WARNSTEDT,
WIDOWED VON BÜLOW, NÉE IMPERIAL COUNTESS VON BAUDISSIN (GRANDMOTHER)

I believe this was a disappointment to my good father, who may have hoped that I, as Senator Martin Jenisch's godson, would have come into possession of the considerable properties which he had founded. In fact, my third name is Martin. But I consider the way I was passed over in those days to be a gracious dispensation of Providence, not only because, as Helmerding used to sing in an old Berlin song, "Wealth alone does not bring happiness," but also because had Kalö fallen to me the sheer burden of the interests connected with it would perhaps have pushed me in the direction of Denmark after all. I thank God that I remained a German.

Before I begin to talk about my uncle Alfred Rücker I should like to recall the brother of Senator Martin Jenisch, my grand-uncle Gottlieb Jenisch. I have known two very ugly people. One of them was the multi-millionaire, Pierpont Morgan. He was disfigured by a gigantic nose, a misshapen nose that resembled a great bulb, or rather a pomegranate sprinkled over with sugar. But his eyes were so intelligent and there was so much humour and wit playing round the finely cut mouth, and the man's whole personality was so significant and at the same time so attractive, that the nose was soon forgotten. There are few people with whom I have found conversation more interesting. He once told me that his father had sent him to Europe, as a young fellow, with a relatively modest sum, to try his luck there. His father gave him only one piece of advice on that occasion: never to do anything against American interests, "for God backs the United States." He, Pierpont Morgan, first went to Göttingen to study mathematics. The professor whose lectures he attended was very satisfied. "I am pleased with you, my young American friend," he said to him a while after, "and if you go on being as industrious as you are, you may become a university tutor some day, and perhaps even a professor." Pierpont Morgan replied that this prospect flattered and attracted him, but he feared that his father had marked him for the banking profesion and that he would have to submit to this paternal wish. "In any case," Mr. Pierpont Morgan concluded, "I would have had less excitement if I had been a tutor in pure mathematics than on the New York Exchange."

Gottlieb Jenisch, the only brother of senator Martin Jenisch was perhaps even uglier than Pierpont Morgan. He had a small snub nose, but large nostrils and large projecting ears, a low forehead, and a bulging mouth. According to the well known utterance of a natural historian, every man resembles some animal. My good grand-uncle Gottlieb Jenisch was like a chimpanzee and would have been welcomed by Darwin. Mrs. Pierpont Morgan not only loved her husband in spite of his nose; she was deeply in love with and very jealous of him. "All women are in love with him," she sighed, "he is such a dear!"

My grand-uncle Gottlieb Jenisch was married to a good and beautiful woman. She had been a Countess Westphalen, whose maiden name was Lützow. She was descended from the family whose most famous scion led "the wild and wayward chase" in the Wars of Liberation, the chase that Theodor Körner sang, and in whose ranks he died a hero's death. It was a successful marriage, and two lovely daughters were born of it. The elder married Count Otto Crote, who before 1866 was the Hanoverian envoy in St. Petersburg and remained an obdurate Guelph even after 1866. The younger married a Count Vitzthum, who for many years was Master of Ceremonies at the Court of Prussia, and at court celebrations he discharged his duties with zeal and skill, duties demanding tact and circumspection. The daughter of Countess Vitzthum was my brother Adolf's first wife, who died all too young. She was as great a beauty as her sister, the Countess Klinkowström. The grand-daughter of the Countess Marie Grote is my handsome cousin, the Baroness Thyra Jenisch. Socrates prayed to the eternal gods on the banks of the Illysus: "Oh, dear Pan and ye other gods who may be here with you, grant me beauty and let my exterior be in harmony with my mind." Even if the gods hear only the first part of this prayer, the ugliest man can at least hope to have beautiful children and grandchildren to delight his old age. He can, above all, hope that a good and loving wife will be granted him.

My Uncle Gottlieb Jenisch was a first-rate sportsman who rode and drove equally well. His house was the noblest on the Binnenalster, on the Alten Jungfernstieg. From his country house on the Elbe, the "Bost," he had a broad view over the mighty stream down to Schulau and Stade. In Mecklenburg he owned the estate of Varchentin, which included a handsome mansion and park. I do not know if Schiller was right when he observed that Nature is always just. She usually grants compensations. What we lack in one direction we usually possess in another.

But to return to my Uncle Alfred Rücker, my mother's younger brother. He had, when quite a young man, been made the London envoy of the Hansa Towns, and was in England well known to the royal family, and especially esteemed by Queen Victoria, a fact he was always ready to remember, as well as by King Edward VII. He had taken some delightful journeys in Italy, Greece, and Spain, partly in company with his friend, the antiquary, Ernst Curtius,

the tutor of the subsequent Emperor Frederick and author of a
widely-read history of Greece. Alfred Rücker died young in his
native town, where he was a Senator. His son Baron Martin
Rücker-Jenisch entered the German diplomatic service and was
in high favour with William II. He was the only diplomat the
Kaiser took with him to Rominten, where, indeed, he is said to
have received permission to shoot a stag, which, in the eyes of
His Majesty, was one of the greatest honours that could be given
to mortal man.

My grandfather Rücker died soon after my birth. I never
knew him. My grandmother Rücker was a good, gentle, and dear
woman. She had suffered the grievous loss of two daughters in
the bloom of their youth, to whom she set up a monument in the
Park at Flottbek, executed by an Italian sculptor in Carrara marble.
We used to contemplate it sorrowfully. My grandmother had
travelled in Italy with my mother in the good old-fashioned way,
in horse-drawn carriages, not in railway trains. They went from
Hamburg to Rome, from Rome to Naples, and from Naples back
to the Elbe. In his able history of the Germans in Rome Frederick
Noack recalls their visit to the Eternal City and the help they gave
to talented German artists there.

In my dining-room at Flottbek there still stands a dancing girl
executed in Carrara marble and a David with his sling in the same
material, which my grandmother brought from the Tiber to the
Elbe. My grandmother's eldest son spent a thoughtful, leisured
life on his Holstein property, Perdöl. As a child I was lost in
admiration of the columns on which the roof of Perdöl rested,
though later I admitted that those of the Parthenon were even more
beautiful. My uncle William did not possess the broad culture
nor the active mind of his younger brother. When he was travelling
in Switzerland my father was asked whether his brother-in-law had
done much mountain climbing. He replied: " To the best of my
knowledge our good William has only climbed the Sluggards-
Horn." This allusion to my uncle's inertia made me laugh very
much.

I have always enjoyed a joke, even when made at my own
expense, as so many have been in the course of my political career.
But I only enjoy really good jokes, and they are rare in German
public life. All in all, I think that my uncle William with his
fondness for peace and quiet, indeed, because of it, was happier
than many others who, like the Greek sage, seek life in movement.
From the Eudaemonistic standpoint he was right. My grandmother's youngest and favourite son, Oscar, died of a malignant

disease in his earliest youth, hæmophilia, a disease of the blood, from which the last Russian Tsarevitch is also said to have suffered. I see my mother's mother before me, an old and completely broken woman, constantly in tears and murmuring, " Oscar, Oscar! He was so good and dear, and such a sweet child, and yet he had to suffer and die so soon."

The country house of my grandmother Rücker lay in the Flottbeker Chaussee. It was a plain-looking house, but far more tasteful in its plainness than the modern buildings, which are mostly overburdened with ornament. Here I first saw the light of day on 3rd May, 1849. Around the house lay a fine park with magnificent old trees, a well-tended lawn, a conservatory, and a wonderful view over the Elbe. My grandmother's park stretched from the beautiful home of the Ritschers, which dated from 1769, to the garden of the Elbe Park villa, which now I occupy every summer. Opposite the park lay the so-called Camp, a big expanse of fields where cows grazed and where stood mighty oaks on which I got my first climbing practice and acquired the freedom from giddiness which I enjoy even to-day. I used to swim with my brother in the Elbe with an old fisherman called Van Ehren in charge of us. This family had lived in Teufelsbrück near Flottbek for centuries. In the afternoon we used to drive in a little donkey cart, our greatest delight, to Altona or Blankenese. We tenderly loved this donkey. Kindness to animals was impressed upon us from childhood. On Sundays we always went to church as all good children should, either down the river Elbe to Nienstedten or up stream to Ottensen. The parish of Nienstedten is said to have been founded soon after the foundation of Hamburg by Charlemagne, and is, indeed, very old. The pastor of the Nienstedten church christened me, and in Nienstedten churchyard when I die I wish to be buried beside my beloved wife.

Few parts of Germany have suffered more from war and the hardships of war than the right bank of the Lower Elbe from Altona to Blankenese. Nienstedten and Flottbek were barbarously laid waste by the Danes and the Swedes, by Tilly and Wallenstein, during the Thirty Years' War, and 200 years later in the " French Period," French and Russian troops behaved there with little less brutality. The sorrowful song of the pious pastor Rist dates back to the time of the Thirty Years' War:

> " Das vormals volle Land is gänzlich aufgezehret,
> Das Vieh hinweggebracht, die Dörfer stehn verheeret,
> Die Flecken ohne Gebäu, die Aecker voller Dorn,

Die Wiesen sonder Heu, die Scheunen ohne Korn;
Die Städte sind verbrannt, die Männer sind erschlagen,
Nur arme Waislein sind noch übrig, die beklagen
Mit Tränen für und für der liebsten Eltern Tod!" [1]

During my Chancellorship I had only to think of the misery and need which Bellona had wrought upon my birthplace in order to recognize that the noblest duty of a German Chancellor, once Germany had been united and the Empire restored, was the maintenance of peace with dignity and honour.

The three graves of which the poet Rückert has sung are by the side of the church in Ottensen. But the graves of the thousands, who were driven out of Hamburg by the cruelty of Marshal Davout, the foreign tyrant, in mid-winter, hungry, naked and destitute, fathers, mothers, brothers, daughters, children, youths, masters, servants and all——these graves:

" *Die rufen weh zum Himmel*
Aus ihrer stummen Gruft,
Und werden's rufen zum Himmel
Wenn die Trommet einst ruft." [2]

Since then we have had French soldiery in the Rhineland and in the Ruhr, we have seen even more brutal, more bestial things than raged in the winter of 1813-14 on the Elbe. The grave of the Duke of Brunswick:

" *Von Braunschweig ist's der alte*
Karl Wilhelm Ferdinand,
Der vor des Hirnes Spalten
Hier Ruh in Grabe fand.
Der Lorbeerkranz entblättert,
Den auf dem Haupt er trug,

---

[1] The land that was once so abundant is wholly devoured,
The cattle carried off, the villages stand desolate,
The plots uncultivated, the fields full of thorns,
The meadows without hay, the barns without corn,
The towns are burnt out, the men are slain,
Only little orphans are left
Who with tears continually bewail their dearest parents' death.

[2] Call piteously to heaven
With their dumb earth, and they shall call
To heaven, when once the trumpet calls.

Die Stirn vom Schlag zerschmettert,
Der ihn auf Jena schlug." [1]

But he foresaw a better future, a day of revenge, the resurrection of Germany, for which his son, the good Prince von Oels, fell at Quatre-Bras. Finally the grave of the singer of the " Messiad " with the inscription:

" *Auferstehen, ja auferstehen wirst du,*
Mein Staub, nach kurzer Ruh.
Unsterblich Leben
Wird, der dich schuf, dir geben." [2]

Our dear friend and playmate was the gardener's son. He emigrated to America later on, and became the director of a mineralogical museum. After my appointment to the Chancellorship I received a letter from him in which he wished me success in my new office. He had, he wrote, become an American through and through, but preserved a good remembrance of his old comrades. To show his friendly feelings he sent me three or four beautiful stones from his museum. Another friend of my boyhood was the son of the Hamburg Syndicus Merck: " Syndicus " was the title given to a Senator who dealt with the external affairs of the " Free and Hansa Town," and directed foreign policy. A predecessor of the Syndicus Merck, Syndicus Gries, once met the literary historian and æsthete, the witty Friedrich Schlegel, who addressed him with the words: " How are you, my dear Grindicus Süs ? " Whereupon Gries retorted promptly: " Very well, Schriedrich Flegel."

The friend of my boyhood, Arthur Merck, went to England later on and turned himself into an Englishman. How many are the leaves, big and small, good and bad, how many are the branches and boughs which the German oak has lost since the days of the migration of the nations?

From my grandmother's house we saw the ships pass by every day, the ships that sought strange seas and far-distant wonderful countries. I longed intensely to go on a sea journey, and my

---

[1] It is the old von Braunschweig,
Karl Wilhelm Ferdinand, who with
Cleft brain, found rest here in
The grave. The leaves are gone
From the laurel wreath that he wore
On his brow, his forehead now shattered
By the blow that struck him at Jena.

[2] Thou shalt arise, yea arise, my dust, after brief rest
He who made thee will give thee immortal life.

joy was great when my father told me that I could go on a new steamer which was making a trial trip the next day, *and* would take me to Heligoland and round the island. I boarded the stately ship one morning full of enthusiasm, at St. Pauli, with my father. The journey to Cuxhaven was completed quickly and without incident. At Cuxhaven we were called to lunch. My father ate with the guests of honour on the upper deck, I with the *dii minorum gentium* down below. It was an opulent spread in the Hamburg manner, particularly the many good and heavy wines. My neighbours kept on filling my glass (I was then fourteen) and encouraged me to go on, by drinking my health. With ever-growing delight I drank glass on glass of sherry, Moselle, Rhine wine, Bordeaux, Champagne, Madeira, brandy. Then I felt a growing need for fresh air and went on the upper deck. There in the distance I saw my father, and went up to him in an exalted frame of mind. But, alas, my gait was unsteady, I could hardly keep on my legs. When I reached him and the dignified Syndicus Merck, I reeled and fell down. " You are dead drunk," my father said to me in a stern voice. The bystanders smiled. My father continued: " Go down below, sleep it off, and don't let me see you again until we are back in St. Pauli." I obeyed, very much ashamed of myself. On the way back from St. Pauli to Flottbek I had to walk ahead of my father so as to prove that I was firm on my legs once more. The next morning he told me that drunkenness was one of the most degraded vices. It was no use citing Noah's example, since that patriarch had wanted to recover from the stress and emotion of the Flood, whereas I had no excuse whatever.

Although this incident was distressing, it was nevertheless a salutary lesson. Distress is a part of the life of all who profit by experience. Drunkenness has remained revolting to me ever since. I am well aware that this admission may annoy and even estrange many of my sturdy fellow countrymen. Did not Georg Christoph Lichtenberg, one of the subtlest German eighteenth century writers, record more than a hundred German expressions for drunkenness? Schopenhauer adds that this is not surprising since the Germans have always been famous drinkers. Karl Hillebrand, the author of the still readable book, *France and the French*, which was published soon after the Franco-Prussian War, and is written with acute insight into both of German and of French psychology, said to me in Florence in 1874: " A German mother feels rather proud when she sees her son come home heavily drunk, but wrings her hands when she hears that he has taken a sleeping partner— a ' bed-hare ' (Betthase) to use an expression of Frau Rath Goethe's.

A French mother is just the other way. She is amused if her son has a ' *bonne amie* ' provided that the liaison is not a lasting association involving him in marriage with some poor girl. But to see her son drunk would disgust her: ' *Fi donc, quelle horreur!* ' " Nearly all German poets have written drinking songs: Schiller the " Punch Song," Goethe the " Table Song " and " Ergo Bibamus." Even the pious Wandsbeker Bote " wreathes the precious ' flowing bowl ' with laurels, and drinks it merrily to the dregs." Of great French poets only Béranger, as far as I know, wrote drinking songs, and even these are not drinking songs in the German sense, but, like the *Chansons du Dieu des bonnes gens*, they have a political tendency, or like the *Bacchante*, an erotic one. For the comfort of those Germans who still believe that a man who has never been drunk is not a man, I will not hide the fact that in my later life I did, two or three times, perhaps, drink more than was necessary for my thirst. I remember two instances:

When I was in the Bonn Hussars I went to the Johannisberg with a good comrade to visit the hereditary Grand Duke of Mecklenburg-Schwerin (later on Grand Duke Frederick Francis III) who was staying in a sanatorium. The Grand Duke was too ill to receive us, but he ordered us to be served with a good meal and even better wines, Johannisberger, Steinberger, Niersteiner, to which I devoted myself with gusto. We took a boat back from Rüdesheim to St. Goar. On the way I would insist on trying to jump into the water, but fortunately I was saved by the energy of my dear friend Carlos Sierstorpff, who, because of his height, was called Murphy, after a famous giant who was on show in those days. On another occasion I wanted to return to Bonn by train after a merry banquet in the " Riese " at Coblenz. To cool my head I left the compartment while the train was in motion and continued the journey on the footboard. A sturdy conductor found me in this situation after an hour and persuaded me to return to my compartment. The French say that there is " *un Dieu pour les ivrogues comme pour les enfants.* " But I can say with confidence that only in a few exceptional cases have I needed this special protection.

CHAPTER IV

My Grandmother in Plön—My Grand-Uncle Wolf Baudissin—the Schleswig-Holstein Question—My Father Leaves the Service of the Danish Government (1862)—He is called to Mecklenburg-Strelitz as Chief Minister (1863).

EVERY year we went from Flottbek to the pretty little town of Plön on the shore of the largest lake in the Holstein plain, where my father went to school and where his mother had been living for many years. She was the only daughter of Count Karl von Baudissin, who had been Danish ambassador in Berlin at the beginning of the nineteenth century. She had seen King Frederick William III and Prince Louis Ferdinand, Hardenberg, Rüchel-Kleist, the beautiful and unhappy Queen Louise, Rahel and Henriette Hertz. Her mother was a Countess Dernath, a family of Dutch origin which had come to Austria, had been raised to the rank of Imperial Counts in 1655, and settled in Holstein later on. The family of the Counts Baudissin, who came from the Lausitz, belonged to the ruling houses which had risen by the profession of arms in the Thirty Years' War. Their ancestor, Wolf Heinrich von Baudissin, fought alternately as a Danish, Swedish, and Saxon Colonel, married the daughter of the Holstein Stadholder Gerhardt Rantzau, acquired estates in Holstein, and died a Lieutenant-General in the Polish service.

The Dernath family died out long ago. They were a proud race who flourished once on the Rhine and on the Danube, in the Netherlands and in Austria, in Bohemia and Hungary, in Holstein and Denmark, but now they sleep in stone coffins. Shall I recall times even more distant than these? The grandfather of my grandmother Susan, that is to say my great-great-grandfather on my father's side, the Electoral Saxon general of infantry and Governor of Dresden and Königstein, Henry Christopher Baudissin, was married to Countess Susan Zinzendorf, a niece of the Moravian. This ancient aristocratic family which flourished in Austria from 1100, and filled the office of Hereditary Grand Master of the Hunt in Austria ever since the fifteenth century, left its home for its religion's sake during the Counter Reformation, and went to Lutheran Saxony. The younger branch of the family returned to

41

Austria and to Catholicism later on. It produced two well-known Austrian eighteenth-century statesmen, both of them Ministers of State and of the Council "for domestic affairs," both of them Knights of the Golden Fleece, the one marrying a Schwarzenberg, the other a Dietrichstein. Their portraits in long full-bottomed wigs which my grandmother left me are hanging in my home at Flottbek. The elder branch of the House of Zinzendorf, which remained true to the Evangelical faith, gave to Protestant Christendom Count Nicolas Ludwig, the exalted founder of the Moravian brotherhood, which aspires to unite all the branches of the different Evangelical tendencies in heartfelt love of the Saviour, and whose precepts I, like every other evangelical Christian, read every day.

My great grandfather Karl Ludwig Baudissin, when he was young, had to leave the Electorate of Saxony because as a cavalry major he had killed a certain Count Gersdorff in a duel, very much as Faust kills poor Valentine: "Now is the lubber tame." After his release from fortress-arrest he was Danish ambassador for five years to the Prussian Court, and died Governor of Copenhagen. His only daughter married my grandfather Adolph Bülow. He, too, had had a duel in his youth in which he shot his opponent. I could have reminded my "die-hard" Pan-German Chauvinists Liebermann von Sonnenberg and Hasse of this in the Reichstag when they said I was not much of a fighter. A brother of my grandmother was Count Wolf Baudissin. A friend of Ludwig Tieck and Augustus Wilhelm Schlegel, he assisted both in their translation of Shakespeare, and himself rendered twelve plays into German, including *King Lear*, *Othello*, *Henry VIII*, *Macbeth*, *Coriolanus*, *The Taming of the Shrew*, *Antony and Cleopatra*, and *Measure for Measure*. Besides Shakespeare, he translated Ben Jonson tastefully, also Molière and Ponsard from the French, and Gozzi and Goldoni from the Italian. Gustav Freytag wrote a good biographical memoir of Count Wolf Baudissin.

I have visited my dear Uncle Wolf both in his town house in Dresden, from the windows of which there was a view of the Grosse Garten, and at Rantzau, his Holstein property, where he used to spend midsummer. He was what the French would call a "*causeur*," just as attractive and captivating in the spoken word as he was clever with his pen. He used to tell me about his diplomatic career when he was secretary to his uncle, Duke Magnus Dernath, who in 1810 was Danish ambassador in Stockholm. While he was there Wolf Baudissin witnessed the murder of Marshall Ferson, who had made the arrangements for the flight to Varennes of Louis XVI, and was a dear friend of the unfortunate

Marie Antoinette. The German sympathies which he openly displayed, made him a personal friend of Ernest Maurice Arndt. In 1813 he was interned as a state prisoner of the second grade in the fortress of Friedrichsort, near Kiel, by the pro-French Danish Government.

I used to listen to my uncle with tense interest when he talked about his daily walks upon the prison wall, which he took under the escort of a sentry. I wondered if I would, in the end, be imprisoned in a fortress if I were to become a diplomat? My great uncle Wolf had whiled away his imprisonment by translating the whole of Dante, a few cantos every day. I was still more interested when my uncle told me about the visit he paid to Goethe at Jena in the Easter of 1809, when he was a student at Göttingen University. He described the meeting with Goethe vivaciously and charmingly in a letter written to his sister, my grandmother. He described how he awaited the great man's coming with the impatience of a child when Christmas is at hand. " When he came at last," the letter goes on, " in a blue overcoat, with powdered hair and without a wig, I was in such a state of wonder and adoration that I completely forgot my shyness. His forehead, nose, and eyes were like those of Olympian Jove. What a handsome face, what a magnificent tanned complexion! And how he talked! How vivid were his words and how animated were his gestures! Hands more beautiful than his are nowhere to be seen. He answered and gesticulated with infinite warmth, grace and charm. The sunlight of his eyes grew so bright, their rays so divine, that if they had been angry their fire would have been unendurable. His accent was that of a South German educated in North Germany. He spoke softly, but with magnificent resonance, neither too quickly nor too slowly. And when he entered the room, what gait and carriage! A born King amongst men! "

When Baudissin with youthful enthusiasm declared that if Zelter and Forkel were to die, the whole art of music would perish, Goethe consoled him with the words: " The really beautiful never perishes, but lives on ever in the hearts of the chosen few, inextinguishable as the vestal flame." He talked for two hours. The next day we went for a walk in the botanical gardens. Goethe praised Fichte's speeches to the German nation, particularly their fine style, and of the Germans he said: " Their fuel is kindling splendidly, but they lack a stove to contain it and hold it strongly together." The stove was made a century later by Bismarck.

Wolf Baudissin kept his health and his capacity for work, his mental power, and his ever-cheerful spirit, as well as his keen

German patriotism, until he died at the age of 89 in 1878. He remained to the last in regular communication with Gustav Freytag, Paul Heyse, and Geibel. Not long after the Franco-Prussian War he received a visit at Rantzau from the author of *Passant* and the *Greve des Forgerons*, the French poet, François Coppée, who dedicated to him the following beautiful verses under the title of " Souvenir de Rantzau ":

> " *Les arbres de Rantzau sont très-bons. Leur ramure*
> *Dans mon âme a versé le repos et la paix,*
> *Et bien souvent, assis dans leur feuillage épais*
> *Ivre de leur odeur, j'ai trouvé l'heure brève,*
> *Et rafraîchi mon front fatigué par le rêve.*
>
> *Pour le parfum des bois, pour la chanson des nids,*
> *Grands aieux des forêts, arbres, soyez bénis!*
> *En vous remerciant de l'accueil favorable*
> *Mon esprit vous unit à l'hôte vénérable.*
> *Près de qui j'ai passé ces jours calmes et doux,*
> *Au comte hospitalier fort et bon comme vous*
> *Qui témoin d'un autre âge, ami des grands ancêtres,*
> *Me parlait en marchant sous les branches des hêtres.*
> *Emu comme à vingt ans de poésie et d'art.*
>
> *Puisse Dieu conserver à ce noble vieillard*
> *L'éternelle vigueur accordée aux grandes charmes,*
> *Et de sa belle vie allonger tant les charmes,*
> *Que bien longtemps encore il promène à pas lents*
> *Sous vos vieux rameaux verts ses jeunes cheveux blancs.*"

The news of the death of my kind uncle Wolf, which came as a great grief to me, reached me one day at the foot of the Parthenon, while I was chargé d'affaires at Athens. My grandmother's second brother had long been in the service of the Danish Garde du Corps. When in 1848 the democratic Eider Danes took the helm at Copenhagen and the independence of the duchy and a provisional government was proclaimed three days later in Kiel, Karl Baudissin joined in the Schleswig-Holstein movement. He fought bravely for the sea-girt land as a general at Düppel, Fredericia, and Idstedt. The third brother of my grandmother, the Court Master of the Hounds, Count Hermann Baudissin, of Sophienhof, in Holstein, lived to an even greater age than his four long-lived brothers and sisters. He died in 1891 in his ninety-third year. He had witnessed both the battle of Jena and the dismissal of Prince Bismarck by the Emperor William II.

His only son, Wolf, who is the same age as myself, studied theology, but, unlike Faust, he never regretted it. He tutored in Strassburg, Giessen and Marburg, and, after 1894, was the successor of the Berlin orientalist Dillman in Old Testament exegesis. He wrote especially about the Semitic religions. He is a very learned person, and impressed me with his knowledge years ago, when we studied together at Leipzig in 1868-9. He certainly attended his classes there more industriously than I did mine. We met frequently in the later years in Berlin during my period of office as Chancellor. He became Rector of Berlin University after my resignation in the winter of 1912-13. He combines profound scholarship with a subtle spirit and a never-failing kindness, and is almost too good for this bad world. He was altogether free from the vanity and place-hunting that are so common in academic circles.

All three of my grandmother's brothers in Holstein were on the German side. But my grandmother certainly was not. She remained until her death at the age of eighty-four, in the year 1874, a daughter of the old regime: strongly legitimist, profoundly religious, opposed to all innovations, unable to understand nationalism and nationalist ideas, utterly distrustful, and, indeed, intolerant of liberal thought. In 1459 Christian of Oldenburg ("Christian the Blessed," as he is called in the History of the House of Oldenburg) became King Christian of Denmark, and with the express consent of the estates of the realm, Duke of Schleswig and Holstein. This was how it ought to be and go on being, in my grandmother's opinion. In fact, the State of Denmark was to remain inviolate. For nearly half a century she used to live in a nice little house in the little town of Plön. Her sitting room was cosy and not too large. It was on the ground floor, and next to it was a dining room not much larger, and a bedroom for any of her daughters who might come to stay with her. On the first floor there were three bedrooms, the first for herself, next to it that of her old and trusted maid, and a third for a white-haired man-servant, who used to like to tell of the scare caused in Holstein in 1807 when the wicked Admiral Nelson bombarded Copenhagen. "Suppose the English admiral were to bombard Kiel," people would whisper at the time, "and Plön and all of us into the bargain."

Male visitors at my grandmother's house were usually accommodated in the attic. I used to get the room which my father had had when he was a boy. He showed me his wash-jug, the contents of which usually froze in winter, for the attics were never heated. You stepped out of the house into a little garden where mallows, knight's-spur, poppies, lilies, mignonette and roses grew. The garden sloped gently up to a bench, where there was a view of the blue waters of Plön lake.

My grandmother was full of life and intellectual interests. As long as she was in tolerably good health she used to invite the masters of the local gymnasium, district officials, and landed gentry to come and spend the evening with her and her daughters. Each one would get a part in one of Shakespeare's plays, in the translation of which her brother Wolf had had such a distinguished share, which would then be read out aloud. In later years she would read to herself in several languages. At a time when people still wrote long letters, she was a voluminous correspondent. Her household was plain and modest, according to modern standards, but it breathed an atmosphere of quiet, order, and contentment. In Plön she was known as the " *Frau Kammerherrin* " (Lady-in-Waiting). She was not the only Lady-in-Waiting at Plön, but she was *the* Lady-in-Waiting, par excellence. " I am going along quietly," wrote Johanna Schopenhauer to her famous son in December, 1807. " Nobody contradicts me and I contradict nobody. No strife or contending in my house; everything goes its even way, as I go mine. Nobody cares who it is that obeys, or gives the orders. Everyone does his share unobtrusively, and life glides calmly by."

My grandmother might have written the same. She left me the correspondence of her ancestors Baudissin and Dernath. A vanished world breathes in these letters, which fill a whole trunk. They are written in graceful French, and deal only with events at the Copenhagen Court; they tell what the King's temper was at the levée, and who had had the honour of being invited to the Jeu de la Reine that evening. Even as late as the second half of the nineteenth century, the Holstein aristocracy was divided. Members of the same family would follow either the flag of Schleswig-Holstein or the " Danebrog." [1]

Of the sons of Count Magnus Scheel-Plessen (who was a cousin of my grandmother's) the oldest Wolf, and the youngest, Otto, remained in the Danish service during the Schleswig-Holstein war and even after 1866, and 1870, the eldest as Danish envoy at Stockholm and the youngest as Danish representative at St. Petersburg. The second son, Karl, opposed the " Eider Danes " before 1864, but within the framework of the ideas of the " Indivisible State." After the peace of Vienna, he headed the deputation which pleaded in Berlin for the incorporation of the Duchy in the

[1] Danish flag.

Prussian monarchy, and became the first Prussian *Oberpräsident* of the province of Schleswig-Holstein. When he was attacked in the Prussian House of Representatives by the Deputy, Lasker, on account of his attitude in the fifties, Bismarck defended him strongly. Prince Bismarck always got on well with the former supporters of the " Indivisible State," but he disliked the semi-particularist, semi-liberal " Augustenburgerism," as he called it. One of the most passionate outbreaks Bismarck ever allowed himself was against the Radical deputy Albert Hänel, one of the last adherents of the Schleswig-Holstein " Landespartei " who had taken up the cause of Duke Frederick of Augustenburg's succession rights.

My grandmother did not like my father's leaving the Danish service in 1862. My father was her only son, and she was deeply attached to him. Her daughter Charlotte, known in the family as Lola, who was born one year after my father, was one of those persons who used to be called " a beautiful soul " in those days. I confess that even now those " beautiful souls " inspire in me a certain fondness, especially when I compare them with the many unbeautiful, malicious, and—what is perhaps worse—vulgar souls of the present day.

My aunt Lola stooped a little. When she sat opposite my grandmother at table, the latter used to say to her every now and again: " *Tenez-vous droite, Charlotte, ma fille.*" My aunt Lola died in the aristocratic Dobbertin Nunnery for Gentlewomen in Mecklenburg, which was founded in the thirteenth century by the Cistercians. It had been handed over in 1572 to the Mecklenburg knightly and land-owning class " for the entertainment and instruction of young Mecklenburg ladies to be good Christians." The thirty inmates of the convent wore a cross of the order on a blue band, the Superior had one in gold, and the others in silver. The convent was situated near a beautiful lake and possessed over four square miles of land, eight villages, fourteen estates and about 200 peasants. Talleyrand said: " *Qui n'a pas vécu avant la Révolution, ne connaît pas la douceur de vivre.*" The ladies of the Dobbertin Cloister, I believe, fully appreciated " *douceur de vivre.*" My good aunt Lola left me a number of valuable English books, among which I still delight to browse.

My grandmother, Suzanne Baudissin, married my grandfather, Adolf Bülow, in 1813. My great-grandfather, Bernhard Joachim von Bülow, of Wendelstorf, Neuschlagsdorf, Retgendorf, Flessenow, Ventschow, Kressin and Düssin, a councillor of Mecklenburg-Schwerin, and Lord High Chamberlain, had six sons. Old Hans

Christoph Ernst von Gagern, relates, in his Memoirs, that when a
nobleman in the good old days felt his end approaching, he assembled his sons at his bedside and made them swear on the pommel
of his sword that they would seek " *Fortune* " in the lands of foreign
lords, but add to the " *Gloire* " of their own House. Whether my
great-grandfather managed to do this I do not know, but in any
case his sons served in many lands. The eldest, Bernhard, and the
youngest, Karl, in Mecklenburg, where the first became, like his
father, Lord Chamberlain, the latter Chief of the Chancellery and
one of the most valiant and original of all Mecklenburg feudal
figures. Frederick became Chief Forester, in Württemberg, under
stout King Frederick, who was a great Nimrod in the face of the
Lord. Henry entered the Prussian service and married Gabriele
von Humboldt, the daughter of William Humboldt. After he
had been Prussian ambassador in London from 1827-1841, and
Prussian envoy to the Federal Diet in Frankfort from 1841-1842,
he took over the Ministry of Foreign Affairs in Berlin in the latter
year. After barely three years of great expectation and intense
activity, he was seized by a stroke of paralysis. He even drew up
his own request to resign. After he had signed it he handed back
the pen to his Legation Secretary, Count Henry Redern, with
the sad words: " A short career." He died a year later at the
age of fifty-three, and was laid to rest beside his father-in-law,
William Humboldt, in Tegel. Rugged German pine trees of the
Marches rustle over his tomb, surmounted by the slender dark
granite column on which is set a statue of Hope, fashioned in
immortal beauty by Thorwaldsen.

My grandfather, Adolf Bülow, went to Denmark as a young
man; he may have done so because his family was on friendly
terms with the House of Bernstorff, which, in the eighteenth
century, provided Denmark with two distinguished ministers.
Count Johann Hartwig Ernst, who was overthrown by Struensee,
deserved praise for increasing the prosperity of the Danish people.
His nephew, Andreas Peter, abolished serfdom among the Danish
peasantry. Both experienced the ingratitude of Princes. The
uncle was expelled from Denmark, and the nephew was harried
out of his post. " There are cases," he declared, when applying
for his dismissal, " when a minister cannot keep his post with a good
conscience. He loses his self-respect if he acts against his convictions. If he can no longer prevent misguided measures he must
not give his tacit consent to them." I remembered these words in
1909, as I drew up my own resignation.

Summoned from Kiel (where he first made himself familiar

with the Danish laws and language) to Copenhagen by Count
Christian Günther Bernstorff, who was Danish Minister for
Foreign Affairs from 1800 to 1810, and held the same portfolio
in Prussia from 1818 to 1832, my grandfather was first placed in
the Chancellery, and later in the Ministry of Finance, and not only
won the confidence of the ministers, but also of King Frederick VI.
In Copenhagen he married Susanna Baudissin, whom he had got
to know at Kiel. It was a perfect love-match. Falling ill from
overwork, he was appointed to Cismar, in East Holstein. He was
only there a year before he died at the age of twenty-nine. The
east coast of Holstein and Cismar was visited by a severe storm on
the night of his death, and my grandmother's hair turned snow-
white in a single night. Her age at the time was not quite twenty-
six. Ten years later she married a second time, becoming the wife
of Hans Adolph von Warnstedt, the Master of the Hunts and
Forests in Holstein.

To her second husband she bore only daughters. My favourite
aunt was the third daughter Elise. She married Count George
von Platen-Hallermund, whose family, Pomeranian by origin, was
raised to the status of Imperial Barons in 1630, and in 1689 to that
of Imperial Counts. The Platen-Hallermund family had been
ennobled into the Westphalian "Assembly of Counts," and
mediatised during the Vienna Congress to please the King of
Hanover, who was also King of England. Their elevation to these
ranks, and even inclusion among the mediatised nobility, enriched,
in my opinion, the Platen family less than the fact that they produced
a poet, Count Augustus Platen-Hallermund, who, although he
could not be addressed as " *Princeps Poetarum Germaniæ* " (as was
inscribed upon his tomb at Syracuse) is one of the greatest among
German writers. I have often visited my aunt Elise and her pro-
Guelph husband at their beautiful Holstein estate at Kaden, near
Ulzburg. He was a brother of Count Adolph Platen, who, when
war broke out in 1866, was Hanoverian Foreign Minister, and,
after the annexation of Hanover, was in charge of Guelph propaganda. Years before 1866 he had been on good personal terms
with Bismarck, which did not prevent the latter from having him
sentenced to several years' imprisonment because of his political
activities. The sentence, it is true, was passed *in contumaciam*, for
Adolph Platen (who, by the way, was a friend of my father's in
their boyhood and student days) had in the meantime left the
country. My father, Bismarck and Platen were all about the same
age; Adolf Platen having been born on 12th December, 1814,
Bismarck on 1st April, 1815, and my father on 2nd August, 1815.

My father's youngest sister married a Herr von Messmer-Saldern, whose father had come to North Germany as a knight in the entourage of the emigré Count of Provence, then later King Louis XVIII. This clever Frenchman succeeded in winning the hand of a rich Holstein heiress, a Fräulein von Saldern. The marriage went very badly. Like a true Frenchman, M. de Messmer never learned German. His wife, to annoy him, would not allow the children to be taught French. The result was that the father and children lived in the same house without being able to understand one another.[1] "A happy family," as the English say in such cases.

My grandmother's daughters held the same political views as their mother, looking back and idealising the good old days. Only once while I was in office were they really pleased with me, and that was when I received the Danish Order of the Elephant, which their grandfather and my grandfather, Karl Baudissin, had also received. In their defence I must add that the Danish Order of the Elephant is in very good taste. An elephant of white enamel supports a red tower on its head, and in the sockets of its eyes glitter two diamonds. It is also one of the oldest of the great European orders, having been founded by King Christian I in 1464.

In Flottbek and in Plön, in Altona and in Kiel, in Rantzau and in Caden and everywhere else in Holstein most political talk was concerned with the Schleswig-Holstein question. Lord Palmerston once declared that this question had been understood by nobody except a German professor who, he added, most unfortunately went mad with the mental strain of it, when about to give the world his results. Prince Bismarck used the extraordinarily difficult and complicated Schleswig-Holstein question to liberate the Duchies from Danish rule, and in so doing, began the masterful policy that led to Versailles via Sadowa and Sedan, and established German unity, a thing that nobody before him had accomplished. He attained his object through a Prussian hegemony, that was exercised by the Imperial and Prussian Government and by the Prussian army, with full and conscientious consideration for the rights and sentiments of the individual states on a federal basis. The Schleswig-Holstein problem, which the National Assembly of 1848, the German Federal Diet and every European cabinet had tried to solve, became the lever with which the genius of Bismarck achieved its purpose. Bismarck, whose work was never more masterly than it was in the days between his appointment to the Premiership

[1] English in text.

and the Peace of Prague, once told my father that it had been a test of strength such as could be endured only once in a lifetime.

The Schleswig-Holstein question became acute with the awakening of national consciousness among all the peoples of Europe. In some the consciousness developed more slowly than in others, in some it was strong, in others weak. In the old days, as Heinrich Voss has said, the Danish ploughman had understood the German, and the German the Dane. Like every great historical movement, the awakening of national sentiment had its dark as well as its bright aspects. The relations between the European states were made more difficult. Despite their self-seeking, their frivolity, and their intrigues, it was easier to arrive at compromises and understandings between cabinets than between peoples who were heated, passionate and often blind. The Austrian monarchy fell because of the exaggerated insistence on nationalism, and Teutonism has lost wide and priceless territories in Bohemia, Carinthia, Hungary, Croatia, Galicia and the Bukovina. The weakness of German national sentiment usually led to the defeat of the Germans in the national struggle, both with the Latin and Magyar races, as well as with the Poles and Czechs.

There were two opposing tendencies in Denmark after 1848: The one state party desired to maintain the Danish monarchy in its complete whole, it wished to keep Holstein for the Danish crown, and for this reason to respect German rights and feelings in Schleswig. The largest part of the Danish nobility, which is frequently of German origin, and the bulk of officialdom, industry and commerce were of this persuasion. The so-called " Eider Danes " laid no weight on Holstein. They would have been glad to have got rid of it like Lauenburg, but they wished to make Schleswig Danish as far as the Eider. At their head stood the fervent Orla Lehmann, a renegade German and cousin of the founder of the German National Party in Holstein, Theodor Lehmann. Only too often were ex-German subjects to be found among Germany's enemies, even in Russia and Poland, Hungary and Bohemia.

In autumn of 1862 my father decided to hand in his resignation as Danish Minister, since he became more and more convinced that in face of the growing influence of Eider-Danish tendencies the duties of Danish Minister were incompatible with his German nationality and outlook. After he had personally handed in his resignation to King Frederick VII, he said to my brother Adolf and me after morning prayers on his return to Flottbek: " I have taken leave of the Danish service, and so now you two are completely and finally German. You do not know yet what that will mean for your whole future, but in time you will understand." I cannot say that my brother and I were greatly affected by my father's announcement. We had always considered ourselves German, we did not speak a word of Danish, and had never been to Copenhagen, which I saw for the first time ten years later. We knew nothing about Danish history, except that Gorm the Old had been the first of the Danish kings, that Canute the Great had conquered England, that the Danebrog fell from Heaven, and that for a long time all Danish kings had been named Frederick and Christian alternately.

Later my father told us about his audience with King Frederick VII. The King received him at Flensburg. My father had stood in great favour with Frederick VII's predecessor, Christian VIII. The old Landgrave Alexis von Hessen-Philipps-thal-Barchfeld told me that not long before the death of the latter (which occurred on 20th June, 1848) he had been commanded to tea at the same time as my father. A lady of the court had declared that Herr von Bülow had beautiful hands. The King had replied audibly: " I don't know whether he has beautiful hands or not, but I do know that he has one of the best heads in my kingdom." Christian VIII was a cultivated and intellectual man. He bore a certain similarity to King Frederick William IV of Prussia, who was a friend of his. His son and successor, Frederick VII, was made of different stuff. He was one of the strangest princes who has ever sat on a throne. His love for romancing and boasting, which I have encountered in other princes also, took a pathological form in his case. When Napoleon III, soon after the birth of the Prince Imperial, created the Helena Medal for all those who had served Napoleon I in the field, Frederick VII asked the French ambassador, Dotézac, who was sitting opposite him at dinner, why he had not received the medal. Very embarrassed, M. Dotézac replied that the medal was in principle only bestowed upon those who had taken part in Napoleon's battles. With a serious expression on his face the Danish King answered: " I will divulge to you a great secret. I took part in the Battle of Waterloo. Yes, really. In the spring of 1815, when I was seven years of age, I ran away from my parents and took part in the battle as a drummer-boy. What I have revealed to you has always been a secret until now."

Frederick VII was married three times, first to a cousin, Princess Wilhelmina of Denmark, and the second time to Princess Caroline of Strelitz. His first wife got a divorce from him after

LUISE VICTORINE VON BÜLOW, NÉE RÜCKER, MOTHER OF PRINCE BÜLOW

nine years, the latter only managed to stand him for five. His third marriage was to a milliner named Rassmussen, whom he raised to the rank of Countess. Among Frederick's other bad characteristics was his drunkenness. Countess Danner, which was the title adopted by the former milliner, also shared this weakness, and was therefore specially liked by her exalted consort. My mother had always refused to allow herself to be presented to the Countess Danner while my father was in the Danish service, and he fully agreed with her attitude. When my father, in 1862, appeared before the last Danish King of the royal male line of the House of Oldenburg, the King asked him in his gruff, friendly tone to sit facing him. The King himself sat at a table on which were strewn a number of long and short pencils. The King spoke German with my father, who did not know Danish particularly well. He asked him why he wished to resign, and begged him to remain, because he had such a good mind. The Danish ministers also wished him to stay on, although they knew that he was an opponent of the Eider Danish tendency, to which most of them adhered. My father retorted that there were two reasons why he could not remain. In the first place he could no longer, being a German, take part in the policy by means of which the Eider Danes were trying to make Schleswig Danish, and, in the second, he was convinced that this policy of the Copenhagen democrats would lead to war with the Germanic powers, a war that would mean the destruction of the old and venerable Danish monarchy. " Do not worry," Frederick VII replied. " Look at this table, the three small pencils represent the Austrians, the Prussians and the other states of the German union who are advancing against me: the two large pencils represent the Danevirke and the earthworks of Düppel, where I shall await them and beat them." The king obstinately clung to this conception. In spite of his peculiarities and weaknesses, Frederick VII was very popular in Denmark proper. Since the House of Oldenburg had succeeded to the throne he was the first national Danish king, and it was on this account that both his domestic peculiarities and his drunkenness were forgiven him.

A few months after my father had left the Danish service with every honour, including the Grand Cross of the Danebrog Order and the Danish title of Excellency, the Grand Duke of Mecklenburg-Strelitz made enquiries as to whether he would be willing to take over the position of Chief Minister at Strelitz, vacant by the death of von Bernstorff. The Grand Duke had heard of my father through his Hessian and Danish relatives, and had even met him once at Rumpenheim. My father discussed the suggestion with my mother in detail in the presence of us children as we sat round the lamp after dinner. He went over the advantages and disadvantages of the new post. A little nook like Neu-Strelitz with hardly 7,000 inhabitants would not be exactly exciting after the animated and interesting life of Frankfort. Since his school and university days he had only lived in the big centres: Copenhagen, Paris, London, Hamburg, Frankfort. But a quiet life had its advantages, too, and boredom was good for the nerves. Without wishing to make Cæsar his example, he said, who would rather have been the first in a village than second in Rome, he nevertheless felt that even the smallest district, if well cultivated, might bring forth precious fruits. Nor could he forget the fact that there was a good gymnasium at Strelitz for his sons. Besides Mecklenburg had been the cradle of his family. So the post in Strelitz was accepted.

CHAPTER V

Mecklenburg—Country, People and Constitution—Neu-Strelitz—Grand Duke Frederick William—The " Gymnasium Carolinum "—Virgil or Vergil ?—First Acquaintance with Berlin (1863)—Journey to South Germany—Summer at Doberan—Düppel and Alsen—Neu- and Alt-Strelitz—My Contemporary Ewald Wohlfahrt—Neu-Brandenburg—Fritz Reuter—Walking Tour on Rügen with the Hereditary Grand Duke Adolf Frederick (1864).

IN the spring of 1863 we set out for our new home, which was in reality our old one. We travelled by train from Hamburg to Schwerin, and from there in a carriage to Strelitz. For the first time in my life I saw real north German country,

> " *Endlos die weissgraue Strasse sich spannt.*
> *Blassgelb und ährenschwer*
> *Dehnt sich ein Feldermeer—*
> > *Norddeutsches Land.*
>
> *Bläulich Wacholdergrün schattet den Sand.*
> *Rübacker lustig glänzt,*
> *Knallrot von Mohn umkränzt—*
> > *Norddeutsches Land. . . .*
>
> *Wolken stehn unbewegt gleich einer Wand.*
> *Fern eine Sense klingt.*
> *Rastlos das Heimchen singt—*
> > *Norddeutsches Land. . . .* [1]

[1] The grey-white road stretches endlessly.
Pale yellow and heavy with the ears of corn
A sea of fields spreads out.
> North German Land.

Bluish green of the elders overshadows the sand.
The turnip fields shine cheerfully, wreathed
Round with bright red poppies—
> North German Land.

The clouds stand motionless like a wall.
A scythe sings far off.
The cricket chirps ceaselessly—
> North German Land.

Sonne stieg dunkelrot nieder and schwand.
Dämmer umschummert es,
Müde entschlummert es—
        Norddeutsches Land." [1]

The landscape was very different from that which surrounds Frankfort, different even from Holstein and the Elbe, and yet it seemed like home to us. At Neu-Strelitz things no longer looked as they had done in the days described by Fritz Reuter. Civilization, which spreads all over the globe, had, although timidly, ventured even as far as Neu-Strelitz since the age when Adolf Frederick IV, the "Most Serene Highness of Mecklenburg-Strelitz" had "resided" with "his dear sister Princess Chrystal, up in his castle at Neu-Strelitz." [2] It is true that conditions in Mecklenburg were still very different from those in the rest of Germany in constitutional respects. Mecklenburg rejoiced in a mediaeval feudal constitution, and was therefore the *bête noire* of German Liberalism. The truth was that Liberalism in this, as in many other cases, judged according to abstract theory, in which it believes as rigidly as Christians who accept the literal inspiration of the gospels do in their dogmas. On the other hand, one of the most famous constitutionalists of the 'fifties asserted that Mecklenburg had the best constitition in Germany. My father, too, was a friend and a defender of guild and corporative representation. I myself have never concealed the fact that in politics I hold no dogmatic beliefs. I once said in the Reichstag that I was no fetish-worshipper and did not practise idolatry. In opposition to Frederick Naumann, who was a doctrinaire of the purest water and had carried his dogmatism from his pastorate into his politics, I pointed out that the welfare and the liberty of the country do not depend exclusively or even predominantly, on its constitution, or even on its electoral system. "Do you really believe," I asked, " that Mecklenburg, so denounced by the deputy Naumann, is much worse governed than a complete democracy like Haiti?"

Every year my father attended the sessions of the Mecklenburg Diet, which met alternately in Malchin and in Sternberg. In this

---

[1] The sun sank dark red and vanished.
   Twilight descends upon it,
   Wearied slumbers:
        North German Land.

[2] Reuter writes Opitz-German, a kind of equivalent to our own Elizabethan "Euphimism": the quotations are as follows: " (mit seiner) Leiwe Swester de Prinzess Christel up sinen Sloss tau Nigen-Strelitz."

way I got to know both little towns, for I was allowed to visit him
in one or the other. Malchin was on the shore of a pleasant lake
in a pretty district which the Mecklenburgers pompously called
" Mecklenburg Switzerland." Sternberg owned a church built
at the beginning of the fourteenth century and dedicated to St. Mary
and St. Nicholas, a beautiful triple-naved early Gothic building.
In the tower of the church there is a much-admired fresco representing the Mecklenburg Diet that met at the time of the Reformation on the Sagsdorf Bridge, near Sternberg. The fresco is surrounded by the coats of arms of the native Mecklenburg families,
among them the fourteen balls of the Bülow device. "*Vierteyn
Klümp in enen Schapen, Seyn dat reckte Bülowsch Wapen.*"[1]

So an old saying has it in Mecklenburg. Unhappily, the now-
so-peaceful little town of Sternberg was the scene of a gruesome
crime in the Middle Ages. The rumour spread in the town that
Jews had been guilty of inflicting " martyrdom " on sacred wafers,
that is to say, of piercing the wafers with a needle. Thereupon all
Jews in Sternberg were burnt alive before the Lucknow Gate on a
hill that is still called the " Jew's Hill." So it was done on 24th
October, 1492, in the name of a religion, the pillars of which are
the Sermon on the Mount and the thirteenth chapter of the first
Epistle to the Corinthians. Nor did the tragedy lack its grotesque
feature, for in the church at Sternberg town a stone in the wall
was pointed out on which were the chiselled marks of two human
feet. The legend was, that after the wafers had been pierced in
the house of the Jew, Eleasar, his wife, driven by unrest and the
qualms of conscience, tried to drown them in the Sternberger Lake.
While doing this she stepped on a stone that lay on the shore.
Suddenly she perceived that her feet were sinking into the stone,
so hurried back, filled with terror. Jews were banished from the
whole of Mecklenburg until the seventeenth century. They were
not allowed to come back to Sternberg until the eighteenth. No
Jews were allowed to settle in Rostock and Wismar when I was a
boy.

My father's Schwerin colleague, the Minister of State, Jasper
von Oertzen, attended the discussions in the Diet, just as my
father did. He was an honest, though somewhat narrow-minded,
man. He shared the cares of government with his eldest son.
When Bismarck got to know them both personally at the time
when the formation of the North German Federation was being
discussed, he said: " I see the father and the son, but I do not see
the Holy Ghost."

[1] Fourteen spheres in one heap are the true Bülow crest.

Neu-Strelitz is the youngest of all Mecklenburg towns, and has neither historical memories nor ancient monuments. How different is Schwerin, where we halted in the journey from Hamburg to Strelitz! Four Bülows had sat in the Episcopal chair of Schwerin: Bishop Gottfried from 1292 till 1314, who completed Schwerin Cathedral, a beautiful Gothic building, and after him his two nephews, the brothers Bishop Rudolph, from 1331 to 1339, and Bishop Henry I, from 1339 to 1347. Finally the nephew of both, the artistic Bishop Frederick, from 1366 to 1375. We admired the tombstones under which these venerable princes of the church had slept for more than five centuries. They are among the most important artistic treasures that Northern Germany can show. The castle in Schwerin is also splendid. Its towers, turrets and gilt cupolas are mirrored in the Schwerin and Burg lakes. Schwerin could not compare even with Ludwigslust, the Mecklenburg Potsdam, not to speak of Rostock, the old Hanseatic town, which at that time still commanded the greatest mercantile fleet of the Baltic. The tower of St. Peter's Church, in Rostock, is the highest in Mecklenburg. The seafarer sees it when still five or six miles from the coast. I heard this when I was a small boy, and later on my dear friend, the poet Adolph Wilbrandt, who was a native of Rostock, confirmed it. Field-Marshal Blücher, to whom Gottfried Schadow erected a magnificent monument, was born in Rostock in the Altbettelmönchstrasse. Blücher, the hero, stands there just as he lives in the hearts of the German people. In his outstretched right he holds his Field-Marshal's bâton, his left rests on the hilt of his sword, and his left foot is advanced. The inscription runs: " To Prince Blücher von Wahlstatt, from his Own People." On the back are Goethe's beautiful lines:

> " Im Harren und Krieg,
> In Sturz und Sieg
> Bewusst und gross,
> So riss er uns vom Feinde los." [1]

Wismar, which lay in the bosom of the Baltic, could not be compared with Rostock as a harbour, but was more interesting than Strelitz because in the Church of St. Mary there was a screen of such admirable work that legend says the Devil helped the smith to forge it. This screen was said to be inimitable, a perfect work of art, made as though of interwoven threads. Even the walled and fortified Friedland, the second town of the Grand-Duchy

---

[1] While watching and waiting, in war, in disaster and in rioting, conscious and great, he tore us from the enemy.

of Strelitz, which was situated not far from Neu-Strelitz, did not excite our imagination more than the capital of the state, our new residence.

Neu-Strelitz, which was founded in 1730, was built in the form of a star with eight points. It is planned rather like Karlsruhe, which was built about the same time. A prince's will had ordained that both towns should conform to symmetrical rather than to picturesque standards. Eight roads radiated from the Strelitz Market Place, where there was a memorial to the Grand-Duke George, the father of Queen Louise. But, in my youth, at least, one of these roads was badly constructed, and another did not run quite straight, which unfortunately spoilt the impression of the whole. The pride of the Neu-Strelitzers was the garden of the castle, with its magnificent avenues of limes and chestnuts, which joined it with the great Schlosskoppel park on the shores of the Zierker Lake, full of quiet shady paths. I spent many beautiful spring mornings there with my little friend Hanne, a gardener's little girl. We teased one another, we played together, picked flowers, kissed one another, bathed in the clear lake as innocent as Daphnis and Chloe in Longo's pastoral novel, which so delighted Goethe and Stendhal. A half-century later the last Grand Duke of Mecklenburg-Strelitz shot himself in this idyllic Schlosskoppel as a result of his unfortunate love for an Italian singer, a "*femme fatale*," who would neither appease him nor let him go. My good little Hannchen was, God be thanked, no "*femme fatale*." I preserve a pleasant memory of her.

When we were free from school during the more agreeable seasons of the year my parents used to take my brother Adolf and me for drives through the countryside on visits to relatives. We drove with two elegant brown horses which we named Cleobis and Biton in honour of the two magnificent youths of Argos, whom, as Herodotus tells in his first book of Histories, Solon the Wise held up to the foolish King Crœsus as examples of truly happy mortals. My great-grandfather, the High Chamberlain of Mecklenburg-Schwerin, Bernhard Joachim von Bülow, was twice married: first to Elizabeth von der Lühe, of the Barnekow family, and secondly to Charlotte von Oertzen, of the Gorow family. The Oertzens and the Lühes, like the Bülows, belonged to what in those days were called "native families." They belonged, as did my own family, to the hereditary Mecklenburg nobility. My grandfather's sisters had married respectively a Herr von Engel, from Breesen, and a Baron von Meerheimb, from Wokrent. Both these families had won their position by the sword. Colonel

Hans Joachim Engel was ennobled by the Swedish King Charles XI, and thereupon received into the Mecklenburg nobility. Henry Mehr, a clever man who had risen from trumpeter to the rank of general in the military service of the Electorate of Saxony was raised to the status of Baron by the Emperor Leopold, and also received into the nobility.

At every visit I was impressed with the prowess of my Mecklenburg relatives and friends as trenchermen. "*Aet du man langsam min Sön, du glövest nicht, wat sich dahldrucken lätt*"[1] was an admonition which the peasants of Mecklenburg often addressed to their sons. The procession of meals during the day of a Mecklenburg peasant was described to us as follows: Early in the morning before starting work in the fields a solid breakfast was eaten, followed at about eight o'clock by a " second breakfast " (called " little lunch "), " *Hochimpt*," or " *Kleinmittag*," equally solid, and accompanied by beer or brandy. When he went back to work again he took with him, as a precaution, lest his stomach should feel a little faint, a good supply of bread and butter. The main meal of the day came at twelve o'clock, and consisted of beef, bacon, ham, potatoes, peas or beans and fresh vegetables, according to the season, the latter however, hardly being included as a filling portion of the meal. At five o'clock came the peasant's equivalent for tea, and when the day's work was, happily, done, the final big evening meal. The proverb " *One is what one eats* " is not unjustified. The Mecklenburgers were and are a lusty race, not very nimble-witted, but men of deep emotions, clear heads, and sober judgment. They are, as the Apostle James said, in praise of his brothers, slow of speech and slow to anger. But when roused to anger, they hit hard.

Mecklenburg is the native city of Gebhard Lebrecht von Blücher and Hellmuth von Moltke, both the sons of local very ancient aristocratic families, of Johann Heinrich Voss and Adolf Wilbrandt. Prince Bismarck said to a Mecklenburg deputation which paid its respects in Friedrichsruh in 1893: " By being a Brandenburger, and a neighbour of Mecklenburg of the Old Marches, and later by being a Prussian and Imperial official, I have had much to do with Mecklenburgers and have found them eminent in ability and industry. Among those deserving of special mention are the Bülows and the Bernstorffs, who have been in our military and civil service, and who have left their mark upon this favoured land between the Elbe and the Baltic."

The Grand Duke Frederick William of Mecklenburg-Strelitz

[1] " Eat slowly, my son, you can't believe how much you can cram down."

was blind. He shared this fate with his cousin and friend King George V of Hanover, with the only difference that the Grand Duke did not try to conceal his blindness, while the King obstinately tried to maintain the illusion that he could see. King George V liked to compliment ladies on their dresses. " You are wearing a beautiful yellow dress," or " That red dress suits you particularly well," he would say to any lady of the Court. Naturally the adjutant attending him had to whisper in his ear who the lady before him was and how she was dressed. Nevertheless, in spite of this weakness, the last King of Hanover was a very estimable person. Of royal appearance and carriage, he was high-minded and generous, but he had an exaggerated and mystical conception of his dignity and of his calling. Baron Hammerstein-Loxten, who was Prussian Minister of Agriculture from 1897 to 1901, and was in his youth in close proximity to King George V, said to me on more than one ccasion that, in spite of many differences, the Emperor William II, in his peculiar and not at all Frederician conception of his royal duties, reminded him of his former master, King George V. Both were inclined towards overweening pride. William II assured his Brandenburgers that he would lead them towards a magnificent future. King George declared, not long before he lost his throne, that the magnificence of the Guelphs would last to the end of time.

The Grand Duke of Mecklenburg-Strelitz was far removed from such extravagances. He was of a sober mentality, with decided knowledge of financial questions. Twice a year he summoned his Berlin Banker, Helfft, to Strelitz and gave him his instructions, which usually led to very successful operations on the Stock Exchange. His view of the world situation (which, because of his blindness, was based on extracts read from the papers by his secretaries) was nearly always correct. He left behind him a great fortune which his avarice had enormously enlarged. When he celebrated his golden wedding, he gave every one of his subjects a taler. Since his land contained scarcely a hundred thousand inhabitants, this wealthy ruler's whim only cost him 300,000 marks. National sentiment in the modern sense of the word was lacking in the Grand Duke. He was a strong legitimist, with conservative tendencies in everything, and fundamentally of the opinion that Germany would have to adapt herself to whatever London and St. Petersburg wished.

His only brother, Prince George of Strelitz, had married the Russian Grand Duchess Catherine Mikhailovna, and had entered the Russian service. The Grand Duke himself was married to an

English princess, the daughter of the Duke of Cambridge. The father and the brother of the Grand Duchess were English Field-Marshals. The Grand Duke was so enthusiastic about his relationship with the English Royal Family that all persons accredited to the Strelitz Court, Chamberlains, and Gentlemen of the Bed-chamber, had to have the " *Honi soit qui mal y pense* " of the Order of the Garter on the gold buttons of their court dress. If the Grand Duke said the Tsar would have wished this or that, it was as if God himself had spoken. For Austria he felt the respect that people who have been well brought up feel for an elderly and very dignified great-uncle. He did not like Prussia, although Queen Louise, one of the noblest women of all times, one of the most touching figures in German history, came of the House of Strelitz and closed her beautiful eyes in the Strelitz castle of Hohenzieritz.

The Grand Duchess Augusta was English to the finger tips, besides being very broad-minded and artistic, and a great lover of music. She was the aunt of Queen Mary of England. The Grand Duke's mother, then nearly seventy, the widow of the Grand Duke George, was a daughter of the Landgrave Frederick of Hessen. She had only to come into a room to make old times seem vivid and actual. Her father, who died at the age of ninety in 1837, had known Frederick the Great, Maria Theresa, the Empress Catherine II and Louis XV. Her husband was the brother of Queen Louise of Prussia. Her only daughter, Duchess Caroline, whose melancholy was attributed to the sad experiences of her marriage with a habitual drunkard and eccentric, was the divorced wife of King Frederick VII of Denmark. She was a gentle, dignified lady, and, in her way, also " a beautiful soul."

My brother Adolf and I developed a deep friendship with the heir to the Grand Duchy, who was only a year older than I was. He was a kind, understanding, lively boy. We used to go for walks with him, and we had dancing lessons together. We danced the Waltz, Polka, Mazurka, Française and Lancers, and the Minuet as well. Even to-day, I find the Minuet more graceful and æsthetic than the Shimmy and Foxtrot.

My brother Adolf and I were put in the Lower Fourth Form in the Strelitz Gymnasium (the Gymnasium Carolinum). The boys of the school met us on very friendly terms. They used to speak Low German together, a language that gives me a feeling of home even to-day when I hear its dear sound. We had many new and interesting things to tell and describe to our fellow pupils, things of which they knew nothing. They confessed that they had never seen a mountain and had never seen a donkey either (at least not one with four legs). They had never been in a railway train. The fact that we had climbed the Feldberg in the Taunus, that we had ridden on donkeys to Falkenstein and Königstein, travelled from Frankfort to Hamburg by railway, impressed them very much, or rather impressed them " *bannig*,"[1] as they say in Low German. We were the only nobles in the form, and were therefore known as the " junkers," though, of course, without the disparaging connotation with which the expression "junker" is applied by people who call themselves Liberal to a whole class which for generations has provided the Fatherland with able and distinguished men, including, to name only a few, Bismarck, Hindenburg, Hardenberg, Blücher, Moltke, Seidlitz, Zieten, Werder, Göben, Heinrich von Kleist, Ulrich Wilamowitz-Möllendorf, Hans von Bülow, Detlev von Liliencron, and a good many others.

The teacher of our form, Professor Ladewig, taught me to appreciate Virgil. It is true that I do not put Virgil on the same level as the blind singer to whose birth seven Hellenic towns lay claim: Ὅμηρος λέξει καί διανοίᾳ πάντας ὑπερβέβληκε so Aristotle wrote. Even the Roman Quintilian had to admit: " *Hic omnes sine dubio, et in omni genere eloquentiae procul a se reliquit.*" But the poet of the Aeneid, the Eclogues and the Georgics does merit a seat at the summit of Parnassus. He deserves more appreciation than he usually receives in Germany. To make him better appreciated, Professor Ladewig, published the Aeneid with learned notes and a commentary. But the pride of his life was to establish beyond doubt that the Swan of Mantua was called, not Virgilius, but Vergilius.

The Head of the Strelitz Gymnasium, the excellent Professor Schmidt, lived to a ripe old age. He died in 1904, and was happy in living to see his one-time Fifth Former become Imperial Chancellor. He was one of the best teachers I met during my school days. It was he that I had in mind when, at a reception given to German high school teachers while I was Imperial Chancellor, I said: " I consider myself to be among those *quibus magistri sui, educatores atque doctores cum grata recordatione in mente versantur.*"[2]

The French language was taught by Professor César Vilatte, who, together with Professor Sachs, published a well-known and excellent German-French dictionary in the Langenscheidt editions. He released my brother and myself from the French classes very soon, because we had as much command of the language as is

---

[1] " No end."

[2] Prince Bülow's *Speeches.* Large edition, vol. iii, p. 256. Small edition, vol. v, p. 251.

possible for non-Frenchmen, and even ran the risk of losing our good pronunciation in the linguistic exercises at the Carolinum Gymnasium. This was not flattering for our stalwart school comrades, but I cannot deny that the language of Racine and Mme. de Sévigné sounded strange when spoken with the broad Mecklenburg accent.

In the year 1863 I travelled for the first time from Strelitz to Berlin with my father. There was no railway connection between the two towns in those days, and the journey had to be done by post-chaise. It was important to get a corner seat in good time. The middle seat was not pleasant, unless you happened to be sitting between two pretty ladies. The journey was very slow and lasted from morning to night. The first station was Fürstenberg. Not far from there was the estate of a certain Herr von Valdoy, of whom legend said that he had experienced the same emotions as Schiller's Knight of Toggenburg, who, with pale face, looks at the window behind which, calm and mild, sits his adored angel. Herr von Valdoy, according to the rumour, felt very much this way towards the melancholy Princess Caroline of Strelitz, who could not rid herself of the sad recollection of her marriage with Frederick VII of Denmark. A longish halt was made at Oranienburg, where we were able to admire a castle built by the consort of the Great Elector. We did not reach Berlin until evening approached.

On the next day I went for a walk with my good father in the Unter den Linden and through the Wilhelmstrasse, where both he and I were to spend long and industrious years. My father looked up his Frankfort friend, Herr von Bismarck, who had been Prussian Premier and Foreign Minister for eight months. While he was talking with the Premier in his study I chatted with his children, who were skylarking in the corridors and on the staircase, the entrance to which was guarded by two sphinxes. When we returned to the Hotel de Rome, where we used to stay, my father told me that he had found Bismarck in a good and brave mood, in spite of all the attacks and some crude slanders which the Democrats had levelled against him. " I shall win through," Bismarck had said to my father, " and I shall be able to deal with the Democrats, provided the King remains true to me—and that he will, for he thinks and feels like a nobleman." The phrase: " He thinks and feels like a nobleman," which I often heard him utter later on, was, in Prince Bismarck's eyes, the highest praise that could be given.

My father and I (it was a pleasure to be in his company) wanted to see mountain scenery again, so we made an excursion to Regensburg, Augsburg, Munich, and back via Baden-Baden. From Regensburg we visited the Valhalla, the "Temple of German Honour," erected by King Louis I of Bavaria. I never dreamed that the time would come when I, as German Imperial Chancellor, would make a speech on the occasion of the unveiling of the marble bust of my great predecessor, Herr Otto von Bismarck-Schönhausen, who was so venomously attacked by the Liberals and so crudely abused by the Democrats. In Baden-Baden I saw Queen Augusta of Prussia for the first time. One evening she visited the Duchess Dorothea Talleyrand and Dino (by birth a Princess of Courland) who was staying in the same hotel as she and ourselves. Two flunkeys, carrying lighted torches, preceded her when she had said farewell to the Duchess and walked down the steps to her suite on the ground floor. Queen Augusta was still a beautiful woman in those days. In her youth the Duchess Dorothea had sweetened the old age of Prince Talleyrand, and in her old age the life of Prince Lichnowsky, who was murdered by the mob on Bornheim Heath, near Frankfort, on the 18th September, 1848.

We spent the late summer of 1863 at the seaside resort of Heiligendamm, near Doberan. It was not as patriarchal as it had been when there was still a public gambling casino there, and the bluff Grand Duke Paul Frederick of Mecklenburg-Schwerin, the husband of Princess Alexandra of Prussia, a daughter of King Frederick William III and sister of our old Emperor William, loved to sit in his shirt sleeves when he held the bank on hot days. But the court still took part in the table d'hôte, which went off in a homely fashion without constraint or special formalities. Doberan had an interesting past, about which my father enlightened me, for he possessed far-reaching historical knowledge and was, in the goodness of his heart, very communicative with us children. He told us that as far back as the twelfth century the Cistercian monastery of Doberan had been founded by the Wendish prince Pribislav II. Doberan once had great wealth, for it had relics that had established its reputation and made it the goal of pilgrimages from Denmark, Sweden, and even more distant countries. Doberan was secularized at the time of the Reformation, and in the year 1793, the year of the Terror in France, the *Épouvantable année de lauriers et de sang grande ombre courronnée*, it became the leading German bathing resort. My father showed me round the church of Doberan, a Gothic building in the form of a cross, in the centre of which there is a steeple of moderate height. In the church he showed me the Bülow Chapel, which was founded "To the memory of his beloved," by the Schwerin Bishop Frederick II, who was descended from the Bülow family. The chapel had been endowed by the monk, Eckhart Bülow. I admired the pictorial representation of a Wendish chieftain over the door, uttering the words:

> " *Stah up—hör*
> *van de Dör!* " [1]

as he threatens a monster with his battle-axe. It evidently represented an energetic missionary who refused to stand any nonsense when it was his business to convert obdurate Wendish pagans. Inside the chapel and under the picture of a Bülow knight, there was the inscription:

> " *Wieck, Düvel, wieck, wieck wiet van my,*
> *Ik scheer my nig een Hoahr om dy.*
> *Ik bün ein Meckelbörgsch Edelmann,*
> *Wat geit dy, Düvel, mien Suupen an ?*
> *Ik suup mit mienen Herrn Jesu Christ,*
> *Wenn Du, Düvel, ewig dösten müsst,*
> *Und drink mit oen söst Kolleschahl,*
> *Wenn Du sitzt in der Höllenqual,*
> *Drum rahd ik: wieck, loop, rönn und gah!*
> *Sünst, by dem Düvel, ick tau schlah.*" [2]

The self-reliance which this Mecklenburger displays in his epitaph, even in face of the devil, the resolution with which he reserves his right to drink like a fish, are in the best spirit of Junkerdom. I may add that for æsthetic reasons I have used the word " straw " in place of a much coarser expression.

In January, 1864, it became evident that my father had spoken truly when, in conversation with King Frederick VII, he warned him against the inevitable consequences of the Eider Danish policy. In February the Danevirke was evacuated by the Danes. On the 18th April, 1864, the Prussians stormed the entrenchments at Düppel. It was the first mighty sweep of the Prussian Eagle's wing for half a century. In Mecklenburg, which had taken a brave part in the Wars of Liberation, there was general enthusiasm.

The Grand Duke's heir shared my ardour. He told me in confidence that his father's attitude towards the war the Germanic

---

[1] Stand up—away from the door.

[2] Away, Devil, away, away, far from me. I do not care a straw for you. I am a Mecklenburg nobleman. What has my supping to do with you? I sup with Jesus Christ, while you, Devil, must always thirst, and I drink raisin soup while you sit amid infernal torment. I therefore counsel you : away, run, run, and go! Else, by the Devil, I'll slay you.

Powers were waging against Denmark was cool, but that his mother, like the upper ten thousand in her English homeland, sympathized with the Danes. In the Lower Fourth Form of the gymnasium enthusiasm was very great, and we sung with full throats:

> " *Ob Meer auch und alpige Halden*
> *Vielmarkig zerteilen die Flur,*
> *Ihr Banner viel Fürsten entfalten:*
> *Ein Deutschland an Herzen ist's nur!*
> *Wohin sich der Sinn uns auch wende,*
> *Millionen, sie schlingen die Hände*
> *Zum grossen Bund, dem ein'gen Vaterland.*" [1]

In the enthusiasm which filled me when the Prussians stormed all the ten fieldworks of Düppel with fierce courage and planted the black-white flag upon them, and when, two months later, they effected the crossing to the island of Alsen, and the Danes were beaten everywhere and driven back on Fünen, I said to my father: " Now we are a great people. We are greater than the English and the French." My father replied gravely: " We have not gone so far as that by a long way. We lack the national consciousness, the national pride of the French and the English. We quarrel among ourselves much too often." In this connection I heard for the first time the cruel words of Goethe that the German is efficient as an individual, but is wretched when taken in the mass.

My father often took his walks with me in Strelitz, just as he used to do in Frankfort. We specially liked to go from Neu-Strelitz to Alt-Strelitz. The road passed over a little hill where a strong wind sometimes blew. When once I complained about this wind, my father replied: " Get used to the fact that strong winds have a habit of blowing across heights. This is as true of the heights of life as of this little hill." My father also once said to me: " He who can govern Alt-Strelitz well will also be able to cope with Neu-Strelitz. And he who has the stuff in him to manage the affairs of the Grand Duchy of Mecklenburg-Strelitz is also capable of governing a greater land. The same capacities are in demand here as they are there. In chess it is the same thing fundamentally, whether the pieces you play with are wooden or silver or gold."

Alt-Strelitz was even smaller than Neu-Strelitz, and had scarcely 2,000 inhabitants. The judge in Alt-Strelitz was the

---

[1] Even if Alpine slopes divide the land into many fields and many Princes unfold their banners, there is only one Germany in the heart ! Wherever we turn, millions join their hands in the great ring, the united Fatherland.

father of my school friend Wohlfahrt, who was born on the same day as I was. We remained friends throughout our whole life. After he had passed his legal examinations with distinction, Ewald Wohlfahrt became Mayor of Alt-Strelitz. When he had shown his abilities in this position he rose to become Mayor of Neu-Strelitz. After he had climbed this rung of the ladder, he wrote to me that there was scarcely anything more that he wished. Providence was, however, so kind to him that after several years employment as Mayor of Neu-Strelitz, he was made a Grand-Ducal Councillor. He had himself photographed in his beautiful uniform, and sent me a copy. I used to regard him as one of the few really contented men I had met. But I had reckoned without the World War and the collapse of the old, happy Germany, which affected even these remote and quiet lives. My friend Wohlfahrt suffered under the misfortunes of the Fatherland, not only because he was such a true patriot, but also because he was fated to see so much of what he had cherished and fostered in his little district destroyed by the upheaval. He wrote to me about this in the spring of 1923: " If you had revisited Strelitz a few years ago, you would have felt yourself at home in the old town of the residency where discipline, order and cleanliness reigned. But now you would be astonished by the deplorable conditions which have existed here since 1919. I regret having to end my life here and daily having to see what I built up with such anxious care being torn down and destroyed. Those who used to be so eager for a single glimpse of his Serene Highness are now the most zealous supporters of the Republic, and have quickly forgotten how much gratitude we owe to our princely House for what it once did, and how much sympathy for what it now suffers. It is really no pleasure for one who was formerly *Consul Loci*, to have to witness and experience all these things; and not merely once, but day after day."

One of our great delights in Strelitz was riding. My brother Adolf and I were mounted on stallions from the Mecklenberg stud-farm, and skylarked about on the big grand-ducal racecourse. The stallions were not easy to ride: they kicked out, shied, bucked, and grazed against obstacles, and took special delight in rearing. We held on grimly to the manes of the great animals, looking like little monkeys clinging to the boughs of trees. But we soon became firm riders by this method. We made such progress that we rode without stirrups, first on a horse cloth and then on an English saddle. Riding without stirrups is a better way than any other to learn how to be on the alert, to maintain a good carriage on horse back and how to control the animal. Another great pleasure was skating,

which we were able to pursue for months at a time in severe Mecklenburg winters. Once as my brother Adolf and I were skating
on the Zierker lake I suddenly fell through the ice. There was a
warm spring at the bottom of the lake and the ice above it was
not strong enough to bear my weight. The water almost came
up to my mouth, but I trod water so as not to go under, and called
out to my brother to lie flat on his belly and throw me a long scarf
which he wore round his neck. In this way he was able to pull
me towards him until we reached a spot where the ice was again
thick enough to bear the weight of us both. We then continued
our run at an even quicker pace, restored ourselves at the other side
of the lake with hot and very stiff grog (which, at least in those
days could be described as the national drink of the Mecklenburgers)
and escaped without a cold.

Our parents allowed us to make excursions into the district
and long tramps as well to our heart's content. On one of these
excursions we chanced upon the " good town of Nigen-Bramborg."
Fritz Reuter was pointed out to us in a little inn in the town of
Neubrandenburg. He sat, very drunk, his head resting between
his hands, before a little wooden table on which stood many empty
bottles. It was known that Reuter had fallen into the habit of
drunkenness during the long sentence of fortress-imprisonment
which he had had to suffer because of the crazy Karlsbad Resolution.
Shortly before his death Fritz Reuter wrote in an album:

" Der Anfang, das Ende, o Herr, sie sind dein!
Die Mitte dazwischen, das Leben war meins
Und irrt' ich im Leben und fand mich nicht aus,
Bei dir, Herr, ist Klarheit, und licht ist dein Haus." [1]

His dear countrymen, the Mecklenburgers and Pomeranians,
will not forget the great poet of the Low German people, the poet
who will live on in the hearts of the whole German nation.

In the summer of 1864 we went on a magnificent walking tour
to Rügen with the good Adolf Friedrich, the heir to the Grand
Duchy, and his Hanoverian tutor, Captain von Petersdorf. We
were able to convince ourselves that in the northern parts of our
Fatherland there are landscapes as beautiful as those in the south
with which we had hitherto been familiar. We bravely tramped
five or six hours a day. At Stralsund we had a look at the winding

---

[1] The beginning and end, O Lord, are thine,
Betwixt these two was Life, and that was mine,
And if I erred in Life, lost in the night,
With you is clearness, and your dwelling light.

road where Ferdinand von Schill, the pious and courageous hero, fell. Over his grave I read Virgil's fitting words:

> " *Magna volluisse magnum.*
> *Occubuit fato: jacet ingens litore truncus*
> *Avulsumque caput: tamen haud sine nomine corpus.*"

Ernst Moritz Arndt had sung to him in his grave:

> " *Dann sattelt ein Reiter sein schnelles Pferd,*
> *Und schwingt ein Reiter sein blankes Schwert,*
> *So rufet er zornig: Herr Schill, Herr Schill,*
> *Ich an den Franzosen Euch rächen will.*" [1]

Before we began our trip to Rügen my father gave me the verses of a now long-forgotten poet, the tender Kosegarten:

> " *Empfange mich, alter Rügard!*
> *Mich lüstet zu schaun*
> *Mit staunendem Blick*
> *Die Riesengräber und Herthas Hain*
> *Die Küsten, die Inseln und das donnerade Meer.*" [2]

The charming gardens of Prince Putbus, who claimed descent from the Wendish chieftain Jaromir, pleased us more than the town of Putbus, which is called the Karlsruhe of Rügen, and with its tedious regularity does, indeed, call to mind the Baden residency.

We were delighted by the magnificent Granitzer forest and by the black, red-lined coats of the people in Mönkgut. We were told about a custom (which, incidentally, is not such a bad one) concerning the girls of Mönkgut who, when they want to marry, do their own wooing and call it the " hunt." " *Se stellt na em ut* "— " she sets her cap at him." On the Stubbenkammer, where Charles XII of Sweden had stood, and on which I stood many years later with William II, we enjoyed a magnificent sunset. We were struck with awe as we gazed upon the Hertha Lake. But what kindled us most of all was the northern promontory of Rügen,

---

[1] A rider then saddles his swift horse,
And a rider waves his bright sword.
He calls angrily " Herr Schill, Herr Schill !
I shall take vengeance on the French for you."

[2] Receive me, old Rügard !
I wish to see with astonished look,
The giant graves and Hertha's grove
The coasts, the islands, and the thundering sea.

Arkona, which we reached after an exhausting tramp through deep sand.

> " *Auf Ankonas Berge*
> *Ist ein Adlerhorst,*
> *Wo vom Schlag der Woge*
> *Seine Spitze borst.*
>
> *Spitze deutschen Landes*
> *Willst sein Bild du sein ?*
> *Riss' und Spalten splittern*
> *Deinen festen Stein.*
>
> *Adler, setz Dich oben*
> *Auf den Felsenthron*
> *Deutschen Landes Hüter,*
> *Freier Wolkensohn!* " [1]
>
> " *Liess der deutsche Kaiser*
> *Fliegen dich zugleich,*
> *Als er brach in Stücke,*
> *Ach, das deutsche Reich ?* " [2]

With these melancholy lines the poet, Wilhelm Müller, celebrated the northern promontory.

[1] There is an eagle's eyrie
On Arkona's hill whose
Peak was split by the
Impact of a wave.

Peak of German land
Willt thou be its image?
Rents and clefts
Split thy firm stone.

Eagle, perch up yonder
On the rocky throne,
Guardians of German land,
Free son of the clouds!

[2] Did the German Kaiser
Let you fly away at the time
When, alas, he broke in pieces
The German Empire?

CHAPTER VI

*The Pädagogium at Halle (1865 to 1867)—Life at the Pädagogium—
Professor Daniel and his Influence—Elocution—Fellow Pupils—
The People of Halle—Politics in Halle—Democracy and Liberalism
—Officials and Academic Circles Nearly all Against Bismarck—My
Confirmation in Halle (18.3.1866).*

WHEN we were back from our Rügen walking tour, my
father informed us that we were to go to another school,
to the Royal " Pädagogium " at Halle on the Saale, at
Easter in the following year. "I am sending you to a Prussian
school as your careers will no doubt be in Prussia some day so
that you will get used to the Prussian manner in good time." At
Strelitz we had got as far as the Sixth Form, but at Halle my father
made us join the Upper Fifth, so that we should not enter the
University too soon. " Good horses," he said, " run in harness
and must be held back, they do not need the whip to drive them
forward." It was hard for me and my brother Adolf to leave our
paternal home. At first we felt very home-sick at the Royal
Pädagogium, into which we were received as boarders. Our
parents, who had probably anticipated this, found some excuse
to make Hopf, who had hitherto been our tutor and was now
teaching my younger brothers in place of us, visit Halle. When
he asked us how we were getting on, we set our teeth and answered:
" Oh, first rate! " All the same, we must have looked pictures
of misery, but it was soon evident that Bismarck was right when
he said that the Prussian jacket rasps the skin at first, but that
it keeps you warmer than any other, and that you cannot do
without it.

We soon felt at home at the " Pädchen," as it was called by the
boys. It was a part of the magnificent Francke Foundation. Above the
main entrance there was a bright eagle aspiring to the sun. Underneath it was a Bible quotation in great, golden letters from Isaiah xl,
31 : " But they that wait upon the Lord shall renew their strength;
they shall mount up with wings as eagles; they shall run and not be
weary; and they shall walk, and not faint." It was in the spirit of this
quotation that August Hermann Francke, who was born in Lübeck
in 1663 and died in Halle, 1727, had established his Foundation

72

in 1698, a work unequalled by any other throughout the whole domain of the Evangelical Church. Once when seven guilders were collected in a poor-box attached to his house he said jubilantly: "That's honest capital! It will have to be used to found some good institute." He began by founding the Poor School, but since teaching alone does not mean education, he also planned an Orphans' Institute, the foundation stone of which was laid in 1698. This was the nucleus around which later everything crystallized. The two Gymnasiums, the Royal "Pädagogium," and the Latin School, the Modern School, a Girls' School, a School for the Sons of Gentlemen, a Girls' High School, a Free School, the big Canstein Bible Institute (where the Bible came from which I received at my Confirmation and still use), a mission, a book shop, a pharmacy, etc. The building in which the Pädchen was installed dated from the days of Francke, and was a solid, practical school building. In front of the Institute was the bronze statue of Francke, that hero of religion, modelled by Rauch. Among former pupils of the school were the pious founder of the brother-hood, Count Nicolas Zinzendorf, and the less religiously-minded poet, Gottfried August Bürger, the Vincke *Oberpräsident* of West-phalia, one of the best of all Prussian officials, who did such splendid work on Prussian reconstruction after Jena, Niemeyer, the University Chancellor, pupil and later director of the Francke Foundation, the poets Albert Knapp, Houwald and Göcking.

The head of the "Pädagogium" was Herr Kramer, the son-in-law of the founder of comparative geography, Karl Ritters. An erudite and impartial teacher and leader, but without the faculty of getting into close touch with his pupils or gaining their confidence. My relations with him remained cold from the day I joined the school to the day I left. The slight coughing and clearing of the throat which accompanied every sentence Kramer spoke seemed to ward off any intimacy. He generally used to hold a gold-rimmed eyeglass in his hand which gave him a somewhat distinguished air, but also removed any tendency to confide in him. A stoutish man in blue dress-coat with bright buttons used to follow him like a shadow. This was the school beadle, Küniger, who spoke with the broadest Saxon I have heard on the lips of any man except King Frederick Augustus III of Saxony. Our class teacher, Dryander, was a genuine philologist. He came from one of the old learned families of Halle which had Hellenised its original name of "Eichmann." This family also produced Ernst von Dryander, the Court chaplain, who, ever, in all circumstances, displayed such moral courage and loyalty. Herr Dryander pestered us with Greek grammar, with the accursed aorist, with optative and similar torments invented to torture his pupils. His acrimony often spoilt my pleasure in the classical authors that we read with him. But I am thankful to him for having made me learn a large number of Horatian odes by heart. My father used to say: " Happy is a man who in his youth has learned much by heart and who has copied out much." I am of the same opinion. What has been impressed upon the memory in youth remains fixed there. It becomes a κτῆμα ἐς αἰὶ to employ a magnificent expression of Thucydides. With regard to copying my father was of the opinion that the best and surest means of acquiring a clear and beautiful diplomatic style in German, as in French or English, was to copy well-written diplomatic dispatches.

None of my teachers exercised so great an influence upon my development as Professor Dr. Hermann Adalbert Daniel, the geographer and theologist of the Royal College at Halle. With the exception of my father it was he who influenced me most. Physically he was rather an astonishing phenomenon. A massive pot-belly, relatively weak legs, and small arms, gave him an uncouth appearance. He had the swaying and dragging gait of a duck, and his pupils, who were very fond of him, good-naturedly nicknamed him " the Waddler." His head, framed in long flowing white hair, was most impressive. His eyes were alive with goodness, love, and understanding, and, above all, with a lofty, sincere idealism. Daniel took great interest in me and his image lives before me even after 60 years. I had almost said " lies before me," since the professor generally used to lie on an old and sadly-worn sofa, while his black tom-cat, which was known to everybody in Halle as " Black Ernest," curled up on his paunch. In honour of this tom-cat Daniel had written an instructive book in justification of the usually slandered feline race. The work was published in Leipzig. Daniel went through a number of the most magnificent classical masterpieces which lay outside the school programme with me, and did not bother me unnecessarily with grammar. We read most of the dramas of Sophocles, the " Prometheus " and the " Persians " of Aeschylus, the " Apology " and some of the " Dialogues " of Plato. Daniel strengthened my love of Homer and Herodotus, but did not work through them with me, because my father had taught me to understand them. Like my father before him, he particularly fostered my keen interest in history, the great teacher, the prophet, who, as it were, foresees backwards. He not only gave me history to read, but also the novels of Goethe. He praised my resolution to learn the first part

of Faust by heart. I had carried out this intention before I left
the college. I can still recite *Faust* even to-day, and a few years
ago I won a wager by reciting impromptu all the verses of *Faust*
in which a certain word had been employed (the word in question
was, if I remember rightly, " leap "). Above all Daniel fostered
my patriotism (the flame which burnt in his own heart), unbounded
love of German manners, of the German language, of German
poetry and philosophy, and of the German land and its people.
The third part of his *Handbook of German Geography* became for
me what the French call " *un livre de chevet*," that is a book into
which you are always dipping. His description of the German-
land, of German hills and valleys, forests and streams, of the
German towns of the north and the south, entered my blood.
In these things I look at Germany with the eyes of my old master.

Politically we no longer agreed when the course of events
brought me under the influence of Bismarck. He was all for
" Greater Germany."

Austria was to him, coming as he did from a small Thuringian
province, dearer than Prussia. The year 1866 hurt him to the
depths of his soul. Even after Sedan and Versailles he could not
get over the separation from Austria. He was a true German who
searched the stars for what was lying at his feet. Daniel was
suspected by his enemies (and who is without enemies?) of being a
crypto-Catholic. I did not believe that this rumour was founded
on fact. He was said to have gone over to the Catholic church
not long before his death in Leipzig on September 13th, 1871.
But, of course, Hermann Adalbert Daniel was a man of wide
understanding. He could appreciate the great and beautiful
aspects of the Catholic Church, and agreed with the proverb:
In neccessariis unitas, in dubiis libertas, in omnibus caritas. Even in
class teaching Daniel took a ready interest in me. One day he
gave us an exercise in public speaking. The boys had to climb
up on the dais and speak there one after the other on a theme given
them by the master without any preparation. I spoke boldly and
respectfully, as I have always done all my life, in my various *viva
voce* examinations, when I made official reports before my superiors,
and later on, in the Cabinet Council, when I made proposals
directly to the Kaiser, in the Reichstag, and in the Diet. When
I came down from the dais Daniel said to me with a smile: " You're
a clever little fellow. You will get yourself talked about." This
praise, instead of delighting me and filling me with pride, put me
into a boyish embarrassment. With an inaudible murmur and a
silly " Much I care " I returned to my seat in the class. Professor

Daniel sometimes made us try to write verse. Every boy had to improvise a poem about his neighbour. My neighbour, Frederick von Oertzen, was a good fellow, but he bore only a very remote resemblance to Adonis, the beautiful darling of Aphrodite, who could not staunch the wound which a cruel boar had torn in his lovely body. Oertzen also had the habit of grinning. I improvised the following hexameters about him:

" In der Wiege dich schauend, laut lachten die Grazien alle,
Sahst sie an, und lachst unaufhörlich seitdem." [1]

By way of apology I hasten to add that these are the only verses that I ever perpetrated in my life. Writing verse had already gone out of fashion in my youth. My father composed many verses that were not at all bad. My uncle Baudissin used to produce witty drinking toasts in verse on birthdays and other festive occasions. In the second half of the nineteenth century politics and economics gripped the Germans so closely that they no longer took delight in such harmless games.

In the " Pädchen " three boys, one senior and two juniors, would have quarters together, consisting of a study and a bedroom. The seniors belonged to the Fifth and Sixth Forms, and the juniors to the lower forms. The latter would now and then get a vigorous smack across their faces whenever they were disobedient, but on the whole, life in the " *cubby hole*," as we called our common apartment, was very agreeable. Earlier occupants of the rooms had carved their names into the desks and cupboards. Among these names were many of historic Prussian families. Among my Halle fellow-pupils Zieten became a Life Guards Hussar, Wurmb a Life Guardsman, Wentzel *Oberpräsident* of the province of Hanover, Benda and Borch, Seebach and Gundlach became what we called " clodhoppers," that is to say, gentlemen-farmers. George von Klitzing was put forward by the " Union of Old and Established Property," and represented the Neumark in the Upper Chamber. He was a turbulent agrarian, and at a session of the Agricultural Association during the campaign over the customs tariff, he declared that I knew nothing more about agriculture than that a goose had two legs and that it is not possible to milk a bull. It was not a bad joke, and I have chuckled a good deal over it.

The twin brothers Ludwig and Adalbert Dohna were strange boys. In addition to all his other peculiarities, Count Ludwig zu

---

[1] All the Graces laughed when they saw you in the cradle; you saw them too, and since then you laugh incessantly.

Dohna acquired such acute neurasthenia later on in life that he
ended in a *Maison de santé*. I saw him for the last time in 1891
at Ostend, where he told me he could only exist if he had an ice-cold
bath in the morning and a boiling hot bath at night. Adalbert
Dohna was a splendid and original character, and many stories
were told about him. When he was doing his year of military
service in the First Dragoon Guards he once took the wrong
direction when the old Emperor was present. The Emperor,
whom no detail escaped at military inspection, shook his head and
inquired after his name. The commander, snorting with anger,
shouted at the regiment as soon as the Emperor had gone: " everything was all right on the whole. Only you, Count Dohna, were
noticed by the Emperor, I can tell you that much! " Dohna
replied with the greatest unction: " Favourably or unfavourably
Colonel? "

Adalbert Dohna took unbounded pride in his name, and indeed
the family of the Burggraves zu Dohna, belonged to the oldest
and the most illustrious amongst the German nobility. Once at
Bonn, the hereditary Grand Duke of Mecklenburg-Schwerin sat
next to Adalbert Dohna, the latter said: " You belong to a respectable, a very respectable family, your Royal Highness, but all the
same, you should not sit next to a Dohna." Later on, when he
was a *Regierungsrat* in Stettin and Breslau he irritated his immediate
superiors all too often by his ruthless outspokenness, but the
Oberpräsidents would never part with him, they all delighted in his
originality. Once at a drinking bout he drank eighty-four glasses
one after the other and lay as though dead for forty-eight hours, but
recovered. He was very musical and played the piano beautifully.
Of all those who were at the Pädchen with me there is only one
living to-day: Franz von Veltheim, now Prince of Puttbus through
his marriage with Countess Marie von Wylich.

> " *Omnes eodem cogimur omnium*
> *Versatur urna, serius ocius*
> *Sors exitura, et nos in aeternum*
> *Exilium impositura cimbae.*"

Next to the big garden of the College there was a little open
air gymnasium, with horizontal bars (on which, standing on our
stiffened arms, we raised our legs to heaven), parallel bars, racks,
and a vaulting-horse. In the garden there was a skittle alley where
we bowled assiduously, with no premonition that the word "bowler "
—" *Schieber* "[1]—would come to have quite another meaning.

[1] " Schieber " is the name given to profiteers in the Republic

Later on in Bonn, in Metz, and in St. Petersburg I was fond of playing the noble game of skittles. In Halle, too, we went riding. The university riding teacher André, an old officer, drilled us on the university riding track in " Spanish step " and " the passade." The horse on which we achieved these feats was called " Marquis."

One of good old André's sayings has stuck in my memory, just as I never forgot that other remark made by our Frankfort doctor, Stiebel, on Schopenhauer. When we asked André in March, 1866, what he thought of the chief of the General Staff, Hellmuth von Moltke, his answer was given in one word, grunted out with the growl of an old half-pay officer: " *Prinzessinnentanzer.*" [1] It is really impossible to characterize the great organizer of battles, the wise, quiet thinker Moltke more wrongly; just as it was not possible to get a falser picture of Schopenhauer than that of his Frankfort contemporary. André's son did much for the development of riding in his periodical, *Der Sport*. At Halle we used to go riding together in the open country, and I took many a hedge and many a ditch with him.

Besides gymnastics, riding and skittles, we used to enjoy swimming at Halle. We had swum in the Maine and in the Zierker Lake, but now we got proper teaching from the good " *Halloren*," [2] of whom legend said that they descended from the mythical Celts. They had not only a monopoly of the salt springs, of which the Gutjahrbrunnen was still being used, but also in swimming lessons. They wore a picturesque costume, short trousers, coloured stockings, a long waistcoat with ball-like silver buttons, and a three-cornered hat. Every year a deputation of the *Halloren* went to Berlin on New Year's Day to present to their Majesties, the King and the Queen, a sausage each and six eggs boiled in the salt spring. As long as I remained Premier they used to gratify me also with these gifts in memory of the instruction I had received at the Pädagogium. Under their expert guidance I assiduously practised swimming on my back, the over-arm stroke, treading water and diving, which was not allowed to become a splash, and above all ducking and swimming under water. After the lesson we used to like to let the cool waves of the weir play over us.

In those days I never dreamt that the pleasant River Saale would one day be the scene of one of the most horrible crimes of the German Revolution. After the November upheaval the Halle mob fell upon Major von Klüber and threw him into the

---

[1] " Fop."

[2] *Halloren*—Workmen in the Halle salt works.

river. The unfortunate man tried to save himself by swimming. The mob threw stones and bits of iron at him, and although he bled from several head wounds, the brave man succeeded in reaching the far shore. There these beasts in human form hacked off his hands when he tried to clamber up on dry land, and he once more sank under the water. Major von Klüber had distinguished himself greatly in the World War. He wore the highest of war decorations, the Iron Cross (First Class) and the Pour le Mérite. He came of an academic family and was a highly educated officer, beloved by all who experienced the kindness of his ways. Even after the defeat of 1870-71 the French army enjoyed the care, respect, the passionate love, and indeed, the downright worship of all the French Parties. In one of his most famous speeches during the first years after the peace of Frankfort, Léon Gambetta called the defeated French army the highest possession, the greatest treasure and the last hope of the French people. In the eyes of the French public Marshal MacMahon was the " *Glorieux Vaincu*," but in Germany there were many who denounced General Ludendorff as the " prolonger of the war." In Germany the Social Democrats agitated, fomented, and incited, consciously and without intermission, in their effort to discredit " militarism " and the security and well-being of the Fatherland, which were founded, above all, upon our armed forces. The results of these suicidal tactics showed themselves at the front in the last year of war and also in the Klüber case.

In politics as well as in religion the parties in Halle were in sharper opposition to one another while I was at school than in most other German university towns. The leader of the Conservatives, the historian, Heinrich Leo, was an out-and-out Prussian, strongly orthodox, and a *Kreuzzeitung*[1] man, as the expression then was. He was widely known for his trenchant similes of the pike in the carp pond, by which he meant Napoleon III; about the scrofulous rabble, *i.e.*, Democrats and revolutionaries; and his " bright, brisk little war " that should tread the scrofulous rabble underfoot. Leo wrote a fine history of the Italian states. His autobiography entitled *Days of My Youth*, reveals a deep love of nature and an original and individual mind.

The trend which opposed Leo at Halle was actively represented by Arnold Ruge, who taught at the College when he was a young man and later on, with Theodor Echtermeyer, edited the *Hallesche Jahrbücher*, of Radical tendency. In 1849 he fled to London,

---

[1] The *Kreuzzeitung* in Germany is roughly equivalent to the *Morning Post* in England.

where he became an associate of Mazzini, Ledru-Rollin, and Karl Marx, and engaged in revolutionary propaganda. But in the spring of 1866 he declared for Bismarck's policy, to the horror of the Democrats, especially the Halle Democrats. His friend Lothar Bucher had already gone the same way. The professor of theology, August Tholuck, represented an intermediary standpoint. He was an ardent protagonist of the " Positive Union." [1] He was more of a pietist than an orthodox man, and was a friend of Daniel's. The Director, Kramer, who shared Heinrich Leo's views, ran the College in a strictly Conservative and ecclesiastical spirit. The *Kreuzzeitung* was the only paper we were allowed to read. But I believe that even if we scholars had been free to choose we should have plumped for the paper at the head of which was the Iron Cross with the surrounding inscription: " Forward with God for King and Fatherland." We were all Conservative to the marrow. I would like to emphasize the fact that there was no antithesis between the nobility and the middle class at the college. We all felt that we were equals.

Once when we Sixth-Formers were on an excursion at Giebichenstein, the formidable castle of the Franconian emperors, where Duke Ernest of Swabia and Louis the Springer had been imprisoned, we wrote some verses in the visitors' book of the mountain tavern of Cröllwitz, opposite Giebichenstein. This was in the spring of 1866. The verses ran:

> " *Nur Ross, nur Reisige*
> *Sichern die steile Höh',*
> *Wo Fürsten stehn.*
> *Nicht Demokraten, Juden und Freischärler,*
> *Denn wer auf die getraut,*
> *Der hat auf Dreck gebaut.*" [2]

Liberal newspapers discovered this crime, and with great pathos and indignation demanded the punishment of the " Junker brats " who dared do such a thing and who mocked " the people " with such impudence. The offence was also too much for Director Kramer. He gave the class a sharp reprimand saying that " apart from everything else, the travesty of the National Anthem was in bad taste and quite uncalled for." No reprimand could have been more just. Not to defend my own and my fellow-scholars' ill-behaviour after so long a time, but to characterize the mentality

[1] A political group within the Prussian Protestant Church, founded in 1876.

[2] Only horses and warriors guard the steep height where the Princes stand—not Democrats, Jews and Freebooters, for he who puts his trust in them has built on dirt.

which then preponderated in Conservative circles, I will call to mind that in the year of destiny, 1866, it was just as usual to misunderstand and under-rate von Bismarck as it was to over-rate the Democratic " carpet heroes," as Bismarck called them. Whoever takes the trouble to read the Parliamentary speeches of Schulze-Delitsch, Waldeck, von Hoverbeck, Virchow, Franz Dumcker and Sybel impartially, or indeed, with sympathy for the defeated and discredited, will be astonished that such a combination of unworldliness and self-conceit, of superficiality and pedantry could make any impression. How was it possible that such phrase-mongering and *naïveté* could have such an effect, and that, too, against the speeches of Bismarck, that were so replete with strength, profundity, and genius?

I believe that nowadays amongst 100,000 Germans, not one knows who Grabow and who Bockum-Dolffs were, although in those troubled times they were famous " men of the people." It is indeed a common fault among German intellectuals that they opposed new tendencies and currents of opinion in a prejudiced, unjust, and often purblind fashion. When the new tendency prevails the same intellectuals march with Corybantic shouts, with wild excitement, and with music and dance before the goddess Cybele. In this connection the historian Heinrich Sybel breaks the record by his attitude towards Bismarck. During the conflict he stood in the foremost ranks of the opponents of the Premier, whom he attacked unmercifully in the House of Deputies. When Bismarck had prevailed Sybel wrote a book in seven volumes about the foundation of the German Empire in which he praised the Premier with the same headstrong emotion with which he had previously denounced him. Sybel's work is mediocre. When Prince Bismarck (to whom the author had handed a copy of the book, accompanied by a pompous address) glanced through it, I heard him say: " If I had the choice between reading this dreary book or hearing its author's calumnies once again, I would prefer the latter." On this occasion Prince Bismarck spoke in praise of Macaulay, Carlyle and Motley.

When I think of the matter retrospectively and clearly, I consider it a misfortune that German Liberalism, and therefore, to some extent, the German intelligentsia, had offered such foolish opposition to Bismarck at the time of conflict. The result was that the greatest of German statesmen to the very end of his life, in his innermost mind, under-rated German Liberalism and its representatives. The blunder made by the Liberals in 1848-9 resulted in the party being regarded as hopeless, incapable, and useless by a

IV.   G

large number of Germans in the second half of the sixties. Mocked
on the one hand by the brilliant Ferdinand Lassalle, and despised
on the other by the powerful Bismarck, German Liberalism, and
with it a good part of Germany's culture, including many of her
professors and jurists, lost too much prestige. In fairness I must
add that during Conflict the Liberals and the Democrats made
a really pitiable show. A minor example was related to me on
one occasion, after I had become a Minister, by an old parliamentarian: Owing to the physical effects of overwork Bismarck looked
worn out and tired one day during a debate in the Chamber.
One of the deputies used the opportunity to insinuate that the
Premier had obviously given up every hope of victory. Bismarck
replied that the orator was wrong, and that he was not giving up
his game for a long time yet. The use of the word " game "
produced a great wave of indignation in the ranks of the jurists
and the professors who sat facing the Premier on the opposition
front bench. Game, game! What frivolity, what cynicism!
The idea of shaking hands with Bismarck sent a shudder down
the spines of the immaculate. Is it surprising that Bismarck did
not think much of such Philistines? I have now and again related
this little incident to English, French and Italian friends to give
them a better understanding of the mentality of a certain section
of my countrymen, and not a small section, either. They completely
failed to see the point. They could not imagine anybody being
angered by the expression: " I am not giving up the game yet."
Is it really so strange that Bismarck regarded such small, pedantic,
theoretical politicians as tinkers, tailors and candlestick-makers?

" *Liegen in Garnison zu Brieg,*
Wissen viel, was Brauch ist in Krieg." [1]

Bismarck led the battle for the prerogatives of the Crown with
heroic courage. On 27th January 1863, he closed the debate
on the address in the House of Deputies with the words: " It
is strange that to-day's debate on this address, which will be
reported to his Majesty, coincides with the birthday of the youngest
heir-presumptive to the throne. In this coincidence, gentlemen,
I see a double invitation: to stand firm for the prerogatives of
the monarchy, and to stand firm for the rights of his successor.
The Prussian monarchy has not yet completed its mission, it is
not yet ripe to become a purely decorative ornament in your
constitutional edifice, it is not yet ripe to become an inanimate

---

[1] They're garrisoned at Brieg.
A lot they know of what's done in war!

cog in the machinery of parliamentary government." Providence
is wise if it veils the future. In those days of violent conflict,
had Bismarck known that the grandson of the monarch for whom
he was battling so wholeheartedly and boldly, that four-year old
Prince William (born on 27th January 1863) for whose future
he was exercising his person and genius, would one day arrogantly
dismiss him and calumniate him, as a servant who had become a
nuisance, it might have been enough to paralyse the energy even
of so great a hero as Bismarck.

I was confirmed on 18th March, 1866, while a pupil at the
College. Pastor Seiler, who gave the confirmation lessons, was
an adherent of positive Christianity. He was a firm believer, and
at the same time a warm-hearted clergyman, who soon entered into
confidential relations with the candidates, acquiring their esteem
and love. The idea of sitting at the table of the Lord and of
receiving the body and the blood of Christ, either for salvation
or damnation, dominated me entirely in the period that preceded
my confirmation. With full conviction and fervour, I repeated
our family prayer that so many of my ancestors, both on my father's
and mother's side had prayed before me: " May thy sacred body,
O Lord Jesus Christ, my Lord and God, be my eternal life, and
thy precious blood the forgiveness of all my sins. May thy holy
Sacrament be not my doom but my salvation and true joy. Make
me, a poor sinner, worthy on thy last day, on the Day of Judgment,
to stand and rejoice on the right of eternal glory. Amen."

Mindful of the admonition of the Apostles (1 Cor. xi, 27-29),
I repeated this prayer as often as I went to Holy Communion, and
shall, God willing, pray it in my hour of death. On the day before
the confirmation we had to go to Pastor Seiler for confession. He
dismissed me with serious admonitions, since, as he said, there
slumbered in me dangerous and evil inclinations and instincts,
besides those that were pious and good. More than other men
must I guard against temptations, abide by prayer, and practise
self-control. He gave me, as my confirmation motto, the first
verse of the first Psalm: " Blessed is the man that walketh not
in the counsel of the ungodly, nor standeth in the way of sinners,
nor sitteth in the seat of the scornful."

I had a painful discussion with my father the day after my
confirmation, as I was returning via Berlin to Neu-Strelitz. He
found my religious emotions too exalted. My mother understood
my mood better, but did not dare to oppose my father. I contradicted him all the more sharply, and, in the end, told him I felt as
though a pitcher of ice-cold water had been poured over my body

after a sun bath. My wise father let the discussion drop. He returned to the theme in Neu-Strelitz. He praised my receptiveness for God's word and the Sacrament, but added that it was not a matter of momentary spiritual emotion, but of an enduring, pious journey through life. He recalled the words of Hegel about the swinging of the pendulum: a too-violent thrust in one direction, even if in the right direction, produces just the same perils as the return swing in the opposite direction.

What he wanted to impress in me was that neither lukewarmness, the shallowness, and lack of fervour on the one hand, nor on the other, excess or excitement were desirable, but always the golden mean which, he, with the experience of his fifty years, recommended to me, a boy not yet seventeen. On my confirmation my teacher, Daniel, presented me with the *Lyra Messianica*, a collection of old church hymns. As a watchword for my life he wrote in it: " See then that ye walk circumspectly, not as fools, but as wise " (Eph. v, 15).

CHAPTER VII

The War of 1866—Appreciation of Bismarck's Policy—Bismarck and Edwin Manteuffel—Prussian Representatives Abroad.

THE tension with which the whole of Germany followed the development of events in 1866 was tremendous, and included even the quiet town of Halle. Certainly nobody then foresaw the great co-ordinated plans, the far-sighted schemes of Bismarck. Everyone felt that an iron hand was guiding events, but nobody had a clear picture of the real aims of our leading statesmen. As now, after six decades, I set down the impressions and memories of my youth, the situation as it presented itself stands out clearly in my mind. I feel it necessary to recall the genius with which Bismarck in 1866 took all the cards in his hands, led the nation's destinies, and overcame all obstacles. I feel it to be all the more necessary because of our sorrowful memory of the disaster brought down on the heads of the German people by the incompetence of the leading statesmen in 1914.

On the 14th March, a few days before my confirmation, the Premier sent that monumental order, which was one of the mightiest declarations that ever flowed from his pen, to the Prussian Ambassadors in the capitals of the other German states. " The interests of Prussia and the rest of Germany are already identical owing to the geographical position. Not only is this our advantage, but it is the advantage of the ' whole of Germany.' If we are not sure of Germany as a whole our position (precisely because of our geographical situation) is more precarious than that of other European states. But the fate of Prussia draws in its train the fate of Germany, and we do not doubt that if Prussia's strength were once broken Germany would continue to take only a passive part in the policy of the European nations. To avert this should be the sacred duty of all German governments, which, with this end in view, should work in co-operation with Prussia. If the German Confederation, in its present form, and with its existing political and military arrangements, should find itself facing any major European crisis, and this, for more than one reason, might occur at any moment, it is only too greatly to be feared that it would fail in its task and that Germany could not be saved from the fate

of Poland." Then followed the most anxious days and weeks
in the glorious progress of the greatest of German statesmen.
On the 9th April, Prussia placed before the Frankfort Federal
Diet the proposal for the reform of the Federal Constitution,
including a Parliament elected by universal franchise.

On the 7th May, when, returning from an audience with the
king, the Premier was walking down the centre-path of the Berlin
Linden opposite the Russian Embassy, two revolver shots rang out
one after the other, in quick succession. They were fired by a small,
dark-haired individual scarcely twenty years old, named Ferdinand
Cohn. He was the stepson of the writer, Karl Blind, who had
fled abroad on account of his participation in the filibusterings of
Struve and Hecker, and was living in exile in London. He was
therefore a deep-dyed Democrat. As he took aim a third time,
Bismarck leaped upon him. Nevertheless, the attacker was able
to fire another shot. Although Bismarck seized him by the chest
and the right wrist, he succeeded in passing his revolver from his
right hand to his left and firing two more shots at the Premier.
Bismarck handed over the criminal to some soldiers of the First
Battalion of the Second Regiment of Foot Guards, who were
marching by the scene of the outrage. The Premier's overcoat
was singed by the burning gunpowder, and was pierced in five
places by the bullets.

Bismarck nevertheless walked home. He looked upon the
failure of this attempt on his life, not only as a special grace of God,
who had miraculously preserved him, but also as a revelation in
the spirit of the Biblical words: " Fear not, for I am with thee,
fail not, for I am thy God." This did not prevent him from asking
von Bernuth, the Chief of Police (who, very embarrassed, called
upon him an hour after the attempt) how it was possible that in
broad daylight and just at the time he returned every day from his
audience with the King, he could be fired upon five times in
succession without attracting the attention of a single policeman.
Very crushed, Herr von Bernuth replied: " I only took over my
post unwillingly. I tried to refuse for a long time." The Premier
thundered: " A long time! Not long enough! " What made
Bismarck most resentful towards the Chief of Police, was that
Cohn should have had a chance of committing suicide in prison.
Bismarck would have found it juster if the assassin had been sent
publicly to the gallows, where, in suffering his merited punishment,
he would have served as a deterrent to others. Many years after
the outrage Bismarck pointed out in the Reichstag that the gravestone of the criminal was decorated with roses and forget-me-nots

by ladies of Democratic persuasion. Perhaps there were some among these ladies who judged political murder less mildly after the assassination of Walter Rathenau.

While the capital was the scene of these dramatic episodes, the pupils of the College followed the sequence of events with indescribable tension. We were indignant that magistrates and deputies of quite a number of Prussian towns had sent addresses to the King appealing for a fundamental change in the system relating to membership of the Government and the dismissal of the Premier, and, above all, opposing the war. The Stettiners groaned that Prussia had lost the sympathies of all Germans, that she was regarded abroad with malicious pleasure, that she was sowing distrust and ill-will, and would never achieve success. The royal town of Königsberg impetuously demanded that the imminent danger of civil war should be averted by the summoning of new men. The Chambers of Commerce played the same tune. The excitement in Cologne was particularly great. The leading " man of the people " there was Classen-Kappelmann. He was, for the time being, very popular. But we laughed in the College when a visitor returning from the Rhineland told us that Cologne's youth had not yet lost its sense of humour, and was singing the following ditty about the " people's hero," Classen-Kappelmann:

> " *Der Mann, der uns noch retten kann,*
> *Das is der Classen-Kappelmann.*
> *Ich han ihn gestern noch in der Flora gesehn,*
> *Da war er so besoffen, dass er nicht konnte stehn.*" [1]

On the advice of the Premier, the King did not condescend to answer the peace-petitions. Breslau alone received special treatment. The municipal representatives of Breslau had sent the King a petition in which, though it is true that they demanded the cessation of the conflict over the constitution and pointed to the widespread discontent prevailing in many quarters on this question, they at the same time declared that Breslau, the capital of the province which would be immediately affected by the outbreak of war with all its vicissitudes, would be second to no other Prussian town in its readiness for sacrifice, as it had proved before in the year 1813. If peace could be maintained Silesia and Breslau would welcome it with joyous hearts. " But should the enemies of Prussia and Germany (as had been the case in 1850) once again try to diminish Prussia's powerful position and humiliate her,

---

[1] The man who can still save us is Classen-Kappelmann. I saw him in the Flora yesterday. He was so drunk there that he could not stand.

Silesia would rather take upon herself all the burdens and sufferings of war than allow Prussia's historic task, the unification of Germany, again to be postponed for decades."

The King's answer, which had been proposed by Bismarck, began: " I give ear willingly to the words which the magistrates and municipal councillors of the town of Breslau have addressed to me. I recognize in them the expression of the same spirit which animated the fathers of the present citizens of Breslau." At the end of the royal communication it was indicated that the understanding between Government and Diet, which the King desired, could be facilitated by the new elections then impending. The King's " Call to my People," which was also drafted by Bismarck, was conceived in the same spirit as the reply to the Breslau petition. It aroused the College to great enthusiasm. " Wherever we look in Germany we are surrounded by enemies whose battle-cry is: ' The degradation of Prussia.' But in my people lives the spirit of 1813. Who will rob us of a single foot of Prussian soil if we are earnestly resolved to guard the conquests of our fathers, if King and people are united closer than ever by the dangers that threaten the Fatherland, and they hold it their highest task to sacrifice blood and treasure in its honour? May God grant us victory, and we shall be strong enough to restore in another, closer, and more sacred form, the loose bond that now, in name rather than deed, holds together the German states, and is now dissolved by those who fear the right and the might of the national spirit."

This call was dated 18th June, the date of Waterloo. Four days previously the Federal Diet had accepted by nine votes (Austria, Bavaria, Saxony, Württemberg, Hanover, both Hessens, Nassau, the sixteenth Curia, namely, Lichtenstein, Reuss, etc.) against six (Thuringia, Mecklenburg, the Hansa towns, Oldenburg, Schwarzburg) the Austrian proposal to mobilise the army of the Union against Prussia. Thereupon the Prussian envoy, Karl Friedrich von Savigny, a friend of Bismarck's youth and later his opponent and first chairman of the Parliamentary Centre Party, replied in fiery words "that Prussia considered the treaty establishing the North German Federation as broken and no longer binding, and would act henceforward as if it were extinguished. Meanwhile his Majesty the King, my most gracious sovereign, will not consider the fundament of the Nation as having been dissolved with the former North German Federation. The Federation will be rebuilt on that national fundament. Prussia stands by this first premiss, and by the unity of the German people, a unity that is raised far above transient forms, and considers it the absolute duty of the German states to find a suitable expression for these forms."

The great Prussian minister's mood in those days of June, when the history and destiny of the German nation began a new epoch, is clearly expressed in a letter he addressed to General, later Field-Marshal, von Manteuffel, which I quote here, since as far as I know, it has not yet been published:

" Your Excellency. Knowing the conviction you expressed on the occasion of the last confidential Austro-Gablenzian peace negotiations, the conviction that we must rapidly make war, wherever war offers itself, for political, military and financial reasons, I was prepared for you to act in the above sense in response to my telegram (number 51), which gave the necessary instructions, and I anticipated important news in the course of yesterday. The news of the friendly tone of the two musicians at the military *chassés croisés* is not in harmony with the mood here that waits the news of the first cannon shot. You said that seizure would trouble certain spirits as being an act of violence, but I answer you in the words of Deveroux: ' Friend, now's the time to shout! ' And if we refrain you not only wreck my European plan out of military courtesy for Gablenz, but you will also find no one in the army, except the Württembergers, who will be able to understand your actions. Every three days costs us two millions, which we simply haven't got, since we, unlike the Austrians, do not live at the expense of our creditors. Every three days are worth another 5,000 allied troops to Austria. The wind is blowing in our favour from all corners of Europe, we are *expected* to act; to-day it is considered natural that we should act, in a week it may no longer be considered so. I had hoped that in consideration of all these circumstances you would play the Yorck[1] a little, but now you have the categorical royal command to act, and if you do not carry out this command as quickly as our whole policy demands, you do Prussia a heavy injury, in my opinion. If we fall back into the swamp of half measures and compromise, it will be very difficult for us to find as favourable a *casus belli* as the present. If there were the possibility of an honest peace I would rejoice heartily. But every hope of that has vanished; the Viennese are leading us by the nose until they and their allies are ready, so that they can strike the first blow or make it appear as though we had been picking a quarrel, when the present impression made by their breach of the treaty in London, Paris and St. Petersburg has

[1] Field-Marshal Yorck von Württemberg concluded the Convention of Tauroppa with the Russians on his own initiative and responsibility in 1812.

vanished.   A few utterances of Gablenz' brother even make me fear that the provocative summoning of the Estates of the Realm will be rescinded before Monday, and then a justification for us to take action will no longer exist, a justification that is as plain as a pikestaff.   The Gastein treaty is either broken or not.   If it is not we cannot begin the invasion even now.   If it is, we can go further. As things are at present, everybody believes the latter to be the case, everybody at home, abroad, and in Vienna.   If we wait the Austrian lie will prevail.   I have just received trustworthy information from South Germany that Austria has not completed her own armaments, and that Vienna has therefore given orders that Gablenz is to put us off with amiabilities.   I shall suggest to his Majesty that as soon as the Diet meets on Monday we put in the demand for the evacuation to Gablenz, independently of the seizure of Holstein, which no doubt will have been accomplished by you on receipt of these instructions.   If the Diet decides upon the proclamation of Augustenburg, it will be your task to prevent it even if by violence, otherwise you would not guard the King's rights.   But I hope to get you the positive order, by Monday evening if you wish it, to force the Austrians to evacuate Holstein at once in this case. I must finish.   Forgive the style of this letter, but your telegram paralysed my nerves this morning, and now they are reacting.   In great haste, but in all friendship, Yours, von Bismarck."

The postscript to this letter written by Bismarck himself was:

> " *Ich that's mit Widerstreben,*
> *Da es in meine Wahl noch war gegeben;*
> *Nothwendigkeit ist da, der Zweifel flieht,*
> *Jetzt fecht ich für mein Haupt und für mein Leben.*
> *(Er geht ab, die andern folgen.)* "[1]

Characteristic of Bismarck is the psychological skill with which he handled General Manteuffel in this moment of greatest tension and excitement during the floodtide of events.   General Edwin von Manteuffel's favourite reading was Schiller's *Wallenstein*. He believed that he had a certain resemblance to Wallenstein, that is why Wallenstein is twice quoted in the letter to him.   The " Württemberger " named in the letter is the General who was then commanding the Guards, Prince Augustus of Württemberg, who, although he was a thoroughly loyal Prussian officer, was not, as a South German Prince, exactly pleased to see the war between Prussia and his nearer home.   If, on the one hand, the full deter-

---

[1] I did it reluctantly, as it still lay in my choice; necessity is there and doubt flies away, since now I fight for my head and for my life. (Exit, the others follow.)

mination and the whole energy of the leading statesman speak in
this letter it must, on the other, again and again be emphasized
with what circumspection, care, and skill he was striving simultaneously to secure the best opening for his country, to avoid set-
backs, and to make the imponderabilia, which he never underrated,
play his game.   No one knew better than Bismarck that energy
alone cannot achieve everything.   He was thoroughly convinced
of the correctness of Horace's warning : " *Vis consilii expers mole
ruit sua* ": strength not led by reason collapses of itself.   Bismarck
proceeded with such energy as had not been displayed in Prussian
politics since the days of Frederick the Great.   But he also strove
to secure all advantages, to avoid the dangers that could be avoided,
to prevent unfavourable incidents as far as possible, and to win
world opinion over to his side.

When France, England and Russia proposed a conference to
avert the outbreak of war in Germany, this piece of intervention
naturally cut across the plans and intentions of the Prussian Premier
in the most obvious manner.   Nevertheless, he hastened to accept
the invitation to enter peace negotiations at Paris.   In a circular
to the royal representatives in Paris, London and St. Petersburg,
he declared that his Majesty the King of Prussia shared the feelings
of the three courts.   He was " very glad " to accept the invitation of
the three Powers.   The Prussian plenipotentiaries in Paris would
get into touch with their representatives so as to discuss with them
the different questions threatening the peace of Europe at the
moment.

Every patriot must feel horror and pain when he considers
how differently the leaders of the empire acted in the disastrous
summer of 1914.   In 1866 Bismarck wanted war, just as, in certain
circumstances, a conscientious doctor believes a surgical operation
to be a necessity, but his tactics were so circumspect, so careful,
and, above all, so skilful, that he showed no weaknesses.   In the
summer of 1914 the German government certainly did not want
war, and the German people just as little.   But Bethmann and his
colleagues operated so clumsily that they burdened us with the
odium of war guilt.   Bismarck in 1866 conducted himself quite
differently.   Despite the pressure of the military authorities, and
although the great Moltke declared that victory depended on the
most rapid initial attack, Bismarck insisted on not declining the
invitations to the peace conference in Paris.   No one was more
convinced than Bismarck of the army's importance for Prussia and
Germany.   His feelings were those of the Prussian officer, that
he was, from his first to his last day of office.   He uttered

the fine and telling phrase that without the army the German Empire could neither have been built up, nor could it have been kept erect.

Nevertheless, he always insisted upon the primacy of politics, that is to say, that in the end political and not military considerations would have to be decisive. He who does the right thing politically is nearly always able to derive an advantage from the mistakes of his opponents. And so it was in this case. Austria rejected the plan of a conference. When the Prussian Premier received the news the French Ambassador, Benedetti, happened to be with him. When Bismarck had read the Viennese dispatch he shouted: "*Vive le Roi!*" It may be said without exaggeration that in the decisive days of 1866 Bismarck did not make a wrong move. The mistakes of French policy at that time are chiefly due to the fact that Napoleon III overrated Austria and underrated Prussia. He wished to perpetuate Germany's dualistic, torn, and disunited state, to weaken Germany as much as possible, and therefore to prevent the absolute victory both of the Austrians and of the Prussians. But an Austrian victory seemed to him the more probable. It is difficult for us to believe this to-day, but in those days the world thought differently; for the world is usually superficial, often thoughtless and not seldom naïve. In 1866 Austria still lived on the memory of her tenacity in the Napoleonic war and of her brilliant victory at Novara. The Prussians had shown courage at Düppel and Alsen, but after all, only against the small and much weaker Denmark, whom they had overthrown with the help of another Great Power. At Bronzell, as well as at Neunburg, Prussia had behaved with uncertainty and almost with timidity. The Austrian monarchy numbered almost 35 million souls in those days, and was the third Power in Europe as regards population. Prussia had hardly 19 million inhabitants. On the Austrian side there were four German Kingdoms—Bavaria, Württemberg, Saxony and Hanover—and in addition to these, Baden, the two Hessens and Nassau, with about 14 millions. Prussia was followed by the Hansa towns, the Thuringian duchies and Mecklenburg (who acted under pressure of circumstances rather than of their own free will) together about a million and a half. Austria and her German allies represented 50 millions; Prussia, with her partisans, hardly 20. So that the scales should not sink too much in Austria's favour, Napoleon III encouraged Italy to take the side of Prussia.

Adolphe Thiers, the French statesman of the nineteenth century, in whom were embodied more than in any other the great and dangerous qualities of the French nation, saw things more clearly than Napoleon III, who was as sentimental as he was imaginative. His speech of 3rd May, 1866, before the French Corps Législatif, is one of the most significant political pronouncements ever made. Not without reason have French historians declared that in this speech spoke the soul of France. The policy of Henry II, Henry IV, Richelieu, Louis XIV, of the Convention, and of Napoleon I, the policy of Poincaré, Clemenceau and Marshal Foch, the conception of most Frenchmen, the policy which builds the power, the well-being, and the greatness of France on the weakness and disunity of Germany were all voiced in it. Naturally it contained the allegation that Prussia was threatening the independence of the Germans (the " German liberty " which had already been taken under the protection of the Bourbon kings), that she intended to build a new German Empire which would be a menace to Europe and intolerable to France. France therefore had to prevent Italy from taking steps against Austria. She must be bluntly and plainly forbidden to do so. After all, had not France sacrificed 50,000 soldiers and six hundred millions on her behalf? Prussia must be compelled to sheathe the sword again.

Thiers's speech was received with thunders of applause from the whole Chamber—the Opposition as well as the majority. Only for a short time did the continuation of the debate prevent the Premier, Eugène Rouher, from reading out a telegram, apparently forged, according to which Italy was stated to have officially pledged herself not to attack Austria. A few days after Thiers's speech Napoleon III hastened to declare in a public manifesto that he, with the majority of the French people, regarded with abhorrence the treaties of 1815, which Thiers wished to make the one foundation of French policy. This declaration did not merely reveal his anger against Thiers, whom the Emperor regarded as his personal enemy. Nor was it merely the unrealistic pronouncement of a fantasist. Napoleon III hoped that, as the result of a war between the two greatest German powers, Prussia would probably be defeated, and would purchase French help by the surrender of the left bank of the Rhine, towards which then, as now, French intentions were directed.

Austrian policy was as clumsy as it had been in 1859, and as it was to be again in 1914. In order to keep the Emperor Napoleon III in a friendly mood, the Vienna Cabinet had promised him that it would surrender Venetia (which Austria had retained after the Franco-Austrian War of 1859), whichever way the war might go. How was it possible in these circumstances that Austria, battling with Prussia for primacy in Germany, did not concentrate all her forces against her German rivals, but instead placed a good and strong Austrian army under the Archduke Albert to fight for a lost cause in the old Campi Raudii in Upper Italy, where German and Roman had so often fought, and where the Cimbri were defeated a century before the birth of Christ? Nearly thirty years later I put this question to an Austrian Minister for Foreign Affairs, Count Kálnoky. I was then a young Minister in Bucharest. As I passed through Vienna from Berlin *en route* for Bucharest, I was nearly always honoured with an invitation to dine with the Royal and Imperial Minister of Foreign Affairs. On such occasions, Count Gustav Kálnoky, who was a well-wisher of mine, used to speak frankly to me about political events of the present and the past in a *tête-à-tête*. When I asked him why in 1866 Austria, which had from the outset renounced Venetia, had nevertheless placed a great and useful part of her strength in Upper Italy, instead of Bohemia, the Minister replied: " In Spain people speak of ' *cosas de España*,' that is of things which only the Spanish understand. There are also ' *cosas de Austria*,' that is, happenings which only a born Austrian can explain. Our Foreign Minister in 1866, the intelligent Count Alexander Mensdorff, wished, as common sense dictated, to make our front against Prussia only. He won over the Emperor Francis Joseph to this view, but when Count Moritz Esterházy, a Minister without Portfolio, but, owing to his relations with the Court and with the clergy, the most influential man in the Cabinet, heard about this he betook himself to the Hofburg and explained to the Emperor that honour and religion demanded that Austria should fight against the Italians: not in order to hold Venetia or to win back Lombardy, since Austria's Italian dreams were now over for ever, but by means of an Austrian victory over Italy to restore to the Pope the territory of the Papal States, unjustly torn from him in 1860, and thus to give him the assurance of the *Patrimonium Petri*. And so disaster took its course."

This Moritz Esterházy, mentioned by Count Kálnoky, who was known as " secret Moritz " on account of his love of backstairs actions and intrigues, was many years later pronounced insane and sent to a *Maison de Santé*, after committing the most objectionable misdemeanours, in Pirna, where he died. His pious wife entered the cloister of the barefoot Carmelite Order at Maierling to do penance for the sins of her husband. The grandson of this Minister was the Count Esterházy, to whom the last Austrian Emperor, Karl, after his accession to the throne in 1916, confided the

Regnum Apostolicum in place of Count Tisza, seasoned by many fights. In this position he contributed appreciably by his folly and inexperience to the final eclipse of the Hapsburg monarchy.

Bismarck in 1866 showed himself a master of statecraft. He left every way open to the last. Shortly before the beginning of hostilities he was in negotiation with the brother of the best Austrian General, the Baron Ludwig von Gablenz (a Saxon by birth) concerning the possibilities of an acceptable understanding between Prussia and Austria. To Bavaria he proposed a reconstruction of Germany on the basis of Prussia's taking over the leadership north of the Main, and Bavaria south of it. To the last had he not destroyed all bridges which led to Hanover. He told the heir to the Hessian Crown, the Landgrave Frederick William, during a visit the latter paid him in the spring of 1866, that he should take steps to prevail upon the head of his family, the Electoral Prince Frederick William, to put himself on the side of the Prussians. When the Landgrave replied that it was too late, and that the final decision (which was bound to go in favour of Austria) was to be taken the next morning in Kassel, Bismarck added: " Pay for a special train to Kassel so as to save your crown." When the Landgrave, who was noted for his avarice, pointed out the cost of a special train, Bismarck answered: " Put your hand in your pocket and spend a thousand talers on a special train. It will pay you to do so, otherwise it will be all the worse for Hessen." The Landgrave answered haughtily: " You forget that 600,000 Austrians stand between me and you."

The mastery with which Bismarck conducted Prussian policy in the fateful year 1866 stands out still more clearly when we remember how little the Premier could rely on the Prussian representatives abroad in those days. The ambassador in Vienna was the Baron Karl von Werther. He was pro-Austrian to the marrow. His wife, a Countess Oriola by birth, was, if it were possible, still more so. After the outbreak of war, when the Austrian Government had handed him his passport and he had to leave his circle of colleagues, a characteristic incident took place. When the Baroness Werther arrived at the Prussian-Austrian frontier, she threw her arms round the neck of the fat Austrian customs officer, who, wearing his cap with the black and yellow cockade, stood chalking the luggage, and exclaimed with tears in her eyes: " In your person will I once more embrace my dear Austria, which I leave with a bleeding heart." She was a sister of the lady-in-waiting to Louise Oriola, whose opinions were quite different. She was a true Prussian, and as long as she was at court she stood up for Bismarck. This earned her the silent disapproval of Queen Augusta, but earned her the favour of our old King William I, as well as Bismarck himself. Bismarck also made use of Baron Werther's exaggeratedly Austrophile attitude in accordance with his own favourite motto: " *Qu'en politique il faut faire flèche de tout bois.*" When he was asked on the outbreak of the war what would happen if the Prussian army were to lose it, he replied: " The King will have to make Werther my successor."

The ambassador in St. Petersburg was Count Henry Redern, a diplomat of the old school in the most extravagant sense of the word. Had he played himself on any stage he would have been a tremendous success. When he was an attaché he had twice failed in his diplomatic examinations (this happened in the first few years of Frederick William IV's reign). Being the son of a Lord Chamberlain, he was often commanded to have tea with the Queen, and was at tea with her Majesty the day he had just failed. The Queen, who knew that he had gone up for his examination, asked him how he had fared. Poor Count Henry Redern was very embarrassed and did not say a word. But Frederick William IV replied with his ready wit: " Our dear Count answered every question so cleverly that the examiners unanimously shouted *da capo, da capo*! " By nature Austrophile, Henry Redern was encouraged in this tendency by his wife, an Austrian by birth and a Princess Odescalchi. When, in the spring of 1866, the situation became more and more acute, the Ambassador in St. Petersburg, Count Henry Redern, replied to all questions concerning the attitude of Berlin: " My King will never allow the white-coats [1] to be fired on."

A few days after mobilization had been ordered in Prussia Ferdinand Stumm, who was then a lieutenant in the 8th Hussars, and later became Ambassador in Madrid, called on Count Redern. When the Count asked him what he was doing in St. Petersburg, Stumm replied that during a holiday in the Crimea he had heard that war was impending in Germany, so he was hurrying back to join his regiment at Paderborn. The Ambassador dismissed him very ungraciously, went to his chancellery, and declared to the secretaries assembled there: " A man called Stumm says we are going to have a war! Incredible! " It was the incredible that happened. Redern shook his head with misgiving over the breaking up of the Federal Diet and over the occupation of Dresden, Kassel and Hanover by the Prussian army. But when the news arrived in St. Petersburg that the Austrians had beaten Prussia's

[1] " White coats," the Austrian uniform.

allies, the Italians, at Custozza, the Prussian Ambassador went to the salon of Princess Kotchubei, the Russian Chief Lady-in-Waiting at the Court, on the evening of the same day and said in his most exalted manner: " *Enfin une bonne nouvelle. Les Autrichiens ont remporté une belle victoire!* " In this case also Bismarck made *flèche de tout bois*. He used the then Prussian military attaché in St. Petersburg, Lothar von Schweinitz (who became Ambassador later on) as the instrument of his policy: the estimable Henry Redern merely served as a screen. In later years he did commendable service as Chief Master of the Robes at the royal court.

In the year 1866 Prussia was represented in London by the ambassador, Count Albert Bernstorff. Both Paris and London were already embassies in those days. Court Bernstorff was six years older than Bismarck. He had been in Munich in 1845, in Vienna (in difficult circumstances) in 1848, and in London from 1850 to 1861. From 1861 to 1862 he was Minister of Foreign Affairs just before Bismarck, and then he took over the London Embassy again. He may not always have agreed with his successor. He may now and then, being the elder and, as he believed, the more experienced man, have shaken his head over Bismarck, but he did his duty as Prussia's representative, and he had a very good position in London. The most important post in 1866 was the Paris Embassy, held by Count Robert Goltz. Bismarck had cultivated friendly relations with him in the 'fifties, but had then broken with him, as he did with many another. Ever afterwards he looked upon Goltz as a personal enemy, which, no doubt, he was. Bismarck used to be fond of relating how in 1866 Goltz summarized his opinion of his chief in the words: " It is my policy this fellow Bismarck is carrying out, but he is carrying it out wrongly." But this did not prevent Goltz from being a very skilful diplomat (in contrast with Werther and Redern) as well as a clear-thinking, decided Prussian.

Bismarck himself once defined diplomacy as " modelling in human flesh instead of clay." Often it was the diplomat's business to persuade people to do things which might not be in their own interests, but which would be of advantage to the diplomat. All those who in the fateful 1866 worked under Goltz in the Prussian Embassy in Paris (Eberhard Solms, Joseph Radowitz, Alexander Lynar, and Major, later Field-Marshal General Walter Loë) have told me that it was above all, thanks to Count Goltz, that France remained neutral in 1866 for as long as we needed her neutrality. Goltz had, it was said, used his great influence both on the Emperor Napoleon III and the Empress Eugénie, as well as on

Prince Jérome Napoléon, and his numerous connections in all circles of society. He also made skilful and energetic use of the Press to dissuade France from intervening before Sadowa. He did good work in the Prussian service. Attacked by an incurable disease, Goltz had to resign soon after the Peace of Nikolsburg, and died before 1870 after a painful illness.

It would be a mistake to believe that Prince Bismarck conducted his policy from 1862 to 1871 according to a programme drawn up in all details and then logically carried out. He adapted himself to circumstances, which he used and exploited with the greatest acumen and with all the insight of genius. In 1862, when he was appointed Prime Minister, he hardly intended to erect the German Empire in the form it took later on, or even a North German Federation in the form it took in 1866. In 1865 he said to Robert Kendell, who had asked him for a post abroad, on the plea that his health was no longer equal to the burden of work in the Foreign Office: " Hold out in Berlin for another year or so, and you will make an excellent Prussian envoy to the Frankfort Federal Diet."

CHAPTER VIII

The Battle of Königgrätz—General von Steinmetz—My Father is Appointed Mecklenburg-Schwerin Minister in Berlin—Cholera in Halle—A Walking Tour Across the Harz (Autumn 1866)—A Visit to my Uncle Baudissin in Dresden—Matriculation Examination (Autumn, 1867)—Puppel—Dulce est desipere in loco.

IMMEDIATELY after the break-up of the old German Federation the Prussian Prime Minister addressed almost identically-worded summonses to Saxony, Hanover and Electoral Hessen, in which, after calling attention to the geographical situation of the three federal states, the reduction of their troops to the peace footing of the 1st of March, and their consent to the summoning of the German Parliament was demanded. On 23rd May Count Bismarck had addressed a dispatch to the Prussian Minister at Hanover, Prince Ysenburg, in which he emphasized the fact that the Prussian Government was not pressing Hanover to conclude a treaty with Prussia, but that the Hanoverian Government should decide for itself what was most to its advantage. The Prussian Government only wanted to know what the character of its relations was then and would be in future. When the Prussian summonses were rejected in Dresden, Hanover and Cassel, the Prussian general, Herwarth von Bittenfeld, invaded Saxony, Generals von Manteuffel and Vogel von Falkenstein crossed the Hanoverian frontier, and General von Bayer occupied Cassel. When the news arrived that Saxony, Hanover and Hessen had definitely turned against Prussia, the Prime Minister, Count Bismarck, walked into his wife's drawing-room and said in a loud voice to Geheimrat von Keudell, who often soothed him with his piano playing: " Keudell, sit down at the piano and play us the ' Hohenfriedberger March.' "

On 29th June the Hanoverian army capitulated at Langensalza after a brave defence. The Prussian *State Gazette* commented on the event: " The fate of the Hanoverian troops, whose renowned past is closely interwoven with the finest achievements of our own army, must fill every soldier's heart with sincere sympathy. The lofty self-denial with which the Hanoverian army, true to the

oath it took, has borne its hard lot, must ensure it the regard of the
Prussian army." Victories were announced in rapid succession—
the battles of Podol, Hühnerwasser, Münchengrätz, Gitschin.
The Prussian General, Bonin, was beaten by the Austrian General,
Gablenz, at Trautenau, but the Prussian Guard was victorious at
Soor and Königinhof, and in three successive days, 27th, 28th and
29th June, General von Steinmetz routed three Austrian Corps at
Nachod, Skalitz and Schweinschädel. Steinmetz was an old
warrior of seventy. He had taken part in the campaigns of 1813
to 1815. He was now known as the "Lion of Skalitz." Later
he proved a failure in the Franco-Prussian War, not as a strategist,
but because of his self-will and obstinacy. He was a difficult
character, and had to be recalled in the middle of September, 1870,
because when commanding the First Army at Spichern, Colombey-
Nouilly and Gravelotte he did not always show precision in carrying
out the instructions of von Moltke. But his achievements in the
Bohemian campaign secure him a lasting place in the history of
the Prussian army. Steinmetz was in every way a splendid, original
character. At the conclusion of the campaign of 1866 he married,
at the age of seventy-one, a seventeen-year-old girl, Fräulein von
Krosigk. The marriage lasted eleven years and went very well.
The Lion of Skalitz spent his honeymoon in the castle of Hohenzollern at the special invitation of his supreme and royal commander.
But the widow could not be blamed for marrying a man five years
younger than herself, Count Karl Brühl, two years after the death
of Field-Marshal Steinmetz. When she died, after five and twenty
years of happy marriage, the widower, in his turn, sought the hand
of a Countess Schweinitz, who was twenty-one years younger
than he. And so equilibrium was restored.

Great was the jubilation in Halle over the Prussian victories.
Itinerant musicians used to draw up before the College and sing
to the strains of barrel-organs:

> "*Der Benedek, der Benedek, der hat es bös im Sinn,*
> *Er wollt' mit seinen Kroaten nach Berlin.*
> *Der Prinz Friedrich Karl, der hat es ihm gezeigt,*
> *Dass ihm in Berlin kein Frühstück wird gereicht.*" [1]

In the streets the students used to sing:

> [1] Benedek, Benedek, plans evil,
> He wants to come to Berlin with his Croats.
> Prince Friedrich Karl has shown him
> That he will get no breakfast in Berlin.

" *Schön schwarz ist der Adler und weiss ist der Schwan*
Drum ist auch schwarz-weiss die Preussiche Fahn'
Und schwarz ist der Teufel und gelb ist der Neid,
Drum ist auch schwarz-gelb des Östreichers Kleid." [1]

With due consideration for the patriotic mentality which underlay these verses, we were not shocked by their undeniable lack of objectivity and logic. But the days of tribulation gave birth also to really fine war songs. There remains in my memory the beginning and end of a song which our director, Herr Kramer read aloud before the sixth form in the spring of 1866.

" *Vorwärts! Vorwärts alle Mann!*
Wie die Väter einst getan!
Zogen wider alle Welt
Unterm alten Fritz ins Feld,
Schlugen alle Welt zuschanden,
Sind vom Grabe auferstanden,
Wolln nun sehn der Enkel Preis.
Vorwärts! Vorwärts Schwarz und Weiss!" [2]

ran the opening verse. And the end was:

" *Vorwärts! ruft Borussia,*
Die schon hundert Schlachten sah,
Die in Freiden und in Krieg
Sich bekränzt mit manchem Sieg.
Von der Memel bis zum Rhein,
Stehn viel Kreuz' und Leichenstein,
Aber all' voll Ruhm und Preis:
Vorwärts! Vorwärts Schwarz und Weiss!" [3]

[1] The eagle is a fine black and the swan is white,
Therefore the Prussian flag is black and white !
The devil is black and envy is yellow,
Therefore the Austrian's dress is black and yellow

[2] Forward, forward, one and all!
As your fathers did before you !
They went out against the whole
World, to battle under old Fritz.
They beat the whole world hollow.
They have risen from the grave,
Want to see their grandsons' fame.
Forward, forward, black and white.

[3] Prussia calls " Forward,"
Prussia who saw a hundred battles,
Who wreathed herself with many a victory,
From the Memel to the Rhine are many crosses and gravestones
But all full of renown and glory:
Forward, forward, black and white.

But the end of the war did not appear to be in sight, and much doubt was expressed as to its final result. South German and Austrian papers explained that Prussia had fallen into a mousetrap out of which she would not be able to find her way again. The Viennese newspapers were still mocking the simian agility of the Prussians, and were confident that it would, in the end, come to grief before the proved efficiency of the Imperial army.

> " *Da schmettert die Fanfare,*
> *Sadowas Tag bricht an.*
> *Wer ist, in weissen Haare,*
> *Der Held dem Heer voran ?*
> *Hell blitzt sein Schwert,*
> *Stark ist der Arm.*
> *Des Königs Arm, der beste*
> *Fährt in der Féinde Reihn,*
> *Er heisse Wilhelm der Feste,*
> *Weil fest sein Königsarm.*" [1]

The victory of Königgrätz had the effect of a thunder-clap on the world, on Europe, and above all on Germany. " *Crolla il mondo!* " exclaimed the Papal State secretary, Giacomo Antonelli, when he received the news. The astonishment which the turn of events at Sadowa caused, even in this considerable and astute statesman, excuses to some degree the lack of foresight which Napoleon III had shown. Perhaps Königgrätz made an even deeper impression than Sedan four years later. Certainly Sedan was more dramatic and bigger, but the victory of Sadowa was even more unexpected. On the Sunday following the victory of Sadowa, Pastor Seiler, who four months earlier had confirmed me, entered the pulpit with the words:

> " *Lobe den Herren, der alles so herrlich regieret,*
> *Der uns auf Fittichen des Preussichen Adlers sicher geführet.*" [2]

---

[1] The bugle sings it out,
The day of Sadowa dawns.
Who is the hero with white hair
At the head of the army ?
His sword flashes brightly,
His arm is strong.
The King's strong arm
Descends upon the ranks of the foe.
He shall be called William the Stalwart
Because stalwart is his arm.

[2] Praise the Lord who so gloriously rules all,
Who led us surely on the wings of the Prussian eagle.

For the first time I heard the rustling of the Eagle's wings in all their power. The sound was in my ears all my life.

Sentiment in Mecklenburg, where I spent my summer holidays, was quite different from that of Prussia. My father, in accordance with his whole outlook, had complained against the breaking-up of the old Federation by the Prussian Premier, although this did not affect his friendship with Bismarck. But he had too clear a political mind and too sure a perception of realities to rock himself in the illusions which the Mecklenburg nobility, and, above all the blind Grand Duke, still harboured. The situation in Strelitz was quite different from that in Schwerin. The Grand Duke Frederick Francis II, a nephew of King William of Prussia, was on Prussia's side with all his heart as well as with his mind. On the other hand, his Minister, Oertzen shared all the prejudices of the Mecklenburg feudal nobility against the powerful north German state, which in their view was too Liberal, too modern, and too militaristic. The Strelitz Grand Duke Frederick William spoke only of " horrible " Prussia. But my father prevented him from allowing his feelings to carry him too far and lose him his crown and his land. My father never thought in narrow formulæ; he had a mind which perceived the living relationships of the world, and was able to estimate antagonistic forces. He was, in other words, a statesman. The anti-Prussian feeling in Strelitz was so strong that even a Lady-in-Waiting of Prussian origin, the Baroness Mary von Bülow-Wendhausen (by birth a Countess Wartensleben) was seized by it. Every day she used to declare at table to her assembled friends that Mecklenburg-Strelitz must declare war on Prussia, which was becoming revolutionary, until finally her aged footman, who stood behind her chair, said in the broadest Mecklenburg accent: " But, Baroness, we mustn't forget our geographical situation."

My father based his arguments on this sensible view when he made it clear to the Grand Duke that he must take the side of Prussia. Thus my father saved Strelitz, but, as so often is the case of Princes, he got no thanks from the blind Grand Duke. The relations between the two gradually became strained. My father took the post of Mecklenburg Minister to Berlin, which was offered to him by the Grand Duke of Schwerin, with a conscience that was all the lighter because Bismarck had informed him that he specially desired him there as representative of Mecklenburg. I will anticipate events by mentioning that in this capacity my father once again saved Strelitz four years later. This was at the beginning of the Franco-German war. The blind Grand Duke replaced my father by a Hanoverian, a Baron von Hammerstein, an out-and-out Guelph, who collected other Guelphs round him. In June, 1870, the activities of these gentlemen were so suspicious that for a time Strelitz was threatened by an invasion of Prussian troops and probably annexation by Prussia as well. My father went to see the Federal Chancellor who, in spite of the tremendous pressure of business which burdened his shoulders in those days, received him with his old friendliness and said to him: " Since you left, some very evil things seem to be occurring in the great port of Strelitz. We could really turn Strelitz into a Prussian province. But this time we will put mercy before justice: firstly for the sake of Queen Louise, and secondly for your sake, old friend. But see that the pig-sty is cleared out."

My father proposed that the ducal heir, who in no way shared the prejudices of his parents against the Prussians, should place himself at the disposal of the King of Prussia for military service. This the Chancellor willingly agreed to. The heir to the dukedom then served on the General Staff of the old Emperor throughout the Franco-German war, and after his accession to the throne in 1904, remained a Federal Prince who was always completely loyal to the Empire.

Cholera came to Halle from Bohemia as to many other German towns, and claimed numerous victims. We frequently met acquaintances while out riding with the younger André only to hear a few days later that they had been stricken down with cholera. Funeral processions were to be seen in every street. The Francke Foundations were spared by the disease. It was attributed by some people to the fact that they lay on a slope so that the exhalations and smells of the town were drawn away from them. But above all, we attributed it to God's Providence, which had held a protecting hand over the work of the pious Augustus Hermann Francke. The emblem of the Foundation, the eagle mounting towards the sun, with the comforting and elevating utterance of the greatest prophet of the ancient tribes (Isaiah xl, 31) had once again proved its efficacy.

A lasting impression was made on my mind by the Austrian prisoners who were brought to the Moritzburg. The Moritzburg which was situated in the north of the town, was an old fortress, which had once been the residence of the Archbishopric of Magdeburg, and was later destroyed in the Thirty Years' War. Since then it had been used for military purposes. The prisoners interned in the Mortizburg used to greet passers-by with cries of " Eljen, Evviva!" " Zivio!" etc., to beg a copper, for which they showed recognition by cheers for Prussia and insults towards Austria in all languages. The brittleness of the Hapsburg monarchy became clear to me then for the first time.

Königgrätz (*Dem König gerät's*—the King succeeds—as they used to say in Prussia in the summer of 1866) was indeed the greatest and happiest day in the life of Prince Bismarck. This victory was the reward of infinite care, great dangers, and heroic courage. Königgrätz also revealed even to the stupidest eyes the genius of the statesman who had ended the conflict over the Constitution in the favour of the Crown. The *Kladderadatsch* published a cartoon on 12th August, 1866, showing a cage to which was attached a tablet bearing the inscription: "*Conflictus intermus*, four years old." The beast of prey in the cage stretches forth its claw that holds a sheet of paper with the word "Indemnity" written on it. In front of the cage is Bismarck, holding a gigantic crown of laurel up to the beast. Inscribed on the laurel leaves are the words: "Königgrätz, Gitschin, Skalitz, Nachod, Aschaffenburg." The *Kladderadatsch* cartoon had the simple inscription: "Picture without many words."

At the same time as he settled the domestic constitutional conflict, Bismarck won the century-old contest between Prussia and Austria for the primacy of the House of Hohenzollern over Germany. The German peoples were to be united under the Hohenzollerns and the Imperial crown was to rest on the head of a Hohenzollern. But it was a good thing that the gods did not reveal all the future, even to the keenest eyes. Who would have prophesied to the Premier, Count Bismarck, on the evening of 3rd July, 1866, that the grandson and successor of the old King William I of Prussia (who, thanks to the masterful policy of his Minister, Otto von Bismarck, was victorious in the battle for German hegemony) that twenty-six years later, William II would with his own hand address a letter to the Emperor Francis Joseph of Austria (who had been defeated at Königgrätz) wounding, humiliating and vilifying Bismarck—a letter that closed the chambers of the Hofburg to the great old man. The prophecy would surely have soured all the joy the real victor of Sadowa felt at his triumph.

In the autumn of 1866 Professor Daniel asked me if I had ever been to the Harz. When I said that I had not, he told me that I must soon remedy this omission, and that I certainly ought to climb the Brocken. "Every German must climb the Brocken, because Goethe wrote *Faust*." I went to the Harz accompanied by my brother Adolf. We marched steadily along the beautiful

roads which cross the Harz. I do not intend to describe the
journey after Goethe and Heine have done so. Nor will I quote
the whole of the ode of Count Frederick Leopold Stolberg, which
we had to learn by heart, and in which he greets the " esteemed
land of the Cherusci," which Dame Nature, out of the prodigal
urn, had endowed with virile ornaments. I will only state that
upon us youngsters, for whom dear Taunus, the Odenwald and
the Black Forest were the most beautiful mountains in the world,
the Harz also made a deep impression. Even in historical interest
it was not inferior to South Germany. The figures of Saxon and
Frankish Emperors rose up before us as we viewed the castles
and the slopes of the Harz, and the grave of the first Henry in
Quedlinburg, as we recalled the old Imperial city at Goslar and
the mediæval history of the German people at Harzburg. The
Brocken could vie with the Feldberg and even with the Altkönig.
Of course, we quoted *Faust* as we approached the summit:

> " *Seh die Bäume hinter Bäumen,*
> *Wie sie schnell vorüberrücken,*
> *Und die Klippen, die sich bücken,*
> *Und die langen Felsenmassen,*
> *Wie sie schnarchen, wie sie blasen!* " [1]

When we were in the neighbourhood of Schierke and Elend,
where Goethe had set the scenes of the *Witches Sabbath*, we smiled
as we recalled that a French translator of *Faust* had recently rendered
this by: " *Le paysage respire la friponnerie et la misère.*" When
we got to the top we had the luck and the satisfaction of getting
a magnificent view. It is true that we could not see the Erzgebirge,
which a Leipzig man we met on the way had held in prospect,
and still less the North Sea and the Baltic, which a man from
Berlin claimed to have seen. But before us lay Magdeburg, the
Thuringian Forest and the Elbe. Our master had urged us to
have a look at the Rosstrappe as well as climbing the Brocken. In
his opinion the view from the Tanzplatz, which we would get
when we emerged from the forest, the view of the granite rocks,
the foaming and roaring Bode, the blue Brocken and the laughing
plain was one of the most beautiful in our Fatherland. He thought

---

[1] Lo now! lo, how swiftly races
Tree past tree! How the gigantic
Crags lean over, and the antic
Rocky snouts that stand in cluster
How they snarl, and how they bluster.
　　　　　　　(*Faust* i. Trans. ALBERT LATHAM.)

the rushing sound of the Bode was like the rustling of the wings of cherubim which the Prophet recognized as the sound of the Lord's approach, the tumult of the Almighty.

In the spring of 1867 we accepted an invitation from my uncle Wolf Baudissin to go to Dresden. Franz Liszt used to say that everybody ought to find his own background. "*Il faut que chacun trouve son cadre.*" In the summer time Wolf Baudissin found his little corner under the oaks and beeches of Rantzau, in winter in Dresden. It was still the Dresden which Herder had made famous as " the German Florence," and which the Vienna publicist, Francis Schuselka, has named the " delicate city of salons " because of the culture and kindness of its inhabitants. This environment suited my uncle perfectly. At his house I met his niece, who was married to the Baron Bodo von Stockhausen. At first von Stockhausen was Hanoverian Ambassador in Paris, then in Vienna, and then High Court Chamberlain to Queen Marie of Hanover. She was a beautiful and intellectual woman. In my father's opinion she had the deepest and most original mind of all his cousins. She published a diary, partly in French and partly in German, which contained many fine observations and reflections. To quote only one of them: " A Frenchman said to me once, ' *Lorsqu' on voyage en Orient, il n'y a qu'un moyen de se défaire de la vermine, il faut être sale au point de la dégoûter.*' " Once while I was vainly racking my mind how I could entertain a visitor and get him to talk, her long-forgotten words came back to me: " There is probably only one way of getting rid of a boring person, and that is to be even more boring than he." Marie von Ebner-Eschenbach wrote profounder aphorisms. But my aunt could do as well as Mechtilde Lichnowsky, the author of several unrhymed dramas.

On the second day of my visit to my uncle Baudissin, a most exceptionally beautiful young woman came into my uncle's salon. I stared at her like the poor shepherds of the valley at the maiden from a strange country.[1] I have no reason for self-reproach on this account, even after so many years and decades, for she was my uncle's grandniece, my cousin Elizabeth Stockhausen, the future Baroness Herzogenberg, of whom Adolphus Wach, the stern jurist, said in his memorial speech after her death in 1892: " To me her beautiful, lustrous, golden hair, her cheerful, infinitely tender, and divinely enthusiastic expression, the high grace of her movements, are the outward manifestations of her soul's perfect beauty, such as the Old Masters reveal when they depict a saint

[1] An allusion to Schiller's poem " Das Mädchen aus der Fremde."

or a virgin angel who smiles down upon us. Her mere presence
was pure harmony, a melody of richest tones, a harmony of the
soul's noblest powers. It was she—this beautiful creature, this
corporeal revelation of the divine. What she was, lived, spoke
and thought, bore the impression of the highest spiritual nobility.
Thus did God create her, a virgin disciple of art, born and not
made. And she ripened, and became art's priestess."

When I first saw Elizabeth Stockhausen at the age of seventeen,
I fell so deeply under her spell, that I dreamed of her for weeks
on end, which she naturally neither observed nor suspected. A
year later she married the well-known musician, Henry, Baron von
Herzogenberg, the most faithful of master Johannes Brahms'
faithful adherents. Max Kalbeck published a correspondence
between Henry and Elizabeth Herzogenberg and Johannes
Brahms. These letters are unjust to the great master of Bayreuth,
but they reveal a lofty disposition. Elizabeth Herzogenberg died
on 7th June, 1892, after a period of suffering, in St. Remo.
There she was buried in a lonely churchyard on the shores of the
blue Mediterranean under laurels, palms and cypresses. Adolf
Hildebrandt adorned her tomb with a marble relief of a female
figure sitting before an organ. The face, in imitation of Donatello's
Saint Cecilia, but with the features of Elizabeth Herzogenberg,
is attentive to the sound of the instrument.

In the autumn of 1867 I took my matriculation examination. I
consider this examination at the age of maturity to be most difficult of
all. The legal preliminary examination was, thank goodness, spared
me. The entrance examinations in Frankfort, Neustrelitz and Halle,
and the subsequent examinations for the Bar and the chief diplomatic examination, seem like child's play to me compared with
the matriculation. We were exhaustively examined in Halle by
Director Kramer, Professors Daniel, Dryander and Voigt, in the
presence of a government official and an education officer from
Magdeburg. The translation of Latin and Greek unseens and the
German essay had to be done in a closed room. After morning
prayers we had to begin on the German essay at nine o'clock.
Tension was great. I saw many white and anxious faces around
me. I myself felt in the best form. One of the candidates
approached me. His name was Puppel. He had already failed
twice in the examination. If he did not get through this time he
would not be able to go in for it again. Besides, the administrative
career which his father had chosen for him would be closed. He
whispered to me: " The German essay is my weakest subject.
If it is too much for me again and I fail for the third time, my

father will kill me. Do help me, I appeal to you! You've got such a ready pen. You can easily write two themes in the time allowed for the paper, one for me and one for yourself. Save me!" I was touched, and told him that he could sit near me.

The subject of the essay was not too easy to deal with. Puppel went pale and looked helplessly at me when it was read out to us. We had to explain the points of similarity and difference between the Iliad and the Song of the Nibelungs fundamentally and exhaustively, and yet briefly and concisely. As quickly as possible, and with the simian agility with which the Vienna Press had reproached the Prussians in 1866, I sketched out an essay for my comrade Puppel. I then turned with a quiet conscience to my own work. But unfortunately the exchange of ideas between Puppel and myself had not gone unobserved by the examiner, who was supervising us from the dais. He swept down on Puppel like a hawk on a dove. He tore my essay out of his hands and, holding it triumphantly up in the air, cried out: "This will be reported to the authorities at once." Then he disappeared. The consternation of the class was great, and still greater was its anxiety as to how the matter would end. After a full hour's delay the examiners returned to the classroom with the education officer at their head, followed by Director Kramer, the inspector *adjunctus* Daniel, and four other professors all "*secundum ordinem.*" The education officer began in a stern voice: "An unheard-of thing has happened. Two pupils have attempted to deceive their examiners. Thank God this outrage has been discovered in time. The pupil Puppel will be excluded from the examination and relegated as well. The pupil Bülow really deserves the same punishment. But owing to the assurance given by the Director and the Inspector that he is a generous-minded youth, who out of sympathy, wished to help his neighbour, the assurance given by his master that he is unusually gifted, twelve hours' detention and a bad conduct mark in his certificate will be adequate punishment for his offence." After the Director Kramer had expressed his deep regret at the occurrence, the masters left the room in the same order in which they had entered.

As my dear Daniel passed by he laid his hand on my shoulder and said: "Hold your head up! You have a flexible nature, and in life you will overcome other difficulties besides this one. Now write a really good German essay. But in future commit to memory the motto I dedicated to you in the ' *Lyra Messianica* ' at your confirmation: 'See then that ye walk circumspectly, not as fools, but as wise '" (Ephesians v, 15).

When Daniel, following the others, had left the examination room, Puppel came up to me. " It's a shame," he said, " that I am relegated and you are not, seeing that you are just as guilty as I." Oh, Puppel, I do not know anything about your fate in later life! I suspect that you entered on a military career in spite of your father's first objections. Perhaps you died a hero's death. If you survived the war I am afraid you never rose above the rank of major. I do not think that you could have attained the rank of general. Whatever your lot, I have often thought about you in my later years.

When Parliamentary parties who assured me of their confidence as long as they wanted to get something out of me, deserted me when they had got what they wanted, and when politicians who seemed my staunch supporters turned their backs on me the moment they were prompted to do so by self-interest or by cowardice, and when subordinates, who had crawled at my feet, betrayed me at the first favourable moment, then, O Puppel, I thought of you. You were not an isolated phenomenon, dear Puppel, you were a species.

When, with the exception of the unfortunate Puppel, we resumed our seats in the examination room, we got a new subject for the German essay. It was: " Our Mediæval Popular Epic as a Great and Magnificent Song of Loyalty." I thought of the admonition which my father had given me a decade before on the high road that leads from Frankfort to Mainz. " Keep up your nerves, sir! " I finished my task before the others, and it got a Class One, a rare thing. The assistant inspector of the High School at Halle, Studienrat Faltin, was kind enough to send me, as the oldest former pupil of the High School, a copy of my essay on my seventy-fifth birthday. I hope it will not be considered vanity on my part that once when I looked at the work I had done so many years before, I did not find it bad. It is true that I realized how right Goethe was when he said that time never breaks up a living organism once it has received its shape. My conversation and the many speeches which I made in my later life, particularly my impromptu speeches, were not infrequently criticized for being too rich in quotation. Even my examination essay of 24th July, 1867, begins with a quotation of Barthold Niebuhr's (that, " the Germans are the Greeks of modern times "), and finishes with a remark of Schiller's " that loyalty is no empty deceit," a remark that was very much to the point. On the following day I had to suffer my punishment of detention. As books were forbidden, I spent the time reciting *Faust*, which, following the advice of my revered teacher, Daniel, I had gradually committed to memory when I was a sixth former.

By way of an epilogue I will now reproduce the letter, which I got from my father when he heard of the offence I had committed in the matriculation examination. His letter does not merely express his kindness of heart, but also his wisdom, which, founded upon experience and knowledge of mankind and character, made him, as Bismarck himself declared, one of Bismarck's most valuable collaborators:

Tuesday, July 30, 1867.

DEAR BERNHARD,

We have been expecting a letter from you for a long time, although we knew that your examination would prevent you from writing on the usual day. Nevertheless, we were very anxious for news. We delayed writing from day to day. Yesterday we got Professor Daniel's letter and yours at the same time. The former came via Neustrelitz, and it told us how you had fared in this trying week. Professor Daniel, whom I shall thank in my reply to-day, writes very charmingly about this great blunder of yours. It is a real comfort to me, my dear son, that you could be saved from the sternest consequences, and I shall refrain from reproaching you after the event, especially as you will have told yourself what there is to be said. And I am glad to say that your exemplary conduct has saved you from a punishment which would have had lasting consequences, even if only the loss of half a year's studies. In this way you yourself have made good what was not at all good. Detention is, I admit, an unwelcome thing. I would have been glad if you had got Number One for conduct this term also, but do not let us grumble at that. There is only one thing, my dear good Bernhard, that I would like you to consider very seriously on this occasion. What you have done, apart from the fact that it is rather superfluous to help a weakling of this kind at all, is not considered wrong in other ways by pupils, and in a moral sense it is rather a sign of your kindness of heart. Nevertheless, it is wrong and unethical, because the examination is a hall-mark given by the State as a guarantee and a proof of a good school education, and is tied up with distinctions and advantages. So that he who helps an unworthy person to pass, commits or connives at a deception, and therefore participates in a falsehood, a thing that cannot have any good results. Therefore let your judgment in all things belonging to this life accord not with appearances or with kindly, unthinking, slipshod ways, but with deeds and with true veracity. You will fare better thus and preserve the purity of your conscience. And how do you know whether Puppel, had you not handed him that unfortunate piece of paper, would not perhaps have passed the examination by his own effort, whereas he has now been relegated? But enough of this, dear Bernhard, I did not want to say any more than would preserve you from similar carelessness in the future. And I am indeed sorry that in these trying days, in which you should have harvested the well-earned fruits of honest labour, should have been spoilt by this episode and that you should have gone through such anxiety. I take it that I may conclude from your sensible letters that you have calmed down again and look forward to the *viva voce* with good courage, the more so as you have had abundant proof of your teachers' good will. I hope that by doing very well in your examination you will be able to mitigate the bad mark in your final report. Mama sends you her heartiest good wishes. Of course, she, too, is very sorry about the whole business, and you know what a dislike her truthful and dutiful soul feels for any tricks etc., committed by the pupils. But she, too, is so sorry that you, who have given her so much pleasure by your school work, have had to live through this disagreeable day, and she hopes very much that you will rest and gather strength. And just one other thing, my dear son. You have always had a certain weakness for rather stupid and careless fellow-pupils who attracted you by their boastfulness. I do not know if the examinee with the stupid name belongs to this category. But I would like to urge you very strongly, now that you are entering life on your own, to keep to the industrious and orderly youths who will be useful to you in your intercourse with them instead of to your weaker brothers.

Yours affectionate,

B. B.

Good Frau von Engel of Strelitz has died at the age of ninety-four. She lived through the great French Revolution, the epic of Napoleon, Maria Theresa, Catharine II and Queen Louise.

I did not leave Halle without sorrowful emotions, although there were certain things which made my departure easier. It was one of the loveliest moments of my life when I burnt my logarithmic tables, with the help of which I had so often solved difficult multiplication and division sums by means of simple addition and subtraction. Clear as the practical advantage of this system was to me, it remained foreign to my nature, as I have no fondness for figures. While I was Cabinet Minister I took part in preparing and presenting a long series of budgets involving thousands of millions, and I always carefully prepared the case for them in Parliament. But it was only the political side of financial bills that stimulated me to independent thought, while I left the purely arithmetical and technical, the advantageous grouping of assets and liabilities and the other budget-balancing arts to my excellent and expert collaborators. An amiable Venetian lady once said to Jean-Jacques Rousseau, as he himself relates, " *O Giacomo, lasciate le donne e studiate la matamatica!* " I felt a certain inclination to do the opposite.

When I left the College I had the feeling which filled me when emerging from the mouth of the Elbe past the red buoys behind Cuxhaven. I saw the open sea before me. A new day beckons to new shores. Nevertheless I was moved when the students sang:

> " *So leb denn wohl, du stilles Haus,*
> *Wir ziehn betrübt von dir hinaus.*" [1]

Halle was not a beautiful town. Those who came from Magdeburg and Leipzig, and above all the refined Dresdeners, used to say humorously that you could smell Halle rather than see it. What they had in mind was the town's atmosphere, filled with saline vapours and lignite dust, and the steep streets with their bad paving, and the dirt, which had become proverbial. But it was not in vain that both Daniel and Thucydides preached to me that mankind owns the land and not the land mankind. I was attached with my whole heart to the people in Halle, especially my dear Professor Daniel. Besides, the surroundings of the town offered many charms. In the far distance beckoned the castles that stand boldly and proudly by the bright shores of the Saale. Often did I wander among them. The two towers of Saaleck, and, high up on a steep wall, the Rudelsburg, the pleasant town of Kösen, Merseburg, with its proud memories of the Emperor Otto the Great, Naumburg, which was beleaguered by the Hussites, indeed, the whole district had entered my heart. I often went on the river Saale.

Our parents had obtained introductions for us to a number of

---

[1] Farewell, quiet home,
We leave you sadly.

reputable Halle families, who gave us a kind reception. A distinguished lady belonging to this circle really took to me. In contrast to my brother Adolf, who had rather a rough nature, I responded to her kindness. On more than one beautiful summer's day I was allowed to escort her to Crölwitz, or Giebichenstein, to the Raven or to the Nightingale Islands. She was a buxom blonde between thirty and forty years old, and it was not easy to row her along. In this respect Hesiod's words proved true, namely, that the path leading to the summit was steep. She had a good, yes a tender heart, and was not stinting with love's reward, when, after our trip on the water, we rested in the friendly shade of the bushes that skirt the Saale, or in the cool room of a country inn. When, after I had successfully passed my matriculation I said good-bye to her and her husband, he handed me a book: *Quinti Horatii Flacci Opera ad exemplar Londinense a Johanne Pine, Berolini* 1745 *Sumtibus Ambrosii Haude, Bibliop. Reg. et Acad. Scient. privil.* As he gave it me he said: " My young friend, my dear wife has told me nice things about you. You seem to be an industrious and able youth, and thirsty for knowledge. But do not forget amid so many praiseworthy qualities that in the spring time of life pleasure should have its due. He quoted, not without solemnity, the lines that Horace addressed to his friend Virgil:

> " *Misce stultitiam consiliis brevem:*
> *Dulce est desipere in loco.*" [1]

His wife could do a lot of things, but she did not know any Latin. She asked to have the Horatian lines translated into our beloved German. With the same feeling her husband declaimed:

> " *Meng in weiseren Ernst wenige Torheit ein.*
> *Süss ist's, schwärmen am rechten Ort.*"

She smiled. It was that *sourire féminin*, with which Alfred de Musset deals in one of his most charming comedies. In the comedy *Il ne faut jurer de rien*, young Valentin van Buck explains to his old uncle what there may be beneath this feminine smile, this *sourire féminin*. Years later I often saw this play in Paris in the Comedie Française. Thiron played the part of Uncle van Buck, Delauney, his nephew Valentin, Mlle. Brohan, Baroness de Mantes, and the pretty Mlle. Reichenberg, her daughter Cécile. When I listened to the reflections of the nephew van Buck on the

---

[1] Mingle a little folly with wiser gravity.
  It is sweet to be rapturous in due season.

sourire féminin I thought of the charming Saale, of my friend who liked to have me row her along, and of her learned husband, who, with a superior air, preached to me the doctrine of Epicurus in the form that Quintus Horatius Flaccus gave it. His Horace is in my library, neatly bound in pigskin.

CHAPTER IX

University of Lausanne (1867)—Vevey—Donna è mobile—Leipzig University—Professor William Roscher—Reading Matter: Influence of the Novel on Knowledge of Life and Human Nature—Walking Tour through Switzerland—Removal to Berlin University—Professor Rudolf Gneist—Death of my Little Sister Bertha—Cure in Bad Oeynhausen (June, 1870)—The Political Situation, the Ems Dispatch.

WHEN I returned to my parents in Flottbek, where they were spending the summer in the little so-called Herrenhaus in Jenischpark, I proposed to my father that I should begin my university studies in Bonn. I had a strong desire either to join the Borussia corps in Bonn, or the Saxon Corps in Göttingen, or the Saxo borrussians in Heidelberg. I would have liked to have gone to Bonn best of all:

> " *zu des Rheins gestreckten Hügeln,*
> *Hochgesegneten Gebieten.*" [1]

My father did not receive my request favourably. He himself had never been a corps-student, and he had little appreciation for a corps-student's life. "You would bloat your belly with beer-drinking, atrophy your mind, disfigure your face with scars and learn nothing." This was certainly a one-sided conception. Not only did the greatest of German statesmen, Prince Bismarck, come from the ranks of the corps-students, but a good many other eminent Germans as well, such men as Rudolf Bennigsen and Botho Eulenburg, Karl Peters and Ernst Bassermann. Nevertheless, it is true that many have sapped their mental powers for the rest of their lives in the students' corps. Taking everything into consideration the army was a better training-ground in the old days for high administrative officialdom and diplomacy.

It was decided that I should spend the first winter of my university period in Lausanne. I set out on the journey accompanied by my brother Adolf. We made a short stay at Frankfort in order to try our luck at the gaming tables at Homburg, which

---

[1] To the long stretched hills of the Rhine
The regions that are most blest.

were then still being run by Herr Blanc, whose money, made in Homburg, and later in Monaco, was to bring him princely sons-in-law and alliances which extended to royal thrones. I won a few hundred guilders, which raised our spirits. The section of the journey from Lucerne over the Brünig to Brienz we accomplished on foot. In Berne we fed the bears, and then went on by foot from the old watch tower in Romont to Vevey. From the Signal de Chexbres I enjoyed my first view of the Lake of Geneva, whither I often returned and for which I yearned still more often.

At Lausanne we were accommodated in the house of Professor Gay, who was University Reader in French Literature. Like most Vaudois he was a brisk and cheerful man who looked on the bright side of life. It is said that the good Vaudois wine puts people in a merry mood. Madame Gay, who came from Aigle in the Rhône district, looked after us very well. There was a view of the lake from the Gays' house. We had a broad panoramic view from the terrace of the old Minster, which, built in the year 1,000, is probably the most beautiful Gothic cathedral in Switzerland. Our favourite walk was to Mont Benon, an excursion which was the pride of all the inhabitants of the town, and, let us hope, still is so.

I cut out all lectures other than those of M. Gay, my host. I discovered some very attractive shops in the Rue du Bourg, where the numerous Englishmen living in Lausanne provided themselves with good tobacco and short wooden pipes. I had smoked cigars in Halle and also in Strelitz. Now I got to know that good English tobacco smoked in a short wooden pipe tasted still better. I enjoyed the pleasure of pipe smoking for forty years, but gave up this vice the day my friend and doctor, Renvers, convinced me that the throat and the stomach were much better off without tobacco. I will not go into the question here whether a man is happier if he has many needs or no needs at all—a matter which has occupied so many philosophers.

Two groups flourished at the university of Lausanne: the Bellettriens, who for the most part came from French Switzerland, and the Zofingers,[1] who were recruited from all parts of the Confederation.

We kept well away from both groups, but entered into friendly relations with a circle of young Swiss, especially Vaudois and Genevese, which in some cases have lasted throughout my whole life. Even in winter we undertook excursions from Lausanne, partly into the snow, and did a little mountain climbing in all directions. We soon got to know the shores of the lake very well.

[1] Swiss student guilds.

I went on foot to Morges, to Rolle, which is surrounded by vine-
yards, to Nyon, with its ancient castle, and to Coppet. While I was
in Coppet I thought of my great-uncle Wolf Baudissin, who in
his youth had been engaged to the daughter of Madame de Staël,
and who later married the Duke of Broglie. The engagement with
my uncle was dissolved because both parties came to the conclusion
that they were not suited to one another. We liked even better to
set out from Lausanne in the direction of Pully, Lutry and Cully
to St. Saphorin, the bells of which ring out so clearly and beautifully.

     Nearly every week I visited Vevey, where my aunt, the widow
of my great-uncle, Senator Martin Jenisch, used to spend the
winter in the Hotel des Trois-Couronnes. Many years later she
bequeathed a great legacy to the town of Vevey, with the help
of which the Jenisch Museum was founded. It contained valuable
pictures, a good library, and an interesting collection of natural
historical objects. I think, however, that my aunt would have
done better to have thought either of her birthplace, Lübeck, or
the native city of her husband, Hamburg. A smart international
company assembled in the Hôtel des Trois-Couronnes, including
many beautiful women. A Spaniard, Frau von X, was considered,
and rightly so, to be the most beautiful. The sight of her involun-
tarily reminded one of the poem Alfred de Musset dedicated to his
Andalusian friend:

> " *Vrai Dieu! Lorsque son oeil pétille*
> *Sous la frange de ses reseaux,*
> *Rien que pour toucher sa mantille,*
> *De par tous les saints de Castille,*
> *On se ferait rompre les os.*"

Her husband was staying in Paris. A young Greek with large,
dark, melancholy eyes was believed to be her favourite. There was
dancing almost every evening at the Hôtel des Trois-Couronnes.

     When I was there on another occasion I noticed that the dark
Greek was much occupied with a fair-haired English girl. I noticed
also that the Spanish girl was observing this flirtation with an angry
eye. As I only knew Frau von X slightly, and had not paid her
any attentions, I regarded the matter with indifference. I was
therefore astonished when she came over to me and asked me to
dance a waltz with her. After we had spun round the big hall
once or twice, she sat down with me on a bench and asked me
about the progress of my studies, and also about my reading. She
examined me keenly and not without intelligence. When I said
that J. J. Rousseau was my favourite author and had declared with

warmth that the *Nouvelle Héloïse* was a magnificent book, she added with a smile: " *Le bosquet de Julie n'est pas loin d'ici!* " She asked me whether I would like to have tea with her at home. Her carriage, she said, was outside, and her villa not far away. It was clear at that moment that the Tempter had appeared to me in the form of a beautiful woman. I ought to have remained unyielding, as St. Anthony did in a similar situation, or, long before that, like the chaste Joseph. But it is not given to everybody to be saintly. It is difficult to become a saint, otherwise there would be many more saints indeed than there are now.

Frau von X was very beautiful, and I was greatly tempted. I accepted the friendly invitation. Indeed, I accepted it gladly. Frau von X took my arm and we went to the door. The Greek, who had been watching us for some time with obvious excitement, approached us. I heard him whisper: " *De grâce! Accordez-moi un instant, écoutez moi! Je ne vous ai pas trahie. Il s'agit d'une distraction, d'une plaisanterie.* " She did not answer. As we stood in the hotel entrance she asked me to step into the carriage first. The Greek stood beside her. He whispered: " *Je vous supplie, ayez pitié de moi! Je vous jure: Si vous ne me pardonnez pas, je me tuerai.* " She had in the meantime taken her place beside me on the seat. She lowered the window of the carriage and, stressing every word, she answered: " *Vous êtes bien trop lâche pour vous tuer. Cocher! Chez moi, et ventre à terre.* "

When I left the villa the next morning and walked back to Vevey I saw a crowd of people in the distance on the quay-side in front of the Hotel des Trois-Couronnes looking out across the lake through telescopes and opera-glasses and gesticulating. When I came nearer I heard that a boat was drifting on the waters without oars and without occupants. On the previous evening the young Greek had hired a boat and had set out alone on the lake. He had not returned. An hour later the news was spread that the body of the poor fellow had been washed up on the shore of the lake near St. Saphorin. He had suffered the death of Leander, but was less fortunate, for his Hero did not weep for him.

While this sad occurrence was being discussed by everyone, my beautiful friend approached me. I rose to meet her in order to spare her feelings. She did not lose countenance for a single moment. She preserved the tranquillity of a marble statue, a tranquillity which even enhanced the Juno-like beauty of her form. " *Je lui ai toujours dit qu'il n'avait pas le pied marin,* " she declared indifferently. The tragic event appeared to make a strong impression upon everybody except the beautiful woman, who had given me hospitality during the night. A good many people proposed that the customary dancing should be cancelled for that evening. She objected to this, declaring: "*Après tout, nous ne sommes ni apparentés avec ce jeune étourdi, ni autrement liés avec lui. Dansons comme toujours!*" She took part in the dance that evening with the indifference which she would probably have shown if, at a bull fight, a toreador whom she had applauded a few minutes before were to fall gored by a bull. This deplorable experience also taught me a lesson. I understood better than formerly Goethe's admonition:

> "*Die Welt ist nicht aus Brei und Mus geschaffen,*
> *Deswegen haltet euch nicht wie Schlaraffen.*
> *Harte Bissen gibt es zu kauen:*
> *Wir müssen erwürgen-oder sie verdauen.*" [1]

A few weeks later I left Lausanne. It was not easy for me to leave the beautiful lake, and I threw a sorrowful departing glance upon the pleasant hamlets, dark woods, green meadows and picturesque châlets. The Wallis and Savoy mountains whose majesty was reflected in the still clear waters of the Lake of Geneva, towered above me. What a contrast there was between the purity of the lake, the beauty of its shores, the harmony of the whole landscape, and the restless, peaceless, evil machinations of mankind who so imperfectly recognize the things that serve their true and eternal salvation.

From Lausanne I went to the University of Leipzig, since my father had refused my request to continue my studies at Bonn. I travelled with Frau von X as far as Basle. At Basle we put up at the Hotel Zu den Drei Königen, from the windows of which there was a beautiful view of the swift Rhine. From there Frau von X travelled to Paris, where her husband was expecting her. We never saw one another again. I heard that she had reached a high place socially and was admired and honoured as a beautiful lady and a brilliant woman of the world. Her daughters made good marriages.

From Basle I travelled to Leipzig, which the student Frosch in the *Auerbach's Keller* named the "Little Paris." Here also as in Lausanne, I only took one set of lectures, those of Professor

---

[1] The world is not made of dough and jam,
Do not therefore behave like gluttons.
There are hard mouthfuls to chew
We must either digest them—or choke.

William Roscher, the distinguished representative of the historical method in political economy. He had a fine mind, and his external appearance corresponded with it. When he entered the lecture hall, scrupulously well dressed, silk hat in hand, placed his elegant walking stick in the corner, adjusted his cuffs, and began his lecture, an atmosphere of the greatest urbanity pervaded the whole auditorium.

I congratulate myself to-day that I attended Roscher's courses and followed his lectures attentively and with reflection. Later on I passed beyond his scope and came under the influence of Adolf Wagner and Gustav Schmoller. But I owe it to his grounding that I acquired a standard of competency that enabled me to guard against exaggeration, one-sidedness, fantastic notions, and fixed ideas. Pencil in hand, I have more than once read his *System der Volkswirtschaft*.[1] The first volume, especially, made a lasting impression. I have filled it with marginal notes and made extracts of whole passages. I also read the *Nationalökonomie des Handels- und Gewerbefleisses*, with interest and advantage. It is more than a " Guide and Reader for Business men and Students," as the author announces on its title-page with a modesty that has become rare nowadays. Everybody who is engaged in public life can learn much from it. When I was still a young man I found in Roscher the weapons with which later on in life I fought those doctrines of the Social Democrats (without being unjust to their aims) which could not be harmonized with the good of the whole community, with the interest of the state as correctly understood, and with the existence of a strong and contented Empire. From Roscher I learned that there is no more a final economic ideal for all time and all peoples than there is one size of clothes to fit all and everybody. He taught me that just as in the cosmos the apparently opposed centrifugal and centripetal forces effect the harmony of the spheres, so in the economic life of mankind both self-interest and conscience form public opinion. He sharpened my perception of the fact that Socialism and Communism are not, as their blind opponents and their blind adherents believe, new and peculiar phenomena of modern times, but a disease which almost regularly attacks highly civilized peoples at a certain period of their existence. He proved from history that from time immemorial the noblest minds and the greatest rascals are to be met with in the ranks of the Socialists. I did not therefore find it so astonishing that in Germany, which has had a very rapid economic ascent, perhaps all too rapid, and which has become wealthy, in some

[1] System of Political Economy.

respects beyond expectation, there have been here and there industrious and estimable workmen, many of whom follow the red flag, and that their flag has been carried before them by leaders who are convinced (at least in part) and are enthusiastic for a noble ideal.

Even when I was quite young I held the view, which I summarized in my first speech as Imperial Chancellor and Premier in the Prussian House of Deputies on 9th January, 1901, in the following words: " In accordance with my whole political outlook I consider it to be the highest duty of the Government in the conflict of economic interests to reconcile existing contradictions where opportunity occurs, in order to effect as just a compromise as possible and to support those who cannot out of their own resources help themselves."

The words of Heraclitus, that " everything flows," are also appropriate to public matters. The epochs in the life of the state follow one another like high tide and low. This became clear to me one fine summer day, in the woods of St. Germain, when thirteen years after I had taken the courses of William Roscher at Leipzig, as a young secretary of the Germany Embassy in Paris, I read the essay which Gustav Schmoller had written in October, 1880, in Strassburg and had published in the *Jahrbuch für Gesetzgebung, Verwaltung, und Volkswirtschaft.*[1]

The eternal poles around which public, social and economic life turns, the contradiction around which battles of domestic politics are fought, are not so much Liberal and Conservative as individualistic and centralistic. The rise of the Prussian State from 1640 to the ascension of the Great Elector, and until 1806, the black year of Jena, was accomplished according to a theory of the state, which, for all its one-sidedness and a certain magnificent ruthlessness towards individual rights and individual freedom, always placed the whole above the part. The regeneration of Prussia from 1808 to 1871 followed in an individualistic sense, amid the spread and advance of liberal thought and outlook. Each of both these great epochs bequeathed a beneficient legacy—the centralistic epoch; the unification of Prussian monarchy, a rigid administration, a model organisation of the army and the bureaucracy; the individualistic epoch and the protection of individual rights, personal freedom and unrestricted movement, the Constitution and Local Government. Bismarck, with the latitude of genius, governed first in the one way and then in the other, and so

---

[1] Prince Bülow's *Speeches*. Large edition, vol. i, p. 176. Small edition, vol. i, p. 234.

created and built up the great and strong German Empire which existed before the World War, a state which combined the old Prussian conservative energy and discipline with generous and liberal German spirit, a state that had not its like in the whole world.

In Leipzig my brother Adolf and I, in accordance with our father's wishes, kept away from the students' corps. The "Meissner" was considered the smartest corps at Leipzig University. Soon after I joined the university two representatives of the corps appeared at our rooms in order to canvass my brother and myself, or, in other words, to persuade us to join the corps. We remained faithful to the promise we had given our father, and refused the request. A young Swiss whom we had got to know in Lausanne, and who, like us, was continuing his studies at the Pleisse, invited us to come to the " beer evening " of the association which he had joined. The excessive beer-swilling every evening repelled us, " pothouse humour " did not appeal to us, the banal tone displeased us, and we did not go again. I preferred to employ my spare time in gymnastics, fencing, and long walks, and, in the evening, to reflection on the notes I took at Roscher's lectures.

Following my old bent, I read a great deal, not only works on history and political economy, but also novels, especially French novels. He who is entering into life learns, as I believe, more about intercourse with mankind, and about practical affairs, more about the ways of the world and the handling of his fellow men, from novels than from the study of the most learned compendiums. Above all, Balzac and Stendhal, Flaubert and Guy de Maupassant, Turgeniev and Leo Tolstoi, and the novels of Disraeli, Thackeray and Bulwer Lytton are to be recommended in this connection. The novels of Gustav Freytag and Berthold Auerbach, Gutzkow and Spielhagen, of Marlitt and Wilhelmine Hillern give kindly glimpses into the souls of German Philistines. But they are not made to serve as a compass for the sometimes stormy passage upon the world's great stream. Theodor Fontane and Maria von Ebner-Eschenbach serve this purpose better. The lack of psychology which is peculiar to many Germans, and which often shows itself in German politics, may be attributed to the fact that the average German intellectual has too few psychological novels in his own language, and therefore reads too much learned trash.

The Countess Sofie Hatzfeldt was pointed out to me in the Leipzig restaurant where I used to have lunch. She did not show any signs of having had so many worshippers in her youth. There was even less indication that of her sons, the elder, Alfred,

would become a prince and a hereditary member of the Prussian
Upper Chamber, and the younger, Paul, an ambassador and a
Knight of the Order of the Black Eagle.   It was also difficult to
believe that the orthodox Catholic and highly moral Countess
Melanie Nesselrode-Ehreshofen, the wife of Count Maximilian
von Nesselrode-Ehreshofen, the Lord High Chamberlain of her
Majesty the Empress and Queen, Augusta, was the daughter of
Countess Sofie Hatzfelt, who in eccentric costume, a big cigar in
her mouth, and her hair dyed red, walked through the streets and
into the taverns of Leipzig arm-in-arm with a Socialist much
younger than herself who, if I remember rightly, was called Mendel
and had recently replaced the greater genius, Ferdinand Lassalle
as her lover.

Nevertheless, she was a considerable woman.   Her nephew,
Field-Marshal Walter Loë, once told me: " When Bismarck had
got into touch with Lassalle, my aunt, the Countess Sofie Hatzfeldt,
who was then still on intimate terms with Lassalle, received a
letter from the entourage of Karl Marx, which expressed the fear
that Ferdinand would let himself be " seduced " by Bismarck.
After she had spoken with Lassalle, Countess Hatzfeldt replied
to the London exiles that they could calm their fears.   Bismarck
was a very considerable man, she said, infinitely superior to the
rest of the Conservatives and reactionaries.   But he did not understand Democracy and the factory workers.   He was deluding
himself (she said) about the consequences of universal suffrage.
Bismarck thought that he could succeed in manipulating universal
suffrage in Germany as Napoleon III had done in France.   That
was a mistake.   Universal suffrage would sooner or later bring
Democracy, the Republic, and Socialism.   The letter of the
Countess Sofie Hatzfeldt in reply to the expressions of anxiety by
the people around Karl Marx ended by stating that Lassalle was
in touch with Bismarck so as to fortify his intention of granting
the universal ballot in the election of the future German Parliament:
" But in the last resort Lassalle will be the gainer by it and not
Bismarck."

In the late summer of 1868 I felt like the student in *Faust*:

> " *Aufrichtig möchte schon wieder fort*
> *Man sieht nichts Grünes, keinen Baum.*" [1]

[1] Frankly, I'd fain my steps retrace,
Within these walls and chambers gloomy.
I'm ill at ease . . .
No green thing, not a tree, I find.
(*Faust*, i.   Trans. ALBERT LATHAM.)

I longed to be back in the Swiss mountains, and before the beginning of the university holidays I had already set out upon a Swiss journey. Here, too, I had no intention of following in Goethe's tracks. I only wish to give a brief sketch of the Swiss travels of a German youth in the year 1868, between Sadowa and Sedan.

I set out with a rucksack on my back containing only the most necessary articles. On top of the rucksack was strapped a raincoat rolled up. Since I did not intend to climb the Matterhorn or Montblanc, I did not make myself ridiculous with an alpenstock ornamented with pictures of Selisberg and Uetliberg, but contented myself with an ordinary strong walking-stick. I sent a small bag on in advance in order to be able to fill up my rucksack with clean things every week. I walked alone for the most part, a habit I have always followed on walking tours since. That did not prevent me from entering into conversation with peasants, shepherds, fishermen, huntsmen and other stalwart Schweizers listed in the *dramatis personæ* of *William Tell*.

I had resolved while on Swiss territory to use only the " *carozza di San Francesco*," in other words, my feet, and not to travel by rail or in the post chaise. From Lucerne, the departure point of my journey, I first climbed the Pilatus, and on the next day the Rigi, and, favoured by the weather, I saw a magnificent sunrise. From Flüelen to Andermatt I chose the way that bold William Tell had recommended to the Duke of Swabia, the unfortunate Johann Parricida. I saw the black Felsentor and the smiling valley of Andermatt. From Göschenen I turned towards the Rhone Glacier and the Furka, and then towards the Bernese Oberland, where I climbed the Great and the Small Scheidegg, the Wengernalp, the Niesen and the Faulhorn. I reached the Rhone valley by way of Grindelwald and Lauterbrunnen, Kanderstag and Leuk. Here walking became very irksome. It was very hot, the road was dusty and the mosquitoes were a torture. But I remained true to my resolution not to make use of a vehicle while in Switzerland. I was compensated after leaving the Simplon road in Visp when, on a shady path close by the rushing grey-white Visp, the Brunneghorn, the Weisshorn, the Rothorn and finally the mighty Matterhorn, stood before me as I arrived at Zermatt. The Riffelalp and the Gornergrat seemed to be the most beautiful spots in Switzerland to me. From here onwards I undertook several climbing expeditions, which were accomplished without great difficulty. Then I went back to Visp. I set out upon the tramp over the Simplon and along the southward roads towards

Italy, in great expectation. The whole landscape stands as clearly before my eyes as though I had crossed the Simplon pass only yesterday. The Lauibach and the gorge of Gondo were passed, Paglino and Iselle were left behind, and Domodossola reached. For the first time in my life I was in Italy.

Goethe in his requiem on Prince Karl Josef Ligne makes Italia approach the bier of this witty *grand seigneur*, whom he calls the merriest man of his century, and speak to him thus:

> *Auch mich hast du besucht;*
> *Du musst's bedenken!*
> *Was ich vergeude,*
> *Niemand kann es schenken.*
>
> *Das Wehn der Himmelslüfte,*
> *Dem Paradiese gleich,*
> *Des Blumenfelds Gedüfte*
> *Das ist mein weites Reich.*
>
> *Das Leben aus dem Grabe*
> *Jahrhunderte beschliesst;*
> *Das ist der Schatz, die Habe,*
> *Die man mit mir geniesst."* [1]

I did not anticipate how many winters I would spend in the Bel Paese. Still less did I suspect that I should find my beloved wife there and with her all my life's happiness.

When I reached the "Long Lake," the *lacus Verbanus* of the Romans, to which we obstinate Germans give the Italian name of *Lago Maggiore*, I went to see the Borromaeic Islands, which Jean Paul in his novel *Titan*, which was much read in those days, described as spring's decorated throne. Although Italy was not in my programme, I felt that I must get to know the *Lacus Larius*, Lake Como, on whose shores I was to sojourn so often during my later life, in Bellagio, and in Cadenabbia, in Tremezzo, and in Torno. When I discovered this enchanting landscape, where for the first time I saw vines and fig trees, olives and chestnuts in

---

[1] Me too hast thou visited;
Thou must bear it in mind!
No one can give
What I lavish.

The blowing of Heavenly breezes, like Paradise,
The perfume of the flowery field they are my wide realm.
Life, from the grave, spans the centuries.
That is the treasure, the possession that is enjoyed with me.

their rich abundance, I understood why, when they saw this garden, our forefathers did not wish to go back to their homeland, which was harsher then than it is now. Politically I must ever deplore this southward migration, since, though it gave a strong ideal and spiritual impulse to the German genius, it nevertheless drained the life-blood of Mediæval Imperial splendour.

I could not resist the temptation to go on to far distant Milan and see the cathedral begun by a great German architect, Heinrich Arler, of Gmünd in Swabia. When in the evening I saw the glorious edifice dedicated to *Mariæ nascenti* with its innumerable spires, statues and turrets bathed in moonlight, and the gilded Madonna on the chief tower, I understood what Italian art under an Italian sky could mean. I took the return route from the Upper Italian lakes by way of Splügen. From Chiavenna to the mountain which forms the frontier between Italy and Switzerland, by post chaise. I sat up on the box beside the driver, who developed his political outlook with Italian vivacity.

For centuries [he said] the Italian people had suffered as much from the French as from the Germans, who preferred now one and now the other and sometimes played them off against each other. The arrogance with which the French had vaunted their services to the Italians after the Franco-Austrian war of 1859 was bound to estrange them. These were the first symptoms of the great change in attitude which subsequently caused Italy, for the sake of her independence and her security, to direct her policy not towards Paris any more, but towards Berlin. My friend the driver complained about the " *prepotenza* " and the " *cattiveria* " of the French.

To complete the journey from the Splügen Pass I again used Shank's Pony. My journey ended at Chur. In the Cathedral of Saint Lucius I saw the gravestone of Jürg Jenatsch, who was murdered in 1639. It was not until many years later, in January, 1896, that I became acquainted with Conrad Ferdinand Meyer's splendid novel, the hero of which is the Graubünden Colonel and liberator. I visited the Cathedral of Chur again in 1917, under the guidance of Bishop Georg Schmidt of Grüneck, who was friendly to Germany and in whose ancient palace I spent an agreeable day with my wife.

I found life in Leipzig less agreeable than ever on my return. The Rosenthal, of which the Leipzigers were so proud, could not compensate me for the Gorge du Chauderon and the Rochers de Naye. All the more did I admire the genius of our great and beloved Schiller, who in Gohlis, the pleasant though humble village at the extremity of the Rosenthal, wrote the Hymn to Joy, his magnificent expression of such an idealism and love of humanity as only Germans can understand.

Early in 1869 I removed to Berlin. I was suffering from an obstinate malady of the throat, and my parents wished to have me near them. It was a case of swollen tonsils and had to be treated with caustic. My parents were living on the first floor of the Arnimschen Palace in the Pariser Platz, where the Academy of Art now stands.

It was here that death for the second time came near me, and pain and anguish entered the house of my parents. The death of my only sister, the twelve-year-old Bertha, opened a deeper breach and made a more painful wound than the one inflicted fifteen years before, when my little two-year-old brother, Waldemar, was called to his eternal home. She was a strikingly beautiful and remarkably gifted child, with great blue eyes and magnificent blond hair, a true German child. She succumbed in a few days to diphtheria, against which no serum had then been discovered. She was brave to the last minute. My father prayed with her the Lord's prayer and the 23rd Psalm (The Lord is my Shepherd). Her last words were a verse from the old Moravian hymn:

> " *Muss ich auch gleich vor andern*
> *Im finstern Tale wandern,*
> *Dein Stab, Herr, and dein Stecken*
> *Benimmt mir allen Schrecken.*" [1]

She closed her eyes on 25th January, 1870. She was buried at the Twelve Apostles Churchyard in Berlin, where my parents and two of my brothers, the General Adolf and Karl Ulrich, also rest in peace.

> " *Schöne Blume, holde, reine,*
> *Christus wollte selbst dein warten,*
> *Drum hat er dich eingepflanzet*
> *In des Paradieses Garten.*" [2]

My father suffered even more severely under this test than my mother. She believed with the firmness of a rock that her

---

[1] Even if I wander in the dark valley, at once and before the others,
Thy staff, Lord, and thy wand take all my fear away.

[2] Lovely flower, dear and pure Christ himself
Wished to wait on thee,
Therefore has he planted thee
In the Garden of Paradise.

child was better in heaven than on this earth. Every dispute with Providence seemed a sin to her. " Thy will be done, oh, Lord! " But she shunned society from that day onwards. My father never got over this sorrow. I am convinced that, during the whole of the nine years that separated his death from my sister's, not a single day passed without his thinking of her and longing for her, even during the six years when he was working with Bismarck at the head of the Foreign Office. I am convinced that when he died he saw his little daughter coming towards him, holding her little brother Waldemar by the hand.

Just as in Lausanne I had attended the lectures of Professor Gay only, and in Leipzig those of Wilhelm Roscher, so in Berlin I followed the counsel of Mephistopheles: " It is best if you listen to one only." But the one that I listened to, Professor Gneist, was not the man who would expect his pupils to swear by every word of the master. In this respect Rudolf Gneist was too many-sided, too volatile, and perhaps also too sceptical. During the period of conflict while Bismarck was Minister, he had offered the strongest opposition. Later on Gneist became a zealous and useful parliamentary supporter of the great man, and developed more and more into an enthusiastic defender of the rights of the sovereign State, a staunch monarchist and advocate of union. It was chiefly his keen-minded dialectic that made him attractive to me.

Once when I was Minister the Berlin *Kladderadatsch* wrote: " To defend the proposition that twice two make five, every good Jesuit can provide one proof, Miquel two, and Bülow three proofs." I wish to indicate that just as rhetorical ability and the orator's temperament are inborn, so also are dialectical and polemical skill. When after my retirement I was reading the priceless treatise on polemics, which until then was unknown to me, in the posthumous papers of Arthur Schopenhauer, I had the feeling which Molière expressed in the *Bourgeois Gentilhomme*. The teacher of philosophy was explaining the difference between prose and poetry. The Bourgeois Gentilhomme asked: " *Et comme l'on parle qu'est ce que c'est donc que cela ?* " The philosopher answered: " *De la prose.*" The Bourgeois Gentilhomme asked further: " *Quoi, quand je dis: Nicole apportez-moi mes pantoufles, et donnez mon bonnet de nuit, c'est de la prose?* " The teacher of philosophy repeated: " *Quoi, Monsieur.*" Thereupon the worthy M. Jourdain replied: " *Par ma foi, il y a plus de quarante ans que je dis de la prose sans que j'en susse rien.*"

What Schopenhauer recommended with regard to handling

the opponent's argument by extending and universalizing it, with regard to the concealed *petitio principii*, to cross-questioning the opponent, to pressing the weak points of his explanations to the *argumentum ex concessis*, the *mutatio controversiæ*, the *retorsio argumenti*, the *argumentum ab utili*, the *argumentum ad auditores*, the *argumentum ad vericundiam*, the *argumentum ad personam*—these were all things I had already employed for a long time and on my own initiative, as occasion demanded, in the debates. I also, to use Jourdain's expression, had been a polemical controversialist without knowing it. Nor have I forgotten the words of Voltaire as quoted by the Frankfort philosopher: "*La paix vaut encore mieux que la verité.*" German politicians who tend to be doctrinaire, obstinate in a party sense, self-seeking and too full of self-esteem cannot be reminded often enough that the domestic peace of the country, mutual accommodation among the occupants of the same house, conciliation among the children of the same mother, must be the first object of all effort. For those of my dear countrymen, who in spite of Bismarck and Goethe, still consider politics as a branch of moral philosophy, I may finally remark that without a certain dose of dialectics, no orator can carry conviction in a parliamentary debate.

In the spring of 1870 my throat trouble appeared to be getting worse, although I had undergone a treatment at Kreuth, an Upper Bavarian Spa, the previous summer. My Berlin doctors had advised me to try a new treatment at the Westphalian Spa, Oeynhausen, and this I arranged to do at the hands of Dr. Cohn, an able and kindly doctor to whom I had been recommended by the great consultant and pathologist, Ludwig Traube. I found my father in a very melancholy mood when, at the end of June, 1870, I said good-bye to him before leaving Berlin. He had not long suffered the loss of his only tenderly-loved daughter, and now came the news that his fourth son, Christian, had, without any perceptible cause, contracted a malady of the eyes. My father was in a state of grave anxiety. Christian, who was hardly yet fifteen, had not only to undergo painful injections, but had also to spend many months in a darkened room, which greatly interfered with his studies. The most modern ophthalmology has, incidentally, superseded this method altogether. Thanks to Christian's mental energy and to his good memory, his excellent tutor, Dr. Emil Oberg, was able to prepare him for entrance into the fourth form by purely oral instruction. Dr. Oberg, who afterwards distinguished himself as Consul at Nish, unfortunately died at a relatively early age. Christian entered the Cavalry Academy at Brandenburg on the Havel, where he passed his matriculation creditably and became an efficient officer of the Second Dragoon Guards, the bold regiment that his brother Adolf had already joined. But in the summer of 1870 his case seemed almost hopeless.

And to fill the cup of my father's sorrows to the brim, my youngest brother, Fritz, suffered a serious injury to the spine. The delicate little fellow had to undergo a prolonged treatment lying on his back.

My father regarded the political situation, especially the state of foreign affairs, with composure. He told me that the Under Secretary in the Foreign Office, Herr von Thile, said to the Austro-Hungarian chargé d'affaires, Baron Münch (our old Frankfort acquaintance, whom I was to meet again seven years later in Athens) that " profound tranquillity " prevailed in the political world, and that nearly all the foreign ambassadors had therefore left Berlin. The Under Secretary himself was thinking of leaving shortly for his usual " cure " in Marienbad. The French Press reported that the French Premier, Ollivier, had declared in the Corps Législatif that at no time had the maintenance of peace been more assured. Wherever one might look, nowhere was it possible to find a problem containing in it any hidden danger. Everywhere the Cabinets had come to recognize that the observance of treaties was the paramount duty of all countries, especially the observance of the two treaties upon which the peace of Europe depended: namely the Paris Treaty of 1856, which assured tranquillity in the East, and the Treaty of Prague, which guaranteed peace for Germany.

In those days the table d'hôte had not been replaced by separate tables at Oeynhausen. The old-fashioned ceremonious manners of the gentlemen I used to meet at lunch there gave me the same sort of pleasure as the Française, the Waltz, or gold snuff-boxes in a ballroom, or at least, so I feel to-day. They were all agreed that no danger threatened peace. King William was said to be old and cautious. The Emperor Napoleon was suffering from kidney trouble. " Lui," as Napoleon III was now known, by virtue of a humorous pun on his Christian name (Louis), was credited with the intention of governing henceforth in a strictly constitutional manner, and had, for this purpose, chosen an enlightened and virtuous Premier in the person of the Liberal Parliamentarian, Emile Ollivier. Neither the one nor the other sovereign, it was said, would run the risk of a war. The Prussian ambassador in Dresden, Herr von Schulenburg, a major of the Fourth Cuirassiers, Herr von Rosenberg, who was as tall as a tree, the Uhlan Cavalry captain, von Willich, and a kindly Cologne patrician, Herr von Grote, were in complete agreement in this view of the situation. " Our generation will never again experience war." This was an opinion I had previously encountered in Berlin, and it was the one that prevailed in our little circle at Oeynhausen. The few foreigners who were staying there held the same view.

Besides two Englishmen, there was an Italian diplomat, Count P, who suffered from advanced consumption of the spinal marrow, and his pretty and coquettish wife, as well as a brilliant Frenchman, Count O., who sighed for the charming Countess, and had accompanied her and her husband from Paris to Oeynhausen. After completing a tour in the Rhineland, the two Englishmen had felt a wish to see the Teutoburger Forest and the Porta Westphalia, the famous gap in the northern part of the Weser Mountains. They had wandered as far as Oeynhausen on this occasion and found it " a charming place." They, too, did not believe that war was possible.

The news that the eldest son of good Prince Karl Anton von Hohenzollern was reported to be elected King of Spain left us all indifferent. Prince Karl von Hohenzollern had for four years occupied the throne of Rumania without the world's having come to an end. He was even on good terms with Napoleon III, of whom he was a fairly near relative. Why should not the elder brother Leopold, whom the Spaniards had chosen, go to Madrid? The excitement in the French Press was not taken seriously, even by Count O.

It was true that the sharp declaration of the Duc de Gramont, the French Foreign Minister, on 6th July, was disquieting. Rosenberg and Willich, the Cuirrassier and the Uhlan, pronounced the French " impudent enough." But Herr von Schulenburg, with the unruffled serenity of an old ambassador, held the view that European diplomacy would, with wise circumspection, avoid all danger of conflagration. Metternich had declared that it was the supreme task of the diplomat to hurry to the spot with a fire-extinguisher whenever a fire threatened. During the Luxemburg quarrel the Chancellor had, it was said, made it clear that he did not want war, and this quarrel had been a much more serious affair than the artificial alarm raised about the candidature to the Spanish throne. He would succeed in maintaining peace this time also. That Count Bismarck remained peacefully in Varzin was counted a favourable omen. And so amid all this frothy talk about the infantile, and in any case insignificant, outpourings of the Paris Press, the week July 4th to 12th passed by. What I heard afterwards justified my belief that in all other parts of Germany the situation was judged exactly as it was in the idyllic spa on the Werra.

On 12th July I went to the railway station with Major von Rosenberg to hear if there was any fresh news. The Berlin express had just arrived and had a stop of five minutes. A traveller handed us a special edition of a newspaper from the window of his compartment. It contained the telegram the Chancellor, Count Bismarck, had sent out to the Embassies of the North German Federation for information and guidance. The circular telegram read:

Ems. July 12.

After the news of the Crown Prince von Hohenzollern's renunciation was officially announced to the Imperial French Government by the Royal Spanish Government, the French Ambassador in Ems presented a demand to his Majesty the King to authorize him to telegraph to Paris that his Majesty the King would give a permanent pledge to withhold his consent if ever the Hohenzollerns should reopen the question of their candidature. His Majesty the King thereupon refused to receive the ambassador again, and has let it be known through his Service Adjutant that his Majesty has nothing further to communicate to the Ambassador.

The so-called Ems Dispatch was perhaps the most brilliant diplomatic move in the political career of the great German statesman. " Whenever the thought of him comes to me I can feel a rustling of wings and the breath of his spirit on my forehead." So wrote Professor Alfred Dove, who was no admirer of Bismarck, to the writer, Gustav Freytag, an opponent of Bismarck's, on 24th January, 1887.

With one single stroke Bismarck had rectified the weakness which the old King had shown in Ems towards the French Ambassador, Benedetti, a pliancy that had gone much too far, though it sprang from the highest intentions and noblest courtesy. Bismarck lifted the contentious question of the candidature for the Spanish throne high above diplomatic wrangling, and proved to the nation that it was a matter affecting Germany's honour. By so doing he kindled a storm of enthusiasm which spread throughout the whole of Germany from Memel to Constance. This enthusiasm found it mightiest expression in the anthem, " *Die Wacht am Rhein*," which, written in November, 1840, and then almost forgotten, celebrated its revival thirty years later. Indissolubly bound up with the memories of the glorious year 1870, the " *Wacht am Rhein* " is enshrined in the hearts of the German people for ever.

Bismarck did not start the war with France: he did not even wish it. If the French nation had agreed to the union of the German states, if it had recognized the equal rights of Germany, Bismarck would never have thought of beginning a war which was to restore to Germany the province of Alsace that had been stolen from her in the seventeenth century. But when it became clear that the French would never allow Germany equal rights, that they grudged us the unity which they had achieved centuries before (with all the tremendous advantages that unity brings), but wished to perpetuate German " liberty," in other words, German disunity, Bismarck was very well able to settle accounts with France, a settlement which had become necessary, not through any responsibility of ours, but through the arrogance and domineering of the French. This settlement with France was arranged without provoking the intervention of the Powers, and indeed, carefully avoided it. Thus the imponderabilia which count far more than any material factors were directed in our interest, the army's path to victory was cleared. " *C'est la diplomatie de Bismarck qui a fait du vrai les victoires allemandes de 1866 et de 1870*," wrote Victor Bérard in the *Revue des Deux Mondes* a few weeks after the outbreak of the World War in 1914. In very truth it was the diplomacy of Bismarck, which, in the last resort, had made possible the victories of 1866 and 1870.

On 15th July the French Premier, Ollivier, submitted an emergency proposal to the Chamber for a credit of fifty millions. His speech ended with the words: " A heavy responsibility weighs upon us, but we accept it with light hearts. Yes, with light hearts, confident in the justice of our cause, and convinced that this war has been forced upon us."

The use of the expression " light heart " (*cœur léger*) did, as French historians and statesmen have repeated over and over again, more injury to France than a lost battle. In the further course of my memoirs I shall have the painful duty of discussing German policy in the late summer of 1914, a policy that yielded nothing in clumsiness and lack of foresight to French policy in the late summer of 1870. On 4th August, 1914, just forty-four years after the crass blunder of the French Premier, Ollivier, the German Chancellor, Bethmann-Hollweg, declared in the German Reichstag that he recognized that he, as the responsible head-official in Germany had committed an injustice in permitting the violation of Belgian neutrality, but that necessity recognized no law. On the very same evening of the day on which he had said these words in the Reichstag, Bethmann, in an audience with the British Ambassador, described the treaty to which, together with other nations, we had appended our signature, as " a scrap of paper " (" *un chiffon de papier* "). The dispute as to which blunder was worse, that of the French Premier or the German Chancellor, will last a long time, but certain it is that both Emile Ollivier and Theobald Bethmann did immeasurable harm to their countries.

CHAPTER X

*France's Declaration of War—Resolve to Join the Army as a Volunteer
—Enlistment in the Royal Hussar Regiment at Bonn—Lehmop—
Rhine Journey to Cologne—Impressions made by Victorious Battles
at Home.*

AS soon as the danger of war became clear and definite I
made up my mind not to stand back when the storm broke
out when it was our people's duty to rally. I wrote to
my father from Bad Oeynhausen. He replied to me in a moving
letter. He said that he understood my youthful emotions. But I,
on my part, ought not to forget my obligations towards my parents.
I was, he pointed out, suffering from a malady of the throat, which
a great doctor, Professor Traube, had pronounced grave, and on
account of which he had sent me to Bad Oeynhausen for a thorough
treatment, which I had just begun. My parents were still suffering
from the shock of their only daughter's death, and she, too, had
died from an affection of the throat. They were in a state of the
greatest anxiety on account of my brother Christian's eye trouble,
and my youngest brother's spinal complaint. I had not the right,
it was pointed out, to cause yet another anxiety to my parents.
In the case of my brother Adolf, who in August had joined the
2nd Dragoon Guards as a cadet and had just received his commission, to go to the front was an evident duty. But I had just
as sacred a duty to subordinate my personal wishes in consideration
for my sorely-tried parents.

I was touched by my father's letter, for its pages spoke all
his love for his wife and children. But I answered at once that I
must stick to my resolution. I should, I said, be unhappy all
my life if I remained at home during this war. I ended with the
Körner's verse: " *Pfui über dich Buben hinter dem Ofen, unter den
Schranzen und unter den Zofen!* " [1] The close of my letter may
have been too emotional, but its motives and tendency were good.

After I had crossed the Rubicon in this letter to my father,
the next step to be decided was where I was to enlist as a volunteer.

---

[1] " Shame on you, fellow behind the stove, hiding behind skirts, clinging to apron
strings."

I hesitated between Bonn and Münster. The tall Rosenberg advised Münster, where his regiment was in barracks. I was drawn to Bonn by my old longing for the Rhineland. After brief consideration I decided on Bonn. I then went to my host, Dr. Cohn. He said to me: " You are strong and well built, supple and sinewy, and developed enough for any exertion. But then, there is your throat trouble! " When I told him I was prepared to take the risk, he said: " If you join up you will first be sent to a reserve squadron and put on garrison duty. I expect you will soon contract an acute inflammation of the throat at Bonn. It is pretty certain that you will do so if you follow in the wake of the other volunteers. Do you really want to take the risk? If so, get on with it. In any case you will have the lasting consciousness of having done your duty towards your country, and on the other hand you might worry yourself to death at the idea of not having done your share in this great war." I still think with gratitude of this good doctor who considered the state of my soul as well as the state of my throat.

Now that all signs seemed to show that the Lord God intended to hang the blood-red mantle of war from the skies, the appearance of Bad Oeynhausen had changed. The stalwart officers at our table stroked their moustaches and looked forward happily to the war. " When the king sends forth his men then everyone is glad," they used to say in 1866. The great majority of the guests at our hydro thought so too. The spirit of patriotism also prevailed among the local population of Oeynhausen. The only exception was a small group of pro-Guelph Hanoverians, who refused to move an inch from their attitude. They had moved themselves from the table d'hôte and were taking their meals apart. There they used to exchange excited words and looks with one another and sometimes clinked their glasses in a way that the all-observing ambassador, von der Schulenberg, interpreted as not suggesting loyalty. The noisiest of these pro-Guelphs was a certain Albert Beckmann, whom I was to meet again nine years later under very different circumstances. In July, 1870, Beckmann was a Guelph agent, who pursued his nefarious activities not only in Germany, but also in Paris, where he had for some time occupied the post of assistant editor of a large French newspaper. Beckmann, like his associate, the Hanoverian Government Councillor, Oskar Meding, who under the pseudonym, Grigori Samarov, afterwards wrote many successful novels of contemporary life, was won over by Geheimrat Stieber, a police official and confidential agent of the Chancellor. After the conclusion of peace Beckmann was allotted to the Imperial Embassy in Paris for special commissions, and for six years I used to meet him every day.

I left Oeynhausen with two prescriptions furnished by the good Dr. Cohn in case I should develop an acute inflammation of the throat. I may say at once that never while the war lasted did I need to make use of these prescriptions. This I owe chiefly to God's grace. But I also see in it a proof that open air and exercise are the best of all medicines. At the station I met Count O., who was returning to Paris via Cologne. He asked me to travel in his compartment. He was a typical Frenchman of the Second Empire, vivacious, communicative, full of confidence in himself, a blower of his own trumpet, and naïvely convinced that " *la belle France* " was not only admired and worshipped by all the peoples of the earth, but that this was only her just due, her right by the will of almighty God and by virtue of " *prépondérance légitime.*" " *Reine du monde, O France, O ma patrie!* " sang the truly French poet, Béranger, only four years after Waterloo. The Frenchman of the old days was, despite all his weakness and failings, not devoid of good fellowship. Indeed, there were moments when he was capable of generous actions and chivalrous motives.

But after the Great War the true Gallic character was revealed. In that war, in which Germany's political leadership was lamentable and utterly devoid either of energy or ability, France, with the help of England, Russia, Italy, Rumania, Serbia, Portugal and finally America, that is to say, with overwhelming military superiority, overcame Germany, not be it noted, by a military victory, but by the massed weight of sheer numbers. Then was revealed what the witty Frenchman, Voltaire, described as that combination of monkey and tiger, which is the Frenchman's character.

Count O. belonged to the old generation, the generation before Poincaré and Clemenceau, before General Degoutte, de Metz and Mangin, who endeavoured to emulate General Mélac, the ravager of the Palatinate under Louis XIV. For a long time afterwards the peasants of the Palatinate called every dangerous dog " Mélac."

As soon as the train was in motion Count O. asked me why I was going to Cologne. When I told him I wished to join up as a volunteer he said to me good naturedly: " *Mais mon jeune ami, vous êtes foutu! Vous et votre armée et votre pauvre pays. Vous voulez résister à l'armée Française ? Mais c'est insensé! Nous avons rossé les Autrichiens à Magenta et à Solferino. Nous avons rossé les Russes en Crimée. Nous aurions rossé les Anglais s'ils avaient osé se mesurer avec nous. L'armée française est invincible, tout le monde le sait."* Thereupon he pulled out one of his visiting cards and with a friendly smile, wrote a few words on it. He was sure that I would fight bravely. But he was just as firmly convinced that I would quickly be taken prisoner, probably wounded, after putting up a stout resistance. For this eventuality he gave me one of his visiting cards, which recommended me to his friends, of whom there were many in the French army. They would treat me well, he assured me. " *Ils seront charmants pour vous,*" he said. Although he was himself a Legitimist, he had a high opinion of Napoleon III. He declared that he had the best political mind, " *la plus forte tête politique,*" that the world had seen since Talleyrand. " *Ah, c'est un rude lapin! Il roulerait le diable lui-meme.*" That Napoleon was ready to meet any eventuality by his uncanny energy was, in his opinion, shown by the events of 2nd December, 1851. " *Il a du poil, au c . . . je vous l'affirme!* " He told me in light vein that he had known the Empress Eugénie well, before her marriage. He had accompanied her to the races and had more than once had supper with her and her Spanish mother in the Café Anglais. " *Quand nous montions le petit escalier tournant, et qu'elle marchait devant moi, je lui pinçais les mollets qu'elle a, du reste, fort beaux.*" At every big station Count O. asked the officials if there was really going to be war. It rather annoyed him never to get an answer from the sturdy officials who stood there stiffly without a word. " *Ils ont de la tenue et de la discipline, il faut le dire. Mais ça ne leur servira à rien. Pauvres gens!* "

The train reached Cologne station at last, and my Parisian friend and I went to the waiting room, which was crowded with people. Newsvendors were selling extra editions of the papers, and everybody wanted to know what they had to say. People were crying out: " Read it out! Read it out! " An unusually tall man, looking like an officer in mufti, climbed on to a table, unfolded a newspaper and read in a loud voice: " The French ambassador in Berlin has delivered the French declaration of war to the Federal Chancellor." There was a breathless silence. Then he lifted up both his arms and thundered: " Three cheers for the King, our good old King William." Everybody joined in the cheers. The women wept. Many men had tears of enthusiasm in their eyes. In a corner of the waiting room stood a number of musicians, probably an orchestra that had been playing dances at a country fair in the neighbourhood of Cologne. In a stentorian voice the tall man addressed them from the table. " Conductor," he called out, " the national anthem! " And the national anthem was sung by everybody present, in a way I had never heard it sung before.

When the sounds of the " *Heil dir im Siegerkranz* " had died away, I looked around for my French friend. He had disappeared. I met him again later in Paris. He did not seem to have any particular wish to refer to our journey from Oeynhausen to Cologne. I myself travelled from Cologne to Bonn, where I put up at the " Star." I heard the students singing the " *Wacht am Rhein* " on the market place until three in the morning. Full of patriotic exultation, intoxicated by the impressions of the day, I fell asleep.

When I woke up next morning I did not see things in so rosy a light. I knew nobody in Bonn. How, where, when, and to whom should I report? Should I be asked if I had received my father's permission to enlist? I had made a fair-sized hole in the money I had brought with me from Oeynhausen. How could I, without the aid of my father, obtain the money necessary for my equipment? Would the doctors detect my throat trouble? Everything was still in the dark. Then I recalled that there was a cornet in the Hussar Regiment at Bonn whose acquaintance I had made at Lausanne two years previously. I had not met him very often then, but I well remembered his fine, calm and capable presence. His name was Bodo von dem Knesebeck, and he was a son of the last Hanoverian ambassador to Vienna. He was also the god-child of Baron Bodo von Stockhausen, the husband of my aunt, Clothilde Baudissin, and the father of my adored (but alas! from afar and only in my dreams) Elizabeth Herzogenberg.

I remembered having heard that Bodo Knesebeck was in the King's Hussar Regiment at Bonn. I resolved to look him up. He received me in his quarters in the quiet and charming way which remained his peculiar quality when at a later date he held the post of Deputy-Master of Ceremonies and *Introducteur du Corps Diplomatique* at the Imperial Court, and, at the same time, did valuable service to the Empress Augusta Victoria, as Cabinet Councillor. The Commander of the Regiment, Colonel Baron von Loë, Knesebeck declared, was so busy that he would hardly have time to receive me. I might try my luck, he thought, with Major von Schreckenstein, who had been entrusted with the command of the reserve squadron.

I at once set out to find him. Max Baron von Schreckenstein was known in the army as " Red Schreckenstein " because of his light reddish hair in contrast with his dark-haired brother, " Black Schreckenstein," who afterwards became Court Chamberlain to the Prince von Hohenlohe-Sigmaringen. Max Schreckenstein was an officer with a brilliant career behind him. Son of a cavalryman, who was Commanding General of the 7th Army Corps and a meritorious War Minister, and of Countess von Hatzfeldt-Trachenberg, he had attained many an interesting command while still a young man. He had fought in Schleswig in 1849, had been allotted, two years later, to General von Hirschfeld's mission to Paris after the *coup d'état* of 2nd December, 1851, was sent to the Prussian Legation in Frankfort for a year in 1854, and had accompanied Prince William of Prussia, the future Emperor Frederick, when he went to England to fetch his bride. He had also fought with the Spanish army in Morocco. In short, he had seen the world. A year ago, after he had received the rank of major and the title of Squadron Leader of the King's Hussar Regiment, he was unfortunate enough to break his thigh-bone in a fall from his horse. He was therefore put in command of the reserve squadron.

" Red Schreckenstein " was reputed to be very successful with the ladies. Even at the age of thirty-eight he already had the appearance of an old roué. Energy and spirit nevertheless shone in his eyes. He received me lying on the sofa, apparently in the worst possible temper which, after all, was natural in the circumstances. Over his sofa was a great copy of Correggio's " Danae," looking forward expectantly to Jupiter's golden shower. The learned art historian, Wilhelm Lübke, in his *Elements of Art History*, considers that the original (which hangs in the Borghese Gallery, not far from the Villa Malta) displays a certain vulgarity, both with regard to pose and to expression. The copy in Bonn certainly answered to this description. The major did not ask me to sit down, but merely said, in a tone that could hardly be described as friendly, that so many volunteers were now reporting that he had neither the time nor the energy to go into individual cases, and that I might just as well go back home again. With rather more vivacity than my age or my modest position in life warranted, I told him that I had not travelled all the way to Bonn—and that against the wishes of my father—to be dealt with in that way. For a moment he flared up, but then looked kindly at me and offered me a well-manicured hand with several beautiful rings on it, adding with a smile: " There seems to be something in you, after all. Can you ride a horse? " I thereupon became polite again, and in a modest tone I replied that I thought I could answer the question in the affirmative.

" H'm! " he said, " then I'll notify our sergeant-major to put you through your paces. Report within two hours to Sergeant-major Wunderlich in the Sterntor Barracks." Two hours later I was on the barrack-square after I had been fitted up with a pair of riding breeches at the first tailor's shop I came across on the way. I showed the sergeant-major everything I could do on horseback—at the walk, at the trot, and at the gallop, and charging at the gallop, in short, all I knew about riding. I volunteered to jump every barrier, too. Wunderlich seemed satisfied. He asked me where I was staying in Bonn, and told me that the major would let me know definitely one way or the other.

In the course of the evening I learned that I was to report again next day at the Sterntor Barracks. I was to be examined by the regimental doctor and then, perhaps, to receive my uniform. Dr. Mayweg, who seemed to be a comfortable sort of gentleman, was obliging enough to tap my chest and feel my arms and legs only. He found everything in the best possible order, and did not look at my throat at all, although I spoke in a husky voice. I was then taken to the stores to receive a uniform. It was one of the really great moments of my life! When I went out into the streets in my close-fitting leather-faced breeches, magnificent yellow-seamed hussar boots, blue hussar tunic with yellow frogs, square fur shako with cockade and chain-metal chin-strap, and broad hussar sabre girded round my waist, I felt like a king. "How much do you want for your old world?" Proud and thoroughly pleased with myself I moved into the little apartment I had taken in the Meckenheimer Landstrasse.

At five in the morning the next day stable-duty began. I was given one of the squadron nags to groom. I had ridden a good many horses in my time, but I had never groomed one. It looks much easier to do than it really is. My nag was very ticklish. It might easily kick its groom on the shins or tread on his big toe, and yet it had to be groomed thoroughly. The horse-comb used by cavalrymen is thoroughly cleaned out so as to obtain the so-called "stripes." The more stripes the better. No occupation could have been better for me than combing my horse.

The day after I was put into my uniform I wrote to my father: "We got our uniforms yesterday morning. I have been busy grooming my horse for two hours in fatigue dress. I feel like a fish in the water, although I am in the open air all day and even sit out in the garden until eleven at night."

I am convinced that a few weeks grooming would do every young man good, especially those German intellectuals who, unfortunately, are often quite flabby, and have converted the old Latin saw "*Mens sana in corpore sano*" into "*In corpore non sano, mens haud sana.*" I also have a pleasant recollection of doing duty in the stables, of the neighing of the horses, of their kicking out and rearing, on which occasions I had to calm them down.

Even those who are naturally efficient make slow progress, particularly when they are young, if they are beginning a new task, unless they get friendly help from time to time. Just as I gratefully remember the Foreign Office officials in the winter of 1873-74 who taught me the technique and the mechanism of the diplomatic service, so, also, do I realise how much I owe to the good sergeant-major of the Bonn reserve squadron who supervised, led, and instructed the young recruits with natural benevolence. Sergeant-major Wunderlich was a splendid specimen of our old magnificent non-commissioned officer class. Severe in expression, never slack in his bearing and always smart, never familiar or jocular, and always grave, he inspired me with respect when he stood before me with his waxed moustache and a thick portfolio in his hand, a respect such as I have never felt for any other chief in the course of my official career, with the exception of Bismarck. I never read *Wallenstein's Lager*, nor saw it performed on the stage, without recalling old Wunderlich in the summer of 1870, whenever Schiller's brilliantly drawn figure of the sergeant appeared on the scene.

> " *Wer nichts waget, der darf nichts hoffen.*
> *Es treibt sich der Bürgersmann träg und dumm*
> *Wie des Färbers Gaul nur im Ring herum.*
> *Aus dem Soldaten kann alles werden,*
> *Denn Krieg ist jetzt die Losung auf Erden.*" [1]

Sergeant Wunderlich did not speak in beautiful verses like Schiller's, but he had the same kind of thing in mind. He must have felt how great was the respect with which he inspired me, for he soon showed me unmistakable goodwill. He proved this, when, after eight days stable duty, he advised me to get a horse of my own. I did not ride badly, he pointed out. I would ride even better on a horse of my own. I had, so he hoped, hung up my civilian clothes for good. I must become a hussar, a King's Hussar: Cadet, ensign, lieutenant—these were the stages he proposed to me. Then I would be on a ladder leading to the highest rank. This career, he thought, would be made considerably easier if I

---

[1] He who ventures nothing may hope nothing.
The civilian, indolent and stupid,
Moves round in a ring like the dyer's nag.
A soldier is fit for anything,
For now war spells the world's salvation.

had a horse of my own. He had heard that a horse was to be had from the Cavalry Captain von Marées in the barracks of the 8th Cuirassiers at Deutz.

The next day I set out for Cologne *en route* for Deutz. I naturally travelled by steamboat, for it seemed prosaic to make use of the train where the beautiful Rhine flowed along. It was a very hot day in August. I had risen at four in the morning. I had seen to the horses, done some drill and sabre practice, and had then gone for a rather too-prolonged morning drink in the Hotel Royal with a number of comrades. On board the Rhine steamer I soon fell asleep in a chair.

How long I had been asleep I cannot say. I only know that when I awoke two beautiful eyes were resting upon me. The eyes were those of a very charming girl who was dressed with modesty and taste. Her figure was full and yet graceful, and her whole person most attractive. She looked at me with an expression of heartfelt sympathy. " You poor child," she said with a sigh, " have you really to go to the war? " I must add that although I had passed my twenty-first birthday three months before, I looked so young that most people took me for eighteen at the most, and many thought that I was only seventeen. I did not like that at all. Mankind, ever discontented, wishes to be older in youth, and younger in age. Still half asleep, I replied in a hurt voice: " I am not a child. I am a grown man and a hussar, and I am going to the war of my own free will." In the meantime I was fully awake, and as she was obviously most attractive and merely seemed amused by my annoyance, I went on talking to her in a nicer tone. There were not many passengers on the boat, and we looked for a seat where we might continue our conversation undisturbed. I told her my name, where I came from and what I was. She told me that she was a disciple of Thalia, that is to say, an actress. She had made her debut on the south German stage as an *ingénue*, and not without success. She was now travelling via Cologne to Berlin, where she had accepted an engagement. She was due to arrive there the next evening and make her first appearance the next day. She prattled on charmingly and guilelessly like a young swallow twittering on the ridge of a roof. She told me more about herself. Despite her youth, the beautiful young girl already had a painful past. She had been a prince's sweetheart for a year. He had been forced to separate from her because his stern father insisted on his marrying into his own class; an ugly princess. The wound this faithlessness had inflicted in the heart of the poor girl was not yet healed. I hastened to explain to her that an unfortunate love affair should be treated homœopathically, according to the principles of Professor Hahnemann, whose monument I had not long previously admired in the Theaterplatz in Leipzig. " *Similia similibus.*" Only a new love affair could effect a cure, I assured her. She did not know any Latin, but she seemed to understand my advice. As the day was drawing to a close we arrived at Cologne. We took a meal in the open air at a little restaurant with a view of the Rhine.

The gusto with which she attacked her frugal dinner—a cutlet with fried potatoes—and sipped cheap Josefshöfer out of a green glass, were a delight to watch. After dinner we walked arm-in-arm along the Rhine and then in the square in front of the " eternal Cathedral," while the moon rose and God lit his stars one by one. We stayed at a hotel which I remembered since my childhood because I had put up there with my parents on the way to Blankenberghe. We were received at the entrance by the head waiter and a maid, who apparently took us for a newly-married couple. The head waiter, whom I boldly informed that our heavy baggage would arrive the following day, showed us into a spacious bedroom, in which stood a great four-poster. The maid whispered to my blushing companion: " Madam will be quite comfortable. Many newly-wedded couples have spent their first night here." The maid and the waiter withdrew discreetly. We stood alone together.

My companion then seemed even more delightful than on the Rhine steamer in the afternoon. I at once observed that she had pretty little feet and fine slender hands. She also had expressive blue eyes and a delicious little upturned nose. Her hair was chestnut brown, " auburn," as the English say. The little smile that played around her mouth and the look in her eyes permitted me to hope that I would not be altogether unattractive to her. Faust says to Gretchen: " Ah, cannot ever I upon thy bosom hang in peace, one brief, one single hour, breast upon breast, and soul with soul commingle ? " And poor Gretchen answers. " Ah, if alone I did but sleep, I'd leave my door on the latch to-night, but we should waken mother " [1] . . . But between me and my little friend there stood no interfering mother.

The morning when we had to part was very sad. After a last passionate embrace, and then another, I took my little companion to the railway station. She called out to me from the corner window of the compartment where she had found a seat: " Don't forget me, and I will never, never forget you." The people on the platform laughed. How coarse people are, we both thought, and

---

[1] *Faust*, i. Trans. ALBERT G. LATHAM.

utterly without understanding for exalted and truly noble emotion ?
But she would not allow herself to be frightened, and, unembar-
rassed by the *profanum vulgus*, threw me kisses, and, as the train
moved out of the station, whispered archly: " Really and truly
you are not the child I said you were on the boat. You are a man,
a charming man, and . . . ." Her last words spoken from the
moving train did not reach my ears. The sweet little head, which
I followed with my longing gaze, soon disappeared.

For long, indeed very long, I never heard anything more of
my little Cologne friend. Not until seven and thirty years *longum
spatium aevi* had gone by, after the successful Reichstag elections
of 1907, did she give me any sign of life. She felt she had to
congratulate me, she wrote in a neatly-phrased little letter, and
at the same time wished to tell me with what interest she had
always followed my successful career. Some years after our
meeting at Cologne (so she added) she had left the stage to marry
an older man, an excellent and highly esteemed person, a rich
banker. Her husband was entirely devoted to her, and she was
very happy with him. Not without a spice of humour she added
that her husband was an unswerving supporter of the Chancellor
Bülow. He had been an enthusiastic supporter of his before the
dissolution of the Reichstag. He had shown his delight at " his
Chancellor's " great victory at the polls by getting a little drunk.
So if the stars are propitious and if too many blunders are not made,
then even the plainest antitheses can in the end resolve themselves
into that harmony which, according to Leibnitz, is the purpose
and the meaning of the cosmic process.

While my sweet little friend's train was rolling onward to
the Prussian capital I looked up the cavalry captain, von Marées,
in Deutz. He at once showed me a beautiful light brown fleet-
footed mare, with star and white fetlocks, which he offered to let
me have at an acceptable price after I had tried her out and jumped
a hurdle or two on her. The good mare bore me from Metz to
Amiens and Rouen, on perilous dispatch rides and dangerous
patrols, and carried me through the battles of Amiens, Hallue,
Bapaume, Tertry-Porcilly, and Saint Quentin. I christened her
" Grete." My little Cologne friend was called Margarete like
two Saints, two Netherland Stadtholders, three or four queens,
innumerable princesses, countesses and baronesses. In our intimate
talks I called her Gretchen, and she agreed to my doing so, all
the more as I could point out how Faust welcomed his Gretchen
with the exclamation (with which I agree): " By heaven, but this
child is fair ! "

In the late autumn, Captain von Marées rejoined his regiment at the same time as I joined mine. He was fated not to return from the war. He fell not far from me near Bapaume, where the 8th Cuirassiers were engaged simultaneously with the 7th Hussars. Captain von Marées was a relative of the much-appreciated artist Hans von Marées, who decorated the aquarium at Naples with tasteful frescoes.

I rode Grete at a smart pace from Deutz to Bonn the same day, and with my squadron the next morning. The exercises on the " sand," as the drill ground lying about half an hour from the barracks was called, pleased me more than stable duty. I rode in the first rank, and Ensign von dem Knesebeck was my squadron-leader. In later years he used to remind me, by way of a joke, how in those days I had to stand stiffly to attention in his presence. I learnt to keep direction and to keep touch. I learnt to grip my nag with my legs, to hold my horse firmly, and to ride without holding the reins, at the trot, gallop, and charge—we learnt everything.

We sang:

> " Die Unteroffiziere an die Flügel,
> Fester Sitz und lose Zügel!
> Die Offiziere vor die Schwadron,
> Seht, jetzt geht's im Trabe schon!" [1]

Then we went to the jumping ground, where we took walls, bars and ditches. Every time a volunteer was thrown he had to pay for drinks. Everybody shouted out " One round due!" As we used to ride back from the drill ground the patriotic citizens of Bonn greeted us with cries of " Lehmop," the old battle cry of the King's Hussars, of whom all Bonn was proud. Where did the cry of " Lehmop " originate? It was famous as far back as 1866, when it was the battle cry of the " Bonn Blues " in the celebrated Elbe army. In peace time when the King's Hussar Regiment rode to the " sand," singing, and in high spirits, the squadron used to pass numbers of tile works, which delivered their building material to the town of Bonn. When more clay was wanted these workmen would call down to their mates in the pit below: " Lehm op!" (Clay up!). The Hussars had taken up this sonorous cry, and whenever they passed a group of tile workers they would cry out a vigorous " Lehmop."

In the year 'sixty-six the ride to the drill ground had become

---

[1] " N.C.O.'s on the wings, firm seats and slack reins, the officers at the head of the squadron. See, they are going at a trot."

a ride against the enemy, and the cheerful morning greeting a battle cry. In 1870 the regiment was first greeted with the cry of " *Lehmop* " by its chosen brothers-in-arms, serving under the same regimental Colours, the 8th Jägers. The cry was taken up afterwards by all the regiments of the Rhenish Army Corps, and when the war was over the whole army knew it.

The King's Hussar Regiment (1st Rhenish No. 7), one of the finest regiments of our old magnificent army, was founded in 1813 by Count Karl Lazarus Henckel, and called the Silesian National Hussar Regiment. Count Henckel, a free mediatized prince, of Beuthen, and owner of the Neudecker entailed estate, had won the " *Pour le Mérite* " in the Rhenish campaign of 1792 and the Iron Cross of the First Class during the War of Liberation. He was badly wounded at Saalfeld in 1806 at the side of Prince Louis Ferdinand. He died in 1864, at the age of ninety-two. He was the father of Prince Guido von Henckel-Donnersmarck, who was well known for his immense wealth, his friendship with Bismarck and Waldersee, and his great financial and industrial concerns.

He died in 1916 at the age of eighty-six, during the World War. The Silesian National Hussar Regiment, which fought victoriously the battles at Dresden, Brienne, Montmirail, Château-Thierry, Laon, and Paris, was, after the war, converted into the 7th (West Prussian) Hussar Regiment, and garrisoned in all sorts of little corners of the Province of Posen, such as Inowrazlaw, Slupce, and Rogasen, where in the opinion of Western and Southern Germans, foxes and wolves wish one another good night. In 1852 the regiment was transferred from the Province of Posen to Bonn in the Rhineland. New Year's Day, 1857, was the most beautiful day in the history of the regiment. On 1st January, 1857, the then Prince of Prussia and future King and Emperor William I, became commander of the 7th Hussar Regiment. He wore its tunic of cornflower blue for thirty-one years. Cornflower blue was his favourite colour. During this long period he knew every officer in his regiment personally. When he became too old to wear the tight hussar breeches and hussar boots he used whenever he passed through Bonn and the officers' corps assembled at the station, to honour his regiment by wearing a hussar sabre instead of the customary infantry sword. Every hussar knew the proud history of his regiment. Everybody longed to honour this past and its illustrious and venerable chief.

While I and my comrades of the reserve squadron were grooming horses and exercising on the " Sand," the first hammer blow of the German War-God fell on Alsatian soil. On 4th August the French were defeated at Weissenburg, and on the 6th at Spichern and Wörth. The enthusiasm of the Rhineland was indescribable. When I look back from the melancholy present to those August days of the glorious year 1870, I feel as though a sad and grey November day had suddenly dissolved before my eyes into a spring landscape. And this joy was justified, not only in the Prussian Rhineland, but also over the whole of Germany. It was the first time for centuries that a united Germany encountered the French hereditary enemy with closed ranks. Even in the War of Liberation, Württembergers and Bavarians, Saxons and Badeners, fought with the French against their own countrymen. At Dennewitz, in 1813, when under General Friedrich Wilhelm Bülow, men of Pomerania and the Marches opposed the enemy's advance on Berlin, they had had to fight with rifle-butt and bayonet, not only against the French, but also against Swabians and Alemanians whom the Corsican despot had compelled to serve in his army. But now, in the Weekly Calendar of *Kladderadatsch*, Rudolf Löwenstein could call to the South Germans.

> " *Wenn einst gepflückt wir haben*
> *Ein Hühnchen mal im Streit,*
> *Ihr Bäyern und ihr Schwaben,*
> *Das war in böser Zeit.*
> *Zu schönrem Streit jetzt stähle*
> *Die Brust sich mutentbrannt—*
> *Ein Herz und eine Seele*
> *Sind wir fürs Vaterland!*
> *All Hass und Hühnchenpflücken*
> *Sei ewig abgetan!*
> *Denkt nicht mehr an die Kücken,*
> *Denkt nur an Galliens Hahn!*
> *Den fasst mir an die Kehle*
> *Und dreht sie um gewandt!*
> *Ein Herz und eine Seele*
> *Sind wir fürs Vaterland!* " [1]

Even mightier rang Heinrich von Treitschke's *Song of the*

[1] Once when we picked a bone together in strife it was an evil day, Bavarians and Swabians.

But now let your breast, burning with courage, steel itself for more splendid strife. We are for the Fatherland as one heart and one soul.

All hatred and all bone-picking be banished for ever; think no more of your quarrels, think only of the Gallic cock, grip his neck and wring it skilfully. We are for the Fatherland with one heart and one soul.

Black Eagle which, written on 25th July, 1870, is one of the most beautiful poems that ever flowed from German lips.

The community of North and South, East and West, sealed with blood on the battlefields of Weissenburg and Wörth, was incorporated in the Victor of Battles, the Prussian Crown Prince and future Emperor Frederick. There was hardly another personality who possessed the qualities which for centuries have been dear to the German heart as he possessed them—purity of soul, constancy of heart, noble pride, and touching modesty, austerity towards himself and goodness to others, complete fearlessness and a delicate sensibility. Wounded men who arrived from Alsace so as to be accommodated in the hospitals at Godesberg and Brühl told the story of the storming of the Geissberg, near Weissenburg. There the French had obtained a footing in a farm surrounded by high strong walls, which they had converted into a natural fortress by making loopholes in them. Under devastating infantry and artillery fire the King's Grenadier Regiment marched up the hill on an exposed path a quarter of a mile long with complete coolness and perfect discipline. The fusilier battalion was in the van, and leading it with raised sword was Major von Kaisenberg, a big, exceptionally handsome officer, who brought home his bride, the beautiful Countess Karoline Strachwitz, shortly before the outbreak of war. The Grenadiers charged shoulder to shoulder. Three captains fell dead. The sturdy standard-bearer, Sergeant Heinrich, was hit by a bullet and the flag fell to the ground. Major von Kaisenberg jumped down from his horse, picked up the flag, and with a mighty shout, led the battalion on at the double upwards past the farm. The flag was shot through and through by bullets and the staff splintered. Kaisenberg seized both ends of the flag and held it high in the air. A bullet felled him to the ground. He got up again, the blood streaming from his wound, and urged the battalion on and on until a final bullet smashed his knee. But his fine grenadiers stormed ahead to gain the hill and take the enemy in the rear. The troops worked forward with stubborn heroic courage along the whole of the line. The battle was won, and with it the first victory in this war. The Crown Prince came to Major von Kaisenberg's death-bed, put his arms around him and kissed him.

Wörth was the first great victory in this war which Silesians and Thuringians, Hessians and Westphalians, Bavarians and Prussians, Württembergers and Poseners, won together. At this battle they at last opened the road to German unity and to the German Empire. When, on the evening of the battle, the Crown

Prince visited each regiment and expressed his gratitude and praise, a worthy Bavarian soldier called out to him: " *Wann wia Eana Sechundsechzig an da Spitz'n g'habt hätt'n, da war'n wia mit dena Malefizpreiss'n schon firti worn!* " [1]

There was truth and deep significance in this simple statement by the good Bavarian. Only after Prussia had united the German races under her leadership and had filled them with the martial spirit of Frederick the Great did the defeated at Langenzalza, Kissingen, and Tauberbischofsheim become the victors of Weissenburg and Wörth.

General Leonhard von Blumenthal, a brilliant strategist, was at the Crown Prince's side as military adviser when he led the Third Army. In 1866 the Prince proved to the General that he was as large-hearted as he was courageous. Shortly before the end of the Prussian war with Austria, Blumenthal poured out his heart in a letter to his wife, an Englishwoman, as many married men, and not only those in high places, are fond of doing. In this letter Blumenthal sharply criticized Prince Frederick Charles, and added: General Gustav von Stiehle, the Chief of General Staff, might not find things easy with so self-willed and obstinate a Prince, but that he (Blumenthal) was in a better position in this respect. The Crown Prince realised that he did not know very much about strategy, and he therefore willingly let himself be guided by his Chief of Staff. The Austrians captured the field-post to which this letter had been entrusted. With malicious delight they published General von Blumenthal's letter. As soon as he heard of its publication Blumenthal reported to the Crown Prince so as to hand in his resignation. Without uttering one single word of reproach, the chivalrous Prince embraced him with the words: " I forgot the letter once and for all, the moment I had read it. I only remember the service you have rendered the army, the Fatherland and myself in this war." Blumenthal returned his thanks to the noble Prince in 1870 at Weissenburg and at Wörth and throughout the whole course of the war. One of the first actions of the Kaiser Frederick, when, a dying man, he ascended the throne in 1888, was to promote Blumenthal to the rank of Field-Marshal.

On the same 6th of August that the French were beaten at Wörth, the Germans stormed the steep heights of Spichern. General von François fell there at the head of the 27th Infantry Brigade when half way up the hill. A shell ripped up his abdomen. The dying man was asked by his adjutant whether he was not

---

[1] If you had led us in '66 we would have beaten the damned Prussians.

suffering terribly. The general threw a glance upon the columns, which, with flags aloft, with cheering, bands playing, and waving their helmets, were storming up the hill. " I am not suffering," answered the dying general, " for I see that the fight is going forwards." The name of General von François lives, like that of Major von Kaisenberg, for ever in the history of the German people.

The hearts of the young volunteers in Bonn beat faster when they heard of such heroism. Our impatience to get to the front naturally grew with our jubilation. We were all desperately unhappy because we had not yet been under fire. The reply to all our repeated requests and complaints was—to our extreme regret—that hussars have to go through three months training in barracks before they can be used in the field. And now came the severest battles of the war, the three battles before Metz, battles which will be told and sung as long as Germans live between the Meuse and Memel, Adige and Belt. No one has described them in a more stirring and powerful manner than Ernst Dohm, in *Kladderadatsch*, on 28th August, 1870.

The news of the battle of Mars-la-Tour brought new cares to my good, already sorely-tried, parents. The Dragoon Guards had attacked in this battle, and two days afterwards the news reached Berlin that my brother Adolf, who was a lieutenant in that regiment, had fallen. Princess Marie Radziwill, a French-woman by birth, who was living near us at the time, often told me later that she would never forget the expression of deep grief, but also the noble control with which my father had said to her, when he met her in the Pariser Platz: " *Toutefois, non pas comme je veux, mais comme Dieu veut.*" Forty-eight hours later a kind telegram from the Chancellor, Bismarck, informed my father that his son was still alive. My brother had ridden on ahead with the first file of his squadron. Arriving at a narrow bridge, he had, under heavy fire, given orders to form three deep and ridden on with his servant, a worthy Pole named Czeslak, and the oldest sergeant, across the bridge. Both fell. My brother escaped with a slight wound. Soon afterwards both Dragoon Guard regiments were ordered to proceed against the French infantry so as to give our infantry a breathing space.

The Third Brigade of Horse Guards was led by Major General Count Wilhelm Brandenburg, a distinguished cavalry general. He was a son of the Premier Brandenburg, whose proud Prussian heart was broken by Olmütz, and whose statue stands in the Leipziger Platz, opposite the monument to General Wrangel. The Premier was a love-child. His mother was the beautiful

Countess Sophie Dönhoff and his father was King Frederick William II. When on the battlefield of Mars-la-Tour a breathless general staff officer shouted to Major General Brandenburg that he must attack the French infantry immediately on very difficult ground, the latter in his distinguished quiet manner drew the major's attention to the fact that this amounted to sacrificing the regiment. The excited major in the broad red stripes barked back at him: " The Horse Guards will be worth the food they eat after all." When he had buttoned up his immaculate white gloves and drawn his sabre, the Major-General Count Brandenburg replied without so much as even a movement of the eyelash: " Oh, that's another matter! Brigade, present arms! Brigade, trot, gallop, charge!" And forward they went, over hedges and ditches, under murderous infantry fire.

In this attack, which had the desired tactical effect of giving our infantry elbow room, the regiment lost both its commanders, Colonel von Auerswald, Colonel Count Finckenstein, Major von Kleist, the handsome brother of the beautiful Duchess of Pless, Captain Prince Henry XVII of Reuss, a brother of the then ambassador in St. Petersburg and subsequent ambassador in Constantinople and Vienna, Count Wesdehlen, Count Westharp, von Hindenburg, the lieutenants von Tresckow, Count Schwerin, Count Solms-Sonnenwalde, and Count Hohenthal. When King William saw the regiment again some days later, tears streamed down the kindly gentleman's cheeks. He could only keep repeating: " So many fine dragoons and fine officers, and both their dear commanders." In the very same hour the Dragoon Guards attacked, the 7th Cuirassiers and the 16th Uhlans " *die Säbel geschwungen, die Zäume verhängt, tief die Lanzen und hoch die Fahnen*,"[1] rode down two French columns of foot and two batteries. Ferdinand Freiligrath, who had crazy ideas in the year of folly, 1848, the year of abortion, insurrections and futile projects, and did not find his way back to the national idea until 1870, when he was an exile in London, immortalized the bugle of Vionville in a wonderful poem, choosing the moment when the commander of the 7th Cuirassiers, Count Schmettow, sounds the muster.

[1] Brandishing their sabres, slackening their reins, their lances down and their flag flying.

CHAPTER XI

Bismarck's Policy in 1870—Austria-Hungary, Italy, England, and Russia—Bavaria's Attitude in July, 1870—Objections of the Bavarian Second Chamber, the Patriotic Attitude of the Upper Chamber—Complete Unity of the Nation—Bismarck's Circular Letter to the Prussian Embassies—Neutrality of Austria-Hungary—Holstein's Mission to Florence.

THE valour of the army shone out in the sight of all. The masterful strategy and leadership of General Hellmuth von Moltke were at once universally recognized. In the General Staff account of the Franco-German war the following pregnant sentences are to be found: " The commander must always keep his main objections in view and must not let himself be diverted by the vicissitudes of circumstance. But the manner in which these objections are to be achieved beforehand can never be described with any certainty."

The spirit of the great Moltke, who led us to victory in 1866 and 1870, is expressed in these words. The misfortune of his unhappy nephew resulted from the fact that he adhered to the letter of the plans of the deceased Count Schlieffen, and even the letter was not carried out consistently and was not even adequately apprehended. In strategy as in politics, and indeed in all things, the words of the apostle Paul are appropriate, namely, that the letter kills and only the spirit gives life.

Not until decades had passed did Germany fully realize how inspired Bismarck's policy was when he left the army free to act in 1870, indeed, not until we lost the World War because of the imperfect leadership of Bethmann-Hollweg and this Empire-wrecking statesman's successors, whom William II appointed—a catastrophe suffered in spite of the achievements of the finest army that ever took the field, and in spite of the self-denial and self-sacrifice which the German people underwent.

In July, 1870, France was bound to Austria as well as to Italy, by agreements which were more precise and binding than the engagements England concluded with France and Russia before the outbreak of the World War. The French-Austrian-Italian coalition, which Paris as well as Vienna had striven for, ever since Sadowa, was initiated by the Emperor Napoleon III's visit to the Emperor Francis Joseph at Salzburg in August, 1867. The Austrian Premier, Count Beust, the Hungarian Premier, Count Andràssy, and the Austro-Hungarian ambassador in Paris, Prince Richard Metternich, were requested to be present at this meeting by the Emperor Francis Joseph. The Austrian Emperor returned the Salzburg visit by a journey to Paris, where a brilliant banquet with hearty toasts was given in his honour at the Hôtel de Ville, which in past centuries had witnessed so much power and pomp, and which went up in flames hardly four years later. Only one meeting had taken place between the Emperor Francis Joseph and King William since the Austro-Prussian war. This was on 22nd October, 1867, at the little Baden station of Oos which the Emperor Francis Joseph had passed on his journey from Vienna to Paris, and whither King William had gone from Baden-Baden, his regular autumn holiday resort.

The interview only lasted ten minutes, and was embarrassing and frosty. The negotiations for a special alliance between Paris, Vienna and Florence began in 1868. As Prince Napoleon revealed ten years later, the Emperor Napoleon III, received the assurance in the personal handwriting of the Emperor of Austria and the King of Italy that, in case of a conflict between France and the North German Confederation under Prussian leadership, Austria-Hungary and Italy would intervene on the side of France " within the space of a few days and without further formality."

In the negotiations for the alliance there were, besides Prince Richard Metternich, amongst the Austro-Hungarian representatives Count Karl Vitzthum, a Saxon diplomat, whom Beust, after having been made Austrian Foreign Minister, had sponsored in the Austrian service. He represented and furthered the plans of his masters with zeal and not without ability, but with a complete lack of loyalty to Germany. A great deal had been negotiated and discussed between the General Staffs of France, Italy and Austria-Hungary, before the outbreak of the Franco-German war.

In March, 1870, the leader of the war party in Austria, who was also the best Austrian military commander, the son of the victor of Aspern, and himself the victor of Custozza, the Archduke Albrecht, arrived in Paris on behalf of the Emperor Francis Joseph, and made definite offers of military assistance to the Emperor Napoleon III to be given by the Hapsburg Monarchy to France in the event of a Franco-German war. Shortly afterwards a French general, General Lebœuf, if I remember rightly, was sent from Paris to Vienna to return the visit of the Archduke Albrecht.

The vindictive rage against the Prussians, who had always been unpopular on the beautiful blue Danube, and the burning desire to win back the lost hegemony over Germany, superseded Vienna's dislike of "revolutionary" Italy, and even her loyalty to the Holy See, a loyalty that had lasted 600 years, and had been put to many tests. The daughter of the Archduke Albrecht, the young Archduchess Mathilde, was to marry the Italian Crown Prince Humbert, and would have done so had she not been the victim of a dreadful accident. The unfortunate girl had, while smoking a cigarette at a ball, set her flimsy evening dress on fire and died in terrible agony.

It was clear that Italy would not co-operate unless she were guaranteed the possession of Rome. Napoleon III could not bring himself to agree to this, especially in consideration of his narrowly religious wife, who had declared: " *Plûtot les Prussiens à Paris, que les Italiens à Rome.*" There were also reasons of French domestic policy—fear of their own clericals at home, especially of the Bishop of Orleans, of the factious Monseigneur Dupanloup, and of the editor of the ultramontane *Univers*, the still more factious Louis Veuillot.

In August, 1867, the Roman question again became acute. Garibaldi invaded the Papal State at the head of a small army of volunteers. Everywhere the inhabitants declared for union with Italy, tore down the Papal flag, and set up in its place the green, white and red Italian tricolour. On 3rd November there was fighting at Mentana between the red-shirts and the French troops which the Emperor Napoleon had sent to the help of the Pope. Garibaldi's volunteers were easily defeated by the French, who were armed with the new French rifle, the now famous chassepot. They were either cut to pieces and disbanded or taken to Rome as prisoners.

On 5th December the decisive debate on the Roman question took place in the Corps Législatif. In reply to the question whether France would allow the Italians to take possession of the Eternal City, Rouher, the most powerful minister of the Second Empire— the "Vice-Emperor" as he was ironically called—replied in three words: "No, No, Never!" In the official account of the debate this categorical declaration was reproduced as follows: "We declare in the name of the French Government that Italy will never take possession of Rome (tumultuous cheers). No, Never! (Numerous shouts of No, Never!) Never will France tolerate such an outrage against her honour and against Catholicism. (Renewed and continuous applause in the Chamber)." In the

HENRY VII, PRINCE OF REUSS (LEFT), AND RICHARD, PRINCE VON METTERNICH
Paris photo. of the 'sixties

vote which followed only seventeen deputies voted against the Government and its attitude on the Roman question. Among the 237 deputies who voted for the Government was Thiers, who was certainly no friend of the Rouher Cabinet or of the Second Empire, but was a relentless opponent of the Italian *Risorgimento*, the Italian national movement which led to the creation of a unified and independent Italy, with Rome as its capital. On the very same day that Rouher's " Never " echoed throughout the world, the Italian Premier, Menabrea, coolly declared to the Italian Chamber in Florence: " Rome is precisely as important to Italy as Paris is to France." I got to know Count Luigi Federigo Menabrea sixteen years later in Paris, where he had, in the meantime, become Italian ambassador. He was a believing and zealous Catholic. " *Les Italiens ont le génie de la juxtaposition*," said Anatole France.

With all the vainglory proper to the French, General Failly, the victor of Mentana, concluded his report on the defeat of the red-shirts with the words: " *Les chassepots ont fait merveille*." In Italy this *fanfarronade* was received with bitterness. Thus the Roman question stood separating the two great Latin peoples. But nevertheless, relations between the cabinets of Paris and Florence remained as close as before. King Victor Emmanuel never forgot the armed help given him by France in 1859. His Foreign Minister, Visconti-Venosta, was frankly a friend of France, and remained so during the period of the Triple Alliance. In north Italy especially, and above all in Lombardy, sympathy for France was still alive and rather widespread. On the whole, it may be said that when war clouds gathered in the summer of 1870, official Italian circles were inclined towards France. On the other hand the Italians have always been accustomed to devising foreign policy with their heads and not with their hearts. It was therefore to be expected in the summer of 1870 that they would regard the agreements made with France as binding only so long as these obligations corresponded with Italian interests of state. This " sacred egoism " was not so frankly expressed in Italy in 1870 as it was in 1915, when it was also " *sacro egoismo* " which in the last resort determined Italian policy, a policy that, with calm calculation, weighed and considered all possibilities, fully aware that the words of the great Moltke: " Think it over first and then act " (and not the reverse) apply to politics just as much as to strategy.

In Vienna the situation was quite different from that in Florence. The Emperor, the archdukes, and the most important of them all, the Archduke Albrecht, at the head (in short, the whole of the high nobility, so influential in the old Austria) could hardly await the moment of revenge for 1866. It was purely for this reason that the most poisonous enemy Prussia has ever had, the Saxon Premier Beust, was attracted to Vienna as Austrian Foreign Minister, shortly after the conclusion of the Peace of Prague. Every other consideration of Austrian policy was sacrificed to the object of restoring the *status quo ante* 1866. This was the reason why the Magyars were, with the utmost precipitation, granted every demand that they had previously repeatedly raised in vain. The Austro-Hungarian monarchy, a clumsy and unmanageable " conglomeration," developed from the old unified state of the Emperor Ferdinand and the Empress Maria Theresa, of Prince Wenzel Kaunitz and Prince Klemens Metternich. Its two halves, Cisleithania and Transleithania, mutually paralysed each other and often had violent public quarrels. Nevertheless, in 1870 the Hapsburg monarchy was still the " Old Austria, rich in honour and victories," and still a great power. The French and Italian friendship, sealed with blood on the battlefields of Lombardy, did not expire for a long time after this.

While, therefore, France was justified in counting upon willing and immediate support in the leading Austrian circles, and in Italy at least on a very benevolent neutrality, and perhaps even on co-operation later on, the North German Confederation founded by Prussia, stood alone and without a single non-German alliance. In 1866 Prussia concluded an agreement of only three months duration with Italy, in the event of Austria's attacking us after the reform of the German Federal Constitution, or picking a quarrel with Italy because of the Italian regions subjected to Austrian rule. On this occasion King William had expressly declared to the Italian negotiator, General Gavone, that he knew nothing could dissolve the ties uniting Italy with France. The result of the war of 1866 did not lead to a lasting consolidation of the relations between the allies of 1866, but rather to an estrangement. This found expression as early as 1866 in irritable arguments about the note sent on 17th June, 1866, by Count Guido Usedom, the Prussian ambassador in Florence, to the Italian Premier, General Alfonso Lamarmora. The note was bluntly disavowed by Bismarck when two years later it was made public. In it the Prussian ambassador warned the Italian Premier that the offensive against Austria must be prosecuted to the utmost, *i.e.*, to the very walls of Vienna, that the power of Austria must be stabbed " to the heart," and that the plan proposed by Prussia for the impending conflagration was war to the knife (*guerre à fond*). The disavowal of Count Usedom's provocation by Berlin Government circles did not allay the embitterment which this missive had evoked in Vienna, nor the displeasure and mistrust occasioned by it in Italy.

Between us and England there was no ground for friction in 1870. English supremacy in industry, trade and shipping was uncontested, and we did not think of building warships. The Queen of England was well disposed towards Germany and remained so to her death, but her eldest son, the Prince of Wales, still only thirty years of age, and who later became King Edward VII, tended the other way. His inclinations and the affections of the future Edward VII were turned towards Paris rather than Berlin. His consort, Queen Alexandra, who had rapidly become popular in England because of her tact and charm, was a Danish princess. Since Düppel and Alsen, she was undisguisedly hostile to Prussia. Germany, all things considered, appeared to most Englishmen a politically negligible quantity, a country only of interest to professors, a State which English politicians could view with indifference, or even now and again with contempt and sometimes with intolerable arrogance. In the course of centuries, England had fought France for world supremacy. Friendly relations had then supervened between the two countries. Even in the days of the Citizen King, Louis Philippe, and even more throughout the Second Empire, these relations came to be known as the " *Entente Cordiale*," and in the Crimea the French and the British had fought shoulder to shoulder. It was to be assumed that the attitude of the English Government towards a Franco-German war would depend, not only upon the course of military events, but also upon the diplomatic skill of the belligerents. If by reason of the near blood-relationship, the Courts of London and Berlin were on more intimate terms than the House of Coburg-Hanover and the Bonaparte family, the diplomatic relations between the Quai d'Orsay and Downing Street were on firmer foundations than those between Downing Street and the Wilhelmstrasse.

Relations with Russia had been the keynote of Bismarck's policy since his accession to office. Not because of any personal sympathy or antipathy, though I will not contest that the old autocratically-governed Tsarist Russia was fundamentally more congenial to Bismarck than Parliamentary England. In this respect Bismarck's views were the opposite of those of most German intellectuals. For Bismarck the decisive factor was the circumstance that the dispute between Prussia and Austria for the hegemony over the German States could not be settled in face of French objections unless the rear was covered by a benevolent Russia, nor the unification of Germany that would arise as a result of this hegemony. The convention which Bismarck concluded with Russia on 18th February, 1863, a few months after his appointment to office, concerning common action in a Polish rising, was used as his spring board for all his further successes. It is eternally instructive to point out that no political resolution, no diplomatic step of the greatest German statesman, caused greater offence to public opinion; no move on the diplomatic chess-board was more bitterly criticized by all liberal and radical minds in Germany than this Convention, from which began the path of victory that led on to Paris, via Sadowa and Sedan.

Two examples may be given: In the debate in the Prussian Chamber of Deputies in February, 1863, on the interpellation of the Polish deputy, Kantak, the Liberal deputy von Sybel, later on of all German historians by far the most zealous panegyrist of Bismarckian policy, declared: " Gentlemen, we have very urgent reasons for protesting against a policy which, from having been free agents, makes us the pawns in a game, burdening us with complicity in a colossal man-hunt, a man-hunt which the whole of Europe views with moral indignation. A minor insurrection in Polish forests is being needlessly transformed into a European question, and once we have let that happen, then, in the nature of things, the main burden of this European question will be transferred from the shoulders of Russia and laid upon ours. It is a policy involving immeasureable sacrifices without the shadow of a prospect of any kind of compensation in any other respect."

The Deputy Simson, who as President of the Reichstag, was present at the proclamation of the German Empire at Versailles in 1871, judged Bismarck, who was on 28th February, 1863, made Prime Minister, as follows: " I do not, gentlemen, demand that a government should always be able to maintain the bold flights of genius, for that would be demanding too much. The more modest demand that it shall follow along the calm sure path of ability and experience, would be more justified. But the admiration we can feel for every tight-rope dancer, merely because nobody falls down, is a pleasure that does not suit everyone's taste."

I may here remark that I, too, especially during the last year of my office, was accused of being a diplomatic tight-rope dancer by many critics, who later were full of confidence and praise for the sure and steady path of foreign policy under the estimable and trustworthy Chancellor, Bethmann-Hollweg. Seldom or never has a minister been more violently attacked, and more sharply calumniated than Bismarck after the conclusion of the above-mentioned Convention between Prussia and Russia. Bismarck did not, however, allow himself to be disturbed or deterred, nor did his pious wife who in those days, so onerous for herself and her husband, found comfort in the old Moravian hymn:

> " *Hier durch Spott und Hohn,*
> *Dort die Ehrenkron!*
> *Hier im Hoffen und Vertrauen,*
> *Dort im Haben und im Schauen.*
> *Denn die Ehrenkron*
> *Folgt auf Spott und Hohn.*" [1]

While Herr von Bismarck-Schönhausen took up a determined pro-Russian and anti-Polish attitude towards the Polish revolt, which earned for him the personal confidence of the Tsar Alexander II of Russia and won for Prussia the sympathies of the " Old Russians," the Vienna Cabinet was pro-Polish and on the side of the Western Powers. Austria harvested the praise of the unperceptive German tea-table politicians. But the St. Petersburg Cabinet could never forget this new affront from the neighbour it had saved in 1849. This was shown in 1866 and 1870. The Austrian attitude to the Polish revolt was not only due to the pressure of the Western Powers, but still more to the sympathies which the very influential clericals in Vienna felt for the Catholic Poles in their fight against schismatic Russia. On the other hand the anti-Polish character of Prussian policy corresponded fully with Bismarck's fundamental views. In this respect Bismarck remained firm and unchanging from the first day of his political career to the last. He always perceived in the Polish Movement the most dangerous enemy to the Prussian state and to German civilization, and acted accordingly.

The debates on the Polish question in February and March of the year 1863 in the Prussian Chamber of Deputies culminated in the final speech by Professor von Sybel on 31st March, 1863. He compared Prussia with a once proud warship, whose sharp keel had ploughed through rushing waves for centuries; her sides often whipped by the stormy winds, were made fast by the iron

---

[1] Here below through mockery and derision,
There above the crown of honour.
Here in hope and trust,
There in possession and contemplation.
For the crown of honour
Follows upon mockery and derision.

armour-plating of the Prussian people's strength, but now with crazy masts that were much too high for her and deprived of the best part of her armour-plating and of her steam power, with Herr von Roon in the engine room and Herr von Bismarck at the wheel, she was venturing out on the boiling seas of European disputes. After this grandiloquent preamble, he said with regard to the Polish question:

> If the man I see opposite me on the Government bench were a man who had already given evidence of any far-reaching insight and sense of justice, I would also ask if his Convention is mindful of the Treaties of 1815 and the right of the Poles, recognised in these Treaties, to live under their own independent constitution, the promise, endorsed by Prussia and Europe, that the King of Poland and not the Tsar of Russia shall rule in Warsaw. (Cheers from the Polish deputies.) What an opportunity this sudden Polish complication might have given our Government to pursue a positive, fruitful, creative policy! If our ministry had itself taken the Polish matter in hand with the frank intention of drawing this old sting out of Europe's heel once and for all, of helping, at last, to heal this old European wound, what a position it might have acquired both at home and in Europe.

This was the spirit in which Theobald Bethmann and Gottlieb Jagow restored Poland, half a century later, amid the applause of political dreamers like Hans Delbrück and Friedrich Naumann, thus committing the biggest mistake (except the ultimatum to Serbia) ever made by any German politician.

By means of the masterly Ems dispatch, already mentioned, Bismarck released the *furor Teutonicus* at home, and created a unified German fighting front. Outwardly Bismarck relied upon the circumstance that the Tsar, touched in his most sensitive spot, that is to say, in the Polish question, would not allow the Austrians to attack the Prussians in the rear while they were fighting against the French, the old protectors of the Poles. Bismarck had hoped all the more firmly for this because the Tsar Alexander II had been deeply insulted on French soil during his visit to the Universal Exhibition in June, 1867, by certain Poles, who had also threatened his life. When the Tsar visited the Palais de Justice, one of the sights of Paris, on 4th June, a young bearded man stepped in his path with the cry of "*Vive la Pologne, Monsieur!*" This staunch fellow, like Heine's Alta Troll, a son of the Pyrenees, was born in the picturesque town of St. Jean de Luz, and was the barrister

Charles Flouquet, who had then not yet reached his fortieth year. Twenty-one years later he became French Premier, but not before he had humbly and sorrowfully apologized in the presence of the Russian ambassador in Paris for his inopportune display of hardihood. Encouraged by Flouquet, the Pole, Berezowsky, forty hours later, shot at the Tsar Alexander II on the occasion of the great review in the Bois de Boulogne. Paris and France had been thoroughly spoilt for the Russian Emperor.

In July, 1870, it was seen how wisely Bismarck had acted when, not without difficulties, he had persuaded his old King to abandon the idea of any territorial extensions in South Germany, but to conclude treaties of defensive and offensive alliance with the South German states against the eventuality of war. These treaties survived the fiery ordeal. Only in Bavaria did this move at first seem doubtful. The decisive step was made by the young King Ludwig II, who, with the same high-minded idealism with which he had offered the hand of friendship to the great German composer, Richard Wagner, not long before, now recognized the *casus foederis*, untroubled by the uproar of the ultramontane and democratic Press, which strongly opposed going to war on the side of Prussia. The population of Munich rendered enthusiastic homage to the noble Prince for his patriotic decision. At the same time magnificent national demonstrations took place in Nuremberg. But there was to be a hard fight in the Bavarian Second Chamber, where the majority consisted of ingrained clerical particularists, who (*lucus a non lucendo*) called themselves the " Patriots."

Prince Chlodwig Hohenlohe, my chief in the Paris Embassy and predecessor in the Chancellorship, has more than once given me a graphic description of the proceedings in the decisive session of the Bavarian Second Chamber. He had been present in the Imperial Councillors' Gallery. The Special Committee had decided, by seven votes against three, to refuse the Government's proposal of a special credit of 5.6 million guilders for the mobilisation of the Bavarian army, and by six votes against three declared for armed neutrality. This resolution was presented by the deputy Jörg, the leader of the " Patriots " and publisher of the *Historisch-Politische Blätter*.

At the very beginning of his speech Jörg had the audacity to persist in declaring that the quarrel between Prussia and France lay outside the realm of German integrity and honour. The whole of the present complication had, he said, originated in the policy of the Prussian ruling house. On the front bench of the Liberals sat the Imperial Baron von Stauffenberg, who was then scarcely thirty-three years old. He came of a family that had formerly belonged to the mediatized nobility in Franconia and Swabia, and one which had been invested with the office of Hereditary Cup Bearer by the Dukes of Alemania. But he was noble in spirit and not merely by birth.

Von Stauffenberg got up, spat, threatened to beat his unpatriotic colleague with his fist, and called him a knave. Unconcerned, and apparently not very sensitive in matters of honour, Jörg went on to say that Prussia might not be able to afford Bavaria any protection in the event of a French invasion, even if she wished to do so. But she did not, he said, wish to protect Bavaria. Many people believed that Prussia deliberately wished to render Bavaria absolutely helpless, so as to be able to swallow her at her leisure. On the other hand, he continued, the Duc de Gramont had solemnly declared that noble France did not intend to acquire one single square foot of German territory, but was ready to give Bavaria a special guarantee that she should possess the Palatinate. After Jörg, in a loud voice, had again expressed the opinion that Bavaria would be badly treated in the event of a victory of Prussia, but never by France, for that would indeed be a blow against French interests, Baron von Stauffenberg, his cheeks blazing with anger, rose to his feet again. He seized a chair which was standing near him, and with a powerful throw, hurled it at the wretched Jörg. The people in the packed public gallery broke into tumultuous cheers. Jörg, whose courage apparently did not stand on a level with his infamous mind, lost the thread of his discourse, and closed with the mumbled rather than spoken declaration that as he was a man who had concerned himself with politics and with the study of public affairs all his life, his opinion was valuable and significant. The war of 1870, he said, was only the logical consequence of 1866, and did not concern Bavaria in the least.

Full of dignity, calmly and firmly, Count Bray, the Premier, replied to the " Patriot " Jörg: " The matter before us is one of keeping or breaking the Treaty. We must declare our attitude toward Germany." The unrestrained applause of the Liberals and Government benches resounded when these words were spoken. The Premier concluded: " I have not lived until now merely to renounce my principles, revoke my signature." After him the Minister of War, the good Baron von Prankh, stood up to speak. Like the Premier before him, he spoke not as a politician, not as a jurist, but only as a soldier, a true Bavarian, an old Bavarian, but also a German. In a manly speech he made a last appeal to the Chamber. " Let us stand by Germany," he said. " Otherwise we are dishonoured and lost." In vain the "Patriots" Dr. Ruhland and Dr. Westermayer, prelate and priest of St. Peter's, Munich, tried to help Jörg, the party chief. In their ecclesiastical capacity they were agitators rather than priests. The former protested against thrusting the sons of Bavaria into a sanguinary war with an enemy who had never given personal offence to the Bavarians themselves. Dr. Westermayer held the sanctimonious opinion that there was a standpoint in morals where care for the hearth and home took precedence over the duty of helping a menaced neighbour. When he uttered this sentence, Westermayer was interrupted by a storm of indignation and shouts of "Shame!" from the Left and the gallery. When he hinted that the Bavarian Palatinate had an urgent interest in Bavarian neutrality in the Franco-German war, the Palatine deputies who were present, protested and cried out that the Palatinate recognized the threatening danger, but wished to be on the side of its German brothers. When the gallery cheered the Palatine deputies, who were patriots in the true sense of the word, the Speaker of the Chamber, Weiss, who was also a "Patriot," threatened to have the gallery cleared, but finally did not dare to carry out his intention.

The Liberal deputies, Fischer, Völk, Edel, Marquardsen, and Barth, drawing attention to the cheers for the Fatherland that could be heard inside the House and came from the crowds outside the Chamber, appealed in fiery words to German patriotism and German honour. The Speaker, Weiss, made a last weak attempt to adjourn the debate because "pressure" was being brought to bear upon the discussion, but after some irresolution, finally allowed the vote to be taken. Jörg's motion in Committee was defeated by 89 votes to 58, and the Government's proposal accepted by 101 votes to 47.

When the deputies left the Chamber, they and the Ministers and Imperial Counsellors were greeted with joy and acclamation by the crowd. As Hohenlohe could observe, Jörg and his close friends did not at first dare to go out into the streets, but chose to wait until the excitement in the town had died down, and then crept home. The Bavarian First Chamber, which had unanimously and without debate voted the credit demanded by the Government, gave a fine example of patriotic sentiment and political insight that made a great impression both in Germany and abroad.

I should like to mention that an old member of the ultramontane Bavarian Party, the historian, Johann Nepomuk Sepp, broke, in 1870, with his former associates, and joined the national cause with word and deed. This upright man, who repeatedly gave me pleasure by his original but well-intentioned letters during my Chancellorship, died in 1909, almost at the age of ninety-three. Shortly before his death he sent me a copy of the book he had written about his journey to Palestine. He had prefaced it with the following profound sentence: " The tree of knowledge is not the tree of life." I must state with especial patriotic satisfaction that thanks to the masterful Constitution which Bismarck gave to the German people, to the wise forbearance with which he dealt with and justified special characteristics in all the Federal States, and particularly in the largest of them, Bavaria, that State in all its parts, Old Bavaria as well as Franconia, the Palatinate, both the Liberals and Bavarian People's Party, remained unwaveringly loyal to the Fatherland during the World War and the difficult years that followed it.

The original sin and curse of the German people, particularism, took on a clerical guise in Bavaria in 1870, but in Würtemberg its mask was democratic. The leader of particularist Swabian Democracy, Herr Karl Mayer, the predecessor and spiritual father of the factious and pettifogging twin brothers Haussmann, and the honourable, but politically incompetent, Vice-Chancellor, Friedrich Payer, raised lamentations in the conclusive sitting of the Württemberg Second Chamber. Germany, without Austria, they wailed, was deprived of her left arm of defence. But since the Bavarian Chamber had given way, nothing remained but to accept Prussian leadership and enter the war. Great political discussions, it was said, were no longer possible, and there was nothing to hope for, save the victory of German arms. The Chamber voted unanimously for participation in the war, and this decision accorded with the patriotic feeling of the Swabian race, which once had borne the vanguard banner of the Empire.

No German state was so directly menaced by a Franco-German war as the Grand Duchy of Baden. Moreover the Duc de Gramont had warned the Baden Embassy in Paris, through his *chef de cabinet*, Baron de Ring, that if Baden entered the war against France, she would be laid waste again, as was the Palatinate under Louis XIV, and not even the women would be spared. " *Même les femmes ne seront pas épargnées* " quoted Baron de Ring, an Alsatian, whom I met six years later in Vienna, when he was First Secretary of the French Embassy. The French were not able to carry out their threat in 1870. But when, fifty years later, they had defeated us with the help of both hemispheres, German women were to learn the infamous acts of which black French soldiery are capable. The threats of Baron de Ring and the Duc de Gramont had no effect on the national sentiment of the loyal Alemanians of the Rhine and their noble Grand Duke Frederick.

The patriotism of the Hessians was not less than that of the Badeners, but the Grand Duke Ludwig III recalled the rueful figure the Princes cut in the days of the Confederation of the Rhine. He said to the French ambassador in Darmstadt, the Count d'Astorg, after 1866: " If the Emperor Napoleon can deliver me from the Prussians, I will cheerfully cede him Mainz." A French proverb says: " *Tel maitre, tel valet.*" Baron von Dalwigk, the Grand Duke Ludwig III's Minister, was worthy of the master he served. When the French declaration of war was sent to the North German Confederation, to which the regions of Hessen north of the Maine belonged, Dalwigk forbade patriotic demonstrations in Darmstadt, on the ground that the French ought not to be provoked, since he feared that within a few days the " red-trousers " might be in the city and their horses drinking in the Darm. When God had crowned our just cause with victory, Dalwigk wavered, and submitted memoranda to Bismarck, whom he had previously hated, urging a fundamental and radical unification of Germany. Bavaria in particular, he argued, could not be allowed to have a special position or any sort of preferential treatment. But about the same time Bavarian troops discovered the secret correspondence that was hidden in a rural estate belonging to the French Minister, Rouher, which showed that the Darmstadt Premier had been in treasonable correspondence with the Court of the Tuileries until the outbreak of war. Dalwigk died despised and forgotten in Darmstadt in 1880. He died only a few months after Heinrich von Gagern, on whose proposal the German National Assembly had decided to offer the hereditary Imperial dignity to the King of Prussia in the Frankfurt Paulskirche on 28th March, 1849. Shortly after this event he allowed himself to be misled by Dalwigk into taking over the post of Hesse-Darmstadt envoy in Vienna, and, after 1866, of working there to promote a greater German policy hostile to Prussia.

For the first time in the course of a long, varied and often tragic history, the German people stood united in the presence of its old enemy, the French. The Princes were united, and the race united from the seas to the Alps. The task was now to prevent Austria and Italy from coming to the aid of France before her main resistance was broken, and so carrying out the obligations they had entered upon. In Vienna the decision was touch and go. Our representative there at the time, General von Schweinitz, often told me in later years that in the summer of 1870 he felt as if he were in the enemy's country at Vienna. Court, society and the Austrian generals made no secret of their pro-French attitude. Beust had set aside rooms for the French Embassy in the Imperial and Royal Foreign Ministry in order to receive friends, agents, and spies, and himself to provide the French with the most direct news. The French ambassador spent the whole day in the Ballplatz, and his secretaries, especially Baron Otto Bourgoing, who was married to a lady of the high Austrian nobility, the Countess Therese Kinsky, dominated the Casino and the Jockey Club. In the Volksgarten, where the distinguished Viennese world used to congregate in the summer evenings, the Prussians met nothing but hostile looks every day; the German representatives had to listen to the anti-German talk of the Archdukes, the most influential generals, such as John, Kuhn, Clam-Gallas, the Austrian diplomats, and even the Emperor himself. The most bitter enemies of Prussia were in the Foreign Office, and were mostly proselytes, like the Nassauer, Max von Gagern, and the Electoral Hessian, Meysenbug, a brother of Malvida, who, as far as anti-Prussian fanaticism was concerned, was even worse than Biegeleben, who came of a strictly Catholic Darmstadt family.

The plan proposed by the French and accepted by their friends in Vienna was that the Austrians should invade Saxony and Silesia. Beust hoped for accommodation and support in Saxony, on account of his old relationships there, but he was completely mistaken. The wise and loyal King Johann, his son, who was equally distinguished as a military commander and a statesman, the future King Albert, the prudent and loyal Foreign Minister, Baron von Friesen, were all unshakably loyal to the treaties concluded with Prussia in 1866, and to the German Fatherland. When a Leipzig newspaper which was in the pay of the French—I believe it was called the *Sächsische Zeitung*—continued to print its pro-French propaganda, even after the threatening speech of the Duc de Gramont and Benedetti's blackmailing attempts in Ems, a party of students arrived at the editorial offices, destroyed the machinery, and beat the paid scoundrels who edited the paper. That had an encouraging effect upon all Saxon hearts. The possibility of a defection by Saxony became as slender as that of an Austrian invasion of Silesia.

The plan discussed by Paris and Vienna, namely that the Italians should push through the Tyrol into Bavaria to prevent the South Germans from joining with the North Germans, and then join hands with the advancing French on the Upper Rhine, collapsed before the strategy of Moltke and the policy of Bismarck.

When General von Schweinitz, in accordance with his duty and the truth, described the really unpleasant situation in Vienna in his dispatches, he received from Bismarck a monumental letter in which he was requested to stop making the King's heart heavy, for his Royal Highness was already bearing a sufficient burden of anxiety. Schweinitz might, so Bismarck suggested, intimidate dear Beust and Company with the threat that if the Hapsburg monarchy were to stab the German people in the back while it was fighting for its life, he (Bismarck) would stop at nothing in his defence. *Flectere si nequeo superos Acheronta movebo.* Schweinitz might try, he suggested, to get into touch with German-Austrian youth, so as to hinder Austria from giving armed assistance to France, if need be by revolts and plots. Bismarck was also successful in getting into touch with the Hungarian Premier, Andrássy, to whom he made it known by a confidential agent that if Germany were defeated by the French through Austria's aid, Hungary would be placed in the dilemma either of re-accommodating herself within the Austrian unified state, in which case she would be governed from Vienna as she was in the Schwarzenberg-Bach's period, or of separating entirely from Austria and then sinking into the Slav-Rumanian ocean. The Magyar race, he thought, would stand or fall by the new Germany.

These intimidating tactics were not without effect. On 20th July, Count Beust sent out an ostensible circular note to the Austrian missions declaring: " If we do not succeed in saving Europe and ourselves from the severe convulsions which are the inevitable repercussions of a collision between two great nations, we desire at least to diminish their force. For the attainment of this object the Imperial and Royal Government must in the present juncture preserve a passive attitude, and the neutrality such an attitude involves. This attitude does not exclude the duty of watching over the safety of the monarchy and protecting its interests in order to be in a position to check every possible danger."

On the same day Beust telegraphed confidentially to the Austro-Hungarian ambassador in Paris: " You will repeat to the Emperor Napoleon and his ministers that we remain loyal to the obligations established in the exchange of correspondence between the two sovereigns at the end of the previous year, and that we shall co-operate, within the limits of the possible, for the success of French arms." Austria's need to consider Russia is pointed out in the strictly confidential dispatch in connection with " the limits of the possible." " We believe that Russia is adhering to her agreement with Prussia in such a way that in certain eventualities, the intervention of Russian armies may be regarded not as possible, but as certain. Paris must not deceive itself: Russian neutrality depends upon our own." Then follows a passage in which the Austrian Chancellor's fears of his German fellow-countrymen in Cisleithania is as clear as his distrust of the Magyars of Trans-leithania: "We must not forget that our ten million Germans see in the present war, not a duel between France and Prussia, but the opening of a national struggle. We cannot conceal from ourselves the fact that the Hungarians will be very hesitant about sacrificing their blood and money for the sake of recovering the Austrian primacy in Germany. Under these circumstances the word 'neutrality,' which we cannot pronounce without deep regret, is for us an imperious need. But this neutrality is only a means; namely the means of bringing us toward the real goal of our policy. It is the only means of completing our preparations without exposing ourselves to a surprise attack by Prussia or Russia."

The dispatch ended with instructions to Prince Richard Metternich to request the Emperor Napoleon again and energeti-cally to withdraw the French troops from Rome as quickly as possible and once and for all. "By such an act of indisputably liberal policy France would remove a weapon from the hands of her enemy and erect a dam against the Teutonic flood which Prussia, as an essentially Protestant Power, has known how to set in motion in Germany, and which fills us with double trepidation by reason of its contagious quality." Beust was a German and a Protestant. His termination of his confidential dispatch (which was published in the *Temps* four years later), the warning against the Teuton flood, the denunciation of Prussia as essentially a Pro-testant Power, revealed Count Friedrich Ferdinand von Beust in all his pitiableness as a twofold renegade.

After the outbreak of war Bismarck sent von Holstein, who was in his close confidence, to Italy. Von Holstein was at that time a Councillor of Legation, and his conspiratorial nature made him very suitable for such a mission. Later Holstein told me, not without satisfaction, that he had succeeded in getting into touch with Mazzini, who had come to Florence *incognito* and in disguise in August, 1870, and had met him late one evening under the arches of one of the bridges over the Arno. Drawing attention to Mentana and to the programme outlined by Rouher in a speech delivered in the French Chamber of Deputies on 5th December, 1867, Holstein showed Mazzini that a victorious France would never allow the Italians to crown the unification of Italy by the annexation of Rome. Mazzini understood, and promised that he would find ways and means of preventing the Foreign Minister from committing " imprudences." Mazzini was able to intimidate Emilio Visconti-Venosta all the more easily because the latter in his youth, before he had become minister and marquis, had favoured radical opinions and had even been the private secretary of the great agitator, Giuseppe Mazzini.

CHAPTER XII

The Battle of Sedan—Napoleon III sends Prince Jérôme to Italy—France's Resistance under Gambetta—Comparison with the German Collapse of 1918—Belgium : Bismarck's Publication of the French Offers made to him at the Expense of Belgium in the " Times "—Effect of the Publication on Public Opinion in Europe and especially in England—Bethmann-Hollweg Forty-four Years Later—Berlin in October, 1870—My First Meeting with Holstein—The Bismarck Family.

THANKS to the energy and foresight of the leading statesman, who missed no chances and calculated every factor, Moltke, the commander, was able to carry out his bold plans. The finest victory in German history, the victory of Sedan, was bestowed upon King William and the German people.

> " *Nun lasst die Glocken*
> *Von Turm zu Turm*
> *Durchs Land frohlocken*
> *Mit Jubelsturm!*
> *Des Flammenstosses*
> *Geleucht facht an!*
> *Der Herr hat Grosses*
> *An uns getan,*
> *Ehre sei Gott in der Höhe!* " [1]

So sang Emmanuel Geibel, the son of the old Hansa town of Lübeck, who had tended and nourished the sacred flame of German patriotism in dreary and apathetic times, often unappreciated and sometimes calumniated. On the evening of the battle of Sedan, our old King William uttered the shortest and most compact, the most modest and at the same time proudest toast that I know, and one which contrasted tragically with the trumpetings the grandson

---

[1] Now let the bells
From tower to tower
Rejoice through the land
With a storm of jubilation
Kindle the shining bonfires.
The Lord has been bountiful to us.
Glory be to God in the highest.

of the old king used to delight in on trifling occasions. Turning towards Bismarck, Moltke and Roon, he raised his glass with the words: " You, Minister of War, von Roon, have sharpened our sword; you, General von Moltke, have wielded it; and you, Count Bismarck have, by the policy you have conducted throughout many years, brought Prussia to the high eminence she enjoys to-day. Let us drink to the health of these three men, to the health of the army, and to everyone who has contributed all in his power to further the success we have achieved hitherto." When the dinner was over, the old King declared in good humour to the Hereditary Prince Leopold von Hohenzollern: " It's really you who've done it all, as the Berliners say. Without you we might never have had Sedan."

Later in the evening, when the guests were seeking their quarters in the darkness, only faintly illuminated by the light of a single lantern, one behind the other in single file, Bismarck enlarged on the King's jocular remark, saying how stupid the Emperor Napoleon, the Empress Eugénie, Gramont and Ollivier had been to pick a serious quarrel because of the candidacy of the Hereditary Prince of Hohenzollern to the Spanish throne, and thus start a war. He added: " If the Hereditary Prince Leopold had really gone to Madrid, his policy would have been Spanish and not German. Perhaps it would even have been anti-German. He would at least have been no different from other Germans who go abroad." Suddenly the Chancellor heard a voice protest. It was the Hereditary Prince Leopold, who, not without irritation, declared that even in a foreign land he would never forget that he was a German, a Hohenzollern, and a Prussian officer. Bismarck begged his pardon. He did not know, he said, that in the darkness he had the honour of walking so close to his Royal Highness, whose patriotism he did not doubt. This episode was told me some years later by the Hereditary Prince Leopold's brother, King Carol of Rumania.

In this case also Bismarck proved right in the end. In the Great War, the second son of this very Hereditary Prince Leopold of Hohenzollern, King Ferdinand of Rumania, by joining the Entente, betrayed the German Fatherland, brought dishonour upon the uniform of the First Regiment of Guards, which he had worn, and exposed himself to the scorn of all Germans. But who could have prophesied the situation of August, 1916, on the 2nd of September, 1870? Who in September, 1870, after the victory which, in its magnitude, contained the same warning as the climax of an Aeschylean tragedy, and which had filled all the peoples of the earth with an admiring awe such as is called forth by some natural phenomenon—a victory that will for ever intrigue the imagination—who in those days could have anticipated the betrayal of 1916?

When I was staying in Tunis in 1884 (I was First Secretary of the Paris Embassy at the time) our Consul, Nachtigal, the African explorer, told me that while he was on an exploring expedition during the winter of 1870-71, he stayed in Bornu, a Mohammedan negro empire in the central Sudan and completely separated from all communication with Europe. The natives told him that according to the reports of Arab traders, a great war had taken place in Europe between the dark-haired French and a fair-haired people. The sultan of the fair-haired people had defeated the sultan of the dark and had dragged him as a prisoner up a high mountain. There the devil had seized the defeated sultan by the hair of his head and had flown away with him into the air. Thus was the battle of Sedan pictured in the imagination of the negroes of Bornu. Thirty years after Sedan, a true patriot, Ernst Bassermann once said to me: "He whose consciousness had been stirred by the experience of Sedan can never become completely unhappy." If the effect of Sedan was so extensive, both then and in the future, how great must have been its first impression! The Councillor of Legation, Baron Allesina von Schweitzer (from 1864 to 1871 Resident Minister of Baden in Florence, and later attached to the German Embassy in Rome, where we were colleagues in 1874-75) told me that on the day after Sedan he unintentionally called upon the Italian Foreign Minister, Visconti-Venosta, unannounced. The Chancellery attendant conducted Schweitzer into the minister's office instead of into the waiting room by mistake. Visconti-Venosta and the French Ambassador, Baron de Malaret, were sitting there opposite one another. The former gave the appearance of being in a state of consternation, the latter was sobbing.

After the defeats of Wörth and Spichern, the Emperor Napoleon III sent his cousin, Prince Jérôme (known humorously as Plon-Plon) to Florence to remind his father-in-law, King Victor Emmanuel II, of the promises given by him to the French Emperor and of the obligations he had undertaken. The King put off his son-in-law for several days. When he became more and more importunate the King informed him that he could come and see him in his box at the theatre. After the first act, he said, he would give a definite answer. The Prince came to the theatre punctually. The first, second, and the third acts were performed, and the King did not show himself. At last one of the King's

chamberlains told the Prince confidentially that H.M. had left
for Aosta at eight o'clock that evening to hunt chamois. When
Prince Jérôme retorted with heat that he would follow on after his
father-in-law, the chamberlain replied with a shrug of the shoulders
that the King never received visits while hunting in the mountains.
When King Victor Emmanuel II, who was a great monarch,
courageous and wily, received the news of Sedan, he declared:
" *Pauvre Empereur! Mais fichtre! Je l'ai échappé belle.*"

How difficult it is for a man to exclude his ego. " *Le moi est
haissable,*" so the great French thinker, Blaise Pascal, teaches us.
But how little do men live up to this maxim! How few men are
capable of suppressing their egotistical wishes and desires, their
selfish impulses, and of thinking only of the great whole! Of
course, I joined wholeheartedly in the jubilation over Sedan
which went on all around me in Bonn. But the thought that in all
probability I would never encounter the enemy in the field
greatly diminished my patriotic pleasure. I wrote to my father
urgently pressing him to make representations to the command of
the reserve squadron that an exception should be made in my
case and I should be sent forthwith to the front, at my own expense.
My father flatly refused my request, and this greatly distressed me.
But the proud patriotism of the French assured my acquaintance
with the battlefields.

Nothing gives a worse idea of the national sentiment and
political insight of Germans of every grade of education than the
paltry criticism often made by our philistines in all walks of life
when they comment on the desperate resistance offered by the
French under the leadership of Gambetta, even after Sedan. In
a celebrated passage of his immortal oration *De Corona*, Demosthenes called to his fellow-countrymen after Chæronea: " No,
Athenians! ye have not done amiss when ye braved all dangers
for the salvation and the liberty of the Greeks. I swear it by our
ancestors who fought at Marathon and by those who were seen in
battle array at Platæa, by the heroes who fought on the sea at
Salamis. Athens granted all these heroes the same honour, and
granted all alike the honour of a state funeral. And it was rightly
done, for they had all fulfilled the duty of brave citizens, though
the lot of each was determined by the Gods." Xavier Charmes,
the most gifted of three gifted brothers, recalled the magnificent
words of the great Greek orator in an article published in a Paris
newspaper after the death of Gambetta. The bold resistance
which France offered after Sedan under the leadership of Léon
Gambetta (so Xavier Charmes wrote in January, 1883) gave the

French the right to remember Austerlitz and Jena, Sebastopol and Magenta, and not to despair of the future.

It was an act of reverence and justice after the victory gained by the French in 1918, that the heart of Gambetta, who had carried France impetuously along with him and had proclaimed " *la guerre à outrance*," should be transferred to the Panthéon in solemn procession. It is with shame and regret that Germans are compelled to admit how different was the mood of large sections of our people after the 1918 revolution, when they were misled by pacifist chatterboxes and Utopian fools.

Abler statesmen than Bethmann-Hollweg and Jagow, Michaelis and Kühlmann would certainly have sought the means of concluding an honourable peace and would have been able to discover it in 1915, again in 1916 and 1917, and even in 1918. But for the army, which fought to the last ditch, both officers and men, from the youngest drummer boy to Hindenburg, Mackensen, Eichhorn, Ludendorff, Below, Woyrsch, Mudra, Marwitz, Scholtz, Litzmann, Krafft von Dellmensingen, to the Crown Prince Ruprecht and Prince Leopold of Bavaria, to the Crown Prince of Prussia and his brave brothers—for Scheer and Spee, Weddigen and Dohna-Schlodien, for all the men in the trenches and the submarines—no praise is glorious enough, no laurel wreath sufficiently rich and beautiful. Yet whereas in Rome, Paris and London, the nation, from the heads of state to the peasants and workmen, makes pilgrimages to the tomb of the Unknown Soldier and lays wreaths and prays there, in Germany there is no national monument erected to the memory of the millions of German heroes in the World War. And when the regimental associations reverently erect modest war memorials, German Communists, reckless scoundrels or bestial idiots, maliciously seek to disturb the humblest memorial celebrations.

When Gramont startled the world by his trumpet blast in the Corps Législatif on 6th July, 1870, England's attitude towards us was cool, while Austria and Italy had concluded far-reaching military agreements against us. How then did it come about that no Great Power attacked us? The supreme merit of Bismarckian policy was the masterly adroitness with which at the beginning of the war he had won over public opinion to our side, and with psychological genius, set all the imponderabilia to work in our favour. It is just these intangible currents of feeling which, as I must here re-emphasize, no politician can over-estimate. Not merely all Germans (with the exception of some unteachable, wrong-headed Bavarian, Swabian and Frankfort particularists) but

LÉON GAMBETTA, FRENCH PREMIER

also a large part of foreign opinion was convinced, after the Ems dispatch, that it was France, who with traditional Gallic arrogance, had provoked us. The result of Bismarck's clever diplomatic manœuvre was that France declared the war, and that the French and not we were made the aggressors. The great statesman knew how to expose the French Emperor before the whole world as guilty of intentions against international law and of plans against the independence and neutrality of Belgium.

In the old days Germans used to talk about the " little model state " of Baden. The fact that Baden had become a constitutional state almost at the same time as Bavaria and thirty years before Prussia, that its Parliamentary life had developed at an early date, with Chamber debates, Chamber speeches and Chamber heroes; that in Baden, by reason of its historical development the land had been divided up into small properties, that no squirearchy and no militarism in the Prussian sense existed there, all this was conclusive for the Liberal mind. The administration was modern, the terms " middle classes " and " society " were virtually identical, and it was the middle class that impressed its character on the administration as well as on the Government. Even the Court, with all its airs of distinction, had something middle class about it, and the Grand Duke Frederick I and his son the Grand Duke Frederick II consciously set the tone of all this. It was typical of the Baden dynasty that when the princes of the line studied at Heidelberg they did not belong to the Saxo-Borussia corps, where the "*fine fleur*" of the Prussian nobility predominated, nor to the Westphalian and Vandal corps, which were patronized by the Holstein and Mecklenburg nobility, with here and there a distinguished member from the Hansa towns, but joined the Swabians in whose tavern the middle-class Badener would sing his " *Altheidelberg, du feine.*"

Just as Baden was the model state in the eyes of enlightened Germans, so has the Kingdom of Belgium been the model country in the eyes of the world, ever since the middle of the nineteenth century. The Belgian constitution seemed to keep the golden mean between liberty and order. Under this constitution the young Kingdom grew to great economic afflorescence and under the device " *L'union fait la force,*" it united two different races, the Latin Walloons and the Germanic Flemings, in one people. Under the watchword of liberty Belgium solved problems that presented grave difficulties and dangerous conflicts to other lands. At Louvain there was a strictly Catholic university which, under the patronage and direction of the episcopate, answered to all the requirements of the Roman Catholic Church better than any other college in the world, not even excluding Rome and Innsbruck. But quite near Louvain, in Brussels, the capital, a Free University was founded where rationalism, materialism and atheism prevailed in a freedom hardly attainable in any other country, and yet without disturbing anyone in a nation which could be called fundamentally Catholic in character.

I remember a conversation which I had in the first years of my Chancellorship with my dear friend the Centrist deputy, Franz Arenberg, and his party colleague, Baron Hertling. We had had a meal *à trois*. After the meal we discussed the old plan of a German Catholic University, which, incidentally, did not mean very much to Hertling. He asked Prince Arenberg, whose parents lived in Belgium, how matters stood in that country. Arenberg replied that a non-Catholic, indeed a fundamentally anti-Catholic university, flourished in Brussels, while an orthodox Catholic university flourished at Louvain. I proposed to Hertling that Ingolstadt should be turned into a Bavarian Louvain, and that the existing university at Munich should be expanded in a " non-committal " sense. Hertling laughed and shook his head: " It would mean murder and manslaughter," he said. " All the Liberals would describe the Catholic university of Ingolstadt as the beginning of a Bavarian eclipse of the sun and as the triumph of obscurantism. And as for a secular university in Munich," Hertling continued, " I would like to hear the interpellations which Messrs. Orterer, Schädler, Speck and Heim, as my Bavarian Centrist friends are called, would address to the Government in the Munich Pranner-strasse if it ventured to do anything of the kind. Impossible! Quite impossible! "

Prince Franz Arenberg shrugged his shoulders and said: " You simply don't know what real liberty and toleration are. There are many things in Belgium that are not nearly as good as they are here in Germany. But in Belgium everyone can seek salvation in his own way. Far more so than in the land whose king coined this phrase.[1] And for this reason little Belgium is still what Talleyrand said it was: ' *L'enfant chéri de l'Europe!* ' "

So Belgium was and remains. The Great Powers had assured its permanent neutrality. On 20th January, 1831, the Great Powers decided in the London Conference that Belgium should be a self-contained, independent state. On 21st May, 1833, a treaty came into existence between England, France and Holland. The other states adhered to this treaty by which Belgium was

[1] Frederick the Great.

declared neutral for all time. Since then Belgium had observed strict and conscientious neutrality in all disputes between other countries, in all political storms that had come upon Europe. The independence and neutrality of Belgium was one of the few fundamental principles upon which the whole world was agreed. All international lawyers had proclaimed it and commented upon it. All diplomats had been familiar with it since their examination days. The inviolability of Belgian neutrality had become part of the *communis opinio* of all who were politically educated.

Thus a great stir was caused—and the effect was like a sudden flash of lightning—when on 25th July, 1870, a few days after the French declaration of war against Prussia, the *Times* published the contents of an offensive and defensive alliance which France had proposed to Prussia during the Luxembourg affair and had secretly proposed again. In this document France declared her assent to the accession of the southern German states to the North German Federation, in exchange for which Prussia was to allow France to acquire Luxembourg, and possibly assist her against any third Power if she were to conquer Belgium. As the *Times* added, Prussia had simply rejected an offer of this kind on both occasions. The *Times* simultaneously published a draft treaty which the French Ambassador in Berlin, Count Benedetti, had submitted to Count Bismarck on behalf of the Emperor Napoleon and the French Government. Articles 3 and 4 of this treaty were as follows:

> Art. 3. His Majesty the Emperor of the French will not oppose a federal union of the Northern Federation with the southern German states, excepting Austria, this union being based on a common Parliament, the sovereignty of the states in question being respected in full measure.
>
> Art. 4. His Majesty the King of Prussia will for his part grant France the assistance of his arms and help her with all his forces on land and sea against whatever power may declare war against her in case circumstances should prevail upon the Emperor of the French to let his troops invade Belgium or conquer that country.

In a decree telegraphed to the ambassador in London and in a circular note to the diplomatic representatives of the North German Federation of 28th and 29th July, 1870, respectively, Bismarck registered the further fact that for four years France had been leading Prussia into temptation by making offers at Belgium's expense, that he had kept these proposals secret in the interests of peace, and had treated them dilatorily. " Since Sadowa," so the circular note of July continued, in an exposition that was very characteristic both of Count Bismarck's general political attitude and of his diplomatic method, besides being instructive for every diplomat and statesman, " France has never ceased tempting us with offers at Germany's and Belgium's expense. The impossibility of considering such offers was never in doubt as far as I was concerned. But I did hold it useful in the interest of peace to leave the French statesmen to their peculiar illusions as long as that was possible without even assenting by word of mouth. I suspected that the destruction of every French hope would endanger the peace, which to preserve was in Germany's and Europe's interests. I did not share the opinion of these politicians whose advice was that war with France should not as far as possible be avoided, because it was inevitable in any case. No one can penetrate the intentions of Divine Providence with regard to the future with as much certainty as this. I always looked upon even a victorious war as an evil in itself, an evil that statesmanship ought to endeavour to spare the nations. I could not ignore the possibility that there might be changes in the policy and constitution of France, changes that would have led the two great neighbouring peoples beyond the necessity for war. Every postponement of a breach would be a step towards the realization of this hope. For this reason I remained silent with regard to the proposals that were made and treated them dilatorily, without ever making a single promise on my part."

Bismarck published his revelations concerning the French plans against Belgium in a great English paper for very sound reasons. The maintenance of Belgian independence was an old axiom of English statesmanship. Even out-and-out pacifists like John Bright, Cobden and Gladstone repeatedly declared that the continued existence of a neutral, independent, and free Belgium was a question of life and death for England, and that, if the need arose, England would have to fight for this question, and had indeed fought for it against Napoleon I for twelve long years. " C'est pour Anvers que je suis ici," Napoleon declared sadly at St. Helena, and it was in every way comprehensible that England would never consent to the seizure of Belgium by another Power. " Anvers dans les mains d'une autre puissance serait une pistolet braqué sur l'Angleterre." This melancholy reflection by the man who had taken the world by storm and had been overthrown, should have been taken to heart in Germany during the World War, when she was agitating for the annexation of the Flemish coast, an annexation that could not be imagined without an endless, weary and bitter contest with England.

The Bismarckian circular dispatch of 29th July, 1870, also contained a sharp and significant snub for the fools who, after the World War, held that during the half century between the Peace of Frankfort and the murder of the Archduke Francis Ferdinand, we ought to have used this or that opportunity to take up the inevitable fight with Russia, France and England as quickly as possible. The impression made upon the English by the revelations published by Bismarck in the *Times* was very strong, and all the more useful to us; for even if the sympathies of the " upper ten thousand " for Paris and La Belle France are left completely out of account, the relations between the French and British cabinets had, as I have often pointed out, been friendly for half a century, and even intimate, in spite of occasional friction.

How was it that Bismarck succeeded not only in securing, but also in keeping, Benedetti's draft treaty in his hands? Count Vincent Benedetti, French ambassador in Berlin since 1864, had been able to acquire the goodwill of the Emperor Napoleon as Secretary to the Paris Congress and ambassador at Turin before he was sent to the Prussian capital. He had also been in favour with Prince Napoleon before his period in Turin, and was one of those who enjoyed the confidence of Princess Mathilde Bonaparte. He was an ambitious and cunning Corsican, but he sometimes forgot the familiar golden rule which the prince of diplomats, Talleyrand, was fond of impressing upon his secretaries: " *Surtout pas trop de zèle.*" Benedetti knew how much value his sovereign had attached to compensation for France ever since Sadowa. He believed that this compensation would be more easily acquired in Belgium than on the German left bank of the Rhine. Therefore he saw in Belgium the fittest object for a transaction with Prussia. At Turin he had seen how Piedmont paid France with Savoy and Nice while Italy was being united. Why should not Prussia also pay compensation, if France agreed to the union of Germany, especially as payment would be made with non-German territory?

As Benedetti always returned to Belgium in every conversation with Bismarck, pointing out that it was a suitable object of compensation, Bismarck, during the course of an animated talk, dropped the remark, in a perfectly natural voice, that it would be much easier for him to consider the whole question of compensation and to discuss it with the old King, if Benedetti himself would suggest the precise draft of the suggested transaction, all the more so as nobody could do this better than the distinguished diplomat who had already employed his skill in drafting at the Paris Congress.

Benedetti, almost as greatly flattered as the raven complimented by the fox, in Lafontaine, immediately transmitted the desired draft treaty to the Prussian Minister. A few hours later he wrote to Bismarck to say that the gentlemen in the Embassy had called his attention to the fact that so confidential a document had been left in outside hands. He therefore requested the return of the draft. Bismarck let Benedetti have his draft back at once, but in the meantime he had had the document photographed. When on 25th July, 1870, the *Times* published the French offer, he was able to allow the facsimile of the draft treaty on Belgium written by Benedetti to appear at the same time. In his circular letter of 29th July, Bismarck also brought to public knowledge earlier proposals, made in May, 1866 by the Emperor Napoleon, for an agreement in which he had proposed an offensive and defensive alliance with Prussia on the basis that Prussia should receive " *une réforme fédérale dans le sens prussien* " and annexations in Germany, " *sept à huit millions d'âmes au choix,*" but for France " *le territoire entre la Moselle et le Rhin, sans Coblence ni Mayence comprenant cinq cent mille âmes de Prusse, la Bavière rive gauche du Rhin, Birkenfeld, Homburg, Darmstadt, deux cent treize âmes.*" That is to say, at least according to French calculations, which were not quite in accordance with reality, nearly two million souls.

Even if the publication of Benedetti's draft treaty was meant for Belgium herself, for England, and for the world, south German ministers like Dalwigk and south German people's representatives like Jörg, were also enabled by the French proposals of May, 1866, to realize that they had not only spoken and acted treasonably, but also very foolishly. In any case, nothing could be more mistaken than to reproach Bismarck for outwitting Benedetti and his master, Napoleon III, instead of letting himself be outwitted by them. The farmer has the right to set a trap for the fox who wants to steal his chickens and his geese. When Benedetti was struggling in Bismarck's trap the fox sought refuge in lies, but he lied unskilfully. In a lachrymose, exculpatory letter addressed to Gramont, Benedetti declared that in his conversations with the Prussian Foreign Minister he had, so as to get a precise impression of Bismarck's schemes, been compelled by politeness to draw up these plans at Bismarck's dictation, so to speak. ·

In those days Europe laughed at Benedetti and Gramont, but Germans do not laugh to-day when they realise the difference between 1870 and 1914. In the summer of 1870 superb diplomatic mastery, caution, circumspection, foresight, resoluteness, patience, energy and skill were on our side, whereas the French diplomats failed. Forty-four years later our statesmen and diplomats, Bethmann and Jagow, Schön and Flotow, Lichnowsky and Wilhelm Stumm, were so eminently unskilful, that our opponents, Isvolski and Sasonov, Sir Edward Grey, and Sir Edward Goschen, Poincaré, Paléologue, Viviani, of whom not one could hold a candle to Bismarck, nevertheless put us in the wrong in all the world's eyes by exploiting our mistakes, and appeared to all the world to have won a moral victory in the World War before the first gun had been fired.

In the middle of October I responded to an invitation of my parents to spend my dear mother's birthday, 18th October, in the family circle in Berlin. My father thought I was looking very well, and even Professor Traube thought that my throat, my *locus minoris resistentiæ*, had survived my recruiting days better than he had anticipated. In Unter den Linden I met Herbert Bismarck, who still limped in consequence of a bullet wound in the leg which he had got at Mars la Tour. He leaned on the arm of a bearded man whose keen, piercing eyes impressed me. He may have been twelve to fourteen years older than Herbert and I. Herbert introduced us to one another: "Bernhard Bülow, a son of the Mecklenburg ambassador, a man whom my father esteems highly. Baron Fritz von Holstein, our truest friend." It was the first time in my life that I met Holstein. I often saw him again. I knew him later as the intimate friend and adviser of Herbert Bismarck, and as mortal enemy of the House of Bismarck. I stood by his death-bed nearly forty years later.

On the day of my first meeting with Holstein I was invited to lunch with Princess, or rather, Countess, as she still was, Johanna Bismarck. She and her daughter Marie, welcomed me in a kindly and hearty manner. The Chancellor's wife was just as natural, as free from shyness, and as homely as she had been in the Frankfort days, and without a trace of artificiality. She kept on urging me and her son Herbert to devote ourselves more assiduously to the very abundant meal and the good Bordeaux wine. She told me that in her native Pomerania they have a saying that eating and drinking keep body and soul together. Otto had always declared that Bordeaux was the natural beverage of the north German, and Otto was always right. He was also right now in insisting on a sterner conduct of the war. She spoke as the women of the Goths and the Franks may have spoken when the horns of battle were blown. Not a stone, she said, must be allowed to remain on another in France. Otto had only one fault, he was much too good-natured. And it was a scandal, she continued, that Augusta, that is to say her Majesty, the Queen, for whom Countess Johanna had as little affection as her great husband, had sent nine cooks to Wilhelmshöhe so as to sweeten the internment of the Emperor Napoleon—the "old horror" ought to have been locked up on bread and water, for it was all his fault that Herbert was still limping, that Billy's best horse was shot under him, and that so many German mothers and widows were going about in mourning. While she was speaking Herbert, who was animated by the excellent claret, struck up his favourite song in a loud voice, Scheffel's song about the Swabian Duke, Krock, who sallied forth from Böblingen to lay waste the whole of Gaul.

Marie von Bismarck was a creature of the utmost purity and kindliness of heart. When we were children we used to play in my parents' garden at Frankfort, where the yellow plum trees stood and from where we could get a view of the Park. Without being beautiful, Marie Bismarck had clear and intelligent eyes and abundant dark hair. In those days she had a slender and pretty figure. She was by nature just as unaffected as her mother, but she differed from her mother in so far as she tried to soften her mighty father, instead of fortifying his by no means inconsiderable tendency towards hatred and anger. Marie Bismarck never knowingly harmed anyone and gave kindly help to many within the scope of her modest influence. She was always a true friend to me, as the following little episode will show :

I remember an evening when I turned up in the Bismarck's drawing room after a rendezvous with a beautiful and elegant friend, who on that day had, unfortunately, been too strongly perfumed with White Rose. The Chancellor had not yet arrived. Mother Johanna was tapping the keys of the piano. I sat down by the side of her daughter. After a few minutes she said to me: "But you are scented. For God's sake go away as quickly as you can, otherwise father will have nothing more to do with you. He took a dislike to Harry Arnim after he came to see us several times and was too strongly scented. Later on when father got to know of Harry's doings, he said: 'I am not surprised. The fellow always stank of scent.'"

I responded to her friendly hint, and took French leave. Great men, too, have their little whims. Wallenstein could not stand hearing a cock crow, Goethe could not stand tobacco, Schiller liked the smell of rotten apples because they exhilarated him, Napoleon was fond of washing himself all over with Eau de Cologne several times every day, Bismarck could not stand perfume. I, myself, never used scent, but I did not mind if women used it.

I was back in Bonn on 30th October, and when I reported for duty to Sergeant-Major Wunderlich at the Sterntor Barracks: " It's a good thing you're there. To-morrow evening two officers, two N.C.O's., thirty hussars (including sixteen volunteers) are going to Metz, where the regiment is in camp. You must go along with them, von Bülow. We are all agreed on that."

My joy at this good news was indescribable. I was so pleased that I could have put my arm round the old sergeant-major's waist and danced the polka-mazurka or Rhinelander with him. Only on one other occasion in all my long life did I feel as great as that—fifteen years later, when, on the ice of the Neva, I got the news that the Holy See had annulled the marriage of the wife of the Prussian ambassador in Dresden, Countess Marie Dönhoff, and thereby made my marriage with her possible—with her whom I loved above all else and who became the joy of my life.

CHAPTER XIII

Back to Bonn—The Front—Bivouac at Metz—First Letters Home—Reconnoitring and Patrol Work—Major Lentze—Promoted Corporal (15.11.1870)—Advance on Compiègne—1870 and 1918.

I NOW set about packing the few articles that a common soldier can take with him to the front. Two woollen shirts, two pairs of woollen stockings, two of woollen pants, a pair of slippers, one little flask of Cognac, some tea and extract of beef, a pair of field glasses, and some writing materials. I also took the New Testament which my mother had given me during my last visit, admonishing me to read God's word assiduously. On the first blank page I wrote the words of St. Augustine: "*Inquietum cor nostrum donec requiescat in te.*"

Before I say good-bye to the reserve squadron I must express the gratitude I owe it for the stable duty I did in the Sterntor barracks and the drill on the "Sand." If I behaved like a man at the front and became a good hussar officer, after returning to the garrison, I owe it to the training I got in the reserve squadron more than to anything else. Major von Schreckenstein did not recover from his badly broken leg for more than a year. He no longer led the reserve squadron. When he became fit for service again he was appointed commander of the 7th Uhlans, and held this position when he died suddenly at Saarbrücken in 1875—an early finish to a life with a gloomy close that contrasted strangely with its brilliant commencement. "Red" Schreckenstein is one of the many whom fortune robbed of happy hours and who passed away before me. In his elegant bachelor home, resting on a sofa beneath the Danæ of Correggio, he received me in no very friendly fashion. He could hardly have thought that the young student who was exhausted by the cure at Oeynhausen, and who stood before him, pale and modest, would, in the course of years, be not only Prussian Premier and German Chancellor, but even a general. I only mention this so that any young man who some day may read these words will not be discouraged by disappointments, difficulties, and obstacles, placed in his way by a hostile, unfeeling world. "Time hereafter changes many

things and puts a period to all," so run the verses in that true and
beautiful song by the pious Georg Neumarck.

In August, 1870, Lieutenant von Stoltzenberg took over
Major von Schreckenstein's command. I found him a benevolent
superior. As I heard later on, he spoke highly of me to the regimental commander who was in the field at the time, and expressed
the conviction that the volunteer von Bülow had the makings of a
good hussar officer. This he also wrote to my father. A grave
internal complaint forced Baron von Stoltzenberg, who had
been with his regiment for eleven years and enjoyed universal
esteem, to hand over the command of the squadron to Second
Lieutenant von Schlichting, in November, 1870. Schlichting was
a good hussar, smart and intelligent, strict when on duty and
easy-going afterwards. He had taken part in the campaign of 1866,
and it was a pleasure to listen to him when he talked about the
invasion of Saxony and Austria, of the bivouac in the Grosse Garten
at Dresden, in the pouring rain, of Hühnerwasser, Münchengrätz,
Prasek, and Königgrätz, and how no Prussian troops had ridden
up closer to Vienna than the King's Hussars on 30th July, 1866,
when from the Hohe Leuthen they saw the Imperial Capital and
the lofty tower of St. Stephen's before them. Since the regimental
flag had gone to the front with the regiment, I took my oath of
loyalty to the King of Prussia on Schlichting's cavalry sabre. No
better man could have administered the oath. We often saw each
other again when I was a Minister. As owner of a big estate in
the province of Posen, Schlichting was a hereditary member of the
Upper Chamber, with whom I frequently conferred about matters
relating to the Eastern Marches. He was not only a true personal
friend, but also a clever political ally.

On 31st October, 1870, at midnight, we entrained at Bonn
station, my light brown mare, Grete and I. Grete was tolerably
comfortable in the cattle truck. But I was wedged in a compartment with many other hussars, all squeezed together like the
Pappenheimer when Max Piccolomini led them in the storm on
the camp at Neustadt. The railway journey from Bonn to Saarbrücken was horribly uncomfortable. Those who do not believe
me should try to hold out for eighteen hours without moving, in
excessively tight hussar's boots in a crowded compartment, in a
train travelling slowly and halting every half-hour. I do not know
what great thinker it was who said that no philosophy could get
over the toothache. I may add that hussar's boots fitting too
tightly are worse than the worst toothache. The good Schlichting,
who led our transport, came to my help in the hour of need. When

he saw me limping on the platform at Saarbrücken, he advised me to rip them open with a pocket knife. " You'll feel better then," he said good-humouredly. Thereupon he took me to the barracks of the 7th Uhlans in a cab, looked over some tall Uhlan boots in the store room, and asked me to pick out the most comfortable pair. The braid was taken from my old hussar's boots and quickly sewn on to the Uhlan boots, so the situation was saved.

Just before my departure from Bonn, I sent my good father a telegram. He was weighed down by many domestic cares besides all the discomfort of an attack of dysentery, from which I also had suffered during my last visit to Berlin. For these reasons he did not like my going to the front, so I wired briefly and concisely: " Proceeding with squadron midnight to regiment direction Metz and Lille, completely equipped, am well and very happy. Please send 200 thalers at once by wire urgent." After a train journey of twenty-four hours we at last reached Courcelles, near Metz. From there we rode to Liéhon, where I slept in the stable with my horse. On 3rd November we reached our regiment at the Château of Groslieu, near Metz. The reinforcements were distributed amongst the four war-squadrons. I was assigned to the first squadron. Metz had capitulated on 27th October. In an army order read out to the regiment the commander-in-chief of the investing army, Prince Frederick Charles of Prussia, did honour to this great event:

On this day an army of 173,000 men, France's best, more than five army-corps, including the Imperial Guard, with three Marshals of France, more than fifty generals, and 6,000 officers, has at last capitulated, and with it Metz, that was never before taken. With this bulwark, which we give back to Germany, immeasurable stores of guns, arms, and war material have fallen to the victor.

Prince Frederick Charles was quite right to emphasise the fact that he and his brave soldiers gave back to Germany the proud fortress which France had taken from us with cunning treachery eighteen years before. The " Red Prince," as he was called in the army, because he was fond of wearing the red Attila of the Zieten Hussars, added in the true Prussian manner: " I acknowledge your bravery with ready gratitude, but not this bravery alone. I esteem your obedience, your equanimity, your cheerfulness, your devotion in bearing hardships of many kinds, almost more highly. These are the marks of the good soldier."

On 29th October the flag with the Prussian Royal Eagle

waved from all the forts of Metz. The commander of the 30th Infantry Brigade, Major-General von Strubberg, had planted it on the main rampart with the words: " In the name of his Majesty, King William, I herewith take possession of this fort, called Queleu. God preserve his Majesty for many long years to come! God bless him! God protect him! Amen! "

On 4th November the 15th division marched through Metz. Our regiment rode at its head. The trumpets blew a fanfare, the standards were unfolded. Proudly and with shining eyes the Regiment of Royal Hussars filed past the general commanding the 2nd Army Corps, General August von Göben, who had halted in the Place d'Armes.

Oh, glorious, splendid days! Days of honour, renown and gladness! My heart bleeds when I think of them now, and then remember the wretchedness and the shame of the present.

After marching through Metz, the Regiment of Royal Hussars went into billets on Mont St. Quentin, whose outlines express so well and characteristically the landscape of the Moselle stronghold. Two years later during my service at Metz I would often visit this hill on foot and on horseback. Our squadron, the First Squadron, had to bivouac during a very cold night. Though I shivered and froze, I was immensely pleased with myself. On 6th November I wrote to my parents from Plappeville :

DEAR PARENTS,
    Please forgive me for not having written until now. I really did not have a moment's time. We joined the regiment on Thursday. I was attached to the First Squadron (15th Division, Royal Hussars Regiment, Rhenish No. 7!!). On Friday we passed through Metz. We marched into the town, into the city, with drawn swords and flag flying. From Metz we went to Chazelles, and from there to Plappeville. I am very well. Our quarters are not bad. I have managed to get food so far. I am in very good spirits. I would be glad if you would send me food, but don't send anything else. I would have to throw it away, for I have not, like my brother Adolf, got three horses, but only two wallets, into which I can hardly cram my shirts and stockings.

On 7th November I wrote again:

    The captain of my squadron, the First, is Herr von Niese-wand, who seems to swear quite a lot. Metz is beautifully situated and surrounded by strong forts. The French have dug trenches along all the roads around Metz, and here and there they have thrown up earthworks. Some of the villages were a good deal shot up, but some looked quite undamaged. The whole country must be very rich. Every spot is cultivated. We marched into Metz through the Porte Serpentinoise, the beautiful gate with different inscriptions in honour of the Duc de Guise. We marched through almost the whole town. The streets are very narrow, the houses high. The Cathedral is fine and in Gothic style. All the shops were open, some of them very elegant. The town swarms with French soldiers. All the ladies seem to be in mourning. The quays on the Moselle are very pretty. Then we rode out to Chazelles, a little village on a slope below Fort St. Quentin. We came here yesterday. Of course we have no beds, though if we are lucky we get sacks full of straw. And we always keep our clothes on, which is not particularly pleasant. I am feeling very well. If you can, send me food. Tablets of chocolate and Liebig's beef extract. It is the best because it is most concentrated, and perhaps a little tin of sardines as well. To-morrow we shall probably advance on Rheims. Under cover of the infantry. Please do not worry about my health, which is very good. A thousand greetings to all. I am well provided with everything. But I would like some provisions. From my billet I can get a magnificent view of Metz with its cathedral and ramparts.

The commander of my squadron, Captain Franz Maria von Niesewand, did indeed shout abuse at everyone and everything. This was because his promotion had been so slow, which annoyed him. He had joined the Dragoon Guards at Berlin as far back as 1849, but in 1852 he had taken up his early studies once again. He had passed his law examination and had worked in the county court at Coblence. After changing his profession once again— and this time the change was final—he was assigned to the 7th Regiment of Hussars as a Lieutenant in 1856. In 1867 he was put in command of a squadron, which he led loyally and conscientiously throughout the whole war. He was hardly two years younger than Colonel von Loë who was about to take over a brigade. Niesewand shouted a good deal of abuse. But he was an excellent fellow. He was a pious Catholic, for which reason the Rhenish nobility called him " St. Francis." I met the excellent Niesewand, who with strenuous efforts had got himself promoted to Commander of the 13th Hussars many years later (he had long been pensioned then) at the fine festival which the town of Bonn gave in honour

of its Blue Hussars on 18th June, 1902. The sturdy fellow, who
had come to be seventy-two years old in the meantime, asked me
if I, as Imperial Chancellor, bore him a grudge, because he had
shouted abuse at me now and again when I was with his squadron.
I replied without a moment's hesitation: " On the contrary, I
thank you with all my heart. If you had not taken me in hand so
firmly and made a real Hussar of me, I would never have become
Chancellor of the German Empire." " St. Francis " was pleased at
this.

When reinforcements arrived in Metz the regiment was
overjoyed to get out of the Moselle valley at last. To its sorrow
the regiment had been given no opportunity of taking part at
Spichern and in the big battles round Metz. During the siege of
Metz it had done reconnoitring work with zeal and vigilance.
One of the regiment's best officers, Lieutenant Deginhard von Loë,
a nephew of the commander, fell at the entrance of Longeau while
reconnoitring. An enemy bullet pierced his temple and killed
him on the spot. But the regiment had not yet done any hand-to-
hand fighting with the enemy. It had not attacked as yet. And
it was attack everyone was eager for. This is what our commander,
Colonel Walter von Loë, who was full of ardent military ambition,
had meant when, not long before the capitulation of Metz, he had
remarked bitterly during a horse inspection: " Though the
regiment may have had no chance of showing what it can do, it
has at least to do its duty and keep His Majesty's kit in proper
order."

After the capture of Metz the task of assuring the investment
of Paris against the north fell to the First Army (to which the
King's Hussar Regiment belonged, being part of the 8th Army
Corps), for General Bourbaki, who had escaped from Metz, was
now forming the French Northern Army. The whole of the
8th Corps, and not least the King's Hussar Regiment, lived in the
hope that after the long and tedious investing duty in the north of
France it would now at last get some " bright brisk " skull-splitting,
as the worthy Valentine in *Faust* describes his military calling.

The advance began on 7th November. The King's Hussar
Regiment was the vanguard of the 15th Division. We marched
through the Argonne forest. The roads were bad, either very
rough or deep in mud. The weather was inclement, cold and wet,
and there was sleet. I had a good horse, the swift Grete, and
consequently I received numerous commands to fetch the divisional
dispatches or get orders there. Since in these parts the population
was very stubborn, and there were a good many *franc tireurs* roaming

the woods, of whose treacherous fire not a few patrols had been the victims, we rode with carbines at the ready. I was only shot at twice. Once a bullet whistled close past my ear. Of course, at night there was no possibility of discovering the person who had fired it. There was nothing to do but imitate the worthy Swabian in Uhland's poem: " keep my pecker up " and " look about me with contempt." But unlike the Swabian, I did not " proceed on my path step by step," but galloped away as fast as possible.

At divisional headquarters I always met with a kind reception, just as I did from the 29th Infantry Brigade (Colonel von Bock) and the 30th Infantry Brigade (Major-General von Strubberg). On one especially cold November night, after a long ride through a snowstorm, I arrived at the quarters of the General Staff Officer of the 15th Division, Major Lentze, at midnight, with a dispatch from the regiment. The major read the dispatch and then said to me: " You have had a long and severe ride. It will take two or three hours before I shall be ready to send you off again. Pull off your boots, and go and lie on my bed and sleep a bit." I drew myself up into a rigid attitude and replied with youthful ardour that I did not feel tired. " Nonsense," said the major, " get some of your sleep done now. A young fellow can always do with some sleep." He gave me a glass of wine, pressed a slice of bread and butter and cheese into my hand, and then I slept until he woke me up. On awakening I was given another slice of bread and butter, this time with sausage on it, and another glass of wine. The major asked me what my name was, talked interestingly and informatively with me about the military situation, and dismissed me refreshed and very grateful. We did not meet again for many years. Our next meeting place was the Royal Palace in Berlin, when he was a General-Commander and I Imperial Chancellor. We were delighted to see each other, and gave full rein to our feelings. The Kaiser observed the warmth of our greeting with surprise. " I know very well," he said to me, " that you are a very fascinating person, but I never thought that you would be able so to subdue the rugged Lentze." It must be added that General Lentze was what the French call " un bourru bienfaisant." He had a reputation for gruffness. But under the rough exterior beat a golden heart, as an obscure young Hussar could testify. He was one of the most able generals of our magnificent army. The leader of the Infantry Brigade, Major-General von Strubberg, too, always treated me particularly well during service in the winter campaign of 1870-71. For this I shall always remain thankful to this honourable general, who came from the Augusta

Regiment, and was close to the person of William I. I often saw
him again when I became Imperial Chancellor.

November 9th, 1870, was an important day in my life. The
regimental commander, Colonel von Loë, summoned me. He told
me first that I had been warmly recommended to him by my
superiors at Bonn. I had, he said, done credit to their recommendations since. I had borne up well during the severe marches through
the defiles of the Argonne Forest, and had carried out my orders
with pluck and intelligence. Would I care to enter the King's
Hussar Regiment as an officer-cadet (*Avantageur*) he asked?
I should have to obtain my parents' consent. I replied that it was
my greatest wish to become an officer of the King's Hussar Regiment.
I hoped that my father would not refuse to allow me this. I was
not able to give any guarantee, I said, because so far I had not
got the necessary consent, and it would be painful to have to
withdraw later on because of my father. But I would do all that
was in my power to prevent my father, who, although he knew
nothing of the army, had an open mind, and was very well disposed
to it, from thwarting my wishes in the matter. The Colonel,
who appeared to be pleased and impressed by my keenness, added
that he, too, would write to my father. He then told me that the
fact that I had studied five terms in the university would be no
hindrance to my future military career, but an advantage. He
mentioned a whole list of generals who had had a university training.
He, himself, had been a student for several terms before he had
taken his commission. He ended with the kindly and jovial
words: " So, my dear Bülow, I hope to make a real hussar officer
of you, a good officer of the King's Hussar Regiment." This was
how Colonel von Loë spoke to me in field-quarters at Charpentry,
near Varennes. It was my first important meeting with the man
who was my example and teacher till his death thirty-eight years
afterwards, and whom I honoured as few other men.

On 10th November I wrote as follows from field-quarters at
Charpentry:

Dear Papa,
    The colonel summoned me yesterday and spoke very kindly
to me. He told me that I had been well recommended to him
from Bonn. He said that he had great pleasure in confirming
the favourable opinion that they had of me in the reserve squadron
at Bonn. He asked me whether you would give your consent
to my becoming an officer-cadet. He said that he would gladly
accept me, for he believed that I had the makings of a Hussar

officer. I said to him that I did not doubt that you would give your approval after I had discussed the factors for and against with you. It would have been too painful for me to have been disavowed by you after I had accepted. In any case, I would not like to take a decision over your head. I myself would be ready at once, I said, and he told me that he would write to you himself. May I beg you urgently, father dear, to grant my request? Please send me your consent in writing, so that then I may enter the regiment as an officer-cadet. We have been doing some heavy marching since Metz, at first in cold weather, to-day in the rain. The battlefield of Gravelotte seemed rather sad in the murky November light. I am (touch wood) keeping well and do not feel at all tired. There is a good deal of talk about an armistice. But as the colonel said to me, none of the generals believe in an early peace. Since we left Metz the neighbourhood has become very drab. Every now and again we pass a wretched village. The landscape is either heath or scrubby grass. We have been marching over hilly wooded ground since yesterday—always, of course, with an advance guard on account of the numerous *franc tireurs*. As I have no map I have no idea where we really are, but I think we are in the Argonnes. Our direction should be towards Rheims. When requisitions are made from the peasants, they complain bitterly. One feels sympathy for them, but there is nothing to be done about it. I didn't have time to get myself photographed in Bonn. Could you have half a dozen copies made of my cabinet size photograph and send one to Countess Bismarck with my compliments and greetings. Since she has asked for one so many times it would be impolite not to do something about it and show some acknowledgment. Please excuse this hurried letter. I am in bed. I went to bed so as to give my clothes a chance of drying. Thousand greetings to all. Please do send me your written consent quickly on a slip. I can only ask you most urgently to let me have it. Please don't let mother worry about me. I won't do anything rash. I feel well, and am in good spirits. God will take care of everything else.

Your devoted son,

BERNHARD VON BÜLOW.

On 11th November I wrote as follows from field-quarters at Bercieux (Marne):

DEAR PARENTS,

Please do send me your written authorisation, somewhat in

this form: " On my son's request I hereby grant him authority to join the King's Hussar Regiment as an officer-cadet." I must have been well recommended to the Colonel by Stoltzenberg and Schlichting, for he offered me what other people can only achieve with the greatest trouble. We are now marching through severe snowstorms. To-day's continued without a break. But all the same, this is better than yesterday's rain. Our section was a wing detachment, and we proceeded for two hours through a wooded mountain-chain over very bad paths. We are now in Champagne. Bercieux is a very prosperous village, which contrasts strikingly with the wretched little places in Lorraine. We passed Varennes, where Louis XVI was stopped on his flight. We all made for the champagne, which only costs three francs a bottle in Epernay and Rheims. It has very probably gone up in price since the first arrivals. I feel extremely well (touch wood). My horse is rather fatigued. Thousand greetings to all. I am very eager for news of you. Please send on your written consent quickly. Perhaps a parcel of food as well. Again a thousand greetings.

Your devoted son,
BERNHARD VON BÜLOW.

The day at Varennes of November, 1870, stands clearly before my eyes. The rain poured down. There was a great square market place surrounded by low houses. Only a few people were in the streets, and they looked at the Prussians inquisitively and shyly. Here, eighty years before, the kindest and most unfortunate of kings had met his fate, the heir and descendant of Hugh Capet, St. Louis, Henri IV and Louis XIV, the *Grand Monarque*, and with it, too, the fate of his proud and beautiful consort, the emperor's daughter, Marie Antoinette, and that of the poor little Dauphin, who in later years was to find comrades in misfortune in the Tsarevitch Alexei Nikholaievitch, Prince Louis Napoleon, and the Archduke Rudolf, who could all bear witness along with him that to be born in the purple does not mean that happiness is assured.

Overjoyed, I wrote to my parents on 15th November, as follows:

Yesterday the Colonel made me a lance-corporal. This ought to decide the matter, for as a volunteer I should only have become a lance-corporal after nine months service. Even so, it's very soon, for as a rule only the cadet period is really counted. Please send me the letter of authorisation soon.

My rise to lance-corporal was my first promotion. This modest step gave me great pleasure. My friend, Missy Durnow, the talented daughter of the Chief Lady-in-Waiting of the Empress Maria Feodorovna, the Princess Helene Kotchoubey, used to say: " *Les petits pois qui ne vous disent rien dans la saison des légumes, vous enchantent comme primeurs.* " That is true all the world over. I was very proud when I stitched on my lance-corporal's badge. On 17th November I wrote from Bétheny, near Rheims:

We marched here yesterday. We are quite near Rheims. From here the town looks very picturesque, especially the cathedral.

Pierre de la Gorce's charming history of the Second French Empire ends with the German occupation of Rheims, the old French coronation-town. Gorce concludes with the words: " *Le soir les soldats allemands se répandirent dans la nef et on les vit, les uns en curieux, les autres en dévots, passer et repasser devant l'autel, ou Jeanne d'Arc avait déployé son étendard, ou les rois de France avaient été sacrés.* " Among these visitors to the Cathedral of Rheims was lance-corporal von Bülow, who entered the cathedral not only as a sightseer, but also as a believer in God, full of reverence for the strength and purity of faith in the hope of heaven which created this magnificent House of God in the middle ages.

After a tiring march of four days we reached Compiègne. During this march increased measures of precaution had to be taken, since the population turned out to be even more turbulent and recalcitrant in its expectation of a speedy return of the Northern Army. We seized and destroyed all available arms in all the main towns and villages. If Rheims incorporated the long submerged grandeur of the old Royal France as did no other French town, Compiègne recalled the brilliance of the Second Empire, which had hardly disappeared even by that time. Generals von Manteuffel and von Göben were quartered in the Château of Compiègne. They had expressed the desire that all soldiers of the 8th Army who might wish to do so should have a chance of visiting the château. I also wandered through the forest of Compiègne with Max Schlichting, who was always of a comradely and friendly disposition towards me. We had no idea that in these miles of woods forty-eight years later the victorious Marshal Foch would meet Matthias Erzberger, sent by the German people to ask an armistice.

CHAPTER XIV

General von Goeben's Army Orders—27.11.1870—Letters from the Front—December Days, 1870—Rouen—Camp at Camon— The Battle near Hallue (23.12.1870)—Christmas at Altonville.

FROM Compiègne we continued our march to Rouen. Before Amiens, on 27th November, there was a battle, which to my sorrow, resembled the battle near Metz during the summer, in that it gave our regiment no chance of attacking. The battle before Amiens also showed us that in the Franco-German war it was often the divisional cavalry's fate only to put the finishing touches to a victory, with no opportunity for the regiment, or even one of its isolated squadrons, to win any more distinguished independent success. The four squadrons covered a space of a mile and a half, and so many orderlies and patrols belonging to each were active all day that the commander only kept a small part of his people in hand. Our first squadron, especially, was wholly broken up into patrols. Hardly a single unit was complete. Colonel von Loë was therefore regretfully compelled to forego any independent action. But he had the comfort, and we with him, that the reliable and lucid reports of the Hussars contributed considerably towards the success of the engagement as a whole. General von Goeben acknowledged this specially several times. In August, 1871, the great commander said to Major Prince Henry XIII of Reuss, who reported to him as newly appointed commander of the Royal Guards Regiment, after having spoken in high praise of the regiment's achievements, that the reliable, nearly always correct, reports of the regiment about the position and strength of the enemy had been of great value to him, that in the end he had such confidence in them that it was enough for him to know that a report came from the Royal Hussars for him to base his operations on it. The regiment, with justified pride, has entered this praise from such lips in the pages of its history.

The victor in the battle of Amiens, General von Goeben, issued the following army order in the night of 27th-28th November, shortly before midnight: " The advancing enemy army has been thrown back on Amiens in to-day's victorious battle of Amiens. I express my thanks to the Army, and shall report to his Majesty on the courage which has been shown once again." The Commander-in-Chief refrained from pursuing the beaten enemy, contrary to the expectation of all. Rouen was the objective which had been assigned by our great military thinker, Moltke, to the First Army after it left the Oise. So the march on the capital of Normandy continued.

On 1st December our army began the westward march on a broad front. The first frost had set in. The streets were frozen hard. During the next few days the cold increased. On 16th November I wrote to my good parents : " Please do not be anxious on my account. I am in the best of health, and my friends say that I am looking better than I did in Bonn. I am also in good spirits and, if it were not for you, the war could go on for a long time as far as I am concerned." Two days later I wrote from Paslys, near Soissons: " I am very well (touch wood). I am fully convinced that I, like all the rest of us, am in God's hands. His will be done, whatever we ourselves may wish. So far as dysentery, etc., are concerned, you really need not be anxious. It is true that there was some danger at Metz. Quite apart from those who were unfit for duty altogether, three-quarters of the regiment were more or less ill. I had a little attack, too, just as I had in Berlin in October. But I got over it splendidly by drinking three strong glasses of Schnapps one after the other. It is still uncertain whether we shall face the enemy soon, as we all hope to do. It is not impossible, for although people think we shall proceed from Compiègne to Paris, it is certain that we shall advance on Amiens against the French Northern Army under Bourbaki. But it does not follow that we shall attack, although I for my part fervently wish that we may. In any case, I am in God's keeping."

On 25th November I wrote from Faverolles, near Mondidier, Département de la Somme:

The day before yesterday I was at Compiègne with Herr von Schlichting, and Count Beissel, a Rhinelander, whom I knew in Berlin. We had a day of rest, and were glad to get out of Janville, which is a wretched hole, where cows and oats are requisitioned amid the wailing and laments of the whole population. Compiègne is a pretty town, a kind of French Potsdam. No doubt others have made this comparison before me, for it is obvious. The shops are quite good, and I completed my equipment by a very fine blanket, which is strapped on the saddle behind, instead of the coat which now we wear. I also bought a little trunk, which the quartermaster takes along for me, and

various provisions, stockings, etc. We had a very good meal in
the Hôtel de la Cloche.   Then we had a look at the château
with Count Sierstorpff, of our regiment, who is orderly officer
with General Manteuffel, and knows all about it.   It is a fine
building in Renaissance style.   The façade facing the town
is not as fine as the one facing the park in which the celebrated
hunts took place.   From there you get a very fine view of the
forest, with magnificent trees, open spaces, that are adorned with
statues, fountains and pretty ponds.   The inside of the château
is, incidentally, more beautiful than the outside.   The big apartments are quite splendid.   Everywhere there are beautiful
paintings and even more beautiful tapestries.   Two pictures in
the entrance hall are especially worthy of notice.   They depict the
attack of the French cuirassiers at Waterloo.   The elegance of
the tables, furniture, chairs and fireplaces, etc., was to my mind
incomparable.   One cannot think of anything more beautiful.
All the rooms, salons and boudoirs are filled with Prussian
officers and men, the latter with big wooden pipes and without
exception shod in nailed boots.   A year ago the Emperor and
Empress would have dreamed as little of this as of Sedan and
Wilhelmshöhe. *Sic transit gloria mundi*. I enclose some photo-
graphs of the château which I bought for you from the caretaker.
Yesterday we left Janville and marched to Auteuil, from which
I was sent with a dispatch to the captain, who sent me on to the
colonel.   The latter was in Ressons, and the staff in Méry.
The Colonel, to whom I gave papa's letter of consent (for which
I thank you very deeply) was very kind.   The French appear
to be withdrawing.   Bourbaki is believed to have entrenched
himself near Amiens.   It is thought that Russia has declared
war on England, France and Turkey.   This is probably a
canard.   Yesterday we saw a balloon which we shot at, unfortunately, in vain."

On 4th December I wrote from Lémon, near Buchy (Seine
Inférieure):

Only a few lines, for it is already late, and I am very tired.
Yesterday we marched to Fromerie, where we had good quarters
and good food at the Hôtel du Cygne, and also made many
purchases.   To-day the order came that our section should
join up with the squadron again.   I received it in a little town
(the name of which I forget) where I was seeing about billets.
I immediately galloped back to fetch the section, which was

far behind with the column. We then went to look for the
squadron, which cost us much trouble. First to the Division,
then to the Staff, then to the squadron which quartered us here
all in a wretched barn. Still Schlichting and I managed to annex
a chicken that now is being cooked. To-day we spent eight
hours in the saddle, yesterday fourteen—and always on the move.
We are five miles from Rouen and already in Normandy. Our
regiment took the advance guard. The French are always
running away. Thousand greetings and best wishes, my dear
parents, to everybody. May God grant us with a happy reunion.

Your devoted son,

BERNHARD.

On 4th December our squadron, as it was galloping along,
surprised a large number of retreating French infantry between
Buchy and Rouen on lumpy farmland, frozen as hard as stone,
and compelled them to lay down their arms. On 5th December,
a magnificent cold winter's day, our staff officer, Major Dincklage
(he is not popular in the regiment because his somewhat stiff
Hanoverian manner does not suit the Rhenish character of the
King's Hussars, but he is an able soldier) proceeded according to
orders with the 1st and 2nd squadrons to reconnoitre in the direction
of Rouen. In front of Rouen barricades and fresh earthworks with
uncompleted trenches showed that the town could only have been
evacuated a short time before, and that serious defence had been
intended. In one of the trenches we found six pieces of ordnance,
which we captured for the regiment. We caught a large number of
Guardes Mobiles. One of them, with true French politeness, paid
me a compliment on my good French while I held him by the
collar to prevent him from escaping: "*Monsieur parle le français
sans accent, je lui en fais mon compliment.*" One of the captured
Guardes Mobiles made a bolt for it at the corner of a street. The
hussar escorting him calmly reined in his horse, put his carbine
to his shoulder, and shot him down at about thirty paces.

Arrived at the suburb of Darnétal, Major Dincklage summoned
the mayor of the place to him. The latter explained that he could
answer for the orderly behaviour of the decent part of the population: "*Mon colonel, les bons citoyens sont sages et tranquilles, ici
comme partout. Mais je ne puis repondre de la canaille. Il y a ici
plusieurs fabriques et par conséquent beaucoup d'ouvriers. Ceux-ci ont
commis des excès apres le depart des troupes françaises. Ils sont bien
capables d'en commettre encore si vous continuez votre marche.*" Nevertheless, the Major went on with his six detachments.

At one o'clock we entered Rouen. At two o'clock we halted in the Place Napoléon surrounded by a shouting, gesticulating and abusive crowd, which did not, however, dare any violence. The great Corsican, whose equestrian statue stood in the square, looked contemptuously and proudly down on the rabble. When the 70th Regiment marched up to the Town Hall scarcely half an hour later, the mob withdrew. Two squadrons of the King's Hussars had occupied the capital of Normandy, with its population of over 100,000, including 20,000 hungry workmen. Our squadron occupied the fine new cavalry barracks, *La Bonne Nouvelle*, in the suburb of St. Sévere. I took a walk along the quays of the Seine in the evening with some comrades. Bright moonlight was playing on the water, and it also glinted on the regimental badges of the King's Hussars as they crossed the great stone bridge over the river. This stone bridge had been opened by the Emperor Napoleon seventy years before, when he was First Consul. At that time he had been received on the bridge by the Prefect of the Seine Inférièure whose cock-sure demeanour had irritated him. After they had crossed the bridge together the future Emperor tried to embarass the *prefet*, who was still very young, by a series of searching questions about the state of affairs in his administrative area. The *prefet* had an effective reply ready for every question. At last the Emperor asked: "*Et combien d'oiseaux ont passé aujourd'hui ce pont ?*" Without losing countenance for a moment the Prefect replied: "*Un seul, Premier Consul, un aigle!*" This *prefet* succeeded well under the First Empire.

Rouen, with its churches, the Cathedral and the Church of St. Ouen, magnificent buildings of the purest Gothic, with its narrow, old-world streets, with the wide and powerfully-flowing Seine, the picturesque heights on the right bank of the river, stand before me in agreeable memory. After the hardships of the long and fatiguing march from the Moselle to the Seine, we were fond of going to the corner restaurant near the quay, where there were wonderful salt-water fish and fresh Marenne oysters. On the day after we had marched into the capital of Normandy I saw the Archbishop of Rouen, Monsignor de Bonnechose, who walked to the prefecture where General von Manteuffel was staying. When the General asked why the Archbishop had not come in a carriage, he replied that his horses, like those of the other inhabitants, had been requisitioned, for which reason he had come *per pedes apostolorum*. The chivalrous General had the Archbishop's horses returned to their owner that same day—an act of courtesy which the French Generals Foch and Nollet, Degoutte and de Metz too

often failed to show when, with the help of half the world, they had
overpowered the German people.

I reported to General Manteuffel once or twice during the winter
campaign of 1870-71. I also repeatedly saw him walk or ride past.
It was my impression that he deliberately assumed the outward
manner of a General of lofty and noble disposition. I have already
mentioned the fact that Schiller's immortal dramatic poem, *The
Wallenstein trilogy*, was his favourite reading. In any case, he
imitated the Friedländer successfully, and all who served and fought
under him looked up to him with trust and reverence as the great
General and unusual man he was. He did the army, Prussia, and
Germany lasting service by bringing new blood into the officers'
corps from 1857 to 1865, when he was head of the War Office
Staff, and later from 1865 to 1866, as civil and military governor
of Slesvig and, still later, in the Franco-German war, as victor at
Colombey and Noisseville, when he was Commander-in-Chief of
the First Army, and especially when he was leader of the Southern
Army, and victor over Bourbaki. As Commander-in-Chief of the
Army of Occupation in France from 1871 to 1873 Manteuffel
treated the defeated French with a consideration that was acknowledged by the French Government and especially by the President
of the French Republic, M. Thiers, in heartfelt letters of gratitude
although this did little to soften the fundamental French attitude
towards us. As Statthalter of Alsace-Lorraine from 1879 to his
death in 1885, the Field-Marshal showed that an eminent General
is not necessarily a good administrative official. By his too lenient
handling of the pro-French elements in Alsace-Lorraine he did
some harm, and was certainly less successful than either his predecessor Herr von Möller, or his successor, Prince Chlodwig
Hohenlohe.

On the 6th December I wrote from Moulinot, near Rouen:

DEAREST PARENTS

On Saturday we shall enter Rouen. At first we counted on a
largish battle, but the French withdrew. The *Garde Mobile*,
which was still in the villages, surrendered without serious
resistance and, as it seemed to me, at times even with pleasure.
I went on patrol with Count Beissel to get contact with the
16th Division, which we succeeded in doing. I then rode back
alone to report to the Major. Many French rifles, caps, and
uniforms lay by the roadside. The French threw them away
so as to steal into the villages as peasants, no one being able to
prove that they had borne the arms. Even a flag lay in the ditch

by the road. I tore it from its staff as a souvenir. When I got back, the squadron had just entered Darnétal, a suburb of Rouen. We were the first Prussians to enter the capital of Normandy, to the great annoyance of the 16th Division, which had reached Amiens before us. General Goeben soon appeared and gave orders to the 10th Infantry Regiment (which had been made famous by Kutschke) as well as the Hussars, to march past with bands playing and flags flying, which looked very pretty and made a great impression on the French.

The attitude of the inhabitants was inquisitive and servile. There had been a riot in the morning, and all the windows of the Town Hall had been smashed. At the street corners the proclamations could still be read according to which Rouen would rather be buried under its ruins than surrender. We reached our quarters towards evening. We stayed in the town, which is a highly interesting place, on Wednesday and Thursday. The Quai Napoléon, with its fine shops, cafés, and hotels, flanks both shores of the Seine. The other streets in the town are narrow and dirty, except for two magnificent boulevards, *de la République* (formerly " *de l'Empereur* ") and " *du Grand Pont* "—which lead from the Town Hall Square to the river. The town Hall itself is big, but of no importance. Very beautiful is the Church of St. Ouen, near by, in Gothic style, with three steeples and a monument to Napoleon I, which is large rather than tasteful, in front of it. The Cathedral, with its chimney-like steeple, also seemed interesting rather than beautiful to me. But the Palais de Justice is superb, and, as I am told, the most beautiful in France. It is in Gothic style, with countless oriels, turrets, and windows. The square where the Maid of Orleans was burned, and her monument, are also interesting. Do you remember with what enthusiasm I once read Schiller's *Maid of Orleans* ? I wept with emotion over the scene where the Maid, locked up in the tower, follows the course of the battle. I must have been eight or nine years old then. Unfortunately, the Captain has sent me on a post relay. I owe this unwelcome duty to my French, which I have to produce on such occasions. An attempt of mine to dissuade him was received very ungraciously with noisy abuse. I am now planted with an N.C.O. and four men in a little village sixty kilometres from Rouen. Our task is to send on the letters to the troops who are marching towards Havre, etc. If the letters are marked with one cross we deliver them at walking speed, if they are marked with two crosses, at the trot, and three crosses, at the gallop (+, ++, +++).

Two men always ride together. In this way I am unfortunately deprived of the prospect of seeing Havre and Honfleur. I have made friends with the curé here, and have had coffee at his house at noon to-day. He showed me the beautiful church built by the Reine Blanche, with the magnificent view of the Seine that flows through wonderful country, many villages with pretty churches, châteaux, villas partly at the water's edge and partly at the foot of the heights that fringe the river on both sides. The curé and I have long talks about religion. He is a mild, kind-hearted priest.

On 19th December I wrote from Montdidier:

DEAR PARENTS,

We have marched back here from Rouen, and our quarters are mostly very bad, but I am very well (touch wood). We passed several little towns like Crèvecœur, Breteuil, and one or two others. We also had one day of rest, but in a horrible hole, where three of us lay on the straw in a goat stall. Montdidier is a somewhat largish town. The population has been very unruly for some time, as it believes that we are retreating and our army before Paris has been destroyed. There are many *franc tireurs* in the neighbourhood. Montdidier, incidentally, is quite a nice little town, with two pretty churches. Amiens is said to have been re-occupied by the French. At least do not let your Christmas be spoiled by thoughts of me, for God be thanked, I am very well.

To entertain my sadly anxious parents I enclosed two French pamphlets which I had bought in Moulinot in my letter: " *Nous allons taper sur le Prussien,*" and " *Je ne voudrais pas être dans la peau d'un Prussien.*"

On 20th December, I wrote from Montdidier:

DEAR PARENTS,

Your cigar-letters are splendid. Please send me a military neck-tie when you can. The weather is mild and fine. We have a holiday to-day. Nothing is to be expected yet awhile, for the Northern Army under Faidherbe is a fraud. Thousand greetings to everybody.

Your devoted son,
BERNHARD VON BÜLOW.

In this letter, which was written three days before the battle of Hallue, Officer-Cadet von Bülow showed that he was but slenderly informed about the military situation as a whole. But perhaps I only wished to calm my over-anxious parents.

On 21st December I wrote from Cayeaux:

> Yesterday we should have had a real holiday. I was under orders to lead a patrol to Roy. But the next day we got our orders and Lieutenant Erffa's patrol, in which I now ride, arrived here with two companies of sixty-fives. The quarters are first rate. We ate and drank to our heart's content. There is a château in the village belonging to a Marquis Doria. To-day I rode to the squadron, and from there to the division and to the brigade. Colonel von Bock, our present Brigadier, invited me to breakfast and was very kind. Yesterday evening Lieutenant Erffa went to Ayencourt, two kilometres away, with two-thirds of the patrol in order to reinforce Lieutenant Knesebeck's patrol there. We are on the alert. The unfortunate infantry have to bivouac in the open. We hope that something will happen to-morrow. The French have occupied the Somme crossings. It is understood that they are to be surrounded and taken prisoner. Amiens has been evacuated by the French and occupied by us again. A thousand greetings to all and a thousand good wishes for Christmas and the New Year. Cigar letters give me tremendous pleasure. Please send me a military necktie when you can.
>
> Your devoted son,
> BERNHARD VON BÜLOW.

Lieutenant Erffa, as he still was then, was a good comrade to me personally, but he put a good many difficulties in the way of my policy of conciliating and not exacerbating the quarrels between the Parties during my Chancellorship, when he was Conservative President of the House of Deputies.

On 22nd December the First Squadron entered Camon, a clean village on the right bank of the Somme, between Amiens and Corbie. I was quartered with my servant in a large peasant house whose owner seemed anxious to show that Bismarck was not wrong when he used to say that wealth has a timid heart. He awaited the billeting of the Prussians with anguish: "*Grâce, Monsieur le Prussien, grâce pour moi, grâce pour ma pauvre femme.*" His wife joined in, sobbing and howling. I endeavoured to calm them both by assuring them that I was not in the habit of eating elderly married couples for breakfast. I said that I did not wish to stay in the house if my presence inspired so much terror. I only desired, I said, a shelter for my two horses, my own and my servant's, and that would be easy to find in the stable close to the house. The only intelligent person in the place was a young girl, apparently a relative of the family. Without losing her head, she explained to the two old people that I did not strike her as wanting to murder them all. I thanked her for her benevolent judgment of my modest person, and added that she seemed to be the only real man in the family. The old man, gradually calming down, agreed: " *C'est bien vrai, Julie a le diable au corps.*" Julie conducted me to the stable. I stretched myself out on my straw bed and slept until the trumpeter sounded reveille.

The morning of the 23rd of December, 1870 broke. The day was clear and windless, with eight degrees of frost. As I came out of the stable into the harness room, Julie was standing there. I then noticed for the first time that she was pretty, tall, well developed, with eyes that spoke of courage and energy, ample raven black hair coiled into a single knot, red lips, and a firm mouth. She asked me if it was true, what they said in the village, that there would be a battle very soon. I replied that it might be so. She said: " *Pour sûr, vous allez vous fair tuer, car je suppose que vous serez aussi brave que vous êtes bon et généreaux.*" I suppose it was the strangeness of the situation, the coming battle with its chances and dangers, and the tranquillity of the early morning that sent these two young people, the son and the daughter of two hostile nations, into an ecstasy. Psychologically it is entirely comprehensible—that much I can say when I look back on it. Our nerves were keyed up. We were not in control of our senses.

I drew the pretty woman towards me. Our lips met. We forgot time and space, which, according to Immanuel Kant, are the only forms of perception, and embraced with passionate emotion. The trumpeter blew the muster. He had blown it for the second time when I tore myself away. I swung myself up on my horse, which my servant was holding by the bridle in front of the house.

I joined the squadron just in time. It was being formed into three detachments so as to make a flanking section to which I belonged as a non-commissioned wing-officer. Lieutenant Knese-beck, who was riding in front of the file, beckoned to me and whispered: " I believe we are going to attack. French infantry are said to be behind the hollow through which we are going to ride." A few minutes later we saw fifty or sixty French riflemen in front of us. Knesebeck raised his sabre, and gave the command. " Advance! Charge! " We twenty hussars brandished our sabres and cried: " Hurrah! " Grete, my light brown mare, easily took

IMPERIAL CHANCELLOR PRINCE OTTO VON BISMARCK-SCHÖNHAUSEN

In his study in the Foreign Office

the broad deep ditch separating us from the French. She was worthy to bear the name of the sweet girl in whose honour I had called her Grete. I pressed both my spurs into her sides, and was the first to land among the enemy. I rode down a Frenchman who was taking aim at me. Moaning and rubbing the small of his back he limped away in the direction of the wood. As I was looking at him I sensed and saw the point of a bayonet close by me on the other side. I perceived an infuriated and distinctly vicious countenance. To-day I am far from objecting to the face of the owner of that bayonet. His expression harmonized with the situation. On the other hand, no sensible person will blame me for striking my opponent across the head with all the might and strength I could summon. He wavered and swayed, tottered, collapsed, gave a death rattle, and was dead.

After I had cast a long glance upon the enemy who had been killed by me, I looked round for my comrades. They, too, had been sturdily at work. Sergeant Zerbe, a west Prussian, made for an enemy sergeant and almost reached him when the latter fired and missed, but skilfully presented his bayonet so that his opponent should run into it. The Prussian sergeant quietly stopped his horse right in front of his enemy, drew his pistol and shot the Frenchman. The hussar Röber, a Cologne boy, had got into a fatal situation. He had tried to ride down a Frenchman, but the latter had driven his bayonet so firmly through the guard of his opponent's sword that he could not withdraw it any longer. The dexterous hussar thereupon threw down his sword, and with it his opponent's gun, took his own loaded carbine and shot the Frenchman down. The most brilliant conduct of all was that of the trumpeter, Rusbild, who had sounded the reveille not long before. He saw a comrade who was lying helplessly under his fallen horse. In spite of the violent fire, he stayed with him until he could help him to his feet. Captain Niesewand, who had arrived meanwhile with two other detachments of the squadron, blew the assembly.

When the squadron had fallen in again, Colonel von Loë came galloping up on a magnificent black horse. We got the order " Eyes right! " The Colonel nodded in a friendly manner which made me feel very happy. Colonel von Loë praised our detachments. We twenty Prussian hussars had got the better of fifty French riflemen. One of our men had been seriously wounded. The five who had been lightly wounded stayed in the saddle. Lieutenant von Knesebeck had his horse shot under him at the beginning of the attack.

Meanwhile the French had occupied the heights, from which

they fired at us vigorously, partly with artillery. As is usual in such circumstances, we executed several movements so as not to offer the enemy a target. Nevertheless, several shells dropped in our neighbourhood. Our sturdy sergeant, John, an East Prussian, and eight other hussars of our squadron, were wounded. It was interesting to observe how a merry and frolicsome attack put a smaller strain on the nerves than quietly waiting under hostile fire. At the beginning, now one hussar, and now another, ducked whenever a bullet flew past, or shell burst in the neighbourhood, but the Colonel would not allow this, and shouted to the squadron: " I forbid you to bow to the enemy. If any of you pay respects to a Frenchman again, the others must laugh at him heartily." No one bowed after that.

Soon afterwards the squadron was led into a protected position by the commander, so as not to expose itself to useless losses. I myself was posted as an observer on a height from where I could follow the artillery duel. The French marine artillery fired well. Our battery, which was under its fire, suffered severe punishment. A shell fragment tore open a gunner's body. The stretcher-bearers dragged him off. He died on the way. They threw a dirty horse-blanket over him, which they had got from a dead French horse that was lying near by. It was not a pretty sight. The first Jäger in Wallenstein's Camp is right when he tells the civilian that war requires an iron heart.

Meanwhile the village of Daours had become a focus of the battle. The massively-built little place, which I visited several times later on during the armistice of Amiens, lies hemmed in between the Somme canal, which flows through its eastern side, and the Hallue, which flows through the western. In a northerly direction considerable heights, with steep marginal declivities, close in the valley that scarcely offers space for a village. Colonel von Löe, to whom General Goeben had entrusted the leadership in the battle on this sector, recognized the fact that the capture of Daours was necessary in all circumstances, although it could only be achieved with the help of the infantry. Thereupon our regimental colours came in sight. It was the 8th Rhenish Jäger battalion. Hussars and Jägers had met each other in front of Böckingen, in the first rendezvous after the march from Bonn. In a short address Colonel von Löe recalled the brotherhood in arms of both units, and closed with the words: " Whenever we Royal Hussars know that the 8th Jägers are behind us, we know that there is nothing we cannot do." Major von Oppeln-Bronikowski replied: " Go ahead, we shall follow, wherever it may be." And so it was.

Major von Oppeln-Bronikowski joyfully declared that he was ready
to storm Daours. Followed by four companies of the 33rd Regiment and two companies of 65th, the Jägers prepared for the attack
on Daours, which was defended with bitterness and obstinacy by
3,000 French Hussars, marines, and troops of the line.

While the First Squadron, which I had rejoined, was awaiting
a favourable moment for attack in fairly heavy fire, twilight had
set in. The position along the line of battle was as follows: The
15th Division had thrown the French back from every Hallue
village. Before the heights, which were held with strong artillery,
could be attacked it would be necessary to wait for the 16th Division,
although it was not numerous enough to surround the enemy. On
that day everything depended upon keeping the positions that had
been captured. And so we did. Repeated attempts at a break
through were repelled by Colonel Loë with the Jägers, and the
33rd and 65th. Daours remained in our hands.

Night had already fallen when the First Squadron received
orders to take up night quarters in Querrieux. We marched
slowly in the direction of the burning village. The horses were
tired and so were we. This was the only time in the whole of my
life that I slept in the saddle. Querrieux was on fire in five places.
Nearly all the inhabitants had fled. The windows and the doors
of the houses had been demolished. As it was bitterly cold and
the later the hour the colder it became, the hussars warmed themselves at burning houses. To my joy I found a stable for my good
Grete and also a half-bottle of wine for myself. I emptied it at
one swig and then threw myself down on the ground in an abandoned
goat-shed. As in my childhood days, I prayed:

> " *Abends, wenn ik slapen gah,*[1]
> *Viertein Engel bi mi stahn:*
> *Twei tau min Haupten,*
> *Twei tau min Feutten,*
> *Twei tau mine Rechten,*
> *Twei tau mine Linken,*
> *Twei, di mi taudecken,*

[1] At night when I go to sleep
Fourteen angels stand round my bed.
Two at my head,
Two at my feet,
Two on my right,
Two on my left,
Two to cover me,

Twei, di mi upwecken,
Twei, di mi wiest
Int himmlisch Paradies,
Un min Vadding un Mudding ok." [1]

And then after this eventful day, while in the distance the sound of the French signals was to be heard in the stillness of the night, I fell into the deepest sleep I have ever known.

On the 24th of December the sun rose in a clear and cloudless sky. The temperature was eleven degrees below zero. An icy north-east wind blew about our ears. The First Squadron held a hollow, west of Windmill Hill, on that early morning. We were able to establish the fact that the French were still holding the positions they held on the previous afternoon. They no longer roused themselves to break through. A number of weak attempts of this kind were abandoned after the first firing from our own advance positions. The heavy fire of the French chassepots and guns did not do us much harm. The continual *va et vient* which prevailed in the French lines seemed to be a proof that the Frenchmen up on the heights (where, owing to the scarcity of villages, they must have bivouacked) had suffered even more from the cold than we down in the valley. I do not know who it was who declared that pleasure in others' misfortune is the only true pleasure. The conviction that the French were even more frozen than ourselves raised our spirits. But what pleased us most of all was that if we had not inflicted a decisive defeat on the far superior enemy in their strong position, our main purpose, the expulsion of the enemy from the immediate neighbourhood of Amiens, would not have been achieved in the battle of Hallue. The Rhine Army Corps had obtained this result with 37 officers and 900 men who had remained before the enemy.

I spent Christmas Eve in a wretched village called Altonville, where, nevertheless, the houses were still standing, in contrast with the shelled villages of Hallue. We discovered a big store of wine in a cellar, and requisitioned some chickens, which were distributed on the basis of one bird for two men. Otherwise our finest Christmas present was General von Goeben's Army Order, in which our leader said that the battle of 23rd December had been a complete success for the black and white flag. But I sadly

---

[1] Two to wake me up,
Two to guide
Into God's Heaven,
And my father and mother also.

thought of my good parents, who would be standing before the
Christmas Tree in Berlin without their only daughter, who had
been taken from them at the beginning of the year, and without
their two eldest sons.

Even severer cold and the same icy north-east wind heralded
the morning of 25th December. My otherwise methodical servant
had left my great coat behind in the field-quarters at Bussy, so that
I had to ride for more than a week in a light raincoat. My comrades
of the First Squadron used to say to me that even many years
afterwards the thought of me and my raincoat in December, 1870,
was enough to make them feel chilly.

On the previous afternoon a patrol led by a Lieutenant von
Steinberg, in which I was riding, had discovered that the hills of
Pont Noyelles were unoccupied. We first encountered fire at the
village of La Houssoye. News that came in during the night
left no doubt that the enemy had begun to retreat. The 30th
Brigade, which had arrived at Daours, received orders to march on
Albert, and to take up positions on the left bank of the Hallue for
the advance via Pont Noyelles. The First and Second Squadrons
of the King's Hussars trotted in the van under the leadership of
the Colonel. Our ride led us over the Franch battlefield. We were
able to convince ourselves of the great strength of the position
held by the enemy. The large number of corpses showed the effect
of our splendid artillery. For the first time I saw a battlefield
covered with corpses immediately after a battle. With the exception
of a few that were horribly mutilated, the sight of the dead bodies
did not leave me with an impression of horror or ugliness. On
the faces of both French and Germans there was the mark of that
inner peace of which Wallenstein speaks when he receives the news
of the death of his favourite, Max Piccolomini: " He is the happier.
He has done with everything. He has finished with desires and
fears. O! He is content! "

But I will not deny that, as we rode over the corpses on that
Christmas morning, despite my war enthusiasm, I thought of the
angel who after the birth of the Saviour, 1,870 years before, praised
God and spoke these words: " Glory be to God in the highest,
Peace on earth, and good-will towards men."

At four o'clock we entered Albert. There we took a number of
prisoners, including two dragoons whom we had surprised. We
put the railway and telegraph in the neighbourhood of Albert out
of action. During this time, Lieutenant von Schrader executed a
genuine piece of hussar work, which he himself describes as
follows:

Early on 25th December I received orders from Colonel von Loë to proceed with my section (No. 3 Squadron) towards Bray and report on the enemy's retreat. After meeting a good many stragglers, with whom I could not bother much beyond disarming them, I suddenly perceived a strong party of Frenchmen who were marching in the same direction as I at a distance of about six hundred paces on my left flank. As I could not leave a force apparently so much stronger than my own section in my rear, I determined to go forward and attack. I noticed too late that the French were posted on the other side of the Somme Canal, which was twenty paces wide and was naturally impassable to us. The canal was rather thickly screened by the prevailing fog, and only became visible at about a hundred paces. There could be no thought of stopping or turning back, for the French would thereby be roused from their apparent consternation— only five or six shots at the most were fired at us—and might have opened a more vigorous fire. There was nothing else left for me to do except to press my spurs into the flanks of my old Vigoreuse, and, galloping close alongside the Somme Canal, shout imperiously at the French company: " *A bas les armes!* "

Now when the French lowered their arms it was naturally not enough for me. What I had to be on my guard against was that the enemy might come to their senses and shoot the whole lot of us down before my hussars, who had been thrown into some disorder by their hurried ride across ploughed land, could arrive and take up their carbines instead of their sabres. I therefore ordered the French to throw their arms into the water, which they did without exception. They were then kind enough to show us a bridge over the canal and even crossed it, so that, without more ado, I could send twenty-five of them back under escort and go on with the reconnoitring I had been ordered to do with the rest of my section.

The resolution, vivacity and imperturbable good humour of Karl von Schrader, who was only a few months older than I, made him a most likeable comrade. After all these years his image still stands sharply before my eyes as he galloped by on his old but still fleet Vigoreuse, with his fur busby hanging back on the nape of the neck, his sabre in hand. We grew to be still closer friends after the war, when we were in the Third Squadron together. How often have we ridden beside one another in the spring of 1872 at the head of our sections, I at the head of the First and he at the head of the Second? Schrader was one of the first who prophesied a great future for me. He had, in his loud voice, already expressed his conviction, after an amicable banquet in Bonn, that I would become Imperial Chancellor. When much later, in the year 1895, during my ambassadorship in Rome, I again met my old friend Schrader (he had in the meantime become Master of Ceremonies) in the house of the Saxon ambassador, Count von Hohenthal, he put me into a state of embarrassment in the presence of the State Secretary von Marschall and the beautiful Countess Lotka Hohenau, by pointing his finger at me and crying out in a loud voice: " Look at Bernhard Bülow closely. He is going to be Chancellor in a few years."

Marschall, a man of great capacity and still greater ambition, who wished to become Chancellor himself, threw me a glance of such irritation and distrust that I could not help laughing. The robust and merry Schrader was shot in a duel in 1896 by the Chamberlain, von Kotze, as the sequel to scandalous events in Court Society such as would have been impossible under William I, but which, under the reckless and flighty William II, boded no good for the future. I will expressly state that Baron Karl von Schrader's attitude in the whole affair was blameless. His opponent, Kotze, had also behaved correctly. Him also I had known in my early years. He was in the same regiment as my brother Adolf, the Second Dragoon Guards. He was a good fellow who, by his deification of William II, acquired the latter's special favour for a long time, which did not prevent his Majesty from allowing him to be arrested and imprisoned instantly when a wholly unfounded rumour made of him the author of slanderous anonymous letters which had caused great excitement in Court and official circles in Berlin.

CHAPTER XV

On Patrol—Battle of Sapignies (2.1.1871)—Lieutenant Count Max Pourtalès—The Battle of Bapaume (3.1.1871)—General von Goeben—Patrol Service Before St. Quentin.

WHEN Karl Schrader executed his brilliant cavalry attack at Bray, the road-junction of Bapaume had become one of the foremost strategic considerations. This important advance post had to be maintained as long as possible, although the forces at the disposition of the German Army for the purpose were very limited, even for defence. The French offensive against Bapaume did not come as a surprise to General von Goeben. He could not have prepared to meet it with greater misgivings. On New Year's Eve, 1870, he reported to the High Command as follows:

> I cannot conceal the fact that as two infantry brigades are necessary at Péronne, I shall not be in a strong enough position to meet an enemy action on a large scale with any prospect of success. Only sixteen battalions are at my disposition on the front.

Since the fighting strength of the battalions of the 8th Army Corps did not, on an average, exceed 650 men, the result was that there was an infantry strength of hardly 10,000 men for a pitched battle against Faidherbe. Moreover, these 10,000 men were to defend a great area.

Between 27th December and 2nd January our regiments' duties became very severe. A *franc tireur's* bullet shattered the good non-commissioned officer, Russ's, thigh near Douai. Lance-Corporal Eulen had his horse shot under him near Mercatel, on the high road leading to Arras, and he himself was taken prisoner after a stout resistance. Colonel von Loë felt it necessary to warn patrols against excessive boldness (which certainly spoke well for the morale of the regiment). This he did through instructions to the officers which read:

> During the last few days it has often happened that the leaders of the hussar patrols who have ridden into the villages

have been received with fire from enemy infantry detachments hidden in the vicinity. Losses of men and horses have been suffered every day thereby. Much as I appreciate the boldness of our men, who, despite all their experience, continue to ride fearlessly into the villages, practical caution demands that we should avoid these unnecessary losses in seeking to break up the enemy's system.

He also declared that in mixed detachments it was the infantry's task to search villages. The most hussars had to do was to find out whether the enemy was hidden in the villages by scouting around suspected areas. Colonel von Loë had not been disappointed with the initiative of his Rhenish Hussars. The individual losses fell off in the next few days. The reports, however, remained reliable and speedy.

On 2nd January the advance of strong French columns was reported. I was just sitting down to a splendid roast fowl to which my lieutenant had invited me. This lieutenant, Count Ernst Steinberg, was the last male descendant of an ancient Lower Saxon family. He combined the good form of the Hanoverians with the cheerful manner of the Rhinelanders, whom he had got to like during the four years he lived in Bonn. Steinberg and I were colleagues in Paris ten years later, he an attaché and I a Secretary of the Embassy. I have seldom known a more likeable man. We got the alarm while I and this best of all fellows were regaling ourselves with the French chicken and washing it down with liberal draughts of local wine. Colonel von Loë formed a half-squadron from a section of the First Squadron (not, unluckily, the section in which I rode) and from the advanced sections of the Second Squadron, and ordered Lieutenant Count Pourtalès to lead it to the heights east of Sapignies, and hold it there at the disposal of the artillery. When, soon after this, our artillery was harassed by French infantry who advanced in strength, the Divisional Commander turned for help to the two hussar sections who were waiting behind a ridge in the ground. Count Pourtalès did not delay a moment. "Forward to the attack! March!" was his order, and the squadron threw itself pell-mell at the enemy, the officers well in front, and behind them the cheering hussars, fifty strong. Those Frenchmen who were not ridden down fled, panic-stricken.

The attack surprised the enemy so much that at first no shots came from their column. Count Pourtalès assembled his hussars and led them back at the trot amid friendly cheers of " *Lehmop!* "

from the artillery, which had at once engaged the enemy and was firing volley after volley. The company of twenty-eighters advanced once more. The French made a momentary stand and then streamed back in complete disorder. General von Kummer used this moment with quick resolution: " The whole will advance," rang the call. The cheering infantry threw the enemy out of Béhagnies with heavy losses at the point of the bayonet. Many prisoners were taken. Two battalions, twelve guns, and fifty King's Hussars had repelled the attack of a whole division. Count Max Pourtalès was made of the same stuff Napoleon I used to choose when he created his marshals. Slim and supple, a smart and bristling black moustache, bold eyes and a smile playing around his mouth, he used to attract the glances of the women and girls in the streets of Amiens and Rouen just as he did in the Poppels-dorfer Allee in Bonn on the Rhine. Son of a Neuchatel father and a Genevan mother, he spoke German with a French accent, but his heart was Prussian through and through. When our regiment reached Tréport in February, 1871, Max Pourtalès led his squadron, the Second, down to the sea, rode into the water with his hussars, and made a little speech to them which began with the words: " Ussars (he could not pronounce an ' h ' correctly) I 'ave led you to the sea." This splendid officer, who glowed with the inward fire of ambition and desire for fame, and who seemed assured of a brilliant military future, fell ill of a grave internal complaint some years after the war, and had to leave the service. Those who knew him could never forget him. The day of Sapignies takes a proved place in the history of the King's Hussars. Count Max Pourtalès was afterwards known as the " Duc de Sapignies " in the regiment.

My good father carefully preserved my letters from the front. When, after his death, I went through his effects, I found that two letters of special interest to me were missing. The one described the rides I took when I was an orderly in November, and the other was my report on the battle of Hallue. I imagine that my father either sent these letters on to my brother Adolf, who was then in the field, or more probably to the Grand Duke George of Mecklenburg-Strelitz in St. Petersburg. The Grand Duke George had married the Grand Duchess Catherine Mikhail-ovna of Russia in 1851, and had entered the Russian service at the same time. Although a legitimist of the purest water, and as such an opponent of Bismarckian policy from 1866 onwards, he, the nephew of Queen Luise, was on Germany's side in the Franco-German war. What my father (who had been a friend of his for a long time) wrote about his impressions, he gladly brought to the

knowledge of the Emperor Alexander II, who, being the son of a
Prussian princess and grandson of Queen Luise, was inclined to
be pro-German, or rather pro-Prussian, in the Franco-German war,
and was interested and pleased in communications from the
Prussian front. But I have my letters about the battles of Bapaume
and St. Quentin to hand. If I venture to quote them, I need
hardly point out that they are not the reports of a general staff
officer, but letters hurriedly jotted down by a young hussar. On
4th January, 1871, I wrote as follows from field-quarters at Cappy,
near Péronne:

DEAREST PARENTS,

Please excuse me for only having written to you twice in a
hurry since Christmas. I hope you are as well as I wish with
my whole heart. I am very well myself, and by God's grace
have come through yesterday's heavy fighting unhurt. On the
25th we set out early in abominably cold weather and crossed
over to the other bank of the Somme. Towards midday our
patrols brought the news that the French had left their positions
near Pont-Noyelles and had withdrawn. Why? That did not
seem very clear, but all the better for us. We were on the alert
about midday and crossed the battlefield to Pont-Noyelles
There the heights which on the 23rd the 33rd East Prussian
Regiment had stormed with fixed bayonets and splendid bravery,
but had been forced to give up again towards evening, lay
before us again. Many corpses were still lying about on the
slopes, some of them quite frozen, most of them looking quite
peaceful. About an hour's ride beyond Pont-Noyelles we got
tolerable billets.

The next day we marched to Frémicourt, by way of two
little towns called Albert and Bapaume. Here we spent three
quiet days, which the horses needed badly. On the third day
I rode out in bitterly cold weather with a requisitioning patrol
I arrived at Montaigne-Notre-Dame, only three kilometres from
Cambrai, where I discovered that the latter town was still
strongly occupied by French troops. On New Year's Day I
marched with Lieutenant von Steinberg's section to Beugny,
half an hour from Frémicourt, where we struck first rate billets.
Two very nice infantrymen were there, a lieutenant and an
ensign. The lieutenant, who was as tall as a tree, was called
Freudenfeld, or something like that. The name of the ensign
I have forgotten. The lieutenant looked after his little comrade
in a most moving way. We had ducks, turkeys, and other fine

things to eat and drank the champagne we had requisitioned. On midday of the 7th we suddenly got the alarm and marched through Frémicourt, which had already been left by the squadron, and from there to the high road leading to Arras. About an hour's march from the town were our batteries. They were firing on the enemy. After a certain amount of infantry fire, which went now this way now that, but was otherwise of no great significance, our section met the Third Squadron, which was in the neighbourhood, and we attached ourselves to it. There was a belief that towards evening the enemy would try to turn our flank, and I was sent forward with a patrol. Nothing, however, was to be seen of the enemy.

About nine o'clock we came to tolerable quarters in Bapaume, and met the squadron there. We left again early at six o'clock (it was quite dark) and arranged a meeting place. Two sections were sent forward to reconnoitre, and about a quarter of an hour later the officers concerned came back with the news that the enemy was approaching in two strong columns. Thereupon we moved left of the high road with a battery and two battalions of the 33rd to engage them. We soon came under severe shell fire, and drew up in a gulley parallel with the high road. From there we could observe the fighting more clearly than either on 27th November or 25th December.

The village to the left of the high road to Arras had been occupied by the French during the night. They had established a battery there which was being excellently served. Soon the shells were flying over our heads, but so high up that they could not do us the least harm. In the meantime the battalion of the 33rds posted to the left of Bapaume, advanced on Sapignies, cheering loudly, and the fight began. The tall lieutenant and the little ensign, with whom I had shared billets in Beigny, were leading their men far away in the distance. Almost in the same minute they both fell like ears of corn under the reaper's scythe. Both were killed outright! We, too, came under fairly strong fire for the French bullets carried a considerable distance. Still, only a few of our horses were shot. I rode as flank N.C.O. of the first troop. A bullet went through the quarter-master's dixie. He was standing behind me. Meanwhile the 33rds had taken the village, but after a quarter of an hour they had to give way to forces from four to five times stronger than their own. The rifle fire grew more and more violent.

We rode up the heights to see what was going on. Unfortunately, we saw how the 33rds had to fall back, singly at first, and more and more. The uninjured were ahead, and kept turning round to shoot, then came the slightly wounded, and then a few severely wounded, who limped along painfully in the rear. The officers tried to halt their men, but in vain. The enemy were too superior in numbers, especially as the French had brought up their batteries and had begun a very heavy bombardment. The two batteries posted left of the gulley also had to withdraw. We were scarcely up on the heights before we encountered very heavy rifle fire. The batteries also began to direct their fire upon us hussars. There was no possibility of attacking a battery and four battalions of infantry. Our squadron was alone. The captain then gave the command to right wheel in sections, and we passed over the newly-ploughed fields at a trot so as to take up a position along the road. Many shells had been falling closely in front of us and behind us, when two exploded in the midst of the section. One exploded so closely in front of us that my horse jumped up into the air and I was bespattered with earth and snow. The sergeant, a Leipzig man named Oskar Becker, who was riding in front of me, had his head torn off by a splinter. It flew into the air with its fur shako, as though it had been blown up. My face and my coat was bespattered with his blood and brains. Otherwise the shells did not do us so much harm as might have been expected. More horses than men were wounded. I raised my sabre and cried out to my men: " Heads up! Courage! " The rushing and bursting of the shells sounded uncanny, and fear, or rather a kind of shiver, ran down the men's spines. But it must be said that not a single man tried to leave the ranks, and that they all kept in line with the other sections as though they were on the parade ground. We crossed the road and formed up twenty paces behind it, near a factory.

The fight had taken an unpleasant turn on our left wing. Our battery drove up into a very heavy fire and shelled the French from this point. The battalion of 33rds, which had lost two-thirds of its men, re-formed and went forward again. The French had not the courage to take Bapaume at the point of the bayonet, although they were four to one, but contented themselves with directing a very heavy fire against the town. Our shells were bursting on the road, one of them dropped quite close to us, hitting an ammunition wagon and tearing horses and men to shreds. Another dropped on the factory near which we were standing. One dropped on the church tower, which looked very comic afterwards.

Meanwhile a dispatch arrived which Lieutenant von Knese-beck was to take to General von Goeben with our section. We passed through Bapaume. We came to the market place, where shells were dropping and which therefore was devoid of human beings. It was a square surrounded by plane trees. Only an old woman was to be seen there. She was digging up weeds and sweeping rubbish away. As we rode by I shouted to her, telling her to take shelter, or else she might be hit by a shell. She answered me with complete apathy: "*Mon bon Monsieur, je suis vieille et pauvre, la mort ne m'effraie pas. J'aime aussi bien continuer mon petit travail, auqel je suis habituée.*" The very unkempt looking dog she had with her also remained in spite of the shell fire. They were philosophers, those two. Knesebeck and I rode to a village some four kilometres from Bapaume, where the General was. Knesebeck took me with him into his room. He was lying in bed. He had had a severe attack of dysentery and still looked very pale. When Knesebeck intro-duced me to him he offered me his hand and said that he had known several namesakes of mine in Hanover (he is himself a Hanoverian). "They were able fellows," he added. He was quite calm, but appeared to regard the situation very seriously. In his ante-chamber, where the orderlies were waiting, it was said that the French had cut off our retreat upon Amiens. Some regarded the battle as lost unless the 16th Division came to our support.

When we returned to the squadron, which had, in the mean-time, been stationed next to our battery right of the high road to Peronne, the battle had already taken a more favourable turn. On the right wing the 8th Jägers and a battalion of the 33rds had pushed the French back and had taken two villages. Bapaume was still held by two batteries and the battalion of the 33rds which had been driven back—they had, incidentally, withdrawn only because they had used up all their ammunition.

At two o'clock General von Goeben appeared on the battle-field and was greeted with loud cheers by the troops who were in action. Everybody thought that things could not now go wrong. He at once ordered the 8th Jägers and the splendid 33rds to storm Tilloy. To support the infantry, our artillery, which we were covering, opened fire like mad. Tilloy was taken at five o'clock. Cheering sounded over the whole battlefield. There is nothing finer in the whole world than Prussian cheers on a battlefield. Meanwhile night had fallen, our battery was still firing on a couple of villages that were held by the enemy, which had begun to burn and looked very picturesque. The result of the battle was fairly favourable in the end. The field was held against forces four times as big as our own, and, above all, Bapaume had not been surrendered.

We did not camp out, but were billeted in a little village that had been totally abandoned. We had nothing to eat except a little chocolate which one or other of us had brought along. At four o'clock sharp we marched out and crossed to the other bank of the Somme to Cappy, a large and prosperous village. Meanwhile Bapaume and Albert had been occupied by the 3rd Cavalry Division, while the 16th Division had also arrived except for those detachments which were still beleaguering Péronne. After we had dismounted in the evening, the captain, who very often complained and was rarely satisfied, came over to me and said: " Your bearing was excellent. You were a fearless N.C.O. and an example to the whole section." He then shook hands with me.

Friday, 6th January, 1871.

DEAR PARENTS,

Yesterday there was no chance of sending off this letter, and I am therefore adding a few words. To-day we marched from Cappy to Bray-sur-Somme, quite a nice little town, where we have found good quarters. Yesterday I received father's kind letter, which pleased me very much with its good news. At the same time I got a handkerchief, chocolate, and cigars, as well as newspapers, for which I thank you a thousand times. Perhaps you will send me another handkerchief, chocolate, and cigars, which will give me great pleasure. The colonel has been very good to me. After inviting me twice to mess with him, which I was unable to do as the squadron was quartered too far away from the Staff, he again invited me when the Staff and squadron came together, and was very kind to me in the mess room. He said he had promoted me to the rank of N.C.O. because of my soldierly conduct in face of the enemy, and that I would have the rank of ensign because of my bravery in the battle of Hallue. But now good-bye, dearest parents. Please do not worry about me this month, which is so sad for us because of dear Bertha. God above, who had always graciously protected me hitherto, will certainly protect me again. Thousand greetings to all.

Your devoted son,

BERNHARD VON BÜLOW.

Among the wounded of the 3rd is a Herr von Sanden-

Tussainen, volunteer in our squadron, who is a cousin of the young Wrangel. He has a bullet in the upper part of the thigh. But the doctor is hopeful so far. Perhaps you will let young Wrangel, whom I send my greeting, know about it. Herr von Sanden is in hospital in Bapaume, and is provided with money. The major has written to his brother-in-law, Professor Aegidi.

Your devoted son,

BERNHARD.

The hope that the volunteer von Sanden would live was not fulfilled. The poor fellow, who had ridden beside me, died soon after he got his wound. His brother-in-law, Professor Ludwig Karl Aegidi, the famous teacher of constitutional law, and publisher of the *Staatarchiv*, was a great savant, but of small stature, and was therefore known familiarly as the "Little Aegidi." From 1871 to 1878 he was in charge of the Press Bureau of the Foreign Office under Bismarck. The Press Bureau then consisted of a chief and an assistant official. Under Caprivi a second assistant was added. During my Chancellorship the chief was Geheimrat Hammann, whom I had taken over from Caprivi and Hohenlohe, with two able assistants, the Councillors of Legation, Esterneaux and Heilbron, constituted the Press Department. Besides these there was also attached to it an army captain, who had been badly wounded in the Franco-German war. His duty was to cut out and paste up newspaper articles that were worthy of attention. I used to say that my Press Bureau consisted of three and a half men. When, after the November upheaval, the three dominating parties, the Social Democrats, the Centre party, and the Democratic party, wanted to give their own people jobs and to establish what the French so beautifully call "*la Republique des Camarades*," the Press Bureau was inflated into a body with a personnel of more than 200. The modest rooms in the Foreign Office were not enough for such a multitude, and the Press Bureau was established in the big Palace of Prince Charles in the Wilhelmplatz, where the gentlemen spent their days usefully, smoking cigarettes and chatting. As far as I can remember, our Press has never had worse guidance nor has our foreign propaganda been conducted so unskilfully as in the first years of the Republican State.

"Young Wrangel," as I called him in my letter to my parents, was the grandson of the Field Marshal. No two people were more different than the old and the young Wrangel. The elder was the re-organizer of the Prussian cavalry who had won imperishable merit. He was an old soldier, who had received the *Order pour le*

Mérite at Heilsberg in 1807, when he was a lieutenant in the Estocq Corps. He had distinguished himself as a colonel at Grossgörschen and Leipzig, and, sixty years later, he wished to take part in an attack on the Austrians in the battle of Trautenau. Under a rough exterior he concealed a very healthy knowledge of mankind. His judgment, although often expressed in comic form, seldom failed to hit the nail on the head. In the November days of 1848, he showed more prudence, and above all, more energy, as Governor of Berlin and Lord Lieutenant of the Mark, than did Prince Max of Baden, seventy years later, and also, unfortunately, than did Colonel-General von Linsingen, who was under the Prince's influence. Young Wrangel was gentle, infinitely polite and rather commonplace. He officiated as Chamberlain at the Royal Office of Ceremonies, and he used to be called " baby of ceremonies." He was a nice and refined man. He died young, after relapsing into incurable melancholy towards the end of his life. In the years before and after the Franco-German war (as I believe I have already stated) my parents lived in the former Arnim Palace. Field-Marshal Wrangel also had an apartment for working purposes quite near to us in the Pariser Platz. As a friend of young Gustav Wrangel, I spent many evenings there before the war, when I was a student and, later on, as lieutenant of hussars.

I do not wish to increase the number of Wrangel anecdotes by adding new ones. I will only take the liberty of relating two, because these are not so well known. There was a handsome regimental commander from Berlin who was distinguished by good looks and smart exterior rather than by real ability. He had been put on the retired list. He turned up in Wrangel's salon soon afterwards. He looked very hurt, and apparently hoped for a few consoling words from the Field-Marshal, and perhaps a few words condemning his retirement as well. Instead of this the old man in my presence kissed him on both cheeks according to his custom, and greeted him with the words, which he pronounced with the broadest East Prussian dialect: " the King, my son, has found a first rate man to take your place."

I hope my lady readers will excuse the second anecdote. The Field-Marshal called at the palace of the Crown Prince to congratulate him on the occasion of the birth of his third son, Prince Waldemar, who died later quite young. The parents had the child brought in and the mother laid the baby in the Field-Marshal's arms. The Crown Prince, who was fond of harmless jokes, turned towards the Field-Marshal and said: " What do you think my third son ought to be? The eldest must be a soldier, and the

second a sailor. I think I shall let the third be a business man."
Thereupon old Wrangel said: "He's already sh . . . . on me!"

On the evening of 3rd January, 1871, General von Goeben
announced in his army orders: "The Kummer Division, supported
by the detachment of his Royal Highness Prince Albert, has
brilliantly held the position near Bapaume against enemies many
times superior in numbers." But the troops of the division, who
for the most part had been through prolonged fighting, were
utterly exhausted. The batteries began to run short of ammunition.
The losses of the division during these heavy days amounted to
10 officers and 30 men killed, 19 officers and 400 men wounded
(some severely) and 150 men missing. General von Goeben
decided not to resume the fighting during the next few days, but
to withdraw the troops behind the Somme for the time being.
General von Goeben is among the few men who have really impressed
me and who have struck me as being truly great. Born at Hanover
in 1816, he entered the Carlist service when he was scarcely twenty
years of age, and fought four years, from 1836 to 1840, in the
Spanish Civil War. A story was told in the army that once when
he had fallen into the hands of the partisans of Christina they had
made him throw dice to save his life. On another occasion he had
been brought to the place of execution and the firing squad had
already taken up its position when he was pardoned by a whim of
the enemy commander. He entered the Prussian service in 1842,
where his qualities soon became conspicuous. He went through
the Baden campaign in 1849, and in 1860 had alredy become a
colonel of the General Staff. In 1864 he commanded a brigade
with great distinction at Düppel and Alsen. In 1866 he commanded the 13th Infantry Division of the Maine Army. In 1870,
when he was hardly fifty-four, he got the command of the 8th
Army Corps. The confidence which his subordinates, from the
generals and colonels down to the last rifleman, had in him was
unlimited, and yet no simpler man was to be met than General von
Goeben.

Of middle height, generally in a bent attitude, so short-sighted
that he had to wear spectacles, he looked more like a professor than
a general.

Behind the modest exterior of the general there was a will of
steel, inflexible energy, and a piercing intellect. His one weakness
was gambling. When he was commanding in wartime he never
gambled, but if the gentlemen of his Staff made up a game on some
day of rest, or if he came upon other officers gambling on a quiet
day, he could look on for hours at a time. This great commander

and great German died in Coblence in 1881, before he was sixty-four years old, when he was commanding-general of the 8th Army Corps. The City of Coblence erected a well-deserved memorial to him. The 28th Infantry Regiment, which the King's Hussar Regiment often met in the war of 1870-71, bore the name " Infantry Regiment von Goeben," in our everlastingly glorious army of old.

On 4th January the march on the Somme began. Our regiment had orders to keep contact with the enemy. One of the patrols of my squadron, in which I rode under Lieutenant von Steinberg, chanced upon a number of French infantrymen who surrendered on the road to Douai and Ecoust. They told us that the main body of the French Northern Army had left the region of Douai and had turned towards Arras. Our first squadron was assigned to the 30th Infantry Brigade. The Second Rhineland Infantry Regiment No. 28, and the Magdeburg Infantry Regiment No. 77 belonged to this brigade, which was led by Major-General von Strubberg. Colonel von Rosenzweig commanded the 28th and Colonel von Zglinicki the 77th. After we had crossed the Somme near Feuillèrs the 30th Infantry Brigade occupied the remoter townships as far as Belloy.

On 16th January, I wrote from Cappy, near Bray:

A thousand greetings and best thanks for your kind letter and the twenty Napoleons which Papa sent me. I hope that you are getting on as well as from the bottom of my heart I wish you may in these days which are so painful to you because of Bertha. What are all the anxieties and discomforts of the present time compared with the misfortune which came upon us over a year ago? God loved her soul; that is why he took her away from this wicked life so soon. We shall know why when the time comes and we meet face to face. In this life we cannot understand. I am well (touch wood). We have to do many patrols across the Somme to Albert and Bapaume almost every day and every night. I have always got through them safely. You will have read in the *Kreuzzeitung* that I have become an ensign. At the moment I do not need any articles of clothing. But, if possible, please send me two handkerchiefs, toothbrushes, penholder with pencil, etc., and perhaps also a map of Northern France and a small (portable and if possible strong) telescope (useful on patrols). A thousand greetings from your devoted son.

Between the battles of Bapaume and St. Quentin, *i.e.*, between 3rd and 19th January, 1871, I did my most interesting patrols. I remember as if it had been yesterday the dark woods right and left of the white high road, the milestones, the silent châteaux in the distance, the whole landscape that bore the mark of an old civilization. The weather was very inclement, the cold often severe, down to ten degrees centigrade below zero, followed by thaws with warm rain. The roads were mostly covered with sheet-ice, and the fields were quite impassable. Riding through the villages in the frost without a fall was not easy. And the man who did fall from his horse stood a good chance of being killed by *franc tireurs* hidden in the villages and sometimes even by the peasants themselves. As the fields were like morasses, it was almost impossible to skirt the villages. But necessity is the mother of invention. Whenever we approached a village we hauled out the occupant of the first large house and requested him very politely (though at the point of a revolver) to show us, at once and quietly, to the house of the mayor. We used to explain to the mayor that he must go with us while we passed through the village. We used to tie him up with a handy piece of rope so that he should not fall down on the slippery village street. If we should be fired at from the village, then, so we told him, we should regretfully be compelled to shoot him, otherwise not a hair of his head would be harmed. In this way we generally got through the villages safely.

Comic episodes were not lacking on these patrols. Once when I was riding through a wood in the pale moonlight, I thought I saw two French infantrymen in the distance in front of me. I drew my sabre and gave the order: " Attack! " I and my two men charged forwards against the enemy. When we reached " the enemy " they turned out to be two stunted oaks. When we got back to our quarters I took good care to avoid telling my comrades of my mistake. A few days later the honest Scharffenberg told how he had attacked a tree instead of a Frenchman, and then it transpired that we had all in turn taken these same trees for Frenchmen.

What a merry mood the ensign and warrant officer who had to do these patrols were in! Patrols at night were even more interesting than those in the daytime. We used to sit at a wooden table in a farmhouse playing cards until one or the other of us had to ride off. We used to play Landesknecht or Tempel, but baccarat, which we called " Makao," was our favourite game. Many of the Napoleons which my good father sent me found their way into the pockets of my comrades. When one of us was ordered on patrol he would give his watch and wallet to the others so that his family would have a souvenir in case anything should happen to him.

CHAPTER XVI

Comrades of the Squadron : Guido Nimptsch, Dietrich Loë, Scharffen-
berg, Pemberton-Ground, Borcke, Beissel von Gymnich, Dietrich
Metternich—Sharpened Intelligence Service—Battle of St. Quentin
(19.1.1871)—East Prussian Fusilier Regiment No. 33—Lieu-
tenant von Deines, Lieutenant Mossner, Captain Rudolphi.

WE young fellows of the 8th Squadron might differ from one another and go our different ways later on. But in those days we were all good friends and ready for any kind of adventure. The man I liked most was Guido von Nimptsch, the stepson of the commander. In the old days before 1848, his father, Paul von Nimptsch, had the reputation of being the boldest and most reckless of all the Silesian Junkers, and that is saying a good deal. He once played a game of *ecarté* with his cousin, Count Feodor Sierstorpff, who resembled him, and was the father of my regimental comrade, Karl Sierstorpff, popularly known as " Murphy " on account of his height. Continued calls of " double or quits " landed him in difficulties. Paul Nimptsch had called " double or quits " once more when Feodor Sierstorpff drew his attention to the fact that he had not enough cash to pay out a possible loss. Nimptsch cooly replied: " Then I declare on my word of honour that if the cards go against me I'll cut off both my ears with a razor." A razor was brought and put on the card table. The cards were shuffled again. Nimptsch played and won. Nimptsch's attitude in the crazy year 1848 was that of the junker in the best sense of the word. He fell into the hands of a revolutionary detachment in a Breslau street. They tied him to a lamp-post, shouting him down as a hated reactionary, and were going to hang him. When the rope was knotted round his neck, he made a sign to show that he had a last wish to express. When ordered to say what it was, he shouted to his executioners: " Hang me so low that you can all . . . ." The mob loosened the knot, but mishandled the Junker in so brutal a fashion that he died from his injuries soon afterwards.

My regimental comrade and friend, Guido Nimptsch, had inherited his father's recklessness, and also, unfortunately, his passion for gambling, as well as the beauty of his mother, the

Countess Franziska Hatzfeld-Trachenberg. Years afterwards the Empress Frederick used to say of him: " Guido von Nimptsch is the best looking man in Berlin." As he was not merely very good looking, but also very intelligent, a splendid military career lay ahead of him, and he had only recently been appointed to duties on the General Staff when one night at the Berlin Union Club he lost a sum at cards far exceeding his means. As his parents possessed no fortune and his rich relatives would not take over the responsibility, there was no alternative left open to him but to resign his commission and go abroad. His sudden departure from Berlin plunged two women into deep sorrow: a society lady who was celebrated for her beauty and her wit, and a delicious *cocotte*, both of whom had been in love with Guido at the same time. In the course of a rather adventurous journey, he travelled from Hartlepool, where he had got a job as a clerk in a coal company, across the Congo and the Panama Canal, where he found another as overseer, from there through Mexico, where he broke in wild horses (he was a first rate horseman), then to New York, where, so it is said, he first earned his bread by driving a truck. Gradually he made his way up in the world again. More than that, he captured the heart of a charming American girl, Miss Lola Bonton, the most celebrated soubrette of New York. He married her and returned with her to Europe. At the same time he became the Berlin representative of a big American insurance company. By his charm and his perfect manners he soon succeeded in achieving a good social position. He lived in happiest marriage until, returning home one evening, he learned that his wife had left the house an hour before. His servant handed him a letter from his beloved wife, which read somewhat as follows: " My sweet Guido. I have never loved any man so much as you, and never shall love any man as much. But unfortunately you have not the means to keep me in the comfort and luxury I expect, and so I have decided to go away with Nostitz, who is rolling in money."

Count Nostitz was military attaché to the Russian Embassy in Berlin. He married Lola, the lady he had run away with, and was transferred to Paris as military attaché after his marriage. The wife of his new chief, the Russian Ambassador, Nelidov, declared that she would not receive Countess Lola on account of her vivid past. The moment Guido von Nimptsch heard of this he travelled to Paris and demanded satisfaction of the ambassador, Nelidov, because his wife had dared to insult the former Frau von Nimptsch. Nelidov, who showed no inclination to stand in front of Nimptsch's pistols, promised that the Countess Nostitz would be well received in his house. "*Toujours chevalresque,*" was the motto of Guido Nimptsch.

Very different from him was the nephew of our commander, Dietrich von Loë. He bore the name " Schlacks." [1] This name referred to his ungainly appearance as much as to his dare-devilry. He would have made a splendid mercenary under Frundsberg. [2] But another nephew of the commander, Count Dietrich von Wolf-Metternich, resembled an eighteenth century French Marquis. He might have danced a minuet in the Great Hall of the Palace of Versailles under Louis XV without attracting any special notice. He was a smart hussar, a magnificent horseman and a bold soldier in the field, always good humoured and always accommodating. When William II and his consort travelled to the Rhineland Province he used to serve the Empress Augusta Victoria as Chamberlain. He was younger than I, and, to my great grief, died soon after the end of the World War. I was always delighted whenever I saw him.

Charles Xavier Scharffenberg was cast in another mould from Dietrich Loë and Guido Nimptsch. The son of a Bremen father who had risen to prosperity in Cuba, and an American mother, he was *bourgeois* in the finest sense of that word. He was capable and conscientious, despised recklessness and frivolity. Like Frau Marthe, in *Faust*, he loved neither strange women, nor the curse of gambling. He esteemed my lively intellect, but found me too indulgent toward Karl Schrader and Guido Nimptsch, whom he described as dissolute fellows, the former as a cynic into the bargain, and the latter as a ne'er-do-well.

Scharffenberg was an idealist. Once when I looked him up with some comrades at his room in Bonn, we discovered a strip of parchment fastened to his desk with the words in large letters: " Do not cast pearls before swine." I said to him casually that by pearls he meant his own sublime ideas and principles, and by swine his comrades. Frank and straightforward as he was, he replied: " Yes, that is true. I fear to profane my ideals if I disclose them to you." Ten years after the Franco-Prussian war he retired to the tranquillity of his idyllic estate in Hessen, Kalkhoff, near Wanfried. He used to delight me during my term of office by his friendly and confiding letters. From the time of his youth he was in close relations with the Dowager Princess of Wied, *née* Princess of Nassau, and through her with Baron Franz von Roggenbach, the opponent of Bismarck, but friend of the Grand Duke Frederick and the Grand

---

[1] " Schlacks "—lout.

[2] Frundsberg—a German mercenary leader, died 1527.

Duchess Luise of Baden as well as of the Kaiser and the Empress Frederick. It is known that Roggenbach was looked upon as the intimate friend of the Dowager Princess and many people even went so far as to say that he was her morganatic consort.

Scharffenberg wrote to me on 6th September, 1909, after my retirement: "In the year 1897 Roggenbach asked me: 'What do you think of Bülow?' I replied: 'From the impression I have always had of him I would say that Bülow is a man who, despite all the frippery of position, family, and wealth, will always remain a real person.' You will remain so after your retirement also." My good friend Scharffenberg suffered the grief of losing a promising son, who was killed in action during the Great War. He delivered a very moving obituary speech. At the disastrous end of the war Charles Xavier Scharffenberg lost heart and died.

The Pomeranian, Richard von Borcke, was a first rate representative of his sturdy native province, and was proud of being a Pomeranian. He used to like to tell a little anecdote which expressed this feeling of pride. After the Battle of Leipzig, where the Pomeranians especially distinguished themselves, the Crown Prince of Prussia and future King Frederick William IV rode over to a Pomeranian regiment and praised the men, adding: "I am proud of you. I, too, am a Pomeranian." It was known that the Crown Prince of Prussia bore the honorary title of "Stadtholder of Pomerania." A worthy Pomeranian rifleman thereupon replied to his Royal Highness: "Yes. Now you all want to be Pomeranians." I corresponded with my dear Richard Borcke until his death during the World War.

The most original character amongst us was undoubtedly the officer-cadet Pemberton-Ground. An American by birth and upbringing, he joined our regiment at the beginning of the war. He hesitated for some time as to whether he should fight for the Germans or the French. He wished to participate in any case. But chose the German side because his grandfather had emigrated to the United States from Baden. He went to Bonn because the Hussar tunic of cornflower blue with the yellow frogs suited him thoroughly. He bore himself sturdily during the winter campaign. When the war came to an end he returned to Chicago and never let anyone hear from him again. Although he was as brave as the others, he did not find it easy to remain calm and unmoved on his horse for hours at a time while the bullets were flying over our heads and the shells bursting around us. He was a devout Catholic, and at such moments he used to promise Saint Anthony that if he remained alive through his merciful protection he would never again frequent certain houses which have only a very distant resemblance to boarding establishments for young ladies. But when the emergency had passed by he forgot his vows only too soon and once again proved the truth of the Neapolitan proverb that when the danger is overcome the saints can be whistled at. *Passato il pericolo, gabbato il Santo.*

Count Beissel von Gymnich's family belonged to the Lower Rhenish hereditary nobility. His disposition was truly Rhenish, and his cheerful spirits never failed. He was very good-natured. I remember once how we were quartered in a cubby hole in a little farmhouse that was too narrow to provide room for more than two people. The quarter-master had reserved the cubby-hole for Beissel and me. The old woman who lived there was told to pass the night in an uncovered shed. She lamented and wept. Beissel suggested to me that we should let her have her room and that we should spend the night in the open air, a proposal to which I, of course, willingly agreed. The old Frenchwoman was greatly reassured, and, when we marched away in the morning, she wished us God's blessing on our long journey. That night in the open air was not, however, the most uncomfortable I experienced in France. Much worse was the sojourn in a disused bakehouse in which I spent two days and two nights in the bitter cold with Dietrich Loë and Dietrich Metternich. Several years after the war Beissel, whose domestic circumstances were happy, was travelling from Bingen to Bonn by railway when, passing through one of the tunnels, a weak report of a shot was heard. When the train emerged from the tunnel Beissel lay dead, with a small hole in his forehead. He had shot himself during the journey through the tunnel. The reason why was never cleared up. The various possibilities that have been brought forward to explain the cause of the suicide have all turned out to be without foundation. " There are more things in heaven and earth, Horatio, than are dreamt of in your philosophy."

While we merry ensigns rode out on patrol in happy mood day and night, in spite of cold and fatigue, the masterful plans of our great commander, General von Goeben, were ripening. He knew that he could make the heaviest demands of his troops in spite of all the hardships undergone by them since the marching off from Compiègne, in spite, that is to say, of seven full weeks of ice and snow, rain and cold, in an unbroken, ever-advancing and ever more arduous campaign. The patrol service was even further intensified in the middle of January. The First Squadron was doing continuous patrol in the region of Albert. We maintained contact with the outposts of the cavalry division. Every three hours patrols proceeded to Flers via Merricourt. We patrolled the region of Daours along the Somme. We found that le Sars and Combles were unoccupied. Bapaume was strongly held and the enemy was in his old advanced positions. We reported that General Faidherbe, the Commander of the French Northern Army, had his headquarters there. On the 16th of January Albert was found to be occupied, and soon afterwards the fact was established that strong French columns were advancing upon Albert from Bray. It was of great importance to find out the enemy's intentions as soon as possible, and to keep to his heels until the moment for battle came. General von Goeben could base his operations on the reports of his cavalry with entire confidence. A part of the credit could be claimed by the King's Hussar Regiment. On 17th January my captain, von Niesewand, received instructions to proceed towards Albert with our squadron and reconnoitre. After a march of over six miles the captain was able to confirm the news brought in on the previous day that Albert had been evacuated and that the enemy had withdrawn on Bapaume.

When General von Goeben received the corroborative reports of his cavalry concerning the evacuation of Albert, he at once ordered the First Army to deploy to the right. The eastward march was exceedingly troublesome. After four weeks of intense, unbroken cold (at times it was as low as eleven degrees Centigrade below zero) a thaw set in, and after the evening of 16th January, warm rain fell on the snow-covered landscape. On the morning of the 17th the streets were covered with sheet ice, but in the course of the day this melted to deep slush. The fields were absolutely impassable. But despite all hardships and bad and overcrowded billets, as well as the short rations that were being issued about this time, the troops were in high spirits. Everybody felt that the French plan of tricking and surprising General von Goeben had completely miscarried. The army was firmly convinced that Goeben would beat the enemy.

I reproduce a letter which I sent my parents on 21st January concerning the events of the previous ten days:

Dearest Parents,

For a number of days we have been continuously on the move, so that it was impossible for me to send you a letter. Since then I have had no news from you either. Please do not be distressed if you receive no news from me. I almost always carry a written letter which I post when I find a chance to do so.

Should anything happen to me, you would hear from the colonel at once. We were in action on the 18th and the 19th. Since the battle of Bapaume we have been scouring around between Bray and Cappy. On the 12th at midday the alarm was sounded at Bray. On this day the French marched into Bapaume, which our troops had evacuated. Thereupon we stayed at Bray, which is quite a nice little town. The Army Corps crossed the Somme and concentrated on the left bank, so that we took over the advanced posts, together with three companies of infantry. This duty was very arduous until the 15th. We had to do a patrol to Albert every three hours, and one to Flers, so that this long and very slippery village (the peasants had purposely watered the streets to make them more difficult for our horses) was a very dubious affair as far as we were concerned. I led the patrol there three times during the day and twice by night, but I always came through safely. On some days I rode close to the French outposts (*Gardes Mobiles*), but they did not fire at me. Whether they were cunning and wanted to entice me, or whether they were just kind-hearted, I do not know, but I expect the former reason is the right one. To cut us off in Flers would really have been very easy. Strangely enough, they only tried to do so once, and not on me, but on someone else. They failed, for he got away just in time. On the 15th the French entered Albert, which the Third Cavalry Division had evacuated without fighting. We were again given the alarm after the French Dragoons had taken two of our men who were patrolling near Albert. The lieutenant who lead them, von Erffa, had a narrow escape. The French, it was alleged, hanged the two Hussars, but I do not believe it. We withdrew to Cappy at noon, but the French did not venture to attack us, and in the evening the battalion entered Bray again. We arrived at Cappy from where we had to send patrols to Carnoy (on the road from Albert to Péronne). On the 16th the French shifted from Albert to Bapaume, as it afterwards transpired, in order to deceive us about their real intentions by a constant shifting to and fro between Bapaume and Albert. Faidherbe went with the bulk of the army to St. Quentin. In the morning of the 17th we marched out as far as Villers-Cotterets. From there we continued our advance on the 18th. Then the battle began. Our squadron was in reserve and only reconnoitred towards evening in the direction of St. Quentin without encountering the enemy.

On the 19th we advanced on Tertry and established contact with the enemy about ten o'clock. We covered the artillery and the infantry. We were able to follow the course of the battle (which went in our favour) very clearly. We attacked St. Quentin on three sides, and the French were terribly cut up by our batteries, which were placed in a semi-circle. Towards two o'clock the victory was already won, but nevertheless, the battle continued into the night. Our infantry attacked in a splendid manner. When a battalion of the 33rd got orders to capture a small wood in which the French had established themselves, they fixed bayonets with loud cheers, while the flag, of which only a pair of black shreds were left hanging, was being unrolled. The major raised his sword with the words: " Let everybody remember he is a Prussian and one of the 33rd." Whereupon they advanced with louds shouts of " *Malheur ! Malheur !* " and quickly drove the French out of the wood.

Our artillery did some splendid firing. It is remarkable how far the French bullets carry, seeing that the French rest the chassepot on their knees when they fire and that these bullets have also a very flat trajectory. Although we had occupied a position with fairly good cover, a number of bullets dropped amongst us. But only two hussars of my squadron were wounded. Towards evening we got orders to march into St. Quentin.

When we arrived there the last of the French withdrew at the other end of the town. After we had found quarters we found thirty *Gardes Mobiles* in a café with their rifles and packs. They all surrendered. The French marines, however, fought very well. On the 20th we marched five miles to Empire (Aisne). To-day a detachment (including myself) has been detailed to escort the Brigadier-General. I therefore have the prospect of a good billet, seeing the brigade is in the habit of choosing out the best possible villages. The road behind St. Quentin was littered with dead, nearly all of whom had bullet wounds in the head. I saw some badly-wounded men who had lain out all night. Nearly all the dead French were young fellows, very well equipped, but mostly small and puny. Some of them had a quite peaceful expression, but some had distorted features. One of them sat leaning against the embankment of the road in the attitude of a man about to fire his rifle, both arms raised. Death must have come instantaneously. Many munition wagons were standing about, the horses having been killed by shells. There was also an unfortunate cow which had been torn to shreds by a shell. A few other cows were feeding peacefully near by. We have done some really strenuous marching of late. On the 17th we marched for ten hours, on the 18th fifteen hours, on the day before yesterday thirteen hours, and yesterday twelve hours. That the infantry can stand this on broken-up roads is a thing that wins my admiration. We have nothing to eat except pea soup when we get to our quarters, but it tastes very good. Please send me two handkerchiefs as soon as you can, some " independences," and a solid cigar-case. Perhaps a little telescope as well, as light and easy to carry as possible. Most of the others have them in opera-glass form. Please send me also the " *Büchsel Collection of War Songs.*" I have got a New Testament. A thousand greetings and best wishes from

Your devoted son,
BERNHARD VON BÜLOW.

The 33rd Prussian Fusiliers Regiment, side by side of which we King's Hussars fought most often, was a brilliant regiment. The 33rds deserved the honour of having the Minister of War von Roon as their chief, one of the greatest men in Prussian and German history. At Bapaume and St. Quentin, as well as at Gravelotte, a great number of officers and men of this regiment sealed their oath to the King and the Fatherland with their blood. The 33rd lost nine officers at Gravelotte, and five more lost their lives at Bapaume. Lieut-Colonel von Henning commanded the 33rd. When I saw him riding through the lines at Bapaume and St. Quentin, Schiller's poem about the Friedländer passed through my mind: " He rode coolly up and down under the blaze of fire, his hat riddled with bullets."

On 24th January I wrote as follows from Sapignies, near Bapaume:

DEAREST PARENTS,

A thousand thanks for your nice letter, which I received yesterday, and which gratified me greatly by its good news. Many thanks also for the newspapers you have sent on to me, and for the cigars (three letters and one parcel), chocolate and gloves. I pray God to give you strength in these agonising days in which our beloved Bertha has fallen ill and died. To-morrow will be the day which is always the most dreadful in the whole year for us. To think back on the time between the 23rd and the 28th is to be unable to understand how it was possible to get over this grief. " *Ich leb' mit tausend Freuden in meines Heilands Hand, mich rührt und trifft kein Leiden, so dieser Welt bekannt.*" [1] That is the only consolation. What could be purer

---

[1] " With a thousand joys I live in the Saviour's hand. No pain that is known to this world moves and touches me."

and more angelic than the soul of a girl of twelve years old, especially of a child so richly endowed, so loving, so beautiful and so kind. If for other reasons I did not believe in eternal life, I would believe in it for her sake. Indeed, the oftener and closer one sees death the greater grows the conviction that it can only be a transition to another life that is better than this.

I am well. We marched here the day before yesterday from Gonnelieu. I also wrote from Gonnelieu, very hurriedly and therefore sketchily, about the events of 18th and 19th. Sapignies is a wretched village, with absolutely nothing to eat in it. We are now putting up outposts who are on the look-out in the direction of Arras four kilometres away. I shall probably be detailed for one of them to-morrow. Patrols rode up to Arras every day. It is said to be occupied by 30,000 men. The Faidherbe Army has been completely beaten at St. Quentin, and has certainly withdrawn on Cambrai in full flight. Still, it has been observed before that the French reorganize their forces quickly, and, besides the rabble of *Gardes Mobiles*, etc., they have a nucleus of good troops, and, above all, a splendid rifle, though they use it badly enough. Gambetta is said to be in Lille. If that is true, the dance will soon begin all over again. It may as well, for all we care, seeing that we now have two army corps, very strong artillery, good positions, and a splendid General. The French are said to have cavalry. We are all burning to meet it face to face. The Fourth Squadron was lucky enough to attack some Dragoons on the 19th. We shall be getting reserves of men and horses on the 1st. We need the latter very urgently. Since Metz we have had fifty-two days of marching and twenty-one of rest; among the latter more than twelve were filled with patrols, etc., so that they do not really count. Of the former, twelve to fifteen were of the kind in which we set out in the early morning before dawn and reached our destination in the evening after dark. We have been in eight engagements—Mareuille, Amiens, Forges-les-Eaux (near Rouen), Pont-Noyelles (2nd January), Bapaume, Tertry, Pouilly (18th January), St. Quentin. We have had every kind of weather in turn—Rain, snow, and wonderful frost. It was certainly worse at Christmas, when the cold made things almost intolerable. Now the weather is really mild. My quarters here are quite good, relatively speaking, enough chickens and wine, and, as I said before, I am in very good health. I do not need any new equipment.

Since Metz the regiment's losses are—three officers, an

acting sergeant, two sergeants and four volunteers severely wounded; an acting sergeant, a volunteer, four non-commissioned officers killed; five or six men prisoners. Of the Hussars eight are dead, twenty to twenty-five severely wounded. Sanden's condition is said to be improving. Many regards to the Countess Wrangel (in an appropriate form) and greeting to her son. Many greetings to Grandmama at Plön. Thousand greetings and best wishes from your devoted son.

Just as Sapignies had provided the opportunity for Count Max Pourtalès to distinguish himself, the engagement at Tertry-Pouilly on 18th January was the day of honour for Ferdinand Rudolphi, the oldest captain in the regiment. He was the only officer who had been in the regiment at Posen and had entered its ranks in Bonn in 1852. He had a narrow escape from faring very badly indeed a year later. King William IV was inspecting the regiment. His Adjutant-General (General von C.) addressed a number of banal questions to the officers in a rather patronizing manner during the inspection. He asked Lieutenant Rudolphi if he was married. "No," answered the lieutenant, "but I esteem the pleasures of marriage very highly." General von C., like many other gentlemen in the entourage of Frederick William IV, had a pronounced pietistic tendency. Only a canting humbug or a pedant could take such an answer from a dashing hussar like Lieutenant Rudolphi amiss, but it enraged General von C. Rudolphi would have had to resign his commission had not his regimental commander, Count Oriola, intervened strongly on his behalf and thus saved the army an officer who won new and rich laurels for the regimental colours on 18th January, 1871, at Tertry-Pouilly, and on 19th January, 1871, at St. Quentin. He combined the 2nd and 4th Squadron under his command on the former date. When on 18th January, the Commander of the 29th Infantry Brigade, Colonel von Bock, ordered Captain Rudolphi to check the hostile infantry's advance against our batteries, the Captain decided to attack at once. The hostile infantry columns, detachments of 150 to 200 men, were marching on the road from Caulaincourt to Beauvois. Using a dip in the ground that ran parallel with their line of march, Captain Rudolphi moved forward at the trot, in troop column, parallel with the enemy's lines. Reaching the same elevation as the enemy with two of his companies, he formed up for the attack at a distance of 400 paces from them. The ditches along the road were taken by the Hussars. They rode cheering, right into the enemy's line, and then went straight through it.

The hostile columns were completely overrun. Part of their men were cut down and the rest surrendered. Far more than a hundred prisoners were collected when fresh companies suddenly coming up quite near to us, began to open a powerful rapid fire upon our squadron. In these circumstances Rudolphi was, with a heavy heart, forced to leave behind the fine bag of prisoners (many of whom, by the way, had been laid low by the chassepot bullets of their fellow-countrymen) and to withdraw from the close fire of the enemy, who came on in ever-growing numbers. The losses of the five detachments consisted of two dead and fourteen wounded. The captain's horse was shot in the back, but the brave animal carried its rider out of the line of fire. As they had charged across the deeply-churned soil of the heavy wet fields, the hussars were bespattered with clay and mud from head to foot, so that they looked like the very devil (as Rudolphi himself declared, not without satisfaction). Only the officers, who had ridden ahead of the others, had remained clean.

On the following day, the day of St. Quentin, Rudolphi had his long-yearned-for opportunity of measuring himself with the French in a cavalry action. In the morning, when he was proceeding from Etreillers with his squadron at a gentle trot, there was a French squadron on the road ahead of him, going back from Roupy towards Dallon, at first slowly, and then increasing its pace. Captain Rudolphi did not intend to let the enemy escape. In a long gallop he went through Savy with the 4th Squadron, and turned to the right in the village on to a field-path which led to the Roupy-St. Quentin road. The enemy cavalry disappeared behind the nearest hill. But after a few minutes the hussars reached the high road and turned to the left in front. Then they approached a hollow into which the high-banked road led. In this area, which was some 600 paces broad, the hostile cavalry was ranged up obliquely across the road. Rudolphi ordered his squadron to slow down in front. Three kilometres were covered at a slow gallop and column of threes. The sunken road did not allow a frontal attack. Rudolphi quickly decided to form two columns and galloped forward to the attack. The French halted to receive them and fired a volley at 150 paces.

I will now follow the account given by my dear war-time comrade, old and devoted friend, General Adolf von Deines, on whose fine history of King William I's Hussar Regiment (1st Rhenish No. 7), I have relied upon in many of my military memories.

At the moment the French fired their volley the old captain's bellowing "Charge!" resounded, and then, amid loud cheering, came the crash. The front ranks of the French were ridden down, the rear ran in full flight towards St. Quentin, with the King's Hussars after them. Captain Rudolphi, who, on his thoroughbred horse, "Lifebuoy," was many lengths ahead of the squadron, rode down an enemy officer while Lieutenant and Regimental Adjutant Mossner, who had joined the attack, charged another with such vehemence that both went over. The Frenchman quickly got up and struck a blow from behind at Rudolphi as he went by. Rudolphi was on his left in a moment and dealt him a powerful blow over the back of the head. A dragoon fired his carbine at Rudolphi at a distance of a few paces, but only grazed the good horse "Lifebuoy." The next moment Sergeant Steenebrügge struck the enemy dragoon squarely across the face. Only when pursuers and pursued arrived at the village of Epine de Dallon, which was strongly held, did Rudolphi rally his men, and then rode back at walking pace. Dead and wounded enemy dragoons lay on the roadside in large numbers, all of them badly cut up by blows given in hand-to-hand fighting. The French Squadron consisted of very muscular, formidable, picked men, on large and heavy horses. They had, according to the country people, been formed as a cover for General Faidherbe that very morning. In this attack about twenty of the enemy were left behind dead or wounded. Those who reached St. Quentin without some memento must have been very few. There was hardly a sabre belonging to the sixty hussars who had taken part in the attack that was not bent or bloodstained.

In this worthy manner did the King's Hussars open the day of St. Quentin. The 4th Squadron was still dressing the line south of Savy when Colonel von Loë arrived with our First Squadron, which had gone ahead of the bulk of the Division. Captain Niesewand now took over the task of reconnoitring at Savy. Fire was opened on us from the little wood east of the village, and we reported that this section was strongly held by infantry. The Brigade Commander, Colonel von Bock, advanced the artillery and let the advance guard deploy. Our First Squadron followed the attacking movement on the right wing under the command of Colonel von Loë. As the 25th Brigade was face to face with strong masses of the enemy, the fight came to a standstill here. In an artillery duel our guns gradually silenced the fire of the French batteries, which were shooting as stoutly as our own. My

First Squadron had to stand for hours in a hollow until General von Goeben, who, until then, had halted on the road to St. Quentin and had from there conducted the battle, ordered our "Colours," the 8th Jägers, as well as two battalions of 28-ers under the command of the Jägers, Major von Bronikowski, to storm the village of Epine de Dallon. At the same time the 29th Brigade and the 1st Division went forward. The enemy was thrown back before our eyes along the whole line.

When darkness came the French were in full retreat everywhere, and our 15th Division stood right in front of the town. The French were obstinately defending its barricaded entrances. Shortly after five o'clock, the riflemen of the 68-ers began to get a footing in the first suburban houses. The battalion and our squadron followed. We reached the market place of St. Quentin. In a short time we took hundreds of prisoners in the streets and houses. Our squadron spent the night in the suburbs of St. Quentin. It was a piquant experience for me to pass the night in a French town of nearly 50,000 inhabitants in which French soldiers were still swarming. We were all filled with the glad feeling that we had completely beaten the French Northern Army. And the latter was in fact hurriedly retreating towards the north. The total exhaustion of the German troops made it impossible to pursue the French that evening. They had been on the move since six o'clock in the morning, mostly across fields, often knee-deep in ploughed land, always in action, and almost entirely without rations. General von Goeben therefore had to postpone the direct pursuit until the next day.

As the day of St. Quentin comes back to my memory, I am glad to think that when I was Imperial Chancellor I had a chance of doing Captain Rudolphi a service. Soon after my appointment to the Chancellorship, I received a letter in which he asked me whether I would help an old war-comrade. He personally attached no importance to a title. He said he had risen from being a volunteer in a battery of howitzers of the 3rd Artillery Brigade, to Colonel and Commander of the Lithuanian Uhlan Regiment, No. 12, honourably and without a title. But for the sake of his sons, he said, he would be glad if he could be raised to noble rank. I used the opportunity when the Kaiser was in a good humour to suggest that old Colonel Rudolphi (of whom I had such a high opinion) ought to receive a title. The Kaiser at once and willingly gave the necessary instructions, and Ferdinand Rudolphi was raised to noble rank on 29th January, 1902, which, as I may remark by the way, was a distinction for the nobility. When I laid down my office as Imperial Chancellor, the first of his sons was in the Emperor Alexander III of Russia's Uhlan Regiment (West Prussian) No. 1, and the other in the Torgauer Field Artillery Regiment No. 74.

I have already mentioned that the Regimental Adjutant Lieutenant von Mossner had voluntarily joined in the cavalry attack of 19th January. Mossner was one of the best officers of the regiment, and I can, without exaggeration, declare that when he was promoted to a higher command, he became one of our most distinguished cavalrymen. He was the son of a Berlin banker who had had the opportunity of rendering devoted service to the Prince of Prussia in 1848, when the Prince was denounced as a "Reactionary" and an "absolutist" during the sad days of March and was compelled to leave Berlin. Kaiser William I never forgot a service rendered him. When he met the banker Mossner two years after his ascension to the throne, he asked him whether he had any wishes that he might fulfil. The banker replied that he had a young son who was considered a good horseman and ardently desired to join the cavalry. The King willingly promised that he would have the young man, who was only just eighteen at the time, admitted to his own regiment, the King's Hussars. Having entered the Blue Hussars in Bonn in 1865, Walter Mossner did not meet with a very kind reception. He came of a Jewish family, and the officers' corps of the King's Hussar Regiment refused to elect him a member. Thus occurred one of the few cases in which William I compelled an officers' corps to receive into its circle a cadet it did not want to accept. The King informed the officers of his Hussar Regiment through the Regimental Commander, that he would consider the non-election of the Cadet Mossner as a personal affront. Having been elected an officer, Mossner at once won the respect of his fellow officers by dealing another ensign, who had been particularly zealous in opposing, a stout cavalryman's blow across the head in a duel. This ensign was Prince Karl Carolath, later on the husband of the beautiful Countess Elizabeth Hatzfeldt. Nominated Lieutenant in February, 1866, Mossner was awarded the Order of the Red Eagle with bars in the Battle of Königgrätz. He was regimental adjutant from 1867 to 1872, and in this capacity he won the complete confidence, the complete satisfaction, the friendship and the personal affection of Colonel von Loë. In 1872 he was appointed to the General Staff, in 1877 Staff Officer of the Life-Guard Hussars, and then their Commander from 1891 to 1895. In 1895 he was put in command of the 3rd Guard Cavalry Brigade, in 1898 became head of the Cavalry Institute, in 1899 Lieutenant-General and Commander of Guard Cavalry Division, in 1903 Governor of Strassburg. Not long before the sad end of the World War, in which he served his country as a Deputy General Commanding, he was awarded the high Order of the Black Eagle by William II. Mossner was, I believe, the last Prussian General to receive the Order of the Black Eagle—a well-earned distinction for a man who had shown his worth in two campaigns, who had been a distinguished Regimental Adjutant, Squadron Chief, Regimental Brigade and Divisional Commander, and, in addition, one of the best horsemen in the army, and who had twice won the great Army races.

By way of supplement to the hurried and somewhat sketchy letter which I wrote to my parents, I would like to add the following: While the battle of St. Quentin was at its height, I received my promotion as ensign, and reported to my commander, Colonel von Loë. He looked at me steadily with his large, serious eyes. He then said:

From to-day onwards you will carry an officer's sword. It shall be yours in well-merited recognition of your proved valour under fire. Never forget the day you reported to me as an ensign. Yesterday, on the same 18th of January on which King Frederick I was crowned with the Royal Crown of Prussia at Königsberg, our gracious Sovereign, King William I, accepted the German Imperial Crown, which was offered to him at Versailles by all the German Princes. German cannons thunder before Paris to-day, on the Lisaine, in the Jura, and here before St. Quentin, in honour of the King and Emperor. Such glorious days as we now live to see cannot often be repeated. What matters is that the spirit of this day be taken to heart, be followed like a guiding star, be always faithfully observed. I expect this from you and wish you luck for your future.

CHAPTER XVII

Armistice of the 31.1.1871—Outbreak of Smallpox—Drill as in Peace Time—Preliminary Peace—Lieutenant of the King's Hussars Regiment (8.3.1871)—The Regiment Marches to Amiens—The Crown Prince Inspects the Parade (13.3.1871)—Town Major of Amiens—Field Letters from Amiens.

ON the evening of the 19th January, Lieutenant Count Karl Sierstorpff was talking to me as he mounted his horse, instructing me to take a dispatch to General von Kummer, when a bullet pierced his shoulder and back, wounding him severely. To the joy of the whole regiment, he could be saved by the surgeon's art. On the 20th of January we started off before eight o'clock. The 30th Brigade (Major General von Strubberg) was the advance guard, our regiment marching at the head. The march in the pouring rain was tedious and wearisome, all the more so as we had to keep to field paths. Colonel von Loë cantered along beside his regiment. To our regret the enemy were nowhere to be seen.

General Strubberg ordered a halt at nightfall. We were billeted in little villages about a mile and a half from Cambrai. Patrols were sent out in the night. I led one of them in the direction of Ribécourt. I found all villages free of the enemy. The peasants told me that the French North Army had passed through Cambrai in complete disruption and had continued its march towards Arras and Douai. Nor did the other columns of our army succeed in reaching the main body of the enemy's forces.

On the 21st we went into billets, where the inhabitants confirmed the news of the precipitate retreat of strong French forces upon Douai and Arras. In the course of the day we discovered that the enemy's main forces had reached the shelter of its fortifications, partly with the help of the railways. In these circumstances General von Goeben allowed the army time to recuperate after the almost indescribable hardships of the last five days. In the evening of the 22nd we reached Bapaume, which was already familiar to us, and took up quarters in the villages of Sapignies, Béhagnies and Favreuil, which were also well known to us.

The following day four more patrols were sent out. I remember one that took me in the direction of Arras. The air was quite clear during these days. I plainly saw the belfry of Arras, the city of Maximilien Robespierre. I also saw a party of eleven or twelve men who were escorting a prisoner in their midst. Peasants, working in the fields, whom I asked for information, told me that this was a " *traître* " who was being led off to meet his well-deserved punishment. To be afraid of spies and to see them everywhere became a mania in France when the World War began, and it was a mania there even in 1870-71. The peasants declared that Arras was full of troops, that General Faidherbe had his headquarters there. Besides patrols, we had to form detachments for the purpose of commandeering supplies. By order of the High Command we formed mixed detachments, who collected contributions in those districts that lay between us and the enemy. Twenty-five francs per head were collected, so that a love of peace might be instilled into those inhabitants who, in part at least, had not yet been injured by the war. We called these detachments our " soothing columns." With a detachment of this kind, consisting of a battery, two battalions, and our First Squadron, Colonel von Loë requisitioned a hundred thousand francs in the canton of Croissiles. The place was unable to pay the required sum at once, but promised to deliver it within three days and, by way of a guarantee, they surrendered five of the most prominent citizens as hostages. The hundred thousand francs were paid within this period. The hostages, of course, went home again.

Now, as before, the patrols and the requisitionings were made very much more difficult by the weather. Dry cold interchanged with heavy snowfalls. The streets, as a rule, were slippery like a mirror. On the 29th January, so it was said, the 15th Division would concentrate near Doullens as General von Goeben was planning an advance towards Arras, Abbeville, and Boulogne. But it was said at the same time, that, according to a telegraphic message which had arrived at Amiens, the artillery fire in front of Paris had ceased in the night between the 26th and the 27th of January, and that negotiations for an armistice were going on.

In the morning of the 30th January the news passed from mouth to mouth that Paris had capitulated. At last there was " news from Paris! " At the same time news of the armistice concluded at Versailles spread abroad. Immediately afterwards French officers came with the flag of truce to negotiate about the line of demarcation. So as to create " an agreeable *status quo*," as he expressed it, General von Goeben ordered certain sections of the army to move forward. At noon on the 31st January, the three weeks' armistice which had been accepted by General Faidherbe, came into force. The French evacuated Abbeville, while we evacuated the Departments of the Nord and the Pas de Calais. A neutral zone of twenty kilometres separated the two armies. In the heavy but warm rainfall we marched in the direction of Amiens and took up quarters in little villages situated north-east and east of Amiens.

Next day we continued our march towards Aumale, a pretty little town to which the fourth son of King Louis Phillipe, who is known both as a general and as a historian, owed his title. Aumale played a part of some importance in French history. Charles the Bold burnt the little town situated on the Bresle which, a hundred years later, offered the wounded Henry IV a refuge from the Liguistes who were pursuing him. *Ce roi galant, qui fit le diable à quatre*, notoriously had a marked preference for the female sex. The women showed their gratitude. Jeanne Leclerc, the most beautiful daughter of the burghers of Aumale let down the drawbridge herself to admit the king who demanded admission.

On 9th February, we arrived at Le Tréport, the harbour town that is picturesquely situated where the Bresle flows into the English Channel. We admired the beautiful church of St. Jacques, and filled our lungs with the sea and spring air. Typhus was raging there, nevertheless, and it robbed us of an efficient Officer of Reserve, Lieutenant Allert. Since the beginning of the armistice the billeting was arranged by the Mairies, and it included our complete board. A German soldier was entitled to coffee and bread in the morning, bread and a piece of meat for a snack at about eleven o'clock, meat, vegetables and half a bottle of wine at noon, some good soup and bread in the evening, and, in addition to this a drop of brandy now and then during the day. It all sounds very nice, but the reality lagged a long way behind these ideal rations. Our people were so very good-natured and satisfied with so little, that excesses against the French population never happened at all, or at least, were very rare. I have often seen our people help the French peasants in their work in the country districts, conversing with them as best they could, holding their children on their laps or playing with them. The peasants were throughout of a peaceful disposition and ardently desired the end of the war. In the towns, even in the smaller towns, a patriotism that sometimes had the intensity of a passion, prevailed, and Gambetta was accounted the saviour of French honour, whereas the country population wished he would go to the Devil.

In the middle of February, our first squadron and the Staff took up quarters in the town of Abbeville, which had once been the

seat of a mighty abbot. Hence the name, "*Abbatis Villa*." Here
our peacetime routine began once more. We did not like it very
much—war service was so much more interesting and exciting—
but by an order of His Majesty's Cabinet, instructions were given
that the reconditioning of the troops should be carried out in every
possible way and with the greatest rigour. I wrote home from
Abbeville:

Abbeville is quite a nice little town, but rather dismal, not
so much because of the war as because of the violent epidemic of
smallpox. But do not be anxious on this account, for I was
vaccinated nine months ago by our famous Doctor Blumenthal
in Berlin. The smallpox, by the way, has spread all over France.
Only one does not talk about it. Let us hope that it will not
reach Germany. Soon after the Battle of St. Quentin I was
billeted in a peasant's house. When I entered the room assigned
to me I saw an oldish man lying in the second bed alongside
the opposite wall. In answer to my question as to whom my
room-mate might be I was told that he was an uncle of the
family's and was suffering from a sick headache. The next
morning it turned out that the poor man had died quietly during
the night. He had died of smallpox.

Wholly unperturbed by the epidemic raging in Abbeville
and the neighbourhood, Colonel von Loë inspected the 2nd and
3rd Squadron during our stay there, Major Dincklage the 1st
and 4th. Although the Colonel was very exacting in every
respect, he was nevertheless able to end his report with the words:
" On the whole the clothing of the regiment and the equipment
of the men and horses is good and fit for war service. The
shoeing of the horses is excellent throughout, the horses of
every squadron are freshly shod. A second set of shoes is in
all the packs and about half of the third set in the wagons."
Thus, after the days of rest, the regiment could anticipate the
reopening of hostilities with complete confidence. Detailed
routine of this kind was not quite the thing the ensigns were
fond of. To the Grand Duke Constantine Pavlovitch is attributed
the utterance: " *Je déteste la guerre, elle gâte les armées*." This
was, of course, the highest expression of stupid pipeclay finicking.
But it is certain that our High Command, when it resumed
peace time service on enemy soil, saw further ahead than the
young ensign who, in the beginning of March, wrote home
grousing: " We are getting more drill than we got in Bonn,
and we do not leave the barracks at all. In the morning, after

stable duty (from five till half past six) we are drilled (from half past eight till twelve), then in the afternoon we are on duty from one till seven o'clock, roll call all the time, inspection, etc. You would hardly realise by looking at the squadron that it had been through a seven months campaign. We always go to church on Sundays when the Divisional Chaplain preaches quite well."

The end of my letter was meant for my mother, who asked in every letter she wrote when I had been to church last. A few days later I wrote: " Our duties are just like garrison duties. Everyone is counting on peace, but everything is being prepared in case hostilities are resumed."

On 24th February I wrote : " Whereas yesterday we still assumed that war would begin again, to-day peace seems assured. It is said that we are going to surrender Metz. This plan does not find very much support in the army, it would be better to have a few more weeks of war, all the more so as the season of the year is very good. The weather has been very fine since the end of January. I haven't worn an overcoat for a fortnight." But there was to be no resumption of hostilities although " it again and again looks as though they would break out once more." In the evening of the 26th a telegram from General von Moltke arrived stating that the Armistice had been prolonged till the 12th of March, and that peace preliminaries had been signed. Thereupon we resumed our mounted drill and went on route marches once again. Then a temporary light peace-time service began—squadron drill and finishing touches to the training of the reserve horses. In the bright warm spring days this drill by the seashore was a recreation. We had a fine time in Abbeville because officers and officials got an extra payment of fifteen francs a day from the French war contributions for the duration of the Armistice. Many of us went to Paris to visit the town which was called *La Ville Lumière* by Victor Hugo during the war and " the Babylon on the Seine " by Germans. On the 6th March the joyful news arrived that the First Army was going to be inspected by His Majesty the Kaiser and King. When, on the 2nd March, the peace preliminaries were ratified, he sent his wife a telegram that ended with words so touching in their modesty: " God has given us this honourable peace. To him be the honour. My thanks with all the deep emotion of my heart to the Army and the Fatherland."

I was made a lieutenant on the 8th of March. A fortnight before I had written to my parents:

I was elected to officer's rank and proposed yesterday.

Considering the circumstances and considering the character of our regiment, the Colonel has had me promoted with unusual rapidity. From corporal to officer in hardly four months! Please write to him, father, and thank him for the goodwill he has shown me and still shows me. He is so very kind to me. He is one of the most intelligent men I have ever met. He can talk on every subject, is very much of an aristocrat and a smart soldier as well.

In the letter in which Colonel von Loë informed my father of my promotion to the lieutenancy, he said: " I am happy to be able to inform your Excellency that His Majesty the Kaiser has been graciously pleased to promote your son to the rank of officer for commendable conduct in the face of the enemy. This distinction is well deserved, since throughout a hard winter campaign he has always given an example of strict fulfilment of duty to all his comrades and subordinates. Besides—and this is a thing to which I attach perhaps even more value in the make-up of my corps of officers—he has won all our hearts by his chivalrous disposition and his amiable and modest behaviour. I do not doubt that when we return to peace conditions and seriously devote ourselves to our professional duties he will, on the basis of his excellent aptitudes and the knowledge and ability he has already achieved, build up a fine military career."

On 9th March the King's Hussar Regiment left the quarters they had occupied for nearly a month on the Channel coast and marched to Amiens, where the 8th Army Corps was concentrated. The First Squadron went into billets in the village of Dury on the road that leads from Amiens to Breteuil, not far from a little river, La Celle. We set about spitting and polishing, for the King's Hussars Regiment was to look as fresh and smart as though it were on peace-time parade in the Hofgartenwiese at Bonn. That day, alas, we were not to see our War Lord and chief of our Regiment, whose venerable figure lived in all our hearts. To his own extreme regret, to the great disappointment of the Rhenish Army Corps, and particularly of his Hussars, the Kaiser had been compelled to abandon the journey to Amiens because he was not feeling well enough, but the Crown Prince came instead on behalf of his Imperial father.

In the morning of the 13th of March the whole 8th Army Corps gathered north-east of Amiens between Altonville and Les Allenbons, together with an infantry brigade made up of the 19th and 81st Regiments, the 3rd Cavalry Division, and the

Prince Albrecht Brigade of Horse Guards. In the first concentration, facing the Amiens-Querrieux road, was the whole infantry,
thirty-one battalions in all. In the second concentration the cavalry
and artillery, and the Guard Hussars were on the right wing,
then came the second Uhlan Guards, next to them was our regiment,
and on our left were the 9th Hussars. The cavalry were formed up
in closed columns by regiments. The Crown Prince arrived at
twelve o'clock. It had been raining heavily until the moment of
his approach. But now that he came galloping up to the Rhenish
Army Corps, the clouds were dispersed and the sun shone brightly
forth. He was riding a black Trakehn horse. He wore the white
coat of the Pasewalk Cuirassiers. As he approached our right wing
Lieutenant-General von Barnekow gave the order and the whole,
Army Corps saluted, the infantry presented arms, the drummers
and the regimental bands joined in, and then a great burst of
cheering from 40,000 German throats roared welcome to the
Crown Prince. How could I ever forget this day, this parade in
the presence of the Crown Prince of Prussia and of the German
Empire, down there in Picardy, close by the steep heights of the
Hallue, where we had fought in the Christmas season in sight of
the old capital, Amiens! How could Germany ever forget the
Emperor Frederick, who throughout his whole life in joy and
sorrow, in every situation, had shown two great manly virtues:
he was sincere to the finger tips, and quite fearless. With shining
eyes, every man in the ranks followed the beloved Royal son, the
victor of Weissenburg and Wörth, as he rode along the lines of
glittering steel. All Germany's past rose up before my spirit:
Theodoric and Alaric, Roland, who fell at Roncesvalles, and
Siegfried, who killed the dragon, the Salic Emperor Henry III
and the Staufen Henry VI.

Like the Emperor Frederick, these two emperors also died
too soon. As our regiment marched past by half squadrons, the
Rhenish Jägers shouted " *Lehm op!* " and the shout was taken
up joyfully by the other troops. And the whole infantry, which
had filed out on the flank, shouted " *Lehm op!* " in one sudden
roar. When the Crown Prince inquired after the meaning of this
exuberant outburst, Lieutenant von Barnekow informed him that
the shout of " *Lehm op!* " was meant for the King's Hussars, and
that this boisterous greeting was the tribute paid to this regiment
for the service it had rendered to other arms. Riding in the ranks
of the regiment on this memorable day were four officers who
much later on were to receive that high distinction, the Order of
the Black Eagle—Colonel von Loë, Lieutenant Mossner, Second

Lieutenants von Deines and von Bülow. A few days afterwards we moved to Salonelle and Saleux via Longeau. Then we were assigned to the mounted detachments by command of the Colonel. Thenceforth we did our training on horseback in the mornings or our mounted drill with the squadron. In the afternoons we did infantry drill or gymnastics.

The Hussars were on quite friendly terms with the peasants in Picardy. They would help them when they worked in the fields. The peasant understood the German soldier when he said "*pain*," "*vin*," "*avoine*," "*foin*." The soldier was fond of repeating the French peasant's favourite expression: "*Malheur, malheur pour nous, malheur pour vous, malheur pour tout le monde.*"

I wrote home about my equipment:

It is very fine, but costs a heathenish amount of money. As soon as I have put my bills together, I will send them to you. For the instruction and benefit of my younger brothers I will describe the chief articles to you: gold embroidered tunic like the one I had when I was a volunteer, only with gold facings, and epaulettes worked in silver, galoons on the sleeves and on the collar, gold rosettes and rippled buttons. The tunic is very beautiful, but unfortunately it costs seventy thalers. The trousers are of the ordinary pattern, only with galoons instead of braid, boots, too, with galloons and rosettes in front. I have had two pairs of boots sent on which I already had when I was at Bonn. I have bought a provisional tunic which is still in good condition, second-hand, for fifteen thalers. It is pale blue with white and black facings. Both tunics fit me very well. The accoutrements are dearest of all, especially the saddle-cloth. But I cannot do without it. The fur cap costs twenty thalers, but is very beautiful. The bandolier is of silver with two big tassels. The frogs have my name worked in gold. Both are very dear, the bandolier not quite so much. The harness and the saddle are the cheapest of all, relatively speaking. The equipment (without horses) will probably come to about 250 thalers. What I would like best would be if I could pay with the little legacy which Uncle Martin has earmarked on my behalf.

I did my best to save my parents unnecessary expense, and was not at all spoilt in those days.

On the 1st April I was appointed Town Major at Amiens. Thereupon I wrote to my parents:

I have been assigned to the Commandant Headquarters at Amiens, where I have become Town Major. This at last means good food and a very good billet. Business is not bad. General Ruville is Commandant. His wife is here too, but she attracts less attention than she would like. The Adjutant is Count Talleyrand, of the 2nd Uhlan Guards, a very nice man. I report to the General at 11.30 and 5.30, and issue the Commandant's orders at 1 and 8 o'clock. On Thursdays and Sundays I issue them when the guards parade. The released French soldiers take up a lot of my time, especially as they are supposed to salute us.

General von Ruville, a smart old officer, who had been in the First Guards Regiment, strictly insisted on this salute. If a passing French officer did not salute him, I had to arrest the delinquent. This sometimes led to moving scenes. Once when I again had to arrest an unfortunate French officer, a lady dashed up to me in great excitement and shouted: " *Homme cruel, vous n'avez donc pas de mère ?* " The crowd yelled and shouted. I replied: " *Mais, Madame, si je n'avais pas de mère, comment voulez-vous que j'aie l'honneur et le plaisir de causer avec vous ?* " The people standing around began to laugh, and the excited lady laughed with them. More serious was the case of a French officer who had struck a sentry on duty who had refused to let him pass a forbidden corridor in the railway station. He was to be shot. General von Ruville petitioned for his reprieve, and it was a long time before an answer came. In the meantime the Frenchman, who was housed in the citadel, was treated in a very friendly manner by all. He had meals with the German officers on duty in the citadel. I had meals with him many times. He could not thank me enough for the good treatment he got. He was reprieved in the end.

General von Ruville came of a family of *émigrés*. The château of his ancestors was not far from Amiens. It was in the same sad condition as the ancestral mansion of Chamisso, the Château of Boncourt. But General von Ruville did not, " with mild and deep emotion, bless those who guided the plough over the land that had once been his." The memory of the ill-treatment his ancestors had received increased his resentment against the French. His adjutant, Count Archambault Talleyrand-Périgord, was in a very awkward situation. He was a Frenchman both on his father's and his mother's side, and the scion of a renowned French family. But when young he came under the influence of his grandmother, the Duchess of Sagan, and went to Prussia. where he joined the army. He was a dutiful Prussian officer, but his heart belonged to France first and last. When the news reached Amiens that the Communists had set fire to Paris, he burst into tears in the presence of myself and General von Ruville.

As soon as the Germans had left Amiens, the Municipal Council decided to re-christen the Place Périgord Place Faidherbe, so as to express their disgust with Count Archambault von Talleyrand-Périgord, who had become a German officer. Archambault Talleyrand who, by the way, was a very charming man, once told me a little incident that was very characteristic of the Empress Augusta. When, on the evening of the 2nd September, the Empress received congratulations on the occasion of the victory of Sedan, she noticed Archambault Talleyrand, whom she knew well and always treated with special kindness, amongst those present. She went up to him and said to him in French how well she understood and respected his conflicting emotions. That was the true Weimar spirit. But I do not believe that an English or French, an Italian or Russian Princess would, in a similar situation, have felt or spoken as the Empress Augusta did. Later on Count Archambault Talleyrand married the eldest daughter of the French Ambassador in Berlin, Viscount de Gontaut-Biron. Bismarck regarded him with disfavour, the Empress Augusta with favour.

In reproducing several letters to my parents relating to military events, I have emphasised the fact that they are not the reports of a member of the General Staff, but the impressions and snapshots of a young hussar. I have given them a good deal of space, as I have to all my war experiences, because it is my wish to do my share in preserving and reviving the military spirit amongst our young people who are now growing up. "He who is unarmed is without honour." If I now reproduce some further letters which I wrote home after the armistice from Amiens about the political situation, I need hardly remark that after half a century I look back with the smile of age and experience upon many of the opinions I had then.

On the 6th March I wrote:

Peace has really come! The French newspapers, which we read with great regularity here, are all preaching revenge: "silence, patience, vengeance!"[1] But the peasants thank God that the war is over. How France will recover with any speed from loss of territory, from loss of lives, from levies and requisi-

[1] English in text.

tionings, from an indemnity of five milliards, and from a bad
harvest and a high mortality caused by all kinds of epidemics,
cannot be foreseen. Surely the regions round Metz, Varennes,
Rheims, Amiens, the whole banks of the Somme, the Seine from
Rouen to Pont Audemer, are ruined for another fifty years to
come! The occupied towns are nearly all overburdened with
debt as a result of the levies. It is impossible to have any idea
of the misery in several regions. But the vitality and tenacity
of the French are very great. We are dining together in the
Commandant's quarters, the General, his wife, Talleyrand, a
certain Dr. Oppler, who is the medical officer of the garrison,
and a certain Lieutenant Schellong, who is auditor here. The
dinner is very good. We have got a cook and an assistant cook,
but meals are rather expensive. Lunch and dinner cost one and
a half or two thalers daily. That is a lot, but not nearly as much
as most of the others have to pay. Since the armistice the
officers are really in a bad way as far as food is concerned. Now
that requisitioning has come to an end, the French charge the
most incredible prices. The officers of two squadrons of my
regiment who are quartered near by, pay two thalers daily and
get poor food for the money. Adolf pays four thalers at Chantilly
now and says the food is not good, either. I do not look as
healthy now as I did during the campaign. Most of us are in
the same case—when we had poor food and little sleep we felt
better than we do now. I ride a good deal. I think I wrote to
you that there are some pretty riding tracks here. I go to
church almost every Sunday with the General. I would have
written sooner if I had not been at Chantilly and Saint-Denis
on Monday and Tuesday. Adolf, who is at Saint-Denis with
his regiment, seemed very well and cheerful. On Monday I
dined with him and his captain, Prince Fritz Wittgenstein, at
Chantilly. I spent the night in a beautiful château where Paul
Bülow is quartered. On Tuesday morning we went for a ride,
and at twelve we took the train to Saint-Denis. From there we
took a carriage to the Moulin d'Orgemont, from where there is
a fine view of Paris. The weather was superb, only it was not
very clear. Nevertheless, the Panthéon, Arc de Triomphe, the
Invalides, Belleville, and Montmartre were quite plainly visible
to the naked eye, while the Colonne Vendôme, the Red Flag of
the Commune, and many other things could be seen through a
telescope. Mount Valérien was firing rather vigorously, and
the southern forts, which were out of view, were replying. At
Asnières, which lay at our feet, nothing was happening. There

was also a very pretty view in the direction of Argenteuil, Saint Germain en Laye, Montmorency, Enghien, etc.

When my brother and I looked down on the fighting between the Parisian Communists and the Government troops from Versailles, just as we might have looked down on the arena in a circus, we did not think that scarcely half a century later the French would rejoice over the street fighting provoked by our Spartacists and Communists at Munich, Dresden, in Thuringia, and in the Westphalian industrial area.

On Whit Sunday I wrote:

At Amiens everything goes on as in peace time, that is to say, quite nicely. There were races yesterday, and in the evening there was dancing at Count Lehndorff's, who is Civil Commissioner here. Two distinguished French families were amongst the guests. I shall be going to Belloy to-day, to the château of a certain Monsieur de Morgan, who is giving us a friendly welcome.

The Civil Commissioner, Count Carl von Lehndorff, was the eldest of three excellent brothers. He himself owned an estate at Steinort, in East Prussia. His second brother, Henry, was the well-known and very meritorious Adjutant-General of the Kaiser William I. The third brother, Count George, did much for German horse-breeding as Master of the Stables and head of the Graditz stud farm. When I was a boy I saw him at a flat race in Mecklenburg. He died shortly before the beginning of the World War, so that he was at least spared the grief of witnessing the collapse of the old happy Germany. When, in the spring of 1871, my father told him how deeply glad he was that peace was restored, Count Carl Lehndorff replied: "You ought rather to regret the advent of peace in the interests of your sons. If the war had lasted another ten years, both of them would have come home as Generals."

The Paris Commune was accompanied by smaller risings in many French towns, particularly Marseilles, Saint-Etienne and Toulouse. In Amiens, too, the workmen were in a state of ferment. The Mayor of Amiens, Monsieur Dauphin, with whom I was on the best of terms, was anxious lest there should be Communist disorders. He wrote to me in this sense and begged me to meet any attempted Communist risings with strict vigilance and, in case of need, with energetic repression. When the Paris Commune had been suppressed by Thiers with that ruthless energy which is usually employed in French domestic conflicts, Monsieur Dauphin called on me and begged me to give him back his letter. If what he had written were ever to become known, he said, then his political future would be wrecked. I returned the worthy man's letter and he afterwards became a Cabinet Minister several times without having the Dæmoclean sword of a disagreeable exposure suspended over his head.

At the end of May I wrote as follows about the impression made by the Paris Commune in the provinces:

> The peasants are very pleased about the destruction of Paris. Everybody is demanding a ruthless, iron dictatorship. Everyone says that France was never better ruled than from 1852 to 1855, when Napoleon III governed by the same autocratic methods as had his uncle. The masses are returning to strict Catholicism, even in the towns. The vitality of France is tremendous. If it were not for the five thousand millions the war would be forgotten in ten years. And then their losses are not as great as ours, they have, especially, lost fewer officers. They had no volunteers, etc. There are some very nice families here with whom I associate. Generally speaking the French are either fanatical haters of the Prussians or totally indifferent towards everything. One would hardly believe how rich the country is, even here in Picardy, which is one of the poorer parts of France. There is village on village, every spot is cultivated, vegetable gardening, for example, is developed as it is nowhere in our country. For two or three miles round there is one villa after another, all luxuriously appointed—greenhouses, hotbeds, the finest lawns, and even on the smallest estates there are hunting grounds and fisheries. On Monday I dined at Belloy, at the château of a certain Baron Morgan; we had the finest melons, strawberries and bananas.

CHAPTER XVIII

Amore Sacro and amore Profano—Ride to Camon—The 8th Army Corps under Orders to March Back—Colonel Baron von Loë—The King's Hussars March through the Eifel to Treves—We enter Bonn (6.7.1871)—Back Home at Klein-Flottbek (20.7.1871).

MY mother very much wanted me to come to Baden-Baden where she was taking a cure for a few days. I wrote to my father on the subject:

Mama suggests that I visit her at Baden-Baden. Unfortunately, this is not possible. Talleyrand is on leave from the 1st, and so far there is no one to take his place. Even when his deputy arrives, I cannot very well ask for leave, even for a short leave, as we may begin our march back any day, and in that case I must put our papers in order beforehand. There are all kinds of rumours about our march back. It still seems quite uncertain whether the Department of the Somme will be evacuated and, if so, when. Some say that only Abbeville, and others say that the whole Department will be evacuated. It is likely that a central point like Amiens will be evacuated at the last moment. But as for our VIII Corps being kept here—the thing everyone is talking about—it is no more than a rumour. Still, we shall probably be amongst the last rather than the first, to leave France. Colonel von Loë seems to assume that we shall soon disband the reserves and then form a quasi-garrison in front of Paris or in the Champagne, though whether for two months or two years, no one can tell. The one-year volunteers who studied at Bonn have been sent back there and, so have the older classes of the rank and file. The result, as far as I am concerned, is that I shall have to remain here at my post for awhile, all the more so as I shall not be able to get away even for three or four days, once things begin to get a bit difficult.

I wrote to my mother on the 2nd June:

I have made the acquaintance of many French families here at Amiens. A certain Monsieur de Neuville, a rich banker with a nice wife and daughter. Another rather nice man is Baron de Latapie, who has a pretty château at Cagny and whose

256

clever wife is said to have played a big part in Parisian Society. I am on friendly terms with the Maire and provisional Prefect of the Somme, Monsieur Dauphin. He is a considerable man and will certainly be an important person in his country. His wife, too, is quite a distinguished woman.

A great friend of mine is Monsieur de Neux, the President of the Philharmonic Society, an amiable man with a nice wife and daughter. I often go to see a certain Mme. de Y., who has a rather insignificant husband, but two charming daughters. It has therefore been a pleasure to be here, and the time has been most agreeably spent. I was invited out somewhere almost every other afternoon and evening. I forgot to mention an Englishman, Mr. Z., who is resident here and owns a large factory. He is intelligent, well-informed, and has a pleasant and beautiful wife. I visited them almost every day. It was much nicer for me this way than having to spend all my time in cafés. The General and his wife have always shown me the greatest kindness. With all his vehemence and his occasional rough manners, the General is a thoroughly kind-hearted man. As a rule a good many people came in the evenings, such as Colonel von Rosenzweig and Major von Koppelow (a Mecklenburg man) of the 28th Regiment, the clever Colonel von Witzendorf, Chief of Staff von Goeben, General Strubberg, our Colonel von Loë, whom the regiment, unfortunately, is going to lose. The most frequent visitor of all is Count Lehndorff, the former Prefect and now Civil Commissioner, who is very kind to me. Unfortunately, his nephew, young Count Fritz Dönhoff, of the 2nd Regiment of Uhlan Guards, a very good friend of mine, has just gone away. But all these people are now leaving little by little. I shall write to you as soon as I hear anything more precise about my own departure. Your obedient son.

In my letter I mentioned Mme. de Y. and her daughters as well as the Englishman, Z., and his wife. I owed my introduction to Mme. de Y. to an excellent Abbé. I have always been fond of discussing religion, provided that both parties observe the maxim which I value so much and emphasise so often: " *In necessariis unitas, in dubiis libertas, in omnibus caritas.*" The good Abbé tried to win me over to his Church. I still possess a Catholic book that was much read in French Catholic circles in those days. It was entitled: " *La Raison du catholicisme par Nicolas, ancien magistrat.*" He hoped more would come of my intercourse with the Y. family, and especially with Mlle. Marie de Y., than this much too wordy and at times rather naïve book. Had one of Heinrich Heine's most beautiful poems not been worn so threadbare by too frequent quotation, I would say of Marie de Y.:

> " *Sie war wie eine Blüme,*
> *So hold und schön und rein.*" [1]

I went for many walks with her and her parents. I was also allowed to accompany her to Mass on Sundays in the magnificent Cathedral at Amiens, which in the splendour and purity of its Gothic style is excelled by few other churches. We stood before the three portals of the church and, hand in hand, admired the groups and images representing the story of the Creation, the Saints and Prophets, the Seasons, the signs of the zodiac, and the professions. The Cathedral at Amiens seemed to me like the sister of Rheims Cathedral. It is indeed hard to say which of the two is the more beautiful. Mlle. Y. took me to the " *beau Dieu*," a Gothic figure, representing God the Father (who is usually depicted as an angry old man) as a mild and benevolent young one. This " *beau Dieu* " could hardly be expected to condemn his creatures to eternal punishment in Hell. The " *beau Dieu* " is the pride of Amiens. I explained to my young friend that the German forest, in which the branches and twigs of neighbouring trees meet and interlace, was the original model of all Gothic cathedrals, including her dear cathedral at Amiens. On the way back from church we talked at length and with animation about religion and religious matters. I made a spirited defence of my Protestant views against the magic of the Catholic liturgy and of the Mass, which is its nucleus, a magic to which I was not unresponsive. But I got no further than " Faust " with his good " Gretchen," who replied to his magnificent confession of faith:

> " *Wenn man's so hört, möcht's leidlich scheinen,*
> *Steht aber doch immer schief darum ;*
> *Denn du hast kein Christentum.*" [2]

In spite of our religious differences, I felt that Marie de Y. was well disposed towards me. But I think I was right in not joining myself to her with an eternal bond. Quite apart from other reasons, I was much too young for such a marriage and much too immature.

---

[1] " She was like a flower, so dear, so beautiful, so pure."
[2] " It seemeth fair in these words of thine,
But yet there is something stands awry,
For thou hast no Christianity."

(*Faust*, i. Trans. A. G. Latham.)

But it was not reasoned considerations of this kind alone that separated me from the dear girl. Titian's best and, in any case his most discussed, picture hangs in the Borghese Gallery at Rome: on the edge of a marble sarcophagus, that serves as a fountain, two women are sitting, one of them clothed, serious and contemplative; the other naked, revealing a superb form, and smiling a mysterious, bewitching smile. A charming boy stretches his arm out into the fountain. The picture is universally known under the name, " *Amore sacro e profano*." If the tender sentiments that bound me to Marie de Y. had the character of *Amore sacro* throughout, I cannot, unfortunately, say the same of my relations with Mrs. Z., relations that were made all the easier because her husband had the excellent idea of leaving Amiens for several weeks and visiting his Scottish home.

As I had not overmuch to do when I was Town Major, I often used to go for rides in the neighbourhood of Amiens. I visited Bussy, Querrieux, Pont-Noyelles and Daours, where we had fought in the winter. I also visited Camon and the peasant's cottage where I was billeted the night before the battle of the Hallue. Julie stood in the doorway, as in the morning of the 23rd December. She recognized me at once, and shook hands with great calm and unconcern. I observed at the first glance that she was in a certain condition. I asked her if I could help her or be of any use to her. She shook her head. Then she told me that she had been married several months, to a farmer, a good fellow. " *Il est un peu rude, mais excellent. Il est bon pour moi, il sera bon pour le mioche, que je vais mettre au monde. C'est un bon gars.*" I asked her if she was angry with me. She again shook her head: " *Nous avons fauté tous les deux.*" I kissed her forehead and rode on, moved, and plunged in grave thoughts. The people, especially country people, are nearer to nature than the educated are. Their feelings are direct, simple and healthy. They are the source from which the upper class, over-educated, sophisticated, sickly with thought's problems, must either derive new vitality from time to time or fade away.

On the 31st May the VIII Army Corps received orders to begin the homewards march. At the same time the King's Hussars Regiment got a piece of news that had been feared and anticipated for a long time. We lost our honoured and beloved Commander, who was entrusted with the leadership of the 21st Cavalry Brigade. The Regimental Orders, in which Colonel von Loë addressed the regiment for the last time, ended with the words: " In the hour of danger and in battle, I have always found you gladly willing to do more than I asked of you, despite hunger and exertion, in cold and ice. For this I thank you, now that I am leaving you, from the depths of my soul. Officers, N.C.O's. and Hussars! When you return to our beloved homeland—I hope it will be soon—and when, in the circle of your families, you call to mind the glorious days of Gravelotte and Boves, of Querrieux and Sapignies, of Bapaume and St. Quentin, do not forget your Colonel, whose greatest pride it is to have lived through those days with you and who will always bear you in faithful memory."

This request of our Colonel's was not really necessary—his image was indelibly imprinted in the breast of all who were under his command in the regiment and in the presence of the enemy.

Baron Walter von Loë was born of the old Rhenish nobility. Everything about him was noble in the best sense of the word. He was a nobleman from tip to toe, but a nobleman without pride of class, without prejudice. He was fondly faithful to his Rhenish home. " I have," he could truly say, " not only been baptized in Rhenish water, I was stilled with Rhenish milk, I am a Rhinelander through and through." But he could not and would not think of the Rhineland as anything other than a Prussian Province, inseparably bound up with the Prussian Monarchy. He was a Prussian to his finger-tips. When the Emperor Frederick, who was very graciously disposed towards him, talked to him once of the time when he was still Crown Prince, of the Imperial splendour of the Middle Ages, and said that the connection between the old German Empire and the new ought to find more outward expression, Loë replied: " Oh, your Imperial Highness, the Imperial dignity is, after all, only a cloak which the King of Prussia has thrown over his shoulders."

In the course of a brilliant military career which he crowned by wielding the marshal's bâton, he was placed before even greater tasks and had ever-growing opportunities of making the remarkable qualities of his downright personality tell. Walter Loë did not compromise in fundamental matters, and yet he was never narrowly exclusive, as Germans too often are. He was not at all obstinate. If a question could not be solved without violence or without a disproportionate risk, he would seek a way out, just as he would look out for a spot where a ditch or hedge could be taken without breaking the neck of rider and horse whenever he reached an impassable ditch or a very high hedge during field drill or a paper chase. He knew no fear, either in the field or in life. He never sacrificed his principles, and yet he was perhaps the only Prussian of high standing who simultaneously possessed the confidence of the old Kaiser and the Crown Princess Victoria, of the Empress Augusta and of Prince Frederick Charles, of the Crown Prince and of Prince William. An intimate friendship of long years' standing united him with the Grand Duchess Louise of Baden.

He was not on good terms with Bismarck. The fault was not his, but lay in the sometimes pathological distrust of the great statesman towards people who, for some reason or other, had aroused his never-sleeping suspicions. After the fall of Prince Bismarck, Loë disapproved of Kaiser William's behaviour towards his grandfather's great servant. " Prince Bismarck," said Loë to me in those days, " should have a place in the Prussian Hall of Glory, together with Frederick the Great and Stein, Blücher and Moltke. Such men should only be approached hats off and not like a boy who throws snowballs at a monument."

Herbert Bismarck wrecked his relationship with Field-Marshal Loë for ever by his behaviour towards Princess Elizabeth Carolath, the Field-Marshal's sister-in-law. " If Herbert Bismarck were not the son of the almighty Chancellor, he would have been summoned before a Court of Honour and would have got a straight dismissal for his behaviour towards Princess Elizabeth. He should in no circumstances have left the Princess in the lurch after he had driven her into divorcing her husband."

This is what Loë told me more than once when I pleaded extenuating circumstances on Herbert Bismarck's behalf. Poor Herbert's innermost feelings corresponded fundamentally with Field-Marshal Loë's stern verdict against him. When he had finally left Princess Elizabeth Carolath in the lurch he wrote to Philip Eulenburg: " I suffer under the overpowering conscious-ness of having betrayed a confidence that was, after all, placed in me and must have been awakened by me! I must continually say to myself that things ought never to have gone thus far. It must be my fault that this has happened! The Princess expected some-thing other of me than I was able to do. How dreadfully it weighs upon me! "

Loë took questions of honour very seriously. No one knew the code of honour as he knew it. Two examples will suffice: During the French campaign, when billeted in the château of a French count in Picardy, Loë, who was then a colonel, carried on the conversation at table with a knowledge of the world that was quite his own. Thereupon the French count allowed himself to be so far carried away as to make an improper remark about the old King of Prussia. Loë got up, left the room, and, through his adjutant, challenged the Frenchman that same evening. When the latter replied that he could not possibly fight a duel with a German officer without exposing himself to the worst reprisals at the hands of the German military authorities, Colonel von Loë sent him a letter to King William the next morning, which he himself had drafted, in which he wrote that as a faithful officer, and adjutant of His Majesty, he begged his Royal Master that he might be graciously pleased to see that not one hair on the Frenchman's head was touched if the latter should, in chivalrous contest, wound or kill von Loë. The French count, when he had received this safe-conduct, called on the Prussian Colonel (being himself a cavalier) and gladly and willingly asked him to forgive the misplaced utterance about King William.

General Loë's attitude in his dispute with the Spanish General Salamanca is better known. The latter had been awarded the Grand Cross of the Order of the Red Eagle when the German Crown Prince, accompanied by von Loë, visited Madrid in 1883. When the Caroline dispute broke out two years later, Salamanca sent the Order to General von Loë (who had, meanwhile, become General Commanding the VIII Army Corps) with an improper letter addressed to the Crown Prince. After he had taken the necessary steps in Berlin, General von Loë sent his Chief of Staff, Colonel von der Planitz, to Madrid with instructions to give the letter back to General Salamanca and quietly, *suaviter in modo, fortiter in re*, enlighten him as to the conception of honour prevailing in the German Officers' Corps and the personal affront offered to von Loë, and, while refusing any *excursus* into the realm of politics and any continuation of the correspondence, to ask for personal satisfaction in accordance with the loyal and chivalrous sentiment of the Spaniard. In case of refusal Planitz was to transmit a challenge to duel with the weapon that was customary in Spain, the sword, and to propose a neutral country, Italy, for example, as duelling ground. General Salamanca, when he met Loë's envoy, Colonel von der Planitz, agreed to everything, took back his letter unreservedly, and declared (as was set down in a protocol in the presence of two witnesses) that he deeply regretted having offended General von Loë by sending him the letter to His Imperial and Royal Highness the Crown Prince. When the Archduke Albert, the victor of Custozza, heard of it, his old soldier's heart rejoiced and he exclaimed: " The chivalrous manner in which Loë had seen this affair through so correctly and energetically increases my respect for him to deep esteem." And Prince Bismarck described General von Loë's action as "right and courageous."

Loë was a true son of the Catholic Church, and did not conceal his convictions, least of all during the *Kulturkampf*. When the Jesuits were expelled from Germany he entrusted his only son to the educational institute, Stella Matutina, at Feldkirch, which was run by the Jesuits. " I used not to appreciate the Jesuits very much," he said, " but now that they are persecuted and banished, I would like to leave no room for doubt about my loyalty to the Church." But even in his relations with the ecclesiastical authorities he always and in every situation remained a Prussian General and a noble. When Field-Marshal von Loë was very advanced in years, a Rhenish nobleman, the Chamberlain von S., was compelled to challenge another gentleman of the Rhenish nobility to a duel. The Archbishop of Cologne declared that if a duel were fought he would proceed both against the duellers and against the seconds with ecclesiastical penalties. Thereupon Field-Marshal von Loë informed the Archbishop that he himself would second Herr von S., and would calmly wait and see whether the Archbishop would excommunicate him. Religious differences were hateful to him, and he would not tolerate them in the army. He was fond of quoting an utterance of General von Petery, who was commandant of Spandau under Frederick William IV and was well known for his original remarks. Petery was a Catholic, his wife a Protestant. When his wife asked him to which church she ought to go on the King's birthday, to the Protestant or the Catholic, the worthy husband answered: " It doesn't matter which of the two Gods you pray to, Minna, it's all the same, as long as you pray fervently for His Majesty."

Field-Marshal von Loë had a great influence upon me in every way. In one of the last conversations he had with me in the spring of 1871, when he was still regimental commander and on the point of leaving for Frankfort, he expressed the hope that I would stay in the Army. He advised me to study Clausewitz. " His book about war and the conduct of war is to soldiers what the *Corpus Juris* is to Jurists and the Bible to theologians." And when I was Imperial Chancellor he said half seriously and half in jest: " I would rather have seen you Minister of War or Chief of the Military Cabinet, but most of all I would have liked you to be commander of our old regiment first."

On the 1st June our regiment began the homeward march on the Rhine under the temporary command of Major von Dincklage. On 4th June I wrote to my parents:

The homeward march is now beginning along the whole line. Two Corps will defile through Amiens: the 8th, which, for the most part, was stationed between here and Abbeville, and the 1st, stationed at Rouen and Dieppe. The High Command will be dissolved and the Command of the 8th Army Corps (General Barnekow) will be replaced by the Command of the 1st Army Corps (General Bentheim). For this reason I have quite a lot to do, and more to write than usual. I have orders to stay here until the 7th of the month and then to follow the regiment. But General Ruville will speak with Goeben and ask if he can keep me here a few days longer, seeing that the whole Department of the Somme will hardly be occupied much longer. And this is quite agreeable as long as I can reach my regiment in time for the triumphal entry into Bonn. But there is no danger that I shall not, for the homeward march will certainly last three weeks.

On one occasion General von Barnekow gave me a lecture that was not only thoroughly justified, but also useful to me for the rest of my life. I had accompanied General von Ruville and his wife to church. When the hymns began Frau von Ruville asked me to get her a hymn book, as she had forgotten hers. I went over to a sturdy musketeer, asked him for his hymn book, and gave it to the General's wife. Thereupon the General von Barnekow said to me with a stern expression: " Give that man back his book. He has just as much right to a hymn book as the beautiful wife of your General." Frau von Ruville was indeed a stately and beautiful lady. Her maiden name was Baroness von Bülow-Stolle, and when she was young she was lady-in-waiting at the Court of Strelitz. The General was much older than she was. He was morose, whereas she was cheerful and gay. It was not surprising that a few years later, when they had left Amiens, she separated from her husband and married a young diplomat.

Before we began the homeward march I had to part from my good Grete. I did not want to expose the bay mare who had carried me so faithfully through the war and had suffered rather in the winter campaign, to the hardships of the march. I left her to Monsieur de Y., who promised me that she would have a good home. No one, he said, would ride her except his daughter. Marie de Y. looked very pretty when she drove her Tilbury with the bay mare, who had been trained by a French stable master. My good father enabled me to buy two other horses. One of them was originally French, and had been captured by a Ulhan. It was a very hardy and efficient animal. The other was a beautiful black mare, a thoroughbred and very elegant. Beyond this, as an officer, I had a right to an army horse, so that I was well provided.

On 12th June I wrote to my parents from Antheny in the Ardennes:

> I left Amiens on Friday morning. On Thursday the General gave me a little farewell dinner and a very friendly and very flattering toast. In fact, he has always been most kind to me, and so has Frau von Ruville. My successor is a certain Herr von der Goltz, Lieutenant of the 10th Dragoons. I was really very sorry to leave Amiens, where I had very pleasant acquaintances, although I must say that I like marching too. In any case, it is healthier to be in the fresh air than to do nothing but write. I have joined the 3rd Squadron with Herr von Böselager (our squadron chief) and two other officers, Jägow and Schrader. I know all three very well, so that we get on splendidly. I went by train to St. Quentin, and from there we marched on via Guise and Vervins, two small and rather nice towns. The Ardennes, where we are now, are a very beautiful district, something like the Harz: many hills, valleys, little rivers and, now and again, ruins of châteaux and monasteries that were destroyed in the revolution. The weather is quite summery. Marching is only pleasant in the morning, after eleven it gets too hot. Our route is Mézières, Sedan, Thionville, Treves. We shall probably have to march as far as Bonn. It is a great pity that in this way we shall see nothing of the triumphal entry into Berlin. But what is the use of complaining?

I took good care not to write to my parents about my leave-taking from Mrs. Z.—a leavetaking that had been very tearful at least on her part. Nor did I write that I very nearly came off badly in an incident that occurred in the train between Amiens and St. Quentin. Perhaps it was because I was so upset by the previous night's farewell to the charming Mrs. Z., that I fell into such a deep sleep that I forgot to get out at St. Quentin. Meanwhile three or four French travellers had entered my compartment at St. Quentin. They did not look at me in a very friendly manner when I woke up at last. They pointed out that I was on French soil which had been evacuated by our troops and was therefore forbidden to Prussian officers, especially those wearing uniform. I replied politely but firmly that the Prussian troops, who were still stationed at Amiens, knew of my departure. If anything happened to me during the journey satisfaction would be demanded not only of the French Government and the railway management, but things would be also made unpleasant for the passengers in this train. After this categorical statement there was a friendly conversation, ending with the pleasant wish that war would not come again so soon. When we came to the next big station, where the public on the platform received me with booing and hooting, I spoke in the same polite, firm manner to the station-master, who understood the situation at once and took me into his room to protect me against all molestation until he could send me back to St. Quentin in an empty first-class compartment of a train going that way, under the special care of the conductors.

On 19th June I wrote to my parents from Bazeilles, near Montmédy:

I do hope that Mamma and my little brothers enjoyed the triumphal entry of the troops in Berlin. We had lovely weather on the 16th. I hope it was fine in Berlin too. We did not get any news about events in Berlin, but I am sure it was magnificent. That we, with all our patriotism, were not able to see anything at all was really a shame. Apparently we are to march as far as Bonn. The marching route to Treves has already been issued. The Meuse enclosed by wooded heights reminds me of north German mountain landscapes. A year ago a novel by G. Sand appeared as a serial in the *Indépendence Belge*. The plot is laid in these parts and the Meuse landscape, through which we have been marching ever since we left Mézières, are very well described in the novel.

On 4th June I wrote from Leinbach in the Eifel:

We have been marching all the time since I wrote you last. From the frontier we went over the Hunsrück to Treves. We crossed the Saar at Conz, where it joins the Moselle. We entered Treves in the streaming rain. The town was beautifully decorated. Prussian flags waved from all houses, there were garlands everywhere and busts of the King and of the Princes. There was a great Germania at the gates, and further inside the town there was a column symbolizing the town itself. The ladies of Treves gave us many wreaths and flowers, but we would willingly have done without them if we could have got better quarters. I was detached from my unit and sent to Metzdorf, a little village close by the Sauer, a rivulet dividing Luxemburg from Prussia. The Luxemburgers are very French, and they shouted abuse at us from across the river, which is only about twenty-five feet wide.

The next day, a day of rest, I employed looking at Treves

with my friend Schrader. Treves is wonderfully situated in the Moselle valley. The Moselle, which flows through it, is fairly wide even here. We admired the Porta Nigra, a strong fortress dating back to Roman times. In the last century the Porta was turned into two chapels in Rococo style. One has been pulled down, but the other exists, at least in part. The arabesques and curves à la Louis XIV look more than usually conspicuous on the Roman façade. We also visited the Roman Baths, which are splendid, but have fallen into decay. In any case the Roman bathing arrangements were better than ours, judging by the great rotunda which is now overgrown with grass and ivy. The Basilica is also said to have been built by the Romans, in fact by Constantine the Great. Its architecture is certainly Roman, but the church itself looks so new that it seemed improbable to us that the Romans could have built it. The former Electoral palace, in renaissance style, is in the neighbourhood, and so is the cathedral which, although very old (dating back to the time of Valentinian I), is rather insignificant. The Hotel Maison Rouge, in which we had dinner, was also noteworthy. It used to be the Town Hall, and still bears the proud inscription proclaiming that Treves stood a thousand years before Rome. Thus Treves is certainly one of the most remarkable towns in Germany, and it was very nice to have had a chance of seeing it.

After leaving Treves we marched through the Eifel. The district is pretty, but pitiably poor. Nevertheless, all the villages received us with flags and fired small mortars. We passed through some very pretty scenery, particularly Manderscheid, with its two picturesque ruins, châteaux that used to belong to the princely family of Salm and were destroyed in the Revolution in 1793. To-day we passed two lakes, which are said to have been the craters of a volcano at one time, in fact the whole of the Eifel is volcanic. To-morrow we shall pass the Ahr Valley, and the day after to-morrow, that is to say, 6th July, we shall enter Bonn. On 2nd November I left Bonn, from Courcelles near Metz, we marched via Metz, Varennes, Reims, Soissons, Compiègne, Montdidier, Moreuil, Amiens to Rouen and Pont Audemer, from Rouen back to Montdidier, from there via Amiens, Albert, Bapaume to Cambrai and then Péronne back to Bray, from Bray to St. Quentin and from there back to Bapaume, from there via Amiens and Mollien-Vidame to Gaille Fontaine and Tréport, from Tréport and Eu to Abbeville, and from there to Amiens, from there to Chaulnes and Péronne and back to Amiens, and from there via St. Quentin, Guise, Vervins,

Mézières, Sedan, Montmédy, Longwy, Thionville, Sierk, Trèves, and back to Bonn at last. During the last few days it has been raining almost all the time, but to-day the weather improved. I shall write to you again as soon as I get to Bonn, and of course, I shall see if I cannot get a little leave. I am quartered here with my detachment in two villages near the little town of Adenar. I have got a very good billet with a most robust old man of eighty-five. He was born as a subject of Count Salm in what was then the county of Salm. He went through the Napoleonic invasions, and from 1810 to 1814 he served in Spain with the 37ième de Ligne. Excuse my bad handwriting and the dirty paper. Your faithful son.

Just as in Treves we were welcomed by big and small, rich and poor, with the same joy and the same heartiness throughout the whole of our march back from the German frontier to the River Rhine in every town and village. I thought of the " Springtime Welcome," which was written fifty-six years previously by one of the noblest German poets, the singer of the war of liberation, Max von Schenkendorf. The poem, entitled " To the Fatherland."

> " *Alles ist in Grün gekleidet,*
> *Alles strahlt im jungen Licht,*
> *Anger, wo die Herde weidet,*
> *Hügel, wo man Trauben bricht ;*
> *Vaterland, in tausend Jahren*
> *Kam dir solch ein Frühling kaum,*
> *Was die hohen Väter waren,*
> *Heisset mimmermehr ein Traum.*" [1]

On 6th July I wired to my mother, who was at Flottbek : " Entered Bonn to-day. Very well. Very best wishes." On 11th July I wrote from Godesberg to my mother:

DEAREST MAMA,

A thousand thanks for your dear, kind letters. I need hardly tell you that I shall do everything I can to get leave as soon as possible. It will not be easy, but I hope to get it, although everybody is wanting leave just now, and in such matters priority of age always counts. I shall ride to Bonn this afternoon and speak to the Major. I shall ask for six weeks, but I do not

---

[1] " All is clothed in green, all is shining in the young light, fields where the herds pasture, hills where grapes are plucked. Fatherland, in a thousand years such a spring hardly came to thee. What our exalted fathers were can nevermore be called a dream."

suppose he will give me more than four. As I said, I need hardly promise to do everything I can to get as much leave as possible and as soon as possible. We have been in Bonn since 6th July. Our reception was very fine, deputations and carriages came to meet us a mile from the town. The town itself is abundantly adorned with flowers, flags, garlands, and fairy lights. All the streets were crowded with people, and we got many garlands and bouquets. I did not hear much of the official speeches, as I am with the 3rd Squadron, and we rode three deep. After the procession through the streets, which ended amid much firing and even more shouting, our squadron proceeded to Godesberg, where we are to stay a fortnight until the barracks at Bonn are put in order. I am billeted in the best hotel and live very pleasantly. Godesberg is a beautiful place, a mile from Bonn and opposite the Seven Mountains. Rich people from Cologne and Elberfeld have beautiful villas there, and there are many foreigners, particularly Dutchmen. The squadron is now being commanded by the new Captain Count Galen, who is very nice. He is a nephew of Bishop Ketteler, of Mainz, and before the war he served in the Papal Zouaves at Rome. On the 6th we had a big dinner at the casino in Bonn, and in the evening the hussars had a banquet. Afterwards the town was illuminated in a really beautiful manner and there was a great firework display in the square in front of the Town Hall. On Friday we had a day of rest as on Catholic holidays. On Saturday the town gave the Officers' Corps a big dinner in the Beethoven Hall, where many speeches were made and everybody was very cheerful. I am content to remain in Godesberg for the time being, as I have nowhere to live in Bonn as yet. It is very difficult to find quarters that are good and not too dear there. Please be assured that I shall do everything I possibly can to get leave soon and see you all again at Flottbek. Best wishes from your devoted son.

On 20th July, 1871, I joined my parents at Klein-Flottbek, and on the day of my return my father entered the following words in his Bible: " God gave him safe return. May He guard and bless the life of our eldest son which He in His mercy preserved throughout this campaign. How can we thank Him enough for blessing his decision so richly, but it was so courageous, and so resolutely carried out and doubly honourable because of his ailing condition, that He has fortified his health and graciously watched over him in battles, difficulties, in the cold of winter, and in danger, given him joy and recognition and to-day granted his return to the place of his birth, to the home from which he went forth into this sanguinary war. We will commend him to God and never forget the mercy He has shown us." On the envelope in which he collected the letters I had written during the campaign, my father wrote: " For the good angel shall keep him company, and his journey shall be prosperous, and he shall return safe" (Tobit, v, 22).

CHAPTER XIX

Lieutenant at Bonn—Preparations for the Law Examination at Greifswald—Prince Franz Arenberg—Chaplain Hartmann—Overwork and Fainting Fit—Professor Wilhelm Studemund—Professor Ernst Immanuel Bekker—Beginning of the " Kulturkampf "—Law Examination at Greifswald (March, 1872)—Pasewalk—Decision to Enter the Diplomatic Service—Leave Taking of the Regiment— At Home in Klein-Flottbek—From Klein-Flottbek to Metz.

AT Klein-Flottbek, in the same villa in the park by the Elbe in which I am dictating these lines, I had a long conversation with my father soon after my arrival. He asked me when I intended entering for my law examination. When I hesitated to give an answer (not because I feared the examination, but because behind his question I instinctively felt his wish that I should do the opposite of the first rifleman in Wallenstein's Camp, and exchange the musket for the pen) my father told me that, in response to my urgent wish, when I went to the front he had empowered me to remain in the army with a view to getting a commission. He had agreed to this on condition that I would subsequently pass my law examination. When I pointed out that I had only studied for five terms, including one term at Lausanne, that is to say abroad, he replied with a kind smile that he had anticipated this objection and had obtained the necessary dispensation for me by consulting the Prussian Ministry of Justice. He ended in a decisive tone: " My dear Bernhard, I expect you to pass your law examination, and pass it with flying colours. You can amuse yourself in Bonn during the summer."

The summer in Bonn was indeed magnificent. Every German who has stood upon the Alte Zoll with the Rhine at his feet, before him the picturesque Seven Mountains, and next to the bronze statue of the old and trusty Ernst Moritz Arndt, will understand me. The summer sun was radiant in the sky, the hearts of the men were beating joyfully after the victorious campaign, the eyes of the women shone with greater lustre and beauty than ever before. The Blue Hussars realised this when they rode up and down the chestnut-bordered Poppelsdorfer Allee, where our regimental band used to play in the afternoons.   Ah! the beautiful summer evenings by the Rhine in the Kleyschen Garden near the Coblence Gate or in the pleasant park of the Royal Hotel, where, gazing upon the German river, we drank " *Schorle-Morle*," a delicious mixture of Moselle and soda water.

The delightful surroundings enticed us to make long cross-country tramps as well as dashing rides on horseback.   We ascended the high tower of Godesberg Castle which, built in the thirteenth century on the site of a Roman Fort by the Archbishop of Cologne, was stormed and destroyed by Bavarian troops in the confusions of the sixteenth century.   The view from the top, upon the mountains and the plain, was extensive and beautiful.   Within the walls of Godesberg was the peaceful God's Acre of the village.   I was so enchanted by the Rhine that I wished I could be buried in Godesberg Cemetery.   We wandered to Plittersdorf, and there in the Schaumburger Hof, ate excellent cream cheese, which was called " *Makey*." We stayed at Waldporzheim and fortified ourselves at the St. Peter and the St. Joseph with the famous strong red wine.   At Altenahr, in Winkler's garden on the banks of the Ahr, we were fond of eating " *Rumpchen*," a small fish prepared raw in vinegar.   And with more solemn thoughts, we walked up to the Apollinaris Church which, visible from afar, rises from the steep declivity of the slatey rock.   The Emperor Barbarossa wanted to transfer the head of St. Apollinaris, the revered Bishop of Ravenna, to Cologne, but when the ship, guided by a mysterious power, stood still with the precious relic opposite Remagen in mid stream, a church was built in the neighbourhood, and the relic was shown there.   The commonplace obtruded near the scene of this pretty legend—the Apollinaris springs, the waters of which were brought into fashion by the Prince of Wales, who afterwards became King Edward VII, and also started the fashion in round Homburg hats.   The Apollinaris Company, Limited, exports many millions of bottles yearly.

We ascended the Kreuzberg church from where, looking northwards, one can view the whole of the Rhine Valley, pleasant villages and hamlets, Bensberg with its cadet school in the old castle, which produced excellent men, like the Minister of Labour Hermann Budde, who died in 1906, the Bergische region and in the background the great and stately city of Cologne with its eternal cathedral.   Even more magnificent was the view from the Drachenfels of the Rhenish plain and the Eifel, the finest view along the whole of the Rhine, a view that enchanted Childe Harold almost as much as did the Castle of Chillon on the shore of the lake of Geneva, and St. Peter's in Rome:

> " The castled crag of Drachenfels
> Frowns o'er the wide and winding Rhine,
> Whose breast of waters broadly swells
> Between the banks which bear the vine;
> And hills all rich with blossom'd trees,
> And fields which promise corn and wine,
> And scatter'd cities crowning these,
> Whose far white walls along them shine,
> Have strew'd a scene, which I should see
> With double joy were thou with me."[1]

When we wanted to cross over to the right bank of the Rhine we used the ferry that passed slowly to and fro across the river, for in those days no bridge spanned the Rhine at Bonn. We visited Heisterbach, a former monastery of the venerable Cistercians, who founded the Mecklenburg cloisters, Doberan and Rhena, which for centuries were connected with my family. Over the gate of Heisterbach was the monastery's coat of arms, a " Heister," that is a young beech, St. Benedict of Nursia, and St. Bernard of Clairvaux standing guardians over it.

" *An den Rhein, an den Rhein, zieh nicht an den Rhein.*" [2]

Thus sang Carl Josef Simrock, a child of Bonn, and my comrades and I agreed with him. By the way, I would not like to give the impression that I only " amused myself " at Bonn in the summer of 1871. In the mornings there was some stiff drill under our new Commander, Prince Henry XIII Reuss, and my Captain, Count Wilderich Galen, would stand no nonsense while we were on duty. All my life I have taken pleasure in some such regular occupation, as I had in those days, within a cadre of serious military duties and with comrades who felt as I did. " *Nulla dies sine linea* " is one of the foundations of my existence. When after my resignation, the days, which had passed so swiftly for decades in the hurry of urgent business, seemed to grow long, I arranged my work according to a programme that embraced wide realms of history, of economics, and of literature. By regularly carrying out this plan I have not only satisfied my desire for activity, but have also opened new horizons and so have fortified my tendency towards the objective contemplation of men and things.

When Lieutenant Bernhard von Bülow galloped along the riding track of the Poppelsdorfer Allee in the afternoons, he may have passed the university tutor, Georg von Hertling, who was six years

---

[1] Quoted in English.
[2] Don't go to live on the Rhine, on the Rhine, on the Rhine!

his senior. Neither suspected that they would sit opposite one another in the Reichstag for twelve years, that the younger would become German Chancellor at the turn of the century, and the elder seventeen years later. In those days I did not even know Herr von Hertling by sight. But I do remember the measured gait and the solemn demeanour of the historian Heinrich von Sybel. He was accounted ambitious, and the students laughed over a couplet composed about him by one of his colleagues: " *Minster wär' nicht übel! So denkt der Herr von Sybel.*" [1]

In September, 1871, I had a rather serious attack of dysentery after the swimming exercise in the Rhine on horseback and in uniform. I was able to return to duty soon, but my father urged me more than ever to pass my law examination. The question now was where to pass it. Amongst my regimental comrades there was hardly one whom I had liked better from the very first than Lieutenant Prince Franz Arenberg. He was to become one of the truest friends I ever had in my life. The House of Arenberg, which received the title of Count of the Empire from the Emperor Charles V, and the rank of Prince of the Empire and subsequently of Duke, from the Emperor Maximilian II, had precedence over all other noble Houses at every German Court. The ancestor of the House, Hartmann von Arenberg, Hereditary Burgrave and Protector of Cologne, fell in battle with the unbelievers as far back as the eleventh century. The family device was " *Christus Protector Meus.*" And the family always remained unshakably faithful to the Catholic Church. Franz Arenberg's mother was descended from the Merode family, which, proud of its descent from the Counts of Barcelona and the Kings of Aragon, disdained to use the princely title of Rubempré and Grimberghe (which had been conferred upon it in the nineteenth century) and wore the device " *Plus d'Honneur que d'Honneurs.*" Franz Arenberg's parents spent the winters in Brussels and the summers in their beautiful country seat on the Meuse not far from Namur. François Arenberg spoke French fluently, almost more fluently than German. But together with his younger brother Jean, he had volunteered to fight for Germany in the war against France, and was a good German and Prussian. He was a true son of the Catholic Church and without any intolerance, one of the kindest and most lovable people I ever met. He was always merry, there was always a joke on his lips, and yet he was industrious and full of knowledge. And he was, above all, an upright and noble character. Even to the present day I regret that I never succeeded in persuading Wilhelm II,

---

[1] " To be a Minister wouldn't be bad, so Herr von Sybel thinks."

who had a wholly unjustified dislike of Franz Arenberg, to appoint him Prussian Ambassador at the Vatican or German Ambassador in Paris or Vienna, positions which, in my opinion, he would have filled admirably. So he had to be content with doing estimable service to his country, to the Government, and to me, his old friend, as an influential member of the Centre Party, particularly as Rapporteur for the Foreign Office Budget.

Once, when I was out riding with Arenberg in the autumn of 1871, he told me that he intended getting several months' leave so as to pass his law examination. After having studied law for six terms, and worked hard at it, too, he wanted to achieve this reward. He said he thought of finding as quiet a place as possible with no social duties to keep him from his work. For this purpose he suggested going to Greifswald. When I objected that Greifswald was the most boring place imaginable, he replied " that is just what I am looking for. Come to Greifswald with me! Haven't you got to pass your law examination as well?" I may add that my derogatory judgment of Greifswald was too hasty and unjust. 1 was soon able to become convinced that Greifswald, situated in very pleasant surroundings, was one of those typical university towns in which quiet and fruitful intellectual activities flourish, a town in which I was to make the acquaintance of able and intellectual men.

I made a last attempt to avoid the law examination altogether, all the more so as I was greatly enjoying the officers' riding lessons which I had begun in October. We rode on English saddles without stirrups. I was able to confirm the experience I had made when I was at school at Neustrelitz, namely that nothing is more conducive to a firm seat and a light hand (the two conditions of good riding) than riding on a blanket or, better still, on an English saddle without stirrups. But my father remained implacable, and I went to Greifswald in November.

My friend Arenberg arrived there before I did and was accompanied by the chaplain of the Arenberg family, Hartmann, afterwards Canon Hartmann, who was his tutor, and had been with him at Bonn. The chaplain was, like his pupil, a very amiable man—full of knowledge, modest, severe towards himself, kind and considerate towards others. He had attended lectures in law at Bonn with his pupil, and in this way become an able jurist. When I arrived at Greifswald he put me through a little examination, the result of which horrified him. " For God's sake," he said, " you have no idea of all the things they will ask you about. You will want at least another year's work before you can risk being examined." I replied that this was out of the question, as I had promised my father that I would pass my examination, and pass it well, in the coming winter.

So I started work. The wisdom of the Indians says: "He who knows all is truly blessed, he who knows nothing can be helped, but he who has only half-knowledge cannot be helped by Brahma himself." That half knowledge is dangerous in politics as in everything else was proved by not a few amateurish Cabinet Ministers after the collapse and in the days of the Republic. Their goodwill and industry were undeniable, nevertheless, they failed in office. At Greifswald I belonged to the second category—I knew nothing of what I needed for my examination, so that I had to make every effort. I got up regularly at five in the morning and worked without a break from six to twelve. I lunched with Arenberg and Hartmann at the table d'hôte in the Deutche Haus. The old-fashioned, homely table d'hôte flourished at Greifswald just as it did at Oeynhausen in 1870. From two to three I talked over what I had studied in the morning with Arenberg and Hartmann. I cannot say enough in praise of the patience with which Chaplain Hartmann, more than anyone else, awakened and developed my knowledge of law and of the related subjects that I needed for my examination.

I used to go out riding from three to five in all weathers, even when there was a snowstorm or sheet ice. I had taken my black mare with me to Greifswald. I usually rode to Eldena, a place situated at the mouth of the little River Ryk. I was attracted not so much by its agricultural school as by the ruins of a Cistercian Monastery destroyed by the Swedes in the Thirty Years' War. The foundation of Greifswald had proceeded from this monastery. The Baltic could be seen from Eldena. Not far from the agricultural school was a grove with gigantic beeches. The people of Greifswald said that this grove was a splendid sight in summer. When I got back to my modest quarters after my wintry ride, I began work again, and, except for an interval for a frugal supper, I usually worked on to midnight. I drank strong tea to keep me awake. I worked about twelve hours and slept hardly five.

I continued this foolishness for eight weeks when, one Sunday, after I had attended divine service in the Marien Kirche (its beautiful pulpit of carved wood was famous in the whole district of Stralsund), I was seized by a severe fainting fit in my room. It happened exactly like the fainting fit I had in the Reichstag nearly thirty-five years later. And the cause was the same—too much work and too little sleep. At Greifswald I fainted in my own little room, and

not in the presence of the representatives of the German people
and crowded galleries, so no fuss was made over the little incident.
I set to work again, after a few days' rest, but took two evenings
off every week. These evenings I used to call on the professors,
with whom I was on friendly terms, and sometimes to play billiards
with the charming officers of the Jäger Battalion. Prince Bismarck
had completed his military service as a one year's volunteer in the
Second Pomeranian Jäger Battalion, at Greifswald, while he studied
at the Agricultural Academy in Eldena at the same time.

I prepared for the examination in my own way. A legal
compendium (the author, if I remember rightly, was named
Bender) guided me like Ariadne's thread through the juridical
labyrinth. With the help of independent thought as well as of
this thin thread, I groped my way through the brushwood of laws
and rights which, as that cynic Mephistopheles observes, drags on
like an eternal disease from generation to generation. When I
could make no further progress alone I sought and found a guide
in the kind Chaplain Hartmann. Of the university professors two
have remained in agreeable memory.

The theologian, Wilhelm Studemund, was a man of unusual
vitality and sparkling intellect. When he began to talk all were
silent (whether at the table d'hôte or during supper) so as not to
miss a word he said. Later on he was transferred from Greifswald
to Strassburg, and from there to Breslau, where he died in 1889,
at scarcely forty-six years of age, when he might still have served
the science which he had enriched by deciphering the palimpsests
of Cajus and Plautus. Professor Ernst Immanuel Bekker made
an even deeper impression upon me. He was over forty when I
made his acquaintance at Greifswald. He died half a century
later, in the summer of 1916, at a very old age. Theodor Mommsen
wrote a distich in his honour when he was seventy.

" *Der Epaulett und Talar verstanden mit Ehren zu tragen:*
Welcher kundig des Rechts dennoch Lateinisch versteht;
Tapfer und klug und beredt, aber den Freunden ein Freund." [1]

As early as 1872 Ernst Immanuel Bekker could look back
upon a varied and interesting life. He was a son of the theologian,
August Immanuel Bekker, who was born in the reign of Frederick
the Great, and died only a few days before the return of the troops
after the war of 1870. After reading the pandects under Karl

---

[1] Who understood how to wear epaulettes and surplice with honour,
   Who, though learned in law, nevertheless understands Latin,
   Brave, clever and eloquent, but a friend to his friends.

Adolph Vangerow, he became officer of the line, and was adjutant of a reserve battalion during the mobilization of 1850. Whenever he spoke of that period he used to add that the weakness and confusion of Prussian politics in those days only increased his gratitude towards Bismarck and, " if possible," his reverence for him. He used to be fond of emphasizing that the conceptions of honour and rank held by Prussian officers had always determined his whole attitude towards life.

While he was in the army he made friends with Count Karl Bismarck-Bohlen, and worked under Otto von Bismarck-Schön-hausen for nearly a year in the Foreign Office, and remained his faithful and devoted admirer ever afterwards. But this did not prevent him from recognising the faults and mistakes of the great statesman. The biggest of these mistakes was, in Bekker's opinion, the introduction of universal suffrage. He wrote as far back as the seventies, " we shall not have to wait a hundred years until everybody will wonder how Bismarck, our great and universally honoured Bismarck, could bring such a thing upon us." Well, Bismarck was only human, after all. And I now remember very well how my friend, Karl Bismarck, said, when I expressed my doubts, that his great cousin had only done it on account of the little Princes, since now they would have to learn how to dance. For this purpose he needed the masses, whom he would dispose of in his own time. He made the same mistake in the *Kulturkampf*. Bekker was a strict Conservative in the old Prussian sense of the term, but he never allowed even his party to rob him of his own individuality and originality. He thought it understandable that the Conservatives should oppose Bismarck when, in the first five years after the re-establishment of the Empire, he followed paths that were economically and politically liberal. But he deplored the fact that certain Conservative politicians allowed themselves to make unworthy personal imputations against the great Minister. Many years later, in 1909, Ernst Immanuel Bekker called the opposition of the Conservatives against the Moderate Death Duties, proposed by myself, and against the necessary reform of the Prussian electoral laws which I had taken in hand at the same time, " ungrateful and unpolitical as well." He had also foreseen and foretold the harmful consequences which these tactics would have for the Conservative party itself and unfortunately for Prussian Germany also.

At Greifswald I experienced the beginnings of the *Kultur-kampf*. On the 18th January, 1872, the first anniversary of the Proclamation of the German Empire was celebrated at a beer-party, in which people from all circles of the town, especially the university professors, took part. During the day, the news arrived that the Minister of Education, von Mühler, had been dismissed. The joy was great. A new and beautiful day is dawning, so they said. The sun of enlightenment, thought and freedom was supposed to have arisen over Germany. Only Chaplain Hartmann shook his head. " It is not for the Church," he said to me as, after the festivities, we went home across the market, with its gabled houses, and passed the Town Hall, " that I am anxious, it is for our German Fatherland. The Catholic Church has survived far worse storms than this, and will survive the quarrel about infallibility which the Liberals exaggerate so stupidly. The Old Catholics are a handful of leaves that fall down from the oak. They do not mean much. But as our whole history teaches, there is hardly anything more dangerous for Germany than religious strife. In the end only Radicals can profit by it." The worthy man was right. The Radicals applauded Bismarck when he opened the campaign against the Catholic Church, but they very soon left him in the lurch.

> " *Doch, ach! Schon auf des Weges Mitte*
> *Verloren die Begleiter sich,*
> *Sie wandten treulos ihre Schritte,*
> *Und einer nach dem andern wich.*" [1]

A well-known democrat, Professor Virchow, coined the phrase about the *Kulturkampf* in the election programme of the Party of Progress in 1873. But not long afterwards the leader of the Progressives, Eugen Richter, concluded election pacts with the Centre wherever he could. The Socialists, the most embittered enemies of the Catholic Church in all Catholic countries, have always striven, both before and even after the collapse of the Empire, to hold the stirrups for the Centre Party in Germany, and the Centre is always ready to requite this service. How could our great Bismarck make such a mistake? Because he understood neither the Catholic religion nor the Vatican. When the fight against the Church was impending, Pius IX's clever, experienced, and quite unprejudiced Secretary of State, Cardinal Antonelli, said to a German Protestant Prince who was visiting him: " I do not understand Prince Bismarck. How can this great statesman make such a mistake? He will not do us any harm. It is very sad that the Pope has lost the Papal States, but this injustice which we have suffered has made us quite unassailable. If Bismarck allows

---

[1] But alas, even mid-way the companions dispersed. They turned their steps faithlessly and one after the other went back.

himself to be so carried away as to victimize our clergy and to persecute our Church in Germany, he will do us good, rather than harm. After all, we have a certain experience in these things and have been persecuted many times in many countries. We know the German Catholics particularly well. Measures, such as those planned by Bismarck, will revive both the zeal of the faithful in Germany and their love for their Shepherd, so that religion can only be fortified and deepened. How can so great a man as Bismarck make such a mistake? *Che peccato!* " Giacomo Antonelli came from the robber stronghold, Sonnino, in the Sabine mountains. He was the son of a neat-herd. He had the clear, sober, elastic, realistic mind that has guided the Vatican through many storms for fifteen hundred years, and had also built up that modern Italy which survives our proud Bismarckian Empire.

Kurd von Schlözer told me in January, 1886, that when he was sent to Rome by Bismarck in 1882, so as to prepare the path for peace with the Vatican, he drank *vino di Orvieto* as he sat in front of a wooden table in an Osteria one fine afternoon with some Prelates who were friends of his. The Prelates sparkled with wit and intelligence, and he said to them: " If Bismarck had drunk *vino di Orvieto* with you just once in the Roman Campagna and had chatted frankly, he would never have committed such a blunder as the *Kulturkampf*." The Prelates smiled, and the oldest monsignore put his hand on Schlözer's shoulder and said: " *Questo bravo ministro di Prussia non è mica un minchione.*" (This excellent Prussian Ambassador is not so stupid after all.) Bismarck was still less a " *minchione* " than Schlözer, but as a rule the things he completely understood were only those he had seen with his own eyes. Abstractions, or the sayings of other people, or what he read did not convince him. Besides, who can ever really succeed? A melancholy question, in which Fate is disguised. Even the greatest men have made mistakes, bad mistakes, but they differ from fools in so far as they do not cling to their mistakes, but pass from error back to truth, so that—to use one of Bismarck's favourite expressions—they can turn the cart before it goes over the precipice.

The public excitement of the *Kulturkampf* did not distract my friend Arenberg and myself from our work. We both worked very hard and sat for our examination in the middle of March, 1872. My impression was much the same as that which I had five years previously at Halle, when I matriculated, and when I took my diplomatic examination later on, namely, that State examinations are not a very sure criterion of the knowledge and attainments of the examinee. My dear Arenberg was a better jurist than I.

But, as I was more skilful in argument and in attack (or what Schopenhauer would call " eristics ") I did better than he did. My examination by Professor E. I. Bekker was more like a debate than an examination. The great jurist who had already given a very favourable report on my written reply to a question relating to lien, examined me with so much brilliance and, at the same time, with such benevolence in the *viva voce*, that all I had to do was to show a certain presence of mind in catching the balls that were thrown at me. It was stated in my certificate, after I had passed the examination, that the law student, Lieutenant Bernhard von Bülow, of Flottbek, had passed with the mark " Good," a mark that was not often given in those days. Arenberg had to be content with " satisfactory." The chairman of the Board of Examiners, the President of the Court of Appeal, Albrecht, and my kind patron, Professor Ernst Immanuel Bekker, expressed the hope that I would take up law as a career, a career that, to Germany's disadvantage, was chosen all too rarely by young men of the nobility, whereas in France, the judge's robe was considered equal to the officer's sword.

The day after our examination Arenberg and I left the good town of Greifswald, which I never saw again. In this way, I only got to see one of the two great sights of the town. These two curiosities were the Croy Carpet and the Swedish Major. The Carpet, which was kept in the University, was a sixteenth century Gobelin representing Luther preaching before the Pomeranian Electoral Family. Unhappily, this Carpet was shown only once every ten years, and had last been exhibited in the spring of 1871. Thus, we would have had to wait ten more years to see it, and this we were not prepared to do. But we did see a second curiosity of Greifswald, the Swedish Major. It is known that Greifswald and New Pomerania were under Swedish sovereignty from 1648 to 1815. " The Swedish Major," as he was universally called, was more than eighty years old in 1872. He had entered the Swedish service in his youth and risen to the rank of Major. Thereupon he resigned his commission and passed the evening of his life in his native town, Greifswald. He had become a good Prussian. But when, according to German usage, or rather misusage there was much grumbling about bad times, he would growl to himself: " Yes, yes, those were good times, under the Three Crowns." Three golden crowns figured on a blue field in the Swedish coat of arms. The Swedish Major was treated with special respect at the table d'hôte in the " *Deutsche Haus*."

On the way back to Berlin we stopped at Pasewalk, which attracted me because it was the garrison of the Second Cuirassiers,

who had covered themselves with glory as Ansbach-Bayreuth
Dragoons at Hohenfriedberg. My favourite march, the finest
music I know, has always been the Hohenfriedberg March. It
was another one of those good things I got from my dear Colonel
von Loë, who used to say that he wished to be buried in the sound
of the Hohenfriedberg March, a wish that was fulfilled at his
funeral in July, 1908. General Christoph Carl von Bülow had
brought about the victory of the Prussian colours by a brilliant
cavalry attack in the Battle of Torgau, on 3rd November, 1760,
when he was Colonel of the Ansbach Dragoons. He afterwards
rose to the highest rank, became General of Cavalry, Inspector-
General, Knight of the Order of the Black Eagle, and what must
have pleased him most of all, Commander of the Ansbach-Bayreuth
Dragoons. We looked for his monument in the Church of Pasewalk,
and we also admired a fine tower which, because of the wide view it
afforded, bore the homely Pomeranian name, " *Kiek in die Mark*." [1]
We walked arm-in-arm across the market place and made plans
for the future. I still had the hope that as a reward for passing my
examination so well, my father would let me remain with the
King's Hussars at Bonn for the time being.

When I arrived in Berlin the next day he destroyed all further
illusions of this kind by informing me that he had definitely decided
upon my future. He had spoken with the Under-Secretary of
State in the Foreign Office, Excellency von Thile, and had asked
him if there was a chance of my being taken into the Diplomatic
Service. Herr von Thile replied that the outlook in this respect
was, in fact, quite favourable. After the victorious war everyone
was going into the Army, whereas our Diplomatic Service lacked
reinforcements. A short while ago, he said, Bismarck had written
to the War Cabinet and asked it to transfer three efficient officers
into the Foreign Office. Of these three officers, I may remark,
only one remained in the Foreign Service—Count Kuno Rantzau,
who at that time was Lieutenant in the 3rd Regiment of Uhlan
Guards. In 1878, he became Bismarck's son-in-law. He showed
tact and dignity in the rather difficult position of son-in-law to
the mighty Chancellor. He was an excellent official to boot, with
more than average ability, a fine character and with all the good
qualities of a Holsteiner—reliable, calm, conscientious and industrious. He did not fail either in the Foreign Office or, subsequently,
when he was Minister at Munich and at the Hague, indeed, with
his charming wife, he won the regard and sympathy of all. There
were good reasons why Holstein and Phili Eulenburg, who worked

[1] Squint over the March.

hand in hand as intimate friends when Bismarck fell and for years afterwards, were hostile to Kuno Rantzau. Holstein was angry with Rantzau because the latter would not go with him along his very tortuous paths or participate in his dubious schemes. As for Phili, he aspired to the post which Rantzau filled at Munich. The two other officers who were ordered into the Foreign Office in 1872 did not stay in the Diplomatic Service. One of them, Herr von Werthern, of the 12th Hussars, for whom a more brilliant future had once been prophesied (either in the Army or in diplomacy) rose no higher than the rank of Commandant of the little fortress of Wesel. The other, Herr von Brandis, a Hanoverian, became Court Marshal at Sigmaringen. *Sic eunt Fata Hominum*—" Ah! if only their paths were not zig-zag!" Thus it is written, not unjustly, in an old family album of the Bülow's under a drawing that represents a zig-zag line.

After the information he had got from Herr von Thile, my father wrote to my Commanding Officer, Prince Henry XIII of Reuss, asking him to have me transferred to the Reserve. He spoke to the same effect with the Chief of the War Cabinet, General von Albedyll. My father told me that he would like me to follow the advice of the Under-Secretary of State, von Thile, and work for a year in Landgericht and the County Council at Metz to begin with. He had, so he declared, made up his mind that I should join the Diplomatic Service, and both he and von Thile believed that the work I should be doing at Metz would be the best preparation for my future and final calling. " I am willing to believe what your patron, General Loë, whom we both esteem so much, has written to me that in time you might rise to be a very smart Colonel of Hussars, but, all things considered, I think that you are best suited to a diplomatic career. You know how fond I am of you. You also know that, as a man of fifty-seven who, like Odysseus, has ' seen many cities of men and learnt many customs,' I have considerable experience. I have thought this matter over carefully. You shall go to Metz. If Prince Bismarck will take you on after a year, then good luck to you in the Foreign Office and the Diplomatic Service." At the same time my father gave me Marten's *Guide Diplomatique*. He was a book-lover, and had the *Guide* beautifully bound in leather. " Diplomacy more than anything else," he continued, " is better learnt by experience than out of books. But whoever wants to become an artist in it must command the technique of this profession. And diplomacy is, I may tell you, not a science, nor, unfortunately, a branch of ethics, but an art. This book will give you some hints."

Armed with my Martens, I travelled to Bonn, where I was to spend another six weeks as a Hussar. I enjoyed these six weeks as much as a last sip of a good wine. We used to drill smartly under the command of Galen, who was an excellent horseman, and we rode every day in the Sprunggarten. Field operations interested me very much. I enjoyed paper-chasing even more. Life amongst my comrades suited me extraordinarily well. Later on I got to know the clubs of Berlin and Vienna, of Athens and Bucharest, of St. Petersburg, London and Rome. But in no club in the world have I felt so much at ease as in our modest mess in the Sterntor Barracks. In no company could there be more harmony than in our officers' corps. Even the unfortunate *Kulturkampf*, which took on ever sharper forms, could not change this. Nothing was ever said by any officer that could have hurt another with different religious beliefs. The Protestant officer on duty would lead his Catholic men to Mass in the venerable cathedral, while the Catholic would lead his Protestant Hussars to the beautiful, newly-built Protestant Church. I will not deny that we Protestants hid our heads with shame when we saw the chaplains walking about in the prison courtyard as a punishment for having read Mass and done their duty. This undignified little war achieved nothing except an increase of the religious fervour of the Catholic population. Giacimo Antonelli had been right, like the clever man he was.

On 11th July, 1872, I became a Reserve Officer of the Regiment. A few days later they gave me a farewell dinner in the casino. The Officer Commanding, Prince Henry XIII of Reuss, drank my health most cordially. When, after the table had been cleared, we stood in the little garden in front of the verandah, I heard my friend Schrader declare in his stentorian voice: " I have said, and I say it again, that Tschoppe will be Imperial Chancellor some day." Tschoppe was the nickname I had in the regiment.

I do not know what made them call me this, and I don't think I ever knew. Nicknames usually come by chance, in some mood, under the influence of wine or by sudden inspiration. Providence has, in its wisdom, so disposed us that man is more receptive to joy and sorrow in his youth than in his old age. At least, to-day it seems to me that I was more sorry to say good-bye to Bonn and my regiment than to leave far bigger towns and wider spheres of activity later in life. I did not see the casino or the Sterntor Barracks again until thirty years later, when I was Chancellor. I left Bonn the day after the farewell dinner. I was very happy when my dear Franz Arenberg informed me of his intention of

THE BIRTHPLACE OF PRINCE BÜLOW IN KLEIN-FLOTTBEK

going to Metz with me. We arranged to be there at the end of August and, if possible, take joint apartments. Meanwhile, I lived at Klein-Flottbek in the Elbe Park Villa, where I go every summer since my retirement. I lived in the room on the second floor, which my kind secretary, to whom I am dictating these memoirs, now inhabits. It is not very big, but has a fine view of the beautiful Elbe.

At Flottbek, which always seemed my real home, I enjoyed the society of my dear parents. I studied Marten's *Guide* under the grave eyes of my father. He commended the *Guide Diplomatique* and explained it to me. I could not have wished for a better teacher. Bismarck knew what he was doing when, in 1873, a year later, he offered him the post of Secretary of State in the Foreign Office. My father was a diplomat of the best school, always very dignified and yet always full of courtesy. When he wished he was lucidity itself, but impenetrable when he did not want his game seen through. Many years after my father's death, which occurred in 1879, Herbert Bismarck gave me the following account of the opinion his great father had formed of mine. " To conduct a policy and see it through to a successful end, as I did from 1862 to 1871, such exceptional gifts and powers are necessary as God grants to very few men. I may say this without arrogance, since grace from on High is also needed. From 1871 our chief task has been to preserve what I achieved in a space of nine years. Strong nerves, a balanced mind, and a skilful hand, are essential for this. The Secretary of State von Bülow possessed these qualities to a high degree."

I arrived at Metz at the end of August, 1872. Franz Arenberg was awaiting me at the station and showed me the way to the rooms which he had rented for the three of us in the Rue des Clercs, later on called the " *Priester Strasse.*" The third of our party was his oldest brother, Philip, who had passed his law examination before his younger brother and was employed at the County Court. He would certainly have made an excellent official on the Bench or in the Administration. But it was his deepest wish to become a priest. His parents were devout Catholics, but they did not want their son to take Holy Orders unless, after long tests, he felt wholly sure of his vocation. Philip Arenberg was one of God's children. In the eyes of frivolous men of the world he was simple-minded, but he was very wise in the meaning of the Sermon on the Mount (St. Math. v, 8 & 9). He placed the Eternal above the Temporal, and the question, how to go to Heaven, seemed much more impor- tant to him than the question as to how he would get on in this world. In our little circle his nickname was "Piel." I was very fond of Piel. A few years after this meeting at Metz he entered the priesthood, and for many years he led a life of humble charity and industry at Eichstätt, in Bavaria, as Canon and intimate adviser of Bishop Baron von Leonrod, who was particularly esteemed by Leo XIII. God gave his faithful servant a peaceful end. He was not yet sixty when he had a stroke during a journey through Vienna just after he had said Mass in the Stephan Cathedral. He passed into the next life without pain and without a death struggle.

Before I say good-bye to the good Piel in these memoirs, I would like to mention an incident which, although without any great significance in itself, nevertheless helped to make the life-long friendship between François Arenberg and myself inextinguishable. One evening, after we had made an excursion to the battlefields near Metz, Philip Arenberg and I went to a little restaurant in the city frequented by German officers. Opposite us sat a Captain who was evidently drunk. After he had stared at Philip Arenberg in a provocative manner, he began talking about hypocrites, who are fit for the pulpit, but not for the army. My dear Piel looked round sadly and helplessly. I intervened, and sharply informed the captain that I thought his behaviour indecent. He replied that he was not quarrelling with me. I answered that I expected people in a place frequented by myself to behave decently, particularly towards a friend of mine. In any case, I continued, I would send my second to him the next morning. Having been dealt with in this manner, the captain got up and went out. When Piel and I got home, the good fellow put his arms round my neck and wept. He wanted to confess why he had not returned the captain's insults. He had as much courage as any officer, he said, and would be ready any moment to risk his life to save another human being or visit the sick at the gravest risk of contagion. But his religion forbade him to fight duels, if only because it horrified him to think of dying without absolution and the Last Sacraments.

As usual whenever there is a duel, the next morning passed amid endless negotiations between the second of Philip Arenberg's opponent and my second, a smart Captain of the 10th Regiment of Dragoons, which was stationed at Metz at the time. The affair ended with the aggressor's asking Philip Arenberg to forgive him, declaring that he had never meant to offend him. I thereupon withdrew my challenge. Next day Franz Arenberg told me he would never forget the way I had stood up for his brother: "*Désormais entre nous c'est à la vie et à la mort.*" He kept his word.

CHAPTER XX

*The Imperial Landgericht at Metz—Rudolf Baron von Seckendorff—
Public Prosecutor Ittenbach—Junior Judge, Magdeburg—A Speech
Before the Metz Jury—The German Theatre at Metz—A Visit
to the Parents of Arenberg at Marche-les-Dames—Work in the
District Council—Cure at Heiden and Reichenhall—My Father
Appointed Secretary of State in the Foreign Office—I Become
Attaché in the Foreign Office—My Father's Advice in the Art of
Diplomacy.*

DURING my duties at Metz I made the acquaintance of two
excellent men with whom I remained on friendly terms for
the rest of my life. Baron Rudolf von Seckendorff, at
that time Imperial Procurator in the Landgericht at Metz, was
descended from an old Franconian family that had given some
excellent men to Prussia, Austria, Bavaria and Württemberg, both
soldiers and civilians. He was born at Cologne, the son of a high
Prussian official, and a Rhenish mother. He combined a strict
sense of duty and unshakable sense of justice with a full knowledge
of *jus aequum* and of the world. When I became, in 1900, Imperial
Chancellor, he was Under-State Secretary in the Prussian State
Ministry. Later he became President of the Supreme Court, and
held that high office for many years, honoured and respected
throughout the whole Empire. My other patron at Metz,
Max Ittenbach, was the first Public Prosecutor at the Landgericht.
He was a true Rhinelander, and was popular both with men and
women by reason of his jovial manner and never-failing humour,
although he showed enough energy when it was needed. Like
Seckendorff, he was an able and eminent jurist. In the course
of years he became Auditor-General of the Army and Navy, Crown
Syndic and member of the Council of State and of the Upper
Chamber. Both Seckendorff and Ittenbach were Catholics.

Amongst the younger gentlemen of the District Council, I
especially liked the junior judge, Magdeburg, who later on rose
to be President of the Province of Hessen-Nassau and, finally,
President of the *Oberrechnungs-kammer* at Potsdam. It would
have been a sign of deplorable superficiality or great narrow-
mindedness on my part, if the course of my life had not imbued me

with the deepest respect for the bureaucracy of the old authoritarian State, a bureaucracy that achieved exemplary things in all branches of the administration and, by self-denial and utter devotion to the State in the years of the revolution, saved the Reich and the Federation from utter collapse.

Amongst the barristers at the County Courts in Metz was a much-discussed, but not uninteresting personality, the advocate Pistor. When he was a young man he had taken part in the Palatine Insurrection of 1849, crossed the French frontier to Metz after the Insurrection was defeated, and become a naturalized Frenchman. His son was a French officer and passionately French. He distinguished himself in the Franco-German war, and afterwards held a high position in the French Intelligence Department, where, if only by his command of the German language, he was said to have done extremely well. In my opinion the French police, from Fouché to Pietri, and from these to the present day, were and are the best, most resourceful and most energetic in the world. Espionage was always well organized in France. As far as intelligence work, spying, and also propaganda are concerned, we are mere amateurs, as the World War has sadly shown. While Pistor, junior, was spying on the Rhine, where he was once caught by our military authorities in company of General Miribel, his father pleaded quite calmly before the County Court at Metz.

When I met him in the winter, 1872-73 on the Esplanade, he asked me if I would care to defend a case. He said he would be glad to entrust me with one in which he was acting officially for the defence. But the case, he added, was as good as hopeless—a Bavarian tramp had killed a Lorraine farmer who had turned him out of his garden where he had been stealing apples. The Lorraine jury would hardly judge the matter mildly. Besides, the defence would have to be made in the French language. I said I was willing to undertake it, and the dossier was sent to me that same evening. It was very thick, but I read it all through carefully, and marked whatever favoured the defence in red, all that would go against my client in blue. I went to bed earlier than usual so as to be as fresh as possible next morning.

The second counsel for the Prosecution spoke of manslaughter with aggravating circumstances, which would have meant penal servitude. He spoke almost negligently for the condemnation of the German defendant by the French jury seemed to him quite certain in any case. When it was my turn to speak I took the offensive at once: " *Le procureur de l'Empereur vous a raconté les faits à sa manière, comme les comprend l'accusation. Je rétablirai la vérité comme c'est le noble office de la défense."* I described a lovely summer morning (for the deed had been done in August)—a peaceful, pleasant, bright landscape, the rich region round Metz, meadows, gardens and fruit trees, idyll! A tired wanderer, exhausted by hard work, who had been tramping through the whole of the night, sees a garden in front of him in the morning and in the garden an apple tree, *un beau pommier.* Praise of the apple tree. I quote Uhland's poem about the " mild host ":

> *" Ein goldener Apfel war sein Schild*
> *An einem langen Aste."* [1]

The wanderer eats an apple, or perhaps two, and then he stretches out to sleep. I quote Macbeth's curse on him who murders sleep:

> " . . . . . Sleep, the innocent sleep,
> Sleep that knits up the ravell'd sleeve of care,
> The death of each day's life, sore labour's bath,
> Balm of hurt minds, great nature's second course,
> Chief nourisher in life's feast . . . . ."

The brutal owner awakens the poor sleeper with coarse words of abuse, perhaps with threats. I quote J. J. Rousseau and the poet of *Tell* to stigmatize such a misdeed. The offended, indeed, the menaced man, snatches a stone and throws it at him who has insulted him or, let us say it plainly, attacked him. " *Le cas de défense légitime était donné, pleinement donné."* By a chance that could not have been foreseen, and could not have been anticipated, the stone hits the man's temple. Death ensues. The German medical expert has certified that the dead man and his brain were in normal condition at the post mortem. All I could therefore do was to quote the evidence of the veterinary surgeon who had also been at the post mortem and express the opinion that the dead man had an exceptionally thin skull. I praise the common-sense of the veterinary surgeon, the man of the people, and hint that the medical officer was one of those experts who cannot see the wood for trees. I only touch on the defendant's nationality in order to express the opinion that for men of honour, like the gentlemen of the jury, the eternal principles of justice and fair play stand high above the passion and prejudices that unfortunately divide the nations. In my peroration I left my place and walked towards the jury, addressing them with raised voice and declaring that I did not

---

[1] A golden apple on a long bough was his device.

adduce extenuating circumstances, but a plain acquittal . . . .
" *Je vous demande l'acquittement pur et simple, et vous me l'accorderez.*"

When I had ended, the judge, who had served in the Court of
Appeal at Colmar, an Alsatian, who had been on the judiciary
under French rule, warned the jury in his summing up: " *Le jeune
stagiaire qui vient de parler, possède le don dangereaux de l'éloquence.
Je prie Messieurs les Jurés de ne pas se laisser entraîner trop loin par
le brillant plaidoyer que nous venons d'entendre.*" I could see by
the looks of the jury that this warning made no impression on them.
They returned after a short discussion and the chairman of the
jury announced the acquittal of the accused. To see what impression this turn of affairs had made upon my client, who was sitting
behind me, I turned round and saw a very astonished face. " I
would never have thought," he said in his Bavarian dialect, " that
you would have got me off. You must give me a few marks now,
so that I can have a gay evening to celebrate my acquittal." Ittenbach, Hamm, Seckendorff, Magdeburg, all my friends on the
County and District Court, offered me their heartiest congratulations. A quarter of a century later, whenever I had to readjust
some *faux pas* committed by his Majesty, Kaiser Wilhelm II, in
the Reichstag, Ittenbach, who often appeared as Auditor-General
in the gallery reserved for the Bundesrat, would whisper maliciously:
" It's nearly as awkward as the case of that Bavarian in Metz."

If Themis favoured me in the Court, Eros mocked me all the
more cruelly soon after. A German theatrical company appeared
in Metz to spread the German language and German culture.
All German officers and officials rightly considered it their duty to
attend the performances of this company (which, incidentally, was
a very good one) in the Town Theatre at Metz. The star of the
company was the *ingénue*. Her name was Ada. She was charming.
She had magnificent blonde hair, she had sentimental and yet
mischievous eyes. She was the favourite of the public from the
very beginning. When she acted the part of Käthchen von
Heilbronn she charmed, in the part of Klärchen she caused enthusiasm, as Gretchen she was unmistakably moving. I did not miss
a single performance. I applauded as though I was the " *Chef de
Claque.*" In spite of my modest budget I used to send her magnificent bouquets at every suitable opportunity, and when, in the part
of Gretchen she whimpered her " Heinrich! Heinrich! " I sent her
a laurel wreath.

The worthy Councillor, Jonas, who looked after the theatre,
introduced me to her. But I was unable to win her heart. Why?
I had a rival. Who was this rival? The comedian of the company.

I felt all the torments of jealousy, a jealousy that was clearly well-founded. I made a last effort. Two days before the German theatrical company left Metz, Ada expressed the desire to visit the town of Nancy. I suggested that we should make an excursion there together. She agreed, but as the train was about to leave Metz station, she turned up, not alone, but accompanied by a colleague, the ugliest lady of the troop, a Bohemian, whose vulgar Czeck accent would have got on my nerves in any case. A more horrible duenna could not be imagined. Nevertheless, I enjoyed the journey. I was pleased to show Ada the pleasant town of Nancy, and to show off my French. I also enjoyed the dinner we had together in an elegant restaurant—her ugly clown could not have offered her anything of that sort.

When we got back to Metz in the evening I was, as the French saw, *gros Jean comme devant*. And yet (so obstinate can a lover be) I turned up at the station the following noon to see the company off. Ada had expressed a wish to possess a lap-dog. I managed to secure a charming dwarf terrier, which I presented to her in a little basket with a pink ribbon round it's neck. She really was pleased and touched. When the train began to move, she kissed her hand at me, but behind her little blonde head there appeared the mocking grimace of the comedian, who, feeling safe at that distance, made a long nose at me. In his posthumous aphorism on the metaphysics of sexual love, Schopenhauer expresses the opinion that to win the favour of a beautiful woman by personality alone is perhaps more pleasing to our vanity than even to our sensuality, since it gives the assurance that one's own self is the equivalent of the person who is cherished, admired, deified above all others. This piece of good fortune was mine more than once in my youth. It is true that the thought of being loved by a beautiful woman for one's own sake, without power, position, wealth, can mightily enhance and strengthen confidence in one's own strength and personality. But Miss Ada taught me that Schopenhauer was also right when in his aphorisms he added this: " it is just because vanity can be so strong an ingredient in love, that un-requited love is so painful, especially when combined with well-founded jealousy." I never heard of Ada again. What can have become of her? " *Ou sont les neiges d'antan ?* " " Where are the snows of yesterday? " So the French poet Pierre Ronsard asked sadly three hundred years ago.

To comfort me—for I was a little put out at first—my dear Franz Arenberg suggested that I should spend a week with him and his parents at Marche-les-Dames, near Namur. It would hardly be possible to think of a kindlier home than Marche-les-Dames, and there was never a more harmonious family circle than that of the Arenbergs. The father, Prince Anton Arenberg, was reminiscent in feature, expression and poise of the portraits which Vandyk painted of princes and nobles in the seventeenth century. Every inch a gentleman! Noblesse within corresponded to his noble appearance. He was a man of great simplicity, genuine kindness, and invariable courtesy towards everyone. One beautiful spring morning as I was walking along the banks of the Meuse with him and his son, we passed several workmen, fishing on the towpath. Every time we passed a workman, Prince Anton Arenberg took off his hat, and with invariable courtesy, asked pardon for the disturbance. He was one of nature's gentlemen, without whose quality name and rank mean nothing.

Princess Maria Ghiselaine von Arenberg, *née* Countess Merode, was a woman of intellect and will power. She had spent several winters in Vienna when she was young. Her mother-in-law was a Princess Lobkowitz, two of her husband's brothers had served in the Austrian army and had married Austrian ladies—the one, Prince Josef, had married Princess Lichtenstein, the sister of the brilliantly gifted Eliza Salm, who for many years was a friend of my wife's, the other, Prince Karl, married Countess Hunyady, the widow of Prince Michael III of Serbia. These family connections did not prevent Princess Arenberg from talking freely about the ignorance and superficiality of the Austrian aristocracy. Jokes about cabmen, so she told me, were the favourite theme of conversation in high, indeed the highest, circles. An especially popular cabman was named Schwan, and puns on the confusion of " Schwanerl " with " Schweinerl " [1] produced bursts of laughter. " *On ne respecte pas l'esprit en Autriche*," she said. " *Et un pays où on ne respecte pas l'esprit est un pays qui baisse.*" She told me that when she was in Vienna she delighted in the magnificent performances in the Burg Theatre, especially when *Faust* was given. Though she could not speak German fluently, she understood enough to follow it on the stage as long as she had the text with her. And she noticed, so she told me, that in Vienna they regularly omitted the scene in which Mephistopheles talked of the church's capacious maw that had devoured whole lands without overeating, and could only digest unlawful goods. On making enquiries, she had been told that this passage had been censored. " *Voyez-vous*," she added " *Voila un délit de lèse-esprit. Certes, je suis très bonne catholique, mais on ne sert ni l'Eglise, ni l'Etat avec une pareille petitesse d'esprit.*

[1] " Little swan : little pig."

Louis XIV le comprit, lorsque lui, le roi très chrétien, permit la représentation du ' Tartuffe' de Molière."

Princess Maria Arenberg rejoiced over Germany's victories, but she was not without anxiety as to our future, and said so repeatedly in those interesting talks which we had in the family circle.

Germany [she said] has won a brilliant victory over France. Now she is the first power in Europe, in the world. But your tremendous successes, which give me real pleasure, if only on account of my sons, are, after all, the work of a few very eminent men, rather than the achievement of a politically gifted and experienced people. I deplore and regret the antagonism between Bismarck and the Catholic Church. None the less, Bismarck is one of the greatest statesmen of all times, and I admire Moltke, Roon, Manteuffel, Werder, Blumenthal and Goeben without reservations. The old Kaiser is one of the most dutiful, wisest and best monarchs who ever sat on a throne. His son is a hero, and at the same time a gentleman to the finger tips. *Tout cela est admirable.* But what about the mass of Germans? Would the Germans be capable, as the English are, of willingly sinking all party interests in the common national interest? Would the Germans, in the hour of need, be capable of closing their ranks to follow the standard bearer, as the French now follow Gambetta, under whom the Papal Zouaves and the Red-Shirts of the Church-hater, Garibaldi, fought shoulder to shoulder? The answer, I fear, is No! Their feeling of unity and subordination of all party views and sectional interests the moment the honour and prestige of the country are in question, seem to me less developed in powerful Germany than in France. German national feeling and German patriotism seem less ardent, less impetuous than French, and as for the majority of your party leaders—*Comparez Virchow et Mommsen comme hommes politiques, comme hommes d'État avec Monsieur Thiers! Richter et Lasker et Monsieur Schulze-Delitzch, Waldeck et Jacoby sont certainement des hommes très vertueux et très honnêtes. Mais vous m'accorderez que, comparés a Léon Gambetta, ce sont des cuistres. C'est surtout la démocratie allemande, qui comme élan patriotique, comme esprit politique, me semble bien inférieure à la démocratie française.*

As Princess Arenberg was speaking I thought of what my father had told me after the storming of Düppel and the crossing to Alsen. I thought of what Goethe said about Germans " miserable when taken *en masse.*"

Princess Arenberg was a niece of Count Charles Montalembert, the great leader of the French Catholics under Napoleon III. She was the cousin of Monsignor Frederick Xavier Merode, who had served in the Belgian army and then under Marshal Bugeaud in the Algerian campaigns, and had won the Legion of Honour. He then went to Rome, studied theology there, was ordained a priest, became Papal Chamberlain and Servitor, and in 1860, Minister of War to Pope Pius IX, and one of the most agressive champions of the temporal sovereignty of the Vatican. In 1865, after the Franco-Italian Convention of the 15th of September, 1864, he was dismissed from the Ministry of War. He died in 1874, as Archbishop of Mitylene *in partibus* and Papal Grand Almoner. Princess Arenberg was the aunt of Count de Mun and of Count Werner de Merode, who stood in the front rank in the struggles of the French Catholics against the anti-clerical policy of Jules Ferry, Gambetta, Clemenceau, Briand and Combes. It could be said of my dear Franz Arenberg that he had imbibed his ardent but always nobly conceived and nobly expressed Catholicism, with his mother's milk.

On 1st March, 1873, I was released from my work at the Landgericht, and assigned to the Imperial District Court at Metz. Here I came under the tutelage of a man who later became one of our ablest statesmen. Count Botho Eulenburg, who at that time was District Governor of Lorraine, was, like many East Prussians, a reticent and outwardly cold personality. But within he was a man of real kindness and fine sensibility. With the indecency particular to German party conflicts, his opponents nicknamed him " the eel," or, when they wished to be particularly malicious, " the slippery eel." In reality, he was a man of principle and sure, firm character. But he was too intelligent not to realize that a nation like ours, always inclined to obstinacy and prejudice, must be guided with a light hand. He was a statesman. I will anticipate matters and say that Count Adolph von Arnim-Boitzenburg, his successor when I was still working at Metz, soon won esteem and confidence by his lively, natural manner and common sense, even though he lacked the brilliant gifts of Count Botho Eulenburg. He was also a very conscientious and able official. His charming wife, Countess Schweinitz, who died young, helped to win the sympathies of the German as well as of the French inhabitants.

I have several times accompanied both Arnim and Eulenburg on their official journeys. Everywhere in Lorraine the District-Governor was received, not only in a correct manner, but almost with enthusiasm. At the outskirts of every village throughout the country the school children would be drawn up in military formation, and always shouted in unison: "*Vive Monsieur le President de la Lorraine!*" Once, when I expressed my joyful surprise at this loyal attitude to a schoolmaster, he answered quite innocently: "*Monsieur, autrefois nous avons crié: 'Vive Monsieur le Préfet de la Moselle! Aujourd'hui nous crions: Vive Monsieur le Président de la Lorraine! Au fond cela revient au même. Nous respectons l'autorité.*" The French Prefect had led, that is to say ruled, with firm and, if need be, a hard hand both under the Empire and the Republic. He would tolerate no political opposition and acted with energy whenever the need arose. But his manners were always excellent—"*Une main de fer sous un gant de velours*," as the great Napoleon recommended. The Reichsland was doubtless better administered by the Germans than it was before or has been since by the French. German mistakes in the Reichsland originated at headquarters, that is to say, in Strassburg and in Berlin. In Strassburg the Privy Councillor von Möller, Prince Chlodwig Hohenlohe, and Prince Karl Wedel, showed the very greatest ability. Field-Marshal Manteuffel (who was very gifted in other ways and had gathered much experience in other posts), the insignificant Prince Hermann von Hohenlohe-Langenburg, and the not very much more distinguished Herr von Dallwitz, all did badly. Was Prince Bismarck right when he converted Alsace-Lorraine into a Reichsland, after we had taken back the Western Provinces which the French had stolen in the period of our lowest decadence? I should not like to be so foolish as to prophesy after the event. Whoever has spent much time abroad, as I have since the World War, and associated with as many foreigners, knows what mockery this kind of superior knowledge *ex post* has brought upon our heads among foreigners more intelligent than ourselves, how ridiculous it makes us appear to them. In foreign countries they laugh at the pompous, unrealistic "historians" like Hans Delbrück who in that doctrinaire manner which we alone will tolerate, explain to us in long-winded, ponderous phrases that if only we had taken the course recommended by Professor X, or Doctor Y, from his study, after the event, with his spectacles on his nose and a long pipe in his mouth, everything would have been different. But he who laughs most is he who has most knowledge of these pedants and knows that they would fail at once if they were put to a practical test, since they lack either the nerve, the brain, or the sureness of touch to carry out even the humblest political plan and perform the simplest diplomatic task. It was Schiller who said that though ideas may live at peace side by side, hard facts clash for ever in space. And Heinrich Heine tells the charming story of the three artists who wanted to paint a camel. The Englishman travels to Africa to copy the ship of the desert on the spot; the Frenchman to the zoological gardens to find his model there. The German constructs a camel out of the depths of his ethical conscience.

I do not want to imitate this German artist, but I may be permitted to say this:

When Prince Bismarck called the Reichsland to life he over-estimated, as he did on several other occasions, the political capacity of the Germans and the strength of their national sentiment. He did not reckon with the fact that the German parties, instead of working side by side for the moral and spiritual re-assimilation of Alsace-Lorraine, could think of nothing except getting as many advantages as possible, all against each, each for himself, in the new province, and with general indifference to the national interest. The two strongest German parties, the Centre and Socialists, succeeded in winning a certain number of seats in the Reichsland. When the French returned to the Rhine the three departments into which Alsace-Lorraine were converted, Haut-Rhin, Bas-Rhin and Moselle, the principle of French unity of " *France une et indivisible*" was put into the foreground. All in all, we would probably have got on better if our great steersman, as the good and kind Princess Johanna Bismarck called her husband, had converted Lorraine into a Prussian province, with Metz as capital, while attaching it to the districts of Treves, and had united Alsace with Baden in an " Alemanian " kingdom, transferring the capital and residency from Karlsruhe to Strassburg, while facilitating and promoting communication between Karlsruhe and the Hagenauer district, Strassburg and Baden-Baden, Wildbad, Stuttgart, Colmar and Freiburg, Mülhausen and South Baden.

In the summer of 1873 I again had trouble with my throat, and I spent some time at Heiden in the Swiss canton Appenzell-Ausserrhoden, where whey is taken medicinally. Heiden is charmingly situated, and the view of the Swabian lake, Lake Constance, is magnificent. But, I was so bored when I was there, that I decided to go to the Bavarian Spa, Reichenhall, where I drank whey and took saline baths in the Achselmannstein Spa amid magnificent surroundings. There, in addition to my regimental comrade, Nimptsch, and his mother and charming sisters, was a select circle of elderly Prussian diplomats. The Chorus of Elders used to sing at Spartan festivals: " What ye are, we were." And the younger men would answer: " What ye have become we wish to be." But when I saw Count Heinrich Redern, Baron Karl von Werther, Count Guido von Usedom, before me, I did not agree with young Spartans, and felt no special desire to emulate these old men.

The best amongst them was Baron Werther. He was the politest, the most correct, and the most peaceful of all men, but it was his fate that war should break out wherever he had been Prussian Ambassador. He was Ambassador in Copenhagen when the Schleswig-Holstein question led to war between Prussia and Denmark. Sent to Vienna, he witnessed the outbreak of war in 1866. When he was transferred from Vienna to Paris the Franco-German war began. The *Kladderadatsch* called Herr von Werther the " Stormy Petrel." Anyhow, he was a stormy petrel with nothing stormy about him. He was in no way embittered and, in contrast to Usedom, he did not grumble at Bismarck, who re-engaged him a few years later, and sent him as Ambassador to Constantinople. Hardly had he arrived there when the Russo-Turkish war began. He was indeed a stormy petrel.

It was my privilege to listen to Count Heinrich Redern, to whom I have already referred in greater detail, when, like Nestor, he told the well-greaved Achæans of the heroic deeds of his youth, and, now and then, related memories of his diplomatic career. He was especially fond of quoting a letter which he had sent from Turin to the Prussian Foreign Minister, Herr von Manteuffel, at the time of the Crimean War. The worthy Heinrich Redern wished to make his young listeners realize how his eagle glance before any other, had foreseen the political future of Count Cavour. His letter to the Minister Manteuffel was worded somewhat as follows: " *Monsieur le Baron, j'ai l'honneur d'attirer l'attention éclairée de votre Excellence sur le premier Ministre de Sa Majesté le Roi de Sardaigne, le Comte Camillo Benso di Cavour. Malgré ses idées un peu trop libérales, Monsieur de Cavour est un homme fort distingué et qui mérite la faveur dont il jouit auprès de son auguste maître. Agréez avec l'assurance de ma plus haute considération l'expression de mes sentiments respectueusement dévoués.*" The political reports of Prussian diplomats were written in French until Otto von Bismarck-Schönhausen took office.

Usedom was married to an Englishwoman, Miss Olympia Malcolm, the daughter of the Governor of Bombay. Her mighty girth did honour to her Christian name, and her originality sometimes degenerated into tactlessness. When Usedom was Prussian Ambassador at Florence, she tried to enter a chamber of the Palazzo Pitti, admittance to which was forbidden. When the

Italian Chamberlain barred her way, she pushed him majestically
aside with the words: " *Io sono la Prussia!* " The daughter of this
marriage, an unusually fine child, was generally known as the
" *Usekathedrale.*" It is said that when her parents had come to stay
in Munich for a time, she had determined to marry King Ludwig II,
but she did not succeed in overcoming the King's misogyny.

While I was staying at Reichenhall I received a letter from my
father informing me that Prince Bismarck had offered him the
position of Secretary of State in the Foreign Office. For some time
he had been uncertain as to whether he should accept the offer or
not. On the one hand he felt that at fifty-eight he was no longer
young enough for a new post of so exacting a nature. On the other
hand, it gave him deep satisfaction to pass the evening of his life,
which had begun in the Danish service, in that of the now glorious
German Empire at the side of the great German statesman who had
re-established it. It was Bismarck's appeal to their old friendship
tested by many different periods, circumstances and situations, a
friendship that had united the two men for a quarter of a century—
which, in the end, made him decide to accept the offer. For this
reason, so he wrote, he had consented.

Soon after my father's appointment was ratified, the Chancellor
asked him how his sons, whom he remembered having met at
Frankfort-on-Main, were getting on. When my father replied
that his second son was Lieutenant and Adjutant in the Second
Dragoon Guards and his eldest working in the District Council
at Metz after having been through the war in the ranks of the
King's Hussars, Bismarck said: "Wouldn't you like to make a
diplomat of your eldest son?" My father pointed out that there
were already three Bülows in the Foreign Service, and that four
would be rather too many. Bismarck replied with kindly humour
that there could not be enough of the species. So I was made an
Attaché in the Foreign Office at the head of which I was to be
Secretary of State twenty-four years later.

The day I arrived in Berlin I met Baron von Brincken in the
Unter den Linden. He was First Secretary in the Embassy at
London then. I had made his acquaintance a year previously at
the Borussen Tavern at Bonn. The excellent man, the image of
the perfect middle-aged diplomat, gave me three good pieces of
advice in the course of our conversation: 1. To join the mess as
soon as possible. 2. To talk little, both in the mess and in Berlin
generally, and never to ask questions (questions would lead to
misinterpretations). 3. To go to parties as much as possible and
dance a great deal, as this would make me popular.

The advice my good and wise father gave me was more serious. His precepts were as follows (I enumerate them because, even if conditions change, men remain fundamentally the same— even the diplomatic novice in defeated, luckless, but re-aspiring Germany, may learn many lessons from these hints):

The strictest and the most rigorous truthfulness in every report.

Report only what is certain.

Report nothing that might turn out to be unfounded later on. Never tell fibs.

No gossip, no exaggeration or over-statement, no over-vivid colouring.

Ne pas forcer la note.

Be especially meticulous with regard to figures.

Point de fantaisie.

Do not paint events more luridly than they present themselves to sober observation.

Care in judgment.

Seldom prophesy, in any case not in reports, at the very utmost only in private letters. Official prophets, star-gazers and fortune tellers, haruspices and augurs, no longer exist. Besides: *Tout arrive, on ne peut jurer de rien, tout change.*

Do not compromise others in your reports. It is neither decent nor clever. Do not write *ab irato.* Prince Bismarck is in the habit of saying that indignation and rancour are conceptions foreign to diplomacy. The diplomat is neither a preacher of penitence, nor a judge in a criminal court, nor a philosopher. His sole and exclusive interest must be the real and downright interest of his country.

Be careful with telegrams. Very careful with the code, which must never be used unnecessarily.

Do not criticize too severely in your reports. *La critique est aisée et l'art est difficile.* Besides the contents of every report can leak out.

Be calm and sober. *Ne prends rien au tragique, tout au sérieux,* as Thiers used to say. And above all, take everything coolly.[1] But always be *en vedette* and look out in all directions.

Calm, balance, self-control. Keep up your nerves, sir! [1] Do not be influenced by sympathies or antipathies.

Do not transmit awkward wishes of foreign governments to Berlin. Leave it to the Foreign Government to make such requests

---

[1] English in text.

through its own representatives in Berlin—they can then be refused more easily. Do not, without being empowered by the Foreign Office, take any steps that might compromise our Government. Remember how badly Benedetti was bitten when he made his " compensation and annexation proposals " to Bismarck.

A clear, concise style, not too long-winded, matter of fact, but not clumsy. " *Tous les genres sont bons hors les genre ennuyeux,*" said Voltaire. Germans forget it far too often.

It is a diplomat's first duty not to be taken by surprise. Politics are dominated by constant change. All things flow. Do not let your imagination run wild. Do not make an elephant out of every gnat. But look upon almost everything as possible and little as certain. Above all, don't let yourself be hurried. The deep secret of our life lies somewhere between excessive haste and lost opportunities.

The chief task of a diplomat abroad is always what Bismarck calls work on human flesh, that is to say, the correct treatment of strangers with the object of realizing tangible, factual successes. Keep in touch with colleagues and do not cower inside four walls like the were-wolf. But at the same time don't let your colleagues tell you any lies or exploit you. *Pas trop de zèle* is a golden rule when rightly understood.

CHAPTER XXI

Work in the Foreign Office (1873-74)—Count Paul Hatzfeldt—His Hints on Dealings with S.D.—Lothar Bucher—Wilhelmstrasse 76 —Evening Receptions in Bismarck's House—Anti-Bismarckian Tendencies in German Society—Unpolitical Nature of the Germans.

AFTER I was called to the Foreign Office my father had me employed for three weeks in the Central Bureau, for three weeks in the Cypher Room, for three in the Secret Record Office, and for three in the Legation Counting House. " Whoever," he said to me, " wishes to live in a house may as well look round the basement and get to know the foundations. Besides, you must learn how to respect our excellent subordinate officials in this bureau." Later on my father assigned me for six weeks respectively to the Councillor of Legation Reichardt in the Trade Department and the Councillor of Legation Hellwig in the Judicial Department, so as to give me a training, a very thorough training, as my father impressed upon these gentlemen.

My father flatly refused to grant my request that I might be assigned to the Political Department at once. He said I would become acquainted with high politics soon enough. Whoever tasted of this solid food prematurely might easily spoil his digestion or never grow to be more than an amateur. In foreign politics, he said, an amateur was the same as a bungler, that is to say, a man who, because he underrates the serious nature and the difficulty of his art, acquires a wrong conception of things and, therefore, bungles them. But even if I did not deal with problems of high politics, I did come into close association with the two most important Councillors of the Foreign Office, Count Paul Hatzfeldt and Lothar Bucher, as early as the winter of 1873, that is to say, when I was still very young.

Count Paul Hatzfeldt was the son of Count Edmund von Hatzfeldt-Weissweiler and Countess Sophie von Hatzfeldt-Trachenberg whom, as I have already related, I used to meet in restaurants and on the promenade between the Grimmaische and Hallische Tor at Leipzig, arm-in-arm with this or that Socialist friend. Count Paul Hatzfeldt showed me great kindness. I owe him many useful hints, all of them adapted to " S.D." (Seine Durchlaucht—

his Serene Highness) as Bismarck used to be called in the Foreign
Office. I made a note of these hints on a piece of paper which has
since grown yellow with age. I found it amongst my papers, and
I reproduce it because the advice it contains is characteristic both
of Otto Bismarck and Paul Hatzfeldt.

1. Never go too far in one direction, in any case never hurry,
if possible be about three crotchets behind time. S.D. is *ondoyant
et divers*, he does not like hounds that dash so far beyond the
quarry that they can no longer take up another scent.

2. Do not put too many " I's " in reports. S.D. can tell for
himself if a matter is well handled.

3. Ask S.D. as few questions as possible. Better write or
telegraph that this or that will be done unless instructions to the
contrary are received.

4. Give a hint at the end of the report that your own opinion
is, of course, subject to the higher judgment of S.D.

5. Things run more smoothly than the novice believes. Take
little disagreeable things and unavoidable annoyances with the
indifference that S.D. himself recommends. S.D. does not like
excited people, still less does he like it when they lose their heads.
Calm, a certain indifference, or even carelessness, please him.

6. A young man who has dealings with S.D. should never
forget that he is a stern, and at times grim, *Pater Familias*. Men
of the world get on well with him, provincial judges badly, professors
worst of all.

Count Paul Hatzfeldt acquired his first vivid political impressions by associating with Ferdinand Lassalle, the brilliant intellect,
who for years had been his mother's lover. It is peculiar that
another man, who was also a very important collaborator of
Bismarck's, the Councillor of Legation, Lothar Bucher, was also
an intimate friend of the same Ferdinand Lassalle. In 1848
Bucher had joined the Radical Left in the Prussian National
Assembly. He pushed his opposition so far as to refuse to pay
taxes, so that in 1849, after the victory of reaction, he had to fly
to London, where he was in constant association with Karl Marx,
Mazzini, Friedrich Engels, and Auguste Ledru-Rollin, the leader
of the French Socialists in the Paris-June insurrection of 1849,
and many other leaders of the revolution. Lothar Bucher also
showed me friendly consideration. He was fond of talking to
me about the time when he was an exile in London. He said that
Karl Marx, the author of the *Communist Manifesto*, was not only
a keen and profound thinker, but also a very fine man, the best

husband and father he had ever known. He also described Giuseppe Mazzini as an unusually noble character. " He could not hurt a fly," he said. When I pointed to the several outrages that Mazzini had organized, Bucher said: " there you touch a problem that would take too long to discuss properly, the problem of the relationship between politics and ethics. It is undeniable that Robespierre was *un homme vertueux*, not merely in words, but in practice, and that many of the so-called terrorists were good, indeed tenderhearted and sentimental men." There was something modest, quiet and almost shy about Lothar Bucher. His relations with women are said to have been always platonic. Even when he was an elderly man he used to pay tender respects to a few widows of high officials, occasionally bringing them bunches of violets.

Paul Hatzfeldt was different from Lothar Bucher, and made anything but a subdued impression. His audacity was equal to every situation and every difficulty. Like Talleyrand, he could say of himself: " *Avec le sourire sur le lèvres et un front d'airain on passe partout.*" And like Talleyrand, he was non-moral, but not at all anti-moral. By all who knew him intimately, Talleyrand was described as amiable, kindly, and considerate towards himself and other people. Towards his subordinates Paul Hatzfeldt was a very benevolent, easy-going chief, never moody in dealing with others, never impatient, least of all aggressive. But ethical conceptions seemed more like conventional forms to these two eminent diplomats, than the commands of a categorical imperative in the Kantian sense. As far as religion was concerned they were content occasionally to observe the outward forms of the Catholic Church to which they belonged. Once when Talleyrand was asked how he could tolerate the presence of a man who was known to be vicious, he answered with a charming smile: " *C'est précisement parce qu'il est si vicieux qu'il m'est sympathique.*" This is what Paul Hatzfeldt might have thought even if he would not have said it. But I would like to emphasize the fact that perversities such as those that poisoned the Berlin atmosphere a generation later were utterly remote from him.

Lothar Bucher never went to the Imperial Court because Kaiser William had declared that he could not receive a former revolutionary, tax-evader, and fugitive. The old gentleman who was so kindly in other ways never had granted an audience to Lothar Bucher, whose name was not allowed to be so much as mentioned in the presence of the Empress Augusta. Paul Hatzfeldt, on the other hand, was held in high esteem by Her Majesty, and His Majesty, too, treated him, if not exactly with inward sympathy, at any rate with great courtesy. When Prince Bismarck fell, Paul Hatzfeldt turned his back on the fallen man, not with tactless haste or exaggeration, but gradually and coolly, although Bismarck had called him the best horse in his stables, and always gave him preference in official matters, even a few years before his fall.

Not long before Prince Bismarck's dismissal, Lothar Bucher resigned from his position as Councillor in the Foreign Office. His enemy, Holstein, had influenced the Under-Secretary of State, Count Herbert Bismarck, who at that time was entirely under Holstein's domination, against Bucher. Lothar Bucher did not like to be treated badly by a chief like Herbert Bismarck, who was so much younger than he was. When Bismarck, deprived of his Chancellorship and courted by very few, retired to Friedrichsruh, Lothar Bucher freely offered him his services and, as is well known, helped his great chief in preparing the *Thoughts and Memories*. For the sake of future diplomats, I will add a piece of advice on diplomatic reporting that Bucher gave me: " The true standard in arriving at a judgment and drawing up a report is always the same. *Facts, sir, facts.*[1] The concrete utterance of any leading man, whether diplomat, deputy, or financier on a definite point, carries more weight than a report on a situation, however excellent the report may be. Do not let modesty suppress your own verdict, let it emerge at the end of your report."

The house in which I worked in Berlin, 76, Wilhelmstrasse, was connected with my ancestors by several memories. In 1818 the Danish Ambassador in Berlin was Count Christian Günther Bernstorff, who was married to an aunt of my father's, Countess Elisa Dernath, and was Prussian Minister for Foreign Affairs from 1818 to 1832. He represented Prussia in this capacity at the Congresses of Aix la Chapelle, Verona, Karlsbad, Troppau and Laibach during the most brilliant period of the Holy Alliance and of Prince Clemens Metternich. His change-over from the Danish to the Prussian service was characteristic of that whole period. His quiet manner, his self-control and great tact had impressed King Frederick Wilhelm III of Prussia favourably. One day he sent for the Danish Ambassador and asked him if he would take over the leadership of the Prussian Department for Foreign Affairs under the Chancellor, Prince Hardenberg, who was gradually getting old and in need of assistance. Count Bernstorff gave thanks for this proof of gracious confidence, but pointed out that he was in the Danish service. Frederick Wilhelm III

---

[1] English in text.

smiled as he drew a letter from King Frederick VI of Denmark out
of his pocket, in which the latter wrote : " To surrender the
excellent Ambassador in Berlin, Count Christian Günther von
Bernstorff, to his dear brother and friend, the King of Prussia, was
a matter of real satisfaction and lively pleasure to him, and it was
as flattering for Bernstorff as it was for the Danish Crown and
Denmark."   Thereupon Count Bernstorff entered the Prussian
service.   A few days later he informed his wife of the change that
had come into their lives, and added that he was already well up
in his new duties.   " You would not believe," he wrote to her,
" how strange it seems to me to hear myself dictating to Prussian
secretaries on Prussian affairs, as though it had always been so."
But his wife was less pleased by the turn things had taken.   She
was particularly grieved at having to move out of the Bernstorffs'
Palace in Copenhagen.   This palace, as is well known, became the
summer residence of the Danish Royal Family.   King Christian IX
often received visits there from his son-in-law, the Emperor
Alexander III of Russia, visits that Bismarck watched suspiciously,
because he knew that Queen Louise of Denmark, although a
German Princess, a Princess of Hessen, was anti-Prussian, and
tried to influence her Russian son-in-law in this direction.

To assist Countess Bernstorff in her housing worries, Frederick
William III, so economical as a rule, gave orders that the long
building, Number 76, Wilhelmstrasse, which at that time belonged
to the widow of the Russian Ambassador Alopæus, should be
bought as the official residence of Count Christian Bernstorff.
The King called this the most beautiful house in Berlin.   Its price
was 80,000 gold thalers, a not inconsiderable sum in those days.
No German should pass by this house without the respectful
thought that here Prince Bismarck worked in his greatest period.
His study was in the upper storey.   The two windows of this are
the third and the fourth from the right next to the middle projection.
It was in the dining room next to the study that Bismarck received
the Ems Telegrams on 13th July, 1870, the telegram he edited
so as to turn it into a trumpet blast.   The Ministerial Council used
to meet under Bismarck in the middle room, and in the study there
used to stand the little mahogany table on which he signed the
preliminary Peace of Versailles on 26th February, 1871.   The
wallpaper of the workroom had small golden crosses on a grey
field, the carpet had bright red and blue with green flowers on a
dark red field.   The walls were prettily patterned with brown
bands in narrow gold strips.   The bedroom, with one window, was
quite simple, and next to it was the dressing-room.

IV.   x

Further towards the back was a second bedroom, two studies and two drawing-rooms which, together with the oval room, sufficed for Bismarck's ceremonial purposes in his great days. The oval room had a coffered ceiling in the Italian taste, and dark yellow walls, on which there were paintings of dancing girls. The legend was that these were a reminder of the famous and much celebrated dancer, Barberina, who, after she had charmed eighteenth century Berlin with her beauty and her art, married the son of a great jurist, the Presiding Judge von Cocceji, who, in 1750, bought her the house which Bismarck was to stamp with the seal of world history. The name of Bismarck had been connected with this house before. Barberina, whose maiden name was Barbara Campanini, sold the house her husband had given her to the Minister of War von Eickstedt, when he died. After von Eickstedt's death his daughter, the wife of the Minister of State von Decken, took charge of it. The two sphinxes that watch over the entrance stairway of the historic house date back to the time of the Russian Ambassador Alopæus, that is, to say, to the beginning of the nineteenth century. They are the work of the sculptor, Pfeffer.

My father once told me that he worked in the room which had served his uncle Bernstorff as an office half a century before. He showed me the porcelain stove of the room with a Prussian eagle on each of its four corners. He had seen the same stove before him when, as a student, he had visited his uncle. My father praised the old Prussian thrift and simplicity. He was fond of quoting the reply which the Delphic oracle gave to a deputation of Spartans who were anxious about the future of their city: " Riches only, riches alone, and nothing else can ruin Sparta."

Count Christian Günther Bernstorff was buried in the little cemetery after his death in 1835. This cemetery used to be in front of the Potsdam Station. It was abandoned a few years ago, but old Berliners would probably remember it still. Whenever I went to Potsdam during my Chancellorship I had a view of this cemetery before I got into the train. When a difficult or unsatisfactory audience with Wilhelm II was impending, I would think of my grand-uncle, who had also had his difficulties and troubles and yet now was sleeping quite peacefully under the green turf, indifferent to the noise of the Potsdamer Platz. " All is over after nine, so actors say," Bismarck wrote to his wife in his Frankfort days. The widowed Countess Elise Bernstorff, my great-aunt, left memoirs that contained much of interest about the period from 1789 to 1835.[1]

[1] *Countess Elise von Bernstorff, née Countess von Dernath.* 2nd edition, Berlin, 1896. Mittler & Son.

I used to pass by the two sphinxes of Pfeffer's when, as an attaché
in the Foreign Office, I visited Countess Bismarck's salon. The
Prince and the Princess told me through my father, that they
would be glad if I would come to see them in the evenings. The
guests would arrive at ten, when the Princess used to be waiting
for them at a large round table on which all kinds of cold dishes
and " *Delikatessen* " were set out; every kind of sausage, sardines,
anchovies, salted and smoked herrings, caviare in winter (usually a
kind present from St. Petersburg), salmon, Italian salad, hard-
boiled eggs, every kind of cheese (from Dutch to Harz cheese), and
countles bottles of beer (genuine, heavy Bavarian beers). Doctor
Ernst Schweninger had not yet imposed his diet on the Prince,
or forced him to drink milk in the evenings instead of beer—in
later years Bismarck used to drink milk instead of beer in vast
quantities. " Everything about the man is vast," a witty Liberal
Deputy once said to me, " even his appetite."

The Prince seldom turned up before eleven. When the
philosopher Hegel saw Napoleon riding across the market place
of the little University town after the Battle of Jena, he said:
" I have seen the universal spirit on a white horse." I never saw
Bismarck enter the room without the feeling that I saw a great
man, a really great man, before me, the greatest man I ever saw or
ever would see. He was all the more impressive because he was
so simple, natural, and free from every kind of pose. This struck
me most of all in Berlin, where so many high officials and Deputies,
once they have reached a certain position, are fond of displaying
a pompous dignity.

The Prince's great courtesy towards all his guests was characteristic of him. Even the youngest he welcomed with a friendly
handshake, usually accompanied by a kind word or a joke. He
nearly always kissed ladies' hands. In after years when he had
to lie on his sofa a good deal because of his gout, he would ask
every lady to excuse him for receiving her in such a position. It
was in the nature of things that when he arrived the Prince should
dominate the conversation. He talked about everything, sometimes
humorously, always with spirit and originality, and never lecturing.
He always produced an impression of superiority, never of vanity.
He spoke slowly, almost haltingly, in a low, cultivated voice.
When he stopped speaking for a while the guests would be silent,
too, so as not to disturb his thoughts. I remember, one evening,
how a certain Prince Henry IX of Reuss, who was present amongst
the guests, suddenly and loudly asked the Prince (after a silence
that had lasted several minutes): " What does your serene Highness

think about our present relations with Russia?" The good fellow asked the question at a moment when there was talk of a disturbance of our relations with Russia. Bismarck looked at the questioner with his large eyes, and then he said: "In all the years I have been in office I have rarely been asked such an un— un—!" We all expected him to say *unheard of*, *uncalled for*, *unmannerly*, or something of the sort. But the Prince, bowing courteously to Prince Reuss, ended his sentence with the words: "such an unexpected question."

Whenever my father was present Bismarck was fond of reminiscing with him about the period when the Federal Diet was at Frankfort, or of discussing problems of Foreign Affairs that were then in the foreground. I remember well how even in those days the Prince described Austro-Russian rivalry as one of the most difficult but as also one of the most important problems of our foreign policy. Bismarck never ceased to be concerned with the relations between ourselves and Russia. On 4th September, 1872, there had been a meeting in Berlin between the Emperor Wilhelm, the Emperor Alexander II and the Emperor Francis Joseph. The moment at which our venerable Emperor displayed his victorious troops to the two other monarchs was one of the highest peaks of Prussian and German history. Without the benevolent neutrality of Russia Bismarck could not have carried out his policy, either in 1866 or in 1870 and 1871. On the other hand, it was clear that if we abandoned the Hapsburg Monarchy to Russia we should drift into a very precarious position. Neither to sacrifice Austria-Hungary nor let ourselves be entangled by her in war with Russia seemed to Bismarck by no means an easy task, but possible of achievement by quiet and skilful German policy, especially if we were clever enough not to oppose Russia in the Dardanelles, but to leave that to others.

It would be a mistake to suppose that the work of Bismarck (who was in the fullness of his powers and at the height of his fame) and his towering human greatness were appreciated in those days. He was attacked from all quarters, in Parliament and the Press, and sometimes in the pettiest spirit. Amongst his opponents were famous men of learning, above all Theodore Mommsen and Rudolph Virchow. Everybody knew that the two first ladies in the land, the Empress Augusta and the Crown Princess Victoria, disliked the Imperial Chancellor no less than did the three party leaders, leagued against him, in the Reichstag—Richter (Radical), Windthorst (Centre), and Grillenberger (Socialist). The good Princess Karl of Prussia, the elder sister of the Empress, was the only member of the Prussian Court (excepting, of course, his old master) really well disposed to Bismarck. When she felt her end approaching in January, 1877, she donned the badge of her regiment, the 7th Westphalian Field Artillery. Thereupon she sent for Bismarck and thanked him in simple, touching words for all he had done for the Royal House, for Prussia and for Germany. She died on 18th January, the Prussian Coronation Day.

In so-called Society, there were endless discussions of Bismarck in the winter of 1873 to 1874. A few days after I arrived in Berlin I dined with the French Ambassador, Viscount Gontaut-Biron. My neighbour was the Captain in the regiment of Cuirassier Guards, Count Conrad Lüttichau, a magnificent type of genuine old-fashioned guards officer—smart as a soldier, dignified in manner and in feeling, and at the same time a good fellow. When we had got to the roast he said to me: " I think we shall be good friends. Cuirassier Guards and Royal Hussars should go together. But you must be clear about one thing—we, all of us, in good society, cannot stand Bismarck." The *Kulturkampf* had laid the foundations for this feeling. The *Kulturkampf* soon led to the breach between the leading statesman and the old Prussian Conservatives. Dissatisfaction with Bismarck was intensified later on, by the ruthless action he took against the Ambassador in Paris, Count Harry Arnim. By striking at him, he attempted to strike at and intimidate the whole *fronde* at Court, and in diplomacy and Society.

When Bismarck entered his drawing-room, I felt the *frisson sacré* that seizes all who can appreciate and understand true greatness, where criticism ends and wonder (τὸ θαῦμα) begins. When Bismarck had retired for the night and I left Number 76 Wilhelmstrasse, passing again before the two sphinxes, I would feel the anxiety that, even in my youth, had afflicted me as to what would become of the German people without him. I only had to follow the debates in the Reichstag, to read the newspapers of all parties, to listen to the political conversations in the houses I visited, to be clear in my mind that Providence, which adorned the German with so many rich gifts and noble virtues, unfortunately made him a Ζῶον ἀπολιτικόν. I had forebodings that we Germans, precisely because of our matter-of-factness, thoroughness and constancy, lacked many pre-requisites for the restless, changeable and variable game of politics. The German is matter of fact. " To be a German is to do a thing for its own sake," said Richard Wagner, and so characterized the essence of the German nature.

The successful politician is seldom matter of fact, is usually an opportunist, and ignores everything save his country's interests. The Englishman says: "Right or wrong, my country."[1] He is penetrated with the conviction as downright and unshakable as it is simple-minded, that what is useful to England is good for the whole world, and that English rule promotes civilization everywhere. For the Frenchman, France is the point around which all his thoughts and opinions revolve. For the clerical Frenchman France is *La fille ainée de l'Eglise* whom other peoples must revere. For the Frenchmen of radical tendencies France is *la mère de la Révolution*, and therefore has a mission, to lead and to dominate the world, or at least Europe, so as to spread democratic and republican ideas. His views, feelings, and traditions always bring the Frenchman back again to the conviction that the *prépondérance légitime de la France* is a condition of true civilization and real, durable well-being throughout the world. Even in periods of weakness, of dissension and impotence, the Italian clung to his beliefs in the primacy of the Italian genius. He looked upon foreigners as barbarians, and from the depths of his soul he would shout his "*Fuori stranieri*!" and schooled his intellectual power under his most fiery patriot who was also the keenest Italian thinker, Niccolo Macchiavelli.

Inwardly the German tends to division, federalism, particularism and even separatism, rather than to combination and concentration. Outwardly we indulge in dreams of the final victory of good over evil, of reconciliation amongst the peoples and eternal peace, dreams which, as history unhappily teaches, are always wrecked by the reality of things and the unchangeable egotism of mankind. As we lack stolid national pride, we are always in danger of allowing Germany to become the Cinderella in the family of nations, because every German wants to put his cloudy doctrines into practice and, above all, promote his particular party interests. There is a malicious Spanish proverb that says: "One Spaniard is equal to a *caballero*, an Englishman is equal to two merchants. A Portuguese is equal to four rogues. One German is equal to eight footmen." There are many Germans who do not even realize that our people, who are by nature so efficient and on great occasions so heroic, has played the part of footmen during many periods of its predominantly tragic history. When, on the 11th December, 1899, I made a speech in the Reichstag[2] in which I said that there had been periods when,

---

[1] English in text.
[2] Prince Bülow's *Speeches* (large edition), vol. i, p. 96; (small edition), vol. i, p. 107.

in spite of all our education and culture, foreigners looked down on us just as the proud cavalier looks down on a humble private tutor, I was not understood by the majority of those good men who represent our people.

In 1863, when I came to Berlin for the first time, the town had scarcely 400,000 inhabitants. The old cathedral was still standing, and so were the houses along the Schlossfreiheit. The military milestone was still on the Dönhoff Platz, but not the statues of Stein nor Hardenberg. On the Encke Platz was the Observatory. The worthy Encke had discovered a comet, Encke's Comet. There still used to be booths on the Lützow Platz. Besides the Linden, there were still some other streets with green trees. There were also streets with open sewers. If I remember rightly, even elegant streets like the Behrenstrasse and the Französische Strasse were crossed by open sewers. The banks of the canal were still grassy. Real Polish Jews still bargained and yelled on the Mühlendamm.

A sandy desert stretched out by the Kreuzberg. Sheep grazed on the Tempelhofer Feld under the care of a contemplative shepherd who knitted socks. Many kites rose into the air in that place. The Berliners were still proud of their Aquarium, of their Peepshow, of the Café Bauer, and Kranzler's confectioner's shops, where elegant guards' officers stretched their long legs and through their monocles approvingly ogled the passing ladies. The Berlin cobbles in those days seemed very bad to me, the cabs worse. The long streets seemed empty, almost desolate, compared with the Neue Wall at Hamburg and the Zeil at Frankfurt. What I liked most when I was a little boy of hardly fourteen were the little booths by the Princess's Palace, where all kinds of wares were offered for sale. Once when my father bought some trifle there, the saleswoman told us that the old King William used to buy humble presents for his family and his entourage from her at Christmas time. Once when she had shown him a rather more expensive article he turned it down and jokingly shook a menacing finger at her and said " You are the serpent of temptation." The loyal saleswoman added: " Our King is the best and kindest man in the world, and yet people will say things against him." When I spent a few days in Berlin, with my family, after my confirmation in March, 1866, some democratically minded visitors at the Josty Café on the Potsdamer Platz said, in our presence, that a sheet of paper had been stuck to the statue of Frederick the Great on the previous day with the words:

" *Ach, alter Fritze, steig hernieder,*
Und sei du unser König wieder,
Und lass in diesen schweren Zeiten
Nur lieber unsern Wilhelm reiten." [1]

In the winter of 1873-4, when I was working in the Foreign Office, Berlin already had the character of a big city, the streets were more alive, there was more traffic. At noon, at the changing of the Guard, the crowd used to throng round the Palace of the old Emperor, cheering him when he showed himself at the fixed hour and nodded in a friendly manner at the corner window, that has since become famous. He could also be seen at the Opera when he sat in his little box and listened respectfully to Wachtel and Lucca. As I said before, I have been impressed by few people in my life, few have made an impression of true greatness upon me. I have very rarely felt awe since, although I am capable of enthusiasm; I have always, ever since my youth, inclined to a certain scepticism. For no mortal did I feel such deep and sincere veneration as for William, our old Emperor and King. And this veneration was felt not only for the Monarch, not only for the King of Prussia, whose victorious son had kissed his hand on the battlefield of Sadowa—it was felt not only for the aged Emperor, who had experienced Jena and Sedan, it was felt for the man who, like no other, possessed the highest virtues of a sovereign: a sense of duty, conscientiousness, firmness of character, inflexible courage, without boastfulness or self-advertisement, true piety without ostentation and mysticism. My veneration was felt for the soldier who was a soldier from top to toe, soldierly to the tips of his fingers; it was felt for a man who was noble and simple, industrious, shrewd to the marrow, never uncouth, and yet never affected.

His mind was not nearly so brilliant as that of his elder brother, King Frederick William IV, but he had that healthy, homely common sense of which a Frenchman said: " *Le génie et le bon sens sont frères, l'esprit n'est qu'un collatéral.*" He was not a genius, but he had all those qualities that make a successful ruler. He had a harmonious and balanced personality, and was a just, a mild, a kindly ruler. He had a very clear perception for the right thing. He knew, above all, how to find the right man for the right place, the most valuable quality a sovereign can possess. The fundamental characteristic of his being, his *qualité maîtresse*, to use an expression of Taine's, was loyalty—loyalty towards others, loyalty towards

---

[1] " Ah, old Fritz, step down and be our King again, and in these difficult times rather let our William take your place on horseback."

himself, loyalty to his office. As he was always loyal to those who served him, they, too, were inflexibly loyal to him. There was rarely a man who worked so hard to perfect himself. His teacher, above all else, was life, all experience, whether sweet or bitter, taught him something, and this to the very end of his days. Like Solon, he could say of himself: " γηράσκω δ'ἀεὶ πολλὰ διδασκόμενος " (" I grow old learning always and much "). There has rarely been a man with such self-control and such self-discipline. His self-discipline engendered his delicate consideration of others, great and small alike. It engendered his kindness and his patience. At heart he was touchingly modest. Once when my father, who was one of the last to pay compliments, expressed his genuine admiration for his modesty, the Emperor, who was eighty years old at the time, replied: " How could I not be modest, seeing that my favourite footman may get a better place than I in the next world if he is worth more than I and does his duty better? "

William I was a kindly, just, sensitive and loyal man, and therefore an ideal monarch. The highest praise he could receive was the fact that his masterful Chancellor had nothing more inscribed on his own tomb than the words: " A faithful German servant of Emperor William I." As I saw him stand at his corner window, I would recollect that in the disastrous year 1848 an insolent hand had daubed the words: " National property " on the very same palace where the people were now cheering him, and that neither this insolence nor this tribute could disturb his inner equilibrium. His noble image will never be torn out of the hearts of the German people, who would deserve the distress and the shame that followed the collapse of 1918 and the Revolution if they were to forget their old Emperor.

When I was first presented to William I at a levee as Attaché of the Foreign Office, he said to me, with a friendly glance at my King's Hussar's uniform: " Your former commanding officer, General von Loë, has spoken well of you. I hope you will make a good diplomat; to be so you need only follow the example of your excellent father."

CHAPTER XXII

Berlin Social Life in the Winter of 1873-4—The Salons: Countess Perponcher, Frau von Prillwitz, Mimi Schleinitz, Countess Louise Benkendorf, Cornelia Richter-Meyerbeer—Chief Chamberlain: Count Wilhelm Redern—The Diplomatic Corps—Die Bonbonnière— Weimar and Potsdam—Summer on the Pfingstberg and in Potsdam.

EVEN if I did not take Herr von Brincken's advice and concentrate most of my Berlin activities on visiting casinos and as many balls as possible, I nevertheless went out a good deal and danced a good deal in this, my first Berlin winter. There were no atrocities like the two-step, the fox-trot and shimmy. The culmination of the Berlin winter season, 1873-4, was a ball in the newly-opened arcade between the Linden and the Friedrichstrasse, to which the Emperor had accepted an invitation. Together with Prince Frederick of Hohenzollern, Count Conrad Kanitz, Prince George of Prussia's Adjutant, with Prince Henry XVIII of Reuss, and with the Austrian Councillor of Legation, Baron Münch, I belonged to the committee that organized and arranged the ball. The lady patronesses were the wife of the Austrian Ambassador, Countess Franziska Karolyi, one of the three sisters Erdödy, who were called the "divine children" in Vienna, Countess Wanda Perponcher, the wife of His Majesty's Court Marshal, and Marie von Schleinitz, the wife of the House Minister. The Emperor stayed till nearly midnight. We danced till three. Few of those who laughed and flirted at this brilliant festivity, who danced the dignified quadrille, the even more dignified lancers, the gallop, the graceful polka, the most spiritual and, there-fore, the most æsthetic of all dances, the waltz, see the light of the sun to-day. *Ou sont les neiges d'antan ?*

Berlin had its salons in those days. Ever since the " *Nouvelle Revue,*" owned by the chauvinistic Juliette Lamber, *alias* Madame Adam, published her essays on the " *Société de Berlin,*" many untrue stories have been spread and believed about the salon of Countess Wanda Perponcher and her sister, Frau von Prillwitz. Who was the author of these libels? From the very beginning suspicion concentrated on the Empress Augusta's French reader, M. Gérard. It was characteristic of German *naïveté* and French

314

astuteness, that the Empress Augusta chose a Frenchman to read to her, thereby making him her intimate, and that a young French writer was accepted by the Germans, although he had been recommended for this post by one of the most ardent of French patriots, the leader of the *guerre à outrance* of 1870-71, Leon Gambetta. The German Republic was, incidentally, even more naïve in this respect than the Empire which, after all, did have some acquaintance with the world. Erzberger and Wirth after him, chose a certain Monsieur Hemmer to receive their confidence and give them advice, a headmaster from Metz, whose sympathies were wholly French—he was placed under arrest soon after the beginning of the World War by the German Military Authorities. His father remained in Metz (which had meanwhile become French) as an official after the war, while his son dealt with the *Arcana Imperii* as head of the Chancellery of the Reich. Monsieur Gérard, after he had been dismissed by the Empress Augusta at last, went into French Diplomacy, where he rose to be an Ambassador. Once, later on, when I met him in Paris, he began to talk spontaneously about the " *Société de Berlin*," and gave me his word of honour *proprio motu* that he had nothing to do with this pamphlet. I could not take this *foi d'honnête homme* of his *au serieux*.

The " *trois sœurs*," Countess Perponcher, Frau von Prillwitz, and the Countess Dankelmann, were kind-hearted, amiable women, and the exact opposite of the description of them in the French skit. They were the daughters of Count Karl Moltke, who acted as Chief Equerry at Neustrelitz when I went to school there. All that went on in their salon was quite *convénable*, although I will not say that the conversation was very intellectual—" *in Geist gemacht*," to use a Berlin expression. During the winter season the conversation turned on petty events of Berlin life, and it may be that there was some gossip and scandal now and again. The Schleinitz salon was different. It was really " highbrow." The host, Alexander von Schleinitz, looked back on a brilliant career. He had been Prussian Minister of Foreign Affairs for a short time in 1848, then from 1849 to 1850, and again from 1859 to 1861. Since then he had been Minister of the Royal House, thereby holding a new and influential post. He was Prince Bismarck's *bête noir*. In this case, as in several others, the great statesman fired cannon balls at a sparrow. That he did not like Schleinitz was understandable. It would be difficult to imagine a greater contrast. With his hair dyed black, even when he was an old man (he died in 1885 at the age of seventy-eight), with his slender waist (which was apparently produced by a corset), his sickly smile, and his rather affected way of talking, Schleinitz was indeed as different as possible from the Lord of Schönhausen.

Schleinitz was Bismarck's predecessor. In those days relations between the Minister of Foreign Affairs, Alexander von Schleinitz, and the Ambassador in St. Petersburg, Otto von Bismarck, were still tolerable. They became very bad when Schleinitz venomously opposed Bismarck in the Prussian Court and did all he could to hamper his policy at a time that was very critical for Bismarck, the spring of 1866, when everything was at stake as far as the great German statesman was concerned. Schleinitz was the special favourite of the Empress Augusta. She drew on him for the arguments with which she tried to set King William against his mighty Minister during that decisive crisis in Prussian history. My friend and comrade in arms, Guido Nimptsch, who was a close relative of Baroness Schleinitz and frequented her house a good deal, told me, that in May, 1866, members of the Austrian Embassy came there every day so as to inform Herr von Schleinitz about the political situation from the Austrian point of view and, on their part, to hear what he had to say of the situation at the Court of Prussia. Bismarck never forgave these intrigues, which he called treason and high treason. On the other hand, the old King, who never sacrificed any servant he considered faithful, would not sacrifice his House Minister. Indeed, later on, a year after the Berlin Congress, he raised him to the rank of Count, which put Bismarck into a towering, extravagant rage.

Marie von Schleinitz belonged to the Trachenberg family, where the different relationships are so complicated that they require a brief survey before they can be understood. The Catholic Prince, Hermann von Hatzfeldt-Trachenberg, abducted the wife of Count Kurt von Götzen, née Countess Mathilde von Reichenbach-Goschütz, who was nine years older than he, in the year 1830. He succeeded in having the marriage Götzen-Reichenbach (which was blessed with three children) annulled at Rome. Of Götzen's second marriage another five children were born. Of the first marriage of Prince Hermann Hatzfeldt with Countess Mathilde Reichenbach were born the hereditary Prince Stanislaus (who was killed not far away from me in the Battle of Amiens on 27th November, 1870), Countess Franziska Hatzfeldt (whose first marriage was with Paul von Nimptsch, and her second with the Field-Marshal General von Loë) and the beautiful Countess Elizabeth Hatzfeldt, who later on became Carolath. A few years after Prince Hermann Hatzfeldt had married the Countess Mathilda Reichenbach he fell in love with the wife of the Prussian Ambassador at the Vatican,

Frau Marie von Buch, *née* von Nimptsch. An attempt to have his marriage with the Countess Mathilde Götzen annulled so that he might be able to marry again was rejected by the Holy See. *Ne bis in idem.* So, with swift resolution, he left the Catholic Church and joined the then newly-founded set of German Catholics, the " Friends of Light," who did not object to blessing his second union. He was excommunicated, but after the death of his first wife, he found his way back to the Church. *Il y a des accomodements avec le ciel.* Of the Hatzfeldt-Nimptsch marriage were born the subsequent Duke of Trachenberg and the Countess Hermina Hatzfeldt, who married the Hungarian Count Edward Teleki. Then, when she had got a divorce from him, she married the Siebenburgian Baron Emile Henning-O'Caroll von Elye-O'Carroll und Oriell. After being divorced from her second husband also, she lived in free love with a gondoliere in the little township of Mestre, near Venice. Princess Marie Hatzfeldt, *née* Nimptsch brought with her a daughter from her marriage with Herr von Buch. This daughter first married the House Minister, von Schleinitz, and then, after his death, the Austrian Ambassador at St. Petersburg and Paris, Count Anton Wolkenstein. I hope that I have now undone the tangle. To show how complicated relationships in the House of Hatzfeldt were, I may also mention that Frau Franziska von Loë was, as Frau von Nimptsch, at once the sister-in-law and the step-daughter of Princess Marie Hatzfeldt. My friend, Guido Nimptsch, could boast of being both the grandson and the nephew of the old Prince Hermann Hatzfeldt.

Before she married Schleinitz in 1865, Marie von Buch had spent two winters in Paris with her grandmother, Frau von Nimptsch *née* Gilgenheimb. There the two ladies were called " *la jeune Buche et la vieille Nymphe.*" When she was married *la jeune Buche* was twenty-five, whereas Schleinitz was fifty-eight. It was clear that malicious tongues in Berlin were busy on this incongruity. It was said that the morning after the wedding day Mimi (for so the young wife was called by everybody, even then) declared, in a rather disappointed voice, to her mother: " so that's what they call marriage! " She was a not undistinguished woman. To begin with her good qualities, she was, as indeed by virtue of her ancestry she ought to have been, a true Prussian, and a true Prussian she remained even when in 1885 she married an Austrian diplomat, Count Anton Wolkenstein, who was Ambassador at St. Petersburg and later on in Paris. She was a Prussian and a Protestant, and both in Paris and Vienna she openly professed her Prussianism and Protestantism. She was a character. This she proved with regard to Richard Wagner, to whose cause she was attached by an inflexible faith, and whose Bayreuth plans she furthered with unflagging zeal. It was thanks to her that the Emperor William I attended the first performance of the *Nibelungen Ring* at Bayreuth. She left the old Emperor no peace until he went there himself, although, as he frankly admitted, he did not in the least understand the music of the future. In her Berlin salon she succeeded in persuading people who, although quite unmusical, were moneyed, to invest in Bayreuth. She was able to persuade the Turkish Ambassador to take ten shares on behalf of the Sovereign. When my father asked the Ambassador later on, how he had succeeded in moving the Padishah to such munificence towards a German undertaking at Bayreuth, he answered quite candidly: " I wrote to the Sovereign that it was good business to start an opera at Beirut, and he has contributed to this purpose with great generosity."

Together with her outstanding qualities, Mimi Schleinitz also had great faults. She was affected in her bearing, her facial expression, her speech, in her whole approach, and often in her very thoughts. Molière's *Précieuses Ridicules* would have welcomed her as their sister. She was very vain and in a way she sometimes called forth ridicule. Like most vain people she was liable to jealousy or envy. Once when her friend, Cornelia Richter said to her that she had a violent headache, Mimi answered: " I have got a headache, too." She was annoyed by the thought that anyone else could offer anything she could not.

Mimi Schleinitz often tried to be on friendly terms with Bismarck and so prepare a reconciliation between him and her husband. Once at the end of the seventies Bismarck dined at the Schleinitz's. After dinner Mimi brought him his long pipe, filled it herself, and lit it with a spill. But if Bismarck really hated someone, a real reconciliation was very difficult. A few days later a paper associated with Bismarck published an article against Alexander von Schleinitz that was no less acrimonious than all the previous ones. The wise old Gerson Bleichröder used to say: " The Prince is like our God Jehovah, who punishes misdeeds without mercy to the third and fourth generation."

Another Berlin salon (it was much more commonplace than that of the Schleinitz's) was that of Countess Louise Benkendorf, *née* Croy. She was the daughter of a Prussian, and a widow of a Russian Adjutant. Her salon was chiefly frequented by diplomats. On the day after the victory of Sadowa she sent an enthusiastic congratulatory telegram to the victor, the old King William. The King, who lacked neither spirit nor humour, replied: " *Je vois avec plaisir que nos victoires ont fixé votre nationalité.*" Prussian by birth, a Russian by marriage, she had from time to time given herself out to be a Belgian, adducing the fact that a part of the Croy family was of Belgian nationality. She had also been chief Lady-in-Waiting at Stuttgart, but later on, when her elder brother was in the Austrian service, she went to Vienna and, as an ardent Catholic, made many pilgrimages to Rome *ad limina apostolorum*. Politically she shone in many colours. Bismarck was convinced that the Countess Louise Benkendorf was an agent of the St. Petersburg Cabinet, and got the means which enabled her to give receptions from the Russian Ministry of Foreign Affairs, so as to influence her guests in favour of Russia, and, above all, to report to St. Petersburg what she had heard from them. Whenever Bismarck wanted a piece of news to reach St. Petersburg inconspicuously, he used to say to one of his secretaries, " you can tell it in the Benkendorf salon to-morrow evening, Gortchakov will then hear it within a week at the most."

I much preferred the house of Professor Rudolf Gneist to the Benkendorf salon, and even the salon of Mimi Schleinitz. Indeed, I preferred it to all the other salons I frequented, not only because the keen minds and sparkling intellect of the host attracted me, but also because I used to meet interesting professors and deputies there, who fascinated me by their conversation, and from whom I could learn. I was also fond of frequenting the houses of Borsig and Hansemann.

During the winter season I used to accompany my parents when they visited my great-aunt, Gabriele von Bülow on Saturdays. She spent her summers in the historic suburb of Tegel, in winter she moved to a comfortable but modest apartment in the quiet, dignified Dorotheenstrasse. There were no richly-loaded side-boards in her home, such as became the usage, or rather, misusage, in Berlin, but only tea with biscuits to dip into it. But the old lady, who gave receptions here, was surrounded by great and beautiful memories. She was the widow of Heinrich Bülow, the daughter of Wilhelm and the niece of Alexander von Humboldt. She was over seventy, even in those days, and was eighty-five when she died. When she was a child she had been to Rome with her parents and there she saw Pius VII and his Secretary of State, Consalvi, and welcomed Canova and Thorwaldsen as friends of the family. Two of her brothers and sisters died in Rome, they rest in the picturesque non-Catholic cemetery near the Pyramid of Cestius. She had lived in Rome on the very same Pincio where I, her grand-nephew, was to find a beautiful winter residence a hundred years later, after my resignation. She spoke Italian readily and fluently in her old age, and when, after my marriage, I introduced my wife to her, she welcomed her, as an Italian, with special warmth, and kept up an animated conversation with her in the best Italian (*lingua toscana in bocca romana*). In 1812, during Germany's darkest days, she had spent a considerable time at Vienna with her parents. Theodor Körner, who was a frequent visitor at her parents' house, took great pleasure in Gabriele, who used to play her part gracefully in the little comedies which he wrote for her on festive family occasions. In July, 1812, he wrote to his relatives: " this graceful child makes the most insignificant things seem significant. She acts my occasional pieces with infinite talent." Körner's first dramatic effort was written for Gabriele. While she acted in Körner's comedies her father gave her instruction in Greek. Four years later, when she was not yet fifteen years old, she was engaged to Heinrich Bülow, who worked under her father as Secretary of Legation. She had been confirmed scarcely six months before. She did not, it is true, marry until four years later. She spent the intervening time with her mother in Rome and in Naples, but remained a good German. In 1817, shortly before her sixteenth birthday, she wrote to her fiancé, who probably feared that she would become altogether Italian: " I feel so tied, and with such strong bonds, to the dear German Fatherland, my whole being and my whole life are, thank God, so strongly chained to it that it will always be dearer to me than any other. I was born in Germany, I got to know and love you there, I became yours there, and you, too, are a German." After climbing Vesuvius from Naples, the fifteen-year-old fiancé assures her Heinrich of her tenderest love in passionate phrases: " I wish I could dissolve in yearning for you, but the peace which your love gives me cannot be driven out of my soul by anything, and so I gladly abandon myself to the sweet and mournful mood in which I feel happy, for in that mood no other feeling of mine can live, save you alone, your inspiring love and my trust in God's goodness, a trust that is doubly confirmed here when I contemplate His works." Her marriage with Heinrich Bülow was consecrated by Schleiermacher in the Church of the Holy Trinity at Berlin in January, 1821. Schleiermacher was the friend and spiritual brother of her father. Nine years later he confirmed Otto von Bismarck, then a schoolboy of fifteen, in the same church.

After Heinrich Bülow, whom I have already mentioned in my memoirs, had been Councillor in the Ministry of Foreign Affairs for several years, he was appointed Ambassador in London in 1887.

PRINCE ALEXANDER MIKHAILOVITCH GORTCHAKOV, RUSSIAN PREMIER

During the fourteen years of his work in London he and his wife became intimate with the Royal Family, and especially with Queen Victoria, who was then still very young. When I was Secretary of State and visited Windsor in 1899, the Queen spoke to me of her very kindly as "my very dear friend, Gabriele von Bülow," and told me how much she loved Gabriele, and how highly she esteemed her husband. Gabriele lost her great father in 1835. In her much-read *Life* [1] the last hours of Wilhelm von Humboldt are described in a passage that is justly famous. Such euthanasia is granted to few people. The lucidity and calm, with which he faced death, made his dying harmonize completely with his whole life, and no more suitable epitaph could be imagined than Schiller's verses in the *Artists*, verses of which Humboldt himself was always particularly fond:

> " *Mit dem Geschick in hoher Einingkeit,*
> *Gelassen, hingestützt auf Grazien und Musen,*
> *Empfängt er das Geschoss, das ihn bedräut,*
> *Mit freundlich dargebotenem Busen*
> *Vom sanften Bogen der Notwendigkeit.*" [2]

During his last hours he said to his daughter Gabriele: "I do not believe that the end of this life is the end of all. My brother Alexander believes that the eternal order of things will remain unknown to us even after death, but I believe that the spirit is the highest of all things, and cannot perish." During his death agony he quoted Greek hexameters. To his daughter he said: "I am not dying yet, for I can see the hair of Venus in all its details." He had been carried into his study, where the Venus of Melos stood. His last words were: "Everything is quite calm, bright, and sunny in me, so that I cannot complain."

Five years after the death of his great father-in-law, Heinrich Bülow was appointed Prussian Ambassador to the Federal Diet at Frankfort in 1841, where, together with Gabriele, he lived in the same pleasant Mainzer Strasse where I was to spend my childhood ten years later. In 1842 he was appointed Minister of Foreign Affairs. In the four years during which he held this office, Heinrich Bülow worked himself to death, just as my dear father did after him in six years. They both died, to use an expression of Bismarck's, on their office stools, like soldiers under fire. Not long before his

---

[1] *Gabriele von Bülow, Daughter of Wilhelm von Humboldt, a Life.* Berlin, Ernst Siegfried Mittler & Son.

[2] In lofty union with Fate, calm leaning on the Graces and the Muses, cheerfully offering his breast he receives the bolt that threatens him from Necessity's gentle bow.

death the Princess of Prussia, who afterwards became the Queen and Empress Augusta, wrote to Gabriele Bülow: " you know that in these grave times I honour Bülow both as the only statesman of Prussia and, at the same time, as a personal friend, which is saying more than I could otherwise express." Heinrich Bülow died on the 6th February, 1846. When King Frederick William IV received the news of his death he said, deeply moved, to Alexander von Humboldt: " It is a real misfortune for my reign. Such lucid ideas, such firmness, such courage when a decision was taken! You, Humboldt, must know it—he was the only Minister who made me feel that he understood me, even when he could not take my view."

On the 18th October, 1861, on the forty-eighth anniversary of the Battle of the Nations, of the Battle of Leipzig, when the coronation of King William I took place at Königsberg, Gabriele von Bülow stood next to Queen Augusta as chief Lady-in-Waiting. Four days later she accompanied the Queen as she entered Berlin. She was aware of the historical importance of that day. She said to her children the same evening that a new era was beginning and, as she hoped and anticipated, an era of real greatness. She was not wrong. After the wild nightmare of 1848, after the weak, tentative and futile attempts to make moral conquests on behalf of the " new age," the heroic, the greatest period of Prussian and German history was to follow. Gabriele von Bülow lived to see her granddaughter Therese Loë appointed chief Lady-in-Waiting to the Princess William, after her marriage with Count Bertram Brockdorff. She died on the 16th April, 1887, and was buried at Tegel, where she was laid between her husband and Alexander von Humboldt.

I often dined at the house of the Chief Chamberlain, Count Wilhelm Redern, who was married to an aunt of my mother's, Bertha Jenisch. He was more than seventy years old at the time. He was the son of a Prussian Lord Chamberlain, and had entered the service of the Prussian Court when he was quite young. He accompanied Frederick William III on a journey to Italy in 1822. He was fond of relating how he was next to the King when the latter was standing on the Posilipus, by Virgil's grave, as he received the news that the Chancellor of State, Prince Hardenberg, had died on the 26th November, 1822, at Genoa. A Prussian Royal Messenger breathlessly brought the King this piece of news. Hardenberg remained in trusted official and personal contact with his Sovereign until his death, that is to say, for a quarter of a century. When the latter received the news of the death of the well-tried and excellent statesman, he said, with considerable equanimity: " quite superfluous to send me a Royal Messenger on this account." The King was fond of speaking in broken phrases. Count Wilhelm Redern ended his story with the words (which he addressed to me): " My young friend, never forget, that there are white people, black people, and Princes. The Princes are different from the other people. The sentiment of gratitude is, as a rule, but weakly developed in them." To-day, half a century later, I must express agreement with this observation. But I will add that the representatives of the people and the parties are not much more grateful.

The older the Chief Chamberlain, Redern, grew, the more he lived in the past. In the end he repeated the phrases which he had acquired in his best period under Frederick William IV, although these phrases were now quite out of date. I remember that in the seventies when, in the presence of Count Wilhelm Redern, who had, meanwhile, become nearly eighty years old, there was talk of the difficult character of the Princess Charlotte of Prussia, the eldest daughter of the Crown Prince and Crown Princess, he replied abruptly: " The Emperor Nicholas ought to be asked what is to be done, he always knows best what we ought to do." He once said to me: " Things used to be easier than they are to-day. In the old days we would simply ask Prince Metternich and later on the Emperor Nicholas, what we were to do, and we always got good advice. Since Bismarck, everything has grown excited and stormy—the best times are over."

If I remember rightly, the beautiful palace of the Redern's, built by Schinkel, stood on the Unter den Linden, where the Hotel Adlon, the biggest Berlin hotel, is to-day. Whenever I go there I think of my old uncle, Wilhelm Redern, his old-fashioned black necktie wound several times round his shirt collar, his long frock-coat, his stiff bearing. His nose was up in the air when he walked, and that is why the Berliners gave him the nickname of " Cloudpusher." His brother, whom I have already mentioned, the diplomat, Count Heinrich Redern, was called the " Bread Monkey," because of his big mouth, which was adorned by a mighty " ratelier." People were not exactly benevolent in old-time Berlin. It is strange that in the greatest period of our history outstanding personalities often got nicknames and were made objects of satire. Things are different under the Republic, whose matadors provoke satires at least as much.

A home in which I felt much at my ease was that of a painter, Gustav Richter, and his wife, Cornelia, daughter of the composer,

Meyerbeer. Until her death only a few years after the World War, Frau Cornelia was a true, dear friend to me. Even her soft voice was sympathetic to me. Her gentleness and kindness created an atmosphere of harmony and peace all around her that made me feel as if I were in an oasis.

The most elegant of the Berlin diplomatic homes was the French Embassy. Thiers, who knew the world and could appreciate what a good social position meant to a diplomat, put aristocrats and representatives of the old system into the most important positions abroad, even after the defeat of France, indeed, to soften the consequences of this defeat, although he strove to preserve and consolidate the Republican form of Government. To London he at first sent as Ambassador the Duke of Larochefoucauld-Bisaccia, later the Duke Decazes; to Vienna the Marquis d'Harcourt, to the Quirinal the Marquis de Noailles, to the Vatican the Baron de Corcelle, to the militaristic city of St. Petersburg he sent General Leflo, to Copenhagen the Viscount de Fériol, to Madrid the Viscount Bouillé, to Berlin the Viscount Gontaut-Biron, who came of an old and illustrious family. As I have already said, the last-named French diplomat soon succeeded in winning the favour of the Empress Augusta. Bismarck was never able to overcome the distrust he felt for this man.

As far as intelligence was concerned, he was far behind the English Ambassador, Odo Russell, later on Lord Ampthill, who combined a very good education and charming manners with political tact and insight. Odo Russell succeeded in winning, not only the sympathy, but also the confidence of, Prince Bismarck. He and his beautiful wife were welcome in Berlin Society. They were equally popular at the Crown Prince's Court and in the Palace of the Imperial Chancellor.

Count Aloys Karolyi represented the Hapsburg monarchy in Berlin before 1866. Herr Otto von Bismarck-Schönhausen, who had just been made Prussian Minister of Foreign Affairs, said to him in 1863 that he advised Austria to shift her centre of gravity to Ofen. Not long after our victory in the Franco-German War, Karolyi came to Berlin for the second time, this time as Austro-Hungarian Ambassador. His successor, Count Felix Wimpffen, had not done much good in Berlin during the intervening years. Bismarck, who had kept up friendly personal relations with Karolyi even in the critical years before the Austro-Prussian War, declared himself in complete agreement with his return to Berlin, but at the same time expressed astonishment that he, a Magnate rolling in wealth, of whom it was said that he kept as many shepherds on his domains as other people keep sheep on their estates, should again take the burden of office upon his shoulders. " Well, it's like this," replied Aloys Karolyi, " in the mornings I go for a ride, in the afternoons I pay visits and play a game of whist at the club, in the evenings I go to parties or give parties myself. Only between twelve and one p.m. did I not know what to do with myself after my retirement. I shall now kill this hour by signing documents in the Chancellery."

The Italian Ambassador, Count Launay, had an excellent political mind. A Savoyard by birth, he hardly spoke Italian at all, and had permission to write his reports in the French language. By disposition Launay was not merely *Italianissimo*, but passionately anti-French. He was the only one of the foreign representatives in Berlin with whom Holstein had an intimate and never-clouded personal and political relationship.

Of all the foreign diplomats, the Belgian Ambassador, Baron Nothomb, was probably the one with the best personal and political position. With no other country were our relations so friendly and so secure as with Belgium. Baron Nothomb's only daughter was married to Colonel von Zedlitz, who had led the second Dragoon Guards at the glorious attack of Mars-la-Tour.

The Russian Ambassador himself always asserted that he came of a distinguished family of *émigrés*. Prince Bismarck, who was not very well disposed towards him, said that Ubril was really the grandson of a French cook whose " *petits pâtés* " were appreciated by Catherine the Great. The Councillor of the Russian Embassy, Arapov, and the Military Attaché, Kutusov, could stand a lot of alcohol. On one occasion, at a Court Banquet, Arapov was put in a merry mood by the wine he had drunk, and he poured a glass of champagne over his own head, saying in a thick, rambling voice: " I am having a second christening, only this time with champagne." Kutusov too rarely came home sober after a dinner or supper. Once when he was in a fairly large party he related how his family was of Pomeranian origin and was originally called Kutus. Thereupon the ready-witted Minister of the Interior, Count Frederick Eulenburg said: " You must have got the ' *sov* ' (' Suff '—drinking habit) in Russia." Baron Mitia Benkendorf, who for many years was the Second Secretary of the Russian Embassy, led a very wild life. He and his wife lived in grand style in Berlin until they disappeared, shooting the moon, leaving considerable debts behind them. The woman sank so low that she ended in a Parisian brothel. She was not particularly pretty and, when several days had passed without her being able to please any visitor, she shot herself and left a letter in which she declared that spurned love had driven her to her death. A French writer did not miss the opportunity of making her the heroine of a novel much read in those days, entitled "*Le pistolet de la petite Baronne.*" It was characteristic of Russian grand ducal frivolity that the Grand Duke Vladimir took this poor woman's husband into his entourage, although it was he who, by his irresponsibility and worse, was chiefly guilty of his wife's downfall. The Grand Duke used to like to take him along on his yearly autumn visit to Paris, and at Chantilly he introduced him to the Duke of Aumale with the words: "*Voici mon ami, le Baron Mitia Benckendorf, célèbre par ses malheurs conjugaux, du reste un homme charmant!*"

Amongst the Ambassadors of the Federal States was the Bavarian Perglas, one of the last representatives of anti-Imperial Bavarian particularism. At Berlin Court celebrations he attached himself demonstratively to the diplomatic corps, and not to the Federal Diet. Once when Bismarck saw him standing amongst the foreign envoys, he addressed him in French. When Perglas, with some embarrassment, replied that he was Bavarian Ambassador and understood German quite well, Bismarck said: "As you always join the foreigners instead of your colleagues of the Federal Diet, I thought you were a foreigner." By way of contrast with Perglas, the Württemberg Ambassador, Baron Hugo von Spitzemberg, belonged to the intimates of Bismarck's home. He and his wife, a daughter of Karl von Varnbüler, who for many years was Premier of Württemberg, were on intimate terms with the Bismarck family even in St. Petersburg, where Bismarck represented Prussia and Spitzemberg Württemberg. Frau von Spitzemberg gradually succeeded in reconciling Prince Bismarck with her father, who, in June, 1866, had replied in the Württemberg Chamber to the question what was to be done with defeated Prussia with the triumphant words: "*Vae Victis!*" Baron Karl von Varnbüler became a zealous collaborator in the great Chancellor's protectionist policy. Like his son-in-law, Spitzemberg, Karl von Varnbüler did not live to see the dismissal of Bismarck. His son Axel von Varnbüler, and his daughter, the widow Hildegard von Spitzemberg, were amongst the first who drifted away from Bismarck after his fall. Axel, who afterwards represented Württemberg as Ambassador and plenipotentiary in the Federal Diet, followed the example of Phili Eulenburg, with whom he had been on terms of intimate friendship ever since they had studied together at Strassburg. His sister, Hildegard von Spitzemberg, attached herself with such enthusiasm to Bismarck's successor that the sarcastic inhabitants of Friedrichsruh would say with a growl that she had set her cap at the old bachelor Caprivi so as to be a Chancellor's wife.

Of the diplomats representing the Federal States in Berlin I liked best of all the Baden representative, Türckheim, and Dr. Krüger, envoy of the Hanseatic towns. Baron von Türckheim zu Altdorf, who had represented Baden in Berlin since 1864, was a sturdy Aleman of the same type as Karl Mathy and Ernst Basser-mann. His keen patriotism and hearty delight in our glorious German Empire, that had emerged from the fiery ordeal of three victorious wars, were doubly beneficent in a city like Berlin, then much too critically disposed, and therefore superficial and petty in its judgments. Dr. Krüger was a forceful Low German, who stood strong and stalwart on solid earth, allowing himself less than anyone to veer with the wind of Berlin scandal.

During the winter the Empress Augusta gave receptions once a week. The apartment of the historical palace where she received was called the Bonbonnière. I have rarely seen guests received in so dignified and yet so kind a manner. It is said that in her early youth the Empress was often conducted by her chief governess to a little wood near Weimar where she had to address a not too commonplace question to every tree in order to train herself for future receptions. Goethe, who saw Princess Augusta of Saxe-Weimar slumbering in her cradle (she was born in 1811), would have been delighted at the bearing and manner of the Queen and Empress. The old Emperor always appeared at his wife's recep-tions. He spoke to each of the guests, always kindly and often with some good-natured pleasantry. When the Empress said good-bye to her guests the Emperor offered his arm to the older ladies and escorted them to the door.

Once when I was standing with my dear old friend, Prince Henry XVIII of Reuss all alone in a small room of the apartment during a soirée at the Bonbonnière, he put his hand into a malachite vase and drew forth a list of the guests which a careless lackey had left there. The Empress had revised the list with a blue pencil. We were sorry to be forced to the conclusion that Her Majesty had crossed out a number of political followers of the Imperial Chancellor and personal friends of the Bismarck family, also a number of the nobility from East Prussia, Pomerania and the Marches, as well as everybody with the name of Stuman. In their stead she had entered other names in the list submitted to her by the Lord Chamberlain, chiefly Rhinelanders, Westphalians and Silesians, most of them Roman Catholic names. Next to my father's name she herself had written the words: " To be invited

with both his sons." The old Empress esteemed my father and
said to my old comrade in arms, the Cabinet Councillor, Bodo
von dem Knesebeck, who was on terms of intimacy with her:
"The Minister of State, von Bülow, is a political friend of Prince
Bismarck's, and has been a personal friend of his for more than a
quarter of a century. I respect his faithful nature. But with his
excellent manners, with his culture, and, fundamentally, with his
whole attitude towards life, Herr von Bülow belongs to Goethe's
time, which is my time." The Empress Augusta always considered
herself a Princess of Weimar, even after June, 1829, when, accompanied by the blessing of aged Goethe, she had followed Prince
William of Prussia to Berlin.

Since in February, 1919, that is to say, in the darkest period
which the German people had seen since the terrible Thirty Years
War and the days of the Napoleonic domination, the cliché which
opposed "Weimar" to "Potsdam" were first spread by empty-
headed talkers, it has been fashionable to contrast these two conceptions. Such superficiality creates confusion of mind and harms
the Fatherland. The truth about "Potsdam" and "Weimar" is
that these are not by any means opposites, but complementaries.
My friend, the poet, Adolf Wilbrandt, has brought Potsdam and
Weimar face to face in a profound though graceful comedy which,
if I remember rightly, is called "*The Under-Secretary of State.*"
A young and clever official and a charming, amiable girl, the daugh-
ter of a professor, feel a mutual attraction and argue about politics.
He says: "I stand by Bismarck, Moltke, Blücher, Fredericus Rex,
Ziethen and Seidlitz, by the creator of our exemplary and model
Prussian administration and our glorious army, by King Frederick
William I, by the Great Elector with whom the re-awakening of
the German people from long political sleep begins." She lisps:
"And I follow Goethe, Schiller, Herder, Lessing." In the end
they understand each other and fall into each other's arms to unite
forever. In the speech which I made at Berlin on the 16th June,
1901, before the National Memorial to Prince Bismarck, I said:

In the political sphere and in the realms of action, Bismarck,
for us, has become what Goethe was for us in the realms of the
spirit, of art and culture. He, too, as Schiller said of Goethe,
has "crushed the serpent that stifled the genius of our Nation."
Goethe has united us in the sphere of education, Bismarck has
taught us to think and act politically. And just as Goethe
stands for ever like a star in our intellectual heavens, so is
Bismarck our guarantee that our nation can never surrender

its equality with other nations, its right to unity, to independence, to power. He has set us an example never to be faint-hearted, not even in times of difficulty and confusion. [1]

And on the 30th September, 1907, I said in the Reichstag [2] that only a combination of old Prussian conservative energy and discipline, with the large-hearted, liberal German spirit, could give the nation a happy future. I have repeated this more than once, and it is as true to-day as it was then. Macchiavelli is right when he says that the nations must always return to the point at which their greatness started. *Ritornare al segno.*

The Empress Augusta was too clever and too wise not to appreciate Potsdam also. But she considered it the task of the Monarchy to exercise a levelling, conciliatory influence. She wished not to stir up political passions, but to calm them. She wanted to heal the wounds which the hard hand of the Iron Chancellor had made. Her guiding star was the saying of Goethe's: " Noble be man, helpful and good."

In the summer of 1874 I lived with my parents at Potsdam, where they had rented a villa on the Pfingstberg, to escape from the heat of the capital. There were some wonderful views from this house. The broad Havel landscape lay spread out before our eyes. The lakes seemed like great silver shields to us. When the day came to an end the sails of the boats that crossed the lake were coloured crimson by the sunset, while hundreds of windows shimmered in the dying light. How glorious was the " New Palace " in Potsdam, the creation of the great King, the house where our dear Emperor Frederick was born, and where he was to bow his head in death. And the Garrison Church where stands the Great King's coffin. How many overwhelming historical memories! And also what a beautiful countryside.

[1] Prince Bülow's *Speeches* (large edition), vol. i, p. 222; (small edition), vol. i, p. 246.
[2] *Ibid.* (large edition), vol. iii, pp. 93-94; (small edition), vol. v, p. 43.

CHAPTER XXIII

Attaché in Rome—Tour of Southern France and Italy—Arrival at Rome (15.10.1875)—Minister von Keudell—Journey to Sicily—Gregorovius—Mommsen—Roman Society—Pius IX and the Kingdom of Italy—Church and State in Italy.

IN the autumn of 1874 my father said to me that in his opinion, now that I had had my first training in the Foreign Office, it would be a good thing if he were to send me abroad. "Where would you like to go?" I answered, without thinking: "To Italy!" My father was kind enough to propose that I should use this occasion to look at Southern France as well. So I started on the journey.

After I had spent several days on the shores of Lake Geneva, which has always remained dear to me, I visited Lyons, Avignon, Nimes, Tarascon, Arles, Marseilles, Toulon and Nice. I read a few good books before I started on my Italian journey: Taine's *Voyages en Italie*, Stendhal's *Rome, Naples et Florence*, and the *Promenades dans Romes*, by the same Stendhal. I read the three volumes which Adolf Stahr, the husband of Fanny Lewald, published in 1847 under the title *Ein Jahr in Italien*, a book that does not seem out of date to me even now, and which I would like to recommend to every German who travels beyond the Alps. I read the *Philosophie de l'art en Italie*, by Hippolyte Taine, and Stendhal's *La Chartreuse de Parme*, with reverence, the finest piece of psychological work that has ever been written about the Italian country and people. When I said good-bye to my father he gave me a last piece of advice to take to heart, Goethe's words: "Delight, pleasure in things, is the only reality and alone brings forth reality—everything else is vain and only renders vain."

In Southern France I was struck by two things—the extraordinary uniformity of France. The people of Provence were the same as those of Normandy and Picardy (with whom I was already acquainted) in their customs, their manners, and their bearing. Everywhere the pensioned officers drank their absinthe in the afternoons, the citizens played dominoes on the tables in front of the cafés, the women went to mass in the mornings, and everybody waited for the newspapers from Paris. I understood how a French Minister of the Interior is able to transfer a Prefect from Lille to Montpellier, from Bordeaux to Nancy, without trouble, and how the French people, if led by a strong hand, has only one will in the hour of decision. That France has always recovered rapidly after every defeat or misfortune is in no small part due to the rigid centralization carried out by Richelieu, the Convention, and Napoleon I, and maintained by all French Governments, and to the French people's inner unity, which has proceeded from this centralization. In the masterful speech which Thiers made on the 19th of February, 1871, in the French National Assembly at Bordeaux, and in which he explained the necessity of peace with Germany, he emphasized, as a reason for not despairing of his country's future in this hour, that was so cruel and terrible, her " ancient and mighty unity." The unity of France is also one of the chief reasons why the French feel the loss of territories more acutely than other nations, particularly more than do the Germans. After the Peace of Frankfort most Frenchmen really felt as though, by losing Strassburg and Metz they had lost one of their own limbs. It was in this manner that a French Minister of Foreign Affairs, Challemel-Lacour, characterized the French mentality since the Peace of Frankfort, though he himself was neither a jingo nor particularly anti-German—he had even known and translated Schopenhauer. Do most Germans feel their losses in the same way—the loss of West Prussia and Posen, which were ours for more than a century, of Thorn and Graudenz and Bromerg, of Danzig and Memel, of Upper Silesia, that was never Polish, of the beautiful town of Strassburg and the fortress of Metz, and the immense losses suffered by the German race in almost all parts of the former Austrian Monarchy?

The second thing I learnt during this journey through Southern France was that although this country had known more violent internal struggles than any other, the French—and I say it to their glory—unite again much more easily than we Germans in common love of their Fatherland. If we except Bolshevik Russia, which is still in full process of development, history has hardly seen greater horrors, more sanguinary internal fights, than France. How much blood flowed under the rule of the Convention? " *Quatrevingt-treize, épouvantable année, de lauriers et de sang grande ombre couronnée!* " So sang the French poet, mindful, in the first instance, of the laurels of victory with which France wreathed herself in those days, and only in the second place, of the blood that was shed in streams. How much blood flowed in Paris in 1849 during the the June Insurrection, and in 1871 during the Commune?

In Lyons I stood upon the Place des Brotteaux. Here, from a balcony, sitting between two half-clothed courtesans and with a plentifully laid table in front of him, Joseph Fouché enjoyed the spectacle of the thousands whose heads fell under the blade of the guillotine that was erected in the square. At the same time donkeys were driven through the streets, and to their tails were tied the ecclesiastical vessels, Fouché, a former monk, being particularly determined to have these profaned. This record did not prevent him from being first Prefect of Police in Paris under Napoleon, and then Minister of the Interior. It is true that Fouché enjoyed imperturbable self-possession. At the great gala banquet that Napoleon gave in the Tuileries in honour of his marriage to the Archduchess Marie Louise, he asked Fouché, who was sitting opposite him and whom he had made Duke of Otranto, with the brutality that was at times peculiar to him: " Est-ce vrai, Duc d'Otranto, que vous avez voté la mort du roi Louis XVI, oncle de l'Impératrice qui est assise à ma droite ? " In a loud, reverberating voice, Fouché replied: " Parfaitment, Sire, et c'est même le premier service qu'il m'a été donné de rendre à Votre Majesté Imperiale et Royale."

Avignon, Nîmes, Toulon and Marseilles witnessed similar atrocities about the same time, 1793. After the fall of Napoleon, the White Terror raged in Southern France, and was not much better than the Red Terror before it—one of its victims was Marshal Brune, at Avignon, who was torn to pieces by the mob. All France forgets these things when the Marseillaise: " aux armes, citoyens formez vos bataillons " resounds. We have never had party fights that were anything like as sanguinary as those in France, but our parties accuse each other of speeches which this or that member of the opposing party made ten years ago.

At Genoa la superba, I thought of our Schiller's Republican Tragedy, Fiesco, as I visited the magnificent palaces of the nobility, Durazzo, Pallavicini, Balbi, Doria. I devoted a week to Florence. Anatole France's beautiful novel, Le Lys Rouge, had not yet been written, otherwise I would have read it before my arrival in Florence, la bella, so as to put myself in the right mood.

Pisa has always had a special attraction for me. Sometimes when I feel run down or have been irritable, I think how beautiful it must be to live in the quiet town of Pisa, to visit the magnificent campo santo in the mornings, where the mural paintings move us so profoundly with the visual representations of the gravity of death, to stroll about on the Lungarno in the afternoons and to look at the river that flows by, calm and still.

I reached Rome on the 15th October, 1874, and put up at the Hotel de Londres, which is the Hotel des Princes to-day, in the Piazza di Spagna. I then paid a visit to the Palazzo Caffarelli on the top of the Capitol, where, exactly twenty years later, I was to pass happy years with my beloved wife during my ambassadorship. In 1874 the Minister von Keudell (Rome was not raised to the rank of an Embassy till later on) received me with a sturdy shake of the hand, but without saying a word. Thereupon lunch was announced. Apart from myself, Captain Otto von Senden of the Second Dragoon Guards, whom I knew well as a regimental comrade of my brother Adolf, was also invited (he had arrived in Rome a considerable time previously).

During lunch Keudell hardly said a word. After we had smoked a cigar in silence he proposed that I should leave for Naples the following day, Naples being a town I ought to get to know as soon as possible. From there, he suggested, I should travel to Sicily, where I ought to spend at least three weeks. I was a little disappointed by this reception my new chief gave me. I had not expected him to talk to me at once about problems of Italian politics, but I had at least counted on some reference to my future task under his leadership and on some sort of official encouragement. When I descended the flat steps of the Capitol past the horse-taming Dioscuri with Otto Senden, I said to him: " Keudell seems to find it very disagreeable that I have been sent to him as an Attaché, for he did not say a word to me. I shall write to my father and ask him to give me another commission. I am sorry to change, for I was so glad to go to Rome, and I hoped I would spend a lovely winter here." Senden smiled and answered: " On the contrary, I thought Keudell was rather talkative to-day. As a rule he talks even less."

Robert von Keudell was indeed one of the most monosyllabic people I ever came across. As long as he was in Bismarck's good books his silence was accounted a proof of a profound mind and intellectual superiority. Later, when he fell into disfavour with the great Chancellor, it was said that his constant silence was also a proof of his complete insignificance. Keudell owed his career not least to the circumstance that when he was a young man he played duets with Fräulein Johanna von Puttkamer. The good and true Johanna always kept her friendship for the friend of her youth, Robert Keudell, even after she had married the great Otto Bismarck. While the latter was Ambassador of Frankfort, Keudell

often stayed with the Bismarcks. He visited them in St. Petersburg
also. When Bismarck became Premier and Minister of Foreign
Affairs, he felt the need to surround himself with a few collaborators
of whom he could be quite sure. He therefore took Robert von
Keudell into the Ministry of Foreign Affairs as well as his cousin,
Count Karl von Bismarck-Bohlen. Von Keudell spent the nine
important years from 1863 to 1872 as head of the Personal Department in the Ministry. Why did Keudell forfeit the confidence of
his great chief? Perhaps the latter was offended because, after
he had married the rich daughter of the former Liberal Minister
of Trade and Finance, von Patow, Keudell was very anxious to go
abroad. It also seems that in Bismarck's opinion Keudell, who had
good relations with writers and publicists, advertised himself too
much. No doubt intrigues with Holstein, who had been Bismarck's
most intimate confidential collaborator ever since 1860, when he
was Attaché in St. Petersburg under him, contributed towards
disturbing their relationship. Keudell himself, at the time when
I worked as Attaché under him, told me that Holstein had persuaded
Bismarck that he, Keudell, had been spreading a rumour in Berlin
that the doctors declared that Bismarck suffered from softening
of the brain, which would lead in the end to imbecility. In any
case, it was a poisonous arrow, which might very well have been
shot by Holstein.

When I worked in Rome under Keudell in 1874-5, relations
between him and his chief were still tolerable on the surface.
Princess Johanna wrote regularly to the friend of her youth. She
had also conceived a great affection for his wife, the very dear and
kind Frau Hedwig. But Keudell no longer felt secure, and would
often say that he longed for peace. For diplomatic efficiency he
was not equal to other German representatives in Bismarck's time
like Paul Hatzfeldt, Schweinitz, Savigny, Goltz, Prince Henry VII
of Reuss. He did not possess the intellectual depth of Lothar
Bucher, or of my father. But he was industrious and conscientious,
and he had the clear common sense of an East Prussian. In Rome
he was universally popular. He was rightly accounted an admirer
and friend of modern Italy. The German colony, which was very
numerous in those days, was enthusiastic about Keudell.

My chief was right in advising me to visit Naples and Sicily.
I do not propose to describe the weeks I passed there in the
autumn of 1874, as I have not the ambition to compete with Goethe.
I climbed Vesuvius on foot, which, in the heat, was a considerable
effort. A fat gentleman from Württemberg who climbed up with
me had a stroke. There were all kinds of difficulties over his

funeral because the Catholic clergy of the surrounding localities grudged the poor Swabian heretic a burial in consecrated soil. At Sorrento I was warned against visiting the mountain height of the Deserto because of the brigands that infested it. In Sicily the post chaise in which I travelled from Palermo to Girgenti was accompanied by mounted Carabinieri. Brigandage had not yet been exterminated on the beautiful island. At Girgenti, I was introduced to the " Circolo Empedocle," which was so called after the most famous son of the town, the philosopher Empedocles. The gentlemen present there were engaged in political conversation. I asked what the people in Girgenti thought of Marco Minghetti, who at that time was Italian Premier. The answer was: " *Una iena alterata di sangue* " (a hyena intoxicated with blood). This expression has stuck in my memory, for it is characteristic of the value, or rather the worthlessness, of judgments coloured by party politics. To-day it is recognised fairly generally that Marco Minghetti was one of the most moderate and wisest statesmen, as well as one of the most cultured and humane men of his time.

When I returned to Rome after my very satisfactory journey through Southern Italy, Keudell offered me a lodging in the Palazzo Caffarelli, where I got a little room in the third storey. The view from there was splendid. As I gradually became acquainted with the envoys of other nations, I heard it said, especially by Austrians and Frenchmen, that in the long run the Pope and King of Italy would not be able to live together in Rome. " *Ceci tuera cela*," said a talkative French colleague, the Viscount de Mareuil. " Either the Pope would excommunicate the King or the King will order the occupation of the Vatican—in either case a big row." The more opportunities I had to inform myself about the status of this problem, the more I realised that foreigners often judge conditions in Rome falsely and that they particularly under-rate the Italian gift which Anatole France has called the " *Génie Italien de la juxtaposition*." A Catholic German lady told me that Pius IX, who was well known as a man of ideas and a good deal of wit, had asked her what she had found most noteworthy in Rome. She naturally answered: " St. Peter's." The Holy Father shook his head. Thereupon she said: " The Forum and the Palatine." The Holy Father again shook his head, and then said with a smile: " The most remarkable thing of all is surely that I, the Pope, King Victor Emmanuel, and Garibaldi, live in Rome together, and that we do not eat one another up." Garibaldi had been elected Deputy just then. I often met him. He had beautiful, kind eyes and a very simple manner. There was something naïve, dreamy, and yet heroic about him.

I had heard from my friend, Prince Franz Arenberg, when we worked together in the Landgericht at Metz, that his uncle, the Papal Minister of War, Count Frederick Merode, had told him the following little incident, which was characteristic of the relations between Church and State in Italy. Pius IX, behind whose chair Count Merode was standing, received a German Catholic Count, who complained about all the sufferings which the Italian movement for unity had brought upon the Church. The Pope listened respectfully, and now and again showed emotion as he nodded assent. When the German gentleman had been dismissed, Pius IX, who forgot that Merode was still standing behind his chair, said to the Italian Chamberlain who was on duty by his side: " *Questo bestione tedesco non capisce la grandezza e la bellezza dell' idea nazionale Italiana* (this German brute does not understand the greatness and the grandeur of the Italian national idea)." From this and similar stories of Arenberg's I had realized, long before I came to Rome, that the relations between the Holy See and modern Italy are rather more complicated than non-Italians assume.

There was much social gaiety during that winter. I danced a lot. During the Ball at the Quirinal, while we were dancing the last lively gallopade, I was unlucky enough to tread on His Majesty King Victor Emmanuel II's toes. I looked into a very angry, very red and very martial face, with huge turned-up moustache. I was careful enough not to beg his pardon, but danced on as quickly as possible. The great King, thank God, never found out who trod on his toes. The finest festival of the season was a fancy dress ball at the house of the Duke Onorato Sermoneta, the magnificent Palazzo Caëtani, a real Roman Palazzo in the middle of the town. It was situated in the narrow, dark Via delle Botteghe Oscure, but inside it had a splendour such as is rarely found in private houses anywhere except in Italy. The Duke was the chief of one of the few families of the old Roman nobility, and traced his descent from Docibilis I, Magnificus, Lord of Gaeta, who lived in the Carolingian period. The Caetanis were Dukes of Gaeta from the tenth century onwards, and presented the Church with two Popes, Gelasius II, in the twelfth, and Boniface VIII, in the thirteenth century. The tomb of Cecilia Metella on the Via Appia, known to every traveller to Rome, belonged to the Caëtanis in the middle ages. They put turrets on the building and turned it into the tower of a robbers' castle, from where, when it suited their fancy, they made raids into the Campagna, and sometimes even

ATTACHÉ BERNARD VON BÜLOW

At a fancy dress ball in the Palazzo Caëtani, in Rome (1875)

defied a Pope whom they considered inconvenient. In his mediæval costume the Duke Onorata looked as though he would throw down the glove before all his enemies the day after the ball. Other costumes, Italian as well as French, English and German, were magnificent.

I was dressed up as one of Wallenstein's cavalrymen, for, being a good patriot, I did not want to put on a foreign costume. When I look round in Rome to-day, I see but few of those who took part in this beautiful ball. Donna Teresa Caracciolo, who was a charming slender girl then, holding the arm of her fiancé, Prince Marco Antonio Colonna, as she stepped through the rooms of the Palazzo Caëtani, has meanwhile become a seventy-year-old *matrona*, but when we meet each other now I delight in her unfading intellectual youth. Alberto Pansa who, while I was attached to the German Embassy, worked as Attaché in the Italian Ministry of Foreign Affairs and wore a magnificent costume at the Caëtani ball, was entrusted with three Embassies during a subsequent course of his career; with Constantinople, London and Berlin. He goes for a walk with me on the Pincio every Sunday in winter, and we exchange old memories. But where are the other dancers of the Caëtani fancy dress ball in February, 1875?

> " *Wo sind sie hin ?   Es pfeift der Wind,*
> *Es schäumen und wandern die Wellen.*" [1]

At another ball that Keudell gave in the Caffarelli, I led the dance. Suddenly the Ambassador beckoned to me and said to me that Her Royal Highness, Crown Princess Margherita, invited our fellow-countryman, Gregorovius, to dance the next quadrille with her. I went to Gregorovius and transmitted this invitation from the exalted lady. He looked at me for a long time, then crossed his arms, and said to me in a solemn voice: " Tell the Princess that Ferdinand Gregorovius does not dance." He put a strong stress on the " not." The little episode seemed to me characteristic of the ponderous solemnity of German men of learning, but it did not diminish my admiration for Gregorovius. There are few German writers whom I have read with as much pleasure as I have read him. My friend, the English Ambassador in Rome, Sir Rennell Rodd, once told me that the American President, Roosevelt, had asked him what reading matter he could recommend for the long journey he was going to undertake, and during which he would have plenty of time to read. Rodd replied without hesitation:

---

[1] Where are they gone? The wind whistles, the waves foam and wander.

" *The History of Rome in the Middle Ages*, by Ferdinand Gregorovius."
I share Sir Rennell Rodd's admiration for this magnificent book.

This reminds me of an utterance of Theodor Mommsen's that
throws a characteristic light on his ironical manner. Mommsen
made the acquaintance of Gregorovius at Rome in the salon of
Countess Ersilia Lovatelli, the sister of the Duke of Sermoneta,
an intelligent, and indeed, a learned lady, and much given to
archæology. The conversation turned on the destinies of the
Eternal City, in which the two great men had met. Gregorovius
related many new things with lively wit and enthusiasm about the
Roman Middle Ages. When he paused for a moment Mommsen
said: " I will tell you something, why don't you *write* a history of
Rome in the Middle Ages?" Perhaps even more characteristic
of the malice which Mommsen commanded is the way in which
he once disposed of Herman Grimm, the nephew of Jacob, and son
of William Grimm. His achievements were not on the level of
the very good opinion he had of himself. He once said in Mommsen's presence that the German post was making astounding
progress under the management of Stephan, and that, a few days
ago, a letter from America had reached him correctly and punctually,
although it had no address except the two words, " Grimm,
Europe." Thereupon Mommsen, with an indescribably malicious
look: " They do not seem to know in America that Jacob Grimm
has been dead a long time." Herman Grimm was married to
Gisela von Arnim, the daughter of Bettina von Arnim, the Goethean
" child." She tried to imitate her mother's originality, but without
possessing her soul and temperament.

During my first sojourn, opinion in Italy was very friendly
towards Germany. This was partly owing to the circumstance
that the tone of the French Press towards Italy was very hostile.
Clericalism, an enemy of the Italian National State, still had great
power in France. Pronounced clericals, like the Duke de Broglie,
the Duke Decazes, General Cissey and Fourton, were in the
Government. The President of the Republic, Marshal MacMahon,
was a true Catholic and a legitimist at heart. At that time all over
France there were constant pilgrimages accompanied by prayers
and demonstrations for the restoration of the temporal rule of the
Pope. The French frigate *Orénoque* was moored at Civita Vecchia
to bring the Pope to safety in case he should need French protection.
As relations between the young German Empire and the Papal
See had grown worse because of the German *Kulturkampf*, and
because Pope Pius IX gave loud and unabashed expression to his
discontent over the German Government's action, Italian patriots

felt themselves doubly drawn towards Germany. But the Italian Government took good care not to imitate Germany's *Kulturkampf* policy, and refrained from all interference in the domestic life of the Catholic Church.

In February, 1875, Pius IX had addressed an impassioned encyclical to the Prussian Episcopate in which he " quite openly " declared to " all whom it may concern," that is to say, in particular, Prussian Catholics, that the May Laws which had been enacted without at all infringing the rules prescribed by the Prussian constitution, were invalid. This signified, if not explicitly, nevertheless implicitly, the release of Catholic Prussian subjects from their duty of obedience to the May Laws. Not long afterwards, Herr von Keudell, with anxious face, told me that he had received an extremely delicate mission from Berlin. Prince Bismarck had written to him that he would no longer put up with the public reproaches and threats uttered by the Pope. Before the seizure of Rome by Italy he would simply have proceeded against the Pontifex Maximus *manu militari*, as, in past centuries, France, the Spaniards and the Roman Emperors of German nationality had done more than once. But now, he said, he would have to hold the Italian Government responsible for the Pope's attitude, and solemnly request it to make him calm down. Keudell felt that it would be difficult to execute this mission, but on the other hand he trembled before his great chief, whose temperament he knew only too well. He decided to carry out his mission that same evening during a Court Ball at the Quirinal. He instructed me, that when he began a conversation with the Minister of Foreign Affairs, Visconti-Venosta, I should stay in the neighbourhood so as to assist his memory when he reported his interview to Berlin.

Emilio Visconti-Venosta, who was forty-five years old at the time, was one of the most calculating and careful politicians I ever came across. I do not believe that he ever did a stupid thing in any sphere during the whole of his life. His family came from the Veltlin and had all the cunning (*furberia*) of the inhabitants of this district, who had to defend themselves alternately against the Swiss and against the Milanese in so many bloody fights in the Middle Ages. He came to Milan when he was young, joined the Radical party there, and wrote newspaper articles in which he called upon the people to pave the streets of the town with the severed heads of the aristocrats. Later on he did not object to being raised to the rank of Marquis. He had, as I have already mentioned, been private secretary to Mazzini. He was Minister of Foreign Affairs four times, the last time in 1896, while I was Ambassador in Rome.

Keudell seized a moment when Visconti was standing alone in a corner of the big ball-room to approach him, followed by myself, the modest but attentively listening Attaché. As they stood facing one another, the honest and essentially warm-hearted German and the cold, cautious Italian, they afforded a piquant contrast. While Keudell spoke to the Minister eagerly, though with visible embarrassment, often halting, and with a red face, the Minister, without moving a muscle of his face, toyed with his long reddish-blonde mutton-chop whispers. When the Ambassador had finished Visconti was silent for at least five minutes, which only intensified Keudell's inner restlessness and embarrassment. Visconti then replied, emphasising every syllable: " I am very much surprised by this unexpected communication, and I must first bring it to the knowledge of the Premier, Minghetti, and His Majesty the King. But I believe that I may tell you the following even now: It is impossible for the Italian Government to exercise pressure on the Pope in the desired direction. It would not only outrage the feelings of the Catholic Italian people, but it would also be contrary to the Guarantee Law of the 16th May, 1871, a law accepted by the Chamber and the Senate, and confirmed by the King, by which the Pope was assured of his position as *independent sovereign* after the incorporation of Rome in united Italy. Article 1 of the Guarantee Law says: ' The person of the Pope (*Sommo Pontifice*) is sacred and inviolable.' But as Italy is most unwilling to forego those good relations which it appreciates so highly with the German Empire, I will, if Prince Bismarck, whom we all admire, insists on his resolve, propose to the Premier and His Majesty King Victor Emmanuel that Rome be evacuated and the Italian capital be transferred to Naples." When Keudell, who plainly felt the irony in the Italian Minister's reply, although he also foresaw that so far the result of his *démarche* would scarcely satisfy Prince Bismarck, became insistent, Visconti wrapped himself in silence. There was nothing left for Keudell save to beat a retreat, followed by myself.

The next day the Ambassador informed the Chancellor by letter as to the course of his interview with Visconti. Prince Bismarck did not return to the subject while I was in Rome. On the other hand, the relationship between the Papacy and Italy as I would like to mention here in advance, was discussed by my father with Minghetti at a meeting between the Emperor William and King Victor Emmanuel which took place at Milan in October, 1875. The Emperor was accompanied by my father, Prince Bismarck had instructed him to give the Italian Premier

a grave warning against further weakness towards the Papacy.
If the Italian Government, so he said, did not show greater energy,
the Italian National State would be destroyed by the plots and
intrigues of the Holy See. When my father spoke to Minghetti
to this effect in Milan, the Italian Premier answered: " We
Italians have had dealings with the Papacy for a thousand years,
and if you will allow me to tell you so frankly—we know it better
than foreigners do, better even than the Germans, whom we esteem
and admire, but who expect everything from learned research and
believe that the historical seminary is the right place to solve big
political questions. I am convinced that without giving way in
vital political questions, though at the same time we show consideration in all religious matters, we shall be on the same quite
tolerable terms with the Papacy as we are to-day, when the great
Prince Bismarck has long since revised his May Laws, and so
begun his retreat."

When it leaked out in the Berlin Press in March, 1875 (it
may even have been published deliberately) that the German
Government had requested the Italian to prevail upon the Pope
to adopt a calmer attitude towards Germany, the Italian Press
declared at once and firmly that no Italian Government would or
could accede to such a German wish. The Italian Guarantee Law
assured the ecclesiastical independence of the Pope. A few days
after the Milan meeting, Minghetti declared to his electorate at
Bologna that it had been said the Milan visit of the German
Emperor could lead to a change in Italian ecclesiastical policy.
That, he declared, was a mistake, Italy's ecclesiastical policy was
founded on the principle of the separation of Church and State.
The result achieved by this principle showed that there was no
reason for changing the policy hitherto pursued. In talking to
my father at Milan, Minghetti had referred to the well-known
words which Cavour had cried out to the monks who brought him
the sacrament when he was dying: " *Frate, frate, libera chiesa in
libero stato!* " I myself lived to hear the Premier Luigi Luzzatti,
a Jew, make a speech on the fiftieth anniversary of the Proclamation
of the Kingdom of Italy, on the 10th March, 1911, a speech in
which the principle of the free church in the free state was reaffirmed
in the most emphatic and solemn manner. Italy has achieved
more than we along this path, more than did our disastrous *Kulturkampf*, welcomed with such exuberant enthusiasm by the good
professors at Greifswald, and no doubt in many other German
universities.

CHAPTER XXIV

The Emperor's Birthday in the Palazzo Caffarelli—Albano—Walks in Rome and Rides in the Campagna—The Crown Prince and Princess—First Meeting with Countess Marie Dönhoff—The Crown Prince's Journey to Naples.

ON the 22nd March, 1875, the birthday of our heroic Emperor, there was a *soirée* in the Palazzo Caffarelli to which numerous German fellow-countrymen, either staying or living in Rome had been invited. Herr von Keudell toasted the Emperor. To hear him speak was a torment. It is always very painful to me when anyone gets stuck in a speech in my presence, but the helplessness of the worthy Keudell was rather more than might be expected on such occasions. He made a beginning and then stopped—the silence lasted several minutes. Then he fumbled a few sheets of paper out of his side pocket. He had the text of his speech neatly written out on them, but could not manage to find the right page. So he stopped again, lost the thread altogether, and began a new and even longer pause. During this an elderly German lady, moved either by sympathy or nervousness, uttered a shrill scream.

When the speech was over at last and the Emperor had been cheered three times, Keudell turned to the ladies and escorted them through the rooms according to rank. In the room where hung the portraits of Prussian Kings and Queens, I met him again. He had offered his arm to a very beautiful woman. She had brown hair, the colour which the English call "auburn." Gretchen, my little Cologne sweetheart, had also had "auburn" hair, but apart from this she resembled the lady clinging to the arm of the Ambassador von Keudell as little as the wild rose resembles the gardenia—which is not saying anything against the wild rose, for the wild rose is a charming flower. The lady who was walking with my chief had strange eyes, eyes that were neither blue, nor black, nor green, but that had an alternating blue, black, or green lustre, eyes expressing pride and obduracy, and then again a profound melancholy, eyes that could give stern, but also coquettish or even tender glances, the eyes of a water nymph. Whoever saw these eyes could realize that this woman had turned many heads, that she

342

had kindled great passions. There was something *nonchalante*, indifferent, and up to a point aloof, in her whole manner, that stimulated. When she was flushed from a quick dance, such as the gallop, a pallor, unusual in German women, lay spread on her shapely oval face. As I watched this beautiful woman, in admiration, my chief said to me: " May I introduce you to Princess Y, to whom you must do the honours of our Caffarelli. Tell her the story of our Palazzo. Now I must go back to the other ladies."

The Princess took my arm, and we strolled round the rooms. I told her the story of the Palazzo, which the Empire was to lose half a century later. " The Caffarelli," I explained to her, " were an old Ducal Ghibelline family, the party true to the Emperor, and dated as far back as the thirteenth century. A Caffarelli fell in the battle of Tagliacozzo as a faithful follower of our poor Conradin of Swabia." My fair companion listened attentively. " You are standing," I continued, " on the Capitoline Hills, on the foundations of an old temple to Jupiter, though at the same time you are surrounded by glorious German memories. In the sixteenth century, also, the Caffarelli followed the German Emperors and for this they were rewarded, when the Emperor Charles V, the great *Carolus Quintus*, visited Rome in the course of his reign. He appointed young Ascanio Caffarelli, who was about my age, that is to say, twenty-four years old, to be his page, and, after he had been in his service for a long time, gave him the southern part of the Capitoline Hills. So far no one has made me a beautiful present like that. When Ascanio, who had been thus distinguished, returned home again in his old age, he had a palace built on his new piece of land by the excellent Canonica, a disciple of the great architect, Giacomo Vignola—this Palace is our Caffarelli, which you delight this evening with your presence. German diplomats have lived here for half a century. The first German of note to stay here was Goethe's son who, It must be admitted, was not so great a poet as his father. It is said that he only composed a single verse in his whole life:

" *Hier steh' ich auf dem Kapitol*
Und weiss nicht, was ich sagen soll." [1]

" The Ambassador to the Papacy, the historian, Berthold Niebuhr, worked here. He wrote a very excellent history of Rome in three volumes, but I won't bore you with that. His successor

---

[1] Here I stood on the Capitol and do not know what to say.

was Josias von Bunsen, whom Bismarck did not like, but who stood high in the favour of Frederick William IV." I led the Princess into a little room next to the big salon. " In this little room," I continued, " a tragedy happened in the fifties. Herr von Kanitz was Prussian Ambassador then, an efficient and generally popular man. Prince Frederick William of Prussia, our present Crown Prince, was on a visit in Rome. He had put up in the Caffarelli. There was to be a big banquet in the evening. All the guests who had been invited had arrived, including Prince Frederick William. Only the host was missing. At last he entered—but how? What do you think he looked like? Why, he wore the costume in which they go fox-hunting in Rome, that is to say, in a red coat, white breeches, top boots and a riding whip in his hand. Naturally everyone was thunderstruck. Only one of those present remained cool, the French Ambassador, Duke Agenor de Gramont. He did not lose his head until much later, on the 6th July, 1870, when he made a stupid, provocative speech in the Parisian Legislative Body. But on that occasion at Rome he was the only one who did not lose his head. He took Herr von Kanitz, who was a personal friend of his, by the arm, and whispered to him that he had something very important and confidential to tell him, and led him into this little room. Kanitz remained there the whole night watched over by the excellent Councillor of the Chancellery, Schulze, who is still living, and whom you can see every day sitting under a palm tree in front of the Casa Tarpeia, with a long German pipe in his mouth. Poor Kanitz, as a matter of fact, has recovered his reason completely. When I sat next him at the dinner last winter, he told me the whole story of his woes, and ended with the words: ' The fact that I tell you all this proves that I am not mad any longer.' "

I also told the Princess about poor Frederick William IV, how, when he was hypochondriac, he found comfort and healing in the sublime grandeur of the Roman ruins when he spent a few weeks in the Caffarelli after he had made his brother William his deputy.

While I was still in the middle of my talk, the husband of the beautiful Princess approached. As unfortunately happens now and then, the husband was in no way the equal of the wife, either in outward appearance or intelligence. She seemed to wish otherwise, when he intimated that it was time to go. She pressed my hand and said she hoped that I would be her cicerone in the next few days and show her not round the rooms of the Caffarelli, but round the Eternal City. I replied that this would be impossible, for I was leaving for Albano early next morning. " And why? " she

asked.   I replied that I wanted complete quiet and solitude to
write a thesis on Italian finance for the diplomatic examination
that was approaching.   She said, with a certain impatience:
" So you prefer your boring examination to my company," and
without shaking hands, she left the palazzo with her husband.
I saw her go with strangely mixed feelings.   Strongest of all was
the impression that a demonic charm had emanated from this
woman whose arm had rested on mine for an hour, and I felt that
fate would bring us together again.   For good? Or evil? Time
alone would show.

Next morning I drove along the Via Appia Nuova, under
cypresses, pines, holm oaks, and olives, to Albano.   I travelled in
an old yellow poste-chaise, between two fat peasant women who
smelt strongly of garlic.   When I got to Albano I found a little
modest *osteria*.   They showed me a room where, apart from the
bed, there was only a table and a cane chair.   But from the window
I had a magnificent view of the Campagna.   On the margin of
this classic landscape I perceived a narrow blue strip, the sea, the
Tyrrhenian Sea.   I bought ink for a few *soldi*, as well as a pen and
the coarsest notepaper on which I ever wrote.   Then I began the
work for which I had brought statistical material with me.   I
worked just as I had done three years previously at Greifswald on
the Baltic.   Only I did not ride in Albano, but strolled about
for an hour or two every afternoon on the banks of the magnificent
Alban Lake.   The work was finished in a week.   Then I went back
to Rome, this time not in the poste-chaise, but *per pedes apostolorum*,
along the Via Appia Antica on a magnificent spring morning.
As I strolled along the Corso in the afternoon I met Princess Y.
Her welcome was not as ungracious as I had expected.   " There
you are, you runaway!   But you won't run away from me this
time!   I take possession of you from this day onwards! " And so,
the following day, we began our wanderings.   As a guide I took
neither Baedeker nor Gsell-Fels, but Byron, Canto iv, of *Childe
Harold*.   I led her to St. Peter's.

" But lo! the dome—the vast and wondrous dome,
To which Diana's marvel was a cell—
Christ's mighty shrine above his martyr's tomb!
Thou, of temples old, or altars new,
Standest alone—with nothing like to thee—
Worthiest of God, the holy and the true.
Since Zion's desolation, when that He
Forsook his former city, what could be,

> Of earthly structures, in his honour piled,
> Of a sublimer aspect? Majesty,
> Power, Glory, Strength and Beauty, all are aisled
> In this eternal ark of worship undefiled."

From the top of the Capitol I showed her the Forum.

> " . . . . and in yon field below,
> A thousand years of silenced factions sleep—
> The Forum, where the immortal accents glow,
> And still the eloquent air breathes—burns with Cicero! "

We walked up to the Palatine. Not far from the " Casino " of the former Farnese Gardens I introduced her to a friend of mine to whom I made many pilgrimages in those days, since of all the hills in Rome the Palatine always had a special attraction for me. This friend was a marble satyr. He stands amongst rose leaves at the entrance to the uppermost terraces. He looks down with amusement upon the people of our age in their ugly clothes, just as he doubtless looked with greater sympathy long ago upon the Roman Consuls, Senators and Prætors in their picturesque togas. I never left Rome without paying a farewell visit to this satyr, and whenever I returned to Rome I always called on him. His divine cheerfulness was exactly the same when I bade him farewell in 1897, before my departure for Berlin, as it was twelve years later, when I called on him again after my return to the Eternal City.

In April, 1875, I suggested to Princess Y. that we should not limit ourselves to the town, but also get to know the Campagna. I managed to get two good Irish hunters. She was an excellent horsewoman, and did not hesitate before any *stagionata* or any hurdle on the Campagna. We rode to the sepulchral monument of Cecilia Metella, and from there to the grove of Egeria, where the amiable and lovable nymph received visits from His Majesty King Numa. Byron has dedicated immortal verses to the Grove of Egeria also.

> " Here didst thou dwell, in this enchanted cover,
> Egeria! thy all-heavenly bosom beating,
> For the far footsteps of thy mortal lover ;
> The purple Midnight veil'd that mystic meeting
> With her most starry canopy, and seating
> Thyself by thine adorer, what befel?
> This cave was surely shaped out for the greeting

Of an enamour'd Goddess, and the cell
Haunted by holy Love—the earliest oracle! "

We liked to take a rest in the Grove of Egeria. I assume that Egeria rarely left her Grove, so that Numa was usually sure of meeting her there. Unfortunately my beautiful Princess had to leave Rome, since her husband was anxious to go to Florence, where he wished to visit some relations. A farewell supper was arranged on the eve before her departure at Spillmann's, a restaurant in the Via Condotti much frequented in those days. Besides Prince and Princess Y., the gentlemen of the German Legation and a few Austrians and English diplomats took part. Although I had had a slight attack of Roman fever, I did not want to be absent at this farewell celebration. Everyone was in high spirits during the feast. While the gentlemen were getting up to put their coats on in the cloakroom, the Princess pushed a slip of paper towards me, and on it I read: " Write to Florence. Don't be ill! I love you." [1] I stuck this delightful intimation into my pocket-book the following day, and over it I placed a little photograph, a wonderful likeness of her beautiful classical head.

" *O zarte Sehnsucht, süsses Hoffen !*
Das Auge sieht den Himmel offen,
Es schwelgt das Herz in Seligkeit." [2]

In the winter of 1874-5 the wish was repeatedly expressed in Italian quarters that the Emperor William I should return the visit King Victor Emmanuel had paid him in September, 1873. On this visit the King was accompanied by his Premier, Marco Minghetti and the Minister of Foreign Affairs, Emilio Visconti-Venosta. Bismarck had taken a liking to the former, but a strong dislike to the latter. After a fairly long exchange of views, there was agreement, both on the German and Italian side that, considering the bad relation between the Vatican and the German Government, and the delicate situation that existed between the Italian Government and the Vatican, a German visit to Rome was out of the question. And, indeed, the visit did not take place until October, 1888, when the Emperor William II went there soon after he ascended the throne, though less from any serious political motive than because of his restless desire to travel.

The last *Roman Letters*, by Kurd von Schlözer, reveal the fact

---

[1] English in text.
[2] " O tender longing, sweet hope, the eye sees heaven open, the heart revels in bliss."

that this first visit of the Kaiser's to the Eternal City was a fiasco for both parties. The young Kaiser ruffled the Pope's feelings by speaking demonstratively and without any particular reason, of Rome as the inviolable capital of the Kingdom of Italy in a toast delivered at the Quirinal. He made matters even worse in an audience with Leo XIII, who had a great deal to say and wished to pour out his heart to the German Emperor. But the Kaiser broke off the conversation in his own brusque, discourteous fashion. William II gave offence to Royalist Italy by arguing about the Parliamentary system and Liberalism in a country which had for years had Liberal and Parliamentary Government. And to make matters worse he hardly condescended to address a single word to the Senators and Deputies, thus putting King Humbert to sore embarrassment. The Secretary of State, Herbert Bismarck, who accompanied the Kaiser in 1888, only intensified his Sovereign's faults and mistakes by his own behaviour. Although he was rich in qualities of the heart and of the head, he was often deficient in tact. This was particularly noticeable on the very difficult Roman terrain.

I now return to the spring of 1875 when, under a wise, dutiful and ever-tactful Sovereign, such mistakes and eccentricities as we experienced in later years were not possible. In the middle of April, 1875, the Ambassador, von Keudell, was informed that the Emperor William would, for reasons of health, have to abandon his intended return visit to Italy, very much to his regret. Keudell was commissioned to place in the hands of King Victor Emmanuel, who was in Naples just then, a letter written by the Kaiser himself, and giving warm expression to his regret. At the same time he was told to inform the King that the German Crown Prince and his wife would be staying in Italy on a fairly long visit, that they would spend some time in Florence, and that from there the Crown Prince would pay King Victor Emmanuel a visit at Naples. When he returned from Naples to Rome, Herr von Keudell told me that he would proceed to Florence on the 23rd of April to pay his respects to the Crown Prince and the Princess. I was to go with him.

We reached Florence on the 24th of April. Keudell and I were ordered to have lunch with the Crown Prince and his wife, who were staying at the New York Hotel. We were first conducted into the reception room, where the suite of their Imperial Highness' was waiting, amongst them the fat, always ill-tempered lady-in-waiting, Countess Hedwig Brühl, and the worthy General Mischke, the playmate in early youth and the faithful adjutant of the Crown

Prince, who had stood by his side at Königgrätz, at Weissenberg, and at Wörth, under shell fire, and was, like his exalted Master, a knight *sans peur et sans raproche*. The folding doors were opened, and the Crown Princess entered. Next to her was an elegant lady clothed in white, who could not fail to strike everyone by reason of her wonderful eyes, black eyes that expressed intelligence, and above all, goodness and feeling. I asked General Mischke: " Who is the little lady next to the Crown Princess? " He replied: " It's Countess Marie Dönhoff, the daughter of Donna Laura Minghetti, and the friend of Her Highness the Crown Princess." I asked to be introduced to the Countess. The General willingly granted my request. The Countess did not condescend to address a single word to me, but I had no time for any reflections on that score, for lunch was served almost at once.

The Crown Princess led the conversation. She was lively, vivacious, and in the best mood. " She is always in a good humour when she is not in Berlin or Potsdam," said General Mischke, who sat next to me, with a sigh. " She has great qualities, rich gifts, character, understanding, and a heart too. But she simply cannot get used to our Prussian ways."

In the evening there was a gala performance at the Teatro della Pergola. I was in a small box next to a bigger one, in which sat Donna Laura Minghetti and her charming daughter, but again not one look was vouchsafed me. In later years my dear mother-in-law, whom I love very much, was always immensely amused when I told her that I would never forgive this cool attitude towards so charming a young man as I must have been.

The next day Keudell entered my room at an early hour. In contrast with his usually calm manner, he was visibly excited. He said he must have a talk with me, for he had just received a piece of news that had moved him deeply, so that he felt he had to pour out his heart to me. Even if I was still very young, he said, I was yet mature beyond my years, and he knew that he could rely on my discretion. " I have asked the wife of the Premier, Donna Laura Minghetti, who is graciously disposed towards me, to sound the entourage of their Imperial Highnesses so as to discover how I stand in their Imperial Highnesses' regard. The result is truly distressful for me. Donna Laura has spoken with the Chamberlain of the Crown Princess, Count Götz von Seckendorff, who enjoys the complete confidence of their Imperial and Royal Highnesses, and is, on the other hand, very devoted to Donna Laura. He told Madam Minghetti quite frankly and quite definitely that the Crown Princess cannot stand me. She considered me a blind follower of Bismarck's, one of those wicked people who are ready for every misdeed so as not to lose Bismarck's favour."

Keudell gave a deep sigh. Then he continued: " And while the Crown Princess considers me a blind Bismarckian, I feel that I am no longer so much in Prince Bismarck's favour as I used to be. I am gloomy about my own future. I feel so happy in Rome, I am so very attached to my position there."

I tried to comfort my chief as best I could. I took the liberty to remind him of Field-Marshal Derfflinger's wise words, namely, that one ought never to get excited over bad weather, woman's moods, and princely disfavour. My well-meant words of comfort did not seem to make a very big impression on him. On the other hand, he seemed to get some satisfaction from the fact that, according to what Count Seckendorff had confided to the wife of the Italian Premier, neither my father nor I would fare any better than he when there was a change of Sovereigns in Germany. *Solamen miseris socios habuisse malorum.* The Princess looked upon the Secretary of State von Bülow as an unshakable admirer of the Chancellor, with whom he had been on terms of personal friendship for many years. Bülow, senior, so she held, tended towards Conservative rather than Liberal ideas, and the son was no better than the father. " Her Highness, the Princess," Keudell concluded, " who, as you know, is Liberal, can stand you just as little as your father."

When I had heard this sad news I felt I ought to pull myself together, so I picked up the book that I had taken with me to read on the journey. I have always found that to read a serious and well-written book is a good means of calming perturbations of the spirit and so recovering inward equilibrium.

The book which I pulled out of my travelling bag in Florence was a novel by Honoré de Balzac, whom I admired very much in my youth and still esteem highly, it was the novel *Le Père Goriot.* I read the book in one sitting. Then I wrote on the first page of the volume the sentences with which Père Goriot ends: " *Rastignac, resté seul, fit quelques pas vers le haut du cimetière, et vit Paris tortueusement couché le long des deux rives de la Seine, où commencaient à briller les luminères. Ses yeux s'attachaient presque avidement entre la colonne de la place Vendôme et le dôme des Invalides, là où vivait ce beau monde dans lequel il avait voulu pénétrer. Il lança sur cette ruche bourdonnante un regard, qui semblait par avance en pomper le miel, et dit ces mots grandioses:—A nous deux, maintenant! Et pour premier acte de défi qu'il portait a la société, Rastignac alla dîner chez madame de Nucingen.*" I decided to imitate Rastignac that same evening, and wrote to Princess Y., telling her that I would visit her in her château in May.

The next morning Keudell told me that the Crown Prince, accompanied by him and by myself, would proceed to Naples, where he would pay King Victor Emmanuel a visit. The long journey from Florence to Naples gave me the first chance I had to approach the Crown Prince closely. When I was in the ranks and halted in his presence at the parade of the 8th Army Corps on the battlefield of Amiens on the 13th March, 1871, the victor of Weissenberg and Wörth, in the uniform of the Pasewalk Cuirassiers, seemed the embodiment of German heroism to me. Now I got to know the kindly, benevolent human being. One felt no embarrassment in the presence of the Crown Prince. He conversed with Keudell about Italian conditions and Italian-German relations. Everything he said was as sensible as could be. He listened attentively to the Ambassador without interrupting him. Whenever he differed he gave calm and clear, but friendly, indeed, almost modest, expression to his views. When the conversation turned to the Franco-German war, he told us several episodes in the battles of Wörth and Weissenberg without boastfulness or pride. He did not mention his personal conduct at all, but only the courage of his troops. He emphasised his peaceful disposition warmly and decisively, declaring that he was entirely in agreement with his father and Bismarck in holding it to be the first duty of the Government and the noblest need of our people to maintain peace with honour.

When the Crown Prince withdrew in the course of the day so as to rest for an hour before arriving in Naples, I began a longish conversation with his two adjutants. They were full of praise for their Prince and I felt that their praise came from sincere hearts. " A lion in battle and at the same time a kind, yes, a soft heart. A stringent moral code, severe and yet no prejudices." They told me that in 1866 and in 1870, the Crown Prince visited the wounded as often as he could, and always endeavoured to let the population of the hostile country feel the rigours of war as little as possible.

I had often heard it said in Berlin that the Crown Prince was no friend of Bismarck's. I was all the more gratified to hear words of appreciation and admiration for Bismarck from the Crown Prince's own mouth. He quoted a fine expression of his uncle's, Grand Duke Charles Alexander of Weimar, who, when Bismarck was once blamed for being a hard man and even worse, replied: " A Michael Angelo should not be measured with the measure of a Watteau." The Crown Prince himself compared Bismarck with

Richelieu. There was a good deal to be said against Richelieu, his behaviour towards Cinq-Mars and other opponents was much to be deplored and blamed, but nevertheless, he remained one of the greatest statesmen of all times. In a low voice he added, turning towards Keudell: " I often differ from Bismarck, especially in questions of home politics. He has opposed me with too much harshness, indeed almost ruthlessly. Altogether, he is not an easy Minister. But we must never forget what our Dynasty and Germany owe him. To part from him would, as things are now at home and in the world at large, be a crime, in my opinion."

We arrived at Naples where the Crown Prince was welcomed enthusiastically by a large crowd. He paid King Victor Emmanuel a long visit, and told us a good deal about it in the evening. The Crown Prince's characterisation of the King was not bad—he called him a chamois-hunter, that is to say, a man with a sure eye and a firm foot, free from giddiness, untiring, undaunted, and yet subtle and cunning when the quarry had to be killed. While he did justice to the King's qualities as a ruler, his own inclinations obviously went more towards the Crown Prince Humbert. " I love him like a brother," he said repeatedly. When the Crown Prince dismissed Keudell and myself at Rome on the journey back from Naples to Florence, he gave me his picture with a kind dedication. This photograph still stands on my writing table.

CHAPTER XXV

My Colleagues in the Legation—Professor Karl Hillebrand—Berlin in May, 1875—Soirée in the House Ministry—My Father on the Political Situation—At Varzin—Visit to the Country—To Ischl via Vienna—Idyll on the Shore of the St. Wolfgang Lake— Salzburg—Lothar Bucher and Life's Problems.

I DID not stay in Rome much longer. I was recalled from the Embassy by an order transmitted by my father to von Keudell. At the same time I got four weeks' leave in order to complete my French thesis on the constitution and the neutral rights of Switzerland. It was not easy for me to part from Rome where amongst other things, conditions in high society had been very pleasant. Herr von Keudell was neither interesting nor was he a man of any importance, but he was a benevolent chief, and I learnt several things from him, particularly in dealing with current affairs. I had a great liking for the first Secretary, Prince Alexander Lynar. He was married to a pretty American, and the marriage had come about in an unusual manner. In June, 1870, as Secretary of the Embassy in Paris, he had made the acquaintance of the charming Miss May Parsons. When, unexpectedly to him, at least, war broke out, he proposed to her in a telegram to Columbus, in Ohio. His proposal was graciously received. It seemed that Miss Parsons thought a German Prince must be very rich, while he had assumed that a young American from Columbus would receive a very big dowry. The slight disappointment that came when the marriage revealed them both as having no fortune, did not, incidentally, prevent its being a happy one.

The two secretaries of the Legation, Herr von Schweitzer and Herr von Hasperg, were both equally harmless. I have already referred to Schweitzer as the Baden representative in Florence. When this post was abolished in 1871, the kind-hearted Grand Duchess Louise of Baden tried to get him a new post in the Imperial Service, and wrote to her mother, the Empress Augusta, on his behalf. This step came to the knowledge of Prince Bismarck, I do not know how. When Herr von Schweitzer hit upon the unfortunate idea of introducing himself to the great

Chancellor at a Court Ball in the Palace at Berlin, the Chancellor addressed him with the words: " So you are the man who in common with Her Majesty the Empress and Queen and Her Royal Highness, Grand Duchess Louise of Baden, is continually putting difficulties in the way of my policy, which I conduct according to the best of my knowledge and conscience! And yet you have the cool im—im—impudence to want to enter the Imperial Diplomatic Service. But I shall not put up with these intrigues any longer."

Schweitzer was an unusually polite and very timid little man. He was so startled by these words that he dropped the opera hat which he held in his hand. His patrons with some difficulty were able to persuade the Prince that the poor fellow was really not working for the overthrow of the great Bismarck; and so he became Second Secretary to the Rome Embassy, where he was usefully employed in making fair copies of Keudell's reports. Whenever the name of Prince Bismarck was mentioned in his presence he was always overcome by a certain discomfort. Herr von Hasperg was a son of the Free and Hansa City of Hamburg, and had risen to the rank of Major in the Hamburg contingent in the days of the Federal Diet. By means of friendly recommendations from his Hamburg friends, who were connected with influential quarters in Berlin, he had succeeded in getting himself attached to the Mission in Rome. Like many Hamburgers, Hasperg was a great gourmet. He was particularly proud of his red wines, which, as a matter of fact, were very good. Once when he had the honour of entertaining Prince Frederick Charles, the great Commander, he placed a Lafitte before him with the words: " Your Royal Highness must drink this wine with understanding."

There was much gossip in the Diplomatic Corps in Rome. My witty friend, Herr von Villers at Vienna, used to say there is gossip in every Corps, in the *Corps de Ballet* as well as in the *Corps Diplomatique*. Gossip in the Roman Diplomatic Corps in those days often turned round the quarrel between the wife of the Russian Ambassador, Frau von Uexküll, and the wife of the English Ambassador, Lady Walburga Paget. Frau von Uexküll's first husband was the Secretary of Legation von Glinka, but she had got a divorce from him so as to marry his chief, the Ambassador Uexküll. Lady Paget had known Baroness Uexküll for many years as Mrs. von Glinka, but demanded, now she had become her colleague, that the lady should be introduced to her afresh, which Frau von Uexküll refused as a humiliation. Lady Paget, who was Prussian—a Countess Hohenthal—was universally unpopular.

Like so many other German women married to Englishmen, she displayed an exaggerated English jingoism after her marriage.

Much amusement was caused by the reply which Madame de Corcelle, the wife of the French Ambassador to the Vatican, gave Pope Pius IX. In an audience which he had granted her, the Pope complained in lively fashion about the split between the " Black " members of society who were for the Pope, and " White " members, who were for the King, a split that prevailed in Rome ever since the Italian invasion. The Ambassador's wife who was famous for her absent-mindedness, comforted His Holiness: " *C'est bien triste, mais tout cela va changer avec la mort du Pape.*"

Of the Germans living in Italy in those days the publicist and historian, Karl Hillebrand, interested me most. He had taken part in the Baden Insurrection of 1849, as a youth of twenty, and after it was crushed, had escaped to France, where he was employed as a teacher of German language and literature in Douay. I visited him when I passed through Florence, whither he had gone after the outbreak of the Franco-German war. Whenever he came to Rome on a visit from Florence, he was usually kind enough to call on me. His book about France and the French is one of the finest psychological studies ever made of our neighbours beyond the Vosges. His essays, published in German and Italian reviews, are also little masterpieces. In our talks in the winter of 1874-75 he gave many a warning against showing arrogance towards our conquered enemy. He emphasised the passionate patriotism of the French, as well as their capacity for following a resolute leader in one united front and without niggling criticism when the hour of danger came. He thought that we Germans somewhat over-rated ourselves since the great victories of the Bismarckian era. Many a worthy German, he said, talked as though he himself had won Sadowa and Sedan and were himself responsible for the policy of 1862—1871. The " Sedan smile " which the German philistine, who used to incline towards exaggerated humility, now displayed whenever he was abroad, was not making us beloved of foreigners. Our gigantic successes were the work of Bismarck and Moltke, two very great and unusual geniuses. Bismarck, so Hillebrand continued, had achieved his shattering success in the face of German public opinion, and against the active opposition of almost all the Liberals and intellectuals. Karl Hillebrand praised the exalted services of the old Emperor who had insisted on the re-organization of the army, and had stood by his great Minister despite the fumings of obtuse Democrats. " It is possible to disagree as to whether the chief merit in creating a beautiful statue is due to the artist, who has fashioned it, or the Mæcenas, who gave him the commission. But what would people say if the marble itself were to declare that it, the real statue, deserved all the praise and recognition?" Karl Hillebrand also said that our people were deplorably unpolitical since they, far less than others, the French, the English, the Italians, knew how to subordinate party views to the general weal, and tended more than any other nation towards the doctrinaire and the ideological. Germans were too "thorough," and sometimes ponderously erudite. I was reminded of what my father and Princess Marie-Ghiselaine Arenberg had said on the same subject and of Goethe's harsh saying that Germans are miserable, taken in the mass.

Herr von Keudell was kind enough to see me off at the station when I left Rome. When I became Ambassador in Rome nineteen years later, the official in charge of documents, the excellent Councillor Stock, showed me a report which he had taken from the archives of the Embassy, which the Ambassador von Keudell had made to Bismarck about myself on 10th May, 1875. In this report it said: " The young barrister, Bernhard von Bülow, has done very well here during his short service; he has punctiliously and efficiently carried out the tasks entrusted to him, and has succeeded in rapidly achieving a good position in high society here. I have no doubt that this official who is very mature, considering his years, will be well able to carry out whatever duties may be assigned to him."

In Geneva, whither I had gone in accordance with my father's wish, I settled down to my French thesis. I found it easier, almost, than the work I had done for my two German examinations. The French language is not only more superficial, but also poorer than the German: one need only compare Goethe's *Faust* with Racine's *Athalie*. *Faust* is like the sound of an organ, *Athalie* like the chirping of a cricket. But this very poverty of the French language makes it easier for a writer who commands it to find the right expression, than in German.

When I reached Berlin at the end of May, 1875, I found an invitation awaiting me, an invitation to a soirée that was being given that evening in the House Ministry, to which their Highnesses the Crown Prince and Princess had been invited. My father had the honour of a long conversation with the Crown Prince. His Highness looked careworn, my father was visibly at pains to comfort him. When the Crown Prince and Princess had retired, and my father and I said good-bye to Mimi Schleinitz, our amiable hostess, he asked me to come for a walk with him in the Behren Strasse, deserted at that late hour.

I asked my father to explain what was behind the alarming articles in our official Press, which were then the general theme of conversation in Berlin, and had put the world in a state of excitement ever since the beginning of April. I must briefly summarise them here. At the end of March the *Kölnische Zeitung*, a newspaper friendly to the Government, published an article in which the precipitate increase of the French Army by the " Cadre Law " was used as an occasion to enlarge upon the possibility of a reconciliation between the Pope and Italy and an alliance between the Vatican, France, Austria and Italy. This " Catholic League " was, according to the *Kölnische Zeitung*, naturally impossible until Count Andrássy, the Austro-Hungarian Minister of Foreign Affairs, had fallen. But his fall, so the warning concluded, was being assiduously prepared in several quarters. On the 8th April, a semi-official Berlin paper, *Die Post*, published a further article under the headline " Is war in sight? " beginning with the words: " For several weeks dark clouds have been gathering on the political horizon." *Die Post* reproduced the " general picture painted in very grave colours " which the *Kölnische Zeitung* had given of the present situation, and added that *Die Post* was far from denying the correctness of the statements " as a whole " made by the Rhenish paper. The dim prospect, so *Die Post* continued, could be supplemented by several details drawn from its own observation. If the question put in the headline: " Is war in sight? " is to be answered, then *Die Post* felt bound to say: " War is indeed in sight, which does not, however, exclude the possibility that the clouds may disperse." A few days later the more than semi-official *Provinzial-Korrespondenz* attempted to assuage alarm, but made no lasting impression, since, not long afterwards, the London *Times* published an alarmist article against Germany, an article culminating in the statement that Germany's industry, trade, finances and social conditions would not long be able to stand the pressure of her military expenditure. But if Germany were to disarm so as to avert her own ruin, France would stand there in menacing readiness. To escape from this dilemma the German military party thought the present moment particularly favourable to ensure a long period of prosperity and peace for the German Empire. The *Times* had expressly described this alarmist article as a " French canard " sent from Paris. But this did not prevent the effusion which was attributed to the French Minister of Foreign Affairs, the Duke Decazes, from being made the most of by all Germany's opponents.

The general tension reached its height on the 10th May, when the Emperor Alexander II of Russia, accompanied by his Imperial Chancellor, Prince Gortchakov, arrived at Berlin for a three days' visit on the way to Ems. Before the Tsar left Berlin he received the Foreign Ambassadors and declared to them that peace was assured. At the same time Prince Gortchakov addressed a communication to the same effect to the Russian representatives abroad, reading the text aloud in the presence of the leading members of the Berlin Diplomatic Corps before he sent it off.

This is how matters stood when my good father, who was visibly still under the impression of his talk with the Crown Prince, walked up and down the Behren Strasse with me from eleven o'clock at night till one in the morning, explaining the situation. I have a very good memory and recollect what he said precisely. He said to me:

If you want to know how things really hang together, I can tell you the following in confidence, but I rely on your discretion. Our great Chancellor has little by little become convinced that the French will never forgive us for their defeat and the loss of Alsace Lorraine, and are at the disposal of every ally who is ready to hazard a war with us. The Russians would, of course, be preferred, but, under certain conditions the English would also be acceptable. On the other hand, Prince Bismarck has gradually received the impression that although we must reckon France a permanent enemy, we have not struck her a really crippling blow so as to render her permanently *hors de combat* in an economic, but especially in a military sense. The hope that the French will destroy one another by internal party conflicts may be defeated by their passionate patriotism and their rigorous centralization. All these thoughts are making the Chancellor uneasy. But you must not therefore believe that he wants war. The Emperor and the Crown Prince, too, will not hear of any war that is not a war of defence. The Crown Prince was very relieved just now when I told him I was convinced we should keep the peace. And as far as Bismarck is concerned, I repeat that since the Peace of Frankfort, he has neither planned nor wished another war. *Vestigia Napoleonis terrent.* But he thinks it would be useful to intimidate the French. He wanted to direct a very powerful jet of cold water, as he called it, in the direction of Paris. It has now transpired that we shall not be able to fight a second war with France without the interference of the Russians, and probably of the English as well. A localized war between the principal European powers, between Germany and France, Italy and France, Russia and Austria, England and France, Russia and England, is hardly possible any longer, because of the highly complex political and economic interests that partly unite and partly divide these States. All of which imposes caution."

Thus my father in the Behren Strasse. Finally he added that Bismarck had unfortunately received news from Stuttgart that a telegram had been sent by the Emperor Alexander II to his sister at Ems, Queen Olga of Württemberg, the day he left Berlin, which read as follows: " *J'ai arrêté l'emporté de Berlin.*" This had annoyed Prince Bismarck, and he was even more annoyed because Gortchakov had been informing a number of journalists and diplomats in Berlin that he had saved the peace of Europe: " *J'ai sauvé la paix de l'Europe.*" When we parted my father added that Gortchakov was not unenvious of Bismarck. Recently when Bismarck, to pacify him, had told him through our Ambassador in St. Petersburg, Prince Henry VII of Reuss, that, now as ever, he considered himself Gortchakov's pupil, the Russian Chancellor replied in sour-sweet fashion: " *Oui, comme Raffael était l'élève du Perugino.*" My father concluded: " there is a danger in the personal relationship between Bismarck and Gortchakov. Gortchakov is simply as vain as a monkey, and as touchy as an old maid. And our great Bismarck is at times too impetuous, too full of rancour and cannot always control his temperament."

I think it was Larochefoucauld who said that weak feelings are stifled and passions are strengthened by separation. A small fire is extinguished by the wind, a big one kindled to brighter flame. When I left Berlin for the château where the Princess Y. was expecting me, I could not but be aware of the fact that I looked forward with great impatience to seeing my beautiful Roman friend again. My feelings for her therefore had withstood the fiery ordeal of a separation. I convinced myself that she felt as I did. We were less free here than in Rome. The proximity of her dull-witted husband was disturbing. But he fortunately was in the habit of going to bed early, and so we were free in the evenings. We used to wander round the old château arm-in-arm. On one side high castle walls, on the other the dark, silent, mysterious forest. In the western heavens shone Hesperus, the evening star, the golden Venus. As I gazed up at this star I raised my hand carried away by my feelings, I whispered: " If I live to be a hundred years old, never, never, never shall I forget this hour, never shall I forget you." Alas! the great poet is right when he says that the Jupiter laughs at lovers' vows. How many has he heard, how few have been kept.

I only stayed in Y. a short time. I had to proceed to Varzin, whither Prince and Princess Bismarck had invited me, more, no doubt, because of their friendship with my parents than of any interest they may have felt for my still very insignificant person. I found the great man in excellent health. Every day he went for a long ride through field and forest with me and his son William. I admired this sexagenarian's robustness.

But his spirits did not seem so satisfactory. I had the feeling that the " war in sight " episode had not left him with a favourable impression. It is true that he spoke contemptuously of " This fuss about the war in sight," but he kept returning to the theme. He talked angrily of the Press Bureau, which had carried out his instructions clumsily, with crudely excessive zeal. He also spoke reproachfully of the Councillor of Legation, Josef von Radowitz, at that time engaged in the Political Department of the Foreign Office. After a banquet at the French Embassy, Radowitz had used threatening language of an incautious and exaggerated character in a longish conversation with the French Ambassador, Gontaut-Biron, and so had given him his chance to write to the Russian Princess Obolenski, with whom he was in touch, that Germany was planning a war of aggression against France. " Josef Radowitz," so the Prince declared, " has all the bad qualities of his father, the great comedian, Josef Maria, and, in addition, he has only to drink one glass more than he needs to lose all control over his tongue. The vanity of Gortchakov, who allows himself to be admired and flattered as an angel of peace by the French Press, has done the rest. I shall never forgive Gortchakov this mischievous trick. I shall pay him back on a suitable occasion."

Herbert was away on a journey, but his younger brother, William, called " Bill " by his family, and all of us, was staying with his parents. I often saw the two brothers together. When I compare the relationship between Herbert and Bill with that between Don Quixote and Sancho Panza, I do not wish to say anything derogatory of either brother, seeing that I had a great affection for both, particularly Herbert. In making this contrast, I have in mind what Richard Wagner once said so finely in a talk with the brilliant and profound Count Arthur Gobineau, the author of the " *Essai sur l'inegalité des Races humaines.*" The master of Bayreuth said to the Frenchman that while Don Quixote was one of the noblest and sublimest figures in the literature of the world,

Sancho Panza was by no means to be despised, since he represented the necessary common-sense of healthy humanity. Bill was not so interesting as Herbert, nor so attractive and warm-hearted, but he was more sober in his judgments, more prudent, and, generally speaking, sensible.

Bill said to me:

> My father is like a lens through which all objects are seen too big. He himself had blown up Eugen Richter, Windthorst, and others, who, compared with him, are only frogs, until they are the size of oxen. The same is true of that vain peacock, Gortchakov. In his rancour against this old comedian, my father should not go too far. After all, he himself is always repeating that good relations with Russia are the pivot of our foreign policy and, to a certain extent, of our home policy also. I rather doubt whether my father can annoy Gortchakov without hurting the feelings of Alexander II.

Before I left Varzin I had a letter from Princess Y. suggesting that we should meet at Ischl, whither I proceeded directly from Varzin. At Vienna, where I arrived on the 3rd July, 1875, the anniversary of the Battle of Königgrätz, I met my friend Baron Münch, a Councillor in the Austro-Hungarian Embassy in Berlin. In the fifties his father had been the representative of Hesse-Darmstadt at the Federal Diet in Frankfort-on-the-Maine. He was, by the way, a relative of George von Hertling, who later became Imperial Chancellor. While I strolled about the Ring and through the Prater with Münch, we talked about old times and the present situation. In his opinion the best guarantee for the security of both countries and of European peace was a strong, firm, friendly relationship between the Hapsburg Monarchy and the German Empire. "The mere fact," he said, "that a good Austrian tells you this in Vienna, on the anniversary of Königgrätz, is surely proof that what used to divide Austria and Prussia has been overcome." Thus did Baron Joachim von Münch-Bellinghausen speak to me nine years after Sadowa as the July sun peeped down on us through the green branches. I did not guess then that only a few years later I would be standing by this good friend's death-bed.

On the 4th July I arrived at Ischl, where Princess Y. was awaiting me in the hotel. When we saw each other again we felt like fiancés on the morning of their wedding. We pressed each other's hands in silence. In the afternoon we went for a drive for several hours to the Gosau Mill. In the evening I threw myself

at the feet of that lovely woman begging, beseeching, imploring.
" No, no! " she said. " Why? Aren't we happy? Why spoil our
love? " She stared at me with frightened eyes, but not angrily.
My passion seemed to scare her. When I asked her why she
shrank from me she put her little hand over my mouth; she was
afraid, she said, of loving me too much. " I seem to have a fore-
boding," she added, " it is as though this love might bring me bad
luck. Great love leads to great suffering, so they say." The day
after my arrival at Ischl, we made an excursion in the brilliant July
sunshine to Strobl, on the shore of Wolfgangs-See. We gazed long
at the bluish green water before we set out on the return journey.
The night was bright with stars, and a mild breeze streamed in
through the open windows of her bedroom. I walked up and down
the room in long strides and almost beside myself. " I shall go mad,"
I kept on repeating monotonously, no longer master of my senses,
over and over again like a litany. At last she got up from the
chair on which she had been sitting. In a low voice, smiling, and
yet with a sad expression in her beautiful features, she said: " It
would be such a pity if such a charming, talented young man were
to go mad merely because of me." And then she sank into my
arms. The whole night long we heard the rushing waters of the
Traun, like Nature's wedding march.

When I got back to my room the next morning, a surprise
was in store for me. A letter had come from my father, containing
the report on the result of my Diplomatic examination by the
Director of the Foreign Office, his Excellency von Philipsborn.
According to this Adolf Wagner had judged my thesis on Italian
finance as " unusually successful both as regards substance and
form." At the moment when I was reading this, to me, very
interesting letter, the Princess entered my room. There was a
liquid sheen in her eyes such as I had not seen in them before.
She held up her lips for me to kiss. " Read this letter first," I
shouted, " the thesis I did at Albano in April about Italian finance
has been very favourably judged by Adolf Wagner, the great
economist." She stared at me and burst into tears. "Ambition,"
she sobbed, " will always be more to you than love." Was she
right? Undoubtedly she was, as far as her own case was concerned.
Nevertheless, the time would come when I was to meet the woman
whose love would be more to me than my personal ambition;
not dearer than the Fatherland, which always and in every situation
has had first place in my regard, but dearer than what men call a
career, more than all outward distinctions and any triumphs of
self-love.

Two days later we moved to St. Wolfgang. Ischl was too much of a fashionable resort for our taste, too restless, and too banal. We preferred St. Wolfgang, with its lake spread out before us with such inviting friendliness, near Strobl. We travelled through the Valley of the River Ischl, between high forest defiles and the towering cliffs of the Looskogel and the Rettenkogel above them. At St. Wolfgang we stayed at the " White Horse," near the steamboat landing stage. Many years later, when I saw the excellently produced *White Horse Inn* at the Berlin Metropole Theatre, I remembered that idyllic spot, St. Wolfgang. With its narrow streets, its confused tumble of houses with their lofts and gargoyles, it seemed like a piece of the middle ages come to life. We often visited the Parish Church in the afternoons, a beautiful Gothic building with a magnificent High Altar that towers up to the vaulted ceiling. On this altar we admired the sublimely-carved wooden figures of the three Magi, above them, life-sized, the Crucified between his Holy Mother and John, next to them the Archangel Michael and some saint whose name was in dispute. Above them, highest of all, God the Father, surrounded by beautiful angels. Mary kneels before the Heavenly Father and receives His blessing. We also admired four worthy bisops, St. Wolfgang of Ratisbon, Pilgrim of Passau, Adalbert of Prague, and a fourth bishop whose name was also in dispute, but whom, in the end, we identified as St. Rupert of Salzburg. This magnificent altar had been built by order of Benedict, the Abbot of Mondsee. It was completed by Master Michael Pucher of Bruneck, in the year of grace 1481. St. Wolfgang owed its existence to the good Benedictine Monks of Mondsee, whom the Emperor Louis the Pious had endowed with the whole region to cultivate it. Bishop Wolfgang of Ratisbon fled hither when his wicked diocesans expelled him. While the fantastic Otto III ruled the German Empire, he led a pious life in a hermit's hut near Falkenstein, until he was discovered and escorted back to his diocese by the penitent people of Ratisbon, after he had founded the Wolfgang Market and worked many miracles there. It was reverence for this Saint that made the Bavarians refrain from imposing war contributions on Market Wolfgang and from quartering troops there during their ruthless occupation of the Salzkammergut in the second half of the sixteenth century. The inhabitants were naturally grateful, and they had a beautiful fountain erected next to their church in honour of their patron saint, Wolfgang. This fountain was cast in the bronze of molten church bells by Master Lienhart Raunacher, of Passau.

No more beautiful frame than St. Wolfgang could be

imagined for the idyllic life which we lived for weeks on end. The worthy citizens of St. Wolfgang bothered as little about us as we about them. No one interfered with us or disturbed us. We walked arm-in-arm along the shores of the lake. We floated on the lake's waters in a slender boat, and I was able to make all kinds of comparisons between the bluish green waves and the nymph-like eyes of Princess Y. We drove to the Falkenstein, where there is a famous echo, and were pleased when the echo returned the nonsense we shouted at it. We sorrowfully examined the " wedding cross " which had been erected on a cliff, in memory of the tragic end of a wedding party that had danced on the ice of the lake and drowned when it broke. The butcher whose bull had gone wild and had jumped into the lake, fared better. This resolute butcher had jumped in after his bull, seized its tail, and so swum to the further shore with it. The " Bull Cross " was erected in his honour. Twice we climbed the Schafberg, which was called " Aur Rigi "[1] in the Salzkammergut. We spent the night in the hay on the summit, and found that at sunrise in the morning the view from the Schafberg was more beautiful than the view from the Swiss Rigi, even if it were not so comprehensive.

I will not conceal the fact that, intellectually, I did not always quite get on with my beautiful friend. She had a preference—a preference incomprehensible to me—for that kind of literature which, to use an expression that does not appeal to me very much, is nowadays called " tripe." She was enthusiastic about Louisa de la Ramée, whose tasteless novel, *Under Two Flags*, had appeared under her pseudonym, " Ouida." She was touched to the point of tears by a novel that was not much better, *Marianne*, by Jules Sandeau, the first lover of George Sand, who was very much his superior. She did not understand my enthusiasm for the *Iliad* and the *Æneid*, for Aristophanes and Tacitus. And when I read *Wilhelm Meister's Apprenticeship*, she began to yawn. I fear that if I had read *Wilhelm Meister's Wander Years* she would have gone to sleep. I cannot say that these differences in our literary tastes disturbed me at the time, but they would have begun to get on our nerves if we had permanently shared one another's lives.

Now, as an old man, and when I think of those days, especially those on the shore of the Wolfgang Lake, I ask myself how I reconciled all this with my conscience. Did I reflect, or had I acted from emotional impulse? Did I reproach myself, or did I find everything as it should be? Quite frankly, I did neither one nor the other! I was in that state of mind which Italian theologians

---

[1] Our Rigi.

call *La Pace del Impio*. If, now and again, I gave any thought to the moral aspect of the passion that filled me, I took comfort in the English proverb, "All's fair in love and war." [1] Besides, since as an officer and a man of honour, I was naturally prepared to give every kind of satisfaction, sword in hand, I had no further scruples. Now that I write the story of my life and allow all events to pass by me in coloured procession, I do not wish to omit this episode. As I said at the beginning of this volume, memoirs are valueless unless they are truthful, suppress nothing, and correct nothing. Even a statesman whose work and life have shown some sense of grave responsibility, may have kicked over the traces in his youth. To drape youth with the mantle of virtue, a self-satisfied recollection of earlier days in the evening of life is a falsification of it. As a part of my autobiography, the episode at St. Wolfgang and many similar episodes may show that a man who takes life and his office seriously can control his passions when the time comes. To-day I say with the psalmist: "Remember not the sins of my youth, nor my transgressions: according to Thy mercy remember Thou me for Thy goodness' sake, O Lord" (Ps. xxv, 7).

At Salzburg, which we often visited from St. Wolfgang, I was to have a meeting which, like a warning voice, reminded me of professional work, creative endeavour, and the gravity of an official position. The scene is still vivid in my memory. My mistress and I had descended from the Gaisberg, where the wonderful view had just delighted us. We were going to drink some wine in the cellar of St. Peter's. Delighted by what we had seen, we entered the inn so full of poetic atmosphere. Before us, obviously sunk in thought, and not even noticing us at first, stood—Lothar Bucher. Of what was he thinking? Of his one-time party friend and comrade during exile in London, Karl Marx? Of his present chief, Otto von Bismarck? Was he, who inclined towards silent meditation, comparing the one with the other? When he saw me accompanied by a beautiful and very elegant lady, he withdrew shyly, while we refreshed ourselves with the good wine of the cellar, happy, glad, and as talkative as children who meet their teacher during their holidays. But the sight of this considerable man who had seen, experienced and considered so much, reminded me of all the seriousness and the stern realities of life. Before me was Berlin, the Foreign Office, my strict father, my present and future sphere of duty. This meeting came like a spring frost.

---

[1] English in text, *i.e.,* "in war and in love everything is fair."

DIPLOMATIC SERVICE

CHAPTER XXVI

Diplomatic Examination—Transfer to St. Petersburg (1875)—Journey to St. Petersburg—Count Alvensleben—General von Werder—The Rasvod—Tsar Alexander II—The Tsarevitch—Andrássy—Balkan Reform Programme—St. Petersburg Society—Slav Women, Russian Girls—Russian Literature.

WHEN I returned to Berlin a few days after the meeting with Lothar Bucher, I could see, from my father's manner, that my somewhat long stay in St. Wolfgang had not particularly pleased him. I had not been quite easy about it myself, but it could at least have been put to my credit that I had not forgotten my work during that idyll. In St. Wolfgang I had prepared what was perhaps the worst part of my task for the diplomatic examination. It had been set me by Professor Gneist and dealt with the rules to be observed under international law by one state with regard to the domestic party conflicts of another. I am rather proud even to-day that in St. Wolfgang I managed to produce something which called forth the following verdict from Gneist, who was obviously satisfied:

> The exposition is of praiseworthy brevity, practical, lucid and fluid in style. The writer's judgment is open-minded throughout. The work deserves to be called very good.

But my father clearly looked more on the debit side of my stay at St. Wolfgang. He refrained from remarks which might have wounded my feelings, but with grave official emphasis, he let me know that he expected my forthcoming diplomatic examination to pass off " smoothly," as he called it. " It would be a fine thing, indeed, if you, son of a Secretary of State, were not to come out of it well."

Impressed by this paternal admonition I worked with renewed intensity and went up for examination on the 15th November. I woke with a very bad headache on that morning—a complaint I often suffered from at that period of my life. When my father remarked on my pallor, I explained it, and he said: " According to Voltaire ' *la migraine est le mal des gens d'esprit.*' Let's see if

IV.   B B

that's true in your case. As a matter of fact, I'm rather glad you have a headache, since with your ready tongue and the gifts God has so graciously bestowed on you it would not be particularly praise-worthy or difficult to face an oral examination. '*A vaincre sans péril, on triomphe sans gloire.*'"

The oral examination passed off as my worthy father expected and hoped. Professors Rudolf Gneist and Adolf Wagner, and the French examiner, Professor Auber, a Frenchman born, all reported that the law student von Bülow had answered the questions on constitutional and international law with an accuracy and prompt-ness which testified to steady application. On subjects dealing with political science and statistics he had revealed an accurate knowledge of the theoretical and economic aspects of the questions, and answered promptly and to the point. He showed the same thorough and exact study of the various historical-political questions addressed him, and had expressed himself fluently and correctly in French. " In view of the aggregate result of the written and oral examina-tions, the undersigned board of examiners consider that Bernhard von Bülow has passed the diplomatic examination with honours, and appears to have prepared himself for the diplomatic service in a thorough and comprehensive manner."

The first to congratulate me, and that in a most hearty fashion, was Herbert von Bismarck. As he knew that I was not up to the mark on account of my headache, he had been waiting in a room close by. There was not a nicer, more distinguished young man anywhere in those days than Herbert Bismarck.

In the summer of 1875, the only daughter of Prince Bismarck, Countess Marie, became engaged to Count Wendt Eulenburg. He was the youngest and perhaps the most gifted of four very gifted brothers, of whom Botho was to become Minister of the Interior and Premier of Prussia, August, Lord Chamberlain and Steward of the Household, and Karl a cavalry General. In the late autumn of 1875 Wendt Eulenburg died of typhus at Varzin, where he was on a visit. I have always regarded his death as a political misfortune. Had he been alive he would have negotiated more skilfully between his great father-in-law and the youthful William II than the over-impetuous and not always tactful son, Herbert. I shall never forget the expression on Prince Bismarck's face as he stood beside the coffin of the young man, who was to have married his daughter, and picked up the decorations that lay upon it—medals of the campaigns of 1866 and 1870. He gazed at them long and thoughtfully. How profound and sad must his thoughts have been! The young girl who was to have married Wendt was as deeply pious as her mother. She told me in a whisper that she feared God must have wanted to punish her for loving her betrothed too well. She mourned him long and sincerely. It was several years before she found peace in a happy marriage with the excellent Count Kuno Rantzau.

A few days after the diplomatic examination my father discussed with me the question as to where I wished to be sent for my first post as Secretary of a Legation. He told me that owing to the severe illness of the Secretary of the Embassy, Count Bernard Wartensleben, there was a vacancy in St. Petersburg. This, he declared, was one of the most interesting places to live in. Count Alvensleben, the present chargé d'affaires, he considered an excellent official, and the right person to teach me. He thought I should find the Ambassador, Prince Henry VII of Reuss, who was at present away on leave, one of the most excellent diplomats it was possible to meet. He had done splendid service in Paris and Munich, as well as in St. Petersburg, while his work during the Franco-German war had been very considerable. If Prince Reuss did not remain in St. Petersburg he would probably be succeeded by General von Schweinitz, and he, too, was an experienced and skilful diplomat, highly cultured and broad-minded.

I asked my father to let me think it over. Consideration for my lovely friend, Princess Y., made me hesitate. She hoped that if I could not remain at the German Foreign Office, I might at least obtain a post in Germany. Dresden appeared to be her ideal. How touchingly egotistical women are when they love! When I told her there was a possibility of St. Petersburg, she burst into tears. A separation of so many miles seemed insufferable to her, and she also feared that my weak throat might suffer in the Russian climate. She considered it harsh, even brutal, of my father to expose me to this danger. In her anxiety and love of me she went to the Prussian Ambassador at Dresden, the amiable Count Eberhard Solms, and begged him to write, not to the Secretary of State, but to Prince Bismarck in person, telling him that he most particularly desired Bernhard von Bülow as Secretary. She admitted to me that she had promised Count Solms, who was no longer very young, but still very gallant, a kiss if her wish were fulfilled. As a pledge and a little on account, she had already allowed him to kiss her forehead. I myself stood like Hercules, midway between ambition and love, though instead of " love " I ought to write "youthful passion." And my ambition was no ignoble one, for I felt that it would be useful for my diplomatic and political education to become acquainted with Russia while still a young man. In one final and decisive conversation I told my father I should welcome my transfer to St. Petersburg.

I left for Russia after a touching farewell scene with Princess Y. In those days, in their somewhat affected manner, the Russian ladies called St. Petersburg " the Palmyra of the north." At the beginning of the war it was changed to Petrograd so as to erase all memories of German culture and language. Now it is known to us as Leningrad. By what name, in another fifty years, will the city of Peter the Great be known? Will her already crumbling palaces still mirror themselves in the Neva's waters? Or will that rigorously logical and integral Marxism, that Bolshevism whose *Tcheka* surpasses in bigotry and brutality all that the Jacobins' " *Comité de Salut public* " accomplished a hundred and twenty-five years ago, have succeeded in wiping out that St. Petersburg, the centre of a mighty Empire, from the days of the great Tsar Peter to those of the little Tsar Nicholas?

Travelling was comfortable in old Russia. This was due to the slowness of the trains. There was no shaking or swaying in the carriages. They ran on a broad gauge, and people could read, write, or play cards (for which Russians have a natural predilection) with comfort in them. Between Wirballen and St. Petersburg were few stations. But if there was a stop it lasted half an hour. The traveller took his choice of the many delicacies the Russian cuisine offers at the station buffets. In old Russia there was always time for everything. Since I travelled as courier, the Prussian Frontier Commissioner was awaiting me at Wirballen, together with his Russian colleague, who bore a title. While I was exchanging compliments with him in French, the Prussian whispered that he wanted twenty-five roubles. He handed them to the Russian stealthily, but the recipient placed them in his pocket-book quite unabashed. Then he announced to us in a charming manner that all frontier, passport and customs formalities were over, and wished me a pleasant journey.

From the frontier onwards there were no more foliage-bearing trees, save for a snow-laden birches here and there. On the stations the gendarmes were wrapped in sheepskins, and their noses and ears bandaged as protection against the already considerable cold. Miserable looking Jews in caftans and curls were huddled in the background, offering, when they thought the gendarmes' backs were turned, cigarettes, genuine Eckau kümmel,[1] and beautiful girls, the last *sotto voce*, and all in a terribly bad German. In this way I saw as soon as I reached Russian soil two characteristic types

[1] An aniseed liqueur.

of pre-war Russian life—police and Jews. The latter trembled before the former long enough, but have got even with them at last, though whether for the good or ill of the country the future alone can determine.

The chargé d'affaires at St. Petersburg, Count Johann Alvensleben was awaiting me at the station. He asked me if, in spite of my long railway journey, I would care for a sleigh drive round St. Petersburg. I gladly accepted his kind offer to give me a general view of the city. My impressions proved to be the same as those I had received from the long journey—a sensation of never-ending monotony. Everything was white. The ground over which our sleigh was speeding, the snowy roofs of the houses, the cupolas of the churches and icicle-hung pinnacles of the towers: the frozen Neva. This universal white merged imperceptibly into the grey sky, so that St. Petersburg, with its blurred and vanishing outlines, appeared the shadowy city of a fairy tale, floating and nebulous, without fixed foundation and indeterminate in form.

I understood the vagueness of many typical Russian faces, the indecisions and uncertainties, the indefiniteness of Russian thought and performance, which persists, whether Peter the Great forcibly calls a new city into being against the deepest instincts of the Russian people, or Vladimir Lenin just as forcibly destroys what two centuries have built up. We drove through the mist past the Winter Palace, where six thousand people were said to live, and which, when it was burnt to the ground, Tsar Nicholas re-built in a few months. And in the winter, too! He rewarded the master builder who did this work and who had begun his career as a Lettish lackey, Kleinmichl, with the title of Count and a wonderful coat of arms with the device: " For zeal have I rewarded you." The reconstruction of the palace swallowed up millions of roubles and cost many people their lives. The cold had reached ten to twenty or even thirty degrees below zero, and the whole building had to be permanently heated to keep the materials from freezing and make the walls dry quickly. This was the spirit in which the Pharaohs built their Pyramids and Tamerlane and Ghengis Khan raised up their pyramids of skulls. We drove along the Nevski Prospekt, the longest and most frequented street of the city, flanked by brilliant shops and sumptuous palaces, and terminating in typical Russian suburb taverns, a nunnery and a churchyard. Glimpses were everywhere to be caught of the gigantic golden needle of the slender Admiralty Tower.

Next day, our military representative, General von Werder, took me to the *Rasvod*. This was a parade held once a week in the big covered and heated riding school of St. Michael. Along one side were ranged the Suitzskys, the adjutants and adjutant-generals so common in Russia. Representatives of all the troops garrisoned in St. Petersburg flanked the other three sides, among them the elite of the Garde-à-Cheval and the Chevaliers-Gardes, reminiscent, with their eagle-crowned helmets, of our Gardes-du-Corps and Garde-Cuirassiers. Picturesque Circassians and wild-looking Cossacks, with their long lances and dreaded whips, stood next to hussars, lancers, and dragoons. The Tsar greeted everybody with a " Good morning, children, are you satisfied with your food and treatment? " Obviously to these gallant warriors the question did not come as a surprise. The troops replied with praiseworthy and unanimous enthusiasm: " We're satisfied with everything and are pleased to do our duty." The Tsar then turned to the suite. I stood at the right wing, next to General von Werder, with whom His Imperial Majesty shook hands. He presented me, and Alexander II looked at me attentively. He had particularly fine eyes, which expressed as much kindliness as is seemly and permissible for a Tsar. These eyes also had that melancholy which is said to be found in those who are destined for an early and a violent death. These expressive eyes were fixed, surprised and questioning, upon my hussar's uniform. Was something wrong with it? Had I forgotten my fur cap? I held it in my right hand. Had I omitted to buckle on my sabre? I had not, and I held it according to orders between the thumb and two fingers of my left hand. Was my sash missing? I felt it, and a quick glance confirmed my hand's testimony. Our old sergeant-major Wunderlich of the King's Hussars would have been satisfied with my smart appearance. Thank goodness! But why does the Tsar gaze so steadily at my uniform? " What is the meaning of this cross you're wearing amongst your decorations? " demanded a deep voice. I replied that it was the Mecklenburg Cross of Merit for distinguished war service. " But that is golden, and your cross is silver," said the rather testy voice of the ruler of geographically the largest realm on earth, the despotic sovereign of a hundred million subjects. I replied with military brevity, decisively, and in a loud voice, that the Mecklenburg-Schwerin cross for bravery was indeed gilt, but that the one of Mecklenburg-Strelitz was of silver. " Very interesting, really very interesting," said the all-powerful Tsar, the *Tsar Samodershets*, turning to General von Werder, and his hitherto severe features assumed a kind expression. " I really didn't know that! " Alexander II spoke German with a hard Russian accent, but fluently, and with obvious pleasure. From that day he invariably addressed me personally at every *Rasvod*, briefly, but graciously, a fact upon which Alvensleben and Werder congratulated me.

According to ancient tradition, only the Prussian-German representatives attended the *Rasvod*, to the exclusion of those of other countries. An aide-de-camp of the King of Prussia had been attached to the person of the Tsar since the wars of Liberation when Prussia and Russia fought victoriously side by side. General von Werder had acted in this capacity since the spring of 1870. Bernhard von Werder was a typical Prussian, a typical military man. He stood stiff as a poker, knees taut, and a backbone as rigid as though he had swallowed a ramrod. He stood there as immovably as at the battle of Königgrätz, when he had commanded the Fusiliers, and earned the rarely-bestowed order *Pour le Mérite*. Forty years later he stood just as erect at the christening of the eldest son of the Crown Prince in July, 1906, when I saw him for the last time. In 1831 he had been a page at the christening of the child who was to become the Emperor Frederick, and did not want to miss the same ceremony with Frederick's great grandchild at the font. The General's upright carriage was the outward sign of his upright mind. He was independent and truth-loving and of singular integrity right through. To these virtues he owed the confidence reposed in him, not only by his own Sovereign, Emperor William I, but by Tsar Alexander II of Russia as well. The Tsar Alexander III, who was not sentimental and did not particularly love Germans, also felt an almost tender affection for Werder.

At the end of the eighties everybody in St. Petersburg knew that Alexander III could not bear the Bulgarian Prince Alexander Battenberg. I need scarcely add that, feeling in high places being what it was, many courtiers sought to please the Tsar by speaking unfavourably of Alexander Battenberg. Once when Battenberg was the subject of attack at the Imperial table, General von Werder, who sat next to the Tsar, said in a loud voice, looking straight into the royal eyes: " And I declare that I love and admire Prince Alexander, for he bore himself well on the battlefield, and was also kind to me personally. Your Majesty should be nicer to your cousin." Everybody was silent, but Alexander III laid his big hand on the Prussian General's shoulder: " Werder, you're the best person at this table." Prince Bismarck did not like Werder, but in this he was wrong. Werder, by his honest and outspoken ways, furthered that friendly relationship between Russia and Germany which Bismarck at heart always regarded as the vital question for us.

Among the diplomats accredited to St. Petersburg I found an old friend. This was Herr von Wind, formerly my father's secretary in Frankfort, during the days of the Federal Diet, and now advanced to the post of Danish Ambassador. He gave me a hearty welcome when I called upon him, and was useful to me in many ways. He presented me to the future Tsaritsa Maria Feodorovna, who was kind enough to remember how we had played together as children in Rumpenheim on the Maine, when she was still the fourteen-year-old Princess Dagmar of Schleswig-Holstein-Sonderburg-Glücksburg. In this way I made the acquaintance of her husband, the future Alexander III, the thick-set, broad-shouldered man had the reputation of being an enemy of Germany. He may have found his father's affection for Prussia exaggerated. He was certainly a less-distinguished man and less internationally minded. But in 1876 I already had the impression that the future Tsar Alexander III was not so much anti-German as anti-foreign altogether, and, following the trend of the times, took pains to be as Russian as possible in manner and appearance.

Not only the Royal Houses, but the nations individually, grew more and more aggressively national with every decade during the course of the nineteenth century. In the fifties Grillparzer had already sighed " From humanity through nationality to bestiality." The World War would have appeared to the great German-Austrian poet as the fulfilment of his gloomy prophecy. But we must not forget that the nationalist movement was furthered less by the Royal Houses which in themselves remained international for a long period or by the aristocracies following their example, than by literature and the Press, by professors and parliamentarians. Above all, we must not forget that in so far as German nationalism is concerned it has been called into being by the pillaging campaigns of the French. After the infamous dictated peace of Versailles every German who has his heart in the right place will pray God to strengthen the sons of Teuto in their dealings with other nations. Not that this prayer should find expression in loud-mouthed vociferations, still less in thoughtless acts of violence, but by placing the Fatherland above everything, above personal ends, above party prejudice and class hatred.

During my first winter in St. Petersburg I often frequented the house of the widowed Countess Protasov. Her husband had advanced under Tsar Nicolas from Commander of the Hussar Guards to Procurator of the Holy Synod—a post equivalent to that of President of the Prussian Protestant Church Council. One morning when Tsar Nicolas, who had been annoyed the day before by the Procurator of the Synod, watched the smart parade of the Hussar Guards under Protasov, he beckoned their commander and said to him: " I appoint you head of the Holy Synod in the conviction that you will keep the bishops, priests and monks in as good order as you have kept your Hussars."

Count Protasov is said to have performed his allotted task quite well. Like all the ladies of St. Petersburg, Countess Protasov and her charming daughter were busy cutting lint during the winter of 1875-76. Why and for whom? For the revolutionaries in the Herzegovina! Twenty-one years after the Peace of Paris, storm clouds were again gathering in the Balkans. On 29th October, 1875, the Russian Official *Gazette* called the attention of the Cabinets of Europe to the complaints and sufferings of the Christians in Turkey, for whom Russia had made too many sacrifices in the past not to have the right to raise a protest now. On 30th December, 1875, Count Andrássy sent a telegram to the embassies of the Austro-Hungarian Empire in London, Paris and Rome, in which he laid down the programme he had evolved, already approved in Berlin and St. Petersburg, of reforms in the Balkan peninsula which demanded the absolute equality of Christianity and Islam. During the winter of 1875-76, harmony between the three Empires was not disturbed. Prince Bismarck regarded this as more important than the fate of Turkey, or even of that of the rival Balkan nations, which he looked upon merely as objects of his own policy. In the same manner the chess-player, shifting his pawns on the board, never quite loses sight of them, but never exaggerates their significance.

Count Alvensleben was a chief from whom I learnt a great deal. He had been trained to show tact and self-possession in the excellent school of his own chief, Prince Henry VII of Reuss. He never showed too much zeal or even excitement, but treated everything with the same conscientious attention. Once when hastily de-coding a Berlin telegram I made a slight mistake. He reprimanded me so sharply that I remembered the lesson during my whole subsequent career. Ὁ μὴ δαρεὶς ἄνθρωπος οὐ παιδεύεται, Goethe placed this motto as preface to *Poetry and Truth*. I regard this axiom of old Menander as one of the wisest precepts ever given. In sincere gratitude and in deserved recognition of his qualities in office I suggested the excellent Alvensleben for the St. Petersburg ambassadorship when I became Chancellor.

Alvensleben, as my chief, stressed the importance of my going into Society. I danced a great deal. I soon learned the mazurka, the national dance of the Russians and Poles. After the minuet and the waltz, whose praise I have already sung (only barbarians could be insensitive to them) the Slav mazurka appears to me the most attractive of dances. The best mazurka dancer in St. Petersburg was neither a Pole nor a Russian, but a German, Prince Ferdinand Wittgenstein. He was a son of Prince Augustus von Sayn-Wittgenstein, who was Prime Minister of Nassau before 1848, and Imperial Minister of Defence from May to December, 1849. Very internationally-minded, like so many German aristocrats of those days, he placed both his sons, Emil and Ferdinand, in the Russian service.

Their handsome mother, Franziska von Schweitzer, was a relative of the Social Democrat, Jean Baptist von Schweitzer, who had been President of the general German Workman's Association from 1864 to 1871. In spite, or rather, because of his eccentricities, Prince Ferdinand Wittgenstein was very much beloved in St. Petersburg. He once bet that he would ride in a troika from St. Petersburg to Perm on the Kama, on the Asiatic frontier of Russia, eat a plate of the very indigestible Russian national dish, a soup called " *Badvinia*," drink a bottle of wine and kiss a girl at every stage where horses were changed. He won his bet.

His elder brother, Prince Emil Wittgenstein, was less original, but mentally his superior. He combined German thoroughness in his work with the " *schirokaia natura*," the expansive Russian manner, which he had assimilated. During the Polish revolt of 1862 to 1864 he suppressed the insurrection in the Russian-Polish Government he administrated, but treated the rebels with humanity and good sense. He was an excellent conversationalist, and was often commanded to table by Alexander II, who appreciated intelligence and humour. His first wife was a wealthy Rumanian heiress, Princess Pulcheria Cantacuzenos. After her death he married a famous Polish dancer, Mlle. Camilla Stefanska. When a prudish German princess asked Emil Wittgenstein how he could bring himself to marry a dancer, he replied: " Do you know the reply Queen Frederika of Hanover once gave a court lady who asked a similar question? This lady was upset that one of the other ladies permitted a gentleman of not particularly good reputation to make love to her. The queen asked the lady if she herself had ever had a liaison with the gentleman. She received a horrified denial. ' Then,' said her Majesty, ' you are not in a position to judge the situation.' And that's why I say now: Whoever doesn't know Camilla can give no opinion as to my marriage! "

Although I wrote to Princess Y. almost daily, I was not impervious to the charms of Slav women. I was clearly too young to live for one set of emotions only. And if, for the moment, I disregard the moral aspect (which I naturally judge differently at seventy from the way in which I judged it at twenty), I still consider it a good thing that I had an opportunity at so early an age of judging the national character of the Poles as well as of the Russians by getting to know their women. Bismarck differentiated between masculine and feminine nations. Among the former he reckoned Germans, English, Scandinavians, Dutch, Swiss, Turks; among the latter the Latins and Slavs. The Polish Princess R. was slender, lithe as a willow switch, dark-haired, with big wondering eyes, imaginative and enterprising, and capable of many things, both good and bad. She was barely eighteen. At fifteen she had been married off to a very insignificant husband. She made me aware that the Poles (and I say it in their praise) are only surpassed by the French when it comes to ardent patriotism. I learned from her, too, that the Pole will always regard the German as his only real enemy. The Princess R. told me so candidly, and though she was kind enough to make an exception in my case (which was very flattering to me) this fact gave her judgment weight in my eyes.

Whatever pedants say, one learns more from life than from all the books ever written, even from those based on " scientific " research.

Countess T., a Russian, and some years older than myself, was no less charming, although quite different. Her husband was not simple, like Prince R., but possessed a mind of such fundamental cynicism as to be unique even for a St. Petersburg *viveur* of those days. She loved her own people, but was not blind to their faults. She quoted with pleasure the words of Alexander Hertsen, the great Russian revolutionary, who said that in Russia twice two sometimes, though rarely, make five, generally three, and almost never four. I owe to her my early acquaintance with Russian literature, with Turgeniev and Grigorovitch (both of whom I met personally later on in life), with Pushkin and Lermontov, Gogol and Gontcharov, and the two really great men, Dostoievski and Leo Nikholaivitch Tolstoi. Everybody knows these names to-day. But in the eighties of the last century I met with surprised and unbelieving smiles from cultured and fashionable people in Paris when I spoke with enthusiasm of Tolstoi and Dostoievski.

I do not want to brand the French of those days with any particular label. Lack of understanding and impatience with any new or not yet understood artistic and literary movements are to be met with in all countries and at all periods. Voltaire despised

Shakespeare, and Frederick the Great the Nibelung Saga. Goethe repudiated Gottfried August Bürger and Heinrich von Kleist. Masterpieces like *Lohengrin* and *Tannhäuser* were damned outright, on their first appearance, by the critics of Berlin and Vienna, and the " Ring " was mocked and reviled at its inception at Bayreuth in 1876 by high-brow publicists. I had therefore full reason to be grateful to my Russian friend who showed me the literature of her country and through it the Russian soul. She pointed out with insistence how many Russian novels, the finest ones especially, had no proper ending. One of the most famous of all Russian novels ends with the hero's journey in a slowly-moving railway carriage into an unknown and nebulous future in a state of acute melancholy, of misery and regret, and, what is almost worse, with a terrible toothache.

Such things happen to Russians in real life. The Russians lack all concentration. " *Lizez Oblomov!* " It contains the whole Russian people. Has the dream of Byzantium, or Tsarigrad, ever materialized? " In the west," said Countess T., " there is talk of a will left by Peter the Great and plans for conquering the world are attributed to us. He never made such a will, nor shall we ever conquer the world. We are like the mists that envelop us when the snow comes for seven months in the year." Countess T. sometimes stood very much on the edge of the social precipice, but always managed to right herself in time. Poor Princess R. toppled over.

We had wonderful rides through the snow and mists of the Russian winter. The delightful families Stronganov, Kreutz, Barclay de Tolly and Vorentsov invited, beside myself, my friend and colleague at the Embassy, Count Augustus Dönhoff-Friedrich-stein. Next to the joy of a long brisk gallop on a good horse in the Roman Campagna or on the shores of the North Sea, I regard a Russian sleigh-ride in a troika with three horses as one of the few real delights of this life, on the unsatisfactory nature of which all serious philosophers are agreed, from King Solomon to Arthur Schopenhauer. Among the young ladies with whom I had the privilege of dancing during my first St. Petersburg winter, two have remained in my memory because they combined in the highest degree those qualities which make Russian girls so appealing—a pure spirit exalted by idealism, the capacity of renouncing those things which temporarily grace life and the selfless devotion to an idea which might even culminate in death for the sake of it.

Young Countess Perovski was a quiet girl, who danced grace-fully, and carried on the customary type of ballroom conversation with her partner, even though her thoughts were quite obviously elsewhere. I gathered as much from the remark she dropped casually, that the world was full of injustice, that people were unhappy and that the only human beings deserving the epithet " good " were those capable of sacrifice for a noble cause. Later she went " among the people " as the Nihilists called it. And when Alexander II fell victim on 13th March, 1881, to a Nihilist bomb, it was she, who, by waving her handkerchief, signed to the waiting assassins that the Tsar was approaching. She was hanged. Turgeniev addressed a poem to her mother in which he praised the young girl who might have trodden flowery meadows, but chose instead the steep and stony path with eyes fixed on a high goal.

My other dancing partner, Fräulein von K., was spared so tragic an end. I had never flirted with her, but was glad to converse with her between dances. One day she asked me rather unexpectedly whether I thought that she and I could be happy together. I thought I was being very clever when I replied that we were both too young yet to think of remaining together for life. I imagined that she, a young girl with no fortune and no connections, was leading on a hopeful young diplomat to make her an offer of marriage. With a tear in her eye, she said: " *Vous vous trompez du tout au tout. J'ai cru un instant que nous pourrions être heureux ensemble. Mais puisque vous ne voulez pas de moi je ferai un parti beaucoup plus brillant que vous.*" Next day I heard that she had become engaged to a man who was highly placed and very distinguished, and a good man, too. I was ashamed of my " *fatuité* " (I know no German word to replace this French expression). I met the girl who gave me this lesson later on in life. We have remained good friends.

CHAPTER XXVII

Ambassador Prince Henry VII of Reuss—Ambassador von Schweinitz—The Radowitz Mission—Alexander II—Tsaritsa Maria Alexandrovna—Catharine Dolgoruki—Duke George of Mecklenburg-Strelitz—Tsar Paul and the Knout—Farewell Visit to Gortchakov (1876).

I DO not wish to create the impression that I lived for the social delights of St. Petersburg only, and did not take my duties seriously. Not long after his arrival at St. Petersburg, the Ambassador, von Schweinitz, asked me to prepare a report for him of the situation in Central Asia, with special reference to Anglo-Russian relations. It was to be done as quickly as possible. I began at once, and worked without stopping from ten at night till eight in the morning. Then I slept for an hour and brought the memorandum to my chief before ten o'clock. He was satisfied with it.

While I was working and studying, dancing and sleighing, the expected change at the head of our Embassy occurred. Prince Henry VII of Reuss, who had been Ambassador until then, got engaged to the eldest daughter of the Grand Duke of Saxony, Princess Marie of Weimar. Owing to her close family relationship with the Russian Court, it was feared in Berlin that she might be placed in a difficult position as an Ambassador's wife. So Bismarck decided to transfer General von Schweinitz, the Ambassador in Vienna, to the post of Prince Reuss in St. Petersburg. After a few years Prince Reuss re-entered the diplomatic service, and in 1877-8, as Ambassador in Constantinople during the Russo-Turkish war (as later in Vienna from 1878 to 1894) did excellent work for Germany. From the days when he first knew me at St. Petersburg, he followed my official career with benevolent interest, and often helped me by his wise advice. He was best man when I married on 9th January, 1886. He was as pleased, six years later, at my appointment to the Roman Embassy as at any personal success. When he left the Vienna Embassy to make way for his successor, Phili Eulenburg, I invited him to spend the first weeks after his retirement at our home, the Palazzo Caffarelli, in Rome, the city which, like no other in the world, teaches resigna-

tion and softens pain. Save for my old wartime general, Field-
Marshal Loë, nobody was more pleased at my rise to the Chancellorship than Reuss. When I fainted in the Reichstag in 1906, the
Prince, who had reached the age of eighty-one, was on his deathbed.
Almost his last words were the wishes for my speedy recovery
and a long term of office, which he desired his sons to convey to
me, " not only for his own sake, but his country's." To the end
of my days I shall remember this with gratitude to a man distinguished both by his birth and character.

Prince Reuss' departure from St. Petersburg was regretted by
everybody there. Both he and Alvensleben were popular and
enjoyed the confidence of Russian Society. On the other hand, the
much-discussed special mission of von Radowitz as Ambassador
Extraordinary to St. Petersburg was a mistake. Prince Bismarck,
annoyed with Gortchakov since the " War-in-sight " episode of
1875, thought that Prince Reuss treated the old Russian Chancellor
with excessive courtesy, too much *en grand seigneur*, whereas
Alvensleben looked up to him rather too much as a superior official
in his capacity as Chancellor. Radowitz, it was intended, should
tell the plain truth to Gortchakov. Josef von Radowitz, still
young, very ambitious and full of courage, undertook the mission
as one that fulfilled his wildest dreams. Besides, he expected a
splendid reception on the Neva, since his wife was a daughter of
Otserov, the Russian Ambassador in Munich, and his brother-in-
law a high official in the Russian Foreign Office, a M. Petersen.
Things turned out differently. Radowitz met with a cool reception
in the St. Petersburg salons. " *Nous ne voulons pas faire des
infidélités a ce bon Alvensleben, ni au très sympathique Prince Reuss,*"
said the ladies of fashion, the " *femmes huppées,*" whose influence
was powerful in those days on the Neva. The Tsar barely noticed
Radowitz. His Chancellor behaved more than coolly. The
" mission extraordinary " was a fiasco.

In honour of the departing Ambassador Reuss, a farewell
dinner *en petit cercle* was given by their Russian Majesties in March,
1876, to which I was invited. Dinner was served in one of the
smaller rooms of the Imperial Palace. There was one picture as
sole decoration on the walls: a parade on the Tempelhofer Feld,
the Emperor William I shows his Prussian regiment, the First
Regiment of Tsar-Alexander-Grenadier-Guards, to his nephew,
Alexander II. But if Alexander, tall and good looking as he was,
made a brilliant impression on parade, it was equally difficult to
resist his charm at close quarters. Without ever departing from
his dignity, he was simple, natural, and pleasant. His conversation

was that of a man of culture, interesting and not devoid of humour.
He was a good talker, and above all, a perfect " gentleman." [1]
Francis Joseph was also that, but Alexander II was intellectually
superior to his Royal colleague in Vienna. He was not as gifted as
William II, but he had better taste and more tact. One must in justice
recognize that no other Russian ruler has done so much for his people
in the way of progress as Alexander II. Russia owes to him the
abolition of serfdom, one of the greatest social measures of all
times, judicial reforms on a European pattern, free local government, relief of taxation, great improvements in the educational
system, relaxation of the censorship leading to a freedom of the
Press which would have been deemed impossible in earlier days
though later it was the very jingoist Pan-Slavs who profited most
by it. Seen beside her husband, the Tsarina Maria Alexandrovna
made a somewhat discontented, down-trodden, and even slightly
offended impression. Although at the time only fifty, she had
entirely lost her looks. And even those who might not have known
that for the last five years she had had a rival, would have seen in
her the wife who was regarded as a nuisance and neglected, if not
entirely spurned. Yet her marriage with the Tsarevitch Alexander
Nikolaievitch had been a love match.

In 1840 the future Tsar Alexander II had followed the custom
of his ancestors for the last 150 years, and made the round of the
German Courts, to look for a wife in the " German stud farm,"
to use a forceful expression of Baron von Stein. He had been
charmed by Princess Marie of Hesse-Darmstadt, who was then
barely sixteen. He did not conceal the favourable impression she
had made upon him from Oubril, the Russian Ambassador in
Darmstadt, and later Berlin. Oubril joined gladly in the praises
showered upon Princess Marie by the Tsarevitch. But he called
attention, in all humility, to what in his opinion constituted a
serious objection to the marriage. Everybody in Darmstadt, he
informed the heir to the throne, knew that the real father of Princess
Marie was not the Grand Duke Louis II, but the master of the
Grand-Ducal Horse, Baron Augustus Senarclens von Grancy.
" Is Princess Marie in the Almanach de Gotha? " asked the
Tsarevitch. When the ambassador admitted that she was, the
amorous prince replied impatiently: " *Alors, de quoi vous mêlez-vous,
imbécile ?* " (*durak*). In the Russian royal family the descent of
the future Tsarina Maria Alexandrovna and Prince Alexander of
Hesse from the handsome Master of the Horse was well-known.
When I was attached to the Embassy of St. Petersburg and, in

---

[1] English in text.

1885 or 1886, drove with the Grand Duke and Grand Duchess Vladimir from Tsarskoie Selo to St. Petersburg, the Grand Duke, who had gone to bed late, fell asleep on the way, and his wife called my attention to his fine, almost classical features. One could see, she said, that her husband was not the grandson of Louis II of Hesse, renowned for his ugliness, but of the handsome Grancy. As a matter of fact, the Senarclens von Grancy were a good family and came from the Canton Vaud, not far from Lausanne, where the ancestral castle stands.

The marriage in 1841 between Alexander II and Maria Alexandrovna remained happy for more than ten years. But the Tsarina had a delicate constitution. She was never able to stand the damp cold of St. Petersburg. She bore the Tsar five tall strong sons and one well-grown daughter. After the birth of her youngest son in 1880, the Grand Duke Paul Alexandrovitch (who was shot during the revolution in 1919 in the Peter-Paul fortress by the Bolsheviks), she was forced by the advice of her doctors to lead a life of retirement, the life of a *monaca di casa*, a term the Sicilians apply to women who are forced to renounce all earthly pleasures. Since then the Tsar had drifted away from her. He fell in love with quite a young girl, Princess Catherine Mikhailovna Dolgoruki. Her parents were members of the oldest Russian aristocracy, but were not in especially good odour. Her mother was said to be an intriguer, her father a " ne'er-do-weel." Tsar Alexander saw little Catherine for the first time in the Smolny Institute for Young Ladies of Noble Birth, which the Tsaritsa Maria Feodorovna, widow of Tsar Paul, had founded on the model of Madame de Maintenon's College of St. Cyr. When the Bolsheviks came to power, the first headquarters of the Tcheka was this same Smolny Institute, surely a fact of which Catherine Mikhailovna in the days of her innocence had never dreamed. When I came to St. Petersburg in 1875 I found everybody of the opinion that Catherine Dolgoruki, who was not yet thirty, had been the mistress of Tsar Alexander for the past ten years. In 1872 she had borne him the first son, which naturally caused considerable agitation in the family of the heir to the throne. In 1873 there followed a daughter. Catherine Dolgoruki did not possess high mental gifts, but it was thought that her simplicity and childish *naïveté* in that sophisticated St. Petersburg environment, had first attracted, then permanently fascinated, the Tsar.

There is certainly no doubt about the fact that Alexander II was much more sensitive on matters touching his young mistress than on any affecting his own person. This was brought home even to the most influential man at the Russian Court, which, as things were in the Russian Empire of those days, meant the chief of the political police of the so-called Third Division, the aide-de-camp and cavalry commander, Peter Shuvalov. A year before my arrival at St. Petersburg Alexander II was informed that Peter Shuvalov, when a complaint was made to him of Princess Catherine Dolgoruki's ascendancy over His Majesty, replied with a laugh that he would soon get even with " that girl." Soon afterwards Count Peter Shuvalov was sent post haste to London as Russian Ambassador.

Near the German Embassy in the Grand Morskaia, lived the Chief Cup-Bearer, Count Hendrikov, whose good and charming wife was a universally beloved and popular hostess. It was reported to the Tsar that she had made a spiteful remark about Princess Catherine. Gendarmes came one day, or rather one night, at her house, left her only an hour to dress and wrap herself in a fur coat, placed her on a sledge, and drove her to one of her husband's country estates in Central Russia, many miles from St. Petersburg, telling her to stay there for the present. This episode recalls Schiller's grim Philip II, who sentenced a lady-in-waiting, the Marquise de Mondecar, to ten years' banishment from Madrid, to ponder over a careless word she had uttered. Countess Henrikov did not have to languish in exile as long as poor Mondecar. After a few months she received permission to return to her palace in the capital. There was an odd condition attached to this permission. For years she had been a friend of our beloved Emperor William I, who from his earliest youth had been closely connected with the Russian Court by the marriage of his sister Charlotte to the Grand Duke, afterwards Tsar, Nicholas I. Countess Henrikov was allowed to return to St. Petersburg on condition that she wrote nothing of these events to the German Emperor.

What happened to Countess Hendrikov was to happen to many ladies of St. Petersburg in much harsher form at the hands of the Bolsheviks forty-two years later. A tragic case is that of Countess Maria Kleinmichl, who told me personally of her experiences. She, too, was fetched by gendarmes from her home one night, hustled into a sleigh and carried off, though in her case the Bolshevik police, who arrested her, did not even let her retain her fur coat, in spite of her seventy years. Nor did they take her to one of her estates, but escorted her to a law court instead, where she barely escaped sentence of death. When, trembling with cold, she begged for her coat on the plea of her age, the Bolshevik in charge of the proceedings, a young rascal barely twenty years old, snapped at her: " You should be ashamed of your age, citizeness Maria Eduardovna! Proletarian women don't live to be as old as that."

I have spoken before of Duke George of Mecklenburg-Strelitz, who had been married since 1851 to the Grand Duchess Catharine Mikhailovna of Russia, and entered the Russian service. Although as a strict legitimist he disapproved of Prince Bismarck's policy, and particularly of the annexations of 1866, he remained on the same old friendly footing after my father had entered the Prussian service, and been nominated Secretary of State in the Foreign Office. I was warmly received in his home. He had humour and good sense. The descriptions he gave me of Tsar Nicholas I and his times were very interesting. His father-in-law, the Grand Duke Michael Pavlovitch, was the youngest brother of Tsar Nicholas. He typified the Byzantine spirit of that era more thoroughly than any other member of the family.

Tsar Nicholas liked tight trousers. Once when his younger brother had ordered a pair of new riding breeches, he said to the French tailor who brought them: " *Si je peux entrer dans vos pantalons je ne les prends pas.*" Grand Duke Michael Pavlovitch was in many ways like his father, Tsar Paul, but did not have the chance to lead the same gay life. Duke George was full of anecdotes of his wife's grandfather. I remember two of them. One is the most flagrant example of despotic absolutism I have ever come across. Tsar Paul was inspecting a cadet school one morning. He noticed a breach of one of his many rules and decreed: " The commandant of the Institute is to have twenty-four hours' arrest." Much embarrassed, the aide-de-camp informed him that he had forgotten to tell His Majesty of the commandant's death which had occurred suddenly in the night. Whereupon Paul replied: " Appoint another and lock him up instead."

To impress the English Ambassador at St. Petersburg, Paul invited him to a parade of one of his Life Guard Regiments, which he intended holding on the St. Petersburg *Champ de Mars*. The Tsar rode at the head of his regiment and commanded: " Gallop! Quick march! " He had a very reedy voice, and though he, himself, galloped ahead, his orders were not understood by the regimental commander, and nobody moved. When the Tsar looked round he found himself alone in the landscape. It was some time before the English Lord, smiling sardonically, could catch up with him. In his wrath the Tsar headed for the regiment and commanded: " Right about turn! March on India! " The commander had the presence of mind to repeat the order and spur up towards some unknown destination. Tsar Paul climbed as high a tower as he could find and surveyed the regiment through a telescope as long as this was possible. In forty-eight hours he had forgotten all about the affair, and the Life Guards crept back to their barracks. But Duke George of Mecklenburg-Strelitz pointed out to me that Paul, in spite of all his eccentricities, was beloved of the Russian people, nor did they mind the fact that he was a tyrant who even, for instance, in snow and mud, expected everyone to kneel to him as he passed. For years after his death the coffin of Tsar Paul had more wreaths " in affectionate memory " laid upon it than that of any other Romanov in the family vault. I myself have often seen pious muzhiks kneel before it, cross themselves, and pray.

When the Slavs in the neighbourhood of Novgorod in the ninth century fell into a state of almost complete anarchy, they sent a deputation to the Norman Varangians with the message: " We dwell in a beautiful and fruitful country, but we cannot govern ourselves. Come and rule over us." This was at the dawn of Russian history, and so the Russians remained under Ivan the Terrible, under Peter the Great, under the great Catherine, and under Tsar Nicholas I. The same is true to-day under the Bolshevik régime. *Plus ça change plus c'est la même chose.* The Russian people love to be ruled by the mailed fist. Not only Duke George of Strelitz and Duke George Leuchtenberg, but in later years the Grand Duke and Duchess Vladimir, told me quite as a matter of course that the wife of Tsar Paul, the Tsaritsa Maria Feodorovna, a Princess of Württemberg, and his eldest son, the future Tsar Alexander I, had known of the plot against the Tsar's life and made no attempt to save him. "*L'empereur s'était rendu tellement insupportable que tout le mond désirait sa suppression.*" The soul of the conspiracy was the Tsar's favourite, Count Peter Louis von Pahlen, a Baltic nobleman, cavalry general, adjutant-general, governor of St. Petersburg and Foreign Secretary. Some weeks previously he had observed that His Majesty was becoming a little mad, and had written to the Russian Ambassador at Berlin, to whom he had to pass on an eccentric royal order: " *Voilà les ordres de Sa Majesté. Vous ferez bien de ne pas vous presser à les exécuter, car la santé de notre Auguste Maître laisse, hélas, à désirer, et les dessins de la divine Providence sont impénétrables.*"

Pahlen, after forming a vanguard of young officers, flag lieutenants and cadets, led them at night to the Royal Palace, opened the gates to them in his capacity of governor of the capital, and let things take their own course. He himself, in gala uniform, with the blue ribbon of the Order of St. Andrew, stood outside the palace gate. If the attack failed he intended to arrest the conspirators with the help of half the company he had left behind, and hand them over to the Tsar, who would praise his loyal servant. If it were successful, he wished to reap the firstfruits of it.

The attempt succeeded. When Tsar Paul heard nocturnal noises, shouts in the corridors, pistol shots, and the butts of the rifles, he hid himself, cowardly as are most tyrants, under his bed. The conspirators poked at him with their bayonets and sabres until he came out and could be tied to the bed-post. Then one of their number went to Count Pahlen and asked what was to be done with the Tsar. Pahlen replied: " *Pour faire une omelette il faut casser les œufs.*" They took this gentle hint, and wound an officer's sash round the throat of the trembling autocrat. Count Subov, the last lover of the Tsar's mother, Catherine the Great, pulled one end of it, General Ushakov pulled the other. The eggs were broken; Tsar Paul was eliminated.

The Russian people, who, as I have said, cherished Tsar Paul's memory in pious fashion, also believed that Tsar Alexander I, who had died at Taganrog in December, 1825, on a journey to Southern Russia, had really lived for many years longer. He had determined to become a monk and expiate the death of his father. For this purpose he had the body of a dead Cossack dressed up in the Imperial uniform and carried with much pomp to St. Petersburg to be buried, after which for many years he expiated his sins in a monastery.

As soon as Count Pahlen learnt that the Tsar was dead, he rode round to all the barracks and heard the troops swear allegiance to Tsar Alexander Pavlovitch. Then he went to see His Majesty's widow, Tsaritsa Maria Feodorovna. On hearing of her husband's death she assumed an expression of great grief, but pulled herself together and informed Pahlen that like the Tsaritsa Catherine, after the death of Peter III, thirty-nine years previously, she intended to take the reins into her own hands. She expected the Ministers to report to her and the troops must be sworn in immediately. With a smile of scorn, Count Pahlen informed her that the troops had already sworn allegiance to Tsar Alexander Pavlovitch, and that the ministers were awaiting his royal commands. The Tsaritsa lost her royal bearing for a moment and burst out: " *Vous avez assassiné l'Empereur, votre Maitre!* " He bowed coldly, without a word, and the ambitious, proud, and handsome woman withdrew to her own apartments. She never forgot this disappointment, although both Tsar Alexander and Tsar Nicholas, her two sons, treated her with the greatest courtesy. As Tsaritsa-mother she took precedence over the reigning Tsaritsa, an order of etiquette which remained in vogue at the Russian Court. Alexander I gave her authority over all welfare and educational institutions, past and future, and until the fall of the Romanov dynasty these were entitled: "Welfare Institutes of the Tsaritsa Maria Feodorovna, at rest in the Lord." Tsar Nicolas gave her great pleasure when, not long after his accession, he made the Life Guards parade before her.

The mother-in-law of Duke George of Strelitz, Grand Duchess Helena Pavlovna, a Princess of Würtemberg, was a highly cultured woman of great character. It was she who expressed the opinion that St. Petersburg was the city of damp streets and cold hearts. During the harsh era of Nicholas her house was a centre for scholars, intellectuals and artists. She was liberal in thought, and supported progressive ideas and reforms wherever she could. But she regretted that young Russia, that is to say the Liberals, devoted themselves more and more to nationalistic ideals, behaving in Jingo fashion at home and abroad, and pursuing with their hatred the Germans in Russia and the entirely loyal Baltic nobility. She recognized Bismarck's genius, even when he was Ambassador to St. Petersburg, from 1859-62, and would often invite him to her house. Typical of the Bismarck of those days is the anecdote told me by Duke George of Mecklenburg-Strelitz. Bismarck and his wife were drinking tea with the Grand Duchess one evening. The conversation was animated. During a pause after Bismarck had talked brilliantly, his wife said to him: "Why, Otto, dear, whatever made you wear your patent shoes? It's only a small party." Bismarck, without a change of expression, replied: "You're right, my heart. The patent shoes are superfluous," and continued his exposé. Duke George said he did not know which he thought was the more admirable—the unshakable self-possession of the husband or the absolute naturalness of the wife.

Generals von Erckert and von Schack were among those Russian generals I met at the Duke's who had left Prussian for Russian service under Frederick William IV, but still retained their German sympathies. To my question whether they thought the autocratic régime in Russia would be of long duration, they replied that they considered autocracy adapted, on the whole, to the traditions, instincts and desires of the Russians. It might last a long time yet, they said, unless a disastrous war aroused the people. The Decabrist revolt of 1825, which nearly led to Liberalism, proved revolutions to be not impossible in Russia. *Kolokol*, the revolutionary organ, edited by Alexander Hertsen in London, found many readers and exerted great influence during the last years of Nicholas and the first of Alexander II. The unfortunate Crimean War certainly hastened, if it did not cause, Nicholas' end, and forced his successor to open his reign with drastic reforms. More lost wars, these generals considered, would bring more radical reforms, and might even lead to a really serious revolution. This prophecy was to find its first fulfilment after the Russo-Turkish war of 1877-78, and proved even more true after the Russo-Japanese war of 1904-5. The end of the Great War completed the process.

During my first years on the Neva there were older Russians who could remember the time when punishment by the knout was practised. It was used for non-political offences, and capital punishment only for political. A contemporary chronicle of Russian customs under Nicholas I, compiled by I. C. Petri, who was neither a wicked Democrat nor a carping critic, contains the following:

> Punishment by the knout is extremely painful. A knout is a heavy whip, some five feet long and half a pound in weight. It consists of a leather thong about as thick as a thaler, two feet long, eight inches broad at the base, three at the tip. The leather, to make it hard and cutting, is soaked in milk and dried in the sun, which makes it flexible like horn or parchment. Eight to ten strokes of a skilful knout-master can cause a miscreant's death if they fall heavily on the backbone. With less vigorous blows a man can be tortured to death by a hundred to two hundred and fifty strokes. The man wielding the knout gets behind his victim, who is bound to a slanting plank; he takes a few steps back and then leaps forward, bringing the knout down as he moves, to give it more purchase. There are four depressions in the plank for arms and legs, and a semi-circular one at the top for the head. Head, arms and legs are bound tightly in these, thus tautening out the muscles of the back.

The brutality of the Bolshevik Soviet system had many examples of no less appalling cruelty in the old Russian régime that preceded it.

My appointment to the St. Petersburg Embassy was looked upon as temporary from the outset. Thus it was that I had to leave the Russian capital in 1876, after five months' stay. Before my departure the Chancellor, Prince Gortchakov, sent for me. He received me in an overheated room, in a very elegant wadded dressing-gown, complaining of a bad cold which kept him a prisoner

to his house.   Behind his spectacles gleamed eyes better described
as cunning than clever.   Bearing and manner were those of a
grand seigneur.   His expression was that of a materialist, sensual,
almost gross.   In a very choice and affected French, he said he
wished me to convey his greetings to Berlin.   " *On me dit que vous
avez beaucoup réussi dans notre sociéte.   Je vous en félicite.   Vous
raconterez à Berlin l'acceuil hospitalier et charmant que les Allemands
trouvent chez nous.   Cet acceuil est conforme aux rapports qui unissent
si heureusement les deux empires.   Cet accord est la clef de voûte de la
paix du monde et le rocher de l'ordre moral et monarchique en Europe.
Puisse-t-il subsister longtemps!* "   The Prince, then seventy-eight
years old, said before I left: " *Vous pouvez dire au Prince Bismarck
que vous avez vu le lion dans sa cage.*"   As I closed the door he
recalled me: " *Et vous transmettez à votre excellent père l'expression
de mon ancienne et fidèle amitié.*   St. Petersburg was the city of
caustic epigrams and the brilliant *jeu d'esprit*—of course, all in
French, and not in Russian.   I was not the only person who heard
Gortchakov refer to himself as a caged lion.   He said the same thing
to Baron Ernest Meyendorff, a Russian diplomat renowned for
his wit, who replied: " *Oui, mon prince, je dirai à Berlin que j'ai
vu cet animal.*"   Gortchakov might have forgiven the joke, but
not the fact that Meyendorff repeated it elsewhere, and that all
St. Petersburg laughed.   In senile spite Gortchakov left Meyendorff to languish for many years as embassy secretary in Brussels.
Much older than I, he was still attaché in Rome when I was
Ambassador there.   Meyendorff said other things the world found
worth remembering.   He paid assiduous court to the lovely
Madame P., the adopted daughter of a rich banker.   He had
taken her as a foundling into his home.   She was somewhat affected.
Meyendorff said to her: " *Ne soyez pas si affectée!   Il n'y a rien de
naturel en vous que la naissance!* "   Women in love will put up
with anything.   Madame P. answered, with a tender glance:
" *Tout le monde ne peut pas être né Meyendorff.*"   The Meyendorffs
are an old and very good German-Baltic family.

CHAPTER XXVIII

Return to Berlin—My Father on the Foreign Situation—Transfer to Vienna—Ambassador Count Otto Stolberg-Wernigerode—Official Vienna, Baron von Schmerling, Prince Richard Metternich, Count Hübner—The Political Feeling towards Germany—Bismarck and the Austro-German Liberals—Count Gyula Andrássy—Revolts in Salonika—Meeting of the Tsar Alexander II with Emperor Francis Joseph in Reichstadt (5.7.1876)—Turkish Atrocities in Bulgaria.

WHEN I arrived in Berlin at the end of April and gave my father Prince Gortchakov's greetings, he said smiling: "The old fool appears to be as vain as he was a quarter of a century ago. *Habeat sibi!* The thing that matters is that petty frictions and jealousies between him and Bismarck do not lead to concrete political differences between ourselves and our Eastern neighbours which might entail unforeseen consequences."

My father gave me a long exposition of the political situation, and concluded with the following axioms couched in his customary brief and lucid form:

1. Prince Bismarck's ideal is, as before, the Three Emperors' Agreement; an agreement between ourselves, Russia and Austria. He desires this agreement for reasons of foreign as well as internal policy. Call it, if you like, a three-horse team, a troika, such as you have seen in Russia. Austria is the third horse.

2. Bismarck is on the whole no friend of alliances. During his finest period, that is to say, from 1862 to 1871, when it is safe to say he did not make a single diplomatic mistake, he only made one alliance, and that a short-time one, the agreement *ad hoc* with Italy for the war against Austria. Bismarck always wants a free hand. He says himself that states and their leaders can only bind themselves, even by the most solemn agreement, for so long as the effects and repercussions of such an agreement do not conflict with the interests of their own country. Certainly, of all other alliances, Bismarck would prefer one with Russia under terms of a mutual guarantee of the *status quo* of both countries. But I fear that Gortchakov will not consent to this. He will say that if Russia guarantees us the continued possession of Alsace-Lorraine, she will surrender her one trump card, the only one with which

she can take any trick in France, as long as the French still hope to win back our Alsatian provinces with her help, whatever French party or form of government may be in power.

3. Within a week or a fortnight, Emperor Alexander II and Gortchakov are expected in Berlin. Bismarck has invited Andrássy to come to Berlin while they are here in person, and get into personal touch with the Muscovites. The Andrássy memorandum of 30th December is to form the basis on which it is hoped to arrive at a practical agreement between the Porte and the insurgents, and so at last get a settlement of conditions in Herzegovina.

4. We shall not take direct part in the coming Russian-Austrian negotiations. But we declare already that we will lend our moral support to any peaceful solution which may ensure tranquillity between our Russian and our Austrian friends. Understanding between Russia and Austria is and remains the condition for every sensible, that is to say, every peaceful, settlement of the Eastern question. Our task must be to support any such understanding with due regard to European conditions as a whole.

As to my personal future, my father said he had intended to transfer me to the Paris Embassy, but that this wish of his had been crossed by Holstein. " Who is this Holstein? " I asked. " I scarcely know him at all, only met him once at Herbert's, and another time at Princess Bismarck's. We barely exchanged a word." My father replied: " Holstein? Well, my dear Peter (he called me Peter in fun when I was a little boy, particularly when we talked in low German dialect) this isn't so easy to answer. Fritz von Holstein came as attaché to Bismarck in St. Petersburg, and at that time he was very raw and callow. But not long afterwards he began to play the same part to our great man as Father Joseph is said to have played to Richelieu." After a short pause my father added: " Holstein strikes me as being sinister. I said so to Bismarck, and warned him against him. The Prince replied that he must have one being whom he felt he could entirely trust. When I said that he could depend on me absolutely, he smiled and answered: ' Yes, but only in good things. Sometimes I have to do bad actions, otherwise who could exist in this evil world? *A corsaire, corsaire et demi.* Holstein is a *corsaire*, and was simply created for devilments. Moreover, beside his qualifications for shady business (*ipsissima verba* of his Excellency), Holstein really possesses a first-class political head, a very strong political intellect. He prevented the Paris trip which I had in mind for you, my son, because he fears that you, as son of the Secretary of State, might

get to hear more than he would care of his intrigues against Harry
Arnim. But you'll learn things in Vienna, too, and get your horizon
broadened.'"

My father told me on this occasion that Bismarck some time
ago had offered to propose him to His Majesty for the Vienna
Embassy if ever he grew tired of the "grind" in the Foreign
Office. He had declined with thanks. Apart from the fact that
my mother, owing to her delicate health since the death of her only
daughter, no longer took any interest in social life, he himself
desired to support Bismarck in the Foreign Office as long as his
own powers lasted. When he no longer felt fit for this work he
intended to buy an estate in Holstein or Mecklenburg and write
his memoirs there. This was the strain in which my good father
talked—whom God was to summon from this earth before he could
begin to think about setting down his memories. He urged me
to lose no time in paying my respects to my new chief, Count Otto
Stolberg, who would be starting for his Vienna post within a few
days. My father had not failed to notice that Princess Y. had
come to Berlin from her country seat as soon as I returned from
St. Petersburg. But with the goodness and the tact that were
second nature to him, he merely hinted that it was my duty to avoid
anything that might cause talk about a lady whom, it was clear,
I respected very highly.

My reunion with my beautiful friend aroused both tenderness
on her side and very stormy and passionate feelings on mine. She
could not conceal from me that she had suffered much under our
separation, which had lasted for nearly six months. I wanted to
atone for the small infidelities on the Neva, born of my juvenile
immaturity and the attractions of the Slav women. We had not
long together, since my new chief, Count Stolberg, let me know
that he was starting next morning for his appointment, and suggested
that I should travel with him. Count, later Prince, zu Stolberg-
Wernigerode, was the head of a mediatized house, which had had
estates in the Harz from time immemorial. The Stolberg arms
contain a black stag in gold and two red trout in silver. The stag
is the pride of the Harz woods, the trout lives in the Harz brooks.
In mentioning the tour I undertook as a schoolboy in the Harz,
I have quoted the lines with which the poet Friedrich Leopold
Stolberg celebrates the fair country of the Cheruskans which
Mother Nature has adorned with a lavish hand and enriched with
every attribute of male beauty. Otto Stolberg was a worthy son
of the Harz. Everything about him was simple, and inspired
confidence. He knew what he owed to his name and his position.

Pride and vanity were foreign to him. He had never striven to
obtain any post whatsoever, and would have preferred to live
privately in the Harz. But in every one of the many offices he
held he discharged his duty with distinction. He was a patriot
through and through, but without narrowness or fanaticism. He
was barely thirty when he became Governor of the province of
Hanover, not long since annexed by Prussia. He held the post
for six years with firmness and tact, not without kindness, always
as a man of distinction. For four years, from 1872 to 1876, he
was an excellent President of the Prussian House of Lords. When
Bismarck asked him if he would care to take on the Vienna Embassy,
Stolberg, who was then not yet forty, replied that he lacked any
form of diplomatic preparation. Whereupon Bismarck retorted:
" You were a young first lieutenant of the Life Guards when you
became a very good Governor of Hanover. As ex-Governor, and
President of the House of Lords, you will be a first rate Ambassador
in Vienna." Stolberg fulfilled these expectations.

At the reception which, like every other new Ambassador, he
held after his arrival, all official Vienna was present. I shall never
forget the sour face with which Baron Anton von Schmerling
entered the Embassy. He was at the time leader of the Austrian
constitutional party and had been founder and leader of the Pan-
Germans from June to December, 1848, under the regent, Arch-
Duke Johann, in Frankfort. Only once before have I seen such
resentment on the face of a statesman; Gortchakov wore just
such a look the day when the Treaty of Berlin was signed in the
Congress Hall of the Chancellor's palace. But with Gortchakov
it was a case of personal spite, of offended vanity, and, as he
declared, ill-treatment. Schmerlin's bitterness had a higher
motive behind it; the failure of his political ideals and aspirations.

With a jovial smile, the absolute type of old Austrian *insouciance*
and gaiety, there appeared Prince Richard Metternich, son of the
great statesman and the handsome Fräulein Antoinette von
Leykam, a Titian blonde. For twelve years, from 1859 to 1871,
as Austrian Ambassador in Paris, the Prince had opposed most
bitterly the Prussianizing policy of Bismarck. A lady who had
known him well, particularly during the summer of 1866, told me
later of the following little trait which, better than the longest
descriptions, displays the charming frivolity of old Austria. He
was staying with the above-mentioned lady when, on the morning
of 4th July, 1866, the news arrived of a devastating defeat of the
Austrian army, in full retreat and beaten on all fronts. He turned

pale, but soon pulled himself together, swept up his coat-tails and sat down at the open piano to strum out a tune.

> " Happy is he who forgets,
> Things can't be helped by regrets."

His father, Clemens, before he became Foreign Secretary, was Austrian Ambassador in Paris, from 1806 to 1809. In this capacity he paid court to Queen Caroline of Naples, sister of the great Corsican. His son, Richard, was devoted to the Empress Eugénie. When in 1871 Thiers became President of the young French Republic, he demanded that Richard Metternich should be recalled, as he was too intimate with the Bonaparte régime and the Bonapartist party. When Metternich paid his farewell visit to Thiers his long coat-tails caught in the door hinge. "*Voyez comme vous êtes attaché à la France,*" said Thiers, laughing as he freed them. " *Il vous fallait pour me détacher!* " retorted Metternich. The aristocrats who ruled the Hapsburg monarchy during the half century which separates Königgrätz from the Great War had not become very much more serious. The Royal and Imperial Minister of the Royal and Imperial house, Count Leopold Berchtold, who let Austria-Hungary slip into the World War in the summer of 1914, spent the first winter after the collapse of the monarchy in a first-class Swiss hotel, where, under the curious eyes of tourists, and to the astonishment of the worthy Swiss, he zealously danced one-steps and Bostons.

The Lord Chamberlain, Prince Constantine von Hohenlohe-Schillingsfürst, was dignified and polite, but rather reserved in his attitude at this reception of the new German Ambassador. He was the youngest of four brothers, all of whom I knew well. The eldest, Duke Victor of Ratibor, was a Prussian nobleman and President of the Prussian House of Lords; the second, Prince Chlodwig of Hohenlohe-Schillingsfürst, was successively Prime Minister in Bavaria, German Ambassador in Paris, Governor of Alsace-Lorraine and Chancellor of the German Reich. The third was the Cardinal, Prince Gustav.

Baron Alexander von Hübner was also present, one of the last upholders of old Austrian principles and ideas. Born Alexander Hafenbrädl, in a modest bourgeois home in the heart of Vienna in 1811, he was summoned to the Chancellery after his marriage with the daughter of the influential Privy Councillor von Pilat, at the age of barely twenty-two, sent as Consul-General to Leipzig in 1844, where he had to watch over the Saxon Democrats, and attached, in 1848 to Archduke Rainer in Milan, where he was nearly assassinated by the insurgents during the *Cinque Giornate*, the first great Italian revolt against Austria. In 1848 he played a discreet but not unimportant part on the occasion of the abdication of the Emperor Ferdinand and the rise of the Archduke Francis Joseph to imperial power. A few years later he was ennobled with the high-sounding title of von Hübner, and sent to Paris, first as Minister and then as Ambassador. It was to him, at the reception of the diplomatic corps, that on 1st January, 1859, Napoleon III addressed that famous remark, which, like the first thunder clap that augurs a heavy storm, preceded the Franco-Austrian war. That new year's pronouncement, and the sudden death four years previously of the Emperor Nicholas are the two most sensational events which I recall from the days of my early childhood. A panic broke out on all the Stock Exchanges of the world in which, especially in Austria-loving South Germany, many small investors lost everything. A suspicion was felt throughout the world that Austria, who by her ingratitude had lost the friendship of Russia in the Crimean War, would now do the same with France, as the result of her unskilful Italian policy. After the Italian war, Hübner was for two months a rather inadequate police chief in Vienna; from 1865-67 he was Ambassador to the Vatican, where he amazed the most pious members of the Sacro Collegio with his ultra-clericalism. If Hübner had ill-luck in politics, his books, written in French on Sixtus the Fifth (*Sixte-Quint, d'après des correspondances diplomatiques inédites*) and his description of a world tour undertaken at the age of sixty-two (*Promenade autour du monde*) are well-written and informative works. Alexander Hübner, who died in 1892 in his native city, Vienna, aged eighty-one, was to have two compensations before his death: his rise to the rank of Count in 1888, and two years later the dismissal of Bismarck by William II. Like all enemies of the new and powerful German Reich, he must have rejoiced over Bismarck's dismissal. Personally he was a pleasant old man, whose clean-shaven face and measured speech were redolent of the Metternich epoch. He was cordial to me whenever we met, either at the Club or in the Prater, and I owe him much interesting information on Austrian history and many tales of old Austria.

The names of the illustrious members of the Vienna Court who appeared at the German Embassy in 1876 are redolent of the great past of the Hapsburg monarchy. Count Folliot de Crenneville, Lord Chamberlain; Count von Grünne, Master of the Horse; Count de Bellegards, aide-de-camp; Major-General Count Bylandt; all belonged to families which had served the

Hapsburgs since the days when they ruled the Netherlands. Many officers attached to the Emperor's person came from the " Reich," as they used to say in old Vienna: the Taxis and the Bechtolsheim from Bavaria, the Wimpffens and Hornsteins from the Neckar, Friedrich von Beck, President of the Emperor's Military Chancellery and later Chief of Staff, and the smart cavalry officer Leopold von Edelsheim, from Baden, the Gablenzes and the Globigs from Saxony, the Kielmannsegges, Löhneisens and Wersebes from Hanover. There were many north Germans at the time in the Austrian army: Lühe and Bülow, Oertzen and Hammerstein.

The political attitude towards the German Reich was friendly on the whole in bourgeois Viennese circles, and was particularly so in the Austrian aristocracy. " Old Plener " was still a power in 1876 —that Ignaz von Plener who was nearly a hundred years old when he died in 1906. He was Finance Minister in the difficult years from 1860 to 1865, and Minister of Economics in the so-called " Citizens Ministry " of 1867 to 1870. An experienced and careful administrative official. A worthy type of these Royal and Imperial privy councillors whom Magyars and Czechs, Slovaks and Poles, the " slave nations," as Hebbel so angrily calls them in one of his poems, all hated and despised. In Germany and especially in Berlin, the " Austrian Hofrat " was the butt of not-always-tactful jokes. Unjustly, since from the days of the great Maria Theresa and the noble and fiery Joseph II, he governed the many-tongued monarchy honestly and painstakingly. The nations with the " wild heads of the Caryatids " owe to him what little of order, cleanliness and culture they possess. In later life I often ran across Ernst von Plener, " old Plener's " son, who was Austrian Minister of Finance from 1893-95, and for many years leader of the Liberals, and with him and his wife, spent some interesting weeks at a Belgian *plage*. She was the clever daughter of a Hungarian statesman, Eötvös, who was Minister of Public Worship many times, perpetual President of the Hungarian Academy, and author of some creditable novels. Her brother, Rudolph Eötvös, was at first Minister of Public Worship, and later President of the Academy in the palmy days of the Transleithanian Magyars. Ernst Plener had been Austrian Embassy Secretary in London, and written good and still readable books on English factory laws and English building societies. I talked with him a great deal on the subject of Austrian conditions.

He, and most Austrian Liberals, often suffered under Prince Bismarck's unfriendly treatment. The epithet, " Autumn Crocus," applied to their leader, annoyed them deeply. This **Dr.**

Edward Herbst,[1] leader of the German-Bohemians, and Minister of
Justice in the Ministry of 1867-71, afterwards leader of the united
Left in the Reichs Council, had aroused the wrath of the great
Chancellor by the opposition he set up to Andrássy's policy of
occupation, the military occupation of Bosnia and Herzegovina,
and the consequent agreement between Cis- and Transleithania.
It is true that the opposition of Herbst did not only annoy Andrássy,
but also the Austrian army, and the Emperor Francis Joseph.
The old Emperor regarded the annexation of Bosnia and Herzegovina as a feather in his government's cap after so many set-backs,
a consolation for many painful losses in the past, a comfort for the
loss of prestige in Germany and Italy, for the surrender of the
magnificent kingdom of Lombardy-Venice, over which the Austrian
black and yellow banner had floated for half a century.   The
Emperor's dislike of the German-Liberal opposition, headed by
Herbst, which was indeed very often petty and small-minded in
its methods, if not in its objectives, led to the fall of the Liberal
Ministry, and assisted Count Edward Taffe into the saddle, whose
" policy of muddlement," so favourable to Czechs and Poles,
made things worse than ever for the Germans.   It is well known
that the autumn crocus is a poisonous plant, with rather pretty
flowers, which blossom in late autumn, and only bears fruit a year
later.   The sharp eyes of genius had seen correctly in his case.
But Bismarck might have expressed it a little more mildly, if only
on account of the Poles and Czechs, who rejoiced over this thrust
at their chief adversary and with him his countrymen.   Bismarck's
dislike of " liberal chamber heroes " and " democratic Philistine-
carping " had made him go too far in this case also.   " What do
you expect? " said my father, when I modestly expressed my
misgivings to him.   " Bismarck's pet aversion against bourgeois
tradesmen in press and parliaments amounts almost to a disease.
Nothing can be done about it.   Our great man always reminds me
of Coriolanus.   Do you remember *Coriolanus?*   We read it together.
Wasn't it in Neu-Strelitz when you were in the second form, or
was it in Frankfort?   Do you remember how Caius Marcius
Coriolanus, whom Shakespeare calls a noble Roman, apostrophizes
the tribunes of the plebs?

' Behold these are the tribunes of thy people,
    The tongues of the common mouth; I do despise them,
    For they do prank them in authority,
    Against all noble sufferance.'

----

[1] Translator's note: *Herbst* = Autumn.

And again:

' What should the people do with these bald tribunes ? '

And how Coriolanus damns the ' double rule ' from A to Z?

> ' Where one part does disdain with cause the other
> Insult without all reason; where gentry, title, wisdom,
> Cannot conclude, but by the yea and no
> Of general ignorance. . . . ' "

In the same strain as my father, clever Bill Bismarck expressed his opinion to me. In Psalm lxii, verse 10, the verse runs: " Surely men of low degree are vanity, and men of high degree are a lie." Certainly men of high degree fail now and then. Dr. Edward Herbst, so harshly treated by Bismarck, witnessed his fall, like Hübner and Anton Schmerling. Herbst and Hübner died in 1892, Schmerling in 1893.

A day after the official reception in the German Embassy I met Count Gyula Andrássy at a little dinner there. He had been the first premier of independent Hungary after Franz Deák had reconciled the Magyars with the house of Hapsburg and made peace between Hungary and Austria. In 1871 he succeeded von Beust as Foreign Secretary of the Dual Monarchy. It was necessary for the balance of power within the Dual Monarchy, as well as in the interests of the general situation in Europe that a Magyar should be appointed Foreign Secretary at the time. So, during the first half of the nineteenth century it had been natural enough in the interests both of Austria and Europe that a great gentleman from the Rhine in " the Reich," Clemens Metternich, should lead, not only Austria, but all Europe also. And it was just as natural that after the revolution of 1848, a fiery Bohemian chevalier, Prince Felix Schwarzenberg, had defended the old monarchy against Italians, Magyars and Prussians. Andrássy had enough sound common-sense, courage and firmness for an independent judgment of what was the main issue in politics. He lacked neither flair nor intuition. He possessed the " Chevalier-Perspective " which Bismarck demanded from the leader of a great state. But he lacked thoroughness and at times stability as well. He despised details too much, the industry that never slacks, which constructs slowly and never pulls down. He was uncultured, and when a very cultured lady reproached him with this fact, he protested: " I am not so ignorant as you imagine. I know, for instance, perfectly well that *Fiesco* is by Goethe, and *Tasso* by Schiller." Count Andrássy had taken part in the revolt of the Hungarians in

1848, under Louis Kossuth. After the insurgents had been suppressed he was condemned to be hanged, and when he succeeded in escaping, his name was inscribed on the gallows in Arad, from which so many Hungarian rebels dangled. I myself heard him say very wittily that the Emperor Francis Joseph had once wanted to hang him on a hempen rope, but had now hung the golden fleece round his neck instead, and he pointed to the Order he was wearing. He would often, perhaps too often, relate how when he fled across the Turkish frontier after the capitulation of Vilagos, an Austrian gendarme barred his way. " I drew my pistol and shot him dead. And now I'm the Royal and Imperial Foreign Secretary." Andrássy was reported to be very vain. But his conceit was so naïve that it never offended. I remember that once at a party the wife of a diplomat expressed her satisfaction over the fact that she had made the acquaintance of the two great men of the century, Otto Bismarck and Richard Wagner. He inquired with a trace of pique: " And I? Don't you think me a great man? "

The fact that at nearly sixty he dyed his hair and beard coal black was all part of this same innocent vanity. Andrássy, on his appointment, had removed all the pronounced enemies of Prussia from the Ministry, who all came from the " Reich," and were mostly converts to Catholicism—Meysenbug and Gagern, Onno Klopp, Biegeleben and Blome. The Pole, Klaczko, had to go, too, whom Beust had furthered. He revenged himself in the corrosive pamphlet, *Les deux Chanceliers*, in which he fanned the flame of Gortchakov's jealousy against Bismarck and defamed Bismarck. The only pillar, and that not a very stalwart one, of the vanished glories of the Beust era, was Baron von Hofmann. He was so full-blooded a Viennese that no Austrian could ever be annoyed with him. As a true son of Vienna he loved ladies, from the bottom of his heart. During my time at the Embassy in Vienna he was prostrate at the feet of a pretty actress, Fräulein J. In the green room of the Burg Theatre, it was said that when, at last, she yielded to his importunities, she had murmured with downcast eyes: " Oh, how you must despise me! " Whereupon the old Baron: " Not at all, we despise each other! "

On 6th May, 1876, the fanatical Turkish mob in Salonika murdered the French and German consuls. This double murder prevented discord between the Powers. From 11th to 13th May, the Emperor Alexander II and Gortchakov were in Berlin, where at the same time Count Andrássy arrived from Vienna. On the day of their departure a long memorandum was published, dealing with the " disquieting " news which kept coming from Turkey, and in which it was stated openly that peace and order could not be fully restored in the Balkan Peninsula until all the unrest was stifled at its source with the calming of Bosnia and Herzegovina. The same day a conference had been held at Prince Bismarck's in which, besides Gortchakov and Andrássy, my father and Baron Jomini (Gortchakov's right hand) took part, and to which the Ambassadors of France, England and Italy were invited. Jomini read out the memorandum over which the three Empires had agreed. Gortchakov expressed the hope that the three other Powers would express their consent as soon as possible, and declared that the goal of the Three-Empire policy was the "improved *status quo*." Bismarck stressed with warmth the importance of agreement and co-operation between France, England and Italy, who signed the memorandum next day.

On 18th May Andrássy made a long speech in the Budget Committee of the Reichs Council in which he stated with considerable optimism that the peace of Europe had actually been ensured by means of the " Berlin Memorandum," and the participation of Montenegro and Servia in the insurrection prevented. He considered it his duty to utter a warning against the " widely prevalent pessimism." Even in those days that pessimism existed which later so annoyed Kaiser William II that he declared that he " would brook no croakers," and suggested they should shake the dust of Germany off from their feet and get out of his country. Twice in this speech Andrássy used the expression " from case to case (*Fall*)." He intended to come to terms with the other Powers " from case to case," as the need arose for it. A witty Viennese actress, Fräulein G., translated this into French by " *Une politique de chute en chute*." She added that she hoped Andrássy would not fall as often as she had done.

At the end of May we sent a German armoured squadron to Salonika. This, if I remember rightly, was the first occasion on which German battleships played any part in world politics. In June, Sultan Abd-ul-Aziz was dethroned. He killed himself soon afterwards with a long pair of scissors which somebody had kindly left for him. His successor, Abd-ul-Murad-Khan was such a cretin that he had to be supplanted by his brother, Abd-ul-Hamid, after a few weeks. Abd-ul-Hamid was the kind of ruler who sat on the throne of Byzantium during the last period of its history, half-cunning despot, half-foolish child, a mixture of slyness and stupidity, cowardly and cruel. For thirty-two years he went in terror of plots, and was constantly threatened by them.

On 8th July, 1876, a meeting took place in Castle Reichstadt between Tsar Alexander, who had brought Prince Gortchakov along with him, and the Emperor Francis Joseph of Austria, accompanied by Count Andrássy. Its results were destined to be of momentous and far-reaching consequence to the history of the world, while to me they would give enough serious work all through my future official life. At first it was only officially announced in regard to the meeting, that Russia and Austria had agreed on the principle of non-interference in the present Turkish troubles, but reserved the privilege, when the fortunes of war should have brought about a decision, of bringing about a confidential understanding with all Christian powers. From Vienna it was proclaimed that the meeting at Reichstadt had " averted every danger " of the war spreading beyond its present frontiers to Europe. On the evening of the meeting Andrássy telegraphed to the then Austrian Ambassador in London, his predecessor, Beust: " Inform the British confidentially as result of Reichstadt meeting that we have agreed to disregard all later suggestions and to retain our present policy of non-intervention. Not till conditions demand it, and in the case of a concrete event, shall further confidential understanding of all Christian Powers be attempted." Beust replied next day that Lord Derby received this intimation with lively satisfaction, and said that he could now declare that no general outbreak of war was to be feared, whose possibility had so disquieted England. The day after his return from Reichstadt Andrássy went to the German Ambassador, Stolberg, and informed him confidentially that Austria had promised to observe a benevolent neutrality in the case of a Russo-Turkish war. In exchange Russia had declared herself in agreement with Austro-Hungarian occupation of Bosnia and Herzegovina in the event of a war in the Near East.

When I first arrived in Vienna I bought, with my father's kind permission, a roan mare, which I rode every morning in the Prater. There very often I met Count Andrássy. He liked my mare, who was an easy goer. He would often ask me to ride with him and would talk to me the whole time. On the morning after his return from Reichstadt, we met again on horseback. With visible pride he said to me: " Stolberg will have told you that I have settled matters with Russia. And I didn't repeat the blunder which Buol made during the Crimean War, when he deeply offended the Russians without obtaining any real advantage for Austria. The acquisition of Bosnia and the Herzegovina is politically, economically and strategically important and pleasing. Bosnia, in particular, is a splendid country capable of high development, with a very fine capital, Sarajevo. We are following in the great tradition of that noble knight, the Prince Eugene." The Royal and Imperial Minister little guessed that a generation later the heir to the Austrian Crown would meet a premature and terrible death in this same " beautifully situated " Sarajevo. Nor did he foresee that this murder would lead on to a four years' war, a world war, the most terrible since the Thirty Years' War that has afflicted humanity, nor that in this war the old Hapsburg Empire, and with it the Magyar supremacy and the Reich of Stefan's Crown, Hungary, would be swept away.

The Turks resemble certain wild animals in one respect. In spite of a kind of good nature they can fly into insensate rage after a long period of passivity. Just as later in the twentieth century they lost many sympathies through their bestial atrocities towards the Armenians, so in June, 1876, they staged a massacre in Bulgaria which caused great excitement in Europe. England, in particular, was roused to intensely indignant protest. The sentiments of the English people are certainly humane. Scarcely any other is capable of such widespread indignation, such deeply-felt horror. But this horror has a way of only letting itself be inflamed in cases where there is no danger to specifically English interests. Gladstone became the mouthpiece of English wrath at the Bulgarian atrocities. He spoke and wrote with the wonderful fluency and a moral sincerity all his own, against the accursed Turkish " atrocities." Indignation meetings took place everywhere. The anti-Turkish agitation which spread throughout England in spite of its somewhat pro-Turkish Tory Government, gave Servia and Montenegro fresh courage. Both declared a war on Turkey, which ended well for the Montenegrins, but not so well for the Serbs, in spite of the strong support of Russian volunteers.

CHAPTER XXIX

Social Life in Vienna—Folk Garden and Prater. Cures in Montreux and San Remo—Transfer to Athens as chargé d'affaires—Christmas in Corfu—Paxos—Taking over the Business of Office in Athens.

AT our Embassy in Vienna I met for the second time Countess Marie Dönhoff, whose lovely eyes I had admired a year ago exactly, in Florence. At the time she did not vouchsafe me a word. This time we saw one another more often. Her husband was First Secretary at the Embassy to which I had been appointed Second Secretary. I perceived with surprise that although she was my own age, that is to say in the first flush of youth, she was mentally far in advance of her years. An Italian, she possessed extraordinary understanding of German literature and the German spirit. She knew Goethe better than most German women, and more than many German men. She had penetrated deeply into my pet philosopher, Schopenhauer. I heard her musical gifts praised on all sides. I was unable to form a personal opinion on this score since, unhappily, I am totally unmusical. But I felt and understood that the whole soul of this rare woman was music. The courage with which she defended the Bayreuth cause, much attacked at the time in Vienna, greatly impressed me.

In her salon, furnished without too great a luxury, but with the finest artistic taste, I met interesting people. I made the acquaintance of the poet Adolf Wilbrandt here, who was to become my lifelong friend. Here, too, I first met Lenbach, the great painter and good man. Here I saw the already more than seventy-year-old Gottfried Semper, the distinguished architect to whom Vienna owes her new museum buildings. When Gottfried Semper, Richard Wagner and Gyula Andrássy were once invited here together, they touched glasses in a toast with a significant smile. They had all been condemned to death in 1849, Wagner and Semper in Dresden, Andrássy in Arad. Here I met Hans Makart, the painter, small in stature but great in gifts and originality. Like Mozart, he haled from Salzburg, but was less amiable than Mozart is said to have been. When he sat once at supper for an hour without saying word next to the witty actress Fräulein Gallmeyer, she said to him at last: "Makart, let's talk of something else." I was delighted with the sparkling verse of old Villers, who had not got any further in the diplomatic service than the secretaryship of the Saxon Embassy in Vienna, but who possessed more wit than twenty average diplomats put together.

Among the friends of Countess Marie Dönhoff, Countess Katinka Andrássy aroused attention by her beauty, and interest by her unprejudiced and independent intellect. She loved her Gyula very deeply. The two had met twenty years earlier in Paris, Katinka as a young Countess Kendeffy from the Siebenbürgen who frequented the Austrian Embassy a great deal, Gyula as an exiled rebel from Siebenbürgen who was spied on by the same Embassy which was to receive instructions from him later. Another interesting lady in Countess Dönhoff's salon was Countess Marie Festetics, the intimate friend of Count and Countess Andrássy and for many years the *dame de confiance* of the Empress Elizabeth of Austria. The Austrian historian, Heinrich Friedjung, told me once later that Countess Marie Festetics knew more important and interesting things about Austrian history in the second half of the nineteenth century than the whole Imperial Viennese Academy of Sciences. Frequent guests of Countess Dönhoff were the four sisters Liechtenstein, as they were called, the widowed Princess Anna Trautmannsdorff, Princess Franziska Arenberg, Princess Marie Kinsky and Princess Elise Salm. The last, in particular, was a faithful friend to my wife and later to me on my appointment to the Roman Embassy, shortly before her premature death. She was one of those Viennese great ladies who combine originality with grace, whose distinction is natural and inborn, so that their tact is never failing and spontaneous, and who, not only in words, but in reality, possessed that much-praised " golden Viennese heart."

I was permitted to accompany Countess Marie Dönhoff from time to time in the municipal park or in the Volksgarten. This People's Garden had been laid out by Emperor Franz (" God preserve Franz the Emperor "[1]) after the German Wars of Liberation for his dear Viennese. They received this proof of royally patriarchal benevolence in the year of the Karlsbad decrees, the introduction of the censorship for Press and books, the dissolution of the patriotic leagues and the prohibition of gymnastic exercises for strengthening body and mind. In spite of this, old Austria seemed filled with the belief that Franz was a great monarch. On his monument in the Hofburg, not far from the Volksgarten,

---

[1] Imperial Austrian National Anthem: " *Gott erhalte Franz den Kaiser.*"

Religion and Peace, Justice and Bravery accompany the ruler who is riding towards his subjects, Art and Science, Commerce and Trade, Agriculture and Stock-breeding, Mining and Smelting kneel in high relief at his feet. As an emblem the words with which the last will and testament of the "good" Emperor's began: "*Populis meis amorem meum*" ornament the front of this grandiose monument which a Milanese, Signor Marchese, constructed—a son of that very city which first raised the flag of insurrection against old Austria. Emperor Franz, for whose preservation the popular Austrian national anthem pleaded so movingly, was certainly convinced that in spite of a flat refusal of all constitutional wishes and liberal ideas, he was really beloved.

In the municipal park Countess Marie Dönhoff was delighted with the smooth lawns, the swans on the lake and above all with the flower beds on both shores of the pleasant Wien, which flows out through the city into the Danube. She always stopped in front of the statue of Franz Schubert, whose music she loved very much. I was pleased with her devotion to the German master, Schubert, with her love of trees and flowers, and her never banal and still less affected, yet always interesting conversation. I remember one expedition made by the ladies and gentlemen of the German Embassy with some Austrian friends of both sexes on the Danube, one fine day in July, to that charming spot, Nussdorf. Countess Marie sat in the bows of the ship. The sun illuminated her sweet, still childish, but very serious face. She wore a Leghorn hat trimmed with cherries. I stood some way from her and could not take my eyes off her. And so in my last hour on earth I shall always see this wonderful woman, the only woman I have ever really loved.

I ask myself to-day how it was that so much charm did not attract me more strongly at the time. I was more in the toils of the Princess Y. than I imagined. She wrote to me daily, passionately, yearningly, always melancholy, sometimes despairing. I visited her nearly every week from Vienna at her country estate. Once when I was there in the autumn I received a telegram from my father in Berlin in which he expressed a wish to speak to me. When I got to Berlin he found me pale and hoarse. The family doctor he consulted diagnosed a catarrh of the apex of the lung, which was not very serious, but needed care and nursing. Next day another examination took place, which ended in the doctor's declaring my further stay in dusty and draughty Vienna a danger to my health, and urging several weeks on the Lake of Geneva, or, still better, the Riviera.

More painful to me than the result of this consultation was the fact that, on this occasion, my father spoke plainly for the first time, without any beating about the bush, of my all too frequent visits to Schloss Y. I had not the right, he told me calmly, but very seriously, though without one word that could have offended the beautiful Princess Y., to compromise, or even risk the woman to whom I was devoted. " There can, of course, be no question of marriage. You are much younger than Princess Y. You only became Embassy-Secretary a year ago. You have no position, and not even any certain prospect of one for the next fourteen to fifteen years ahead. You have no personal fortune. Apart from your love you have nothing to offer a lady who is accustomed to wealth and luxury and the best of everything, who possesses her castle in the country and her town house, pearls and diamonds and all that heart can wish. I do not speak of your duty as a Christian. But as a man of honour it is your duty to be frank with a woman whom you would uproot from conditions in exchange for which you can offer nothing adequate. To be true—above all else true to oneself—everything in life depends on that." My father asked me to give him my word of honour that if I went to the Lake of Geneva or the Riviera, I would not permit Princess Y. to visit me there. Still less was I to be allowed to visit her. " You must part. It is not only I, your father, who ask this of you, common-sense, honour and duty, all demand it."

The letter I wrote that night to the Princess was a difficult one to compose. I told her with a certain amount of exaggeration, but quite sincerely, that seldom or never had a being been so torn between his honour and love as I. I thought with the eighteenth-century French Marquis: " *Ma vie à madame.*" But like him, I was forced to add: " *Mon honneur à moi.*" If I let matters come to a divorce between her and her husband I should, I wrote, not only be acting foolishly, but dishonourably, since I could offer her no assured future. Had I been in a position to do so I would not have hesitated one second to have begged her to unite her life to mine. But to ruin her without any such alternative—no, I could never do that, either from motives of honour or love. In reply I received a telegram in which the Princess implored me to talk things over with her in person. Our talk lasted till four o'clock in the morning. It was very painful for both of us. The Princess was less annoyed than I had expected but she sobbed and wept unceasingly. *When Women Weep* is the title of a well-known and very charming comedy. In this case, however, it was a tragedy. I promised my friend to write her every day. But here, too, though

the spirit was willing, the flesh was weak. Our correspondence
tailed off gradually.

I will anticipate a little and mention how, when I was summoned
to the Congress in Berlin in 1878, Princess Y. wrote and invited
me to visit her in the country. I did not answer the letter, nor ever
saw my lovely friend again till twenty-five years later. As is often
the case with women of the clinging sort, and unhappily married,
she had sought consolation in a new love and accepted the ardent
devotion of a very fine young man, who possessed some excellent
characteristics, both good and brilliant, but lacked the one which
is perhaps the most important for this life, the French call it *esprit
de conduite*, and the ancient Greeks called it μῆτις. Accustomed to getting his own way always and everywhere, he had
urged her to leave her husband, in the firm intention of marrying
her immediately afterwards. But after the divorce, in the first
careless ardour of their new passion, they took a long journey
together which set people gossiping. Now that things had gone so
far there was nothing left for her salvation but a speedy marriage.
For this step, which his parents opposed, her new lover had not the
strength of mind. And so once again the profound dictum
of Honoré de Balzac was proved true, that once a woman leaves
the railway track of social convention she breaks her neck.

I had become Imperial Chancellor when I saw Princess Y.
again. I was spending a short vacation in the Italian town where
she had lived since her divorce. Her sister, whom I met by chance
on a walk, asked me if I would not call just once on the Princess.
When I entered her flat I felt like Faust when he visits Gretchen
in her cell. She was not living in a cell. But when I looked at the
two little furnished rooms, "*camere mobiliate*," in which she had
been dreaming her life away for the past twenty years, I shuddered.
Faded curtains, a threadbare carpet, dingy wallpapers, as sole
ornament on the wall a mediocre picture of her father, the only
article from her luxurious home that she had been permitted to
take away after her divorce. I had heard already from several
quarters that she had had a hard struggle financially, since her
advisers had carelessly omitted to see that any provision was made
for her on her divorce; her former husband refused to pay one,
and her own relatives showed no desire to help her. So-called
"society" in the town had turned its back on the poor woman
with all the harshness and hypocrisy everywhere shown by "decent
people." Her German relatives did not want her to live with them
after the scandal her story had caused. I did not find her much
changed physically. She still had the same *svelte* figure, slender

white hands, and tiny feet. She still had the same syren's eyes, whose iris shimmered from blue to black and had turned so many heads. But instead of the former steely pride her features expressed, to-day, a helplessness, a hopelessness, a mute desperation which touched me deeply. She asked me in that familiar voice which seemed to come from another world: "Do you remember that it is twenty-five years since we saw one another last? That is a long, long time—a quarter of a century. Where are you to-day? And where am I? How is it possible that we never met again? Had you forgotten that bluish-green Wolfgang's Lake? And Ischl? And the murmuring of the Traun? We might have met again as good friends." There are situations in which, as Nietzsche recommends, it is best to be silent together. But at last I could bear our mutual silence no longer. "Every evening," I said, "two expresses leave the same station at the same time in Berlin. For half an hour, as far as Zehlendorf, they run side by side. Then one branches off to the west and one to the east. The traveller in the first train is in Cologne in the morning, the other in Breslau. Next evening one is in Paris and one in Warsaw. The day after the western traveller is in Biarritz, and the other in Moscow. On the third day one is in Madrid and the other in the Urals. And the Urals and Manzanares are a very long distance away from one another." It sounded very commonplace. In any case it had no effect. She was still silent. I began again: "Wilhelm von Humboldt put it very well when he said that what happened to one mattered less than the manner in which one bore it." This quotation had still less effect. Ah, philosophy never yet dried one tear. Her sister, who had accompanied me, gave a sign that it was time for me to go. I kissed both the Princess' hands and turned to the door. At the moment I went out she gave me a long deep glance of tenderness. She had been brought up a Catholic, but from her youth had been indifferent to religion. In spite of that she made the sign of the Cross three times in my direction. I never saw her again. She lived for twelve years longer. Not long before the beginning of the Great War death released her, after a life which for more than thirty years had resembled death.

I will return to the living, of whom Schiller said that they are always right, and will pass to Montreux, where the doctors and my good father had sent me in the autumn of 1876. Once there I determined to draw up a plan of studies and to stick to it as faithfully as to the inhalations and throat paintings of the treatment. I read two books which made a permanent impression on me: *The History of Civilization*, by Buckle, a work which swept several wrong ideas from my brain and accustomed me to sober reflection and inductive methods of thinking. I read at the same time Taine's *Philosophie de l'Art*, his *Histoire de la Littérature Anglaise*, and the first volume of *Origines de la France contemporaine*, that masterly exposition of the ancient régime. Henry Thomas Buckle and Hippolyte Taine are two authors whom one should always read again from time to time so as not to grow mentally rusty. Above all, pencil in hand, annotating every page and pondering every sentence, I read Ludwig Hahn's monumental work on the political life and activity of Prince Bismarck. I lived quite close to the lake in a little room from the windows of which I could see my old friend, the Dent du Midi. Happy as I was on my dear Lake of Geneva, I moved down to San Remo as soon as it grew colder. I stuck to my plan of reading and learning, but added Renan to my list of authors. There I read his *Essais de Critique et de Morale*, including the fine essays on Baron Silvestre de Sacy, the distinguished Orientalist who, after the fall of the first Empire, was one of the leaders of the rising Liberals, on Victor Cousin, the founder of the school of eclecticism, on Augustin Thierry, one of the greatest French historians, great, not only on account of his scientific attainments, but as a stylist for his clarity and good taste. One of the best things Renan ever wrote is his essay on Lamennais, and the political swing over about the middle of the nineteenth century of the Roman Curia, which has always had a flair for what is to come, from its former aristocratic monarchistic standpoint, to the understanding of democratic aims and ideas, and tolerance, where these appeared to be useful, even of republican institutions.

Renan has often stimulated me. I did not let myself be robbed of my belief in Jesus Christ and His Word by his criticism of the Bible, but I regard him as one of those French prose writers whom one should recommend, especially to Germans. Here they can learn that thoroughness does not mean heaviness, and seriousness need not imply pedantry. They can learn irony, that polite, penetrating irony to which we Germans are so sensitive, perhaps because we do not know how to wield it. One need only compare the finely edged polemics of a Renan with the coarse insolence and gross expression which German men of letters delight to hurl at each other, proud of their honest sincerity and their rigid scientific method. Characteristic of the value which the French set on purity of style was the fact that during the Great War they did not make any Member of Parliament or Professor head of their propaganda department, but Marcel Prévost, one of the most brilliant writers of France. He is the author of *Lettres de Femmes*, of

Nouvelles Lettres de Femmes, Demi-Vierges, and other delightful novels which many a German critic relegates to the realm of pornographic literature. But unfortunately French propaganda during the war proved more efficacious and far-reaching than the many learned works approved in academic seminaries, pamphlets and newspaper articles by Hans Delbrück and Werner Sombart, Haller and Lasson, Meinecke and Troeltsch, Breysig and the brothers Weber, etc., to whom readers abroad paid small attention, or even ignored.

Next to Taine, Buckle and Renan, I read by preference the *Maximes* of La Rochefoucauld, the *Pensées diverses* of Montesquieu and the *Oeuvres choisies* of Vauvenargues. I had them bound together and wrote on the front page as warning and admonition two maxims of Vauvenargues: " *Les gens vains ne peuvent être habiles car ils n'ont pas la force de se taire,*" and " *L'activité porte les hommes à la gloire, les petites talents, la paresse, le goût des plaisirs, la vanité, les fixent aux petites choses.*"

On my walks around San Remo I carried this compendium in my pocket. When I had climbed to the White Madonna della Costa or to the Madonna della Guardia on the Capo Verde whence, with an effort, in clear weather one may spy out the island of Corsica, a little dot on the far horizon, I took out my book and received with redoubled pleasure in these surroundings the wise teaching of men as experienced as Montesquieu, Vauvenargues and La Rochefoucauld. I sauntered during these months on the Corso of San Remo. I little suspected that twelve years later this road would be the Via Dolorosa of our dear Emperor Frederick, who was to suffer dreadful physical pain, and, still worse, appalling mental tortures, here. And with him was to suffer Germany, deprived far too soon of the noble and intelligent Prince.

I mixed very little with the invalids in the San Remo Kursaal, just as in former times I had rarely made friends when travelling. The only exception I made in San Remo was for a twelve or thirteen-year-old crippled and sickly girl who had only her delicate and not wealthy parents to take an interest in her. I taught the child draughts, and played with her of an evening in the reading room. I told her fairy tales, too, fantastic Oriental stories and our own dear German Grimm alternately. When I entered the reading room the child looked up with big expectant eyes, and when I had to say good-night, she made a little curtsey and seemed very disconsolate.

I came back from the Madonna de la Guardia one day in December to my hotel and found a letter from my father informing me that I was transferred to Athens. This letter added that Herr von Radowitz, the Imperial Ambassador at Athens, had been summoned to the Foreign Office as assistant; the Embassy Secretary, Herr von Hirschfeld, had to be transferred to Constantinople, where a reinforcement of staff was necessary owing to our having accepted the task of looking after Russian interests. I was to go to Athens immediately to take over the leadership of the Ministry. Wise and kind as ever, my father added that it would be useful to my diplomatic education to take an independent post while still young. The future attitude of the hitherto neutral Greek Kingdom and the Hellenic elements in the Turkish dominion would not be without significance for the result of the Russo-Turkish war. I should find an opportunity for writing interesting dispatches. I must keep my eyes open and my nerves under control. *Toujours en vedette*, but without *excès de zèle*, so that he could be " again " satisfied with me. My father, who had always had interests outside politics, stressed his hope and expectation in this letter that Athens might assist my mental development. He reminded the young man of the words of Goethe he had quoted to the boy and recommended me to test myself by the diamond shield of the Greeks at the foot of the Acropolis, to discover what I still lacked, not only culturally, but in every way.

At the end of December, 1876, I left San Remo, the Odyssey in my pocket, with a view to the approaching sea journey which was to lead me towards Homeric shores. The parents of my little friend to whom I had taught draughts and told fairy tales had asked me not to let the child know of my approaching departure, since that would make her so unhappy. They would tell her after I had gone that the great Bismarck had ordered me to leave immediately for the beautiful city of Athens to see that the restless and troublesome Greeks behaved themselves. I rather incline to the belief that the affection of this poor, sick, crippled girl was deeper and purer than that of those society ladies, whose ever-repeated sighs and recriminations may always be soothed by applying the same quite local remedy.

The day before Christmas I left the loveliest spot of the Ligurian coast. I travelled via Porto Maurizio, Alassio and Savona to Genoa, the city in which two years before I had first encountered the magnificence of Italian architecture and the magic of Italian nature. Genoa *la Superba*, the city where Christopher Columbus and Giuseppe Mazzini first saw the light, where Camille Cavour was a young artillery officer in barracks, where even Christian Friedrich Nicolai, that perfect representative of the smugness of the Berlin small *bourgeoisie*, was forced to own that Genoa certainly was more beautiful than even the boldest imagination could have anticipated. From there I proceeded via Bologna and Ancona towards Brindisi along the coast of the Adriatic, still unknown to me; that Adria celebrated in the songs of poets throughout so many centuries, which in our own days Gabriele d'Annunzio, in despite of Austria, called " *amare Adriatico*," and where to-day, after the collapse of the Hapsburg monarchy, Jugo-Slavs and Italians eye one another so suspiciously.

A rolling and reeking Greek ship brought me in the night from Brindisi to Corfu. But evil Greek odours and with them sea-sickness, vanished when Corfu dawned on the horizon in the morning. It lay dull as a shield in the darkly-heaving flood, just as in the days of the Odyssey. I admired once more the plastic unattainable heights of Homeric description of nature. Proud and steep, over mountains and sea loomed the island. On the landing stage at Corfu Consul Fels was waiting, in whose house we spent a pleasant German Christmas. No section of the German people anywhere welcomed the reconstruction of the German Reich, a strong German Reich, more fervently than did Germans living abroad. The petty criticism and priggish doctrinaire foolishness with which certain Germans at home marred the joy of others in this new and splendid Reich created by Bismarck was scarcely understood by these Germans who only saw Bismarck's creation in far perspective in the stark majesty of its outline. Next to the Consul there stood a Greek captain. His name was Kokinos. The mistrust this name aroused in me by its fatal similarity to *coquin* soon showed itself to be without foundation. Kokinos was a tireless and willing guide for my three days on Corfu. The island did not greet the beholder's gaze with the same dewy freshness as it had in the days of Nausicaa. But no melancholy Empress Elizabeth had as yet built the Achilleion and raised a memorial to her unhappy son and to Heinrich Heine, her favourite poet, in this castle. No Emperor William II had as yet descended upon the isle of the Phæaceans with his unrest, his pretentious suite and his not-always-happy architectural ideas. The worthy Kokinos led me towards the Cape of Canone, through such luxuriant olive groves as I had never seen before, over green meadows where asphodel bloomed, scenting the air. He showed me the spot where Her Royal Highness Princess Nausicaa had rested graciously to await the King of Ithaca who, clothed in only a leafy bough, which he held closely before him, was permitted to approach her stark naked and deliver a well-sounding speech, received most graciously.

Those were happy days. Captain Kokinos showed me, with much the same pious belief as Italians display their relics, and the Wartburg custodian the ink spot made by Martin Luther, the Phæacean ship turned to stone by Poseidon before the eyes of the terrified Phæaceans as punishment for their rescue of Odysseus, hated of the sea god. This ship has become in the course of centuries a delightful little island, covered with splendid cypresses and called Pontikonisi, which means the isle of mice.

After a few days' stay Consul Fels and Kokinos saw me on board the boat from Corfu, a Trieste-Lloyd steamer, and the journey proceeded. Paxos came into view. I thought of the legend of Pan's death. It was in the days of Tiberius when a Greek merchant-boat on the way to Italy was becalmed near this island. It was evening. The passengers talked and laughed and drank. Suddenly there came a voice from Paxos calling the steersman, an Egyptian named Thamos. General surprise. The worthy Thamos was quite flummoxed. He answered the third call hesitatingly. Whereupon a hoarse voice called from the land: " As you pass Palodos report that great Pan is dead." Everybody trembled. They wrangled as to whether or not to obey. Thamos, a prudent, God-fearing man, decided that if the wind were favourable he would pass by Palodos. But if he were again becalmed he would regard this as a sign from the gods and obey the mysterious voice. When the ship neared Palodos the wind dropped again. All sails hung limp. Whereupon Thamos called from the stern-post, loud as he could, " Great Pan is dead! " There came a mighty outcry, an astonished wailing and weeping, as though from a whole crowd of people. The Emperor Tiberius, an evil tyrant according to Tacitus (though Professor Adolf Starr has suggested that he was an excellent ruler) heard of this incident. He grew uneasy, and summoned a commission of philosophers which, however, like most commissions, dissolved without having accomplished anything. Already to the Emperor Augustus, his step-father, the approaching end of the world had been prophesied. When old Augustus, with natural curiosity, asked the Sybil of the Capitol, who was known to him, who would be his successor, she replied: " The divine son of the virgin will come from Heaven to overturn the altars of idols and establish his Kingdom in the world." On the spot where Augustus heard these words he erected an altar with the inscription: " *Haec ara filii dei est.*" This, according to the legend, is the origin of one of the oldest and most remarkable churches in Rome, the church of *Santa Maria in Aracœli*, where at a side altar is displayed the " *santo bambino*," in whose honour Italian children, with the oratorical gifts of this people, declaim florid speeches at Christmas time. The idea that the birth of Christ was already mysteriously announced during the reign of the Emperor Augustus was firmly fixed in the minds of mediæval men. Scholastic philosophy saw in the fourth Eclogue of Virgil an indication of Christ's birth.

> " Ultima Cumæi venit jam carmicia ætas ;
> Magnus ab integro sæculorum nascitur ordo.
> Iam redit et Virgo ; redeunt Saturnia regna ;
> Jam nova progenies cælo demittur alto."

In reality this Eclogue is a charming pastoral song which Virgil, like his friend and colleague, Horace, a flatterer of the great ones of this earth, laid at the feet of his exalted patron, the Consul Pollio, when an heir was born to him. How surprised the worthy Consul would have been had he been aware of the significance which future ages would attach to this poem in honour of his child sleeping in its cradle, and most probably recompensed with a few gracious words and gold pieces. The most vivid imagination is unable to picture the result of any present event significant or trivial in its bearing on the future.

While I was exchanging reminiscences and observations such as these with a few German philologists and archælogists who were, like myself, proceeding to Athens, we had touched Zante, flower of the Levant, rounded the Peloponnesus, and reached the Piræus. I beheld the Pentelikon, the Hymettos, the Lykabettos, the Acropolis and the Parthenon. Now as a living reality I saw what had occupied my mind so often from my earliest childhood, and graven itself on my imagination through drawings and copperplates. But I was too conscientious a German official to lose myself entirely even in these enchanting impressions. My first steps were directed towards the Imperial Embassy, there to take over documents, cashbox and official archives, to inform the Foreign Office by wire of this fact, and so proceed to study the situation on the basis of my predecessor's report of it. I gained a fairly comprehensive picture from these, as well as from the material sent me in Foreign Office dispatches and cuttings, taken from the European Press.

CHAPTER XXX

The Near Eastern Crisis (1876-1877)—King George of Greece—The Diplomatic Corps in Athens—The Princess of Wales' Visit to Athens—The English Squadron—Death of the Austrian Minister, Baron von Münch—The Russians March into Rumania—Trip to Olympia—Excavations—Professor Ernst Curtius—The Grecian Monarchs at Tatoi.

THE situation had become considerably more acute in the Balkan Peninsula since the summer. Unrest and tension were increasing everywhere in Europe. On 6th October my father had addressed a fairly long memorandum to the representatives of Prussia accredited to the German federal governments. Against the attempts of foreign mischief-makers to entice Germany out of her calm and cool reserve, the directions for her future policy were laid down as follows: After the open enmity displayed by Servia and Montenegro towards the Porte, all Powers had at first agreed " for the present " to hold fast to the principle of non-intervention, and not to precipitate events. Following the observance hitherto customary in the Near Eastern question, Germany could do no other than join in this tendency. The moment for ending a war which might possibly threaten the peace of Europe appeared to have arrived, in the opinion of several Powers, when " unheard-of atrocities " were directed by the Turks against the Christian peoples of the Balkans. Particularly as it had become more and more apparent that, though on the whole greater successes had attended Turkish arms, none of the warring parties had been strong enough to overcome the adversary completely. Convinced that under such circumstances an end must be put to the bloodshed, an action demanded by the public opinion of all the countries in Europe, the Cabinets of these countries had unanimously accepted the task of mediation offered them by Servia and Montenegro. This had begun with an attempt to influence Constantinople towards ending hostilities. Although this had not succeeded in bringing about a definite armistice, the efforts of the Powers had at least by the second half of September secured a cessation of hostilities both at the Servian and Montenegrin seat of warfare. All Powers agreed that this *temporary suspension* seemed the proper moment to obtain the acceptance of peace proposals, and so bring about a formal armistice. But unanimous as was opinion on this one point, the views of all the Powers were widely divergent as to methods. For Germany's policy adherence to the agreement with "our closer allies" was the determinating factor. It would fall to us to play the part of benevolent mediator between the two equally friendly Powers, Russia and Austro-Hungary, who were concerned in a far higher degree than ourselves with the fate of the Ottoman Empire and its population.

This document closed with the words: "Little as we may fail to recognize that the present situation in the Near East offers serious and difficult problems for the European Cabinets, we yet have every reason to hope that the elements making for understanding will be strong enough in the future, as in the past, to prevent discord between the Powers themselves. We particularly incline to the hope that Russia and Austria, both linked by geographical position, historical tradition, and ties of blood to the destinies of the Turkish Empire, may arrive, in spite of partial differences of standpoint, at a balance between duties and considerations, which each of them can regard as decisive for the satisfaction of its political and material interests."

On 31st October the Russian Ambassador in Constantinople, General Ignatiev, addressed an ultimatum to the Porte declaring that if, within forty-eight hours no effectual and unconditional armistice of from six weeks to two months had been concluded on all fronts, and the Turkish commanders had not issued stringent orders to cease all military operations immediately, the Ambassador and the Embassy staff would be forced to leave Constantinople. The Porte was frightened and agreed to an armistice for two months. This firm Russian action in Constantinople was in harmony with the Tsar's personal attitude.

On 2nd September, 1876, the Tsar Alexander II had granted an audience to the English Ambassador, Lord Loftus, in his country residence, Livadia. Loftus had been Ambassador in Berlin, where Bismarck used to call him "Lord Pompous" on account of his conceited manners. The Tsar informed the Ambassador that he could not longer reconcile it with Russian honour, interests and dignity to tolerate the excuses, prevarications and *mauvaise foi* of the Porte. He ardently desired not to dissociate himself from the European Concert, but the present state of affairs was unbearable. If Europe were not ready to act with decision and energy, he would have to do it by himself. Alexander II had expressed his regrets that England still cherished "imaginary

suspicions" against Russia's policy, and displayed constant fear
of her designs. He had repeatedly given solemn assurance that
he desired no conquests, nor in particular harboured the slightest
wish to annex Constantinople. All the rumours of an alleged
" last will and testament of Peter the Great " and the Empress
Catherine's aspirations were pure fiction. Such intentions had
never really existed. He himself would regard the conquest of
Constantinople as a misfortune for Russia. Neither in his nor in
his father's reign had there been any question of such a step.

In 1828 Tsar Nicholas had given his proofs of this, when he
had halted his victorious army four days' march away from the
Turkish capital. Alexander II gave Lord Loftus his " Sacred
word of honour " that he cherished no intention of acquiring
Constantinople and that, if it should ever prove necessary to
occupy a part of Turkey, such occupation would only be " temporary." As for the suspicion so widely entertained in England
that Russia was planning a future conquest of India, he declared
this to be simply absurd. It would be impossible to conquer
India. And he had neither the desire nor the intention of possessing
Constantinople.

This last constantly reiterated statement was naturally to be
taken *cum grano salis*. It was not a downright lie, nor was it a
mere fib. The Emperor Nicholas I, more determined than his
more sentimentally disposed son, had written on the margin of a
memorandum of the Russian Foreign Office containing the reasons
compiled by Count Nesselrode for the conquest of Constantinople:
" The possession of Tsarigrad (the Russian name for Constantinople)
would bode no good fortune for Russia. Constantinople could
not be a mere provincial capital like Odessa or Kiev. A third great
capital city on a par with St. Petersburg or Moscow would imply
a weakening of Russia." The end of this royal comment concluded: " I, myself, would never make this mistake. God preserve
my successor from doing so."

The German Reichstag had also concerned itself with this
Near Eastern crisis. My father was obliged on 8th November
to take an open stand on the question of Germany's position. The
Bavarian Centre Party's member, Dr. Jörg, a grim particularist,
whose unpatriotic behaviour in July, 1870, I have already mentioned,
called Germany's policy towards the Balkan tangle " shortsightedness," and " weakness." This Near Eastern embroilment was the
consequence of the wars of 1866 and 1870, and the resultant
" complete " destruction of the balance of Europe. Armed to the
teeth, the German people now saw its most vital interests sacrificed

in spite of intolerably heavy armaments. It was time to lay aside the burden of arms so that the German people could breathe again. Failing this we should soon be drawing our last gasp in the shortly approaching war which would decide the future of Europe. My father answered the partly foolish and partly perfidious statements of Jörg to the effect that German policy was above everything one of peace. We never interfered in other people's affairs, but had only our own German honour and interest in view, especially in matters which did not immediately concern us. That had been the policy of the German Reich hitherto, and so it would continue. Our attitude to all the Powers was based on confidence and esteem. We should see to it that we retained this esteem and confidence. Germany was and would remain the bulwark of peace. And this bulwark would be all the more solid the more the Government could depend upon possessing, deserving and retaining the trust of the nation and its representatives. With the approval of the great majority of the Reichstag, the National Liberal member, Braun (Wiesbaden), expressed his approval of the statements of Secretary of State von Bülow and his confidence in the foreign policy of Prince Bismarck. "And if we support this policy," concluded Braun, "we are doing our duty better than those who, though without being certain that the Capitol is in danger, think they ought to rescue it by cackling." The end of deputy Braun's speech called forth lively applause and great amusement from the majority of the Reichstag.

The day after my father had spoken in the Reichstag, the English Premier, Benjamin Disraeli, the Earl of Beaconsfield for the past two years, made an important speech in the House of Lords. He enveloped himself, to use the language of Ferdinand von Walter, in *Kabale und Liebe*, in the whole pride of England. Peace, he explained, was a peculiarly English policy. England is not an aggressive power, because there is nothing she desires. But on the other hand, there is no other country so well prepared for war. What England wants is nothing more than to maintain the mighty Empire she has built up and which exists as much through personal sympathy as through might. England would never wage war save in a just cause. Her resources were endless. Should she ever begin a campaign the arms would never be laid down until justice had been done. The English Prime Minister's speech breathed, from the first word to the last, that spirit of imperialism, that peculiar English nationalism, sponsored by Benjamin Disraeli, the grandson of a Jew who had come to England from Venice.

A day later the Emperor Alexander II made a grandiloquent speech before the nobles and city fathers in Moscow full of the inflated egotism of the autocrat. He began by distributing approval and disapproval among the Serbs and Montenegrins The Serbs got a bad report, the Montenegrins a good one. They behaved, "as ever," like true heroes in the unequal struggle. He could not, "unfortunately," say the same of the Serbs in spite of the many Russian volunteers in the Servian ranks, who had shed their blood for the Slav cause. The Tsar was aware that, like himself, the whole of Russia was deeply concerned for the sufferings of their brothers in race and religion, but for a ruler the "true interests of Russia" came first. He desired to spare Russian blood "to the very last." But if the Powers did not succeed in obtaining guarantees from the Porte for a concrete improvement of the treatment of the Christians in the Orient, it was his firm intention to act independently. He was convinced that in that eventuality all Russia would rally to his call, convinced, too, that Moscow, as always, would set the good example. "God help us to fulfil our sacred mission." Ten years later the head of the Russian Foreign Office, Baron Jomini, who had accompanied the Tsar and Gortchakov to Moscow, told me the following story about this speech. The Emperor had proceeded in a peaceful spirit to Moscow, and had promised his Chancellor, Prince Gortchakov, who stayed behind in the railway carriage while he went to the Kremlin to speak if at all "*très-sagement, sans aucune imprudence.*" The sight of the enthusiastic Moscow nobility, the memories evoked by the Kremlin, and, in fine, the whole atmosphere of Little Mother Moscow had overcome him, with the result that he had made this imprudent speech. One more proof of the dangers of autocracy, unless the autocrat is very reflective, cautious and a master of his nerves.

Prince Bismarck had already expressed his opinion. He did not choose the Reichstag for this purpose, but his own dinner table. At a dinner party to which he had invited the presidential committee of the Reichstag he spoke of Near Eastern affairs with sovereign ease. He did not doubt that peace would be maintained. Should war break out, however, Russia and Turkey would soon be weary of the struggle. It might then be possible for Germany to act with success as mediator. To give Russia advice now would be imprudent; it might irritate the Russian people, and that would be far worse than a temporary misunderstanding with the Russian Government. England would be unlikely to wage open war with Russia, but rather a semi-official one like Russia in Servia. If Austria were drawn into the war and was placed in a dangerous position it would be Germany's place to fight for Austria and for the upholding of the present state of the map in Europe. Germany was the leaden weight which made the toppling figure stand up again. Austria possessed great vitality, greater than many thought. He himself (Bismarck) told Lord Salisbury of this when they met a short while ago, and this would be proven should the Emperor Francis Joseph ever address his people. In a semi-official despatch from Berlin, the *Augsburg Gazette* gave a resumé of Prince Bismarck's after-dinner speech as follows: "Germany will try to keep peace above everything, but should war break out, will localize this war, and if in the course of it Austria's interests be threatened, she will step in to defend Austria."

My clever friend in St. Petersburg, Missy Durnov, used to say there existed two kinds of truth for diplomats, the truth they expressed in speeches, conversations and memoranda, and the truth which they kept to themselves. This truth Madame Durnov called " *la vérité de derrière la tête*! " I do not believe I am wrong when I say that Bismarck would not have been displeased to see Constantinople occupied by the Russians. Nor would he have minded in the least if the English had sent their fleet into the Dardanelles. He found Count Andrássy's policy a limp one, and said four years later in my presence to his son Herbert: " They tell you that in every Hungarian there's a Hussar and a lawyer. Well, in the year 1877 Andrássy acted more like a lawyer than a Hussar." But Prince Bismarck was far too wise a man to let such " *pensées de derrière la tête* " ever appear in the foreground, however indirectly. In his remarks the main outlines were set out by which I had to judge the attitude of the Greek Government to the Near Eastern crisis and estimate the true significance of the surface complexities of the Greek domestic situation.

A few days after my arrival in Athens I was given a special audience by King George. He welcomed me as a friend of his first youth, since we had met when we were both very young in Rumpen heim and Frankfort. The King, during my whole stay in Athens, never failed to show me the same complete confidence and friendship. He had inherited the unshakeable calm of King Christian IX of Denmark, his father, and the penetrating intelligence from his mother, Louise of Hesse. Like his father, he was a perfect " gentleman." [1] This impressed the Greeks, of whom it cannot be universally said. His wife, Queen Olga, was a daughter of the Grand Duke Constantine of Russia. She was a Russian through and through, very orthodox, an excellent woman, a trifle naïve. She asked me

---

[1] English in text.

once in the course of a long conversation, if it were really true that her great grandfather, Tsar Paul, had not died a natural death. She had read this in some French book, but did not believe it could be true, since her history master had always told her that Tsar Paul had died in his bed as a devout Christian and excellent sovereign, beloved of his people and relations. I was obliged to inform Her Majesty that Tsar Paul had been strangled by his aide-de-camp, and that his wife and son had had knowledge of the conspiracy. The marriage between King George and Queen Olga was a very happy one, although, like his brother-in-law, King Edward VII of England, the King of Greece permitted himself an occasional relaxation. When, in this respect, even after his marriage with Princess Sophie of Prussia, the third daughter of the Emperor Frederick, the son followed his father's erring footsteps, the young Princess asked her father-in-law's advice as to how she should act under the circumstances, King George, with great seriousness, replied: " You must consult your dear mother-in-law; she will be able to give you the best advice on this point."

I met Queen Olga again long after this, many many years since the days when I had been chargé d'affaires in Athens. She spent the winter of 1924-25 in Rome, at the Hotel Eden, opposite Villa Malta. She had aged by half a century in the meantime. Her husband, King George of Greece, had been murdered in Salonika ten years earlier. Her son, King Constantine, was dethroned and died in exile. Her grandson, King Alexander, had died a mysterious death in Tatoi. All her Greek relatives were dead or exiled. Her Russian kindred had had no better fate. An utterly broken woman stood before me. She spoke of the happy past with sorrow, told me I had looked so young as chargé d'affaires in Athens that they had nicknamed me " the child." I had to reply that, alas, I was rather an old child nowadays. The collapse of the Russian throne had affected her more than the fall of the Greek dynasty. She had always considered the latter rather precarious, but had believed, as in the Gospel itself, that the Tsarist throne was impregnable.

In the diplomatic corps I was most in sympathy with the Hon. Stuart, the English Minister, and his secretary, Mr. Wyndham. I have always preferred the society of my English colleagues. Of all foreigners I consider the English most reliable, the sincerest friends, and the easiest people to get on with. The Englishman can always be trusted: he possesses both good manners and tact. The Russian Minister, Saburov, was a typical Slav, brilliant, flexible, insincere and entirely undependable. " *Il ment quand il ouvre la bouche*," said Mr. Stuart of him. He had married a German, a Countess Vizthum, honest through and through, austere and virtuous, in short a pattern of female rectitude. " *C'est la vertu dans toute son horreur*," he used to say of her. She was still in love with him, and therefore it amused him to annoy her whenever and wherever he could. At dinners he had large floral decorations placed on the table between himself and his wife so that he need not see her boring face. It delighted him to have the roast on the menu described as " *Dinde à l'ambassadrice*," nor did he conceal of which " *ambassadrice* " the " *dinde* " reminded him. He naturally was no model of marital virtue. He had succeeded in winning the heart of the wife of the Italian Consul in Piræus. Women in those days wore what the French called a " *cul de Paris*," the Germans a " puff," the English a " bustle." Under the bustle of his adored Consul's lady, Saburov poked the love letters he wrote to her. One day the Consul, her husband, fished out a missive from this queer letter-box. There was a duel in which the righteously outraged Consul shot the Russian Minister through the arm. Saburov's later career was successful. He became Russian Ambassador in Berlin, but Bismarck soon found him unreliable, while the Russian Foreign Secretary, Herr von Giers, also realized that Saburov was intriguing against him. The Emperor Alexander III, who was of upright nature, decided: " *Saburov est une dangereuse canaille qu'il faut supprimer*." He was recalled from his Embassy in disgrace and disappeared into the darkness of the Russian senate. I had many interesting talks with the Turkish Minister, Photiades. He was a Greek, like many officials of the Porte, who zealously and not unskilfully maintained that the Greeks were better off under Ottoman rule. In this way, by reason of its higher cultural standards, Hellenism might spread through Asia Minor, assimilating Bulgarians, Servians and Rumanians. If Turkey disintegrated the Hellenes would become the prey of Rumanians and Slavs.

To a foreign onlooker, Greek party politics seem like a satire on parliamentary government. I was often reminded of these Greek governments when, after the fall of the German Monarchy, the parties then in power, Centre, Democrats and Socialists, began to take their first tottering steps. In Athens, within forty-eight hours, I witnessed the formation of three Cabinets. One after another they received a vote of no-confidence, and were forced to retire. The absolute dependency of all government employees on the party in power for the moment went so far that as soon as a new Cabinet took office, even the official concessions to boot-blacks, who carry on their craft at every corner of the dusty Athens streets, were withdrawn and redistributed.

What attitude did government and people adopt to the decisive question: " Shall Greece follow Rumania's example and enter the war against Turkey on the Russian side, or would it be better to keep neutral? " The Greeks, both Government and people, wished to gain as much as possible and risk as little as they could. When a Greek politician with all the oratory and pathos of the lineal descendants of Aeschines and Demosthenes exclaimed in the presence of Tissot, the witty French envoy: " *que les Grècs voleraient très prochainement à la frontière!*" M. Tissot dryly remarked: " *Ils voleront où et quand ils pourront, certainement, mais ils ne voleront pas à la frontière.*"

In the spring of 1877 the Princess of Wales came to Athens on a long visit to her brother. She was fond of roller-skating, and a graceful performer on the skating rink which was constructed in the palace garden. I often had the honour of skating with her. She possessed then the same charm and graciousness she had had as a child and kept to her old age. Later in life I often met Miss Charlotte Knollys, her plain but very intelligent lady-in-waiting. Soon after this the Duke of Edinburgh, Queen Victoria's second son, put into Greek waters for some weeks, with the fairly large English squadron which he commanded. The officers of this squadron did not conceal their anti-Russian sentiments. When once on board the flagship, there were many strictures passed on the Russians, the Duke, with a certain irritation, begged his officers not to forget that he himself was married to a Russian—the only daughter of Tsar Alexander II. Very respectfully and quietly, but quite unmoved, an English officer replied: " I know, sir. I would not like to be married to a Russian lady." [1] The English-man knows how to combine good manners with complete independence and, upon occasions, the greatest *sans-gêne*. Among the officers of the squadron was Prince Louis Battenberg, a son of Prince Alexander of Hesse-Darmstadt, by his morganatic marriage with Countess Julie Hauke. Even in those days Louis Battenberg had already become quite English; at the outbreak of the World War he so completely renounced his German home as to change his German name into the English " Mountbatten, Marquess of Milford Haven."

When the Princess of Wales left Athens, I accompanied her, together with the Austrian Minister, Baron Münch, and the Italian Minister, Count Maffei, as far as the Piræus. It was a fine

[1] English in text.

June morning. Although the fishermen on the shore warned us against bathing, we could not resist a plunge into the clear waters, and we swam about in them for an hour or more. But the Greeks had not warned us in vain. Three days later Münch fell ill of a high fever. He soon grew so much worse that I sent for a Catholic priest, whom I asked to give him the Last Sacraments. Münch, who for some years had been chargé d'affaires in Berlin, was thought very highly of by Bismarck, who had liked his father, the Darmstadt Minister in the Bundestag. The poor sick fellow knew that he would soon be given the Austrian Embassy in Berlin, and could talk of nothing else in his delirium. Even while the priest was murmuring the prayers for the dying, Münch lay muttering: " I want to get to Berlin! Away from here, away from Greece! To Berlin!" His voice trailed off at last, and his breathing grew fainter and he died. His family, in memory of him, gave me a pretty water-colour of the Parthenon, which still hangs in my bedroom in the Villa Malta. It was the last thing on which his eyes had rested.

Of all the Queen's beautiful Court ladies the loveliest was Fräulein A. Her wide blue eyes reminded me of Pallas Athene; her beautiful figure of the Caryatids of Erechtheion. I liked her very much, and often called on her. We went for long walks together. Indeed, I seriously considered whether I would not suggest to her that she should join her life with mine. There was much to be said against this proposal. I was not at all sure whether she would get used to conditions of life in Germany. When her Pallas-Athene eyes were not resting on me I felt she was very uneducated. What would my parents have said to a Greek daughter-in-law? But she was lovely, very lovely. A chance meeting in the street influenced my decision.

> " Maid of Athens, ere we part,
> Give, oh, give me back my heart,
> Or, since that has left my breast,
> Keep it now, and take the rest,
> Hear my vow before I go—
> Ζώη μοῦ, γὰρ ἀγαπῶ."

Thus runs one of Byron's finest poems. When I was out one day with my English friend, Mr. Wyndham, in the streets of Kephissia, a monstrously fat woman approached us. She waddled like a duck. Wyndham introduced me. What she said was not to the point. But the odour of garlic was the worst of all. When she left us Wyndham said: " That's Lord Byron's Maid of

Athens!" I stared after the waddling old woman whose silhouette appeared twice as ugly in the limpid Greek air. And yet Byron had sung of her:

> "Athens holds my heart and soul:
> Can I cease to love thee? No!"

I was sobered, and renounced the idea of leading a Greek bride to the altar.

In April, 1877, the Russians marched on Rumania. In May the Danube principalities declared war on the Porte. After Tsar Alexander II had taken up headquarters on the Prahova in the Rumanian town of Plojesti, the main Russian army crossed the Danube. In the middle of June, the Russians under General Gurko, crossed the Shipka Pass, and Russian headquarters were transferred to Trenovo, which, in the Middle Ages, had been the capital of Bulgaria. The Turks, on the other hand, occupied Plevna, on the Russians' right flank. They gathered there under the brave Osman Pasha, who for a short time revived the old military prestige of the Half-Moon. In September the attack upon the Turks by Russians and Rumanians under command of Prince Carol was resumed, with many casualties. When the Russians were unsuccessful, the Greeks asked us neutral powers to protect Hellenism in the Ottoman Empire, now threatened by Turkish savagery. Secretly they were rejoicing in the Russian misfortunes. The Greeks left us in no doubt that the continuance of the Turkish Empire and the *status quo ante bellum* would be more welcome to them than too strong a position of the Russians in the Near East.

Already during the summer the English and Russian Ambassadors at the Porte, Elliott and Ignatiev, had passed through Athens on their way to Constantinople and on the way back again. No greater contrast can be imagined than that between these two diplomats. Elliot, with his calm indifference, was a good representative of that insular self-consciousness which, perhaps because it is as natural as the colour of one's hair or the size of one's feet, inborn, and accepted as such, is less irritating than the inflated vanity of some Frenchmen, or even than the, at times, rather pedantic love of being in the right, of many Germans. Ignatiev was much more lively. He was even *affairé*. He ran from pillar to post, assuring the French, English, Italian and Austrian Ministers and myself (Germany's representative), one after another, in rotation, that our various interests were, and continued to be, his chief concern. He assured the Greek Ministers that he wished nothing better than the materialization of the "great idea," the μεγάλη ιδέα of reconstructing the Byzantine Empire, and for this, and this only, had he been working, the Turks that he meant well by the Porte and was doing all he could to free it from the unfortunate position in which it found itself in owing to disobedience to Russia. He laid on his colours so thickly that neither Christian nor Mussulman believed him.

In the summer of 1877 I went to Olympia, where for two years past, excavations had been carried out under German leadership, and at Germany's expense. I was accompanied by two scientists. A sage to the right hand and the left, and the worldling in the middle. The younger of these professors was Count Hermann von Solms-Laubach, professor extraordinary of botany at the University of Strassburg. He was interested only in his special branch of learning, botany, and I cannot understand to this day why he ever went to Olympia. The elder, Professor Ernst Curtius, was in his forty-sixth year at the time. He had been tutor of the Emperor Frederick, was the author of a three-volume Greek history which had run into seven editions, and of a distinguished work on the Peloponnesus. He was also Director of the antiquarian department in the Berlin Museum and permanent secretary of the Philological-Historical section of the Berlin Academy. He was not only a famous archæologist, but a charming man of distinguished manners, and stimulating conversation. Only one thing about him disturbed me: his ceaseless, carping criticism of Heinrich Schliemann who, after having carried out successful excavations in Troy since 1870, was now beginning his search for traces of the accursed Atrides and striving to unearth their treasures. It pained me that a German intellectual of the type and reputation of Curtius should do his best to stigmatize as a bungler and charlatan such a passive, naïve, yet not the less fine, enthusiast as Schliemann, a man filled with holy zeal for knowledge. It was not necessary to be a diplomat to see that every word he spoke breathed jealousy against the successful rival in the archæological field.

When I stood at last on the flat plain which is bounded to the north by Kronos Hill, to the south by Alpheios, and its tributary, the Kladeos, I felt removed from all earthly woes. Here stood the temple of Zeus, Olympian Zeus. Pausanias of Magnesia, who visited Olympia nearly two hundred years after Christ's birth, has described the temple of Zeus to us in his Periegesis, a species of classical Bædeker. The statue of the God was in the Cella. Zeus was shown seated on a throne of cedar-wood, inlaid with ebony and richly ornamented with precious stones and sculptures. The face of the figure, the naked part of the torso and the feet were made of ivory. The curls of hair and beard were of fine gold. In one outstretched hand Zeus held a statue of the Victory, also of fine gold, in the other arm there was a sceptre fashioned of an assortment of precious metals. The cloak that covered the lower part of the god's body was also of gold. But according to the description of Pausanias, the power of the figure itself superseded all the wealth of the costly materials, and the magnificence of the temple. It was the most perfect materialisation of the god-head as the Greeks visualized it. "He is unhappy who has not viewed the Olympian Zeus," ran a Grecian proverb. This Olympian Zeus, together with the gold and ivory statue of the Athena Parthenos on the Acropolis, was the masterpiece of the greatest Greek sculptor, Phidias, of Athens. When he created it he had in mind the mighty verses of the Iliad:

> "Thus spake Kronion and beckoned with dusky brows
> And the ambrosian curls of the king flowed forward
> From the divine head; the heights of Olympus trembled."

In Olympia I parted from my two learned companions to visit Arcadia, Messenia and Lakonia on horseback. These people of the Peleponneseus pleased me as much as the politicians in Athens had displeased. I have seldom seen more hardy and industrious people than the Greeks who ran beside my horses. Their only food seems to be onions, a few dried figs, and a handful of rice. When, after hours of steady travelling over steep and stony paths, we halted at midday, they were disturbed neither by the Homeric sun's fiercely burning rays nor by the bugs that crawled by dozens on the matted hair of their chests. The *retsinato* seemed to taste like a banquet to them. May I here be allowed a remark in parenthesis. I cannot understand how heroes like Achilles and Diomedes, such a dandy as Alcibiades, or even Odysseus, who could bear such privation, ever refreshed themselves with *retsinato*, that horrible resinous wine. The assertion that the nectar with which the immortals quenched their thirst must have been this same *retsinato* which tastes like turpentine, is blasphemy. In Arcadia I was delighted with the oak forests which reminded me of my German home; in Messenia, with the olive, fig and orange groves and the fruitful fields of grain.

I stood with admiration before the ruins of the Temple of Apollo in Bassæ. But Sparta surpassed all previous impressions. Chateaubriand relates that when he arrived in Sparta he called out three times in a loud voice: "Leonidas!" Less theatrically disposed than the author of *René*, I contented myself with the views from the bridge that spans the Eurotas, of the chain of Taygetos and with reading on the spot the description of the Battle of Thermopylæ, in the seventh book of Herodotus. I thought of the inscription on the grave of the fallen Spartans:

> " Go, tell the Spartans, thou that passest by,
> That here obedient to their laws we lie." [1]

I know of no finer tribute to military courage and civic loyalty. From Sparta I went to Argos, Nauplia and Corinth. But Sparta remained the most vivid impression of my whole Peloponnesian trip.

In the autumn of 1877 I spent a pleasant week with the Grecian royalties at their mountain castle, Tatoi, the summer residence of their Greek majesties. There had once been the Attic Demos, of Dekeleia, which the Lacedemonians occupied on the advice of Alcibiades, exiled from Athens, and therefore enraged against her. The last part of the Peloponnesian War was called after this event the Dekeleisian War. On this famous soil we passed our time in innocuous *jeux de societé*. Once when Queen Olga who, as niece of Queen Marie of Hanover and brought up by her, was not exactly a lover of the Prussians, was asked whether, and how much, she loved the Emperor William, she answered tactfully: " I love him as my great-uncle." The witty Russian *chargé d'affaires*, Radovski, asked in what respect Prince Nicholas of Montenegro differed from Prince Milan of Servia, answered promptly: " *L'un est un aigle, l'autre un milan.*" (A *milan* is a kite).

As Christmas, 1877, approached, the King invited me to spend the German Christmas Eve, which, of course, comes before the Greek festival, with him and his family. I spent the evening alone with the royal couple. He told me frankly of his difficulties. It was one of the many unpleasing qualities of the Greeks that they made their sovereign answerable for everything. If war were to break out his subjects would consider him responsible for sacrifices and losses. But if Greece remained neutral, and in consequence got nothing at all, that would make him even more unpopular.

No real enthusiasm for war was to be observed in Greece during the whole of 1877. The war loan of ten million drachmas voted by the Chamber in December, 1876, and opened for subscription in January, 1877, was only partially subscribed. " The Hellenes are a great, a very great people, to-day as in days of yore,"

---

[1] Ὦ ξεῖν', ἀγγέιλον Λακεδαιμονίοις, ὅτι τῇδε κείμεθα, τοῖς κείνων ῥήμασι πειθόμενοι.

said a leading Greek politician, Herr Deligeorges to me, " but, alas, we are bankrupt." A cabinet formed by Deligeorges in March was followed, in May, by a second Kommunduros ministry, and this again by Deligeorges, supported by the two former premiers, Zaimis and Trikupis. This reminded me of one of the games I played as a child, Musical Chairs, or General Post.

Then I smiled, but can smile no longer, when I reflect that under the German Republic, particularly in its first years, things were no better, than in Greece half a century earlier. They were even worse, since in June, 1877, Athens succeeded at least for the time being, in forming a coalition of the chiefs of all the political parties, Kommunduros, Deligeorges, Zaimis and Trikupis.

CHAPTER XXXI

Peace of San Stefano (March, 1878)—Summons to the Secretariat of the Berlin Congress—Athens in retrospect—Berlin in June, 1878—Attempts on Emperor William I—Hödel and Nobiling—Dissolution of the Reichstag and new Elections—The Socialist Law—My Father on the Berlin Congress—Dangerous Inflammation of the Throat—The First Session of the Congress.

AT the beginning of January, 1878, the Russians crossed the whole Balkan frontier, occupied Philipopolis, and marched on Adrianople. The moment seemed to have arrived when Emperor Alexander II would realize the century-old dream of the Russian people, and plant the crucifix of the Orthodox Church on the Hagia Sophia. But the Emperor had left the camp and returned to St. Petersburg in December, 1877. His longings for Catherine Mikhailovna Dolgoruki gave him no peace. His brother, the Grand Duke Nikholai Nikholaievitch, was obliged to remain as Commander-in-Chief of the Russian Danube Army at the seat of war, though he, too, could scarcely await the moment of return. A Polish dancer was expecting him on the banks of the Neva, who had already cost him and Russia considerable [sums. Both the Emperor and his brother persuaded themselves that an occupation of Constantinople might perhaps lead to a European war, and would in any case put obstacles in the way of a reunion with their loved ones at home. In contrast to Hercules, they chose service at the skirts of Omphale rather than the fame that rewards great deeds.

At the end of January, 1878, an armistice was concluded between Russians and Turks in Adrianople; two months later, in San Stefano, an idyllically situated little town on the Sea of Marmora, a preliminary peace was concluded between them. On the Russian side this was signed by Nikholai Pavlovitch Ignatiev and Alexander Ivanovitch Nelidov. The last-named became Ambassador five years later in Constantinople, and went in this capacity afterwards to Rome, and so to Paris. He died there in 1910, and Isvolski was his successor. By the Peace of San Stefano Rumania, Montenegro and Servia were declared independent, and the two last-named considerably enlarged. Bulgaria remained tributary to the Porte, but was given a Christian Prince, a constitution of its own, and its boundaries extended as far as the Aegean. The Porte had to pay an indemnity of 300,000,000 roubles to Russia. Turkey was forced to give up the Dobrudja, the Scythia Minor of the ancient Romans, to Russia. The Russians intended to cede this sparsely populated and badly irrigated plain to the Rumanians, as a poor compensation for the fruitful and thickly populated Bessarabia, which Russia, by the Treaty of Paris in 1856, had been obliged to hand over to the Danube principalities. Alexander II, a dutiful son, regarded it incumbent on him to win back Bessarabia, which had been wrested from his dead father.

When, early in 1878, my Greek friends heard that negotiations for an armistice and peace were *en train* between Russia and Turkey, there was excitement for the first time at the foot of the Acropolis. The coalition cabinet was forced to resign. Kommunduros formed a new ministry, with a warlike programme; valiant and active defence of Hellenism, of oppressed and threatened brothers. The Ministers made martial speeches, and the deputies tried to outdo them in this respect. The King could only do the same, and " war," as Kommunduros proudly stated, " became the *mot d'ordre* from hut to palace." The Chamber voted a further credit of ten million drachmas. The government determined that 12,000 Hoplites should march into Thessaly. But the military enthusiasm of the Greeks had nothing of the fire with which their ancestors had fought at Marathon and Platea, and later at Chäronea. It was a flash in the pan. The Greek troops gained only insignificant advantages in Thessaly, and were timidly supported by members of their race there. I, like every other representative of the Powers, was assured by the Greek Government, that it had never really wanted to make war, only to send a few troops into Thessaly to keep order there, and prevent unrest, which the Porte was, unfortunately, too weak to quell. The Greeks were like the man in the comedy who begs his friends to hold his coat tails, so that he cannot jump out of the window into the street. When we, as representatives of the Powers, had soothed the Greek Government by declaring our benevolent attitude towards their desires, the Kommunduros Cabinet determined, in February, 1878, to withdraw most of their troops from Thessaly. A large majority of the Greek Chamber approved this inglorious retreat. More important in relationship to the political stage of the world than these insignificant doings in Hellas were the negotiations, carried on in the spring of 1878 in London, between Russia and England. On the English side the principal was Lord Salisbury, to whom the Premier, the Earl of Beaconsfield had entrusted foreign affairs in the place of Lord

Derby, who was too undecided for him. His antagonist was the Russian Ambassador, Count Peter Shuvalov, who knew Alexander II better than anybody else. He knew that the long war had wearied the Tsar, and hoped to please him by reaching an amicable understanding with England. Although versed for many years in the knowledge of princely mentalities, he forgot that though princes are always pleased to be extricated from a difficult situation, they are not always grateful to their rescuers. Prince Bismarck spoke the truth when, later, he more than once expressed his satisfaction at having played the part of " honest broker " by furthering Anglo-Russian understanding. He was certainly right when, in the speech attacking the Reichstag member, Eugen Richter, on 6th December, 1876, he declared that he would never advise any active participation of Germany in Near Eastern entanglements, as long as there was nothing more at stake for us than would be worth the sound limbs of one Pomeranian musketeer. It is another question whether it was wise of Prince Bismarck to negotiate, in his capacity as broker, entirely with Peter Shuvalov, and completely ignore Gortchakov, whom, early in May, he had invited demonstratively to Friedrichsruh. By his attentions to Shuvalov, Bismarck hoped to impress the Tsar with the fact that here was a suitable substitute for Gortchakov. This, as I have said elsewhere, was a mistake, for the reason that Shuvalov was already out of favour with the Tsar, since he had brought down the wrath of the royal mistress upon his head.

At the beginning of May, 1878, I received a telegram from my father which relieved me from my post at the Athens Ministry and summoned me to the Secretariat of the Congress, which was to meet in the middle of June at Berlin. Pleased as I was at this decree, I was sorry to leave Athens, but grateful to my father for having extended my diplomatic education by entrusting me for a year and a half with the control of a fairly important Ministry, in stirring times and not always under easy conditions. This had done me far more good than any independent studies, however intensive. For the first time I understood what Bismarck meant when he called diplomacy " traffic in human beings," that is to say, a form of action in which tact, flair and the knowledge and art of treating human nature, are all necessary. To-day I still believe that apprenticeship in Greece has been of political value to me ever since. But apart from this, I had received some lifelong impressions, of a non-political kind, in Athens. As I gazed at the semi-circle of the Dionysos Theatre, embedded like a shell in the Acropolis, with mountains and sea in the background, the figures of Aeschylus, Sophocles and Aristophanes came to life. I could read in my quiet room of an evening of Prometheus bound, the Persians, Philoktetes and Antigone, with more understanding and pleasure than ever before. I had visited the Theatre of Dionysos, with Aristophanes in my hand, and watched the orchestra people itself with the creations of the greatest of all comic writers. How typical, gross and straddle-legged there stands the immortal demagogue of the *Knights*, in whom, from tanner Kleon to our own days, the leaders and spoilers of the people of every age and nation are personified!

> " It is for that, that you're the man of the day,
> Because you're vulgar, low, plebeian,
> You've that in you a demagogue must always have
> A roaring voice. Shop-keeper, you're a scamp
> Right through. In short, a statesman every inch."

On the green shores of the Ilyssos under the plane trees that look no different from those which gave shade to Plato, I read the *Apology*, the *Theatetos* and the *Georgias*. How gladly I opened *Œdipus at Kolonos* of an evening, when I had spent the morning on the Hill of Kolonos, once a sacred spot, and green with grape, olive and laurel, and where now a monument is set up to the German philologist, Ottfried Müller, who died in 1840. Of modern poets, besides Goethe, I could only read Friedrich Hölderlin, who can charm us in every country, every situation, and every circumstance. In Hölderlin, the Swabian, there breathes the spirit of old Hellas more strongly than in any other modern.

Soon after my arrival in Athens I had bought a Turkish pony who bore me gaily to the sea, to the oldest port of Athens, the Phaleron, and to the marble quarries of the Pentelikon. I went by sea to Aegina, past the tomb of Themistocles, the most moving simple grave in the world, just as the mausoleum of Theodoric at Ravenna is the most noble princely monument. In the evening I stood in Aegina—amid the red poppies, and the broad leaves of pungent-scented asphodel, on the ruins of an ancient Greek temple. Aegina arouses great memories. It is the isle of Aeakos, the son of Zeus and grandfather of Achilles, and therefore, as the worthy Grand Duke Karl Alexander of Weimar would say, " *un monsieur très bien apparanté.*" On such expeditions I always carried a book in my pocket. This time I took Goethe's poems. Countess Marie Dönhoff had given me the book a year ago in Vienna, after she had read out to me, in a low voice deep with feeling, the song to the moon:

" *Füllest wieder Busch und Tal*
Still mit Nebelglanz,
Lösest endlich auch einmal
Meine Seele ganz." [1]

Why did her picture suddenly rise before my eyes among the ruins of the Athene Temple while the moon rose in the heavens and the blue Saronian gulf shimmered between the temple pillars? I saw her slender figure plainly, her small sweet face, her wonderful eyes. But she was far away, far as the moon which still fills wood and vale with floods of white mist.

" *Was von Menschen nicht gewusst,*
Oder nicht bedacht,
Durch das Labyrinth der Brust
Wandelt in der Nacht." [2]

More easily than from Aegina and Salamis, Erechtheion and the Parthenon, did I part from the people I met in Greece. After the death of Münch nobody had been more than an acquaintance among my diplomatic colleagues. I parted still more easily from the talkative Greek politicians who dreamed of the new Byzantine Empire and the new rise in general well-being to which they imagined this would lead, than from the *corps diplomatique*. The parting from two German scientists who had been my favourite companions in Athens was more difficult to me. Professor Ulrich Köhler, head of the Archæological Institute, introduced me to Thucydides, his chief study and his most admired writer, whom I learned to look upon as he did. The director of the Athens Observatory, Professor Julius Schmidt, an Oldenburger, was called Moon-Smith, because every time the moon was visible he stood in his observatory before the telescope and studied its surface. In 1856 he had already written a standard work on the moon. In 1866 he published the result of his observations in selenography. While I was in Athens he constructed a map of the lunar mountains at the behest of the Prussian Ministry of Public Instruction and thanks to its financial aid. He was not only a distinguished astronomer, but a profound

[1] Who floodest wood and vale
With misty silvern sea,
Setting adrift my soul
In its entirety.

[2] That which no human dreams
Nor soul ponders,
Through the mazes of man's own breast
In the night wanders.

thinker. I often went to see him at his observatory, to discuss Kant
and Wilhelm von Humboldt, as well as to hear of the mountains
of the moon, zodiacal light and earthquakes. I owe it to " Moon-
Smith " that I even then was able to get some insight into the
depths and breadth of Kant's philosophy. I also heard from him
many a good and clear exposition of Goethe. With my father and
Professor Hermann Adalbert Daniel in Hallé, " Moon-Smith " was
the greatest educational influence on my life. It was strange that
the man who had thought so much on the tremors of the earth's
crust and volcanic eruptions should have had a childish fear of
thunderstorms. He had furnished a room in the cellars of his
house, where he felt he could be most safe from the darts of Zeus.
When the sky threatened and grew dark he withdrew to this
fastness.

I paid my last visit to the Acropolis, stood for the last time
before the solemn Parthenon, the graceful Erechtheion, looked
down on Athens, on the ancient olive woods of the Kephissos plain,
on the Pentelikon and the Hymettos, on Salamis and Aegina, on
the bold promontory of Sunion, and the far mountains of Peloponnesus. The day before my departure I was received in a long
private audience by the King. " I hope," he said to me, " that
you are taking back pleasant memories of myself and my country.
Give your father my heartiest greetings. He is an old friend of
my mother's, and corresponded with her for many years. There
are people who declared that it was he who drew up the London
Protocol of May, 1852, which declared my father the heir of the
childless King Frederick VII for the Danish succession. Be my
spokesman with your father, and as far as possible with Prince
Bismarck." During the Congress-negotiations in Berlin I carried
out this commission. King George remained my benevolent patron
till his death. Whenever he came to Berlin he called on me. I
succeeded in patching things up between him and the Emperor
William II, who had formerly been ill-disposed towards him, but
who, impulsive as he so often was, was full of enthusiasm for the
Greeks and their King after acquiring the Achilleion in Corfu.

When I arrived in Berlin, in June, 1878, from Athens, I found
my father, like everybody else, very much shocked by attempts
on the life of our venerable Emperor. When on 11th May, 1878,
he was driving with his only daughter, the Grand Duchess Louise
of Baden in an open carriage along the Unter den Linden, towards
the Tiergarten, a miserable youth, a plumber's apprentice, Hödel,
from Leipzig, fired at him from a revolver. The first shot missed
its mark, as did the second, which the would-be assassin fired into

the crowd who pursued him. In court Hödel displayed a revolting mixture of cynical impertinence and cowardly lying. Three weeks later more shots were fired at the sacred head of the Emperor, and this time they were accurately aimed. The noble old man, who knew no fear, drove out on Sunday, 2nd June, towards the Tiergarten as usual. It was an open carriage, and he exchanged greetings on all sides, headed for the Brandenburger Tor, through which the army he had trained had marched victoriously three times. Suddenly he collapsed, streaming with blood. From the window of a house in the Unter den Linden a double-barrelled gun had fired two well-aimed shots. It was buck-shot, and had injured head, shoulders, both arms and his right hand. The Emperor who throughout his whole life had never lost his self-control, retained it even now. Truly great, in dignified calm, he returned to his palace, supported by his bodyguard. The doctors, summoned immediately, with the great surgeon Bernhard von Langenbeck at their head—who came to the palace in his slippers so as to lose no time—declared that it was doubtful whether their skill could save him at his great age—eighty-one. More than thirty pieces of shot had to be extracted one by one, many of them in dangerous spots. Had the Emperor been wearing the officers' cap instead of the helmet which he wore punctiliously, according to regulations, every Sunday, he would have been killed. It was the helmet which shielded his head from the force of the impact. A great wave of shame and wrath surged over the German people. Immediately after the attack the frenzied crowd tried to tear the would-be assassin limb from limb. Our worthy police force rescued him at the risk of their own lives by forcing back the crowd. If Hödel was a ne'er-do-weel son of the rabble, Dr. Karl Nobiling appeared on the scene as an intellectual. He had turned to the Socialist Party early in life, and at a time when they exercised a great influence on the half-educated and immature. Had he lived during the French revolution he would certainly have been one of the Hébertists, and taken his seat as member of the Commune between Raoul Rigault and Théophile Ferré. Later he would have acclaimed Karl Liebknecht and Rosa Luxemburg as his spiritual brethren.

Indignation was very deep throughout all Germany at these wicked crimes of the spring of 1878. Popular feeling was roused as it never had been since the days of the Franco-German War, nor was I ever again to witness such a violent expression of popular wrath. This atmosphere was very different from that of a generation later, after the attempts on Eisner, Haase, Erzberger and Rathenau. Certainly, every murder is and remains abominable. Nobody with decent feelings can ever condone or even pardon the political murderer. Nor would any man of ordinary humanity withhold his pity from the victim. But Eisner and Erzberger, Haase and Rathenau were the impermanent figures of a revolutionary epoch, and the three first-named were certainly dubious characters. None of them had achieved anything serious. In a hundred, perhaps in fifty, years, their memory will be faded and forgotten. The Emperor William I, the good old Kaiser, will remain in the heart of the German people, a living memory like Charlemagne or Frederick Barbarossa, since he embodies the finest, proudest, happiest, and most glorious days our nation had known since the Middle Ages. As to his personal characteristics, I know of nothing more moving or noble than the words the old man spoke on his recovery, on 7th December, 1878, when he received the mayor and city fathers of Berlin: " Providence permitted that a heavy blow should strike me. I regard my preservation as a warning to me to look into my life and see whether I have so fulfilled my duties so as to merit being saved from death."

It was natural that Bismarck should make use of the atmosphere created by these attacks to dissolve the Reichstag and proceed to new elections. These gave the Conservatives of all shades the victory in many districts over the Left Wing of the National Liberals and Liberal elements. With the penetrating insight of genius which can see at once what mere talent, not to mention the vulgar crowd, the *profanum vulgus*, fails to perceive, Bismarck, as far back as the middle seventies, had seen through the hollow pretension of the Marxian doctrines, and realized their especial danger to Germany. Our German love of theory for its own sake, the weakness of our national sentiment, often expressed in high-flown ideology, had honestly persuaded the German working man of the truth of the Marxian doctrine of " class war," the solidarity of the international interests of " the workers," to which all other duties and considerations must be subordinated. French, English and Italian working men, when they acknowledged its rigid and narrow precepts at all, accepted the teachings of Marx with the unspoken reservation that their country's interest should not be affected by them. The German is willing to sacrifice his own welfare and that of his Fatherland on the altar of nebulous theory. But was that law against the dangerous aims of Socialism, which in the autumn of 1878 was laid before the newly-elected Reichstag and passed by it with a large majority on 18th October, the right was of protecting our people from the grave dangers with which the Social-Democratic movement threatened it?

Like Napoleon, another great man of action, Bismarck at times overestimated the power of Might. He did not want to acknowledge that strength alone is powerless against spiritual movements, that it is just as impossible to suppress a revolution in thought as it would be to compress the air which one enfolds between the palms of the two hands. Although Social Democracy was based on a very vulnerable scientific theory, and in some cases an already exploded doctrine, the movement, in spite of all its exaggeration and the very real danger it contained for the welfare of the German people, was in many cases the expression of the understandable and even justifiable aspirations of our working class. What was more, the anti-Socialist law bore plainly the mark of having been worked out by the bureaucracy of some department of state, like the anti-Catholic laws of the *Kulturkampf*. The powers it gave to the police-chiefs of the larger cities—powers of which they took full advantage—to drive Socialist agitators out of the district, only resulted in the spread of the pernicious erring doctrines into areas where they had hitherto been unknown. Now, just as in the *Kulturkampf*, there were many martyrs to conviction, and the law strengthened the movement it strove to abolish. Another proof that secret intrigues and agitation are more dangerous than any open criticism and control through public opinion.

On 13th June the first session of the Berlin Congress took place. Prince Bismarck greeted the delegates in a short address, after which he was elected President of the Congress on the motion of Count Andrássy. That evening, in the white saloon of the venerable Berlin Palace, and surrounded by all the Princes and Princesses of the Royal House, the Crown Prince gave a banquet to every member of the Congress, as deputy for his father, who was still confined to his sick bed. His Highness, with characteristic tact, had caused the canopy over the throne to be removed from the hall and in its place hung Winterhalter's large portrait of the Emperor and King. The Crown Princess, who never denied or forgot her Fatherland, had had placed before herself and her husband the great silver centrepiece which came from the first London Industrial Exhibition. During the meal she called Lord Beaconsfield's attention to this superb piece of work. The Earl smiled, consciously flattered. The royal lady had brought from her English home, together with many other good things, an understanding and a love of the arrangement of flowers and fruit. Nothing more charming could be imagined than the great baskets of dark red and paler roses, the pyramids of cornflowers and geraniums, which graced the table, set out this time on the window side of the hall so that Winterhalter's picture should be in the best light. Soon after the beginning of the banquet the Crown Prince rose and gave the following toast in French: " The Congress assembled in Berlin has begun by expressing its wishes for the recovery of His Majesty the Emperor, my illustrious father. I thank the representatives of the Powers for this expression of sympathy. In my father's name I desire to see your efforts crowned by such an agreement as shall be the firmest basis for a universal peace. In the name of His Majesty I drink to the Sovereigns and Governments whose representatives are gathered here in Berlin." Prince Bismarck, who had composed this speech, expressly requested that the Congress should be addressed in the French language.

After the banquet I walked with my father across the Linden and down the Wilhelmstrasse to the official quarters of the Secretary of State at the Foreign Office, where I was staying with my parents. Later it became the Reich's Treasury.

Bismarck, my father told me, did not like the idea of the Congress. " The older he gets the more he dislikes the duties of representation. Added to that is fear of the unpleasant memory the Congress may possibly leave behind it. It is not impossible that the Russians or the Austrians or the English may leave the Congress in a huff, and Bismarck, who called it and who presides over it, may be made responsible for their disappointment. But since our prestige has suffered through the two abominable attacks on the Emperor, he feels it necessary to do something to restore it in the eyes of the world. Contrary to his habit he is carrying out in this case a policy of prestige. On the whole, it would have been better if the Congress had been held in Switzerland, in Lucerne or Interlaken, or even in the city of the lagoons. In Germany, of course, only a German can preside. But since Bismarck himself thinks it imperative for us to come through the Congress without injuring our relations with Austria, England, or above all, Russia, we ought to have arranged it in such a way that Russia could be given the Presidency, without any loss to our prestige. This might have been done by arranging that a Congress held in Berlin should choose our Chancellor as president, and that then he himself might have suggested that the eldest, most experienced and wisest of the delegates, that is to say, Gortchakov, take over the actual management of the negotiations. Then Gortchakov's vanity would have been satisfied, the Tsar's egotism, and the Russian

national sentiment.   Above all, had this been done, the Russians
would have borne the brunt of responsibility for the final result
of the Congress.   Well, let us hope that the genius of our great
Bismarck has once more directed everything, in the best possible
manner.   But we should be more careful of the *amour-propre* of
Gortchakov.   He has, after all, as Chancellor of a great Empire,
played a significant part for over twenty years.   At present the
thing he wants most is a chance to retire with dignity, and if
we like we can help him to do so.   He said not so long ago to
one of his assistants, Councillor Hamburger, who repeated it
to me, " *Je ne veux pas m'en aller comme une lampe qui file, mais
comme un astre qui se couche.* "

Thus my father on 13th June, 1878.
In the night of 13th June I awoke with violent pains in my
throat.   I thought I was choking, and struggled for breath.   Unable
to say a word, much less call out, I looked about for a stick and
banged on the floor as heavily as I could, since my brother Alfred's
room was under mine.   He came up quickly, saw that I was in a
bad way, and sent for our family doctor, Geheimrat Leyden.
Leyden considered it necessary to consult Langenbeck, the famous
surgeon, immediately.   Meanwhile a table was drawn up to my
bedside with a number of requisites for an operation laid out on it—
knives, scissors, sponges and lint.   My brother, to whom I signed
to give me particulars of what was going on, explained: " Leyden
thinks it will be necessary to perform a tracheotomy to save you
from choking.   I signed for pencil and paper, wrote down instructions to Alfred to fetch me my brief bag, and had the love letters
which it contained burned before my eyes.   In the meantime
Langenbeck had arrived.   Like all great doctors, he inspired a
feeling of safety and perfect calm.   During the Franco-German
War he had been surgeon-general of the army.   When he had
examined me thoroughly, he said: " Leyden, I don't consider a
tracheotomy absolutely necessary.   Perhaps we can avoid it.   The
condition for this is that the swelling should abate of its own
accord.   That can only happen if you manage to get a few hours'
quiet sleep."   Kindly, but seriously, he added: " Your father tells
me you were with the King's Hussars and went through the winter
campaign with them.   I had a son in the same regiment.   (A son
of the great surgeon had indeed served with the King's Hussars.
Later on he became commander of the Second Army Corps.   I
met him in this capacity when I made the speech at the christening
of the liner, *Deutschland*, in January, 1900, at the Vulcan Wharf in

Stettin.) All King's Hussars have good nerves. I expect of you that you sleep now like a top for several hours." He laid his hand on my head and went. I turned my head to the wall, prayed " Our Father," and soon fell asleep.

In the meanwhile my good mother had asked General-Super-intendent Büchsel, the Vicar of St. Matthew's Church, of which we were members, to pray for me. She often reminded me of the fact that I took a turn for the better at the very moment when Büchsel had begun to do so. And she always added: " The effectual fervent prayer of a righteous man availeth much " (James v, 16). When Langenbeck came back after a few hours he was satisfied with me. " It's better," he said. " Now we'll make a good incision in both tonsils and the uvula." This he proceeded to do. Then Langenbeck took a little box containing four fine strawberries from his bag. " His Majesty the Emperor sends you these," he said. " I have just told him of your illness. He wishes you a speedy recovery and sends you these straw-berries from the dish of fruit which they brought him for his breakfast at his bedside this morning. Our old gentleman spoke very kindly of you. He remembered that General Loë, your former commander, had praised you to him." When I look back on my severe illness of 1878 I say with good Joachim Neander, the friend of the great pietist Spener:

" *Lobe den Herrn, der künstlich und fein dich bereitet,*
Der dir Gesundheit verliehen, dich freundlich geleitet:
In wieviel Not
Hat nicht der gnädige Gott
Uber dir Flügel gebreitet? " [1]

Twelve days after my illness I was at my work again. I still looked very pale, and when I went up the stairs to the first storey in the Chancellor's palace, Herbert Bismarck had to support me. He had inquired after me every day during my convalescence in the kindest manner. Now he told me: " You'll be pleased to hear what my father said when you were so ill: ' Let's hope young Bülow pulls through. He's the most gifted among the younger diplomats. And, what's more important than talent, he has tact.' "

In the first session of the Congress at which I was able to be

---

[1] Praise the Lord Who artfully and gently prepares thee,
Who gave thee thy health, and guides thee with friendship,
In how great need
Has not the loving God
Spread His wings over thee?

present Gortchakov made a speech which proved that Bismarck was not wrong when he called him a very great comedian. Gortchakov had not been present at the first session on account of illness. Now he appeared, supported by two lackeys like Lord Chatham a hundred years ago when, after the defeat of the English at Saratoga, he had himself carried to the House of Lords to protest against weakness and a dishonourable peace. There was no further likeness between the great and earnest English statesman and the vain schemer who represented Russia at the Berlin Congress. When Gortchakov had taken his seat he declared in perfect French that he felt obliged on this, his first session of the Congress, to make a few remarks inspired by his love of truth and of his country, emotions which all his life had determined his actions. During the last sessions, from which he had been absent, his colleagues had conceded in Russia's name, more than he had ever intended they should. At this Gortchakov bowed, with a sarcastic smile, to Count Peter Shuvalov and the Russian Ambassador in Berlin, Baron Ubril. Tension vibrated through the Congress. General uneasiness was observable. Gortchakov went on to say that he understood the loyal feelings of his colleagues too well to raise any objection to the concessions they had felt it their duty to make. He only wished to affirm that mighty Russia only made such sacrifices because of her love of peace, just as she had waged the whole war to help the Near Eastern Christians. Russia was pursuing no selfish or no secret ends. As she had fought for civilization and Christianity, so now she made even greater sacrifices on behalf of the restoration of peace. Nobody would question the prowess of the Russian Army, which had won such brilliant victories. But Russia wished to show the world that she willingly exchanged laurels of victory gained at the cost of so much precious blood, for the palm of peace.

Deep silence greeted this speech. The members of the Congress eyed one another in astonishment. Bismarck, who hated phrases, smiled sarcastically. Beaconsfield, who knew no French, was having the Russian Chancellor's speech translated to him. Then he rose and answered, in an exceptionally pleasant voice, whose inflexions were those of a great orator, bowing towards Gortchakov: " I am convinced that I am interpreting the sentiments of this Congress when I express the profound admiration with which the speech of my noble and illustrious friend has filled me. I am happy in the reflection that it was the desire for peace which influenced Russia's decisions during the last negotiations. In the name of this Congress now listening to me, I should like to acknowledge this fact, and I hope that our further proceedings may be instigated by such noble sentiments."

In the absence of Gortchakov, the regulation of the Bulgarian question desired by England and Austria had been accepted by Shuvalov and Ubril. Russia gave up her claims to a uniform Bulgaria on the north and south of the Balkans to the Aegean, such as the Treaty of San Stefano had foreshadowed, and contented herself with a Bulgaria north of the Balkans. The southern portion of that New-Bulgaria was to be organized under the name of East Rumelia. England and Austria wished to conserve Turkey in the south of the Balkans as a vital force. In return for this two important concessions were made to Russia: Danube fortresses were to be razed, but all, including Varnas, to be handed over to the new principality of Bulgaria. Sofia was also given to Bulgaria, from which point of vantage the Balkans could be easily circumscribed. Looking back, observers can see plainly how frequently even experienced diplomats may be deceived as to the results of their decisions. At the Berlin Congress the Russian delegates supported all Bulgarian aspirations with the liveliest and most untiring zeal. They were inclined to regard every contradiction as an offence directed against Russia. Barely a decade later Russia was to regard Bulgaria as an enemy, and during the Great War, Bulgaria fought against her. "No weaver knoweth what he weaveth."

On 28th June, at the beginning of the session, Count Andrássy read out a long memorandum pointing out that for more than a year Austria had had to suffer by the insurrection and unrest of states contingent to her frontiers. Austria-Hungary had had to receive more than 150,000 Bosnian fugitives, who obstinately refused to return home as long as their country was under Turkish rule, since the Turks neither gave them protection nor any means of making a livelihood. Turkey appeared to be incapable of keeping order in her provinces, which were in an indescribable state of misery and revolutionary agitation. There was danger that this unrest and misery might spread to the Slav population of the neighbouring Hungarian monarchy. Should the Congress permit of such conditions continuing it would assume a very grave responsibility for the future peace of Europe. Count Andrássy concluded: "I do not demand that Bosnia should be annexed by Austro-Hungary. I only urge the Congress to make some decision. Should this appear in any way practicable, Austria-Hungary will endorse it."

Whereupon the Marquis of Salisbury rose. He, too, read out

a memorandum in which he declared England to be convinced of the justice of the remarks of the first Austro-Hungarian delegate. Since his noble friend Count Andrássy repudiated the open annexation of Bosnia and contented himself with a covert annexation, he suggested that the Congress should move that Austria-Hungary be given the order to occupy Bosnia and Herzegovina and administer them. It was in the interests of Europe to place these states under the direct protection of a great Power. " This Power can only be Austria-Hungary, the nearest neighbour of Bosnia and the Herzegovina. Austria-Hungary would seem to be indicated as the right Power to make an end of the insurrection."

On behalf of France, Waddington joined in the English suggestion with enthusiasm. He pointed out that this settlement was compatible with the legitimate interests of Turkey. The Italian delegate, Count Corti, declared his acceptance, though without much enthusiasm. He felt that the Italian people, accustomed to profit by every major European complication, would be dissatisfied with him if he returned to Rome with empty hands. Prince Gortchakov, who had concluded the Reichstadt agreement two years before with Count Andrássy, expressed his complete satisfaction: " *La motion anglaise relative à la Bosnie et à la Herzegovine rentre dans les vues générales de la Russie, et je lui donne mon entière adhésion.*" I heard at the time that it had been arranged by letters between Austria-Hungary and Russia during the Congress, that Austria-Hungary, if it appeared to be in the interests of peace in the Balkans and of Europe, could, with the agreement of the Powers, change the occupation into an annexation. The English suggestion was adopted unanimously by the Congress. Only the Turkish delegate made a shy protest. He was put in his place by Lord Beaconsfield, who did it with sarcasm, and by Prince Bismarck, who was almost rude. Nobody in the Congress hall guessed that the incorporation of Bosnia and Herzegovina was a dangerous gift, and that thirty-six years later the collapse of the old Hapsburg monarchy would be traced to it.

On 29th June the Congress settled the Greek question. France and Italy moved that a frontier rectification take place on behalf of Greece, if possible with the agreement of Greece and the Porte, eventually through negotiations with the Powers. England displayed some hesitation as to this, but soon overcame her doubts. Russia supported the Franco-Italian suggestion unreservedly. The poor Turks, whose opposition was gradually weakening, temporized with the excuse that they lacked instructions. On the evening of 29th June Prince Bismarck said in his wife's drawing-room in my presence, laughingly to my father: " The concessions to Greece were an act of courtesy toward your eldest son, who, by the way, did his business in Athens very well."

The first days of July, in which the Servian, the Montenegrin and the Rumanian questions were settled, were of the greatest interest. All three principalities were declared independent of the Porte, which had already agreed to this by the Treaty of San Stefano. In the three newly-created states equality of all religious faiths was enjoined by a French demand. This last decree was specially directed towards the Rumanians, who demanded from the large number of Jews within their frontiers the observance of all duties laid upon citizens, yet systematically denied them all political rights. Prince Bismarck agreed whole-heartedly with the French suggestion. He pointed to the German constitution and declared that German public opinion demanded that the principle of equality for all religious faiths which prevailed in Germany should be applied also to Germany's foreign policy. Servia was given Niš, Montenegro Podgoritza, but neither had a port on the Adriatic. Left in the lurch by all the Powers, Rumania was obliged to give up Bessarabia again to Russia. In return she received the Dobrudja, a tract of land from Silistria to Mangolia, on the Black Sea, and the Snake Isle. In a well-turned speech, but in vain, the Rumanian Premier, Bratianu, appealed to the " *Grand Conseil Européen et particulièrement aux illustres représentants de Sa Majesté l'Empereur de toutes les Russies, dont nous avons eu si souvent l'occasion d'apprécier l'ésprit élevé et le cœur magnanime.*" This fulsome compliment had no effect upon either Count Shuvalov or Prince Gortchakov. Prince Bismarck vigorously supported the Russian demand for Bessarabia. He even insisted that negotiations upon this point be accelerated. He hoped that the Danube principalities would be content with the recognition of their independence. " *L'œuvre du Congrès,*" he stated, " *ne saurait à mon avis, être durable si un sentiment de dignité blessée subsistait dans la politique à venir d'un grand Empire. Quelle que soit ma sympathie pour l'état de Roumanie, dont le Souverain appartient à la famille Impériale d'Allemagne, je ne dois m'inspirer que de l'intérêt général qui conseille de donner une nouvelle garantie à la paix de l'Europe.*"

Russia's obstinate, and at long last successful, policy, directed towards the re-conquest of Bessarabia, wounded the Rumanians deeply. After all the help which the Rumanian army under Prince Carol, who was both brave and skilled in warfare, had given the Russians during the Balkan war, Russia's action against her former allies seemed an act of the grossest ingratitude. From that day onwards Rumania's sympathies were directed towards the Triple Entente, and more particularly towards Germany. During the period when I was Minister in Bucharest ten years later, it was possible for us to conclude an advantageous commercial treaty with Rumania, and after that a political alliance, which assured us of Rumania's co-operation if ever Russia should attack us. Only the crass mistakes of our policy in the summer of 1914 could sever the bond which for more than twenty years had bound Rumania to Germany.

CHAPTER XXXII

Bismarck and Gortchakov — Signing of the Berlin Agreement (13.7.1878)—Shuvalov and Gortchakov—Privy Councillor von Holstein—An Engagement in the House of Bismarck—Biarritz, Dr. Adhéma—Books read.

THOSE were great days in Berlin in 1878, so taken for granted by everybody, as though the German Reich never could be otherwise than powerful, feared and respected by all the world.

Prince Bismarck presided over the Congress with technical virtuosity. What Antonio says of the Pope in Goethe's *Tasso*, that he saw great things great and small things small, was true of Bismarck in his leadership of the Berlin Congress. He overlooked nothing of importance, had an attentive ear for every reasonable question or representation. He understood how to disregard everything superfluous, disturbing, or time-wasting. "Prince Bismarck directs the Congress," said one of the English secretaries to me, "like a very good driver his coach-and-four. He is a most skilful whip." [1] Even when Bismarck spoke in French he was the great debater who had no equal in the German Parliaments for quick-wittedness and trenchancy. All members of the Congress agreed that the comparatively speedy procedure and finish were due to the supreme authority and personality of Prince Bismarck.

It is painful to reflect that in spite of such masterly direction the net result of the Berlin Congress was to change our situation for the worse; that it did not influence our future advantageously. This was due particularly to the senile touchiness and vanity of Gortchakov, though also to Bismarck's wrong treatment of him. In this regard an interview had a very bad effect, which Bismarck, at the instance of von Holstein, always anti-Russian in sympathy, granted to the *Times* correspondent in Paris, M. Blowitz, who had been sent to Berlin for the Congress. Blowitz was a journalist in the grand manner, and in any case one of the cleverest and most inventive publicists that I ever came across. Like Kautski, to whom the revolutionary government opened up the Government archives after the November revolution, Blowitz came from

[1] English in text.

Bohemia, and his real name was Oppert. This he had changed, since he did not like the sound of it, for the more euphonious one of his birthplace. Drifting to France, he became a tutor in the house of a Marseilles merchant. He succeeded in winning the heart of his pupil's mother, a fact which has always surprised me, in view of his appearance. Women are ever incalculable. On a pleasure-boat in the harbour of Marseilles, Blowitz and his adored one are said to have thrown the sleeping spouse overboard and calmly let him drown, in much the same way as Zola, in his thrilling novel, makes Thérèse and her lover behave to poor Monsieur Raquin. Oppert-Blowitz owed his position in Paris to Thiers, whom he supplied with valuable information, during the first stirring years of his presidency, and for whom he gained the public ear in England through the megaphone of the *Times*.

Like everybody else in a public position, Blowitz had intrigues to combat and difficulties to overcome. Once, as he affirmed by Holstein, whom he himself considered the greatest living intriguer, he had been denounced to the owner of the *Times*, Mr. Walter, in such dark terms that Walter decided to go to Paris and look into matters for himself. Suddenly he appeared in Blowitz's presence. Without for an instant losing his self-control, Blowitz invited him to lunch next day *à la fortune du pot*, as he said emphatically. When Walter appeared in the elegantly appointed flat of Blowitz, he found all the accredited ambassadors in Paris and the Papal nuncio waiting there to welcome him. Blowitz said carelessly to the editor: " *Mon cher ami faîtes la maîtresse de la maison et prenez place en face de moi.*" They sat down to lunch—Mr. Walter between the English and the German Ambassadors, Lord Lyons and Prince Chlodwig Hohenlohe. When he left he begged Blowitz to accept a very considerable increase in salary. A man in such a social position was worth his weight in gold. At a banquet which I gave to the International Press Congress, held in Berlin a year before my resignation, I related a personal experience of mine with Blowitz. " When I was at our Paris Embassy at the beginning of the eighties," I said, " I asked Herr Blowitz one day in a melancholy mood, because my promotion seemed so slow—they call it ' lieutenant's melancholy' in the army—whether he thought I should have any chance in journalism. ' I can get you a job at once,' answered Blowitz, ' at thirty thousand francs a year.' That increased my self-confidence at the time, and the thought gives me pleasure even to-day." [1] It was in the nature of things that Blowitz

[1] Prince Bülow's *Speeches*. Complete ed., vol. iii, p. 332. Abridged, vol. v, p. 260.

as a naturalized Frenchman should consider French interests first, and then, as correspondent of the *Times*, be careful not to wound English feelings. He soon perceived the personal tension between Bismarck and Gortchakov during the Berlin Congress, and rubbed publicist's pepper in a wound which obviously delighted him. In the report of his single interview with Bismarck, which he worked up bit by bit into a positive volume of correspondence, in the *Times*, he put into Bismarck's mouth unfriendly, even malicious remarks anent Gortchakov.

The personal feelings of influential politicians, whether or no they be Ministers or the heads of states, deputies or publicists, their likes and dislikes, above all, their aversions, always affected the relationships of the Powers, and so the future of the peoples. This will always remain the case, since human beings remain the same at heart whether they tread the slippery parquetry of Courts, or frequent their pet public-house for a game of cards of an evening.

It was Gortchakov's misfortune that once, when he appeared in Princess Bismarck's salon, the hound, Tyras, ran between his legs and knocked him completely over. But that this trifling event should have been given publicity by the Press and been smugly elaborated to ridicule the eighty-year-old man was neither in good taste, nor was it wise. Bismarck spoke the truth when, in many speeches and manifestos directed to St. Petersburg, he declared that he had zealously upheld Russia's interests at the Congress, and felt he had deserved the St. Andrew Order with brilliants had he not already possessed it. But it is precisely to political life that the axiom of the Greek sophists applies—that appearances are often more important than realities. The outraged and, in spite of his great age and physical decline, unfortunately still-intriguing, Gortchakov, was successful in inspiring the Russian public with the belief that at the Berlin Congress Bismarck had betrayed and injured Russia's interests.

After Bismarck—*longo sed proximus intervallo*—the most notable of all members of the Congress was without doubt Disraeli. It says much for the large-mindedness of the English nation that the grandson of a Jewish immigrant from Venice should not only have risen to the status of English Premier, but also have become the leader of the proudest aristocracy in the world. The Marquis of Salisbury and Lord Odo Russell, both scions of old historical families which had already been renowned under Queen Elizabeth, willingly played second fiddle to Disraeli. But it says something, too, for the attraction and the powers of assimiliation of the English that there was no more English Englishman than Benjamin Disraeli.

OPPERT-BLOWITZ

Correspondent of *The Times* in Paris and at the Berlin Congress

Charles Louandre remarks in his fine study of Tacitus, dedicated to the great French historian, Augustin Thierry: "*Aux yeux de Tacite tout le mouvement de l'histoire n'a qu'un but, la grandeur de Rome, au delà de cet horizon il n'y a que le vide et le néant.*" Disraeli was as much the Englishman as Tacitus the Roman. English—English to the backbone! Every one of his words was meant for the English public. English interests only, English wishes and advantage inspired his acts. Though outwardly amiability itself, he paid, in reality, no attention to any un-English feeling or point of view. His outward appearance was peculiar. He wore lovelocks like a Galician Jew. Far from denying his Jewish origins, he gloried in them. When an attempt was made in the House of Commons to slight him, young Benjamin Disraeli had answered that he was happy to belong to that race whose outward form our Lord and Saviour had worn while He was upon earth. He had been christened in the Christian faith at twelve years of age. Disraeli paid great attention to his dress. He was always very smartly dressed, in the latest fashion, a true British gentleman. The Earl of Beaconsfield was the only one present at the Congress-sessions who did not use the French language; he spoke it as little as he did any other foreign tongue, and scarcely understood a word. In this respect he was like Matthias Erzberger, though this was the only point of similarity between the English Lord and the member for Buttenhausen. The speeches of the Earl of Beaconsfield were translated into French in the Secretariat of the Congress for the protocol. He never altered anything in the translations, but said, smiling: "I am glad to have said such nice things." Bismarck started out with a prejudice against Disraeli. But Queen Victoria, too, had once had strong feelings against him, and he had succeeded in winning the favour of Her Most Gracious Majesty. Even Bismarck soon fell under his spell. "Dizzy," as the English called him, was a greater winner of souls. Andrássy paled beside him. But in spite of many gaps and some weaknesses, the Hungarian had a sense of situation. He knew how to seize the moment in Berlin, and recognized that he could do nothing wiser than to hand over his country to Bismarck's direction. His colleague and future successor, Baron von Haymerle, was a nervous royal-and-imperial bureaucrat who annoyed Bismarck just as much as the smart and elegant Andrássy pleased him. In regard to Haymerle, but still more in regard to the irritating yet irresolute policy of Austria towards her many nationalities and her weaker neighbours, Bismarck used to tell a story of his own youth. He once went into an English gunsmith's to buy a revolver, and had taken up a delicately-wrought, but small specimen. The salesman recommended a larger size, with the remark: " A small bullet excites a man, a strong bullet stops him." [1]

The Italian delegate in Berlin, Corti, made a big mistake through being over-clever. In the course of a long conversation Bismarck made the remark that the propitious moment had now come for Italy to lay her hand upon Tunis. Corti thought he was being very cunning when he replied: " *Vous voulez donc nous brouiller avec la France.*" If Corti had seized the opportunity Italy would to-day possess the best and most promising piece of land on the North African coast.

The French delegation played the most modest part at the Congress. Not that it was slighted or even neglected by the Germans. On the contrary, it was precisely the French delegates who were treated with special courtesy and kindliness at Court and in Berlin Society. Prince Bismarck, too, was always particularly polite towards the French. But the French delegation was not a brilliant one. The first member of it, Waddington, was English by birth. A naturalized Frenchman, he was a French patriot through and through. But he lacked the traditional attributes of the Frenchman. He looked like a scholar and spoke and acted like one. Once at a big dinner in Paris, when he sat next to Sarah Bernhardt, she did not catch his name, and asked Gambetta, who sat opposite her, who her boring neighbour was. The great Tribune replied with a smile: " *Ne faites pas attention à lui, c'est un numismate.*" Waddington had a good knowledge of coins and was a keen collector. The second French delegate, M. Desprez, director of the political section in the French Foreign Office, was an elderly and dignified, but very modest and reserved official. The third French delegate was the French Ambassador in Berlin, Count St. Vallier, a clever and skilful diplomat of distinguished family, but sickly, which influenced his behaviour in public. Born of a legitimist house, he changed his politics under the Second Empire. Under Napoleon III he was an intimate visitor of the Tuileries. After Sedan he had gone over to the Republic. We have experienced such changes in opinion after the fall of the monarchy in Germany, not only among counts, but even among professors and mayors. In France such lack of character aroused more feeling than in our country. His social position was not all too good at home, and so St. Vallier looked depressed. The time was to come when Frenchmen abroad were not so modest in their bearing as they were in 1878.

I felt an involuntary pity for the Turkish delegates, and for

[1] English in text.

that reason a certain kindly feeling. Turkey was only the passively suffering object of negotiations. For hours it was debated which of her limbs could still be lopped off. Nor was she adequately represented, since no *bona-fide* Turk was anxious to be present at the dismemberment of the Ottoman Empire, and the Porte had dispatched as its principal delegate a Turk from Magdeburg. His name was originally Karl Detroit; he had run away from his home in the capital of Saxony as a little boy, shipped as cabin-boy at Hamburg, and absconded again at Constantinople, where he became a Moslem. He was brought up in the house of Ali-Pasha, the future Grand Vizier, whose special protection won him no good reputation. Mehemed-Ali, as the young Magdeburger called himself, had a brilliant military career in his new home. During the Russo-Turkish war he had had high commands, and was esteemed an efficient soldier. But Bismarck could not forgive him his apostasy from Christianity and could not be persuaded to treat him with politeness. He was also avoided by our officers. Soon after the end of the Congress he met with an honest soldier's death. He was sent to Albania, where an insurrection had broken out in November, 1878, and was massacred by the rebels. He was the first member of the Congress to leave this world. The second Turkish delegate, Alexander Karatheodory, was a Phanariot, that is to say, he came from that light-house quarter of Constantinople where the remains of the old Greek aristocracy had settled after the invasion of the Turks, and from whence so many dragomen of the Porte and so many Hospodars of Moldavia and Wallachia were recruited. He gave an impression of calm and intelligence. He may have told himself inwardly that the Greeks of the Orient who had weathered so many storms since Sultan Mahomet II captured Byzantium and rode his battle charger up the steps of the high altar in St. Sophia, would manage to survive the Berlin Congress. Only the third Turkish delegate, the Ambassador of the Sublime Porte in Berlin, Sadullah Bey, was a national Turk. It is a shattering thought that forty years after the Berlin Congress the German Reich and the German people were to undergo in Versailles far more terrible treatment than the Turks in Berlin in 1878; a truly ruthless mishandling. When the Treaty of Versailles was forced on Germany and Hermann Müller, the Social Democrat, signed the shameful peace, together with Catholic deputy Bell, there was—as every German must tell himself again and again until the hour of justice dawns for us—not the slightest attempt to negotiate its terrible conditions.

On 13th July, just a month after the beginning of the Congress, the peace treaty, the *Traité de Berlin,* was signed in the large hall of the Chancellor's Palace, which has borne the name of Congress Hall from that day. Anton von Werner caught the moment and held it fast in a well-known painting which hangs in Berlin City Hall. After my father's death the Berlin City Fathers sent a photograph of this picture to my mother with a kind letter. It depicts the moment of signing the treaty, a great historical event, with a faithfulness that coincides with my personal memories. Towering over everybody else like a fir tree among larches, Prince Bismarck stands in the centre of the picture. With demonstrative heartiness, he is clasping the hand of Count Peter Shuvalov, who wears the magnificent uniform of a Russian aide-de-camp. Count Andrássy stands behind Prince Bismarck in a smart Hussar uniform, but rather as one who has placed himself under the protection of a stronger personality. Prince Gortchakov sits in an easy chair, but in an easier attitude than I ever saw him in. He does not look nearly as poisonous as, according to my remembrance, he actually did look, on 13th July, 1878. Lord Beaconsfield, somewhat bent, seems to console him. My father, Prince Chlodwig Hohenlohe and Waddington are all depicted seated. The poor Turks are huddled like sheep in a storm at one end of the long table on which the Treaty was signed.

On the evening of 13th July the farewell dinner to the Congress was given in the White Hall of the Royal Palace, for which 150 invitations were sent out. Prince Bismarck sat opposite the Crown Prince and Princess, Andrássy to the right of him, then Beaconsfield, Shuvalov, Károlyi, Salisbury, Ubril, Russell and my father. On Bismarck's left sat Waddington, Corti, Karatheodory, St. Vallier, Launay, Sadullah, Desprez, Mehemed-Ali, Hohenlohe. The Crown Prince, on whose right was seated the Crown Princess, and on his left the Grand Duchess of Baden, made the following speech in French:

> The hopes which I expressed a month ago in the name of the Emperor to the distinguished statesmen assembled for the Congress have fortunately been fulfilled. The work of peace so earnestly desired by Europe is the crown of your efforts. As interpreter of the sentiments of my illustrious father I am happy to do honour to the wisdom and the spirit of reconciliation which had brought about this great result. The agreement which has been accomplished will be a new pledge for peace and general well-being. The support of Germany is assured to all in advance who aim at securing and preserving these two great

BENJAMIN DISRAELI, EARL OF BEACONSFIELD, ENGLISH PREMIER

benefits. In the name of His Majesty I drink to the well-being of the sovereigns and Governments whose representatives signed on this memorable date the Treaty of Berlin.

I sat next to Herbert Bismarck. Full of excitement and with a proud expression, he said to me: "This is a great day. Four years ago that wretched cooper's apprentice, Kullmann, shot at my father and wounded him on his right wrist. To-day my father has signed the Berlin Treaty. In 1814 the European Congress gathered in Vienna. In 1856 the Peace of Paris was signed. Now it's the Berlin Congress and to-day the Peace of Berlin. *Prosit*, old Bülow!"

Both for Count Peter Shuvalov's own official position and for later developments of world-history, it would have been better if the count had not delayed his departure from Berlin as long as he did. Count Shuvalov was a clever, skilful, amiable and distinguished man, but like so many Russians, he worshipped more than was fitting at the shrine of Aphrodite Pandemos. On one of his evening walks in the Friedrichstrasse which he undertook with such *sans gêne* and which the Berlin police supervised so discreetly, to prevent any unpleasant incident, he had made the acquaintance of a too-facile lady, from whose arms it was difficult to entice him. Thus it came about that Gortchakov got back to St. Petersburg and the presence of the Emperor Alexander II before him, just as in the old low German fairy tale the hedgehog was there quicker than the hare. My friend, the Russian aide-de-camp, Baron von Ungern-Sternberg, related to me many years later the meeting between Peter Shuvalov and the Tsar. "I was on duty that day," said Ungern-Sternberg, "Peter Shuvalov came into the aide-de-camp's room with his head held high and highly pleased with himself, and desired to be announced to His Majesty. '*J'ai remporté un beau succès*,' he said to me. '*Le Traité de Berlin est conforme aux vrais intérêts de la Russie. J'ai sauvé la paix qui est assurée pour longtemps sur la base d'excellents rapports avec l'Allemagne, l'Angleterre, la France, l'Autriche, avec toutes les puissance. Notre auguste Maitre sera content de moi.*' That is what Count Peter Shuvalov said. He was summoned in to His Majesty. Ten minutes later the audience was over. He appeared again in the aide-de-camp's room. What a change had passed over him! If the scene had not been so tragic and, as I am convinced, such a misfortune for my Russian Fatherland and the world, I should compare Count Peter Shuvalov to a poodle who had a pail of water thrown over it. He was quite beside himself, white as a sheet. With a trembling voice and every sign of the deepest agitation, he whispered to me: '*J'ai été calomnié d'une manière infâme auprès de Sa Majesté. C'est ce vieux Gortchakov, ce vieillard pourri et méchant, qui ma joué ce sale tour.'* I shall never forget the genuine wrath and deep resentment visible in the words and the expression of Count Peter Shuvalov. It was a scene which, played on the stage and by good actors, would have been a most howling success." Thus the description which Baron von Ungern-Sternberg gave me of the incident. A year later Count Shuvalov was recalled from his post in London, and finally pensioned off. He did not die till 1889. During my second stay in St. Petersburg I often saw him and spoke with him a great deal. He looked back on an eventful life which had given him every opportunity to observe the moods and capriciousness of princes.

During the Berlin Congress I grew more closely acquainted with Privy Councillor Holstein. He sat on the Committee of the Congress. The heads of this were a German, Herr von Radowitz, Ambassador in Athens, summoned to the Foreign Office for this purpose, and a Frenchman, First Secretary of the French Embassy in Berlin, Count de Mouy, on excellent terms with one another. As long as the Congress lasted there was harmony between Radowitz and Holstein, who had been friends till then. The squabble came later and its cause was characteristic of Holstein. When the Congress broke up, the Powers concerned in it all decided, with the exception of the poor Turks, its victims, whose reserve in the matter was understandable, to bestow Orders on the members of the Committee. Radowitz, already a Minister, received a number of Grand Crosses, Holstein only a few Commander's Crosses, *i.e.*, not stars to wear on his breast, but only crosses round his neck. Instead of taking the standpoint of Ludwig Uhland, who on 18th October, 1816, the anniversary of Leipzig, speaks proudly in one of his finest poems of " princely councillors and court officials with dull stars on their cold bosoms," Holstein took this as a deadly insult. He had been placed lower than Radowitz, his junior. And from that day on he followed him with pathological hate. His rage was all the more senseless because, since the Arnim case, he had never been out into Society, never put on a decoration, and did not even possess evening dress.

The house of Bismarck in the quarrel between Radowitz and Holstein ranged itself on the side of the latter. The Prince had never really forgiven Radowitz for being the son of his father, the leader of the union policy which he had hated since 1850. I have heard Prince Bismarck himself admit that when in November, 1850, he heard the news of the resignation of the Minister, Radowitz, he had drunk a whole bottle of champagne, for sheer joy. The

Prince considered Holstein as true as steel and regardless of all warnings, continued in this belief till 20th March, 1890. The worthy Princess Bismarck did not like Radowitz either, on account of his waxed moustache, his raven-black, romantically-combed locks, his eyeglass, and his habit of talking a great deal. " He gossiped." She liked his Russian wife still less. On the other hand, she treated Holstein like a son of the house, in memory of the fact that she had done so twenty years previously when he was attaché at the St. Petersburg Legation. Herbert Bismarck, too, had been, for as long as he could remember, under the influence of the " faithful Fritz," as Holstein was called in the Bismarck's home. Young Herbert was impressed, not only by Holstein's perfect French, but by his acute perceptions and breadth of vision. Holstein was above all his superior in cunning.

These good opinions of Holstein in the house of Bismarck were not entirely shared by the sober Bill, but he was the sole exception. Holstein, who had eyes for everything, and observed all that went on, had devoted his attention to me at an early stage, less, probably because of my own importance than because I was the son of a Secretary of State, and personal friend of Bismarck. During the Congress he took every opportunity to show me small attentions. Once in this first stage of our acquaintanceship, I had a long conversation with Bill Bismarck about Holstein, as we took a trip to Stralau by boat. " You want to know what I think of Holstein ? " asked Bill, in his comfortable way, as he smoked one cigar after another, and drank one glass of beer after another in a country inn. " Well, that's a complicated matter. Holstein has been a great friend of ours for many years. Father thinks him exceptionally useful and places implicit faith in him. Mother spoils him and gives him the best bits at table. As for me, I don't deny his great talent, nor his brilliant French and English, nor his quickness and cleverness. I will only hope that if ever he's put to the test Holstein really will show himself true as steel, as Herbert thinks and expects. But there are two things which do not please me about him. He suffers from an almost pathological delusion of persecution. As he is very sensitive and suspicious, this delusion is constantly finding new fuel. And so he is always working up my father, who, in any case, is suspicious enough, and always irritable with people, to-day against one, and to-morrow against another. On the whole I consider Holstein a disintegrating element." Thus Bill Bismarck, while all around us Berlin boating trippers of both sexes splashed one another with water and bombarded each other with fruit stones.

Not long after the close of the Congress Holstein came to see me in my room. Having described Radowitz to me as an utterly incompetent official, he proceeded, with much circumlocution, to talk of my father's position and my own future. My father was doing himself harm, not only with Prince Bismarck, but also in the eyes of the public, by protecting a charlatan like Radowitz, who went about everywhere saying he had the Secretary of State in his pocket, who only existed thanks to his work and intelligence. I myself should do better not to back the horse Radowitz. My father ought to send him back to Athens as quickly as possible. The Chancellor would not make any objections. The Oriental section administered by Radowitz could be taken over by myself. I should do it much better than he. I answered vaguely, and told my father next day of our conversation. He shook his head. " Cats can't leave off mousing, and Holstein can never stop intriguing. He's developing by degrees into a really dangerous schemer. That is the opinion of Bucher and also of Clemens Busch. Unfortunately the Prince hasn't really very much love for Radowitz. But I shall continue my protection, and can only hope and believe that the Prince will let me have my own way as he does in nearly all personal matters. Radowitz is an industrious, well-informed and talented official. It is nonsense to suggest that you could replace him, though you might, perhaps, in eight or nine years' time. But you aren't far enough yet. Besides, as you've often told me, you have no desire to be appointed in the Foreign Office. I shall send you to Paris as Second Secretary. But say nothing of this to Holstein, who, it seems to me, won't want to have you there." Holstein reverted several times to his plan, but I turned it down.

Though my father very rightly did not want to hand me over to the Oriental section just yet, with a permanent post for which I was still unready, he employed me during the three months after the close of the Congress, one after another, in every section of the political department of the Foreign Office. This was very useful for my development. I had to work hard and spent my time in reading dispatches and documents so as to penetrate as far as possible into the aims and methods of Bismarckian policy. " Genius cannot be copied," said my father to me. " Nothing could be more foolish than to imitate Bismarck. But what one can learn from him is insight into the realities of politics and his disgust of theory, which has always been so dear to us Germans. Bismarck will not hear anything, either, of the scientific method which has been so much puffed in Germany. Politics for him are not a science, but an art.   Once and for all and above all, learn from our great Bismarck his conscientiousness in big as in little things, his care, his reflection, a passionate unswerving patriotism, his unshakable devotion to Prussia, to the German spirit, the monarchy and the army, to all that has made us great and alone can keep us great."

At the end of September Geheimrat Leyden was of the opinion that I ought to take some sea-bathing to overcome the last traces of my dangerous inflammation of the throat.   Since at that advanced season of the year bathing in the North Sea was inadvisable, I was sent to Biarritz.   Before my departure I was present at a dinner at the Bismarck's given in honour of the engagement of the only daughter, the thirty-year-old Countess Marie, to Count Kuno Rantzau.   My father, who possessed the gift, now rare, of proposing a well-turned toast, even extempore, expressed his and all our good wishes to the engaged couple, in words that came from the heart and went to the heart.   The good Princess Johanna wept with emotion, and the Prince embraced and kissed my father.   A friend of the Bismarck house, the distinguished Goethe-critic and annotator Gustav von Loeper, said to me: " That was the pure essence of Goethe, and fell like balm on my ears."   That day's couple had a happy marriage in store for them, which lasted nearly forty years. I have already mentioned Count Kuno and Countess Marie.   She was simple, bright, plucky and good hearted; he simple, reliable and intelligent.   He died during the Great War.   She is living still at Dobersdorf, her husband's estate in Holstein.   As a child she saw Frankfort and the German Bundestag, St. Petersburg during the first period of Tsar Alexander II's Government, and Paris during the most brilliant time of the Emperor Napoleon III.   She witnessed the heroic ministerial career of her father from the first to the last day, and saw his fall.   But she still had to suffer the collapse of his proud creation, the German Reich, the fall of the old and glorious Prussia, the end of so much happiness, fame and greatness.

At this family dinner-party Herbert Bismarck was as brilliant and high spirited as could be.   But I got the impression that he did not always exert a favourable influence on his father.   " Bismarck," Holstein would say, with his usual acrimony, " egotist to his finger-tips, he sees in his eldest son the prolongation of his own ego."   Herbert did not love the Crown Prince.   He complained too loudly, and too freely, certainly often very unjustly, of him.   In Kleist's *Hermannschlacht* the chorus of bards addresses the following magnificent lines to the Cheruscan prince:

" *Du bist so mild, o Sohn der Götter,*
Der Frühling kann nicht milder sein;
Sei schreklich heut, ein Schlossenwetter,
Und Blitze lass dein Antlitz spein! " [1]

In these words Heinrich von Kleist might also have addressed
the Emperor Frederick, who in battle was terrible to the enemies
of Germany, but mild as a German spring day in his private
capacity.   More justifiable were Herbert's complaints in 1878 of
the Crown Princess.   He exaggerated when he declared that in
the whole of Germany she only loved the Spa Homburg von der
Höhe, beloved of her countrymen and the Apollinaris water first
made fashionable by her brother, the Prince of Wales.   Certainly
the Crown Princess would have done better during the period
when her husband was deputizing for his sick father not to interrupt
the conferences of the ministers so often, to fetch the Crown Prince
for his " constitutional walk." [2]   Not without wit, and also not
quite without reason did Herbert suggest that the Prince Consort
would scarcely have dared to disturb the audiences of English
ministers with her most gracious Majesty the Queen in such a
manner.

On the way to Biarritz I stopped several days in Paris.   The
French capital was quite given up to the Great Exhibition which
the President of the Republic, Marshal MacMahon had opened
with great pomp on 1st May, 1878.   I did not visit it.   I think
it an admirable thing that technicians should attend international
exhibitions and make studies there, since they can have no other
means of making comparisons and so judging of their own progress.
But whoever, like myself, is not an expert, may confess that, leaving
aside all " cant " (I must be permitted the excellent English
expression), nothing is both so tiring and so boring as an exhibition,
and in particular an international exhibition.   The sight of a fine
picture, the reading of a good book, give me far more inner satisfaction.   The success of this particular exhibition was very flattering to
French vanity.

The Prince of Wales was present at the opening ceremony,
and made a speech in which he gave exaggerated utterance to his
love of France.   The heir to the English throne had been an
enthusiastic " lover of France " from his earliest youth.   Germany

---

[1] Son of the gods, how mild art thou,
  Spring cannot be milder.
  Be terrible to-day with thunderbolts,
  Nor Jove himself be wilder !
[2] English in text.

he had always disliked. The fault lay with his father, Prince Albert of Saxe-Coburg-Gotha, a man of exceedingly high moral qualities and education, who, although filled with a sense of the importance of his position as Prince Consort and politically quite English in thought, had yet remained in many ways a German Philistine. As such he supervised the education of the future King of England, who could never rid himself of the impression that the word " German " was identical with narrow-minded moral preaching, drilling, and brute force. If he found a man to be dull, clumsy and uncouth, he would say of him: " He is as tiresome and tedious as a German professor." If a lady seemed to him to lack all grace and elegance, he compared her with a " German *Frauchen*." Prince Edward was strengthened in his views by two women closely related to him: his charming wife, who as a Dane could not bear Germany or the Germans, and his sister, the German Crown Princess and future Empress Frederick, who in the Potsdam she disliked, yearned after her (as she imagined) freer, and certainly more splendid English home, seeking, like Iphegenia in Tauris, the land of the Britons with her soul. The Prince of Wales was clever enough to notice that he pleased the English more and more by adopting the manners and outward appearance of a typical Englishman. He heard on all sides that his father had been respected in England, but remained an object of dislike because, as the Earl of Granville once expressed it, he possessed all those German virtues which the Englishman cannot abide, and set against them none of those vices which can best be described as English. The Prince of Wales had declared the freeing of the sea-washed Schleswig-Holstein, as a result of the war of 1864, to be a moral blot on German history. He had thought in 1866 that Austria was fighting for right and justice, and displayed his sympathies with France so clearly during the Franco-German war that the Prime Minister, Gladstone, spoke to him seriously about it, and, in the end his worthy mother was obliged to take him to task. It was clear in 1878 that the Paris Exhibition was not only a success in itself, but had given the French their chance to show, only a few years after defeat and the bloody civil war of the Commune, with two months of Socialist rule in Paris, all the vitality, flexibility, and above all, constitutional sense of the nation, so firmly anchored in ardent patriotism. All European nations vied with one another to testify their sympathies with France. Besides the Prince of Wales, the second son of King Victor Emanuel, Prince Amadeus of Italy, had come to Paris to represent his father.

After a short stay in the French capital, I continued my journey by the Spanish express and arrived, apparently well, in Biarritz. But next morning I awoke in a fit of choking, like the one that had befallen me in Berlin not long before. Though the band was playing gay Offenbach melodies outside my window, the southern sun shining into my room, and the Atlantic roaring below, I felt very miserable indeed. I struggled for breath and thought I was near death by suffocation. I rang, a doctor was summoned. Among those doctors to whom I am still grateful, I must reckon, beside my true friend Renvers and my doctor friend in Oeynhausen who, in spite of my somewhat unsatisfactory state of health, did not forbid me to volunteer, Dr. Adhéma of Biarritz. After one glance down my throat he took a sharp pair of scissors from his breast pocket and made an incision in uvula and tonsils. The swelling of the tongue, he declared, would go down again without an incision. For the present we need not worry about that, nor about my lips or eyes. He had been an army doctor in his youth and served against Abd-el-Kader, the Emir of Mackara, under Bugeaud, the popular Marshal, celebrated in the famous soldier song of the "*casquette du père Bugeaud*." Such swellings of the throat had often come his way during his years of service, as a consequence of a sudden and great change of climate. He thought my two attacks were the result of the swift change from the climate of Greece to that of Berlin and then four months later the journey from Berlin to the mouth of the Adour.

As I had promised my father to keep him quite truthfully informed of my state of health, I did not conceal this inflammation from him. I ended my letter with a quotation from the Roman poet who addresses the goddess Fortuna in these proud words:

"*Laudo manentem: Si celeres quatit*
Pennas, resigno quæ dedit, et mea
Virtute me involvo."

My father replied that he venerated and understood the Stoic attitude of mind. But he would prefer it if, during an illness, I called upon God and His only begotten Son. There alone could comfort and aid be found, and true peace for the soul. *Inquietum cor nostrum donec requiescat in Te.*

Dr. Adhéma, during his long medical practice, had had a very famous patient—Monsieur de Bismarck-Schönhausen, who was then Prussian Ambassador Extraordinary and plenipotentiary at the French Imperial Court. During a not very serious indisposition which had befallen Bismarck while staying in Biarritz he was treated by Adhéma. But the Prussian Minister told the good

Adhéma nothing of the conversations he had had with Napoleon III, which were to smooth the path for him towards Düppel and Sadowa. The Prussian had certainly made a tremendous impression on him. " *Il avait beaucoup d'esprit, beaucoup de vivacité, un grand entrain, énormément d'aplomb. Il était très persuasif. Les femmes étaient enchantées de lui. Les hommes aimaient à dire qu'il n'était pas un homme sérieux. Il nous a assez prouvé, hélas, qu'il n'était que trop sérieux.*" I wrote to my father about Adhéma, who told Bismarck about it. Bismarck, who had a stupendous memory, sent greetings to his Biarritz doctor for me to deliver, saying that he remembered him very well. Adhéma was pleased to think that the great statesman had not forgotten him, but in a way which spoke volumes for the strength of French patriotism, begged me to tell nobody that the German Chancellor had sent him his regards.

I made some wonderful trips from Biarritz, where I hired a small pony carriage with two lively little horses which I drove myself. I drove to Bayonne, from whose quay I had a fine view of the mouth of the Adour and of the Atlantic Ocean. The downfall of the great Napoleon began here when he forced King Charles IV of Spain to abdicate and set his brother Joseph on the throne, as the Emperor, Charles V. I drove to Saint-Jean-de-Luz, on the Bay of Biscay and to the Spanish frontier at Hendaye; to Fuenterrabia on the Bidassoa and Irun. I bathed till late in the autumn. I have scarcely read so much anywhere as in those two months at Biarritz. I followed the words of our great King Frederick, " *Bücher sind kein geringer Teil des Glücks. Die Lektüre wird meine letzte Leidenschaft sein.*" (" Books form no small part of happiness. Reading will be my last passion.") I read again the *Confessions* of J. J. Rousseau and the *Contrat Social*. So as not to become enmeshed in the sophistries of that powerful tempter, Jean Jacques, I added the volumes, just then appearing, of *Origines de la France contemporaine*, by Hippolyte Taine, one of the most profound and lucid of the great French historians. I re-read Labruyère and La Fontaine, and the novels of Voltaire, and Victor Hehn's splendid book on domestic plants and animals. Above all, I read Treitschke, whose *German History*, together with the *Speeches of Bismarck*, have become the basis of my political thought and feelings.

CHAPTER XXXIII

Transfer to Paris—I take up my Duties—The Ambassador Prince Chlodwig Hohenlohe—Paris Society—Gambetta: His Attitude to the " Revanche " idea and to Social Questions—General Galliffet—Waldeck-Rousseau, Scheurer-Kestner.

AT the end of November, 1878, I reported in Paris as Second Secretary of the Imperial Embassy. I had spent two days on the way at Bordeaux and Tours respectively, and convinced myself that both towns were just as boring as Lyons, Rouen, Amiens, Bayonne, Grenoble, Clermont-Ferrand, Nancy and all the other French provincial cities known to me. Bordeaux, the biggest town in the west of France, and the fourth largest of the country, reminded me through its situation of Hamburg and Cologne. But how much more beautiful are the old and the new Jungfernstieg than the quais of the Garonne! How much fuller of pulsating life, more grandiose, is the harbour of Hamburg, than that of Bordeaux! And the twin-towered cathedral of Tours can measure itself just as little with the eternal cathedral of Cologne as the city of St. Martin with the German city which has so many hundred churches and chapels. But historical memories are as significant in Bordeaux as in Tours. Bordeaux, the Roman Burdigala, with its villas on the slope overhanging the stream, its vine-clad hills, had been sung already by the Roman poet Ausonius, Prefect of Gaul, and Consul. Fourteen hundred years later, the Girondists marched from here to Paris, where they were to leave permanent traces in the history of their country and of the world. In Tours a gay Court life had already developed in the eleventh century, and had helped to lay the foundation of the century-long supremacy of France in the realm of elegance, good taste and fashion, a reputation from which this country has derived not only cultural and economic profit, but political advantages as well. Bordeaux and Tours played a part even in the French history of our own day. When Paris was cut off from other countries by the enemy, the French Government sent a delegate to Tours. Here, in this capacity, Léon Gambetta assumed the dictatorship in 1870, and in barely four months, by general levy, reinforcements from Algiers and what was left of the old army and navy, got together nearly a million men. *Aux armes citoyens!* If Gambetta could not raise fourteen armies out of the ground like the Convention, he still managed to place four in the field, the Loire Army at Orléans the Eastern Army at Besançon, and two armies against which I fought as a young Hussar: the Western Army at Rouen, and the Northern Army at Lille. In Bordeaux the French National Assembly assembled which set its seal on the peace concluded between the German Reich and France on 10th May, 1871.

In Paris I was most kindly received by my new chief, whom I had met already in Berlin during the Congress. Chlodwig, Prince of Hohenlohe-Schillingsfürst, Prince of Ratibor and Corvey, Ambassador from the German Reich to the French Republic, Knight of the Prussian Order of the Black Eagle, Royal Bavarian Crown-Colonel-Chamberlain, was a *grand seigneur* to his finger-tips and by birth and rank. At the same time one can scarcely imagine a more modest bearing than his. There was something almost shy about his manner. Not as though he were lacking in dignity. He never forgot that his house owed its origins to Duke Eberhard von Franken, the brother of the German Emperor Conrad I. This pride formed, so to speak, his moral backbone in any difficult situation. As Bavarian Premier and Foreign Secretary he had a difficult task from 1867 to 1870, in opposing the clerical-particularistic opposition in the Bavarian Chamber. These clerical particularists, who, comically enough, called themselves " Patriots," were rough and coarse and did not mince their words. They were certainly lacking in that decency which Schiller praises in the *Nadowessian* " when he still saw the light." Prince Chlodwig Hohenlohe was no orator, nor did he become one later, as Chancellor. When forced to parry an attack he could only stammer out a few words, which he would read from a piece of paper handed him by one of his subordinates. Under such circumstances he bore the onslaught of the " Patriots " for weeks, an owl in the crows' cage, to use a Bismarckian phrase. When, many years later, I met the Bavarian Ambassador in Berlin, Count Hugo Lerchenfeld, who had worked at that time in the Bavarian Foreign Office, I asked how Prince Hohenlohe ever managed to support this situation, and Lerchenfeld answered:

Well, you see, he felt such an inner contempt for these parliamentary soap-boilers, that their anger and vituperation made as little impression on him as dirt thrown by street urchins. He came out of the Chamber in a pleasant, or at least perfectly tranquil frame of mind.

Prince Chlodwig retained this *aequa mens* even in the face of opposition and enmity on the part of his peers.

After he had been overthrown as Bavarian Premier, he spent a few months in Vienna with his youngest brother, the first Lord High Steward Constantin Hohenlohe. He was received coolly by the Viennese aristocracy. He was not only reproached for his inclination towards the hated Prussia, but also, and perhaps still more, for his friendship with Döllinger and his opposition to the dogma of Infallibility whose significance for the relationship between Church and State he had already pointed out before the meeting of the Council, in a circular note which became famous. His own sister-in-law, Princess Constantin Hohenlohe, told me that he paid no attention to the cold attitude of Viennese Society and behaved in their drawing-rooms as though he were surrounded by love and veneration. A sister of Prince Chlodwig was married to Prince Karl of Salm-Horstman, a Pietist of the deepest dye. He had had a model of the New Jerusalem, of which one day he hoped to be a citizen, fashioned in papier mâché, according to the specifications in the Apocalypse, and carried this work of art about with him on his journeys. I have seen with my own eyes how Prince Chlodwig gruffly refused to allow his brother-in-law, with this model in his hand, to enter the railway carriage in which he and I were seated. But he dearly loved his sister Elise. She was what used to be called " a beautiful soul," and he listened gladly to her advice and her suggestions. Speaking of her brother, she once said to me: "The text of the Sermon on the Mount applies to Chlodwig: 'Blessed are the meek, for they shall inherit the earth' (Matthew, v, 5). My brother owes all his worldly success and everything he has attained to that meekness, which, allied with patience, overcomes everything." There was some truth in this observation. But besides his meekness and his patience, Prince Hohenlohe possessed an exceptional tenacity, great tact, calm and balanced judgment. He was too great a gentleman ever to run after anybody, but he offended nobody and never definitely refused anybody anything. My cousin, Adolf Bülow, who was later Commander-in-Chief, first of the Rhenish, then of the Baden, Army Corps, and Military Attaché in Paris, at the time when I was Secretary there, characterised my new chief with the words: " If you went in to the old gentleman just as you are and said to him that you wanted the Order of the Black Eagle, he would not look at you in an astonished manner, nor throw you out, but answer kindly: ' I must see what can be done about it for you.' But on the other hand, it is as good as impossible to make him do anything he doesn't want to.   He flutters away like a little bird that won't let itself be caught."

The wife of Prince Chlodwig Hohenlohe, Princess Marie, was a remarkable woman. She was the only daughter of the Russian Prince Ludwig of Sayn-Wittgenstein, by his first marriage with the daughter of Prince Dominikus Radziwill, of Olyka, Nieswicz and Mir. The way this marriage occurred was characteristic of the manner in which the Emperor Nicholas I ruled. The Tsar did not wish that the enormous estates of Prince Radziwill should remain in Polish and Catholic hands. So he appeared suddenly and unexpectedly in the Radziwill castle, Werky, in Lithuania. " You have an only daughter," he said to the Prince. " I decree that she is to marry my aide-de-camp, Wittgenstein, who is seated in the third carriage behind mine. The wedding can take place in three weeks' time, and I shall very graciously be present at it." In vain did the frightened Pole, who did not at all like the idea of marriage with a Russo-German and a Protestant, make a few lame excuses. Nicholas brooked no opposition. The marriage was solemnized in his presence. Princess Marie Hohenlohe and her brother, Prince Peter Wittgenstein, future Russian Imperial aide-de-camp, were the fruits of it. She was permitted to profess the Catholic Faith of her mother; the son had to be a Protestant.

He became a *viveur* on the very grandest scale in St. Petersburg, Paris and Nice, whose inheritance, the great Lithuanian property, Werky, Prince Chlodwig Hohenlohe contested for many years at the Russian Court, and with the St. Petersburg Ministry of the Interior. Princess Marie was " *grande dame* " to her finger-tips, especially in her attitude of indifference towards public opinion and social conventions. Her only passions were hunting and homeo- pathy. She shot chamois, though she preferred shooting wolves, and best of all, liked shooting bears. She shot more bears during her lifetime than many a famous St. Petersburg bear-hunter. Once, when hunting a chamois, she fell into a crevice, and was only many hours later dragged out again with ropes, much bruised and scratched. She would often risk her life in a bear hunt, and would make the journey from Paris or Strassburg to Lithuania simply to shoot a bear whose appearance had been announced to her by telegram.

Though she did not enjoy it so much as hunting, the homeo- pathic treatment of patients who came to her with their ailments was also a great pleasure in its way. In Schillingsfürst and in Aussee in Salzkammergut, where she possessed an original but charming villa, furnished like a peasant's cottage, both natives and

visitors were constrained to let themselves be treated by her. More
than once in my own case she effected quick cures of influenza and
stomach trouble. But perhaps I should have recovered again even
without her little white pills. She treated me with motherly kindness, introduced me into Paris Society, where her rank and distinction had soon secured her a high place. I do not know whether
she always kept all the ten commandments, but the eleventh she
certainly obeyed: she never let herself be bluffed. Once at one
of her weekly receptions a German lady, of the well-known Frankfurt
banker family of Bethmann, married to M. Nottinger, a Swiss,
who had naturalised himself a Frenchman, and, with all the zeal
of German renegades, become more French than the French,
said to her in my presence: " I would have come before, but none
of my French friends knew your address." Without the flicker
of an eyelash, the Princess replied, extremely haughtily: " The
people I want to see know when I am at home. I'm always very
glad not to see the others." She took me nearly every evening into
the " *grand monde*," as it is called. Prince Chlodwig read the
evening papers at home, wrote dispatches and made notes for his
memoirs, which on their publication years later, were to arouse
the ire of William II.

Although scarcely eight years had passed since the war, I
frequented most of the houses of the Faubourg Saint-Germain, the
aristocratic quarter of Paris. The clever Countess Laferronnays
once said to me: " *Vous voyez combien vous êtes bien acceuilli un
peu partout. Si vous recontrez par ci, par là quelqu'un qui vous fait
mine grise n'oubliez pas que nous avons été, hélas, vaincus. Si nous
avions été les vainqueurs, nous serions à vos pieds.*" That was well
meant, but not quite correct. I hear that Parisian Society, now
that France, in league with the whole world, has conquered us, is
more unpleasant towards Germans than after the French defeat
of 1870-71. Machiavelli appears to be right when he says that
people can be won and ruled in two manners, either by fear or by
love. Fear is the more certain.

More interesting than the general run of salons, as banal in
Paris as elsewhere, were two houses which received me with a
kindness I have never forgotten. The Director of the Banque de
France, Georges Pallain, was a sincere and warm-hearted French
patriot and an extremely acute man of finance. He was also an
author of delicate perceptions, who edited the correspondence
which Louis XVIII conducted with Talleyrand during the Congress
of Vienna, and had written an interesting essay on Mirabeau. At
his house for the first time, I met the three brothers Charmes, all

three gifted publicists, whose articles in the *Journal des Débats* and in the *Revue des deux Mondes* were widely read.

Here (*i.e.*, in Paris), too, I made the acquaintance of the brothers Cambon, of whom Paul became Prefect in Lyons and Ambassador in Madrid and Berlin. They introduced a young journalist to me of whom they said he had "*un drôle de passé*," but a fine intellect and style, and burning ambition. His name was Camille Barrère. As a young enthusiast he had played a part in the Paris Commune, and was at the time on the staff of the *Père Duchesne*, which took up the tradition of Marat during the Commune. It was alleged that Barrère had written the notorious article in which *Père Duchesne* demanded the head of the Archbishop of Paris, Darboy. The Archbishop really was shot by the Communists. Barrère, however, thought with Falstaff that "discretion is the better part of valour," and fled to London just in time in May 1871. There he not only managed to wipe out the remembrance of his past, but learned to speak English perfectly, and enlarged his political horizon in the grandiose English *milieu*, a fact which was of great advantage to him in his later diplomatic career.[1]

I have also a grateful memory of Count Roger du Nord. He was then already an old man. France is especially famous as the country of well-dressed and *piquante* women. I should prefer to call it the country of the well-preserved, experienced and clever old gentlemen. Count Roger du Nord had been one of the closest friends of Adolphe Thiers. He used to call him "*le sauveur de la France*," and regarded him, together with Cardinal Richelieu, Colbert and Prince Talleyrand, as one of the greatest French statesmen. He placed Henri Quartre above all three. Over his desk there hung a fine picture of France's most popular king,

---

[1] [PUBLISHER'S NOTE.] At our request His Excellency Monsieur Camille Barrère, late French Ambassador in Rome, has supplied the following comments on the above passage :

1. "I never was introduced to him in Paris by my friends the Cambon brothers. It was only several years later that I met him first at Prince Bismarck's table when I was French Minister in Sweden.

2. "Paul Cambon is dead. But his surviving brother, Jules Cambon, not only denies the aforesaid introduction, but emphatically denies that he or his brother ever spoke to Prince de Bülow concerning myself on any occasion.

3. "I never was on the staff of the *Père Duchesne*. I never wrote an article in that paper nor anywhere else, asking for the execution of the Archbishop of Paris, or, thank Heaven, of anybody else.

4. "Last and least. The author of the *Memoirs* states that having gone to England in 1871 (I was then 19 years of age) I 'learned to speak English perfectly.' As a matter of fact, I was educated from my infancy to the age of 13 years in English schools. The English language was to me a second mother tongue."

showing his entry into Paris after he had declared " *que Paris valait bien une messe.*" Once when the old Count was looking at the picture, he said to me: " *Voilà le vrai génie politique! La politique demande des concessions et des combinaisons.*" He praised, in Thiers, his political vision, courage and energy. In 1859 he had not cared for the French-Austrian war, and prophesied that the " so-called " liberation of Italy would give France an inconvenient neighbour, particularly on the Mediterranean. Thiers, in his speech of 3rd May, 1866, which ranks among the greatest political speeches ever made, prophesied that the war between Prussia and Austria then impending, might have unpleasant consequences for France, in the case of a Prussian victory. He perceived at the right moment the danger to France of Cavour and Bismarck. When Napoleon III, with Ollivier and Gramont, declared war on Prussia and the North German Alliance in the most awkward manner in July, 1870, he alone spoke the language of reason before a vituperative Chamber which constantly interrupted him. During the war, through the journeys which, in spite of his advanced age, he made in winter to St. Petersburg, Vienna and Rome, he enlisted sympathies for France, and in the end, through concluding peace at the right moment with Germany, saved her future. But his greatest achievement was the energy with which, in the spring of 1871, he overthrew the Socialistic revolt of the Commune. When Thiers ordered thousands of rebels to be put up against the wall and shot, when he exiled thousands of others to New Caledonia, he secured for his country the possibility of a peaceful and normal internal development, just as a doctor saves the life of his patient when he orders an operation at the right moment." So Count Roger du Nord. But I think it is a striking proof of French civic sense and good statesmanship that they count Thiers the surgeon who ordered for this bloody operation, among their greatest statesmen, and that Paris and many other cities have since his death erected countless memorials to him. The German sings " *Deutschland Über Alles!* " But the Frenchman places France, her interests, her status in the world, her greatness and her reputation really " *über alles.*" It was in just this respect that Adolphe Thiers was a real, a typical Frenchman. Before and after 1871 he never ceased to believe in the " *Prépondérance légitime de la France,*" in the divine decree, that France should be supreme in Europe. He was, on the whole, inaccessible to religious feelings, a disciple of Voltaire. But there was something religious in his belief in his country.

At Count Roger du Nord's house I met Gambetta. He was forty years old at the time. At the first glance there was nothing impressive about him. He was too stout for his middling height; his movements were abrupt and undistinguished. Jules Grévy and Jules Ferry, Waldeck-Rousseau and Freycinet displayed more dignity in their bearing. Like the Cyclops of the Odyssey, Gambetta had only one eye. But the story that he had injured the other himself so as to escape military service was the miserable calumny of his enemies. He had lost the eye in an accident as a child. On the whole, however, the outward appearance of the man who had led the *Défense nationale* was not exactly distinguished. Gambetta on the tribune of the Corps Législatif was very different to Gambetta in evening dress, in a salon. He was a born orator, in the Roman sense, in the same tradition as Danton and Mirabeau, Jaurès, Castelar and Crispi. He had a deep, strong, resonant voice, which could boom out whenever he wanted it to, and the broad and dominating gestures that go with such voices. His features were lively and expressive. His powerful lungs and ready tongue had won him a place of honour as a young student in the Café Procope, in which so many Frenchmen, who afterwards became famous, made their first oratorical flights. The student Gambetta had, of course, lived in the Latin Quarter, in the Rue de l'Odéon, in the same little hotel in which the writer, Alphonse Daudet, his junior by two years, occupied a garret room. Years later Daudet, in *Numa Roumestan*, perhaps his best book, was to describe with an acrid pen the figure of the southern French demagogue who conquered Paris. The story of Gambetta's having had to borrow a few sous to pay for his supper from his fellow students is untrue. He received from his respected father, an Italian herb-dealer in Cahors, the very adequate monthly sum of 300 francs, quite enough to live well in the Latin Quarter. On the other hand, I am willing to admit that though he may not have been a needy Bohemian, Gambetta must certainly have looked like one in his youth, both in the Café Procope, and later, when he had become a lawyer and migrated to the right bank of the Seine, using his deep voice, in the Café Madrid, to collect about him a crowd of admiring listeners. Even in the days when I met him, I was struck by his neglect of his appearance. His dress coat fitted badly. His shirt rose from the confines of his waistcoat, like a curtain blown in the wind. " *Sa chemise bouffait.*" His tie was crooked. All that would have impeded his progress in England, where dress is considered so very important that Disraeli prophesied a fine future for a Member of Parliament making his début, because he wore his eyeglass " *like a gentleman.*" [1] Though the Frenchman

---

[1] English in text.

is not nearly so particular as the Englishman how a man looks, he is all the more sensitive to his gifts as an orator. The Germans lay stress neither on the one nor on the other, but judge the politician according to his ethical standing and his general attitude towards the problems of world philosophy.

Léon Gambetta, like Napoleon, like Cardinal Mazarin the successor of Richelieu and continuer of his work, like Maréchal de Retz and Cardinal de Retz, was of Italian origin. His grand-father had come to France from Genoa. His father, who had been born in Italy, spoke French to the end of his days with a pronounced Italian accent. Gambetta *père* ran a shop which sold medicinal herbs, and called it " *Au port de Gênes.*" When Gambetta *fils* was already a famous man, one could still read on a shop-sign in his native town, Cahors, capital of the department Lot: " *Gambetta, Herboriste, au port de Gênes.*" Was Gambetta of Jewish origin? It is often said that he was. His features would not belie Jewish blood. His facial angle was Jewish. But if Gambetta really was a Jew it would merely be another proof of the political gifts of the Jews, already illustrated by Disraeli, Daniele Manin, Luigi Luzzatti, Karl Marx and Ferdinand Lassalle, not to mention Moses and King Solomon.

The dinner at Count Roger du Nord's, at which I met Gambetta stands out vividly in my memory after so many years. The worthy Count was a great gourmet. There were huge truffles, magnificent *Truffes de Périgord*, boiled in champagne and served with the best butter, about the most indigestible fare one can imagine. I admired the appetite, with which Gambetta attacked these truffles. In the size of his appetite he resembled Bismarck. He drank Chambertin with them, a heavy Burgundy. After dinner he came towards me, put his arm through mine, sat down on the sofa and motioned me to sit down beside him. He was what Italians call " *Simpaticone* " to a high degree. More than merely that; his was a great nature. He began at once to speak of his attitude in the Franco-German war, and it was quite natural that he should. The admirable energy with which he led France, already beaten at Weissenburg, Wörth, Spichern, Colombey-Nouilly, Vionville, Mars-la-Tour, Gravelotte-Saint-Privat, Noisseville and Sedan, after Sedan and the capitulation of Metz, after the siege of Paris, and in the last desperate fights, was the basis of his position in France. It gave him a standing which was possessed by no other Frenchman of his day. He was not only a patriot, he was *the patriot*. He was not only nationally-minded, as all Frenchmen are, with very few exceptions, he was the Nationalist *par excellence*—just as Clemenceau during the last year of the Great War was the upholder of the *Guerre jusqu' au bout,* so was Gambetta in the winter of 1870 advocate of the *Guerre à outrance.* It had been his energy, his enthusiasm, his belief in his country which prolonged war and resistance by four months, and which assured him a place in the heart of the French people, as in the proud history of France. Even in December, 1870, Hippolyte Taine, that critical spirit mistrustful of all hero-worship, wrote to a friend: " Even if we are crushed, Gambetta will in any case have saved our honour. Through him France will be more highly respected in future." For that reason, when France, albeit with the help of two hemispheres, emerged victorious from the Great War, the heart of the man who prolonged the war of 1870, Gambetta's heart, was brought from Nice, where his body is buried, to repose in the French temple of fame, the Paris Panthéon.

In short, trenchant and lucid phrases, Gambetta, at our first meeting, described to me his action and behaviour after Sedan as Member of the Government of National Defence. " France," he told me, " had sunk to her knees. But I said ' *Debout et marche!* ' Whoever governs France in great moments," he continued, " has the sensation of holding a thermometer; a pressure of the hand suffices to make the thermometer rise or fall. At such moments, at the great moments, one can do anything with France." (*Dans ces moments, dans les grands moments on peut tout faire de la France.*) He then spoke of the relationship between Germany and France. I should no doubt have been told how soon after the end of the war, with its unhappy results for France, he had said in regard to *la revanche* that " one must always think about it and never speak of it." That was still his opinion. People were annoyed with him in Germany for having spoken of the " *Justice Immanente* " of history. It did not follow that a war between France and Germany was unavoidable or even imminent. Smiling, he added " Look at Rome. When the Italians entered the Eternal City through the breach of the Porta Pia, it was generally believed that Pope and King could not live together in the same town. People quoted our good Victor Hugo: ' *Ceci tuera cela.* ' Now you see, Pope and King are living quite peacefully side by side in Rome. They do not love one another, but they do not scratch out each other's eyes. Of course, the Pope hopes that he will live alone again in Rome one of these days. And the Italians hope that he will in the end make complete peace with them. But at present they manage to agree *tant bien que mal.* Between France and Germany many future possibilities are thinkable, many ' *combinazione,* ' as the Italians say.

You know the expression: ' *La France désire la revanche, mais elle veut la Paix.*' The first part of this phrase is only true with reservations, the last is absolutely correct."

The modern Social Democratic movement, whose prophet, Karl Marx, spread Communist doctrines from London, and which was already represented in the German Reichstag by Bebel and Liebknecht, was absolutely repudiated by Gambetta. He had just as little understanding of it as, eighty years earlier, the Jacobins had had of Babeuf, whom they sent to the scaffold. " I deny," Gambetta said to me emphatically, " that there is such a thing as a social question. There are only social questions which one must attack in series, one by one, case by case (*qu'il faut sérier*). At his electorate in Belleville, who had greeted him with whistling and shouts when he propounded this " series " theory in an election speech, he had shouted in a voice of thunder: " You are drunken slaves! But I shall know where to find you in your dirty hovels and to seize you by the throat! "

After Gambetta had asked me to call on him, he shook my hand warmly, and turned to the other guests. Of these he treated General Galliffet with the greatest intimacy, entirely as a personal friend. The Marquis de Galliffet, Gaston Alexandre Auguste Galliffet, not yet fifty at the time, was a brilliant soldier. The musketeers immortalized by Dumas in his tale of the days of Louis XIII must have looked like him, and so must the *Talons rouges* under Louis XIV and Louis XV. He had distinguished himself by surprising bravery, even as a young officer. In Mexico a fragment of shell had torn his body open. He seized the intestines that pressed out beyond the walls of the abdomen with one hand, and forced them back until medical aid arrived. It was said that from that day he wore a silver belt round his middle. He had headed smart cavalry attacks at Reichshofen (Wörth) and particularly at Sedan. When the general in command at Sedan asked him whether he dared lead the regiments once again in the attack, he had replied: " *Tant que vous voudrez, tant qu'il vous plaira, et tant qu'il y aura un homme et un cheval!* " He had distinguished himself later in the fight against the Paris Commune, this time, however, displaying the brutality which is often associated with French heroism. General Galliffet told me himself that evening at Count Roger's, that after the Commune had been suppressed he had given the order to place every insurgent against the wall and shoot him. He had had every workman shot whose hands were blackened with powder. " It is possible that among those shot there were a few whose hands had got black by other means than through powder. But at such moments one cannot be *méticuleux. Il ne faut pas y regarder de trop près.*" To justify his ruthless treatment of the Communists of 1871 Galliffet could cite General Cavaignac, who in 1848 swamped the June rising of the Paris workmen in streams of blood, and yet remained for the French "*un glorieux soldat.*"

The friendship between Gambetta and Galliffet was certainly in no way disturbed by the fact that many of the faithful electorate of the People's Tribune in his old constituency, the *arrondissement Belleville,* had been mown down by command of the Cavalry General in May, 1871. The flexible nature of the Frenchman and especially his admirable patriotism, bridges all political differences, and unites, at the decisive moment, even the bitterest enemies on the common ground of love of country. When the leader for many years of the clerical Legitimists of France, Count de Mun, died, at the beginning of the war, a highly patriotic obituary speech was made at the grave side by Edouard Vaillant, the last surviving "*communard,*" and one of the most brilliant workmen's leaders, though this General of cuirassiers had been highly instrumental in suppressing the Commune in May, 1871. When in the last stage of the Great War, Clemenceau was preaching *guerre jusqu' au bout,* just as Gambetta had in the winter of 1870-71, the most clerical General of the army, Castelnau, was announced. " *Je suis celui qu' on appelle le ' Capucin botté.' Et je viens me mettre entière- ment à votre disposition.*" The Premier, atheist and enemy of the Church *par excellence,* asked: " *Êtes-vous patriote ?*" The General: " *Jusqu' à la mort.*" " *Alors je vous donne l'accolade.*" And they wept in one another's arms, for joy and misery. And we Germans ? Nor did Gambetta when he took over the reins of Government in 1881, hesitate one instant to place the most reac- tionary and monarchistic officer of the French Army, General Miribel, at the head of the General Staff.

During the dinner at Count Roger du Nord's, Gambetta had directed my attention to the deputy, Waldeck-Rousseau. Only thirty-two years old, eight years younger than Gambetta, he was outwardly very different from him, a tall and slight man with a quiet, regular featured and very earnest face, and cold eyes. He was gracefully, even smartly, dressed. On the tribune he was less impressive, using a resonant, rather sharp and incisive voice, that carried far. He spoke, as they so rarely do in France, without gestures, but in the tones of the parade ground. He was never emphatic, though at times sarcastic, slightly supercilious. The Chamber did not impress him in the least. His speeches were short and pregnant, but perfect in their form. When Gambetta introduced us he said to me: " *Ce jeune homme sera un jour la dernière cartouche de la République.*" This prophecy was to be fulfilled. When Waldeck-Rousseau was called to the Government in the summer of 1899, he saved France, brought to the verge of civil war through the Dreyfus affair, and the feeble policy of his predecessors. He did not satisfy entirely either the pro- or anti-Dreyfusites, and this is generally the fate of a sensible policy. But he restored internal peace by pardoning Dreyfus and remitting all the penalties suffered by those implicated along with him. At the same time, in spite of the impassioned resistance of the Right, he passed the law directed against the religious orders, in view of the fact that the six years of Dreyfus troubles had been caused by clerical intrigues. On the day in which he passed this law, in June, 1902, he resigned from the Government, conscious of having piloted the French ship of State through storm and stress safe into port. Two years later he died, not yet fifty-eight years of age, of cancer on the liver.

While Count Roger's other guests treated me with particular friendliness, only one, Senator Scheurer-Kestner, showed a coldness towards the German intruder. But this senator, with his fair hair and blond beard, tall and broad-shouldered, looked exactly like a German himself. He came of the well-known Mülhausen family of industrialists, and was a grandson of the charming Charlotte Buff, who as a girl of twenty had turned the head of our greatest poet. She has been immortalized as Lotte, in the *Sorrows of Werther*. In her human form she married the official, Johann Kestner, and became the grandmother of the Chauvinistic Frenchmen, Senator Scheurer-Kestner, who later fearlessly supported the cause of Dreyfus, and was more French than the French. It is an old trait of the Germans that they develop the most fiery patriotism and are the greatest Nationalists when they have become naturalized in a foreign country.

The kind Count Roger du Nord often invited me to dinner. Each time I met interesting people from whose conversation I learnt, and whose wit rejoiced me. The old Count once made a true and profound remark to me about his Fatherland. "France," he said to me, " *est la fille ainée de l'Eglise et mère de la révolution.*" That is our advantage in foreign policy, since we can play the red or the black card at will. Gambetta was of the opinion that ' we could even play both at once.' Although six years before in his famous speech at Saint-Julien, he had given as the French *mot d'ardre* ' *le cléricalisme, voilà l'ennemi,*' and only a year previously

he proclaimed to the clerical ' *cabinet Broglie*,' in the Chamber that
France would not let herself be ruled by priests, he worked outside
the French frontiers to protect ' *la clientèle catholique de la France.*'
Anti-clericalism, Gambetta decided, is no article for export.   ' But
at home the gulf between revolution and Church has been the main
subject of our party quarrels for the past fifty years, and will still
lead to many a fight.'

Gambetta had kindly asked me to visit him sometimes.   Every
time I did so I left him with the feeling of having spent an enjoyable
and profitable hour with a very notable man.   His opponents
accused him of being superficial and, with particular pleasure, of
ignorance.   He was always being reminded with scorn and horror
how once he had mentioned the French defeat at Crécy as one of
the many French victories and " days of glory," and the slip was
brought up against him with more complacency than intelligence.
In reality, he had not only read a great deal, but stored up the
fruits of his reading in a wonderful memory.   Whenever I went
to see him he asked me a number of questions about Germany
and conditions there, with which he was imperfectly acquainted.
I tried to explain our constitution to him, its intricacies aroused
his astonishment.   He could only understand with difficulty why
Bismarck had not unified Germany in the same fashion as Cavour
and his successors had managed to create united Italy.   He could
see that the German Bundesrat was intended to represent a Conservative element, in contrast to the Reichstag, elected by universal
suffrage.   " *Ah, voilà!   Le Conseil fédéral a les fonctions très utiles
et très nécessaires qu' exerce chez nous le Sénat.*"   But the very complicated relationship between Prussia and the Reich passed his
powers of comprehension.   His whole habit of mind, based on
Latin clarity, " *la clarté latine*," and on abstract French formulæ,
rebelled.   When I told him that the French constitutional arrangements resembled a well-laid-out garden, such as that of André
Lenôtre in Versailles, but that ours were like a German forest,
he replied that he much preferred Lenôtre's garden.   He was
firmly convinced that a centralized country possessed more motive-
power than a federally-organized one.   " *La force de la France
réside dans son unité, dans sa centralisation.   Nous la devons à Richelieu,
le grand cardinal que j' admire par-dessus tout, à son successeur Mazarin,
à Louis XIV qui mérite le surnom ' le Grand ' pour l'énergie avec
laquelle il a maintenu et fortifié l'unité de la France, à la grande Convention, au grand Napoléon.   Tous ils ont centralisé.*"   When I
repeated these observations to Prince Bismarck, he said: " A
centralized country is certainly easier to govern.   Whether such a

centralization is more pleasant for those who are being governed is another question. In any case, it is not possible in Germany. It is contrary to all German usage and predilections, to our virtues and our vices—to our whole history."

When he was discussing this same subject with my father, the Prince said: " The French are more easily governed than the Germans. In spite of all the revolutions in which their temperament finds its outlet from time to time, they have more respect for the authority of the State than we have, more State-consciousness, more sense of statesmanship. The French are not such petty bourgeois as the Germans. Above all, they are more patriotic."

CHAPTER XXXIV

*Marshal MacMahon—His Resignation (29.1.1879)—Jules Grévy—
Bismarck's Attitude towards France—The Three Jules—M. de
Freycinet—The Staff of the German Embassy—Thielmann, Philip
Eulenburg—Friedrich Vitzthum, Nicolaus Wallwitz—The Babylon
on the Seine ?—A Dream.*

I WAS introduced by Prince Hohenlohe to Marshal MacMahon,
President of the Republic. I had met in the forty-eight-year-
old Marquis Gaston Alexandre Galliffet a young and brilliant
cavalry general; in the seventy-year-old Marshal MacMahon I
made the acquaintance of a grim old fire-eater who had already
borne arms under Charles X. He looked magnificent, with his
white pointed Vandyke beard and the deep bronze of twenty years'
service under the African sun of Algiers. A *mot* he had never
uttered had made him celebrated. He is said, on receiving the
order to evacuate the Malakov Tower, which he had taken by
storm (it was undermined and might go up in the air at any minute)
to have answered: " *J'y suis, j'y reste.*" But the Marshal repeatedly
explained that he never said any such thing. " *Je m'exprime
d'habitude plus simplement,*" said the old trooper, " *Les grands mots
ne me vont pas.*" But this really fine phrase, so pregnant in its
heroism and its brevity, became the basis of his brilliant career.
Because of it the French forgave him that march to Sedan which
ended so unfortunately. Through it his name has become historic.

There are sayings which cling to a name for ever. Besides this
" *J'y suis, j'y reste,*" the " *Pæte non dolet* " of the noble Arria to
her husband, Cœcina Pætus, is one of them, and so is the
" *Vorwärts* " of old Blücher, and the " *Hier stehe ich, ich kann nicht
anders* " [1] of Doctor Martin Luther. There are, of course, other
sayings which leave a permanent stain on the character of those
who uttered them. In this category belong the " *Cœur léger* " of
Emile Ollivier, and the " *Fetzen Papier* " (Scrap of Paper) of
Theobald von Bethmann. Though " *j'y suis, j'y reste* " appears to
be apocryphal, some of the more absurd utterances attributed to
MacMahon in Paris seem authentic. To a black cadet at the
Military School at St. Cyr, who was pointed out to him at an

---

[1] " Here I stand and can do no other."

IV.   I I

inspection as peculiarly efficient, he is alleged to have said: " *c'est vous le negre ? Très bien. Continuez, mon ami, continuez!* " It is said that at a naval review at Toulon he gazed long at the Mediterranean and then exclaimed: " *Que d'eau! Que d'eau!* " The remark which caused most amusement was one he made while inspecting a military hospital, at the bed of a typhus patient: " *Fièvre typhoide ? Mauvaise affaire, très mauvaise affaire! Un homme en meurt, ou il reste idiot pour le reste de sa vie. J'en sais quelque chose. J'ai eu la fièvre typhoide en Algérie.* " Such tales as these are also reported of the excellent Grand Duke Alexander of Weimar, who was more cultured than MacMahon, but just as candid.

It was not easy for his Ministers to discuss politics with Marshal MacMahon. One example: Some semi-official Paris newspapers had permitted themselves particularly offensive language towards Germany and the German Government. Prince Hohenlohe had protested to the Foreign Secretary, the Duc Decazes, pointing out that Prince Bismarck would not stand such insults for long. Decazes replied suavely that the Marshal-President would express his regrets to the German Ambassador in person if the latter would do him the honour to be guest in his box at the *Grand Prix de Paris*. And when Hohenlohe accepted the suggestion, the Marshal did, indeed, approach him very solemnly : " *Croyez-moi,*" he said to him, " *Je suis légitimiste dans l'âme. J'ai commencé ma carrière militaire en servant le bon roi Charles X. Ma famille a toujours été fidèle aux Bourbons. Je ne les ai pas oubliés. Mais les difficultés, les nécessités politiques! Il faut marcher lentement, très doucement.*" Prince Hohenlohe did not lose his accustomed calm, but he could not refrain from telling the Duc Decazes that this assurance of the President of the Republic had not quite fulfilled his expectations. " *Le crétin!* " groaned Decazes, " *Il vous a dit ce qu'il devait dire à M. de Carayon-Latour, le chef de ceux qu'on appelle les chevaux légers, le chef du parti des légitimistes purs, qu'il fallait calmer et rassurer. Je suppose que le Maréchal aura exprimé à M. de Carayon-Latour ses regrets pour les attaques que certains journaux dirigent contre le Prince de Bismarck.*"

The worthy Marshal was prone to confusion. When he was created Duke of Magenta on the battlefield, on 4th June 1859, he announced this good news by telegram to his wife and signed " Malakov." In his gratified excitement he had mixed up the tower of Malakov with the battlefield of Magenta. His wife was a member of the old and distinguished family de la Croix de Costries. His eldest son married a Princess d'Orléans. The Marshal's retirement from office was as clumsy as his whole political behaviour. Gambetta, in 1877, had told him bluntly that, if he opposed the desires of the French people to consolidate the republican form of government, he must either, " *se soumettre ou se démettre.*" Instead of choosing one way or the other, the Marshal did both. First he submitted and then he resigned.

Through those interesting weeks during which the Marshal resigned, I acted as chargé d'affaires, although, at the time, I was second secretary to the Embassy. Prince Hohenlohe had gone to Berlin for an investiture, and Herr von Thielmann, the First Secretary, to Nice and the Cote d'azur. On 29th January, 1879, the banker Erlanger sent me a message that he had something interesting to tell me. When I arrived he showed me a letter in which the aide-de-camp of the Marshal-President, the Marquis d'Abzac informed him confidentially that MacMahon would lay down his office as President of the Republic next day. " Wire that immediately to Prince Bismarck. It is a political star-turn." It was very kind of Baron Erlanger to enable me in this way to be the first to transmit this important piece of news. I have said elsewhere how my kind and clever father had pleaded in Frankfurt-on-Main for the admission of Baron Erlanger to the Diplomatic Club although the great Baron Karl von Rothschild had declared that " *en somme* " Erlanger was only " *un misérable juif.*" This shows that kindness does not always go unrewarded even if it seems insignificant.

This news of the resignation of Marshal MacMahon, Duke of Magenta, and his replacement by the lawyer Jules Grèvy was received with satisfaction by Bismarck, who was glad to see this *bona fide* Republican at the head of France. Quite rightly he regarded this change as a significant consolidation of the Republican system of government, on the part of our western neighbour. Only after the resignation of the Marshal in 1879 did the French Republic become a reality. That suited the wishes and policy of Prince Bismarck. He was firmly convinced that a democratic and republican France would be more peaceful than a monarchist one. This estimate was right up to a point, since a republican government in France had less temptation to seek distraction from inner troubles in war abroad. On the other hand the great statesman's expectation that a republican, as opposed to a monarchist France, would be incapable of forming alliances, was not fulfilled. He underestimated the vitality and flexibility of France, as well as the powers of attraction of its brilliant capital for nations and the heads of states. Moreover he laid too much stress on the legitimist principles of European sovereigns. The days of the Holy Alliance were over.

The Prince of Wales was not the mystical Tsar Alexander I, King
Victor Emanuel was not as rigid as Nicholas I. Even the entirely
autocratically disposed Alexander III, who loved neither revolution
nor republic, allied himself with France, though not before Caprivi,
Marschall, and Holstein, with the approval of William II, had
denounced the Re-Insurance Treaty with Russia, concluded by
Bismarck, and, by announcing this step, abruptly and discourteously,
pulled out the corner stone from Bismarck's structure. Even after
the Republic had consolidated itself not only abroad but at home,
the European princes still visited Paris, just as for decades they had
visited the Paris of the Bourbons, and that of Orleans and the
Bonapartes. The heir to the English throne and the Russian
grand dukes set this good, or rather bad, example to everybody else.

If Prince Bismarck had expected that a republican France would
be less dangerous from the military point of view than a monarchist
one that too proved to be an error. Bismarck was judging French
democracy too much by the pattern of our own. He looked at
German democracy, at Schulze-Delitzsch and Rudolf Virchow, at
Johann Jacoby and Waldeck, who felt as pacificists, who detested
everything military in the depths of their souls, and who were
enthusiastic about international fraternity. But French democracy
was differently constituted. And French Socialism very different
from that of Germany, as Millerand, Viviani, Briand, and Albert
Thomas, showed their German comrades during the Great War and
after it. There can be no doubt that Jaurés, upon whom many sentimental Germans had set their hopes, even if he had not been murdered in 1914, would have behaved just as patriotically as his friends
and party comrades. Even Gustave Hervé did not stand back—
he who had declared before the war that the French flag belonged
on the dung heap. Obeying the law of the swinging pendulum he
transformed himself into just such an out-and-out Chauvinist, as
previously he had been a peace-monger. The traditions of French
democracy are chauvinistic, and nationalist. The " Marseillaise " of
which Lamartine said quite rightly " *qu'elle reste gravée à jamais
dans l'âme de la France* " was their lullaby in infancy. Danton had
led the Republican army on Belgian and German battlefields,
Gambetta on the Loire and on the Somme. The army was as dear
to French democracy of all shades of opinion as to every other
Frenchman. Gambetta had said that the army was the last hope,
and must be the first thought, of every good Frenchman. When
Thiers looked over the gold rims of his glasses at the troops parading
past him in June 1871 in Longchamps after the bloody suppression
of the Commune, tears ran down the face of the old patriot—tears

of joy and enthusiasm. These were the troops who had only just returned from German prisons, and in six weeks of a hard siege and fierce street fighting, had overthrown the Socialist rebellion. When, at the end of the Great War, the radical Georges Clemenceau was asked by his admirers what kind of a memorial his grateful country should raise to him after his death he said he would like to be depicted standing at the edge of a trench out of which French soldiers " *les poilus* " are acclaiming him as their leader in a fight " *jusqu'au bout.*"

Prince Bismarck was also mistaken in believing that a Republic in France would be so weakened by inner political dissensions, strikes, and revolutionary unrest, as to be unable to take military action. The French Republic has understood very well how to maintain internal peace with a firm, and if necessary, with a hard hand. Towards strikes it has acted more severely than any German government. After the end of the miners' strike of 1905 the French Ambassador in Berlin, Jules Cambon, expressed his astonishment and his sincere admiration of the fact that this gigantic revolt had been settled without bloodshed. " At home, in France," he added " they nearly always shoot when there's a strike." In this respect one of the most illustrious French statesmen, Adolphe Thiers, had set a good example to his successors. A few years after he himself had taken part in the July revolution against Charles X, he sent, in his capacity of Home Secretary of King Louis Philippe, the workmen of the Lyons quarter, the Croix Rousse and the Rue Transnonain in Paris, who had erected barricades after the pattern of 1830, mercilessly to the scaffold. Seventy years later Clemenceau showed the same flexibility as Adolphe Thiers before him. A strike had broken out in the south of France. As is usual the masters had taken on unorganized workmen when the trade-unionists had " downed tools." Such strike breakers are known in France as " *les Jaunes.*" When it came to skirmishes between strikers and blacklegs the military company which had been ordered to the spot intervened, the commanding officer gave orders to fire and several workmen were shot dead. The officer was himself slightly hurt by a stone. The Premier regarded it as his duty to go and see after matters in person. When he arrived on the spot a workmen's deputation received him and asked him to attend the funeral of the dead comrades. Clemenceau brusquely replied that he did not join in doing honour to law-breakers. Then he demanded to be driven to the hospital where the wounded officer lay. When he arrived, he drew the badge of the Legion of Honour from his pocket, decorated the officer with the " *accolade* "—that is to say, he embraced and kissed him. When, a few days later, these events were mentioned in the French Chamber of Deputies, Clemenceau was reminded of the speeches he had made more than once on behalf of the strikers, in struggles between masters and men. He replied with as much *ésprit* as common-sense: " *Alors j'étais de l'autre coté de la barricade. A présent je suis à la tête du gouvernement et responsable de l'ordre et de l'avenir de la France. J'ai agi en conséquence.*" The French Republicans did not care to offer Germans the spectacle which the drunken Helots gave to Spartan youth.

Ever since it came into being the Third Republic has kept order in France with unshakeable firmness. But this fact did not put Harry Arnim in the right when he maintained to Bismarck that a monarchist France would be better for us than a French Republic. We lived at peace with the French Republic for over forty years, although it did not do us the favour of offering our democratic children an example of how not to do things, and this in spite of the fervid patriotism of the Republicans and even of their quiet hope of revenge. Had our diplomatic leaders been less unskilful, and kept their heads in the tragic July days of 1914, we could have lived still longer at peace with Republican France.

Of the " three Jules " who played a part in France after the war—Jules Simon, Jules Grévy, and Jules Ferry—Grévy was the least important. His outward appearance reminded me of those old Berlin advocates who shine in court by reason of their sound common-sense, calm, and juridical penetration and, in their clubs, by their humour and occasional dry jokes—who don't mind a comfortable game of " *skat* " when politeness demands it, and will, even risk a hand at *L'hombre* with old ladies. Grévy wore, like many of his legal colleagues, white side-whiskers which the French call *favoris*. His upper lip and chin were clean-shaven, his head completely bald. He looked the typical lawyer, and any actor who copied his make-up would have been certain of success. He could have remained President to the end of his days if his son-in-law had not ruined him politically. Many a politician has been wrecked by his wife, many another by his sons, but, as far as I know, Jules Grévy is the only one whom his son-in-law has on his conscience. This son-in-law's name was Daniel Wilson. He was the son of an Englishman; very rich, a man about town, who had purchased the historic castle Chenonceaux where he gave brilliant parties. Chenon--ceaux was even more picturesque and in any case more distinguished than Schwanenwerder near Berlin where, under the Republic, the big men of the Social-Democratic Party were wont to amuse themselves. Wilson was filled with political ambition. He founded a daily paper, *La petite France*, in which he attacked Gambetta and, after his death, Gambetta's friends in the party. He made use of the privilege appertaining to the President alone, of sending not only his own private correspondence but the *Petite France* unstamped. He had received from a shipowner in Le Havre a hundred thousand francs for his newspaper enterprise and obtained the red ribbon of the Legion of Honour for the donor. Jules Grévy, a good *bourgeois* father in every way, had not wanted any separation from his only daughter Alice. But Alice could not part from her beloved Daniel, and so he came and lived under his father-in-law's roof in the Elysée palace, and dragged old Grévy to ruin along with him. Jules Grévy laid down his office in December 1887, three years after I left Paris. He was just eighty years old. He died a year later in his home in the Jura. He had the satisfaction of seeing Gambetta, whom he detested, die before him.

Jules Ferry was not less a simple *bourgeois* than Jules Grévy. He was less attractive than Leon Gambetta, in contrast to whom his nature was rather petty. He came from the east of France, from Saint-Dié in the Vosges department, where his ancestors had been honoured citizens for generations. He was tall, fair, broad-shouldered with angular movements. Gambetta who did not specially care for him, had said of him that had he adopted a military career he would have been a Ney or a Murat. It was difficult to believe that in his youth this serious man had written a satirical brochure which had been the foundation of his rise, and his great political career. The fantastic tales of Hoffmann are better known and more popular in France than at home in Germany. Under the title of " *Les contes fantastiques d'Haussmann* " Ferry, a year after the collapse of the Empire, published a sharp attack against the Seine Prefect, Haussmann, who had modernized Paris under Napoleon III rebuilding on an enormous scale, which led to equally colossal debts. The pun *comptes* (bills) and *contes* (tales) brought Jules Ferry fame in a night. The Tonkin expedition made him for a time the worst hated man in France. When, in 1885, the false news of a heavy French defeat at Lang-Son in north-eastern Tonkin reached Paris, the Premier, Ferry, had to climb a ladder and get over the wall between the Palais Bourbon and the garden of the Foreign Office, to escape the mob who were waiting outside the Chamber of Deputies to tear him in pieces. No French statesman had to suffer more under the stupidity and injustice of the *turba mobilium quiritium* than Jules Ferry. He was accused of an affection for Germany. I myself heard scornful shouts of " Bismarck " directed at Ferry in the street outside the Chamber of Deputies. In reality Jules Ferry was a Chauvinist of the deepest dye. He was one of the founders of the Patriot League. France owes the acquisition of Tonkin and Tunis to him. His enemies declared he had let himself be enticed by Bismarck to Tunis and Tonkin to distract the mind of the people from Alsace-Lorraine, embroil France with Italy, and destroy the French army. In reality he saw further than Bismarck, who hoped to a certain extent that big French colonial acquisitions would console the French for the loss of the three eastern departments. Ferry knew that French thoughts would always return to Strassburg and Metz. But in the meantime, under the benevolent auspices of Germany, he annexed large tracts of land, with a fine future promise.

It was not easy to negotiate with Ferry as I had to do during my period as chargé d'affaires. With every word one felt his intense hatred of Germany. He saw snares everywhere, even where they never existed. But I managed in the end to get on, even with him, by cultivating absolute calm and courtesy and sticking to essentials. Sometimes he would talk quite amiably with me on other subjects than current political affairs. His was a despotic nature and in his heart he despised plain democracy. Fraternity, and in particular international "*Fraternité*," he declared to be a silly phrase, "*Egalité*" to be nonsense, because impossible, and "*Liberté*" only permissible in so far as it did not interfere with the interests of the state. Like Gambetta, he demanded "*une France blindée et cuirassée*," a France secure and armoured, and insisted even in 1885, that the French nation, both at school and by a conscription law of the utmost severity, must be militarized to the very marrow of its bones. His will ended with the words: "I desire to be buried in Saint-Dié, within sight of the blue line of the Vosges (*la ligne bleue des Vosges*) so that I can hear the plaints of Alsace as long as it is severed from France, and its joy when it is again united." From the standpoint of France he deserves the memorials raised to his memory, some by those very same people who attacked and overthrew him during his life—in Tunis, in Haifong, the port of Tonkin, and his birthplace Saint-Dié. His bitterest enemy was Georges Clemenceau who attacked him nearly as viciously as he attacked Gambetta.

If Ferry was the embodiment of a strong and robust eastern Frenchman, Monsieur de Freycinet was a slenderly built, extraordinarily amiable and polite son of the south of France. He was nicknamed "*la souris blanche*" but a firm soul dwelt in his frail body. Throughout the winter of 1870-71, he had been military adviser to Gambetta. As competent a judge as the German military attaché in Paris, Adolf Bülow, told me that Freycinet, an engineer who had never been a soldier, when called upon at the age of barely forty-two, to organize the French defensive, showed greater military capacity under the most difficult circumstances than many highly experienced generals in a less critical position. Relationships between the Embassy and the Freycinets were good. Prince and Princess Hohenlohe associated with the Freycinet family on friendly terms, and the Prince once said, jokingly to me: " We could really build the bridge between France and Germany by arranging a marriage between Phillip-Ernst and Mademoiselle de Freycinet." Phillip-Ernst was the Prince's eldest son. All such small amiabilities did not prevent Freycinet's working with particular zeal to bring about an alliance between France and Russia. That his efforts were successful was not only due to his skill: it was the fault of those at home who did not wish to renew Bismarck's Re-Insurance Treaty.

The First Secretary of our Paris Embassy, when I came to Paris as Second Secretary, was Legationsrat von Thielmann. Bismarck's well-known saying, crude in form but right in substance, that the mating of a Teutonic stallion and a Semitic mare does not always produce bad results, had been in reference to two German diplomats, the attachés Thielmann and Berchem. Both had Jewish mothers, both had the Christian name of Max, both were industrious and fond of their work. Both were rather too zealous, a trifle loud, and not always tactful. Bismarck had said also of them: " Berchem knows everything, but Thielmann knows everything, even better." When Count Berchem in his youth was sent to Stockholm, as chargé d'affaires, he wrote almost daily dispatches about Swedish political events and economic conditions, about the blue lakes and the feudal castles of Sweden, the value of which was not always consonant with their length. Prince Bismarck said: " Berchem seems to think he's discovered Sweden." Baron Thielmann's first aim was to know everything better, and to instruct others. One small incident which occurred in the summer of 1881 between him and the French Foreign Secretary, M. Barthélemy Saint-Hilaire, remains unforgettable. The Ambassador, Prince Hohenlohe, was staying in Aussee, in the Salzkammergut, Thielmann wanted to see Algiers and so, for the period of his absence, introduced me to the French Foreign Secretary, as deputy chargé d'affaires. Barthélemy Saint-Hilaire was already long past seventy. He was a Professor at the Collège de France. He was accounted a distinguished scholar, and was extraordinarily polite and charming. He gave a slightly garrulous description of the great French colony, which the German diplomat was about to visit. At almost every sentence Thielmann, forty years his junior, interrupted, to point out errors in the Minister's colourful but somewhat verbose account. The latter said to him at last: " *J'ai cru vous être agréable en vous faisant part des impressions que j'ai rapportées moi-même de notre belle colonie africaine. Mais comme vous en savez plus long que moi, je n'ai plus rien à vous dire et vous souhaite bon voyage.*"

Thielmann was a great traveller, whose trips through North, Central, and South America, are described in his almost 600 folio size work, *Four Ways Through America.* But he was no diplomat, if by diplomat is to be understood a person who has the art of getting acclimatized in a foreign country, establishing relations, making friends, and thereby gaining influence for himself and enlisting sympathies for his country. In the further course of his career he won for himself the reputation of uncommon capacity in financial and economic questions. But the expectations aroused by his appointment as Secretary of State in the Treasury, in 1897, were not fulfilled. *"Méfiez-vous des spécialistes,"* Thiers used to say.

The Third Secretary of the legation was Count Philip Eulenburg whom I met for the first time in Paris. He was called " Phili " by all his relatives and friends. He was two years older than I, and extraordinarily good-looking. Tall, with fine, somewhat melancholy eyes, and a pleasant, melodious voice, his manners were of the finest, always natural without being either familiar or stiff, so that his bearing was truly aristocratic. His entire personality was of that type which the French call " *Charmeur.*" Intellectually he was a dilettante through and through, in every branch. He despised technique and believed only in inspiration. He was very musical, played the piano, sang, composed, and wrote verse, but all this without taking any model or studying any rules. In a Paris *salon* he asked the great singer, Pauline Viardot-Garcia, in my presence, whether he might play something to her and that " something " one of his own compositions. She listened attentively and said: " *Vous avez un joli talent, mais je vous engage à étudier le contrepoint.*" Phili blenched and said no more. On the way home he poured forth his anger in violent complaints of such stupid criticism. " I shall take care never to study counterpoint," he said, " it would only lame the wings of my genius." Since I am quite unmusical I did not contradict him on this point, but in other fields I have had many a friendly dispute with him. It was especially in the realm of politics that I repudiated the " inspiration " that does away with experience and technique from the outset and considers itself the only method to follow. And in matters of art I quoted Goethe:

" *Natur und Kunst, sie scheinen sich zu fliehen*
Und haben sich, eh man es denkt, gefunden;
Der Widerwille ist auch mir verschwunden,
Und beide scheinen gleich mich anzuziehen.

Es gilt wohl nur ein redliches Bemühen!
Und wenn wir erst in abgemessenen Stunden,
Mit Geist und Fleiss uns an die Kunst gebunden,
Mag frei Natur im Herzen wieder glühen.

So ist's mit aller Bildung auch beschaffen:
Vergebens werden ungebundne Geister
Nach der Vollendung reiner Höhe streben.

Wer Grosses will, muss sich zusammenraffen:
In der Beschränkung zeigt sich erst der Meister,
Und das Gesetz nur kann uns Freiheit geben." [1]

To my sorrow Phili paid no attention to the Goethe I so venerated. He used to say that there was more true poetry in the *Hälmchen
und Gräschen* (Little Blades of Grass) than in all Goethe's epigrams.
The *Hälmchen und Gräschen* was a collection of lyric poems written
by his niece Kalnein, barely eighteen years of age. Eulenburg
placed Josef Maria von Radowitz above Bismarck; Frederick
William II he preferred to old Fritz (Frederick the Great). He did
not like strong characters at all, since these, he had found by experience, were most disagreeable in close contact. But on the other
hand he felt himself to be so soft and weak-willed that he needed
stronger people to lean upon. Our mutual friend, the very gifted

[1] Nature and art may seem to shun each other
And yet, before we think it, they have found each other.
Even my unwillingness has left me
And now both seem to attract me equally

It needs only a real effort,
And if, in hours of concentration,
We have given ourselves, with toil and thought, to art,
Nature may flow untrammelled in our hearts again.

Such is the nature of all training
In vain do half-formed spirits
Strive for the perfection of clear summits.

Who aspires to greatness must concentrate his strength
By limitation the master first reveals himself.
And only law can give perfection.

Karl Dörnberg, who died of diphtheria in St. Petersburg at far too early an age for the good of the diplomatic service and of his country, had given him the nickname of " Philine." Alfred Berger, the witty director of the Hamburg Theatre, who went later to the Vienna *Burg Theater*, compared him to an onion which reveals itself layer upon layer.

I have seldom seen a more charming domestic life than Philip Eulenburg's. His wife adored him. The children looked up to both parents with affectionate admiration. As an official Phili was no use. Thielmann seized upon this fact, first to instruct him, then to badger him and to make his life as unpleasant as possible. So it went on until I pointed out seriously to Thielmann the enormity of his behaviour. My championship of poor Phili laid the foundation of our long years of friendship. If, from the first day he approached me with enthusiastic, charming devotion, he inspired me also with the most congenial feelings. All my life, in my youth as well as in my old age, I have been susceptible to charm and *esprit*. I soon fell under the spell of " Phili " Eulenburg and I have never ceased to respond to it. Next my good and faithful Franz Arenberg, and together with Herbert Bismarck and Friedrich Vitzthum, Philip Eulenburg is, I think, the friend who has been nearest my heart.

In obedience to family tradition Philip had entered the Gardes-du-Corps in Potsdam as an ensign in his early youth. He was little use either as a soldier or an official. But military discipline is more severe than that of bureaucracy. Phili often described his years in Potsdam as the most horrible time of his life. When the Franco-German War broke out his commander left him behind, as unfit for field service, with the reserve squadron. After the submission of Strassburg he succeeded, through his family connections, in getting himself attached to the service of Count Friedrich Alexander von Bismarck-Bohlen, just appointed Governor-General of Alsace. Here, for the first time, he displayed his uncommon gift of knowing how to treat people, and had soon gained an influence over his chief, who obtained for him the Iron Cross, a very rare distinction in those days, although " Phili " had never been at the Front. At the end of the war, with the help of his clever and sensitive mother, who adored her eldest son and who, indeed, was the only feminine being he ever loved passionately, Phili managed to get his father's permission to doff the cuirass of the Gardes-du-Corps and devote himself to a civilian's career. With praiseworthy industry he matriculated at Strassburg several years after he had left school, passed his first law examination, and was entered in the diplomatic service.

His sister Adda, who afterwards married Count Karl Kalnein, had formed a close friendship with Marie Bismarck. He himself made friends with Herbert. With the fine psychological understanding that characterized him he managed things so skilfully during Herbert's conflict with his parents, at the time of his love-affair with the lovely Princess Elizabeth Carolath, that young Bismarck regarded Phili as the only friend who could understand his love, and what he suffered, whereas Prince and Princess Bismarck saw in him the clever mediator, who could persuade their son to renounce his love. Even the poor deserted Elizabeth bore him no grudge since he wrote her such kind and touching letters.

In Paris my lucky star led me into the society of two people of my own age who were to become my life-long friends. Both were Saxons, " native and elected," as Prince Bismarck used laughingly to say of the sprigs of old Saxon nobility. Friedrich Reichsgraf Vitzthum von Eckstädt, heir of the entail Schön-Völkau, Reibitz and Sausedlitz was a nobleman from top to toe. Tall, fair-haired and blue-eyed, he looked a *grand seigneur*, and he was one. He would stoop to none, but was good and kind to everybody. His bearing was as assured on the parquet of court receptions, as when he presided at a meeting of the Chamber or at an agricultural congress. He was my colleague as Embassy secretary in Paris and St. Petersburg, and my subordinate as Secretary of the Legation at Bucharest. When in after years I became Chancellor he was a valuable assistant to my domestic policy, since he was president of the first Saxon Chamber, and Saxon Marshal-General. I have often visited him in his fine castle of Lichtenwalde, so romantically situated on the banks of the Zschopau, on a steep incline. It was from here that Harras, the bold knight, ventured his leap into safety into the grim depths below, as described by Theodor Körner, himself a Saxon:

> " Da hält er auf steiler Felsenwand,
> Hört unten die Wogen brausen.
> Er steht an des Zschopautals schwindelndem Rand
> Und blickt hinunter mit Grausen.
> Aber drüben auf waldigen Bergeshöhn
> Sieht er seine schimmernde Feste stehn,[1]

[1] Then he reins up on the steep wall of rock
Hears the waters roar beneath
Stands on the giddy edge of the Zschopau valley
And looks down with a shudder—
But, over yonder, at the summit of the woody hill
He sees his shimmering castle

Sie blickt ihm freundlich entgegen,
Und sein Herz pocht in lauteren Schlägen.

Und der kühne, grässliche Sprung gelingt,
Ihn beschützen höhre Gewalten;
Wenn auch das Ross zerschmettert versinkt,
Der Ritter ist wohlerhalten;
Und er teilt die Wogen mit kräftiger Hand,
Und die Seinen stehn an des Ufers Rand,
Und begrüssen freudig den Schwimmer—
Gott verlässt den Mutigen nimmer." [1]

Fritz Vitzthum was very popular in his home. In the whole district of Lichtenwalde, right and left of the Zschopau he was called " Our Count." The November Revolution, as will be remembered, took a peculiarly ugly form in Saxony. But nobody attacked the master of Lichtenwalde, even at the time when the " Free State " of Saxony was governed by Comrade Zeigner. And when the Communist Max Hölz was busy in Saxony and, like Schinderhannes, a hundred and twenty years earlier on the Rhine, pillaged castles, mansions, and parsonages, Lichtenwalde remained unharmed.

Count Nicholas Wallwitz was, like Fritz Vitzthum, secretary at the legation in Bucharest when I was at the head of it. Later on as Minister in Teheran, Luxemburg, Hamburg, and Stockholm, he did fine work. Above all he gained a very good position as Minister in Brussels, securing the confidence, both of the Belgian Court and the Belgian Government. Many things might have turned out differently if this conscientious, far-seeing, and skilful diplomat had been left at the important Brussels post. In 1896 Nikolaus Wallwitz married my dear step-daughter, Countess Eugenie Dönhoff. She has been an excellent and understanding wife to him in all his diplomatic posts and is now his most trusty help in the management of their Pomeranian estates in these difficult post-war conditions.

---

[1] Its sight is friendly in his eyes
And his heart thumps loudly.

And the bold, fearful leap succeeds
Higher powers protect him,
What though his steed sinks down shattered
The rider is safe.
And he breasts the stream with a strong hand
His kindred stand on the bank,
Joyfully they welcome the swimmer,
God never forsakes the brave.

After the victorious war of 1870-71 it became the fashion in Germany to speak of Paris as the Babylon by the Seine. This was a gross exaggeration. In all big cities vice gains a foothold and it is uglier in London and New York than in Paris. It is doubtful, in my opinion, whether, in the years preceding the war, Berlin was not more reminiscent of the city of Nabopolassar and Nebuchadnezzar than Paris, where wit and grace redeem the worst aspects of sin. I will not pretend that I lived like a Trappist in Paris. My dear friend, Franz Arenberg, always liked a certain tale of a young French officer who owned up to various transgressions of the sixth commandment in his confession. Although he had confessed two or three such errors the confessor still persisted: "*Est-ce tout? Vraiment tout?*" Whereupon the young man replied: "*Mais, mon père, je ne suis pas venu ici pour me vanter.*" Augustine, great and holy man, closes the description of his sins with the cry "*Felix culpa!*" He was pleased at the greatness of his transgression for it led him to repentance and showed him the illimitable depths of divine mercy and divine love. My feelings after six months in Paris resembled more those of Tannhäuser when he said to Madame Venus:

> "*Euer Minne ist mir worden leid,*
> *Ich hab in meinem Sinne,*
> *O Venus, edle Jungfrau zart,*
> *Ihr seid ein Teufelinne.*" [1]

Since I could not go on a pilgrimage to Rome I sought comfort and consolation with a good and warm-hearted woman, who looked after me with the tenderness of a mother and, at the same time, the devotion of a beloved mistress. Countess D. lived apart from her husband without being actually divorced from him. She was about forty— the woman Balzac has celebrated. She was a woman of the world to her finger tips but not conventional, natural and at the same time distinguished. I compared her often to Madame de Warens which flattered her at first, for she had a high opinion of the genius of the great magician Rousseau. But when, impelled by my comparison, she took up the *Confessions* again, and discovered that Madame de Warens had had intimate relations with her lackey, Claude Anet, that she was not even content with this condition of affairs

---

[1] Love has left in my heart
The sense of slaughter
Fair Venus, methinks,
Thou art Satan's daughter.
(*Tannhäuser* libretto.)

and that Jean-Jacques was proud of being the third in this alliance, she seriously forbade me to make such a comparison. As we had found one another without passion so did we part without pain. My visits to her grew rarer till they ceased, and little by little my correspondence with her ceased too.

Nearly thirty years later I was reminded of her again in a strange manner. It was not long before my resignation from the Chancellorship that I had a strange dream. I dream very seldom. This dream however was as vivid and plastic as those old Homer mentions. Suddenly Countess D. stood before me in the flesh, quite unmistakably. It was her face, her voice, her expression. "*Enfin je vous revois,*" she began in the most natural manner, "*Il y a bien longtemps que nous ne nous sommes plus vus. Pourquoi ne m'avez vous jamais écrit? A moi qui vous aimais bien?*" I replied with some embarrassment, but without shame: "*J'ai eu tort, très-tort, ma chère amie. Mais si vous saviez combien ma vie a été agitée J'etais si occupé. Mais si je ne vous ai pas écrit, je ne vous ai pas oubliée.*" She gave me her hand and disappeared, like the dream figures in Homer, through softly agitated air ἐς πνοιὰς ἀνέμων. When I sat down at my writing table next morning in the Chancellor's palace I took up a writing block and wrote on a quarto page: " Cipher bureau. Please inform me in time of the next royal messenger's journey to Paris as I want to send a letter by him." Before I could carry out my intention of writing my friend a letter, I learnt from a Paris newspaper, which I was reading over my morning tea, that Countess D. had died the night before. Her death, said the paper, left a genuine gap in Paris society, where she had enjoyed much affection and general esteem.

I refrain from all comment, and will only state that I have never had anything to do with spiritualism, somnambulism, clairvoyance, hypnotism, or telepathy, that every form of occultism has always lain quite outside the scope of my experience. For the rest I will point to what Schopenhauer has said in regard to dreams and visions, both in his principal work *The World as Will and Idea* and in his *Parerga and Paralipomena*.

CHAPTER XXXV

The German colony in Paris—Count Guido Henckel-Donnersmarck—
The Païva-Henckel Palace and its guests—" Count " Kessler—Cure
in Ems (July 1879)—Emperor Wilhelm I—Empress Augusta—
Return to Paris—The clerical constitution in France—Jules Ferry
and Paul Bert—Disquieting news of my Father's health—Journey
to Berlin.

THE roving spirit of the German is shown by the fact that for centuries past there have been German colonies in Rome and Paris, in Copenhagen and in London. The German colony in Paris had not at first suffered particularly under the Franco-German War. The police of the Empire let the Germans in Paris fairly well alone. But when, on 4th September 1871, the Republic was proclaimed, many German families were repatriated, and all Germans placed under police supervision. In contrast to the imaginings of naïve Germans, French democracy, from the first Republic, has mostly presented a nationalist and chauvinist aspect towards foreigners. It was, indeed, Gambetta who, in September 1870, insisted that measures taken against the Germans should be carried out with brutal energy. In spite of this a great part of the old German colony came together again in Paris when the war was over.

The best known German in Paris was Count Guido Henckel von Donnersmarck whom Thiers described as " *ce gros banquier allemand qui habite les Champs-Elysées*," and about whom the concierges in the *Avenue des Champs Elysées* would relate that Bismarck, for services rendered, had given him a part of those five milliards which France had had to pay as indemnity to victorious Prussia. Count Guido Henckel was, physically as well as mentally, a man of striking personality. Very tall and broad-shouldered, in those days with a large black beard, of ponderous movements and with sharp eyes, mostly with a sarcastic smile at the corners of his mouth—a man whom all eyes followed when he walked along the boulevards. He embodied strength and did not belie his appearance. Perhaps for this reason he gave the name of " *Kraft* " (strength) to the second son born of his second marriage. A realist through and through, rarely susceptible to sentimental ideas, here and there

humane in his actions, more from a sudden mood rather than from
ethical motives, in general full of scorn for humanity and the individual, he was a not very pleasing type of those masterful employers
who did so much to embitter their employees and thereby to widen
the social breach.   But he was a man of business on the very largest
scale, with one of the clearest and most penetrating heads for
economic affairs I have ever met.   Cecil Rhodes and Pierpont
Morgan were mentally his peers.   To discuss economic questions
with Guido Henckel, or inspect an industrial plant with him, was
instructive in the highest degree.   Albert Ballin, certainly qualified
to judge, said to me more than once, after a conference with Guido
Henckel: " He is the leading industrialist and at the same time the
cleverest banker we have in Germany."   There was only one industrialist whom Ballin regarded as the equal of Count Henckel in
both mind and will-power—Hugo Stinnes.

Count Guido Henckel was forty-eight years old when I came
in closer contact with him in Paris.   He was the son of Count Karl
Lazarus, whom I have mentioned as first commander of the National
Hussar regiment, which fought with honour in the Wars of Liberation, and out of which, later, the King's Hussars were formed.
From the very first Bismarck had thought highly of his capacity.
But there was no really confidential relationship between them as
long as Bismarck was in office.   The great man, who was suspicious,
and forgot with difficulty, bore a secret grudge against Henckel on
account of the intimate relations that had once bound him to Harry
Arnim.   Guido Henckel was one of those who were not always
spoken of kindly in the house of Bismarck before Bismarck's fall.
but who, nevertheless, stood by Bismarck out of office, and remained unswervingly loyal after the overthrow of the Titan.   Guido
Henckel was a life-long friend of Count Alfred Waldersee, the
future Field-Marshal; on the other hand throughout his whole life
he was the object of Holstein's fanatical hatred.   Count Guido,
Baron of Beuthen, heir to four entailed estates, nine freehold
estates in Upper Silesia, eight estates in Russian-Poland, hereditary
cup-bearer of the Duchy of Silesia and hereditary member of the
Prussian House of Lords, would have seemed destined for the stereo-
typed life of a Silesian magnate had he not been drawn out of the
ordinary social rut by the god *Amor*.   The most remarkable thing
about Count Guido Henckel was his wife.   Born of poor Jewish
parents as Sarah Lachmann in Neisse, in 1826, she had been seduced
and deserted in her early youth.   After many vicissitudes in Poland
and Russia she was noticed in Moscow by the French pianist H.,
and taken over from him later by a Russian Prince D., who brought

her to Paris. When the Russian Prince died she became destitute
and lived the miserable life of a street-walker. It was said in Paris
that one evening in the Champs Elysées a *Sergeant de ville*
spoke to her roughly, and even knocked her down with a brutal
shove. As she stumbled miserably to her feet again she is said to
have sworn to herself to build a fine palace to mark the spot of her
direst shame. In any case soon after her deepest degradation, her
luck changed. She met the rich Count Guido Henckel, four years
younger than herself, whom she controlled completely till her death
in 1884. Since neither her family name nor her Christian name
pleased either of them she exchanged the latter for the better sounding " Blanche " (the White, the Pure). At the same time Count
Henckel bribed a ruined Portuguese diplomat to marry her, and so
she became the Marquise Blanche de Païva.

Bismarck who, even before the Franco-Prussian War, had heard
of Count Guido Henckel's capacity, asked him to come to headquarters after Sedan, and told him that he had been chosen for
Metz as soon as this town should have capitulated. Henckel has
often told me that even then, in September 1870, Bismarck had said
to him in confidence that Metz must become a German city. As
Prefect of Metz Henckel cut a good figure. Two years later,
when I was working at the courts of justice and at the prefecture in
Metz, a worthy Metz citizen said to me: " *Le comte Henckel! Ah,
voilà un préfet qui nous plaisait! Il se promenait dans un beau phaéton
qu'il conduisait lui-même. Il avait à côté de lui sa maîtresse, une cocotte
très-chic. En somme, un homme fort distingué.*"

Henckel was summoned to grand headquarters for the armistice
negotiations in Versailles. In contrast to Bleichröder who was of
the opinion that France could at most pay a milliard war indemnity,
Henckel maintained, more accurately, that so rich a country could
afford five milliards with ease. He based this calculation on a brilliantly written memorandum, composed during the night in a few
hours, and with only the Almanach de Gotha, on which to found his
statistics. Certainly his magnificent memory came to his aid.
When Prince Bismarck asked Henckel, after the peace, whether he
would care to be Prussian finance-minister, he refused any official
position whatsoever, with the excuse that he was about to contract
a marriage which would stand in the way of any form of office.

He married, in October 1871 in Paris, the Marquise de Païva
whose Portuguese mock husband meanwhile had shot himself, and
lived with her for thirteen years very happily in the magnificent
palace which Countess Blanche had built for herself in the Avenue
des Champs-Elysées, on the same spot where she had once been so

mishandled by the *Sergeant de ville*. I often dined with Count and Countess Henckel. The numerous and elaborate dishes reminded me of the banquet of Trimalchio, which Petronius describes so well. Conversation at table mostly turned on the food. "*Comment trouvez-vous ce potage?*" one of the guests would ask his neighbour. gravely. And the reply was just as solemn: "*Avant de répondre à une question aussi importante il faut réfléchir mûrement. Ce potage me rappelle un potage que j'ai mangé, il y a bien des années chez le Duc de Morny. Mais l'inoubliable chef de notre ami Morny avait une manière d'assaisonner ses potages que le chef de ce bon Henckel n'a pas encore attrapée.*" And the other would console his neighbour: "*Espérons qu'il y arrivera avec le temps. Et alors ses potages seront aussi parfaits que ceux qu'on mangeait chez Morny.*" I need scarcely say that such a mixture of gluttony and dullness did not particularly please me, and yet there were brilliant people among the guests of Count and Countess Guido Henckel. I am thinking here of Henry de Houssaye, on the staff of the *Journal des Débats* and the *Revue des Deux Mondes*, who had written a fairly good essay on that libertine genius Alcibiades, and later published interesting studies on the *Campagne de France* in the year 1814 and the Battle of Waterloo. He was an intimate friend of the Countess Blanche. She had asked him for a suitable phrase as inscription for the splendid onyx staircase of her palace. Henry de Houssaye improvised immediately: "*Le vice comme la vertu a ses degrés.*" In French the word "*degrés*" means the steps of a stairway as well as grades and nuances in a moral sense.

A frequent guest in the palace was the inventor of modern business journalism, Emile de Girardin, who was more than seventy years old at the time. He boasted of having founded fourteen newspapers during his life, and enumerated these with unction from time to time. He had defended the July monarchy in the Conservative *La Presse*, the second Empire in *Liberté*, Gambetta in the *Défense nationale*, and suggested a federalist re-grouping of France in the *Union francaise*. During my time in Paris he edited *France*. Emile de Girardin had been involved in the most unsavoury stock-exchange speculations. Under Louis Philippe the government had quashed the proceedings pending against him for fraud. As quite a young man he had forced Count Alexander Girardin, the chief huntsman of King Charles X, to recognize him as his natural son, by bringing a case against him which stirred up much scandal. He had once been the husband of a woman who stood morally far above him, the witty and vivacious authoress, Delphine Gay. He had shot that noble idealist, Armand Carrel, in a duel. Carrel had placed himself at the head of Paris journalists who protested against

the July "*ordonnances*" of the Polignac Ministry, and so brought
about the July revolution and July monarchy. It was Girardin's
boast that in every one of his daily leading articles he launched a
perfectly new idea. "*Une idée par jour*" was his motto. In his
bearing, his appearance and conversation, he was cynicism personified.

General Fleury was another interesting personality. As a young
man, having gambled away his fortune, he became a Spahi in
Algiers when he was twenty-two, behaved with gallantry and was
promoted squadron leader. In 1848 he came in close contact with
the then President of the French Republic, Louis Napoléon, who
needed people of his kind. Fleury and Morny prepared the *coup
d'état* of 2nd December 1851 and carried it through with prudence
and energy. Created aide-de-camp of the Emperor, senator and
master of the horse after the proclamation of the Empire, he enjoyed
the full confidence of Napoleon III as well as that of the Empress
Eugenie, whose special favourite he was accounted. Emile de
Girardin once told me in confidence at Henckel's, after he had
drunk a good deal of excellent Château-Margaux, that General
Fleury was really the father of the Prince Imperial. "Fleury," he
added, "is at least a Frenchman, whereas the real father of
Napoleon III was a Dutch admiral." In the autumn of 1869
General Fleury was appointed French Ambassador at St. Petersburg. In this capacity he saw the outbreak of the Franco-Prussian
War, the collapse of France, the thunderbolt of Sedan. I heard in
Paris at the time, and later on from French diplomatic colleagues,
that when Fleury heard these sad news he was speechless at first.
Then he vented his feelings in a military oath which will not bear
repetition, and at last gave his opinion: "*C'est égal! Nous nous
sommes bien amusés.*" This frivolity of the Bonapartist adventurer
was on a par with the *insouciance* with which, as I have already
related, the Austrian cavalier, Prince Richard Metternich, received
the news of his Fatherland's defeat at Königgrätz.

In the midst of her Paris guests Countess Blanche Henckel von
Donnersmarck did the honours. She was terrible to look at.
Monstrously stout and *décolleté* nearly as far as her waist, painted
and powdered, hung with diamond necklaces and ropes of pearls,
she sat there looking like an Indian pagoda. But she was a woman
of high intelligence. She spoke both German and French with a
Yiddish accent, but what she said was worth hearing. It was said,
and I believe with truth, that her husband never began a business
enterprise nor risked a big speculation without consulting the
"Païva," as she was still called in Paris. When the Païva died, in

1884, Count Henckel, as he afterwards told me himself, stood by the bier, laid his hand on the coffin, looked round at the assembled relatives, and said to them: " It is the proudest thought of my whole life that the woman who lies here consented to marry me and was my loving wife for thirteen years." With a sarcastic smile Guido Henckel added: " And all my cousins, nieces, and nephews bowed down before the rich uncle."

If Guido Henckel and his wife were reminiscent of Balzac characters, another member of the German colony in Paris, the Hamburg merchant, Adolf Kessler, was proof of how an obedient husband can climb rung after rung of the social ladder, with his wife's help. There is a delightful poem by Béranger which begins with the words:

> " Mon epouse fait ma gloire,
> Rose a de si jolis yeux."

A fortunate husband tells how he owes his promotion to the friendship of a senator, who would scarcely have noticed him had it not been for his wife's pretty eyes:

> " Quel honneur!
> Quel bonheur!
> Ah! Monsieur le sénateur.
> Je suis votre humble serviteur."

Frau Kessler, who was of Anglo-Indian descent, had, like Béranger's Rose, very pretty eyes. Nothing was more natural than that the courtly aide-de-camp, Count Heinrich Lehndorff, one of the most faithful paladins of our old Kaiser, should pay her every attention, though of course " de la façon la plus convenable," whenever he met her in Ems. He also granted her dearest wish by suggesting that her worthy husband should be ennobled with the prefix " von." But the proverb that appetite comes with eating, applies as much to social life as to food. Frau von Kessler longed to be Countess von Kessler. Nor did she conceal this burning wish from my dear friend Prince Henry XVIII of Reuss when, a year later, again of course, en tout bien et en tout honneur, he paid her his court in this same Ems. He did not manage to procure her the Prussian count's title, but succeeded in persuading his cousin, Prince Henry XIV of Reuss (younger line) to raise Herr von Kessler to the status of count of the principality of Reuss. This had sad results for the German petty princes as a body, who were forthwith forbidden to award any titles in future. The four kingdoms were unanimous in making this decision. But the worthy

Kessler, who had entered life's arena as clerk in the business house of Auffmort, remained " Count " Kessler, of the Reuss- Greiz- Schleiz and Lobenstein house. The only drawback was that outside the realm of the principality of Reuss, with its population of barely a hundred and fifty thousand souls, his title was not recognized— and that Prussia in particular ignored it. This did not prevent the son of the Reuss (younger line) from accrediting Count Kessler abroad in a diplomatic capacity as " Count," under the Republican régime. His mother certainly showed that she could not merely captivate distinguished Germans. Among her later adorers was General Boulanger who, however, preferred in the end Madame de Bonnemain, on whose grave he shot himself in Brussels on 30th September 1891.

In July 1879 I was sent by my excellent Paris doctor, Dr. Monod to Ems, to strengthen my throat, still my *locus minoris resistentiae*, by bathing and drinking the waters. A few days after my arrival there our dear old Kaiser arrived for his usual cure of three weeks duration. Nothing could have been more simple and unassuming than his life and behaviour in Ems. Whoever sat and breakfasted on the so-called " Mushroom," a little terrace opposite the Kurhaus, could see the eighty-two-year-old sovereign at a window of the modest suite he occupied, bent over a pile of documents at the hour of nine in the morning, when he started his day's work. He never raised his eyes from his desk, and would himself open the envelopes of the letters before him, and seal his own. He often made notes. He would cut off the blank pages of any communications and lay them in a drawer for use as scribbling paper. Ems was the only place where the Kaiser wore mufti. He wore a long black frock-coat, a white waistcoat, a tie he tied himself, and light trousers. Every year these trousers led to a little difference of opinion between the Kaiser and his old valet. The valet insisted that a new pair of trousers were necessary. The Kaiser, who was never mean where it was necessary to maintain his personal dignity, and who, where he saw real need, was really generous, would always suggest that the Ems trousers might be turned. He sat at his writing-table till twelve o'clock when he took a little walk on the promenade. In the afternoons he worked again from three to five, sometimes till six, or later. On the promenade he would stop and talk to acquaintances, always pleasant, sometimes with a joke, always perfectly natural, without stiffness or any suggestion of pose, though his bearing was never anything but royal. With ladies he was courtly and gallant without a trace of senile fulsomeness, but acting on the principle of Louis XIV, in all other respects so different a character, that good manners should make a man raise his hat even to a housemaid.

Not long after the Kaiser's arrival I was commanded to dine. After the meal the old gentleman entered into a long conversation with me about French conditions. My father had submitted the dispatch in which I had reported the conversation with Léon Gambetta, already mentioned. The Kaiser, in his kindness, had written a marginal note on the edge of my dispatch: " I congratulate the father of the Paris reporter on the lucid and sound description of his experience." The old gentleman harked back to this dispatch. He asked me a number of questions, to find out what I thought about the general attitude in France, and the possibility of a fresh war with France. His questions were clear and precise, every word bore witness to the finest of those many fine qualities he possessed: sound common-sense. He listened attentively as I developed my view. He never interrupted. When I expressed the basis of French opinion in the words: " *La France désire la revanche, mais elle veut la paix,*" he asked: " And when will the wish be stronger than the will in France, and when will the will follow the wish?" I replied at once: " When we make war with Russia." With a grave face the old Kaiser answered: " That is my opinion also."

During my cure in Ems I was invited to dine one evening with the Empress and Queen, Augusta, who was staying in Coblenz, and who was sixty-eight years old at the time. She was already very bent, but her eyes sparkled with their old fire. It was impossible to hear her speak without thinking of Goethe. In contrast to the Frenchman and the Italian, the German only too often fails to realize the beauty of his native speech. It is at once the profoundest and tenderest of all languages, the unsurpassed medium of philosophy and lyric poetry. The Empress Augusta spoke a noble German such as I imagine Frau Charlotte von Stein must have spoken. What was sometimes criticized as affectated in it, was a sense of form which, half a century earlier, Germans had begun to under-value. She was extraordinarily cultured. Her privy counsellor, my old war comrade, Bodo von dem Knesebeck, collected under her guidance the finest and profoundest thoughts of great writers of all nations and periods—the best anthology I know in German. The Empress gave it as foreword a quotation from Goethe's *Years of Wanderings*: " Great thoughts and a pure heart—that is what we ought to ask of God."

The Empress Augusta had too much tact to criticize my great chief in the presence of a young official in the Foreign Office, and

EMPEROR WILLIAM I AND HIS SISTER, THE GRAND-DUCHESS
ALEXANDRINE VON MECKLENBURG-SCHWERIN, AT EMS

spoke of him with perfect courtesy. But she repeated what she had often said to my father, whom she valued, that in her opinion, even if we regarded France as irreconcilable, we must never forget the *suaviter in modo* towards our neighbour. " Do not let us make the mistake of offending other people's pride—the mistake which did such harm, both to Napoleon I and Nicholas I." Then she went on to speak of the internal policy of Prince Bismarck, which she regarded with even more distrust than his foreign aims. " You must know through your father," she said, " how much I regret these clerical-political entanglements. I have seen their harmful effect only too clearly in the Rhine provinces which are specially dear to me. It is hard for me to understand how a statesman of such genius as Bismarck could first of all introduce universal suffrage, and then cause these religious troubles, which can scarcely end in a success for him. Let us hope it does not come to that with the Socialists too! Many Liberals had serious misgivings about this universal suffrage without any limitation, any precaution, men like Twesten, Gneist, Schultze-Delitzsch, and Sybel. Both Savigny and Windthorst had serious doubts."

In August I returned from Ems to Paris where, in March, the Minister of Education, Jules Ferry, had declared war on the Catholic Church in two decisive pieces of legislation, both of which had been foreshadowed by Gambetta, in the previous autumn. The first of these drafts modified the construction and the powers of the Supreme Educational Council, in an anti-clerical sense. The second deprived the Catholic universities of the right to bestow academic degrees which the pro-clerical bill of 1875 had given them, and reorganized higher education. Free institutions were no longer permitted to use the title of " university " or " faculty," and no member of a non-recognized religious faith was allowed to teach in France. According to the draft of M. Jules Ferry the board of education was, in future, to consist of fifty members, who must all belong to the state-approved teaching body. The clerical element which had hitherto belonged to it—four archbishops or bishops—was eliminated. The application of Par. 7 of the law concerning the freedom of higher education meant that twenty-seven male institutions with a pedagogic body of nearly two thousand members, were no longer permitted to teach in France. Among them were the Jesuits who possessed twenty-seven establishments, with more than eight hundred members of the order. The number of pupils in those eighty-eight houses were computed at seventy thousand. The female establishments which were forbidden too, to teach, numbered annually two hundred thousand schoolgirls. It is natural that the clerical party in France was greatly stirred by these educational laws. The Cardinal of Bordeaux opened the campaign with a long pastoral letter; the Archbishop of Paris followed with a moving appeal to both Chambers, a storm of petitions against the Ferry bills was let loose. In Paris a " General Committee of Petitions for Educational Freedom " was formed.

At a dinner at the Swiss Ambassador's Kern, I made the acquaintance of the deputy, Paul Bert, who had drafted the reports for the Education Bill. My seat at table was next to his. He explained his point of view to me with great vivacity and complete frankness. Prince Bismarck, he said, whose great talents he did not intend to belittle, had manœuvred wrongly in the so-called *Kulturkampf*. He had waged war against the Roman See, against the Bishops, and even against the lower clergy. The Holy See, since the Italians had freed it from the burden of temporal power, was unassailable. " *Le Pape peut se cacher derrière le dos des ministres italiens qui sont aussi fourbes que lui. Aussi Pape et Italie s'entendent comme larrons en foire.*" To shake the Bishops out of their inertia was useless, and the *curés*, nearly all democrats, must be left alone as far as possible. " *Nous ferons la guerre au bon Dieu et nous réussirons.*" The main thing is for the State to get a hold on the schools, and through the schools, on the youth of the country, and its future. Religious instruction must be abolished in the state schools. At most it should be permissible to give religious instruction outside the ordinary curriculum and the school building, by members of the faith in question who, however, would have to obey the orders of the school governors. Only the children of those parents who had sent in a special application should take part in this religious instruction. The members of religious congregations, orders, and associations were to be excluded from the schools, just as much as those ordained in the faith. Members of religious orders should only be allowed to inaugurate and conduct free schools, if they had passed the state examination, and if their order were recognized by the state. Paul Bert finished his exposition by saying that his aim was the abolition of religious instruction and the expulsion of members of religious orders. The last-named were more dangerous to the state than the ordinary cleric. " *Il faut laïciser la France.*" The existence of the Republic and the international position of France were dependent upon this. This goal would not be attained in a day, but at long last, albeit after a difficult struggle. The Republic would accomplish it. The opposition to the schools-bill had not much real significance. It found no support among the masses. " *Chez nous le grand rire de Voltaire a balayé depuis longtemps la superstition. Notre religion à nous sera le patriotisme. Un patriotisme ardent, intransigeant, capable de tous les élans, prêt à tous les sacrifices. Cela vaut mieux que les mômeries des capucins et les impostures des jésuites. La science nous éclaire et nous guide, l'amour de la patrie nous anime, nous vaincrons."*

At the end of August I received a letter, which made me feel very serious, from my mother. She wrote that my father's health was causing her great anxiety. On the advice of the family doctor he had taken a cure of several weeks in Gastein, which had not suited him at all. He suffered from sleeplessness, bad headaches, and, what worried her most, fits of giddiness. My mother asked me to come to Berlin as soon as possible. Having requested leave of absence and obtained it, I arrived in Berlin, where my brother Adolf, who was first lieutenant of the First Lancers at the time, met me at the station. His account confirmed only too surely the fears of my good mother. Professor Wilms, head of the big Bethanien hospital, summoned in consultation on the advice of the family doctor, did not conceal from my brother, in private, his opinion that my father was much in need of a long vacation, after six years of overwork. Professor Wilms had said to my brother: " If you want your father, who is hardly sixty-four years old, to live for another ten or twelve years, you must make him resign from office and live in the country for his health only, far from all politics. If he insists upon staying in office he must take a rest for at least six or eight months." My brother added that so far my father refused to listen to any talk, either of retiring or taking a holiday.

When I saw my father I found him physically much run-down. He looked very pale. He was mentally very clear and composed. There could be no talk of resting, he explained calmly and decisively, since our foreign policy stood at a turning point which might be decisive for the whole fate of our Fatherland and of the rest of the world, for many years to come. " You know," he continued, " that personal relations between Bismarck and Gortchakov have been strained for the past four or five years. The chief fault lies with old Gortchakov, of course, with his senile vanity and his spiteful malice. But our own great helmsman must take some share of the blame. As you saw yourself, he treated Gortchakov too badly at the Berlin Congress. His demonstrative preference for Peter Shuvalov was a mistake in tactics. Violent as he is, Bismarck, to punish Gortchakov, goads on the Russians in all Balkan questions, and that after declaring for fifteen, or, indeed, for five-and-twenty years, that Prussia pursues no active policy, and above all no anti-Russian policy, in the Near East. The good old Kaiser, in his quiet and sensible way, regrets and condemns these temperamental outbreaks of his great Chancellor. But the older he gets the more difficult it is for him to oppose his brilliant and tempestuous adviser. The Kaiser is just about to proceed to the big manœuvres in Königsberg. Since Alexander II happens to be in Warsaw just now, His Majesty has sent Field-Marshal Count Manteuffel there to greet him. I think this is very sensible, since Manteuffel possesses the confidence of both monarchs."

The next day the news arrived that the two Emperors had met in Alexandrovo, a Russian frontier townlet, opposite the Prussian city of Thorn. The meeting passed off well. In a letter to Bismarck, who was taking the cure at Gastein at the time, Kaiser Wilhelm had written in his frank way, among other things: " The Tsar has said that two monarchs can manage to understand one another if Bismarck ' *avec son tempérament fougeux* ' will not always keep picking quarrels with old Gortchakov." He, Kaiser William, had opposed this erroneous view and hoped to have convinced and calmed his nephew. Bismarck, ever suspicious and imaginative, saw in the Imperial letter the proof that on the Russian side they were working to bring about his downfall; that his supposed enemy, Manteuffel, in league with the " enemies of the Reich," Clericals and Democrats, supported such intrigues, and that the old Kaiser was already wavering. His suspicion and wrath were increased by an interview given by Gortchakov at the Hotel de l'Europe in Baden-Baden, his favourite resort in the autumn, to a Frenchman—and a member of the *Soleil* staff at that; that is to say of the press most hated by Bismarck. Gortchakov complained of the attacks launched against him by the German official press—at a man of eighty-one years of age who had directed Russia's foreign policy for the past twenty-four years. A newspaper inspired by Berlin had declared that his policy walked on stilts. Doubtless he, Gortchakov, owed such insults to his friendship for France, which he had never concealed. He had already said to M. Thiers and to Duc Decazes what he would now say again to the present French statesmen: " Be strong! That is indispensable for your own security and for the European balance of power." Gortchakov said further to the Frenchman, that he did not take Prince Bismarck's economic policy, uncomfortable though it was for Russia, amiss, since the Germans had every right, in economic matters, to regard German interests only.

With regard to the meeting at Alexandrovo the Russian Chancellor had said: " The two monarchs love and respect each other very deeply, and this will certainly suffice to overcome many difficulties and so smooth over the slight differences which might arise, here or there."

CHAPTER XXXVI

Preparation for the alliance with Austria-Hungary—Bismarck in Vienna—Opposition of the Kaiser Wilhelm I—My father on the alliance with Austria—Signature by Wilhelm I (15.10.1879): My father's request to resign—Bismarck visits him—Death of my Father in Frankfurt-a.-M. (20.10.1879)—Kaiser Wilhelm's sympathy—Funeral in Berlin—The winter in Paris—At the Hohenlohe's.

THIS, broadly speaking, was the position when Prince Bismarck made the alliance with Austria-Hungary. He operated with the quick and impressive decision in which he surpassed every other monarch and statesman of the nineteenth century, with the sole exception of Napoleon I. After repeated conferences with the Austro-Hungarian foreign secretary, Count Gyula Andrássy, who visited him at Gastein, the German Chancellor went straight to Vienna. The Emperor Francis Joseph interrupted his hunting and received, at the Hofburg, the mighty man who had driven Austria out of Germany, to place on the brows of a Hohenzollern the German Imperial Crown which a Hapsburg had worn for nearly six centuries. After Bismarck had, in Gastein, come to an understanding with Andrássy as to the contents and form of the agreement, the Emperor Francis Joseph signed the treaty, as agreed upon by the two ministers, after a long conference with Bismarck. Only the signature of the German Emperor was now lacking. But it was very hard indeed to obtain it. Wilhelm I, before his departure from Berlin for his annual autumn visit to his daughter, the Grand Duchess Louise in Baden-Baden, had several serious interviews with my father. My father, although physically in very bad health, summoned his last energies together, in truly heroic fashion, to persuade the Emperor of the necessity of signing. My father said to me before he set out to this difficult task:

> Once Bismarck has reached an agreement with Andrássy in Gastein, and asked for and obtained the signature of the Emperor Francis Joseph in Vienna, the matter must be settled. Quite apart from the standpoint of my personal connections with Bismarck which would prevent my leaving my admired and beloved friend in the lurch at this decisive moment, and seen

509

quite objectively—we shall have placed ourselves in an impossible position if Emperor Wilhelm refuses to sign. Bismarck would, of course, resign, and this would lead to unbelievable confusion and agitation all over Germany. What would become of our relations to Austria? We should have thrown over the bride, after a public betrothal, just before the wedding! Russia, annoyed and suspicious, but not really intimidated, would turn against us. And the French! That would be chaos! So we must plunge into the current and hope that our great captain will soon, with his customary skill, steer us into calm waters again.

Firmly resolved to stand by his old friend Bismarck and support him in this difficult hour, my father, with absolute selflessness, though with more inner doubt than ever before as to the wisdom of the path Bismarck had chosen, resolved to follow him along it.

As I sat beside his writing-table my father summed up the position, half in monologue, and half for my benefit. I can endorse every word of his thesis, which has remained in my mind with peculiar vividness:

Bismarck's attack against Russia has been launched *ab irato* and therefore I consider his move towards Austria too abrupt. I say this *sine ira et studio, quorum causas procul habeo*. I stood in the Pan-German movement for many years of my life. Before I came to Berlin in 1867, Prussia was not particularly beloved by me. You will remember that, just two decades ago, in 1859, during the Franco-Austrian War, my heart was entirely with the Austrians. When you, as a little boy in Frankfurt, brought me a special edition with the false news, afterwards contradicted, of a great Austrian victory at Magenta, I gave you a guilder for sheer joy. During the same war Bismarck, as Prussian Ambassador at St. Petersburg, certainly rejoiced sincerely over the Austrian defeats in Lombardy. Your mother always showed a preference for wearing black and yellow at the time. Outside Prussia everybody in Germany was enthusiastic for old Austria, so rich in honours and victories. Four years later the military convention concluded with Russia for co-operative action against the Polish insurrection, was the starting-point of Bismarck's great career, which led us via Königgratz to Versailles. Without benevolent Russian neutrality our victories in 1864, 1866, and particularly 1870-71, would have been impossible. If our official press now tries to prove that Russia, by displaying benevolent neutrality towards us in '66 and '70, was only acting in her own interests, from purely egotistic motives, this is not quite the truth. In any

case it does not apply to the Tsar Alexander II. His fondness
for Prussia can be traced back in great measure to the love and
veneration he bore his uncle, King Wilhelm, to his pious memory
of his dead mother, Princess Charlotte of Prussia, to the memory
of the brotherhood-in-arms of Prussia and Russia from 1813 to
1815, and to the intimate relationship, through many decades,
not only between both dynasties but also between both states.
Bismarck is now purposely ignoring the ties of sentiment which
any practical politician should always take into consideration.
We should remember the personal conduct of Alexander II
during the whole Franco-German War, the hearty congratulations he sent his old uncle after every German victory, the Cross
of St. George which he not only bestowed on his Prussian regiments, but distributed through the whole German army. To
this day every year in Krasnoje-Selo the Tsar toasts the Prussian
Guard and the Tsar-Alexander-Grenadier Guards on the 18th of
August, regardless of the presence of the French military attaché.
The Prussian Guard covered itself with glory at Saint-Privat; to
be colonel of the Tsar-Alexander-Grenadier Guards is the pride
of his life. I repeat that I consider it right to be friends with
Austria, but I could have wished it to be done in a less spectacular
way. Now, it is precisely the man of genius whose mistakes are
as excessive as his merits. *L'homme a les défauts de ses qualités.*
Bismarck lets himself be so carried away by his wrath as to
believe that Alexander II, prompted by Manteuffel, has been
trying to blacken him in the eyes of William I and, to some extent,
actually succeeded. As though our good old Emperor were not
loyalty itself towards his great Chancellor!

To overcome the Emperor's opposition to the alliance with
Austria the Vice-President of the State Ministry, Count, afterwards
Prince, Otto zu Stolberg-Wernigerode, was sent to Baden-Baden.
Stolberg, who, as I have already related, was a kind chief to me in
Vienna, and later till his early death, a very kind friend and patron,
often told me how difficult it had been for him to overcome the last
scruples of the old Emperor. In his excitement the old man,
usually so calm and collected, once banged so hard upon the table
that the ink spurted up out of the ink-pot. In a touching manner
the good old Emperor recalled all the many dear memories, which
bound him with Russia; the friendship of both his parents for
Alexander I, his own life-long friendship for Nicholas I, the faithful
affection which his nephew Alexander II had always shown him.
Yet at the same time he would insist that his objections to so swift

and so unexpected a change of our policy were certainly not merely due to sentimental reminiscences, nor indeed to any feelings whatsoever. " On the whole, and *tout bien pesé*, we have always been wise to keep friends with Russia," the Emperor repeated several times. And Stolberg added: " In spite of all my friendship for Austria where I was very happy as ambassador, I could not rid myself of a feeling that a wisdom, ripened by sixty years of experience, spoke in his words." At last, on 15th October, William I signed the agreement with Austria. Shortly after having signed he said bitterly to his faithful aide-de-camp, Count Heinrich Lehndorff. " When I think of my brother-in-law Nicholas, of my sister Charlotte, of Tauroggen, Kalisch and Breslau, of Möckern, Gross-Görschen, Bautzen, Kulm and the Battle of Nations at Leipzig—when I think of all that, I feel like a traitor."

Acting on his principle that, when necessary, all dogs must bark, Prince Bismarck, to break down the opposition of the old Emperor, had organized a mighty press campaign. I worked in the special press-department organized for this purpose, which Radowitz conducted. The aim of this campaign was neither to intimidate the Russians nor please the Austrians. It was to give the old Emperor the impression that the whole country, from Meuse to Memel, wished the alliance with Austria, and approved it. To this effect we, Radowitz, little Professor Aegidi, the intelligent Legation Secretary Rudolf Lindau and I, composed " letters to the editor," emanating from all parts of Germany, which were submitted to the Emperor as expressions of public feeling. For all his common-sense and sagacity, his cleverness and perception in many matters, William I was almost naïve when it came to the modern press-campaign and publicity nonsense. He really believed he was listening to the voice of the people when this manufactured correspondence was laid before him. When we headed them as coming from the Rhine we expressed our dire forebodings that should the treaty not be achieved the green Rhine waters might not be secure from French attacks, and this caused alarm from Mannheim to Düsseldorf. In other letters, purporting to come from Munich, Stuttgart, and Dresden, the ancient sympathies of the Bavarians, Swabians, and Saxons for the Danube-Germans were recalled; in "messages" from the provinces of Eastern Prussia, we painted the " Cossack" menace in grimly realistic colours. The mastery with which this press-storm was organized showed Bismarck's iron hand in the velvet glove.

No sooner had the Emperor signed than my father summoned me, and told me to hand over his personal application to resign to Prince Bismarck, whom he had requested by telegram to receive me.

The Prince welcomed me in his study which was later to serve myself and my wife for nine years as our dining-room. He told me to sit down opposite him. I, the scarcely thirty-year-old Legation Secretary, sat and watched him—tall, broad-shouldered, with his heavy bushy moustache and bushy eyebrows, his wide, severe, penetrating eyes, the greatest German statesman of the nineteenth century, one of the greatest statesmen of all times, the mighty man of genius. When he had carefully read my father's request to resign, on the grounds of ill-health, he handed it back to me: " There can be no question of your father's resigning," he said, " not even of leave of absence for more than three months. Your father is indispensable to me." With all a son's anxiety, I answered, more emphatically and excitedly than I should have done: " Your Highness, my father cannot and must not, remain in office. His life is at stake. I have promised my mother to be firm." For a moment the Prince looked at me with astonished, rather angry eyes. The corners of his mouth twitched. I faced his wrathful gaze and repeated: " My father must get out of the treadmill, at least for this whole winter. I promised my mother not to come back till I had accomplished that."

The Chancellor's expression changed. His eyes grew kind, almost soft: " It does you all honour, Herr von Bülow," he said to me, " that you uphold your mother's wishes so steadfastly. Please give her my regards. But now think of me and my position! As successor to your father only two diplomats are in question, Radowitz and Paul Hatzfeldt." He criticized both very sharply, almost too sharply. I am modifying the expressions he actually used. Bismarck has said himself that his sense of gratitude was poor, and his tendency to blame, strongly developed. " Radowitz," he said, " is untrustworthy. Nobody has ever known where his father came from—whether he was a Wallachian, Slovakian, or Hungarian Jew. Anyway, Radowitz *père* was pupil in a French military academy and fought at Leipzig on the French side. Later he managed to worm his way into the good graces of Frederick William IV, who, like his grandfather, Frederick William II, had a weakness for adventurers. Our present Radowitz has a drop of decent blood in his veins through his Prussian mother, a Voss. He grew up in more settled circumstances than his father, but there is no depending on him." (He spoke more strongly.) " He has no fortune, and has a Russian wife, flighty and *mondaine*. He is a good worker, but he has no head for politics. Paul Hatzfeldt has a head for politics. But on the other hand he is ignorant and lazy. He lacks principle. If you want to see the lack of principle expressed in a human face, look at Paul

Hatzfeldt." The Prince was silent again; then he continued. " When you are older, Herr von Bülow, you will see how few people can be both intelligent and decent. The good people are generally fools, and the clever are often worthless. Your father is both clever and skilful, a man of honour and at the same time a nobleman through and through. That is why I find it so hard to dispense with him." The Prince dismissed me with the remark that he intended to visit my father shortly in Potsdam. He would telegraph the hour of his arrival. He did not want to be fetched from the station and would only see my father in my mother's presence. He promised not to tire or excite him.

Next day the Prince drove on the Pfingstberg at Potsdam, up to the villa where my parents lived at this time of the year. He was unaccompanied. He went straight up to the room where my father was lying in bed. He embraced and kissed him and began to talk to him and to my mother, who was sitting at the foot of the bed, reviving memories of their time together in Frankfurt on which, he said, he looked back very much as Adam and Eve must have looked back on their lost Paradise. " In those days we were young and happy, now we are old and irritable—at least I am." He told my father that he could not possibly pass on his application to the Emperor, or support it. His Majesty would not accept it. " He thinks as much of you as I do. That is to say a great deal. Go away on indefinite sick-leave and stay away as long as is necessary. You know how glad we shall all be when you come back again." Again he embraced my father and kissed him on both cheeks, kissed my mother's hand, and left the house. On his return to Berlin he invited me to dinner. With the naturalness that never deserted him he told me he never remembered having paid a sick-call in all the time he had been in office, except to a member of his own family. " Certainly never to any colleagues! " He found my father better than he had feared. He was full of hope for him, and certain that he would return from Cannes, where he intended to recuperate, perfectly cured, to his and our relief. The next day my father took the sacrament from the hands of General Superintendent Büchsel, our friend since we had moved to Berlin.

On 17th October my father travelled with my mother, my youngest brother Fritz, then fourteen years old, and myself, to Frankfort, where we intended to spend the night before proceeding further to Cannes. Of all our Berlin friends and acquaintance only one came to the station to see us off, the deputy, Edouard Lasker. My father shook his hand with the words: " I am so touched and pleased that it should be you, our lives have lain so far apart."

Lasker answered simply and cordially: " I always respected your Excellency, and I wanted to show this by coming here to wish you a pleasant journey and a happy return. What binds us is stronger than that which separated us."

On the journey to Frankfort my father dozed a great deal though, in the intervals, he talked with my mother and myself as clearly and lucidly as he ever had. He said to me: " Much which has pre-occupied me, or even grieved me, during my life seems to me to-day to be insignificant compared with the one thing necessary— the thing which our Lord Jesus Christ impressed upon Martha." My mother smiled sadly: my father had often compared her to Martha, who had many burdens. " One thing is necessary," repeated my father several times, " that the will should submit and love grow zealous and pure." Before we reached Frankfort my father asked me to buy a really handsome bouquet for my mother, at a flower shop which he remembered from his Frankfort days, since the next day, 18th October, would be her birthday.

He had a stroke that same night. When we reached his bedside he was unconscious and speechless already. The doctor, hastily summoned, declared his condition to be hopeless. My father did not appear to suffer. Nor did he die till the early morning of 20th October. The expression on his face was peaceful, the high and finely-domed forehead stood out powerfully. My mother closed his eyes. Next day the following letter, written by the Emperor in person, arrived from Baden-Baden:

> Apart from yourself, my dear madam, and your family, nobody, I believe, in Prussia, has more right to mourn your husband than I. I regret his loss most sincerely—and since I cannot express to you what it means to me, what must you and yours be feeling! Not only have I lost a statesman; I have lost a friend, who possessed my entire confidence, and who always, with rare devotion and perfect tact, could choose the right course, and follow it resolutely. It is not easy to replace so many good qualities, all united in a single person, and at my great age such losses are hard to bear. May God help you sustain the heavy blow with resignation. Though sympathy may ease your pain the Almighty alone can heal your wounds.
>
> Your deeply moved,
> KING WILLIAM.

Soon afterwards I received the following telegram from Prince Bismarck:

von Bülow, Secretary of the Legation: Have read your telegram with deep pain. I beg you to convey my heart-felt sympathy to your mother. Next to you and yours the loss hits me worst, personally and officially.

von Bismarck.

Later, in memory of his great father, Herbert Bismarck gave me the original of this telegram, written in Bismarck's own hand.

In the course of the afternoon I received a wire from the aide-de-camp, Count Lehndorff, from Baden-Baden, in which I was informed that the Emperor would pass through Frankfort on his way to Berlin, between twelve and one that night and, during the ten minute stop, would receive me in his compartment. The Commander of Frankfort, General von Loucadou, called for me at midnight to take me to the station. When the royal train came in Count Lehndorff approached me and said: " The Emperor is expecting you in his carriage. He has sat up on purpose, because he especially wants to express, in person, his deep sympathy with you, your mother, and brothers. Get into the train."

The Emperor gave me his hand. In the days which followed upon my father's death I received many proofs of sympathy. But nobody spoke so heartily, so kindly, so simply and yet so royally to me, as did our old gentleman. He praised again the distinguished official and personal characteristics of my father, his strict attention to duty and warm heart, the firmness of his principles, his conciliatory and well-balanced character. When the train's approaching departure was announced to him he said: " Always keep your father's example before your eyes and walk in his ways, and all will be well with you."

Three days later the memorial service for my father took place in St. Matthew's Church, which my parents had attended ever since they came to Berlin. The Emperor was there and all the princes of the royal house. My brother Adolf and I awaited His Majesty in the porch. We were asked to sit next to the royal princes. Prince Karl, who belonged to a generation which insisted on military correctness, said to me as he pointed to his son, the brilliant Prince Friedrich Karl, " He hasn't got his proper boots on again." The Commander of my brother Adolf's regiment, the highly influential Count Alfred Schlieffen, later chief of general staff, was also present. I can still see him in front of me with his severe and thoughtful face, with the monocle. When the Emperor arrived he went straight to my mother, kissed her hand, and took his seat beside her. The memorial service, read by General-Superintendent Büchsel, went straight to my heart and consoled me. His address was inspired by that steady faith which transcends human sorrow, and points to a place where all tears are dried. " Do not weep, dear Frau von Bülow," he said, turning to my mother—this true shepherd who as a village pastor of the Marches, had filled his office so nobly before he was made General Superintendent: " Why need you weep? While you are weeping here your dear husband from above is looking down on you lovingly. He is far happier than we on earth."

When I had helped my mother move house to Potsdam, where she now intended to live permanently, I returned to my Paris post. Before I left she had a message from her uncle, Count Wilhelm Redern, the Lord High Chamberlain, who informed her on behalf of His Majesty, the King and Emperor, that, in memory of her husband, her second son, Adolf von Bülow, first lieutenant in the First Guard Lancers, had been nominated personal aide-de-camp of Prince Wilhelm of Prussia, the future wearer of the Prussian crown.

When I arrived in Paris my chief, Prince Hohenlohe, asked me, with his usual kindness, to stay with him at the Embassy since, doubtless, I desired during my mourning, to live quietly and not to be worried, and this would be much easier under his roof. His mother-in-law, Princess Léonville Wittgenstein was staying with him and his youngest son, Prince Alexander, who was then seventeen years old. I look back with pleasure on those quiet evenings in the winter of 1879-80 which I spent there. Princess Léonille, the second wife of Prince Ludwig zu Sayn-Wittgenstein, was a woman of distinction. A Russian by birth, a Princess Bariatinski, she had turned to the Catholic Church from inner conviction, and clung to it with fervour though without any narrowness or bigotry. To her death in 1918, at the age of 103, she remained my kind friend and patroness.

Another guest of Prince Chlodwig Hohenlohe during this winter was his former official, Baron von Völderndorff, an unusually cultured and intelligent man, who possessed literary tastes and had written a number of interesting historical essays. We would often go for walks in the Champs-Elysées. Once as we crossed the Place de la Concorde we discussed the domestic situation in Germany and the difficulties encountered by even so great a statesman as Prince Bismarck in dealing with the stupidity and the pettiness of the German parties. " But what is to become of us soon, when Prince Bismarck is no longer there? " I asked. Baron Völderndorff replied that the destiny of an ever expanding population of over forty millions must not be determined by one man, even though that man were so great and possessed of so much genius as our Bismarck. "But who is to replace him?" I asked. "I see nobody." Völderndorff answered that nobody could, or would, replace Bismarck. But we must learn to do without such a Titan. If, before long, the great misfortune should befall us of losing Bismarck, Prince Chlodwig Hohenlohe would be the right successor. At the moment we reached the Pont de la Concorde Baron Völderndorff continued, after a pause: "And I know of another successor, not for to-day, but in twenty years time. Yourself." I replied: "Till now I thought you a good kind-hearted man. But now you remind me of the witches in Macbeth. ' Hail to thee, Thane of Glamis! Hail to thee, Thane of Cawdor! ' " He smiled, but still maintained his opinion. Alexander Hohenlohe told me later that, soon after my arrival in Paris, his father had said to him: "Keep an eye on young von Bülow, he may be Chancellor some day."

On 14th July 1880, the day on which, ninety-one years earlier, the Bastille had been stormed, and which was declared a national holiday after the final victory of the Republican constitution, a great parade took place in the Bois de Boulogne. The President of the Republic gave new flags to the representatives of every regiment that had fought on the field of Longchamps. Inscribed on them were the names of victories won by the French Army: Rocroy, Fontenay, Valmy, Jemappes, Arcole, Rivoli, Marengo, Austerlitz, Jena, Wagram, Isly, Inkermann, Magenta, Solferino, Puebla. Thus was the consciousness of its great military tradition kept alive in the French people, as the duty of every patriotic, intelligent, and resolute government proscribes. I was present at the magnificent spectacle in the President's box. The troops marched past in good order. The enthusiasm of the thousands of onlookers was indescribable. Certainly France desired peace, henceforward as before, but the proud spirit of a people, nationalistic and chauvinistic to the marrow, had re-asserted itself after the disorders of the *année terrible*, and Frenchmen gazed with love and boundless confidence on their army.

Gambetta expressed this sentiment when he declared, at the brilliant naval parade which took place in August at Cherbourg, that the passionate enthusiasm of the French people for its army, the incorporated strength of the whole nation and recruited from its purest blood, sprang from the need to reinstate France in her former great place in the world. This speech was not ignored in Germany. Emperor William I, never given to flamboyant speeches, but who would not tolerate them in others, made a speech to the army on 2nd September, 1880, the tenth anniversary of Sedan, very effective in its calm dignity. He gave praise to the French for the excellent qualities of their army but warmly thanked the men who had led our German soldiers in the glorious days of 1870-71, at the same time recalling the memory of those whose lives had secured us victory. His last thought, he said, would be for the army. Let it always remember that great successes can only be obtained so long as soldiers remain true to the dictates of honour and duty, always keeping the strictest discipline, never slackening their preparation for war, nor disregarding any detail of training that could give a sound foundation to the whole structure.

On 10th November, 1881, after a debate which had criticized the Tunis expedition, the Premier, Jules Ferry, resigned. The President of the Republic, Jules Grévy, entrusted Gambetta with the formation of a new cabinet. Gambetta followed these instructions, like Schiller's princess dowager of Messina, obeying necessity rather than personal inclination. He would have preferred to have held back a little longer. But he felt that in view of the growing dissatisfaction with his secret dictatorship (*gouvernement occulte*) no other choice remained to him than to come forward to the footlights. Everybody expected a great cabinet (*le grand ministère*). But he did not succeed in forming one, since none of the outstanding politicians to whom he turned, Jules Ferry and Léon Say, Henri Brisson and René Goblet, Humbert and Tirard, showed any disposition to join forces with him. Even Freycinet, his trusted coadjutor in the government of national defence, refused him. So with quick decision he formed a cabinet of his personal friends. Waldeck-Rousseau became Minister of the Interior, Rouvier, so often mentioned in later years, of Commercial and Colonial Affairs; Gambetta himself took over the Foreign Secretaryship, together with the Chancellorship. As Under-Secretary of State he nominated one of his intimates, Eugen Spuller. This was the son of an immigrant from Baden, but born on the Côte d'Or, where the best Burgundy grows, and so a Frenchman of the deepest and most chauvinist dye. That did not prevent the opposition scoffing at the " Badener " and suspecting him. As his Chief of Cabinet, Gambetta chose Herr Joseph Reinach, the son of Jewish parents and born in Frankfort but who, on settling in France, developed such passionate nationalism as is still displayed by him to this day.

Shortly after forming the new cabinet the German Embassy gave a big dinner in Gambetta's honour. The new Premier greeted me with his old friendliness. He looked tired and worn. Henri Rochefort, who had once fought shoulder to shoulder with Gambetta against the Second Empire, was now his bitter enemy. He had so libelled the resident governor Rousten, sent by Gambetta to Tunis, that this official was forced to bring a suit against him. At the trial much of an unpleasant nature came to light, and this led to fresh attacks on Gambetta. When he took me aside after dinner he said to me: " You see how infamously I am attacked and by what low creatures! " With a melancholy smile he added: " I once prophesied to you, my young friend, that you might one day stand at the head of your country's government. Should this ever happen never forget that politics are a dirty business, and that one cannot think badly enough of most politicians, especially if they are parliamentarians." When Prince Hohenlohe asked me next day what impression I had received of Gambetta I answered: " *Il a du plomb dans l'aile.*"

France is a country where, since Voltaire, Beaumarchais and Paul Louis Courier, good epigrams have played a large and sometimes a devastating part in politics. Since he had been Minister Gambetta had been made the target of many bad, but some excellent, and in any case, poisonous verbal arrows. One has stuck vividly in my memory. In a lively session of the Chamber the Minister of Defence, Campenon, wished to make a speech at a moment which seemed inopportune to Gambetta. To prevent his colleague speaking Gambetta laid his hand on his shoulder. A Socialist called out to the Minister of Defence: " *Obéissez à César.*" When he was called to order for this remark he said: " *Je retire César et je mets Vitellius.*" Since that day Gambetta was called Vitellius by the opposition-press, in reference to the most unworthy of all Roman Cæsars, notorious for his reputation as a *debauché*.

The German democrat likes to ape the " man of the people " by his uncouth manners, and sometimes his intolerable vulgarity. In contrast to this the democrats of Rome and England have always had the tendency to emulate the manners of good society, its customs and, now and then, the more presentable of its passions. Gambetta, who had coined the words " *République Athénienne,*" wished, by his way of life, to remind people of Pericles rather than Cleon. In a country which prides itself on being the home of Brillat-Savarin, and of the most sophisticated cooking, he laid stress on having a good cook. The name of this cook was Trompette. In many articles and caricatures Trompette was made bitter fun of, as the " body-cook " of the former Tribune of the People.

On 26th January, 1882, the Chamber voted against Gambetta's proposed revision of the Constitution. At once Gambetta resigned and Grévy entrusted Freycinet with the formation of the government. He constructed a cabinet in which Léon Say, Jules Ferry, and Humbert took office, who had not wanted to bow down before Gambetta. The coalition which overthrew Gambetta was led by Clemenceau, who had contrived a *rapprochement* to this end between the extreme Left and Right. Freycinet who, not without intention, adopted a manner in marked contrast to Gambetta's haughtiness, made his bow to the Chamber with a humble speech in which he declared that the new government was full of "*déférence*" for the People's representatives, without whom they could do nothing.

A few weeks after his fall Gambetta asked me to come and see him. I found him far more cheerful and looking much better than he had as a Minister at that dinner at the German Embassy. He said with a smile: " It is nice of you to come and see a dead man. But I am only in a trance. I am thinking of acting like Lazarus who arose from his grave to the great astonishment of his sisters, Martha and Mary. I am only forty-four years old. The future lies before me." Thus Gambetta in March 1882. Victor Hugo has said: " *L'avenir est à Dieu.*" Léon Gambetta had not included that " *Media in vita* " in his calculations. He lived scarcely a year after his fall. In the middle of December 1882 he died of a wound, self-inflicted, in his modest little country house in Ville d'Avray, near Paris. All sorts of fairy tales are circulating even to-day about this accident. The real facts, as told me by several friends after his death, are much less romantic. Their stories are identical in substance. For over ten years Gambetta had loved a charming and clever woman, Madame Léonie Léon, who had been separated from her husband for a long time. She had fallen in love with Gambetta on hearing his impassioned speech against the Plebiscite, from the gallery of the *Corps législatif*. Gambetta would gladly have married her. But as a Catholic she did not want to marry a second time before her first marriage had been dissolved by the Papal Chair, and this seemed impossible. While Gambetta was walking in his garden with Madame Léon, a small revolver, which he was holding in his hand, went off without any movement on either his or her part. The bullet penetrated the palm of his hand and the lower arm. While he was keeping his bed because of this accident a chronic inflammation of the appendix from which he had suffered for years past, entered an acute stage. The abscess broke and led to peritonitis and so to his death. A surgical operation at the right moment could have saved his life as the doctors told me at once. He died on New Year's night, 1883.

The memorial service took place on 7th January. I have seldom seen a more imposing demonstration. Here, too, as at the funeral

of poor Werther in Goethe's immortal romance, there followed no
priest, but hundreds of thousands of mourners of all parties and all
social grades.   Immediately behind the coffin there walked Paul
Déroulède, President of the League of Patriots and author of
Chants d'un soldat.   He waved his arms excitedly and shouted
" *Quand même! Quand même! Vive Strasbourg! Vive la revanche!* "
The burial could not take place in Paris, since Gambetta, *père*,
an *emigré* from Genoa to France insisted that the mortal remains of
his great son should find their last resting-place in Nice.   A national
monument to Gambetta the patriot, leader of the *Résistance à
l'outrance*, prolonger of the war of 1870, was raised in front of the
Louvre, built by Charles V, the Wise, the old citadel of the French
rulers, added to by François I, Henri IV, Louis XIV, Napoleon I
and III, and so intimately connected with French history.   It is a
full-length statue with head thrown fiercely back and hair waving in
the breeze.   The stiffly outstretched hand points to a far-off goal.
It points to Strasbourg and the Rhine.

CHAPTER XXXVII

France's former reigning families—The houses of Bonaparte and Orléans—The Duke of Aumale—Espionage—The Corps Diplomatique—Monsignor Czaki—The Prince of Wales in Paris.

DURING my period of office in Paris the members of France's former reigning families had not yet been forbidden to live in their country. One did not notice much of the house of Bonaparte. The Prince Impérial, once called " Lulu " by his father's enemies, had succumbed miserably in South Africa, at the age of barely twenty-three, in a skirmish with the natives. His mother, the Empress Eugénie, overcame her feelings and visited Paris every spring, staying in an hotel from which she could look out on the spot where once the Tuileries had stood, and where her son had played merrily as a boy. She lived to see the Great War and a year before this visited my mother-in-law, Donna Laura Minghetti, in her home, the Villa Mezzaratta, near Bologna. They had never met since the outbreak of the Franco-German War in July 1870. When the two old friends met again after so many great events the Empress burst into tears and sobbed aloud. She had buried the strongest, the only hope of her house, since the other living Bonapartes gave little promise for the future.

After the death of poor " Lulu," Prince Jérôme Napoléon, " *Plon-Plon* " had become head of the house of Bonaparte. By his freethinking attitude and even more by the cynicism with which he paraded his godlessness, he had become the *bête noir* of all religious circles in Paris who, in the France of forty years ago, exercised more influence than to-day. His scandalous private life only served to increase the general disgust which his cowardice in every French war, the Crimean, the Franco-Austrian, and the Franco-German, had occasioned among all classes and political parties. But " *Plon-Plon* " was by no means lacking in brains. I met him several times. Outwardly, at least, he had an unmistakeable likeness to his great-uncle, and was not without a trace of his genius. Herbert Bismarck recognized this when he met " *Plon-Plon* " at the house of my mother-in-law in Rome, in the winter of 1892-3. The son of Prince Jérôme Napoleon, Prince Victor, born in 1862, had the reputation of being a fool. As late as 1848 the illimitable prestige of the name Napoleon had made possible the reconstruction of the Empire under the fantastic and weak Napoleon III. Thirty years later the dynasty of the great Corsican, as far as human estimates may be trusted, had vanished for ever from the scene.

In contrast to this the Orléans family appeared in the first half of the 'eighties to have a better chance of returning to power. It lived undisturbed in Paris, and I often met members of it socially. The head of the house, the Count of Paris, scarcely forty at the time, took more after his mother, a Mecklenburg princess, than after his French father, the brilliant Duke Ferdinand of Orléans, who lost his life in a carriage accident in 1842. The Count of Paris made an impression of solidity and culture, but not in any way of brilliance. He lacked the frills which the Frenchmen love. His brother, Duke Robert of Chartres, reminded one more of the ancestor Henri IV *qui fit le diable à quatre*. The Duke had the reputation of a *bon vivant*, had borne himself well, under an assumed name, in the war of 1870-71, as a private soldier and, during my time in Paris, commanded a regiment of cavalry as a plain colonel. Duke Louis of Nemours was deaf as a post and quite immersed in Brazilian interests since his son, the Count of Eu, had married the daughter and heiress of the Emperor Pedro II of Brazil. The same was true of Prince François de Joinville who had also married a Brazilian princess. Duke Antoine de Montpensier, husband of a sister of Queen Isabella II of Spain, had become a Spaniard since his marriage. The Duchess Sophie d'Alençon, who had been a Bavarian Duchess, a sister of the Empress Elizabeth of Austria and of Queen Maria Sophia of Naples, was a pleasant woman, and would always greet me amiably in German. In 1897 she died in a great fire when she shamed all the men by her courage and presence of mind.

The most notable member of the house of Bourbon-Orléans was the Duc Henri d'Aumale, born in 1822. He honoured me twice with an invitation to his magnificent castle at Chantilly. There he did the honours of this historic seat of the Condé family as a *grand seigneur* should. He treated me, a young man, with the same perfect courtesy as did his guests the generals, and the members of the Académie-Française, to which he belonged, and later bequeathed Chantilly. In escorting me round the castle he called my attention to a life-size portrait of his grandfather, Duc Louis-Joseph-Phillippe d'Orléans, who joined the Jacobins during the revolution, voted for the death of his cousin and king, poor Louis XVI, and was soon afterwards guillotined himself. As he showed me this picture the Duc d'Aumale said smiling: " And do you know how Philip Egalité died? Before he mounted the tumbril he ordered his last breakfast: three dozen of oysters, the best Marennes, two cutlets, a bottle of Chablis. Do you know how he was dressed? He rode to the guillotine in a green coat with a white *piqué* waistcoat, yellow breeches, and boots shining like a mirror. ' *Et violà mon grand-père le citoyen Egalité.*' Thus had the famed Duke of Orleans entitled himself. The great English historian, Carlyle, has described it to us: *Mon grand-père était un bougre, mais il n'avait pas froid aux yeux.*" Among the guests in Chantilly were two literary men: Edouard Pailleron, author of the comedy *Le Monde où l'on s'ennuie*, in which the drawing-room philosopher, Caro, was satirized in the wittiest manner, and Victorien Sardou. Pailleron's mockery was justified. I was present myself when the pseudo-philosopher Laro damned our great philosopher, Schopenhauer, from A to Z, at Princess Monia Urusov's, and it was discovered afterwards that he had scarcely even read his principal works. Victorien Sardou, also a literary guest at Chantilly, has left more lasting traces behind him than Pailleron. His comedies *La famille Benoîton* and *Nos bons villageois* are masterpieces, and even to-day not out of date. His *Rabagas* is, perhaps, the best and most penetrating thing written since Aristophanes against sleek democracy and dishonest demagogues.

Let me relate how I met a real spy, socially, at least, if not officially. *Homo sum; humani nihil a me alienum puto.* The military attaché of the Embassy, Major von Villaume asked me one day if I would do him an important service. "It's rather a shady business," he said. Villaume was the grandson of a Frenchman who had become a Prussian in rather peculiar circumstances. He had been Voltaire's private secretary at the time when he quarrelled with his great patron, King Frederick II of Prussia. In his rage against Voltaire the King had the secretary arrested and brought before him. The Secretary appeared in a very smart suit. "How did you come by such a fine suit, such elegant cuffs, such a first-class *jabot*?" demanded the King. And the wretched Villaume answered promptly: "*Voilà comment M. de Voltaire aime à habiller ses gens.*" The great Frederick, pleased by this self-assurance, told Villaume he would show him that the King of Prussia treated his secretaries even better than the malicious M. de Voltaire, and took him into his service. His grandson, Major von Villaume was a very efficient officer. His request to me was rather a delicate one. A Rumanian had applied to him, who offered proofs that the French General Staff had organized a far-reaching espionage service in the Rhineland and to this end had established relations with German N.C.O.'s and minor civil servants. Major von Villaume added that his flat was

so carefully watched that it would be impossible for him to receive
the Rumanian himself. Would I place my apartment at his disposal? I did so, and received the Wallachian in the fashionable
flat I rented during the years 1880-1884—Rue Montaigne, 71.
He was able, as it turned out, to prove to Villaume that the French
emissaries had succeeded in prevailing upon a number of disloyal
Germans to betray important official secrets. The guilt of the
culprits was proved beyond a shadow of doubt and they were condemned to long terms of hard labour. I had several talks with the
Rumanian in obedience to my principle of gathering information
wherever it is to be found and so enlarging my horizon, and improving my knowledge of human nature. He told me many details of
his stirring career, how espionage is done and the best way of
managing not to be caught. His chief field of activity was in the
railway stations where it is easiest to scrape up an acquaintance.
When finally he bade me good-bye the Rumanian gave me his card
with the words: " One can never tell whom one may need and
what for. Once a humble mouse helped a mighty lion in his hour
of need. If I can ever be of use to you you may call upon me to do
anything I can for you." I made no use of this offer. On the other
hand I possess a nice stick which he gave me as a souvenir of his
personal regard, begging me to keep it in remembrance of him.

The diplomatic corps in Paris was very numerous. Bismarck
often said jokingly that Paris seemed to be the only really healthy
diplomatic post. In all other cities the diplomats complained of the
climate and needed a change of air. It was only in Paris that they
felt really well enough to remain. Paris was, and is, a wonderful
city, after Rome, the one place in the world where foreigners can
live most pleasantly. Whoever is in search of historic memories
and the masterpieces of art must go to Rome, Byron's " city of the
soul," where " the laurel grows high under the blue heaven." But
whoever wants to enjoy the ever changing spectacle of political life
and live in a town where the highest human possessions are contested with wit and passion, where public life is richer in dramatic
moments than in any other country of the world, must go to Paris.
I need scarcely say that to me, as a German and a Prussian, the
Brandenburger Tor is more worthy of veneration than the Arc de
Triomphe or the Triumphal Arch of Constantine, and that the
statue of our great King Fredericus Rex is nearer my heart than
Napoleon's Column. This is only *pro domo mea*.

The most distinguished and at the same time pleasantest figure
among the non-German diplomats in Paris, during my stay there,
was the Russian Ambassador, Prince Nikolai Orlow. He had lost

an eye as a young officer in the Crimean War, at the storming of Silistria. The black bandage over the empty socket gave this tall man a soldierly air and made him one of the most interesting figures in society. Prince Orlov had for years been a close friend of Prince Bismarck, and the friendship was based on mutual esteem. Princess Orlov, a distinguished and charming woman, was, with the exception of the Grand Duchess Helena Pavlovna, the only woman with whom Prince Bismarck liked to talk politics. Among the secretaries of the Russian Embassy were two with whom, in later life, I often came into close contact. Count Kapnist was afterwards to become Russia's representative at the Papal court, and so Ambassador in Vienna; Count Michael Nikolaievitch Muraviev Legation Secretary in Berlin, Minister in Copenhagen, and finally Russian Foreign Secretary.

As Prince Orlov was the pleasantest figure in the Paris *corps diplomatique*, so was Count Beust, the Austro-Hungarian Ambassador, the most miserable. He looked as though he never washed himself. In spite of this he thought himself a handsome man and was especially proud of his small feet. He arranged himself when seated so that people could see them. At parties he sometimes sang to his own pianoforte accompaniment, a song written and composed by himself, on the subject of his resignation as Austro-Hungarian Chancellor, with the refrain:

> " *Mein Herz bleibt den Freuden, den Lieben getreu,*
> *Verzeihung den Feinden, der Kampf ist vorbei.*" [1]

In reality the writer of this sentimental ditty had never forgiven his enemies, in particular Prince Bismarck. He stirred up feeling wherever he could in Paris against the German Empire and even carried his treachery so far as to be a frequent guest in the *salon* of Germany's greatest enemy, the notorious Madame Edmond Adam (Juliette Lamber), who edited the chauvinist *Nouvelle Revue*. As chargé d'affaires I had to visit him occasionally. He would not talk willingly on current political affairs, which did not interest him, but always reverted to the period 1848-1866. He was positively scurrilous in his remarks upon events in those days. With reference to the fact that the Beust family came from the neighbourhood of Havelberg, in the province of Brandenburg, and that Bismarck is alleged to have had the idea in the 'fifties, of becoming minister to the blind King George V of Hanover, he said to me: " If I, Beust,

---

[1] My heart remains true to all I called friend,
My foes are forgiven, the fight's at an end.

had been leading statesman in Prussia and Bismarck Hanoverian Minister I would have treated him even worse than he treated poor Count Adolf Platen." He did not appear to feel how absurd this suggestion was. Beust was not given his deserved retirement till 1882. The reason for this was an incognito visit of the Empress Elizabeth of Austria to Paris. On her return she told her exalted husband, the Emperor Francis Joseph, that he could not permit himself any longer to be represented by a ridiculous and, at the same time, malicious person as Count Friedrich Ferdinand Beust in any European capital. The First Secretary of the Austro-Hungarian Embassy under Beust was Count Agenor Goluchowski. We were destined to be Ambassadors at the same time in Bucharest and, at the same time too, Foreign Secretaries of our respective countries.

The English Ambassador, Lord Lyons, was next to Hohenlohe and Prince Orlov, the most distinguished Ambassador in Paris. Like most Englishmen he judged everything, in questions both important and insignificant, solely from the English standpoint. At a big dinner in his house he placed the attaché of the German Embassy, Hereditary Prince Erni von Hohenlohe-Langenburg, higher than all French Ministers and even above the other Ambassadors. He explained this by the fact that Hohenlohe-Langenberg was a great-nephew of Her Majesty Queen Victoria, and therefore had precedence of everybody else. During my period of office in Paris two men were ambassadors who had played a great part in the history of their country. General Enrico Cialdini, Duke of Gaëta had fought against Austria in 1848 and 1859, beaten in 1860 the Papal troops, led by the French General Lamoricière at Castelfidardo and, in 1861, forced the fortress Gaëta, the last refuge of the Neapolitan Bourbons to capitulate. Count Menabrea in the 'sixties had been Minister, first of the Naval Marine and then of Public Works, from 1867 to 1869 an excellent Prime Minister. Like Blanc, Pelloux, Barral, and other leading men of modern Italy, and like the Italian dynasty itself he came from Savoy. Of his secretaries, Avarna was destined to be Ambassador in Vienna, and Bollati in Berlin. Both were exemplary loyal, clever, and skilful diplomats. The Spanish Ambassador Duke Fernan Nunes was an odd character. By birth an Italian, member of the Lombard noble family, Falco d'Adda, he had, through his marriage with a wealthy Spanish heiress, acquired the Spanish nationality and with it the Spanish *grandezza*. He was deeply interested in young ladies of the ballet. " *J'aime*," he used to say, " *à protéger les beaux arts*." As his wife was very distinguished but very ugly his departures from the path of marital rectitude were not taken amiss. He was not at all interested in politics. When I lunched with Fernan Nunes at the Prince of Wales' three days after Gambetta had taken over the reins of government, and it was discovered that the Spanish Ambassador knew nothing of the formation of the Gambetta Ministry, the Prince of Wales laughed heartily.

As a diplomat I have always been true to the principle of frequenting the representatives of the smaller countries, since from them one often receives the best and most authentic information, because they arouse less suspicion. Four of these gentlemen were specially kind to me: the Danish Minister, Count Moltke-Hvitfeld was not exactly fond of Germans but, in memory of old connection, with my father, he was kind to me. To the Greek Minister Brailas-Armeni, I had been recommended by King Georgios. The Dutch Minister, Baron Zuylen, was friendly towards Germany and so was his strictly Calvinistic wife. In the house of the Brazilian Minister, the old Viscount Itajuba, I was accepted as a relative, as his handsome daughter Olga had married my mother's youngest brother, Senator Alfred Rücker.

The most interesting personality of the *corps diplomatique* was, for me, the *Papal nuntius*, Monsignor Czacki. He was a member of an old family of the Polish nobility domiciled in Volhynia but, as is always the case with non-Italian prelates in the service of the Papal Chair, had become completely Romanized. In one of his most delightful novels, the *Anneau d'Améthyste*, Anatole France has drawn a masterly portrait of a *Papal nuntius*, Monsignor Cima: " *A quarante ans il avait l'air d'un adolescent malade. Quand il baissait les yeux, sa face était celle d'un mort. Le coude droit dans la main gauche et la joue reposant inclinée dans le creux de la main droite, il avait une grâce presque funèbre qui rappelait certaines figures de bas-reliefs antiques. Son visage au repos était voilé de mélancholie. L'on disait à Rome qu'il avait le mauvais oeil.*" This portrait was in many respects that of Monsignor Czacki. In particular the *nuntius* Czacki might have served the French novelist as model for the skill with which his Monsignor avoided uncomfortable questions, and refrained from expressing any definite opinion. But the *mal 'occhio* so dreaded by the Italians Czacki did not possess. Association with him did me no harm, but stimulated, and taught me many things. This Romanized Pole had become an excellent exponent of that Papal diplomacy which, in some respects, is the best in the world. He was natural and simple, and at the same time extremely reserved. He never gave way on questions of principle, but in all other things was as accommodating, and as opportunist as possible. Although the relations of the French government to the Catholic Church were already very strained he treated the anti-clerical French ministers and parliamentarians with the greatest amiability. I have often seen him sitting on the sofa and smoking cigarettes, in animated conversation with Jules Ferry, Freycinet, Spuller, and Paul Bert. French clerics he would treat superciliously, as I observed when I visited him: "*Ces gens-là par leur fanatisme étroit et lourd qu'ils appellent foi, gâtent les meilleurs, les plus fines combinaisons. J'en ai pardessus la tête.*" Monsignor Czacki was a great admirer of Prince Bismarck. He had told me already at our first meeting that it was his dearest wish to meet the greatest statesman of the century, as he called him, and to discover with him a *modus vivendi* between Germany and the Church. "*Avec un si grand homme on trouve toujours une combinaison. L'Eglise s'est arrangée avec Clovis et avec Napoléon I. Elle s'arrangera avec le Prince de Bismarck. Du reste, Léon XIII ne demande pas mieux que d'arriver à un arrangement avec votre grand Chancelier.*" Monsignor Czacki became a Cardinal. He died in Rome, where he was buried in the old church of Santa Pudenziana, which according to tradition, is the most ancient in Rome. Legend tells how the Apostle Peter lived in the home of Pudens the Senator, and erected a house of prayer there. The bronze tomb of Cardinal Czacki, who died in 1888, represents him lying there in life-size effigy. From time to time I visit this venerable church which belongs to the so-called Cardinalist Churches and to which Czacki was appointed on obtaining the red hat. The bronze statue is so like him that I seem to see this prince of the church, whom I respected so highly, before me in the flesh, when I approach it.

Probably the most intelligent of the heads of the foreign missions in Paris was the Belgian Ambassador, Baron Beyens, who had been working there for almost a generation. He was suspected of being of Jewish origin, and was certainly clever and industrious. His wife, a Spaniard, like Fatinitza in the charming opera of Suppé, could boast of having seen and experienced a great deal. She once said to me: "When I was young I turned the heads of ambassadors. Now I am old I have fallen in love with an Italian attaché who might be my son and who flees from me, like Hippolyt from Phaedra." She was an "*apassionata*," as the Italians say in their picturesque language, of a temperamental woman. The son of this marriage was Belgian Ambassador in Berlin when the Great War broke out. In this capacity he unfortunately had the opportunity of observing, at close quarters, the pitiful awkwardness and superficiality of our diplomatic leaders at that time and was able to report it in detail to his government. During those first August days of the tragic year 1914 he said to an Italian diplomat, who soon afterwards repeated his words to me: " The German army is the best in the world. The German nation is wonderfully disciplined and organized. But no nation can win a victory that is led by such statesmen. That gives me hope and courage for the result of this war."

Nearly every year the Prince of Wales appeared in Paris which he preferred to any other city of the continent. He associated with all circles—with the princes of the house of Orléans whom he treated as relatives, and the sons of the house of Rothschild whom he treated as friends, with politicians and *bon vivants*, with the dowagers of the Faubourg Saint-Germain, and the ladies of that world which Alexandre Dumas *fils* called " half." He invited me regularly to luncheon when he came to Paris as a friend of his brother-in-law's, King George of Greece and, as he had the kindness to say, a youthful playmate of his wife. He conversed with me every time with much intelligence and acumen. The personal friendship he showed a young diplomat was maintained to the day of his death by the future King Edward. It did not prevent his so-called " policy of encirclement," but broke the shafts of many barbs, rounded many corners, eased many things, and hindered the worst.

It was my greatest pleasure to visit the museums and galleries of Paris, which are unique in their way. This habit of mine was to lead to the happiness of my life. It was the spring of 1883. I, as so often happened in the Louvre, was in the *Salle Carrée*, in front of the " Marriage of Cana " by Paolo Veronese. I met two ladies whom I had not seen for a long time, but recognized at once. One of them was Donna Laura Minghetti, the other her daughter, Countess Marie Dönhoff. The mother, in spite of her fifty years was still youthful and strikingly beautiful. The daughter seemed to me even more charming and graceful than in Florence and Vienna. I listened with admiration to the mother as she showed me one picture after another, explaining and interpreting it without pedantry, quite spontaneously, but with an unfailing sense of artistic values. I could not look enough upon the beautiful eyes, the slim, charming figure, the exquisite grace of the daughter. The mother understood no German. The daughter spoke the most delightful German I had ever heard. I found, both during our walk, which lasted an hour, through the halls of the richest picture gallery in the world, and afterwards in the Tuileries garden, that she knew Goethe and Schiller, Hölderlin and Kleist, Schopenhauer and even Immanuel Kant almost better than I did myself. I could not share in her enthusiasm for Richard Wagner, Beethoven, and Bach, as I am unfortunately unmusical. But I respected her delight in German composers. As a German indeed she pleased me very much. We arranged to dine together that evening in Café Brebant, and from there, for an expedition to Fontainebleau next day.

As we went through the halls of the palace built by King François I, through the Cour des Adieux and the beautiful woods, Donna Laura Minghetti told me that her daughter was about to obtain a divorce from her husband, Count Karl Dönhoff. Madame Minghetti assured me that neither had the slightest cause for reproach. Count Dönhoff was the perfect *galantuomo*, a good and distinguished man. But time showed that the two characters were too unsuited to make a happy marriage possible, not to speak of the difference of age and nationality. The divorce would take place by mutual consent in the greatest privacy.

When, on the day before she left Paris, I asked Madame Minghetti when she and her daughter would return, she said that it would not be for some time. But she proposed to spend a few days with her daughter in Genoa at the beginning of September. I asked Countess Marie's permission to write to her, and we corresponded zealously throughout the summer. She wrote just as she spoke: never vapidly, never conventionally, with neither affectation nor *sous entendu*, always naturally. Perfectly sincere, perfectly candid. One felt that she only said and wrote what she really felt, and that she never pretended anything; that lying and hypocrisy were not only hateful but impossible to her. Everything about her was genuine. I had never met such kindness accompanied by such a fine intellect. For the first time in my life I experienced real yearning, real hope, and real sorrow, real joy and real pain—I felt real love.

In Genoa I asked her what I had already longed to ask in Paris but had not had the courage—would she ever be able to make up her mind to marry again. She was silent for a long time, and then she gave me her hand with the words: " In any case—nobody else." From that moment I knew that I too could never love anybody else. From that day on to marry her became the aim of my life, the only woman I have ever loved supremely, with all the tenderness and all the passion of which a human being is capable.

DONNA LAURA MINGHETTI

After Lenbach

CHAPTER XXXVIII

Advancement to the First Secretaryship—Chargé d'affaires—Alfonso XI in Paris—Princess Monia Urusov—Dr. Landsberg—Visit to Rome —Pietro Blaserna and Marco Minghetti—Naples, Cape Miseno— Journey to Tunis—Dr. Gustav Nachtigal—Algiers—Dr. Julius Fröbel.

WHEN, at the beginning of September, 1883, my chief, Prince Chlodwig Hohenlohe, went on his usual holiday to Aussee, I had not long before been promoted to the First Secretaryship of the Embassy. I had been really delighted at this advancement, though not quite so much as I was at the button which marked a step upwards in my military career in the King's Hussars—but certainly it pleased me more than many a bigger jump later on. The chief reason for my satisfaction was the fact that, as First Secretary, I had the certain prospect of controlling Embassy matters as chargé d'affaires independently, for a long period every year. And that was what I was eager for. I wanted to " be active " as the ambitious diplomatic débutant calls it, when he has to face the footlights alone for the first time.

When my ambassador left Paris the world was peaceful, and nothing pointed to stormy weather ahead. The death of Count de Chambord, last member of the elder line of the house of Bourbon and of the legitimate line in France, was only of importance to France herself, and only of slight importance even there, owing to the increasing consolidation of the Republic. Alphonse Daudet had written his novel *Les Rois en exil* which ends with the melancholy phrase: " *La royauté, une grande vieille chose-morte.*" This Daudet regarded kingship—as a magnificent corpse. At that time this seemed true only of France. The capture of Huë, the capital of Annam, was another success of the French Republic. In case the French should grow too cocksure the *Norddeutsche Allgemeine Zeitung*, the organ of Prince Bismarck, directed, in the middle of August, a particularly forceful cold douche at the " nonsensical " anti-German tone of the French press, which might eventually lead to war.

In spite of this nobody believed that the visit of King Alfonso XII of Spain could bring about unpleasantness. King

533

Alfonso after having been present at the German manœuvres in Hesse and been appointed on this occasion chief of the Prussian Lancer Regiment, No. 15, garrisoned in Strassburg, wished to return home via Paris. Things turned out badly. When the King drove from the station to the Spanish Embassy, he was received in the " *capitale de la civilisation* " with cat-calls, shrieks, and cries of scorn, not only by the mob in the street, but more especially by the fashionable mob in the windows of the clubs, the big hotels, and elegant restaurants. Immediately on his arrival the King received the *corps diplomatique*. His bearing was regal. To me, the German chargé d'affaires, he said, pointing to my King's Hussars uniform, in a loud voice and in the French language: " I am pleased to see a Prussian uniform. I am proud of the fact that His Majesty the King and Emperor, your royal master, bestowed a Prussian uniform upon me. Here people seem annoyed about it. That leaves me quite indifferent." Prince Bismarck took this incident calmly. He wired to warn me that it was for the Spaniards to raise complaints and demand satisfaction. These complaints were made very timidly. The only " satisfaction " given was that President Grévy expressing his cold " regrets," first to King Alfonso and then to the Spanish ambassador. Charles V and Philippe II would probably not have been satisfied with this. But the French had again showed that they were still, to use Tocqueville's expression, " *la plus brillante et la plus dangereuse des nations de l'Europe*," the spoilt children, who do as they like and are never punished.

When I look back on my nearly six years in Paris I have pleasant memories of my friendship with a Russian Princess and a German journalist, neither of whom possessed any social position, money, or other outward attractions, but were both people well worth knowing for their outstanding qualities.

Princess Monia Urusov had settled in Paris to educate her children. Her mother, daughter of a very wealthy Russian landowner, the Chamberlain Maltsov, had been for many years the intimate friend of the Empress Maria Alexandrovna. Her husband, Prince Urusov, was governor of one of the eighty-nine Russian governmental districts. She had quarrelled with her parents. Her husband, an enthusiastic disciple of the great Leo Nikholaievitch Tolstoi, thought it his duty, after reading the *Kreutzer-Sonata*, to cease conjugal relations with his wife. Monia Urusov was very original, at times eccentric, as so often happens with Russian women. But she was an idealist in the truest sense of the word. She sacrificed all conventions and material interests to her somewhat Utopian ideas. She was deeply intellectual. She knew Shakespeare as well as Molière and Pushkin. It was a pleasure to converse with her on literature. She was not beautiful, and still less elegant, and cared not at all for her appearance, so that there could be no question of my making love to her. She had a good influence over me in keeping me as far as she could from things superficial and frivolous, and calling my attention again and again to the true sources of permanent happiness, the heart and the mind. She gave me a Shakespeare which stands on my writing-table to-day. In it she wrote: " To thine own self be true."

At her house I often met Ivan Sergeievitch Turgeniev, a great writer and a very pleasant man. He was free from that vanity which at times makes the most brilliant French *causeurs* the most impossible people. Nor did he display the pedantry of so many intellectual Germans, who are all too fond of lengthy dissertations and whose dogmatism only too easily turns the conversation into an argument. Turgeniev spoke as he wrote, clearly, profoundly, and gracefully. He was, politically, not much inclined towards Germany. But his admiration for German philosophy and literature, and especially for Goethe, was boundless. He said to me once that in one of Goethe's lyric poems there was more true poetry than in all the *Odes and Ballades*, the *Orientales*, the *Rayons et Ombres*, and the *Contemplations* of Victor Hugo. He made fun of the extraordinary vanity of Hugo, who was, in his opinion, over-rated in France. Hugo had once said to Turgeniev that he did not find the much admired *Torquato Tasso* of Schiller so particularly fine. When Turgeniev modestly called his attention to the fact that *Torquato Tasso* was written by Goethe and not Schiller, Hugo replied, shaking his head with an Olympian gesture: " *Quand on s'appelle Victor Hugo, on n'est pas tenu à connaître toutes les médiocrités d'Outre-Rhin.* Alexandre Dumas *fils* was not far behind Victor Hugo in his good opinion of himself. It was merely that the latter manifested his pride in a pompous and priestly manner, Dumas with cynical impertinence. Once when Dumas sat down next to Princess Urusov at one of her evening parties, he asked her whether the thought of having such a famous writer at her side had not turned her head and whether she would fall on his neck. Monia replied: " *Du tout! Car ce qu'il y a d'un peu propre en vous, je puis l'acheter chez Hachette pour trois francs cinquante.*" Turgeniev and Princess Urusov agreed that, although Russia must not introduce the parliamentary system overnight, it was necessary to arrive at constitutional government as soon as possible. Otherwise a revolution would sooner or later be unavoidable. Should this break out it would be cruder, more brutal and destructive, than the great French revolution had been.   Turgeniev for many years was devoted to the singer whom I have already mentioned, Pauline Garcia, as ugly as she was witty, the wife of the art critic, Louis Viardot.   Husband and adorer were the best of friends.   A tale went the rounds that when the temperamental Pauline was allowing a young pianist to make love to her too openly Turgeniev said anxiously to Viardot: " *Il faut ouvrir les yeux.   Pauline est en train de nous tromper.*"

The journalist, Moritz Landsberg, was a sickly little old man. He lived on the third floor of a modest tenement house near the Gare Saint-Lazare.   He suffered from a painful affliction of the bladder.   I often sat by his bed and listened to his reminiscences of Paris which were as many-sided as they were stimulating.   He had settled long ago in Paris and was one of the oldest of the German journalists there.   He had known both Heine and Börne well, and admired, as I did, " the pine-tree that stands alone in the north, solitary on a bleak height," and the *Pilgrimage to Kevelaar*.   But he had no admiration for Heine the man: Heine had received a regular subsidy from the French secret funds under Louis Philippe, for his pro-French propaganda.   He had also pestered Napoleon III for money, but had met with a refusal.   " Spotty and dirty " was how Landsberg described Heine the man.   On the other hand he spoke of Börne with respect.   He did not deny that in his case, as so often happened with German publicists and historians, the critical gifts were greater than the creative talent.   He thought his attacks upon Goethe not only unjust but absurd.   (" A vicious pug barking at the moon.")   But taken all round Ludwig Börne had been a decent fellow, honest and sincere.   In spite of all his roaring he was a patriot; Heine had been a renegade.   Dr. Landsberg was an Israelite.

In the early days of March 1884 love drew me to Rome.   I had asked Donna Laura Minghetti's permission to make this journey, telling her I set great store on an interview with Signor Minghetti. Donna Laura replied that her husband would be delighted to renew our acquaintanceship.   Both he and she, however, wished that my visit to Rome should attract no attention.   As a divorced woman her daughter had to be doubly careful, and to avoid all gossip. Donna Laura suggested I should avoid the big Roman hotels and stay at the house of one of her friends, the senator and professor of physics, Pietro Blaserna, in the *Istituto fisico* on the Viminal, Via Panisperna.   It was thus I came to know the distinguished scientist who remained my true and wise friend until his death during the Great War.   Blaserna came from Görz on the Isonzo.   As an Italian, born under Austrian rule, he had studied in Vienna and

Berlin, and spoke fluent German. He was a close friend of our great naturalist, Hermann Helmholtz, whose classic works he had translated into Italian, and whose enthusiastic disciple he was. With him he was accustomed to spend the summer in the Engadine. It would be hard to imagine a pleasanter, more intellectual atmosphere than that prevailing in the house of the good Blaserna. Great book-shelves hid the four walls of his study from floor to ceiling: reviews and pamphlets covered the floor. But in the middle of the room stood a large cage in which canaries fluttered happily from perch to perch, drank out of the little bowls in the corners, or pecked at the leaves which their good master, who cherished them like a father, had poked in through the wires. " I never married," he said smiling, " these are my children." During the three days I stayed in Rome I had many an interesting and, for me, instructive conversation with Blaserna. Unlike most Italians he spoke rather slowly, but what he said was all worth hearing, whether he gave an address in his capacity of President of the *Academia dei Lyncei*, Italy's most distinguished academy, or spoke as Vice-President of the Senate, or lectured before a large audience of eager students, or only carried on friendly conversation.

The day after I arrived in Rome I was received by Marco Minghetti. He was in his sixty-sixth year. He came from Bologna and, like many north Italians, had fair hair and red cheeks. He was tall and well-built, a statesman and man of letters, with the manners of the man of the world. He could look back on a great political past. In 1848 he had been minister of Pope Pius IX on the first and only occasion when the Curia had tried to make peace with the movement for *Italia unita* by placing itself at the head of it. When this attempt failed owing to the impatience of the radical element of the Italian nationalist party, and the indecision of the Pope, Minghetti had withdrawn into private life and devoted himself to the management of his estates and his national-economic and literary studies. He would relate, with pleasure, how, when in the middle 'fifties, Pius IX visited Bologna, between the revolution of 1848-49 and the French-Piedmontese-Austrian War of 1859, he summoned Minghetti and received him with all his old kindness. Before he asked him to sit down the Pope looked behind all the curtains and said with Italian naturalness and *bonhomie*: " I'm looking to see if any Jesuit has hidden himself to listen to our conversation. The Jesuits have many good qualities but they are very inquisitive. I should not be surprised if I once discovered a Jesuit in the *cesso*." The *cesso* is that discreet spot whither even the most highly placed are accustomed to go alone. Minghetti had tried in vain to reconcile Pius IX with the Italian national idea. This reconciliation was the goal and ideal of many distinguished Italians: Gioberti, Azeglio, Tosti, Manzoni, Cesare Cantu, Rosmini.

Marco Minghetti was, to the end of his life, a glowing Italian patriot, and practising Catholic. In 1859 he had been the secretary-general to Cavour, in 1860 his Minister of the Interior. He had stood beside the death-bed of Cavour on 6th June 1861, and heard how the great Italian statesman, one of the greatest statesmen of all time, exclaimed to the monk who gave him the last sacraments: "*Frate, frate, libera chiesa in libero stato!*" From 1863 to 1864, and again from '73 to '76, Minghetti himself had been Prime Minister. He had been overthrown by the Piedmontese because, by the terms of the September convention with Napoleon III, the Italian capital had been removed from Turin to Florence. In 1876 the Florentines overthrew him. They were annoyed that Florence had got into debt owing to the expenses which it had had to incur as the capital. So difficult is it to satisfy the mob! Whenever the Prussian State Ministry were about to debate a financial measure, my clever colleague, Johannes Miquel, would say, with a sarcastic smile: " It makes no difference how we approach it, we shall be grumbled at anyway." Minghetti had retained a great political position even after his resignation as premier. He was respected by all parties, even by the ministers of the Left; by Crispi, Depretis, Nicotera, and Saracco, whom King Victor Emanuel II had called to office after his fall. He was considered the greatest Italian orator of his time. Generally he spoke extempore, but always in perfectly finished periods. Cicero must have spoken like that, save that the violence which the greatest Roman orator displayed towards Catilina, Verres, and Antonius, was far removed from the always temperate Marco Minghetti. Minghetti possessed a marvellous memory. Once when he lectured on Dante, in Bologna, he not only dispensed with a manuscript but did not even need the *Divina Commedia* to refer to, since he knew it by heart, from the first canto to the last. Tasso, Ariosto, and Virgil were also firmly fixed in his mind. When he died the *Imitation of Christ*, to which he referred again and again, of Thomas à Kempis, lay under his pillow.

In the spring of 1884 Marco Minghetti spoke to me as follows:

My dear step-daughter Maria, whom I love as though she were my own daughter, has told me of her wishes and intentions. I will be quite open with you, candid and precise with the *clarté latine* which I respect so much. I do not doubt but that you are a charming young man, since my wife and my daughter assure

me of it in unison. And just as little do I doubt your feelings for
Maria. But no marriage can be built up on sentiment alone.
You are the same age as my Maria, still young, scarcely thirty-
five. You are now First Secretary of the Embassy, upon which
I congratulate you. That is very nice, but as a position it means
nothing yet. As you have told my wife, with a frankness of which
both she and I highly approve, you have not much money. All
these are obstacles which a man can overcome. But there is
another which is, for the present, quite insurmountable. My
daughter is divorced from Count Dönhoff by law, but not by the
church. A second marriage will only be possible if the first is
declared annulled by the Papal Chair. Without this annulment
re-marriage is completely out of the question, either for Maria,
myself, my wife, or any other Catholic.

When Minghetti saw that these words not merely distressed but
even overpowered me, he gave me his hand with the words: " I do
not know why, but although I know you very slightly, I like you
and trust you. I promise you to do all I can to get the annulment."

In the evening Donna Laura told me not to despair. She was
a courageous and broad-minded woman. " Marco will manage
the annulment if one point can be found to start from," she said.
" He is very much liked and respected by the Vatican. Everything
will depend on direct negotiations between himself and ' ces messieurs ' at the Vatican without German interference, either by the
German ambassador at the Quirinal or the Prussian Envoy to the
Vatican—neither Keudell nor Schlözer. We Italians get on much
better and quicker among ourselves than when strangers try to
interfere between us." Donna Laura told me then that she and her
daughter intended to go to Naples for a few days, and that they
would be glad to meet me there. I replied that I asked nothing
better. I had obtained six weeks leave, for a journey to Tunis and
Algiers, since a first-hand knowledge of these towns would be useful
to me as First Secretary of the Paris Embassy. Naples could be
taken en route.

After taking a cordial leave of good Professor Blaserna and his
canaries, I set out for Naples. Donna Laura and her daughter were
staying at the Hotel Tramontano. We first visited Santa Lucia,
where Donna Maria had been born in the Palazzo Acton, and from
there we went to the church of the nobility of Naples, S. Domenico
Maggiore, where her father, Prince Domenico Camporeale, was
buried, and where I admired the figures in relief of the miracle of
the crucifix by Toma de Stefani. Close by, in the monastery, there

had lived and worked, in the thirteenth century, Thomas Aquinas, the greatest of the Scholastics, the *Doctor Angelicus* and *Doctor Universalis*, whom Leo XIII raised to the position of the first Catholic theologian and patron saint of all Catholic schools. In the same monastery, three hundred years later, another Dominician, Giordano Bruno, was educated, destined to a less successful career than his brother monk of Aquino. After many errors of false doctrines, he was burned as a heretic in Rome, on the Campo dei Fiore, where, nowadays, they hold a weekly rag-market and English globe-trotters and German tourists eagerly hunt for antiquities.

In Naples, from the Villa Nazionale, we enjoyed one of the finest views in the world. We dined in the evening at Figlio di Pietro's, at the foot of Posilipo, by the shore, off spaghetti and *frutti di mare*. Next day we visited Virgil's tomb. But I sought in vain the inscription which, as a boy, in the second form at Neu-Strelitz, the worthy Professor Ladewig, who taught me to love Virgil (according to him, Vergil), had often told me of:

> " *Mantua me genuit, Calabri rapuere, tenet nunc*
> *Parthenope: cecini pascua, rura, duces.*"

We drove further along the coast to Baiae, once an ultra-fashionable bathing resort, the Brighton or Biarritz of Imperial Rome. "*Nullus in orbe sinus Baiis praelucet amoenis!*" (Nothing in the world equals the lovely bosom of Baiae) says a rich Roman in Horace who wanted to settle there. We reached Cape Miseno. The pious Aeneas buried his chief trumpeter Misenus there. Virgil set the stamp of immortality on this tomb in his four lines:

> " *At pius Aeneas ingenti mole sepulcrum*
> *imposuit, suaque arma viro remumque tubamque*
> *monte sub aereo, qui nunc Misenus ab illo*
> *dicitur aeternumque tenet per saecula nomen.*"

It is from here that one gets the most perfect view of this Paradisal country. Before us lay the Gulf of Naples, Gaëta, and the chain of mountains that surrounds them. Around us, lakes and bays, tongues of land and narrow isthmuses, the shimmering blue Mediterannean and the refulgent sky overhead. Fronting the sea a medieval watch-tower raised its head. Full of the joy of standing side by side, we swore that never-ending love, which is the highest of all earthly happiness, the love that surmounts all barriers and obstacles. "To surrender one's whole self and feel a bliss that must be eternal! Eternal! It's end would mean despair. No—no end! No end!"

Next day I left via Palermo for Tunis. The resident governor, Paul Cambon, whom I knew already, and to whom I had a letter of introduction from the French Foreign Secretary was on vacation. In his stead the First Secretary of the Residency, Monsieur d'Estournelles received me. We remained in friendly touch till the outbreak of the World-War, which destroyed so much. Shortly before I resigned the Chancellorship he came to see me in Berlin and there delivered a tactful and clever lecture on the motives and the aims of a sensible pacifism. If only we had all heeded his words! Instead, the malice of the one, the stupidity of the others, involved the whole world in war.

In Tunis d'Estournelles asked me where and how I had prepared myself for this North African journey. I replied: "Only with Flaubert, with *Salambô*." He answered: "*Bravo, vous ne pouviez trouver un meilleur guide pour ici.*" Thanks to Flaubert and his splendid descriptions, ancient Carthage rose again before us. We could sense the *Génie de Carthage* in whose honour, at the end of the book, Havas the Fool, with his left arm around the waist of his wife Salambô, raises the bowl of wine in his right. D'Estournelles took me north-east of Goletta, the port of Tunis, there where the narrow tongue of land is penetrated by the sea, to the spot where old Carthage stood. It lay about a mile north-east of Goletta, on the headland between the sea and the lake of Tunis. Here, before the eyes of the younger Scipio, the birthplace of Hannibal, conqueror of the Romans, went up in flames after desperate resistance, and the watcher was moved to the point of tears by this vision of the transience of all things human. On the ruins which strewed this place sat Marius, half a century later, and the trembling slave did not dare to lay hands on the conqueror of the Cimbri and the Teutons.

D'Estournelles did not deny that there were far too many Jews and Italians in the residency of Tunis. "They absolutely predominate here," he said. "There were only a few French before we marched in, and the number has not appreciably increased since then." The superior numbers of the Italians did not appear to cause d'Estournelles anxiety. "We French," he explained, "are not colonisers. That doesn't matter as long as we dominate others by military superiority, and so keep the administration in our own hands. This is now the case and so it will remain as long as we keep our position in Europe."

D'Estournelles was on the best of terms with the German consul, Dr. Gustav Nachtigal. The little I know about the interior of Africa I owe to this distinguished man. He had crossed Africa in all directions and told me the most enthralling tales of Tibesti, Bornu, Kanem and Borku, Bagirmi and Wadai, Darfur and Kordofan. Soon after our meeting in Tunis, Nachtigal was sent as Imperial Commissioner to the coast of upper Guinea. He placed Togo and the Cameroons under German protection. On the return journey he died, in the spring of 1885, too early for our colonial policy and for the Empire. I was lunching with Bismarck when the Prince received news of his death. Bismarck laid the telegram aside with the thoughtful words: " A pity! He was full of energy but prudent as well. A loss." Nachtigal came from the district round Stendal, from the home of the Bismarck family.

D'Estournelles wanted me to pay my respects to the Bey of Tunis. Dr. Nachtigal supported this desire. Both were of the opinion the Bey would be offended if distinguished foreigners visited Tunis—" The home of peace and happiness " as the capital was called officially—without calling upon him. This also in former times had been the standpoint of the petty German princes, as Dr. Nachtigal observed. Accompanied by Nachtigal and D'Estournelles, I drove to the Bardo, the residence of Mohammed Es Sadok. Slender palm trees, their leaves glittering in the sunlight. raised their heads, right and left of the track, in the wide plain, We met herds of camels which, for the first time here, I saw outside the Zoological gardens. The Bedouins who led them looked most dignified, in their long *burnouses*, with their hoods, and their flowing beards. They reminded me of Old Testament patriarchs. . . . Thus must Abraham and Isaac, Jacob and Laban, Moses and the Prophets have looked. Mohammed Es Sadok, short, stout, short of breath, with a great bald head and dull eyes, looked far less venerable than his subjects. When my two companions had addressed him, eulogizing my excellent qualities, the ruler of the Tunisian realm handed me the Grand Officer's Cross of his house. He murmured something about the brilliants which went with this decoration, and so made his gift doubly valuable. When, later on, I wanted to make a present of the diamonds of the ridiculous order, which I had never worn, to my wife, it was discovered that they were imitation.

Everywhere in Tunis I met Jews. Nachtigal computed the number of Israelites settled in so-called Barbary, in north-west Africa, between the Mediterranean and the Sahara, in Algiers, Tunis, Morocco, and Tripoli, at a million. There were more Jews there at that time than in Germany, not to mention England, France, and Italy. Nachtigal who, although not an Israelite himself, was deeply interested in the history of the Chosen People, declared that the Jews form one per cent. of the earth's population. The sum total of

all Jews was fourteen millions. Of these five millions were in
Russia, three millions in the United States, three millions in Poland,
two millions in the Ukraine, a million in Rumania, five hundred
thousand in Germany, nearly as many in Hungary, three hundred
thousand in Bohemia, nearly three hundred thousand in German-
Austria, two hundred and fifty thousand in England, one hundred
and fifty thousand in France, barely forty thousand in Italy. I do
not know if these figures, which I noted at the time, are correct
to-day. In any case it seems undoubtedly true that there are far
more Jews in eastern Europe than in the western countries. Most
of the American Jews must also have migrated from the Near East.
The Jews of Barbary had come to Africa from Spain and Portugal,
some two hundred thousand strong, when the Inquisition drove
them from the Iberian Peninsular. They were not much better
treated by the Mussulmen than they had been by the Holy Office.
Till the French occupation they were not allowed either in Tunis or
Algiers, to pass a mosque without taking off their shoes. They could
scarcely appear in the street without being spat at and insulted.
There was a certain consolation for the Jews in the fact that the
Mohammedans, like the ancient Romans, scorned the Christians
even more, since the latter were only a sect of the former. Moreover,
as Nachtigal assured me, the clever children of Israel had, as once
in Egypt, and later in many other countries, managed, even under
the Beys, to obtain a.dominant position, in spite of all oppression
and persecution. All money affairs were in Jewish hands. They
were the treasurers, secret writers, and interpreters of the Bey, kept
his jewels and diamonds under lock and key, and controlled the
Mint. They were the doctors and apothecaries of the ignorant
nation which had no talent for the exact sciences.

I heard dreadful tales of the cruelty which had prevailed on the
North African coast before the French took possession of it.
D'Estournelles may for obvious reasons have exaggerated, but
Nachtigal also knew something of it. The smallest offence was
punishable by flogging, which was carried out with an ox-hide whip.
The strokes were counted on a rosary. More than 999 strokes
might not be given according to the Koran. But no delinquent ever
got so far, particularly if, as was permitted, the strokes were inflicted from in front. It was a popular custom to bury those con-
victed of serious crimes up to their necks in sand, and let any passer-
by aim at their heads. Or else their nostrils, mouth, and ears would
be filled with gunpowder, and set light to. Some criminals would
be sewn up alive in the hide of a dead ox, or bound to the tail of a
mule which was then urged on to a gallop. The *Lex Talionis* stood

high in honour. A Jewish cook who was discovered to have sold human flesh, baked in oil, was cut, bit by bit, into little pieces, which were thrown into boiling water one after another and flung to the dogs before the eyes of the dying man. But enough of horrors.

From Tunis I drove to Bone, which is still a favourite seaside resort, and which once, as Hippo Regius, was the episcopal seat of Saint Augustin, whose *Confessions* I have read again and again. In Constantine, the capital of eastern Algeria, built on a ledge in the rock, and surrounded by a deep ravine, I made the acquaintance of a high Catholic dignitary, a worthy and an intelligent man, who willingly gave me his impressions and experiences. He did not believe in the danger, or even in the possibility, of a native revolt in Algiers and Tunis. The natives were too well aware of the numerical superiority and better technical equipment of their French masters. That did not imply that the Arabs were pleased with the French supremacy or were even satisfied. In reality they longed for the Beys again, although their rule had been a barbaric one. It very rarely happened that any Arab went over to the Christian religion in spite of the advantages this would have brought him. Strangely and sadly enough there was far more evidence of the opposite. When, on occupying Tunis, the French troops marched into Kairuan, the old capital of Arabian Africa and one of the sacred spots of Islam, with splendid mosques and schools of law—they had found Mohammedan anchorites in the surrounding district, and among them former French officials and officers. How a Christian, a European, could ever bring himself to live like a hermit in the wilderness, or let his judgment be so perverted as to lose himself in the tenets of a religion which stands far below Christianity, neither my priestly friend nor I could explain.

From Constantine I took the diligence, via Batna and El Kantara, to Biskra. Here in the society of two young French officers, with whom I went out riding, I learnt to know the desert. The vastness of the horizon, the uniformity, the deep silence, the seriousness of this aspect of Nature made an overpowering impression on me. I could understand why Christianity, the Jewish religion, and that of Islam were all developed in the desert. It leads to concentration and meditation. It increases our sensibilities, and gives wings to the imagination. Only the sea and the high Alps are comparable to it. When I expressed my rapture to my companions, they interrupted me. " You wouldn't talk like that," they said, " if you had to spend a few summers here, as an officer. For a civilized human being the desert is hell. *Ni plus, ni moins!* Every summer one or two officers are driven to shoot themselves from sheer melancholy, caused by the dreadful heat and monotony. What keeps the majority of us going is a sense of duty, and the fact that we know that whoever has been through this, abstaining from alcohol and, steeling himself body and soul, will be fit for any future hardships and capable of facing any danger."

These officers were the first people I ever heard express the opinion that her north African possessions did not mean a military weakening of France, as was generally supposed in Germany, but rather a considerable reinforcement. North Africa was an inexhaustible reserve of healthy, tough soldiers, who made good fighters. All that was necessary was to provide such men with bold and energetic leaders. " If you supply the sexual needs of the native, and give him officers who lead him with revolvers in their hands, you can storm hell with him." Often in opposing the false views held by German military men, and especially by William II, that the extension of the French possessions in northern Africa was more harmful than useful to France, did I remember these direct conversations on " *la force noire de la France*." My military companions agreed with my priestly friend in Constantine, in regarding as out of the question any serious revolt in Tunis or Algiers. The military value of the Foreign Legion was set very high by all the Frenchmen I met, officers as well as officials. Of course these " *enfants perdus de la civilisation moderne* " had to be subjected to iron discipline. But under firm leadership they were just as formidable as were the mercenaries of medieval times. The French Foreign Legion was presumed at the time to number twenty thousand men. It was supposed that at least fifty per cent. of the legionaries were Germans. According to old French tradition the Legion was used by preference as cannon-fodder. The desert climate, with its dreadful summer heat and acute cold in winter, decimated the ranks of the legionaries. The annual total losses of the Foreign Legion were computed at seventy per cent.

Algiers, where I finished my African journey, was almost a disappointment for me after Carthage and after the desert. In any case the " White City " did not fulfil the expectations which my reading of *Semilasso*, by Prince Pückler-Muskau, had aroused in me. But in Algiers too I made a not uninteresting acquaintance. The German Consul, Dr. Julius Fröbel, made a modest, shy, almost diffident impression. Nobody would have guessed the stirring past on which this octogenarian could look back, and from which one could learn that in the much-despised early-Victorian world there was far more romance than in our more sensible, but also, more prosaic age. Julius Fröbel was brought up by his uncle, Friedrich

Fröbel, the famous pedagogue and founder of the Kindergarten, in Keilhau, near Rudolstadt. From Keilhau he went to Zürich, where he received the chair of mineralogy at the Polytechnic. When he became a naturalized Swiss he gave up his professorship and placed himself at the head of the radical party of the city on the Limmat. He founded the *Literarische Comtoir* to publish revolutionary works forbidden by the censorship in Germany, and which Fröbel spread abroad with passionate zeal. When he was arrested on a propaganda tour in Cologne and exiled from Prussia, he found a refuge in Dresden, became more and more radical in his views, and was elected to the Frankfurt parliament in 1848 as a red Democrat, In October 1848 he went, with a friend in the party, Robert Blum, to Vienna, to present the revolutionaries in that city with an address from the Left in Frankfort. At the end of October he took part as captain in the fights of the Viennese revolutionaries against the imperial troops besieging the city. After the fall of Vienna he was arrested, together with Blum, and condemned by court-martial to death by hanging. That was doubtlessly the most dramatic moment of his life. Robert Blum was shot, as is well known. Julius Fröbel was pardoned at the last moment, by Prince Alfred Windischgraetz, to whom one of his aides-de-camps had pointed out that Fröbel, once in a speech or pamphlet, had expressed himself in favour of an Austrian hegemony for Germany. Windischgraetz, indeed, permitted Fröbel to return to Frankfort where, in June 1849, he was present at the exodus of the Rump parliament to Stuttgart. After this he lived, first at Cuxhaven, then on Heligoland, and emigrated, in 1849, to America. There he established a soap factory in New York, went bankrupt, moved to Nicaragua, took part in a commission which was to investigate the possibilities of building a canal, went to San Francisco where he published a newspaper and, when this too was a failure, came back to New York. Here he married the Countess Caroline von Armannsberg, whose father, Count Ludwig Armannsberg was in turn royal Bavarian Minister of the Interior and of Finances, President of the Regency of the newly-founded Greek state, and even Hellenic Vice-Regent, and who ended his days in Munich as Councillor of the Bavarian Crown.

Fröbel returned with his wife to Germany, joined the Pan-German party and established in Vienna a semi-official journal, the *Messenger*. With Julius Fröbel arose the idea of the Frankfort Convention of Princes, for which he won support from the Emperor Francis Joseph, through his brother-in-law, the Hereditary Prince of Thurn and Taxis. At the same time he had worked for a reform of Austrian commercial policy in the direction of free-trade and of his own social theories in which he, as he confided in me, kept the middle way between Rodbertus and Lassalle. In 1866 he took over the editorship of the Würtenberg *State Gazette*, but gave it up after a year and founded the *South German Press* in Munich, in which he fought for Bismarck's policy, and in so doing accomplished his transition from the Pan-German to the Little-German-Prussian party. After he had sold the *South German Press*, which, by the way, paid as little as other earlier enterprises, for a fair price, he went in 1873 as Consul to Smyrna in the service of the German Empire. From Smyrna he had been transferred to Algiers.

Julius Fröbel received me with the suspicion which, in his adventurous life, had clearly become second nature to him. When I had managed to calm his fears that I had come to Algiers to supplant him he presented me with his principal work: *The Economics of the Human Race in regard to the Unity of ideal and practical Interest*. Then, timidly at first, but gaining gradually in confidence, he began to relate his impressions as Consul in Algiers. On the basis of his practical, clear, and profound observations of conditions in North-West Africa, I wrote in one night a memorandum, which the Ambassador, Prince Hohenlohe, handed in later to the Foreign Office. The general political impressions of my tour to Tunis and Algiers I summed up in a long letter to Holstein.

CHAPTER XXXIX

Visit of Herbert Bismarck to Paris—Invited by Herbert Bismarck to London—The Ambassador Count Münster—Mr. Gladstone—Marriage of Adolf von Bülow in Nienstedten (1.7.1884)—Transfer to St. Petersburg—At Prince Bismarck's in Varzin.

SINCE I had advanced to the position of First Secretary of the Paris Embassy Holstein had become increasingly interested in me. At this period, when they were still intimate friends, Herbert Bismarck said to me once of Holstein: " Holstein possesses uncommon flair. He can feel whether a young diplomat is a ' rising man ' or not, before the fellow is clear about it himself. And this, too, makes him valuable to my father." Holstein not only interested himself in my dispatches and official activities, but tried to approach me on social ground as well. When, after my promotion, I came on leave to Berlin, he invited me to Borchardt's. As we drank the excellent claret (Holstein was a gourmet) he explained to me that he felt for me almost as a father feels for his son. My father, not long before his death, had asked him to look after me, he said. " When I am no longer there," he had said, " keep a protective hand over my eldest boy." Holstein said all this with a slight tremolo in his voice. I believe there was even a tear in his eye. Was there any truth in the story? I doubt it. Though my father had respected Holstein's great gifts, his knowledge of languages, his quickness at repartee, his immense capacity for work, above all, his political sagacity, he had never trusted Privy Councillor Fritz von Holstein.

Back in Paris in May, 1884, I received a letter from Herbert Bismarck, at the time First Secretary at the London Embassy. He advised me of an approaching week's visit to Paris, where he hoped to have a good time with me. I found him on arrival much better and happier than two or three years ago when he was still quite dominated by his unhappy passion for Princess Elisabeth Carolath, dissatisfied with himself and the whole world, and in the most pessimistic of spirits. He astonished me now by the staying power he displayed, sitting up till all hours, in the Café Anglais or at Voisins, drinking heavy Romanée-Conti and extra-dry champagne, to appear at lunch next morning in the best of condition and finish a bottle of port. I invited him frequently to small suppers with French friends, who liked him. He did not speak French very fluently but had an original way of expressing himself and found an apt expression for everything he wanted to say. I remember one excellent lunch at the Café Voisin to which, beside the clever and charming Count Adrien Montebello, came Camille Barrère, the future ambassador in Rome, and the brothers Cambon, both destined to become ambassadors. The Frenchmen admired the drinking capacity of this young German giant, but also his humour and his gift for repartee. I introduced Herbert to Francis Charmes, later of the *Revue des Deux Mondes*, who was particularly pleased by his keen intelligence. I also took him to Versailles. When I showed him the regal courtyard where the statue of the *Roi-Soleil* is surrounded by those of sixteen French generals, from Bayard to Masséna, and, as later we walked through the picture gallery, dedicated to the fame of France (*à toutes les gloires de la France*) which glorifies all the victories of the French army throughout the centuries, all the splendours of " *la gloire* " with none of the shadows, I pointed out the boundless vanity of Frenchmen, which makes the German, inclined to moral reflections, shake his head, but which is, at the same time, the source of their unquenchable ambition, of the indestructible French vitality, and above all, the passionate French patriotism. Herbert said: " All this here is all nonsense! Those are *tempi passati*. We mustn't allow the French to bluff or impress us. They are really done for ever." In contrast to his great father, Herbert, both as the Secretary of State and even more later as Embassy Secretary, had from his youth been inclined to sweeping political statements.

Not long after Herbert Bismarck had returned from Paris to London, I received a letter from him in which he invited me in a manner as pressing as it was cordial, to come over for a few days. Not only would my visit give him personal pleasure but he thought it would be useful officially for me to have a look at London and establish relations there. He suggested that I should stay with our mutual friend, Count Friedrich Vitzthum, Second Secretary of the Imperial Embassy, who would be glad to put me up in his comfortable and charming house. I accepted at once and in two days left for London, via Boulogne. My train passed Amiens, and I thought of the days in December, 1870, when I was billetted at Camon, fought at Querrieux, Pont Noyelles, and Daours, and later, in the fine May of 1871, rode in the woods of Longeau. I arrived in the English capital at an interesting political moment. In English home politics everything, in February 1884, was centred

round the Franchise Reform Bill, which Gladstone had brought
before the Commons at the end of February, and which, at a single
stroke, would nearly double the electorate. The Lords were opposed
to this reform and fought it with skilful tactics. They did not make
the mistake of the Prussian Conservatives during the last years of my
chancellorship, when they rigidly opposed every reform of the
Prussian voting system. More clever, more statesman-like, and
more patriotic, the English Conservatives, and with them the House
of Lords in which they had the majority, declared that the extension
of the franchise was in accordance with their own wishes. But they
made the not unreasonable demand that the new division of parliamentary seats, which Gladstone wished to postpone, should be included in the first draft of the Bill so that both parties might see
clearly what they stood to gain or lose by the whole measure. The
Lords were unable to secure fusion of the two measures in one and
the same bill. But since they determined not to pass the first till
the second had been laid before Parliament, Gladstone suggested a
compromise. He came to an understanding with Lord Salisbury,
the leader of the Tories and the majority in the Upper House, and
made such concessions as were absolutely necessary to satisfy them,
though these did not go far enough to endanger the liberal majority
in the Commons. Lord Salisbury accepted the compromise and the
great reform was assured. Once again the hereditary political
wisdom of the English—what King Frederick William IV described as " traditional common-sense "—was brilliantly vindicated.

In foreign politics attention was focussed on the mission with
which General Gordon had been entrusted in the Soudan. The
whole of England trembled for the fate of its beloved and respected
General Gordon.

My first visit in London was, of course, paid to the Ambassador,
Count, later Prince Münster. He was eccentric, both physically
and mentally. Very tall and thin, he had a disproportionally large
head, which reminded me of a giant pumpkin on a long stalk.
Münster used to waggle this head. This gave him a look of pride
and indifference, as though he cared for nothing and nobody, combined as it was with a pendulous lower lip, and dull eyes. In this
respect he was a typical specimen of the old Hanoverian nobility,
whose aristocratic stiffness exceeded any other in Germany. Yet
there was no denying that this haughtiness was allied to other
more solid qualities. Münster had unshakable self-confidence and
great common-sense. His talk was as odd as his appearance. He
did not conceal his contempt for the Foreign Office under Bismarck,
to whom he was wont to refer as the " Central Ox." He paid no

attention to Foreign Office criticisms or even to reprimands from
Bismarck himself. When he once received a written censure from
the " great Otto," as we in the diplomatic career used to call him,
he said indifferently, and in the very presence of Herbert Bismarck:
" How annoyed he must have been when he dictated this! "

On the first evening I spent with Münster he had a friendly
dispute with Friedrich Vitzthum about an Anglo-German question
which was being discussed at the moment. Münster liked Vitzthum
although, or perhaps because, he did not conceal any opinion he
had of him. " I know very well," said Vitzthum that evening to his
chief, who had again made derogatory remarks about German officials and university professors, " that you, Excellency, are of the
opinion that an English lord of twenty-one, who has rowed and
played cricket at Oxford or Cambridge is cleverer than all the
German bureaucrats and intellectuals put together." With perfect
calm Münster said, smiling: " And so he is, my dear Vitzthum.
So he is! Politically a young lord of that kind is cleverer than all our
professors and privy councillors! " When the topic came up that
he and Bismarck had been colleagues in St. Petersburg from 1859
to 1862, Münster said, not without unconscious humour: " It was
easy enough for Bismarck with the strong Prussian army behind him
to win a good position for himself in St. Petersburg. But that I, as
representative of little Hanover, made such headway there—that
means something." When we returned from the Embassy to
Vitzthum's house Herbert summed up his opinion of Münster in
the criticism that his education, his marraige with an Englishwoman,
and all his preferences, had made an Englishman of him, so that he
saw everything through English spectacles. He would therefore
only be of use to us as long as we had no serious differences with
England. If this remained the case, and Berlin watched and controlled him, Münster was in his right place in London, for the
English liked him and had complete confidence in him. It was
only the Prince of Wales he did not get on with, but that was because the Prince was not only anti-German at heart but could not
forgive what he considered to be Münster's treason towards the
Hanoverian royal house. As an old Hanoverian and son of a
Hanoverian dignitary, who had been ennobled by the house of
Guelph, Münster, according to the opinion of the heir to the British
throne, should have remained loyal to the Guelphs after 1866.

During my London visit Münster was kind and polite to me.
Many years later he resented being obliged to resign, at the age of
eighty, and really quite senile, with the diamond order of the Black
Eagle to console him. At the time of my London visit he asked

me whether I would not like to be transferred as First Secretary to London since Herbert Bismarck was going to leave this post. I should be very welcome as First Secretary. I was suited to London and would carve out a good position for myself there.

Münster introduced me to the Prime Minister. The Right Honourable W. E. Gladstone, M.P., First Lord of the Treasury was already seventy-five years old. From his twenty-fourth year, that is to say for fifty-one years, he had been a member of the House of Commons. Already half a century ago, in 1834, under Sir Robert Peel, the upholder of Catholic emancipation and pioneer of free trade, he had been Under-Secretary of State in the Colonial Office, and in 1868, Prime Minister for the first time. Gladstone had not the fascination of Disraeli, the father of English Imperialism. He did not exercise that charm, which had made of Benjamin Disraeli the most popular Prime Minister since Palmerston, either upon Queen Victoria, who greatly preferred his rival Beaconsfield, or upon the English people which showered on Disraeli as many and as constant favours as did his exalted mistress. In Disraeli's honour the primrose decorates the buttonholes of English Nationalists to this day. But William Gladstone was also an exceptional personality. I was struck by his large eyes, deep and earnest, which spoke of enthusiasm, sincerity, and the zeal of the missioner. He had an exceptionally pleasant voice. I am far from judging him by the words he exchanged with a man forty years his junior. But I understood that he impressed his countrymen by qualities which were English in the best sense of the word: his deep seriousness, efficiency, capacity for enthusiasm, conscientiousness, and loyalty to his convictions. Gladstone changed these convictions occasionally, but believed as firmly as in the gospel in whatever he said at the moment. A lady once wrote to Disraeli the same question that the good Gretchen asks of Faust: "Now tell me, what is your religion?" Disraeli replied that a wise man never says what he thinks about religion. Gladstone was in far closer contact with it. He read, meditated, and commented on the Bible. There is an enchanting picture by Lenbach, depicting William Ewart Gladstone discussing exegesis with Ignaz Döllinger. Gladstone looks out reflectively into space; Döllinger ponders with folded arms. Gladstone had very much of the theologian in him. He was always thinking in terms of the Bible. Disraeli was something of a sceptic. Gladstone was easy to shock. Before the formation of the Italian national state he had scolded the government in the kingdom of Naples, and in the Papal States as being a "denial of God." After the Turkish excesses in Bulgaria he raged against the "unspeakable

Turk." But like the majority of his countrymen Gladstone would only get indignant when his wrath did not seriously interfere with English interests. He was not always proof against the reproach of hypocrisy into which statesmen fall easily who take up an ethical standpoint, and yet wish to defend the interests of their country.

There have been few statesmen so convinced of their own infallibility as William Gladstone. My friend Harding, called " The Professor " in the English diplomatic service, on account of his profound and exact knowledge—not to be confused with the future Under-Secretary of the Foreign Office and Viceroy of India, Hardinge—told me once of the following little personal trait. He was invited to dine at Gladstone's. The great man held one of his customary monologues, explaining how in the Balkan Peninsular there existed only two nations, the noble Greeks and the hateful Turks. Harding, who knew the Balkan Peninsular from personal experience, modestly, almost shyly, called his attention to the fact that millions of Slavs were living on the south-eastern peninsular, Croats, Serbs, and Bulgars, as well as Rumanians and Albanians. As Harding was quoting the statistics and characterizing these various nationalities, their past, their culture, and aspirations, a footman handed him a note. It came from Mrs. Gladstone who had written : " We never contradict Mr. Gladstone."

Almost every day, Münster himself would drive me, in his perfectly conducted four-in-hand, to one or other sporting event. Herbert gave a supper in my honour before I left, in Richmond, to which, besides the witty and brilliant Lord Charles Beresford and his charming wife, he had invited the Home Secretary, the Minister of War, Sir W. Vernon-Harcourt, and the Marquis of Hartington, later Duke of Devonshire. Sir Charles Dilke, President of the Local Government Board was also present at this little dinner. Not long since he had found the way back to Monarchism from a not quite academic Republicanism. This exceptionally gifted man, who, with his book, *Problems of Greater Britain*, became one of the pioneers of the present British Empire, which rests on a federal basis, ruined himself later, socially and politically, through an affair with a woman. Another time Herbert invited old diplomatic colleagues and friends among whom I remember the Frenchman d'Aunay, later the friend and confidant of Clemenceau, and his ambitious and coquettish American wife, the clever and historically well-versed Mr. Bapst, the Dane, Falbe, the Hungarian Hengelmüller von Hengervor, and the Russian Niki Adlerberg.

When I bade farewell to Herbert he presented me with a handy little revolver and the humorous advice to " shoot on sight " anybody who crossed my path inimically. This revolver still lies on my writing-table in the Villa Malta. I left London with every hope that, during the course of the summer, I should take Herbert Bismarck's place as First Secretary, and so get a chance to know England better, which I had liked so much from this short visit.

On 1st July, 1884, I had four days leave for the wedding of my brother Adolf to our cousin, Countess Carola Vitzthum. The ceremony is still vivid in my mind. The wedding took place on the Lower Elbe, where I was born, in the old church of Nienstedten, whose pastor had christened me, and in whose quiet churchyard I hope to be buried. It would be difficult to imagine a handsomer couple. He thirty-four, she barely twenty. He tall, slight, muscular, with earnest, almost austere features and large thoughtful eyes; she with beautiful though rather melancholy eyes, a pretty figure, girlish, slender, and full of charm. She had been maid-of-honour to the Empress Augusta, who had a good influence upon all the ladies of her court, using them, as Goethe suggests, to steep their minds in all that is good and beautiful. It was a love marriage in the full meaning of the word. She looked up to him with tender admiration and affection; he was passionately in love with her. Barely two years later Carola died in her second child-bed. Thirteen years later Adolf was killed in a riding accident.

> " *Was sind Hoffnungen, was sind Entwürfe,*
> *Die der Mensch, der Vergängliche, baut?* " [1]

During the breakfast, which took place in the Bost, the pleasantly situated country house of the bride's parents on the Elbe, under oaks, limes, and beeches, in Dockenhuden, where the river flows in a broad stream, I received a telegram from the Foreign Office announcing my transfer to St. Petersburg and stating that I was to take up this new post immediately, as the Imperial Ambassador in St. Petersburg, General von Schweinitz wished to begin a vacation which, for family reasons, could not be postponed. This was how I left Paris. I had believed that within a few days I should leave the Elbe for the Seine. Instead of this I never saw Paris, where I had lived six years, again. What are hopes, what are plans!

Together with these orders from the Foreign Office I received a telegram from Varzin, in which Prince Bismarck expressed the wish to see me and invited me for a two-day visit. Next day I went straight from Hamburg to Varzin, where I had last been nine years previously. I was received in the friendliest manner by the Prince,

---

[1] What are hopes, what are plans
Built by man, the transient?

the Princess, and Bill Bismarck, who was in his father's personal service. The Bismarck home was patriarchal in the best sense, not only as between parents and children, but between the host and his guests. Like every real genius Bismarck was not to be classified merely under one heading such as " the greatest Junker," any more than Moltke could be called only a strategist or Goethe " the writer of *Faust*." But, in his inmost heart Bismarck was a Prussian nobleman and officer, a German farmer, and the father of a family. The Princess asked at once after my mother, of whom she was very fond. The Prince gave me his hand with the words: " It must be five years since your father died, but I miss him as much as on the first day."

The Princess pressed me with delicacies with which the dinner table at Varzin was as well provided as in Berlin. When she tried to persuade me to take a second and third glass of heavy Kulmbach beer, a present to the Prince, he stopped her with the words: " I imagine that Herr von Bülow, who is very like his father, save that he is slighter, only takes a moderate amount of alcohol, which I find praiseworthy, although I myself take the opposite point of view." Conversation turned on the social life in Berlin. The Princess was enthusiastic about Frau von Spitzemberg, the wife of the Württemberg Minister there, who had been her friend for over twenty years, ever since their time together in St. Petersburg, and whom she had always found loyal. The families related to the Spitzembergs, the Varnbülers, Hofackers, Erffas and Belows, were also praised though, on the other hand, the " horrible, unbearable, affected Mimi," the wife of the minister Schleinitz was violently attacked. The great Prince smiled approvingly and stated that he found the husband, Count Alexander Schleinitz, was " almost as unbearable " as Mimi. When Bill took me to my room at midnight he said, humorously, with a satisfied smile: " There's not so much scandal talked anywhere as in our house." I told him that things looked differently in the lion's cage to what they did in the sheep-pen or in the barn-yard.

As I sat next morning in my room, eating a very large and excellent breakfast, the Prince entered. He sat down opposite me with the words: " Don't let me disturb you, go on eating your eggs. I hope they have been boiled properly." Then he continued, " You are probably furious at being sent to St. Petersburg instead of to London? London is certainly pleasanter to live in. And I don't suppose it's easy for you to leave Paris. However you feel, you are putting a very good face upon it and not acting the injured party, and that's always the cleverest thing to do." I replied that I found it extremely interesting to think that I should soon see the Finnish bay and the frozen Neva again, after having just ridden over the desert at Biskra. The Prince nodded and then began to talk foreign policy.

Our policy is and remains a policy of peace. We have no reason to want a war, and I do not see what we should have to gain by one. The annexation of German-Austria, or the Baltic provinces, or even any Dutch or the Swiss territory, would only weaken us. And so-called "prophylactic" wars, that is, the policy of attacking somebody else so that he may not grow a little stronger and attack first, I consider, as did your father, who would have told you this, not only un-Christian but politically foolish as well. What did Napoleon I ever accomplish with his "prophylactic" wars? One can always begin a war but one never knows how it may end! Three times God has given us victory. That was a great mercy. But to let it come to a fourth war, without pressing reasons, would be tantamount to tempting Providence. It is in our own interests to keep the peace. Of course we must keep our sword sharp. Our political position, power, honour and wealth we owe in the first place to the army. The army also ensures monarchical government as the only solid basis of the realm, of order and our growing prosperity. The pivot of our position, and with that of our whole policy, the point on which things turn, is our relationship to Russia. The French will only attack us if we let ourselves get embroiled with Russia, but then are certain to do so. As for the English, they have no reason at all for attacking us, even if they are beginning to envy our industrial and commercial progress. The Englishman is like the dog in the fable, who cannot bear that another dog should have a few bones, although the overfed brute is sitting before a bowl full to the brim. An English attack would only be thinkable if we found ourselves at war with both Russia and France, or did anything so utterly absurd as to fall upon Holland or Belgium, or block the Baltic by closing the Sund, or some nonsense of the kind, which is out of the question. For us, therefore, St. Petersburg is now the most important diplomatic post. That is why I have transferred you there. London and Paris are observation posts. In countries where, in the long run, parliament decides matters, the diplomat cannot accomplish much. In a country where things depend in the first place upon the sovereign it is different. Even the greatest autocrat never acts according to his own ideas, even if he sometimes thinks he does. He will always have a wife, a mistress, brothers, aunts, cousins, favourites, aides-de-camps and chamberlains, who influence him to a greater or a less degree. Then the diplomat can do positive and concrete work. We have, thank God, got rid of Gortchakov. His successor, von Giers, is not a heroic figure, but is well disposed. I consider him honest, and far preferable to Gortchakov. I look upon Alexander III as loyal too. That he is not so well-disposed towards us as his father is not a misfortune. Alexander II was steeped in the traditions of the Wars of Liberation, and for that very reason he was so sensitive about anything which he mistakenly considered to be a departure from the principles of the Holy Alliance. He was like a woman who, because she was once very much in love with her husband, goes on suspecting him all his life and continually plagues him with her jealous question: " Do you love me ? " I believe that a calm and neighbourly relationship is quite possible with Alexander III. But point out wherever you can in St. Petersburg that nobody can know how a military clash between the three imperial powers might end. One thing is certain: The three dynasties, the three monarchs, would probably pay the penalty and the only real victor would be the revolution. Napoleon said on St. Helena, that Europe, after his fall, would be either Cossack or Republican. I believe that if the Prussian and the Cossack ever come to blows Europe will become Republican. The ticklish factor in our connections with Russia is of course Austria. We cannot let Austria be overrun and shattered. But just as little must we let ourselves be dragged into war by her. To manœuvre between these two crags is a matter of skill and a clear head, much the same qualities as are necessary to prevent two trains meeting in a head-on crash. The pointsman must keep his eyes open and have a steady hand. The most difficult to deal with are the Magyars, because they are so violent. They are our best support In our relationship towards the Hapsburg monarchy, but, at the same time, they are those who most incline to exaggerated suspicion and imprudence. Besides, God in His wisdom has so arranged it that the peoples of the Near East, which, as we know begins on the high-road to Vienna, cannot abide one another. The Magyars and the Rumanians, the Croats and Serbs, the Turks and Bulgarians, the Czechs and Slovaks, the Greeks and the Albanians hate each other even more than they hate the German.

I had listened with the closest attention, and with boundless

admiration. But I did not let my breakfast be interrupted and ate
my eggs, the toast, and a smoked herring, which the kind Princess
had ordered to be brought me, in comfort. That afternoon I went
for a walk with Bill, he said to me: " You will be glad to hear that
my father said some nice things about you. It pleased him especially
that you went on calmly eating your eggs, ' He has good nerves,'
he said, ' He pleases me altogether.' "

Prince Bismarck did not return to the questions of foreign
policy. Next day, on the other hand, in my presence and in the
bosom of his family, he expressed some violent opinions of his
domestic enemies. He did not want in the least to govern autocratically, he said, although the reproach was daily levelled against
him. Real autocracy would be very different from the present
government in Germany. He was perfectly well aware that, in
Germany, in the second half of the nineteenth century, absolutism
and autocracy would be impossible, apart from the fact that such
government had never been one of his ideals. But a parliamentary
régime seemed to him just as impossible. Our parties possessed
neither the patriotism of the French nor the sound common-sense
of the English. Under the circumstances he did not understand
what benefits the German Liberals promised themselves from the
" inauguration of responsible ministries of the realm," which they
had lately adopted as part of their programme. As long as he remained in office he would never countenance such a thing. Considering the political incapacity of the average German, the intellectual parliamentary system would lead to conditions such as had
prevailed in 1848, that is to say, to weakness and incompetency on
the top, and to bumptiousness and ever new demands from below.

I should like to mention the following as a footnote to my visit
in Varzin, since it is typical of Bismarck's friendship for my father.
Three years after the resignation of Prince Bismarck, in the spring
of 1893, the publicist, Hans Blum, the eldest son of the agitator,
Robert Blum, shot by court-martial by the Austrians in 1848 in the
Brigittenau, near Vienna, gave, in an essay, an account of conversations with Prince Bismarck, in which he repeated alleged unfavourable remarks made by the Prince about my father, whom he was
said to have accused, among other things, of too great harshness
towards his subordinates in office. My brother Christian, captain
of the 2nd Dragoons, who met Herbert Bismarck soon afterwards
in Sorrento, asked him the rights of the affair. On 31st March,
1893, Herbert Bismarck, who had returned to Schönhausen, wrote
me:

Your brother Christian will have written you about our

conversation in Sorrento. As soon as we had the somewhat troublesome Italian journey behind us I wrote to my father on the subject during my leisure in Fiume, and found on my arrival here, three days ago, his answer. The following passages will be of interest to you. On the first page he says: " I talked to Blum freely because his parliamentary activities, at the time of his father's death, had brought him into closer contact with me. He was not a stranger to me, and he made loose and clumsy use of my frankness. As far as I can remember, however, the name of Bülow did not occur in his indiscretions. To criticize Bülow *à la* Blum never entered my head. Bülow was such a kind and loyal friend that he might have had far more unpleasant qualities as an official than I ever found in him. I would never have parted from him with any other feelings than those of kindliness, and so I proved to him when he was ill, and I visited him in Potsdam. I believe he was the only person I ever went to see in that way." I am glad to be able to let you know of this passage in my father's letter, since I know it will satisfy you. I add nothing to it, because I have already spoken to your brother about it, very warmly and thoroughly, and imagine you are already aware of this. In Rome we had the pleasure of meeting Donna Laura several times in her old health and kindly spirits. She has quite won my wife's heart. In old friendship,

Always yours,

H. B.

Almost forty years after I had visited Prince Bismarck in Varzin, Frau von Schmoller, widow of the famous political economist wrote me on 10th June, 1922, that she had been friends for a long time with a Frau von Zitzewitz, who was born a Puttkamer, and whose parents had been relatives and friends of the house of Bismarck. The letter continued:

In Varzin, a long time ago, a cousin of Princess Bismarck, a Frau von Puttkamer-Varzin, was saying to the Prince, who was in a bad humour at the moment, and would have liked to be rid of everything official, that he had no successor, to which he agreed. She went on to ask him whether he could think of anybody for the future and he was silent for some time and then said: " Yes, I know of somebody, Bernhard Bülow. He is Legation Secretary at present. He'd be able to do it one day." The young daughter of Frau von Puttkamer, who was the present Frau von Zitzewitz remembered these words of Prince Bismarck when the appointment of Prince Bülow was made.

From Varzin I travelled via Stolp, Danzig, and Königsberg, to my new destination. In Königsberg I made notes, almost verbatim, of my Varzin impressions. These notes are the basis of the above description. That same night I wrote a long letter to Countess Marie Dönhoff in Rome, in which I told her how painful it would be for me to be so far away from her as St. Petersburg. She was still living with her mother in the Piazza Paganica. But neither space nor time could ever separate me from her, I said. She replied by sending me the German translation of a poem by Leopardi. The poem is called "Love and Death." In German it runs:

" Das Licht erblickten einst zur selben Stunde
Als Brüder Tod und Liebe.
So Holdes blüht im irdischen Getriebe
Nicht mehr, wie diese, noch auf anderen Sternen.
Denn von der einen stammen die
Lieblichsten der Freuden,
Erquickend auf des Lebens Meer die Herzen,
Der andere tilgt die Schmerzen,
Die Übel allzusammen.
Als Kind, von Reiz umstrahlet
Und anzusehen erfreulich,
Nicht so, wie sich das feige Volk ihn malet,
Begleitet er zuweilen
Den kleinen, zarten Liebesgott getreulich.
Da sieht man sie gesellt die Welt durcheilen,
Zum Trost für weiser Herzen einsam Schmachten.
Und weiser wird niemals ein Herz erscheinen
Als das des Liebenden, noch mutbeseelter,
Das Leben zu verachten,
Und nie so gern ertragen wir Gefahren
Für andere Herren als für die Herrin Liebe.
Die deine Hilf erbaten,
O Liebe, sehn, erwacht zu höherm Triebe,
Den Mut, und klug in Taten,
Nicht in Gedanken bloss, wie sonst sie pflegen,
Sind dann die Menschenkinder allerwegen.
Erwachen, die da schliefen,
Die Regungen der Liebe,
Aufs neue wieder in des Herzens Tiefen,
Da meldet seltsam sich zugleich mit ihnen
Ein lebensmüdes Sehnen nach dem Tode.
Nicht weiss ich wie. Doch allen so erschienen

Ist dies als echten Liebens erste Wirkung.
Vielleicht erschreckt das Auge
Sodann die Öde dieser Weltumzirkung,
Vielleicht ist schal die Farbe dann den Blicken
Des Menschen, ohne jenes
Unendliche und Neue,
Das einzig ihn vermöchte zu beglücken!
Und grossen Lebenssturm um seinetwillen
Sieht er voraus und trachtet
Nach Ruh, strebt, in den Hafen sich, den stillen,
Zu flüchten vor dem wütenden Verlangen,
Das ihn gewittergleich erfüllt mit Bangen.
Und dann, wenn überwunden
Ihn ganz die Macht, die hehre,
Und in der Brust ihm tobt zu allen Stunden
Das Leid—oh, wieviel Male
Ruft dann sein Herz, das schwere,
Herbei den Tod, zum Trost für seinen Kummer!
Wie oft des Abends und wie oft im Strahle
Des Morgens, stets noch unerquickt vom Schlummer,
Meint er beglückt sich, wenn's vergönnt ihm wäre,
Nie wieder zu erheben
Vom Lager sich, nie mehr das Licht zu schaun!
Und oftmals bei dem Klang der Totenglocke,
Beim Liede, das geleitet
Den Menschen hin zu des Vergessens Auen,
Da hört man ihn mit Seufzern
Den Glücklichsten beneiden,
Den er so sieht von dieser Erde scheiden.
Sogar das Volk, das roh und unbelehret,
Der Landmann, unerfahren
Der Tugenden, die Bildung nur bescheret,
Das Mägdlein auch, dem sonst der Mut zu schwinden
Beginnt beim blossen Nennen
Des Todes mit emporgesträubten Haaren:
Er wagt, aufs Grab und auf des Todes Binden
Den Blick zu richten, fest und standhaft Eisen
Und Gift erwägt es, ruhig,
Gefasst nun lange Stunden,
Und klar wird ihm die Schöne
Des edlen Tods im Geiste, dem unweisen,
So sehr erzieht zum Tod die Menschensöhne
Der Liebe Zucht. Und oft, wenn schier unsäglich

Herangewachsen ist die Qual im Herzen,
Dass ird' scher Kraft sie nimmer deucht erträglich,
Dann weicht dem Stoss der Schmerzen
Der schwache Leib und obsiegt solcherweise
Die brüderliche Macht des Todes—oder
So stark ist im Gemüt der Sporn der leise
Des tiefen Liebesdranges, dass gewaltsam
Mit ihren eigenen Händen
Der rohe Landmann und das schwache Mägdlein
Ihr ird' sches Los vollenden unaufhaltsam.
Die Welt bespöttelt solches Los—sei Frieden
Und hohes Alter ihr doch stets beschieden!
Den heissen, den beglückten,
Den mutbeseelten Geistern
Gewähr das Schicksal einen von euch beiden,
Willkommen Herrn und Meistern
Und Freunden dieser Menschheit,
Die nichts in All an Macht so kann erreichen
Als das Verhängnis. Du, den vom Beginn
Des Lebens an ich rufe stets und ehre,
Mit wandellosem Sinne,
Du, holder Tod, der einzig
Mitleidig auf dies Dasein blickt, das schwere,
Wenn je du dich gepriesen,
Von mir empfindest, wenn, Göttlicher, dich jemals
Ich zu entschäd 'gen strebte
Für Undank, den dir schnödes Volk erwiesen,
O säume nicht mehr, komm mit raschen Schritten
Und schliesse diesem Lichte,
Nun endlich weichend längst entwöhnten Bitten,
Mein düstres Aug, o Herrscher dieses Lebens!
Wann immer ich nicht flehe mehr vergebens
Und du zu mir herniedersenkst die Schwingen-
Gewappnet, hoch die Stirn,
Wirst Du mich finden, mutvoll stets begegnend
Dem Schicksal, nie die Hand, die ich in meinem
Unschuldigen Blute färbt und mich getroffen
Mit geisselschlägen, rühmend oder segnend,
Wie Sklavensinn der Menschen tut seit lange,
Abschüttelnd jedes Hoffen, womit die Welt, die bange
Sich kindisch tröstet, jede
Beschwichtigung, vom Schicksal nichts erwartend
Als dich und heiter stets entgegensehend

Dem Tag, wo nach erfülltem Lebenslose
Mein Haupt zur Ruh sich legt in deinem Schosse."

AMORE E MORTE

Ὸν οἱ θεοὶ φιλοῦσιν ἀποθνήσχει νέος

Fratelli, a un tempo stesso, Amore e Morte
Ingenerò la sorte
Cose quaggiù si belle
Altre il mondo non ha, non han le stelle.
Nasce dall' uno il bene
Nasce il piacer maggiore
Che per lo mar dell'essere si trova;
L'altra ogni gran dolore
Ogni gran male annulla.
Bellissima fanciulla,
Dolce a veder, non quale
La si dipinge la codarda gente,
Gode il fanciullo Amore
Accompagnar sovente;
E sorvolano insiem' la via mortale,
Primi conforti d'ogni saggio core.
Nè cor fu mai più saggio
Che percosso d'amor, nè mai più forte
Sprezzò l'infausta vita,
Nè per altro signore
Come per questo a perigliar fu pronto:
Ch'ove tu porgi aita,
Amor, nasce il coraggio,
O si ridesta; e sapïente in opre,
Non in pensiero invan, siccome suole,
Divien l'umana prole.
　　Quando novellamente
　　Nasce nel cor profondo
　　Un amoroso affetto,
　　Languido e stanco insiem con esso in petto
　　Un desiderio di morir si sente:
　　Come non so: ma tale
　　D'Amor vero e possente è il primo effetto.
Forse gli occhi spaura
Allor questo deserto: a se la terra
Forse il mortale inabitabil fatta
Vede omai senza quella
Nova, sola, infinita
Felicità, che il suo pensier figura:
Ma per cagion di lei grave procella
Presentendo il suo cor, brama quiete,
Brama raccorsi, e porto

Dinanzi al fier disio,
Che già, rugghiando, intorno intorno oscura.
 Poi, quando tutto avvolge
 La formidabil possa,
 E fulmina nel cor l'invitta cura,
 Quante volte implorata
 Con desiderio intenso,
 Morte, sei tu dall'affannoso amante !
 Quante le sera, e quante
 Abbandonando all'alba il corpo stanco
 Sè beato chiamò, s'indi gammai
 Non rilevasse il fianco,
 Ne tornasse a veder l'amara luce !
 E spesso al suon della funebre squilla,
 Al canto che conduce
 La gente morta al sempiterno obblio,
 Con più sospiri ardenti
 Dall'imo petto invidïò colui
 Che tra gli spenti ad abitar sen giva
 Fin la negletta plebe,
 L'uom della villa, ignaro
 D'ogni virtù che da saper deriva,
 Fin la donzella timidetta e schiva,
 Che già di morte al nome
 Sentì rizzar le chiome
 Osa alla tomba, alle funeree bende
Fermar lo sguardo di costanza pieno,
Osa ferro e veleno
Meditar, lungamente,
E nell'indotta mente
La gentilezza di morir comprende.
Tanto alla morte inclina
D'amor la disciplina. Anco sovente,
A tal venuto il gran travaglio interno
Che sostener non può forza mortale,
O cede il corpo frale
Ai terribili moti, e in questa forma
Pel fraterno poter Morte prevale;
O così sprona Amor là nel profondo,
Che da se stesso il vilanello ignaro,
La tenera donzella
Con la man violenta
Pongon le membra giovanili in terra.
Ride ai lor casi il mondo,
A cui pace e vecchiezza il ciel consenta.
 Ai fervidi, ai felici,
 Agli animosi ingegni
 L'uno o l'altro di voi conceda il fato,
 Dolci signori, amici
 All'umana famiglia,
 Al cui poter nessun poter somiglia

Nell'immenso universo, e non l'avanza,
Se non quella del fato, altra possanza.
E tu, cui già dal cominciar degli anni
Sempre onorata invoco,
Bella Morte, pietosa
Ta sola al mondo dei terreni affanni,
Se celebrata mai
Fosti da me, s'al tuo divino stato
L'onte del volgo ingrato
Ricompensar tentai,
Non tardar piu, t'inchina
A disusati preghi,
Chudi alla luce omai
Questi occhi tristi, o dell'età reina.
Me certo troverai, qual si sia l'ora
Che tu le penne al mio pregar dispieghi,
Erta la fronte, armato
E renitente al fato,
La man che flagellando si colora
Nel mio sangue innocente
Non ricolmar di lode,
Non benedir, com'usa
Per antica viltà l'umana gente;
Ogni vana speranza onde consola
Sè coi fanciulli il mondo,
Ogni conforto stolto
Gittar da me; nul'altro in alcun tempo
Sperar se non te sola;
Solo aspettar sereno
Quel di ch'io pieghi addormentato il volto
Nel tuo virgineo seno.

Under these splendid lines Countess Marie had written, in a firm hand: "Without you, I prefer death; with you, life."

CHAPTER XL

St. Petersburg (July 1884)—Taking over—Death of Gortchakov and Skobelev—Imperial Secretary Polovtsov—Herr von Giers—Meeting of the Emperors at Skierniewice, preparation for the Interview with Bismarck in Berlin—Journey to Skierniewice—Emperor William I, Tsar Alexander III, and the Emperor Francis Joseph—Warsaw— The Consul-General von Rechenberg—Count Fersen—Count Dmitri Tolstoi—Pobiedonoztsev—Countess Kleinmichl—Madame Durnov —General Tcherevin.

I HAD left St. Petersburg in March, 1876, wintry, dark, veiled in mists, covered with ice and snow. I returned now, in July, 1884, to a St. Petersburg of light white nights and the heat that lay heavily and oppressively over the Neva. Prince Alexander Mikhailovitch Gortchakov was no more. He had resigned two years previously at the great age of eighty-four. The cynicism which had been typical of him all his life did not desert him when he left office. He received a deputation from the Foreign Ministry, who handed him a very appreciative, ceremonial farewell address, in the name of all the officials who had served under him during his twenty-six years of office, an address couched, according to his taste, in the most bombastic terms—with the filthy and cynical words: " *Une bonne nouvelle pour commencer. J'ai eu ce matin une excellente selle. Voltaire a dit que pour un vieillard c'était là le seul vrai bonheur.*" A year later Gortchakov died in Baden-Baden. To the last moment he was a lecherous old man, an unpleasing spectacle from whatever angle one looked at him. Already during the Russo-Turkish War he had aroused unwelcome attentions every evening in Bucharest by applauding all the obscenities of French café-chantant singers. Death overtook him in the bed of a priestess of *Venus vulgivaga*. The frightened girl hurried to the police, who, naturally enough, wished to avoid all public scandal. It was arranged that the body of the Russian ex-Chancellor should be moved to the hotel where he was staying. The corpse was therefore laid in a big washing-basket and covered with soiled linen. This was how the mortal remains reached the hotel; a priest of the orthodox church made the further arrangements.

566

The end of Gortchakov is reminiscent of the death of General Mikhail Dmitrievitch Skobelev, conqueror of the Teke-Turkmenen, victor of Khiva and Kokan, hero of Geoktepe, Lowatz and Plevna, who died in a Moscow house of ill-fame. Blind drunk, he had had himself bound in a fit of masochism to a door and ordered the inmates of the establishment to whip him till the blood came and take no notice of his screams and protests. When the women, weary of the flagellation, ceased their labours, a syncope had put an end to the life of the not yet forty-year-old general. The editor of the *Moscow Gazette*, Mikhail Nikeforovitch Katkov, chief exponent of a reactionary, absolutist and strictly nationalist system, was sent for, and he made arrangements for the quiet removal of the body of Russia's most popular general, since Suvarov, to the Church of the Redeemer, situated within the Kremlin, whose golden lattices and gold and silver vessels were famous throughout Russia. Even those who were not prudes and Pharisees had to own in face of these two deaths—old Gortchakov and young Skobelev, a popular general and a statesman—that the sophisticated and brilliant façade of fashionable Russian life, hid a mass of brutality and corruption. The rumour which was circulated immediately in the French press to the effect that Skobelev was the victim of a dark German intrigue was, of course, an absurd invention, which would not even have done credit to a shilling shocker. The death of Skobelev was by no means a matter of rejoicing for us. There were equally good, even better, generals in the Russian army. But the Russian court may very well have breathed a sigh of relief at his demise. It had been hinted that Skobelev was not free from ambition to act the part of Russian Bonaparte. He had said to a pretty French governess, to whom he had paid court: "*Vous serez ma Josephine.*"

I arrived just in time in St. Petersburg to take over affairs from von Schweinitz, the ambassador, who left next day for Germany. When I went to see him I found with him Polovtsov, the Imperial Secretary. This high official was a typical Russian. Yet another proof of the contention of Marquis Adolphe Custine, the friend of Rahel and Varnhagen, who, in his book about Russia, published eighty years ago, expressed the opinion "*que la facilité de faire sa carrière préservait la Russie des Tsars d'une révolution générale.*" Polovtsov was of modest birth and had gambled away the little money he possessed as a minor *tchinovnik*. Russians adore card-playing. Polovtsov, on the verge of ruin, used his last roubles to procure the outfit of a gentleman and set out to pay court to the first rich heiress he could find. Her fate had also been a strange one. She was the adopted daughter of the banker Stieglitz, and had been

found outside his house, a new-born infant, wrapped in coarse nap-
kins one cold winter's morning by the *dvorniks* (porters). Stieglitz
came from Hanover. The story goes that long ago two small, but
intelligent, Jew boys left the city on the Leine to seek their fortune
in the world. One went to Hamburg, and became the ancestor of
the flourishing banker family of Heine, with branches there and in
Paris. The other had gone to St. Petersburg and founded the
banking firm of Stieglitz.

When Polovtsov left, after an animated conversation with
Schweinitz and myself, the ambassador said to me: " You have
brought a valuable gift with you to St. Petersburg. You speak very
good French. That is the key to the heart of the St. Petersburg
Upper Ten. Now you only need to make love to the feminine
leaders of St. Petersburg society and the game is yours." When I
replied that for various reasons I felt very little desire to do that, the
sophisticated general smiled. " So much the better. You know
your Goethe? It is just the man who doesn't seem to care a bit
about making an impression who does so, " *ob er reizt, ob er rührt der
beleidigt, der verführt.*" [1]

A few days later I went to Gatchina, the favourite castle of the
Tsar Alexander III, not very far from St. Petersburg, gloomy, but
easiest to protect from Nihilist attacks. As German chargé d'affaires
I had to present myself to the Foreign Secretary, Herr von Giers,
whose custom it was to reside in Gatchina when the Tsar was in
residence. Nikholai Karlovitch von Giers, sixty-four years old at
the time, made a very poor impression outwardly. Grey before his
time and badly dressed, and round shouldered, he did not possess a
quarter of the aplomb of Shuvalov, or Orlov, Lobanov, or Ignatiev.
He had begun his career in the consular service and then been
ambassador in Berne and Stockholm. His enemies declared that he
was of Jewish extraction and that his real name was Hirsch. In
reality, his grandfather, a minor Swedish nobleman, had come from
Sweden via Finland to Russia. Giers was not popular in Russia and
he knew it. " My family," he would say, " bears on its escutcheon
a small fish which is swimming against the stream. Such is my own
fate." With all his unimpressive appearance, Giers was the best
and wisest Foreign Secretary that the Russian Empire had had since
Nesselrode. Three years later the Grand Duke Vladimir said to
me once in a confidential talk: " At one time, like everybody else,
I used to grumble about Nikholai Karlovitch. But since he explained affairs in a very candid and detailed talk with me, I am

---

[1] " The lover who seems not to care whether he annoys them or moves them—
angers; and seduces."

convinced that neither Russia nor especially the imperial house, could have a better minister and adviser than Giers."

At our first meeting Herr von Giers invited me to take a walk with him. While we were crossing the park he said, in his dull, toneless voice: " I have heard of you through Orlow and Muraviev, and you also left a good impression behind on our St. Petersburg society, from your first stay in Russia. My son and my dear daughter-in-law—she was Dutch and, alas, she has died since then —were received with the greatest kindness by your parents, years ago in Berlin. I can talk to you confidentially. We need peace, and have no interest in making war. *Voilà une base solide pour être d'accord.* All depends on nothing being done on either side which might arouse unnecessary suspicions." After a slight pause the minister continued: " My Tsar wishes, above all, to be left in peace. It is not true that he was an enemy of Germany. He is as little inimical to Germany as he is friendly towards the French, the English, or the Spaniards. He is quite different from his father, grandfather, and great-uncle—Alexander II, Nicholas, and Alexander I. Our present Tsar, Alexander III, is Russian, and only Russian. He dislikes everything foreign. If that is remembered in Berlin we shall be able to get on very well together." Although I had a communication for Herr von Giers in my pocket I thought it better not to rush matters. I made my adieu, content with this pleasant impression that he had confidence in me.

Soon after my arrival in St. Petersburg Bill Bismarck wrote me privately to say that his father thought a meeting of the three Emperors very desirable, after all the misunderstandings of the last years. This was fixed for the middle of September, the place, one or other Russian palace between the Prussian frontier and Warsaw. I could set about sounding the *terrain.* If my suggestions met with any success the Ambassador, von Schweinitz, when he returned to his post, would present the official invitation. Since Giers had asked me to visit him again soon, " *non pas on chargé d'affaires, mais en ami,*" and wished to introduce me to his family, I drove out a few days later to supper in Gatchina. Madame von Giers was a Rumanian by birth, a Cantakuzene, from the famous Phanariot and Hospodar family, a dignified and kind woman. One daughter, visibly the father's favourite, was suffering from tuberculosis. The doctors held out little hope. She sat now, pale, with feverish glittering eyes, at the dinner table. When she had withdrawn I told her parents how terribly my own had suffered from the loss of their only daughter. Herr von Giers himself took me to the station. I thought it better to take Mephisto's advice to the scholar in

Faust and seize the moment. Without any finessing I told the minister what Bill Bismarck had written to me. Giers reflected for a moment and then said: " I am grateful to you for your frankness. I, too, would like to see a meeting of the three Emperors, for their own sakes, for the sake of their mutual relationship, and also to impress the gallery. I will see what can be done." Soon afterwards Herr von Giers asked me to come to the Ministry and told me that his sovereign had accepted. " *Sans enthousiasme! Il ne s'emballe guère. Il ne perd jamais son équilibre, son phlegme, si vous voulez. Il accepte, mais à la condition qu'on ne lui demandera pas de prononcer un discours. Il a horreur des discours.*"

When I reported this reply I got a telegram from the Chancellor inviting me to Berlin for a few days. The Emperor Francis Joseph had, in the meantime, declared himself satisfied, both with the meeting and the place selected, the royal hunting box, Skierniewice, in the government of Warsaw. Our Ambassador, von Schweinitz, had returned to his post. Arrived in Berlin I was invited to dinner by Prince Bismarck. There I met Prince Wilhelm, who greeted me with almost boisterous friendliness which was, however, due less to me than to my brother Adolf, who had been for four years, his aide-de-camp, and so become his personal and much-esteemed friend. Prince Bismarck, whose suspicions never slept—and this was understandable enough after the many unpleasant experiences he had had in his heroic life—stared for a few seconds in surprise and not without mistrust, at the Prince and myself. Then he took me aside and asked me my impressions in St. Petersburg. I answered: " When I was last in St. Petersburg, during the winter 1875-6, we were living on the best of terms with Russia. This love-match has now become a marriage of convenience." The Prince, who obviously agreed, smiled and answered: " That may be so." Then he said that he wished me to be present at the meeting of the three Emperors in Skierniewice. I was to be included in the Imperial suite. He himself would take his two sons so that they saw something for once. As Prince Wilhelm left he said, with regret, that he could stay no longer since " unfortunately " his parents were expecting him. The Prince replied in the very formal tone he had at his command when he wished: " I beg Your Royal Highness to lay my most humble devotion at the feet of your exalted parents." The Prince, who had obviously expected a reply in the same tone as his joke, looked dumbfounded.

Next morning we left for Skierniewice. In the railway-carriage the eighty-seven year old Emperor told stories of his former visits to Russia. He had a particularly vivid memory of one he had paid sixty years ago, to his sister Charlotte, and her husband, the Grand Duke Nicholas Pavlovitch. In paying his respects to the reigning Tsar, Alexander I, the Tsar had told him in confidence that on his (Alexander's) death not Constantine, his second brother, but his third brother, Nicholas, would ascend the imperial Russian throne. Constantine had refused the succession, not only because of his morganatic marriage and ill-health, but because he was " *un origin-al.*" The Emperor William continued: " I spent the evening of the day on which this confidence was made with my sister, and my brother-in-law Nicholas. When I saw them together in their comfortable home I said to myself: ' Ah, you poor things, you don't know what evil is in store for you! ' " The Emperor William went on to speak of his childhood. He spoke quite simply, without vanity, very like Wilhelm von Kügelgen in his *Memoirs of an old man's youth*, or Walter Scott in the *Tales of a Grandfather*, or Guizot in his *Histoire de France racontée à mes petits enfants*.

Among other things the Emperor related:

By ancient tradition the Prussian princes must be enrolled in the army on their tenth birthday. At the same time they receive the Order of the Black Eagle. At Christmas, 1806, my father led me under our very modest Christmas tree in Memel and said: " By rights you ought not to become an officer until your birthday, 22nd March 1807. But since I do not know how things will stand with us then, or where we shall be, I name you lieutenant from to-day and confer on you our Order. Remember always to honour both order and uniform." I put on the little uniform, made to my childish measure, and wore a Prussian uniform for the first time. My beautiful mother wept bitterly.

We crossed the bridge over the Vistula near Thorn. We passed Thorn. Hermann Balk, probably the greatest Grandmaster of the Teutonic Order, had founded Thorn and colonized the neighbourhood with Westphalians. Thorn became one of the most flourishing trading cities of the north. Barely two hundred years later the degenerate Teutonic Order concluded the disgraceful Peace of Thorn, by which the Order ceded half its territory to Poland and took the other half as fief from the Polish kingdom. And in the eighteenth century Thorn was to be the scene of one of the worst defeats in German history, and at the same time, one of the cruellest deeds of violence. Here, in the market place the worthy burgomaster Rösner, together with nine equally innocent and honourable German town-councillors, was beheaded merely because some students of the evangelican college, constantly provoked by those of the Polish Jesuit Seminary, had at last defended themselves, and so provoked a tumult in the course of which, driven to desperation, the German citizens had stormed the Jesuit stronghold of their oppressors and tormentors. And along with this judicial murder the chief evangelical church of Thorn was wrested from the Protestants and given over to the Catholics, while the Evangelical college was banished a mile outside the town. Even now, as I write these lines, the old German city of Thorn languishes again under the barbarous yoke of the Poles.

On the evening of 15th September a gala dinner took place in the castle of Skierniewice. Our old master sat between the Tsar and the Emperor Francis Joseph. No more pure and typically Russian face and appearance could be imagined than those of Alexander III. He was a perfect Slav. " If," said the Ambassador, von Schweinitz, "you were to dress the Tsar Alexander in a peasant's coat, a shirt worn over his trousers, with shoes of linen bast, he would look exactly like any Russian peasant." This, although Alexander III had not a drop of Russian, but only German, blood in his veins. I add here that the English royal family, which is also of pure German origin, looks quite British. *L'influence du milieu* is therefore often more significant than any inherited racial characteristics. While Alexander III, at the gala banquet in Skierniewice, looked as though he could scarcely await the moment to rise, the Emperor Francis Joseph gave an impression of dullness and fatigue. His lustreless eyes gazed, far away, over the table, into the distance. Of what was the Hapsburger thinking? That once, then scarcely nineteen, he had overthrown the Magyar rebels with Russian aid, conquered the Piedmontese with Russian reinforcements, and humiliated Prussia? Did he think that, during the Crimean War, he had rewarded the Russians for their help by ingratitude and so provoked Russia's dislike, both of the Hapsburg and the Hapsburg policy, which they opposed from the Crimean War till the Emperors met in 1872? Thirty-three years older than Francis Joseph, forty-eight years older than Alexander III, the Emperor William seemed in his peace and wisdom like the patriarch of the great European family, he alone seemed capable of guiding the rulers and the peoples.

After dinner the famous Warsaw ballet appeared. The graceful and lovely dancers gave a bright note to the solemn company. At the same time, commanded by the Tsar, came thirty or forty Polish princely families, to do homage to the Emperors. The Prussian aide-de-camp, Prince Anton Radziwill, himself a Pole, whispered to me: " There are few among these Warsaw nobles who have not had fathers, grandfathers, brothers or cousins in Siberia." Next morning a conference took place between the leading statesmen of the empires. Herbert Bismarck took my arm and laughed. " We'll stay in the next room to the conference chamber. That isn't eavesdropping, it's improving one's mind and showing interest. That man in the corner there need not disturb us. He's a detective. In this damned country one is never safe from Nihilists and bombs." At a square wooden table sat Prince Bismarck, Herr von Giers, and Count Kálnoky. In his exposé, given in conversational tones, Bismarck reminded the others of the last meeting of these three Emperors in Berlin, 4th September 1872. Was it not, after so much friction, advisable, in the interest of European peace and the maintenance of the Monarchist form of government in Euope, to reflect again that the aims of revolutionaries could be furthered by dissensions between the three great Northern Powers? The three together would lose far more by a defeat than any of them would gain in the case of a victory. Prince Bismarck suggested that the three Empires should pledge themselves to a benevolent neutrality, in case one or the other of them should be attacked by a third power. In the longer conversation that followed it was fully agreed that, above all things, it would be necessary to treat incidents in the Balkan Peninsular, of which there would always be plenty, with tact and goodwill on both sides—the Austrian as well as the Russian. Petty conflagrations must be stamped out not fanned into a blaze. It was essential for Austria-Hungary and Russia to check the all too zealous procedure of their Balkan agents, who, for the sake of local squabbles and rivalries, often ignored the main objectives of their cabinets. " *Jamais trop de zèle.*" This golden rule of Talleyrand, said Prince Bismarck, might be impressed on their subordinates in office most insistently, by his honoured colleagues.

In Skierniewice I made the acquaintance of two Austrian diplomats, with whom I often came in contact later. Legation-Secretary Baron Aloys Lexa von Aehrenthal was chief of Kálnoky's cabinet and possessed his entire confidence. At that time he was openly a friend of Russia, in contrast to Goluchowski, Khevenhüller, Hengemüller, Pallavicini and many other Austrian diplomats. The Austro-Hungarian Foreign Secretary, Count Gustav von Kálnoky, was not so brilliant as the late Count Gyula Andrássy. But he, too, wore Hussars uniform, and pleased Prince Bismarck better than his predecessor, the colourless, lustreless wooden Viennese bureaucrat Haymerle. Kálnoky was short with a snub nose. My friend, Princess Elise Salm-Lichtenstein, said of him in her droll Viennese way: " Gusti Kálnoky with his little nose in the air looks a real housemaid." Kálnoky was a trained diplomat, experienced and careful. He stuck to the old motto of his family: " *Nec timide, nec tumide*." At heart a thorough black-and-yellow[1] Austrian, he understood how necessary it was, in the interests of the Monarchy, to keep on good terms with its various nationalities. His family came from Transylvania and belonged to the Szekler hereditary nobility, though, under Maria Theresa, several branches had migrated to Moravia. That made it easier for the minister to receive deputations, either Cis- or Transleithain. Kálnoky, who had been Austro-Hungarian Ambassador in Russia before he became Foreign Secretary, rightly regarded the maintenance of good relations with Russia as vital, both for his country and the peace of the world.

After a hearty farewell from Herbert Bismarck I returned to my post, via Warsaw. I found kindly guides in Warsaw where I spent two days: the German Consul-General, von Rechenberg, and the Russian captain, Count Fersen. Rechenberg took me to the quondam Polish royal palace (Zamek Królewski), with the historic Reichstag halls, and the Brühl palace. I liked best the charming castle of Lazienski, situated on an island in an artificial lake, surrounded by a delightful park. In Rechenberg I met another eccentric. Julius, Baron Rechenberg gave his age as seventy. In reality he is said to have been over eighty even at the time. In any case he had fought on the Greek side in 1824 at Missolonghi. The Poles feared Rechenberg, partly because they knew that he knew them and their crooked ways, partly because, to make himself appear more splendid, he told them that he was in constant direct correspondence with Prince Bismarck. When once in the Warsaw Club he read out several highly interesting passages of a letter, received from the great Chancellor, an inquisitive Pole looked over his shoulder to discover that Rechenberg was not reading from any letters of Bismarck but from a hotel bill. What he gave forth to the admiring circle as Bismarckian wisdom, though improvised, was not at all devoid of *esprit*. The results of Rechenberg's years of Polish experience, which he gave me copiously, were summed up in the following axioms:

1. The Poles have not really given up one of their pretensions, either to Thorn or Kulm, Posen and Gnesen, Upper Silesia or the Ermel district.

2. Every concession to the Poles increases their demands.

[1] Black and yellow were the Austrian colours.

3. No policy of pin-pricks, especially in the schools question, but an energetic land policy.

4. Above all no shilly-shally.

When I was Prussian Prime Minister and had to deal with the problems of our eastern frontier I often remembered these axioms.

Count Fersen was serving at the time in the Guard Lancers, garrisoned in Warsaw. His father was a Baltic Russian, his mother a Prussian, daughter of General Rauch, for many years the military attaché at the Russian court. A thoroughly loyal Russian officer, though at the same time popular in Polish society, Count Nicholas judged the Poles in much the same way as Rechenberg: " Poland is a strong link binding Russia and Prussia," he said, " But of course only as long as a sensible policy is followed, both in Berlin and St. Petersburg. Prussia and Russia are as solidly at one in their views of the Polish question, as they are on the subject of revolution. But if ever we Russians, Germans, and Austrians fall out, the Pole will rejoice as *tertius gaudens*.

At the station, on the journey from Warsaw to St. Petersburg, I met the Russian Minister of the Interior, Count Dmitri Alexandrovitch Tolstoi. Sixty years old at the time he had been chief of the Holy Synod twenty years earlier. Through his strict supervision of the universities he had made himself generally hated, and still more so, perhaps by his passionate preference for the study of the classics. A year before the murder of the Tsar Alexander II, Count Tolstoi had been retired under the liberal regime of Loris-Melikov. A year later, in 1882, Alexander III placed him at the head of the Ministry of the Interior, which he guided for three years with a firm hand. Count Dmitri Tolstoi to whom Herr von Giers had introduced me in Skierniewice, asked me politely to take a seat in the carriage reserved for himself. He himself began to speak of the bitter attacks to which he had been subjected, because of his love for Homer and Virgil, Horace and Thucydides. He hoped that, in intellectual Germany, there was more understanding of his educational ideals than in Russia. When I announced myself a convinced believer (as indeed I was) in classical education, the ice was broken. In this I still agree with Count Tolstoi who soon went on to tell me of internal conditions in Russia. He related, not without humour, how, a few weeks ago, he had visited that highly intellectual Nihilist, Miss Vera Figner, a general's daughter, in prison. As an active and courageous agent of the Nihilist executive committee, this lady had been, directly or indirectly, concerned in many bombing outrages. For two hours he had argued with her,

"*Vous savez, nous autres Russes nous adorons bavarder.*" On leaving Miss Figner he had said to her, " I am sorry to have to leave you, Vera Petrovna. If only I could stop two hours longer I should convert you to loyalty to the State." She had answered at once: " And I equally regret your having to leave me, Dmitri Alexandrovitch. If you had stayed another two hours I should have made a Nihilist of you."

The minister capped this piquant story with a very intelligent and considered dissertation on Russian affairs. He did not deny that, in Russia, pure autocracy would not be tenable in the long run. But western European parliamentarism was still less suited to his country. The Russian people would understand just as little how to deal with the ballot-box as a rough and clumsy peasant with a fragile child's toy. Count Tolstoi said, I would often remember it many years later—after the outbreak of the Russian revolution: " Every attempt to introduce west-European parliamentary methods into Russia is doomed to failure. If the Tsarist system which, in spite of its shortcomings and weaknesses, all of which I admit, has held Russia together for centuries, should collapse, Communism will take its place, nude and crude Communism, *le communisme pur et simple, le communisme de M. Karl Marx, de Londres, qui vient de mourir and dont j'ai étudié attentivement et avec intérêt les théories.*" The minister continued:

You ask again and again whether I really believe that the present Russian form of government whose failings are patent, can be maintained. No! Certainly not! But between a Utopian parliamentarianism, quite unsuited to Russia, and Communism, which destroys and ravages everything, there is a third alternative: the extension of the Semstvos. These were established twenty years ago as district councils, representative of local and provincial interests in the old-Russian government districts. The members of these provincial conventions are elected by the towns and country communes for three years. They are concerned with the development of agricultural industry, and with local trade, the upkeep of roads and bridges, the poor, and the public health. They have to keep up the elementary schools, can control and abolish the evil practices of the bureaucracy, all-powerful until 1864. The Semstvos are supposed to arouse and further the peasants' interest in administration and public affairs, which is, of course, still very undeveloped. They may burden us financially but they have proved a blessing, and a really educational force all over Russia. We ought to continue to develop along these lines!

The doubtless very cultured Minister had grown more eloquent and animated, almost enthusiastic. I allowed myself to ask him the modest question—is it not advisable, even before the full extension of this splendid Semstvo project, to create those guarantees for personal freedom, justice, and religious tolerance, which have existed so long in all other European countries? "Certainly!" replied Count Tolstoi, "Oh, of course! But first of all we must abolish Nihilism. *Nous sommes dans la bonne voie.*" I was too well brought up to tell a statesman much older and more experienced than myself that he was moving in a vicious circle. Through his all too draconic police system he only strengthened the revolutionary movement, which it was his whole ambition to crush.

I met Count Tolstoi several times again. He was always equally friendly. In his house he introduced me to the most powerful man in Russia next the Tsar, at least in the eyes of the Russian people, Constantine Petrovitch Pobiedonoztsev, chief pro-curator of the Holy Synod and fifty-eight years old at the time. Outwardly he had a certain resemblance to the consistorial president, Immanuel Hegel, the son of our great philosopher. Outwardly! and as much as any Russian can look like a German. I had often seen Hegel's son who, like myself, attended the services of St. Matthew's Church in Berlin. Pobiedonoztsev was one of the most cultured men I have ever met. His learning was not merely many-sided, it was profound. He knew our literature thoroughly, and considered it far finer than the French. He not only quoted *Faust* but even Schiller's *Letters on the Æsthetic education of Humanity* and *Wilhelm Meister's Wanderjahre*. His standpoint to-wards religious problems he used to describe to me more or less as follows: "One of our greatest thinkers, Soloviev, called the Catho-lic Church, Peterine, the Evangelical, Pauline, and the orthodox, Johannine. The Orthodox Christian is soft and yielding: he would like to embrace all humanity." When I could not suppress an incredulous smile Pobiedonoztsev continued, with arms uplifted, and the exalted air of an apostle full of his mission:

But it is so! It really is so! Just see how millions of orthodox believers have been seduced by the cunning Jesuits and led to a union with the Roman church and apostasy from their own! What trouble we have to win them back! Just think how hundreds of thousands of Russian peasants deserted Orthodoxy and founded a sect, merely because a few copies of a Protestant prayer-book came into their hands, the *Hours of Meditation*, com-piled by Heinrich Zschokke. Even to-day, these Stundists give

IV.   P P

us trouble, we who, before God, the Tsar, and Russia, are responsible for the unity of the religious belief in the Russian people. The Russian is so pliable of temper and so yielding that only by consistent severity and, if necessary, by harshness, can the religious unity of Russia which God desires be protected, upheld, and assured.

My chief, General von Schweinitz, had been right when he pointed out to me the great social and also, as things lay, political influence possessed by women in old St. Petersburg. The first Society leader I met there was Countess Marie Kleinmichl, who had been born a Countess Keller. She was the daughter of a German-Russian father and a Serbian-Polish mother, but was herself most at home in St. Petersburg. She only felt well in St. Petersburg air. Only St. Petersburg affairs interested her. It was a horrible stroke of destiny that this clever and charming woman should have been forced by the Bolshevists to end her days in exile, after her farms, her Petersburg palace, and her country house on the islands, had been seized and she herself literally stripped to her chemise. In 1884 she shone as a star on the social sky. I learnt a good deal from her conversation. She made me see that Russia, at the core, was democratic. A small example: she had quarrelled with her brother-in-law, a Count Kleinmichl, but was still good friends with a cousin, a Prince Dolgoruki. Both applied for the office of Marshal of the Nobility in her district. Countess Kleinmichl invited the influential nobles of the province and said to them: " You have the choice of a Kleinmichl or a Dolgoruki. It is painful for me to have to say it but the truth is that the family Kleinmichl is descended from a Finnish lackey whereas the Dolgorukis can trace their pedigree back to Rurik. As noblemen you cannot hesitate." The guests replied: " Why deceive us Maria Eduardovna? We want a Marshal who has good credentials with the Tsar. That must be Kleinmichl since his grandfather was raised from lackey to count. Dolgoruki cannot boast of that."

The Countess Kleinmichl was liberal-minded, in the Western sense, and had been confirmed in her views at the court of the Grand Duke Constantine. The Grand Duke Constantine Nikolaievitch, second son of Tsar Nicholas, was called the Russian Louis-Philippe in St. Petersburg *salons*. People went so far as to maintain that he had had a hand in the murder of Tsar Alexander II. Certain it is that, as regent in Warsaw in 1862, he had played an ambiguous part. At Countess Kleinmichl's house I made the acquaintance of a number of fallen great ones: Loris-Melikov, Valuiev, Abatsa.

Count Loris-Melikov, an Armenian, had for a few months been chief of the executive commission and so Dictator of Russia. He had persuaded Alexander II demoralised, as I have said, by palace quarrels and repeated attempts on his life, that, if he would grant a Liberal constitution, he could enable the Tsar to marry his mistress, the Princess Catherine Dolgoruki, and even get her crowned Tsaritsa. The murder of the Tsar Alexander, which took place on 13th March 1881, put a bloody end to all these plans and projects and the glory of Loris-Melikov was over. He was Armenian and a Russian proverb says: " A Greek equals two Jews. An Armenian two Greeks." If Loris-Melikov was accounted cunning and unreliable, as no doubt he was, Valuiev made a pleasing and dignified impression. Count Peter Alexandrovitch Valuiev had accomplished much towards the abolition of serfdom, as Minister of the Interior, between 1861 and '68. He was pro-German and an honourable and humane statesman. He had also written a readable novel called *Lorin*, which he gave me in the German translation and which still forms part of my Roman library.

If, now and then at Countess Kleinmichl's, representative figures of a former epoch, that of Alexander II, opened their melancholy hearts to me, at Madame Durnov's—" Missy," as she was called by her friends and relatives—I met all those in favour under the reigning Tsar. Missy Durnov was one of the most interesting women I have known. An intelligence sharp as a scalpel, great charm, a perfectly natural manner, but always and in everything a great lady. If I understood the Russia of Alexander III I owe this to her in the first place. In her fine palace on the Neva I made friends with the most influential man in the entourage of the Tsar Alexander III, the aide-de-camp, Tcherevin. He was responsible for the Tsar's personal safety, which he guarded successfully. This was all the more praiseworthy and astonishing since Tcherevin was seldom perfectly sober. I have known many a tried and proven drinker in our own dear Fatherland, and in other countries, but nowhere and never have I met such an out-and-out toper as Tcherevin. After dinner, which, in St. Petersburg, was eaten as a rule at nine o'clock, he would sit down in the club, or wherever else he happened to be invited, to drink aniseed liqueur out of a claret glass. This lasted till twelve, or even one a.m. With unsteady steps he said good-night, drove home, and drank there till daybreak, bad Caucasian local wines out of a tumbler. After a few hours sleep he put his head, with the drooping moustache, under the ice-cold jet of a pump, and drove to Gatchina to the " *Daklot* "—the audience with the Tsar. The Tsar liked him. He valued his loyalty, the faithfulness of a Newfoundland dog, his sound common-sense, his unbounded courage. He had proved more than once that he was equal to any situation. One of the many supplicants whom Tcherevin had to interview daily—a black-haired Armenian—had pointed a revolver, with his right hand, at the general and handed in a petition with the left. Like lightning Tcherevin seized the hand of the would-be assassin and twisted it round with his iron fist, till the wrist broke. Then he handed over the unsuccessful murderer, bleeding and howling, to the Cossack detachment he had summoned, and the man was hanged in the course of the day.

It was not easy to remain friends with Tcherevin, who would keep insisting on my taking him home at midnight, already very drunk, and keeping him company there till five or six in the morning, during all which time I was forced to drink the abominable Caucasian wine, which he swallowed in such unbelievable quantities. But in his cups Tcherevin, who knew all that was going on, let out many things and much that was interesting. Sometimes he was really witty. "*Voilà le secret de la situation*," he said once in a thick voice, "*L'Empereur—est—peu—intelligent. Mais il est immuable comme un roc. Il veut la paix, fermement, fortement, absolument. Il veut la paix pour plusieurs raisons. Une de ces raisons est que l'Empereur déteste monter à cheval pour des raisons physiques, à cause d'une hernie.*" Tcherevin, like Giers, also said: "*L'Empereur n'aime pas les Allemands, mais il n'aime pas mieux les Français et les Anglais. Prenez en votre parti. Par contre, l'Empereur aime les monarchies, il déteste les républiquæs. Bonne chose pour vous. Faites-en votre profit.*" On many a night that state of mind which the German student describes as "howling misery," overcame Tcherevin. Then he would sob and hiccough and speak of his children. He had had three by a St. Petersburg courtesan and loved them tenderly, although they were probably not all his. He was having them educated in Strassburg in a German school, and would also speak, with feeling, of their mother. He possessed, to a high degree, that "*Shirokaia natura*" (the expansive nature) that Russians love. I owe to General Tcherevin, not only useful and interesting sidelights on Tsar Alexander's psychology—to which as Prince Bismarck had impressed on us, we had to attune ourselves, since, in practice, everything depended on him—but he spoke in a kindly manner of me to the Tsar and Tsaritsa with the result that both of them treated me with distinction.

CHAPTER XLI

Afghanistan, the Anglo-Russian conflict—Prince Bismarck's seventieth birthday—In Bismarck's home (1.4.1885)—Conversation with Herbert Bismarck—Bulgaria and Prince Alexander Battenberg— Summer 1885 in St. Petersburg—Annulment of Countess Marie Dönhoff's marriage by the Papal Chair—Marriage in Vienna (9.1.1886).

THERE was no doubt about the fact that, in Russia, in spite of the apparently unshakeable foundations of the present system, as typified by Alexander III, Dmitri Tolstoi, Pobiedonoztsev, and Tcherevin, the revolutionary fire was smouldering under the surface. There was no lack of alarming symptoms. In spite of all the watchfulness of the police, revolutionary pamphlets were passed from hand to hand in the *salons*, according to both Countess Kleinmichl and Madame Durnov. Plots were discovered at the universities in which even the professors were implicated. A few weeks after the meeting of Skierniewice, a case was tried in St. Petersburg which resulted in numerous executions by hanging, and still more banishments for life to the Siberian mines. Tcherevin seemed to me to be most disquietened by the fact that officers of the Ismailov Lifeguards had been arrested for revolutionary conspiracies and had to be " sent away." On the other hand it relieved and pleased him to think that at last the chief conspirators, for the murder of Alexander II, had been arrested, in particular the old conspirator, Lopatin, who was called, in Nihilist circles, " the father of the revolution " and accounted the most energetic of them all.

In the spring of 1885 the latent differences between Russian and English interests in Central Asia entered an acute stage. I had written a long memorandum on the subject eight years ago, as youngest secretary of the St. Petersburg embassy. Even should this crisis, to use a phrase of Herbert Bismarck's, end like the shooting at Hornberg, it would, none the less, be significant. In the spring of 1875 it had been shown that neither England nor Russia was willing to permit a new weakening of France by Germany. Ten years later it was clearly visible that neither England nor Russia desired to weaken one another, in order to make of Germany *tertius gaudens*. The leader of the English Conservatives, Lord

Salisbury, had used a much sharper language towards Russia during the Afghan conflict than Mr. Gladstone and the Liberals. Salisbury went so far as to accuse the Russian government of continually breaking its word. In May 1885 at the opening of a Conservative Club, he had added: "What does one call a man who cannot pay what he owes in private life? A scoundrel or a bankrupt!" After the fall of the Gladstone government in June, 1885, Salisbury became Prime Minister and showed himself as conciliatory towards Russia as his predecessor, declaring, in November, that nothing stood in the way of good Anglo-Russian understanding. There was room in Asia for them both. The two Danish sisters, the Empress Maria Feodorovna of Russia and the Princess Alexandra of Wales, had done a great deal to bring about this swift *rapprochement* between "the whale" and "the bear." Both ladies had inherited the Danish-Hessian dislike of their mother, Queen Louise of Denmark (born a Princess of Hesse), for the new, strong and prosperous German Empire.

Did Prince Bismarck desire a military skirmish between Russia and England in the spring of 1885? In any case his magisterial good sense, which seldom erred in regard to foreign politics, prevented his letting any such wish be noticed. Herbert Bismarck, less careful than his father, permitted himself some careless remarks as the Afghan crisis reached its height. In the company of foreign diplomats he exclaimed: "If England and Russia come to blows it'll be a pity if any misses its mark!" This remark was reported in London and came to the ears of the Prince and Princess of Wales, who used it to the advantage of their endeavours to bring about a compromise between Russia and England. When, at the acutest stage of the Afghan crisis, Herr von Giers said anxiously to his sovereign that Russia must either be prepared for a big war or give way, the Tsar, as Giers told me later, answered: "I shall not give way and there will be no war." Alexander Alexandrovitch was right.

The Afghan crisis had aroused anxiety on all European stock exchanges. Particularly in Berlin where the Russian commitments were heavy, much money was lost. In one part of the press bitter reproaches were levelled against Bismarck because he had not warned stock exchange and public in time of the possibility of a conflict between England and Russia. Bismarck retorted that it was a matter for the stock exchange and the speculating public alone, to play *à la hausse* or *à la baisse*. If he, as leading statesman, had raised a cry of alarm it would have looked as though he either desired to restrain England and Russia from carrying on their business in any war which seemed to them worth while, or to set them against each other " like two butchers' dogs." Reserve was the correct policy for Germany to observe during this conflict. I may add here that nineteen years later just such another silly criticism was made of me as Chancellor—*i.e.*, that I had not pointed out the possibility of a Russo-Japanese war.

In the middle of March, 1885, I received a letter from Herbert Bismarck. He supposed I should want a holiday in the spring after a trying official and social winter. Could I try and arrange to be in Berlin on 1st April, his father's seventieth birthday? To have taken part in this festival would be a proud memory for me throughout my life. I accepted the invitation gratefully and gladly. And, heaven knows, I never forgot that day, nor shall I ever forget it. Never has a German statesman been so honoured and acclaimed by the best part of the nation, nor was any German worthier of such homage. Certainly the leaders of the opposition, Eugen Richter, Ludwig Windthorst, and August Bebel, stood aside in grudging dislike. But their electors took part in their thousands in the honours showered upon Bismarck without letting themselves be disturbed by the reflection that most of Bismarck's successes had been achieved against the will of their leaders and accompanied by their incessant wrangling. The Genevese publicist, Victor Cherbuliez, who, under the pseudonym Valbert, wrote rather anti-German, but clever, articles on German conditions in the *Revue des Deux Mondes* and other French papers, once described a German Democrat of the 'eighties, who had gained such a reputation in his provincial home-town by his constant grumbling criticisms of Bismarck, that his fellow-citizens elected him to the Reichstag. Once there he took the first opportunity of attacking the hated statesman with all the power of his lungs, and his rich store of democratic platitudes. When Bismarck, at the close of the debate, settled up with adversaries he did not answer the attacks of the provincial Mirabeau since they were too insignificant to notice. When this became known in the home-town great excitement ensued. " What! Our member not even vouchsafed an answer by the great Bismarck! What an idiot he must be! Because Bismarck does know best in the long run!" The stupidity of " Hödur," the elector who always lets himself be gulled by the sly Loki, with his horn spectacles on his nose and the index-file on the desk, has seldom been more amusingly caricatured. And one of the subtlest spirits of the day, the author of *Sparrows Lane* and *The Hunger-Pastor*, Wilhelm Raabe, wrote: " German nation? Nonsense! German-speaking or chattering mass of population moulded for a short moment by a few very great men into the form of a nation! To-morrow these men may be dead and the mass will disintegrate again, and foreigners come in again from all sides to fill their pockets, raising up and sustaining the ancient freedom of 'good old Germany.'" An unjust criticism as far as it is applied to the great mass of the German people, peasants and workers and the industrious middle classes. But an only too justified complaint against German intellectuals who lack the ardent patriotism of the Latin as much as the unshakable national pride of the Americans and English and so slip back again and again into vain introspection, blind doctrinairianism, and obstinacy.

On the evening of 31st March, 1885, a torchlight procession marched through the Wilhelmstrasse past the Chancellor's palace. Bismarck stood at the window of a corner room on the first storey of the left wing. So that those outside might see him plainly, the doughty Herbert held a lamp over his father's mighty head during the whole march past. Joy and enthusiasm shone in the eyes of the torch-bearers. The expression on the features and in the eyes of Prince Bismarck was indescribable. The impression this countenance made on me on that evening, 31st March 1885, I only received again from the Hamburg statue of Bismarck, by Lederer.

On the morning of 1st April, 1885, the Prince replied to congratulations in the big hall of the Chancellor's palace. In the same hall where, seven years earlier, the Berlin Congress had convened and in which, thirty years later, the fatally deluded Bethmann was to promise to a Polish deputation, the resurrection of the Kingdom of Poland. If Prince Bismarck, on the evening of 31st March, 1885, reminded me of the heroes of German legend—of Dietrich, Bern, Hagen, Tronje—at this reception in his home, his simplicity and naturalness of manner reminded me of a *junker*, from the Eastern Elbe, receiving a congratulatory deputation on his twenty-fifth anniversary as Sheriff, or on his silver wedding. Among those who congratulated on 1st April 1885, General von Pape, the hero of Saint-Privat, pleased me most. It fell to him, in the name of all present, to raise three cheers. He was so entirely a soldier that in his speech he constantly referred to Prince Bismarck as "State Chancellor" instead of "Imperial Chancellor"—probably a reminiscence of Hardenberg whose name had still resounded in his childhood. He spoke without oratorical effort, without making points or phrases, but in the same quiet voice with which he had commanded the Prussian infantry of the Guard, at Saint-Privat.

In a personal letter which Emperor Wilhelm wrote accompanying a copy of Werner's picture *Proclamation of the Empire at Versailles*, he said:

> It is my heartfelt wish to express to you how thankful I am that such a wave of gratitude and homage to you is passing over the nation. It warms my heart that these sentiments find such wide-spread expression, since it does credit to Germany in the present, and strengthens our hopes for her future, that we show ourselves so conscious of truth and goodness when we honour our great men. You, my dear Prince, know how deep a trust, how sincere an affection and sense of gratitude dwell in me at all times! I am therefore telling you nothing in this letter which I have not said often enough before, and I think this picture will show your descendants how conscious were your Emperor and King, and his whole house, of what they had to thank you for. With such thoughts and feelings I end these lines. Till death and after,
>
> Your grateful and faithful
> Emperor and King
> WILLIAM.

Bismarck had once said that he had cut his name for all time in the bark of the German oak; this letter from his noble master must have shown him how firmly it was engraved in the heart of every German worth the name. With pride the German nation can boast that the intimate friendship which existed between its two greatest poets, Goethe and Schiller, is unique. But just as unique is the relationship, ideal to its deepest core, between our old Emperor and the great minister who calls himself with such modest pride on his tombstone, " the loyal German servant of his master."

A few days after his father's birthday celebrations Herbert invited me to a " jolly " evening with him at Borchardt's, his favourite Berlin restaurant, in the Französischestrasse, and one which he had every reason to favour. He wanted to hear my opinion of Russian conditions, and that in detail. I will only give an extract from my exposé. I said approximately the following: " As long as the heavy hand of Alexander III is extended over Russia everything will remain as it was. The giant empire is still asleep." In his novel *Virgin Soil* Turgeniev's hero, the Nihilist Neshdanov, bends over a three-legged table in a poverty-stricken room and, by the light of a tallow candle, gives vent to his political feelings in a poem the last verse of which runs:

" A glass of brandy in your hand
Holy Russia, my fatherland
Feet on the Caucasus, head at the Pole,
A deep, deep sleep envelops your soul."

Russia sleeps. But will she always sleep? And if there is an awakening, what then? The sixteen-year-old heir to the throne, whom I saw and observed on various occasions, makes a distinguished, cultured impression, but seems very gentle, almost delicate, and by no means energetic. The inference, as the Prince is always impressing on us, is that we must aim, politically, at conciliating Alexander III, with whom I am convinced we can live very well in peace and friendship. After him I feel that a revolution in Russia will be just as possible, even more likely, than any Russian attack on the Central Powers. All this, of course, provided that we in the Wilhelmstrasse continue in an adriot and careful policy.

When I felt that between Herbert and myself there had grown up, in the course of the evening, that indefinable atmosphere of sympathy, friendship, and confidence, which draws young men together, I let him know my resolve to marry Countess Marie Dönhoff. He had already heard of it. Perhaps from Holstein, to whom I had written on the subject a year before. Perhaps through gossip, which nobody, and especially no beautiful and intelligent woman, can escape. But apparently he had not taken the matter seriously. When he realized that I meant what I said he seemed surprised, embarrassed, and at first, dumbfounded. Two conflicting emotions possessed him. On the one hand there was his desire to show me he was my friend; on the other a very understandable envy that I was to know a happiness denied him, the happiness of living all one's life at the side of the woman one adores and building up a new life for her. He had loved Princess Elizabeth Carolath passionately. He loved her still and, I believe, never ceased to love her. He could never rid himself of a feeling that he failed in the one great love of his life, that his behaviour in this crisis had neither been wise nor quite correct. Through the memoirs of Prince Philip Eulenburg, a number of details concerning this romance have been made public which, at the time, were only known to a narrow circle. At last, after a long silence, he said:

I know Countess Marie Dönhoff. She is a gifted, a truly good, and an uncommonly charming lady. But she is a foreigner and we should and must keep to the principle that our diplomats should not marry foreigners. Besides she is a Catholic. She is divorced from her first husband and this husband belongs to our diplomatic service. She is a friend of the Crown Princess, of Mimi Schleinitz, of Cosima Wagner, Frau von Helmholtz, and other women who hate my father. I do not think that my father will give his consent to such a match. I cannot even advise him to. I shall even advise with all energy against it.

As I look back on that conversation with my dear friend and contemporary, Herbert Bismarck, I realize acutely how little any human being is able to see how the future will turn out for him, nor how he may act in time to come. Herbert married Countess Marguerite Hoyos, whose mother was pure English and her father half Austrian, half Hungarian. His eldest son has married a foreigner, the Swede, Ann-Marie Tengbom. But I could not prophecy this on that evening at Borchardt's. I did, however, say to Herbert that Countess Marie's friendships with the Crown Princess, Cosima Wagner, Frau von Helmholtz and Countess Schleinitz, were based on artistic tastes and had nothing to do with politics. To object to her foreign origin seemed to me especially petty in her case, since in culture and outlook she had become completely German. As for Catholicism I myself was certainly an evangelical Christian, but without any narrow bigotry. If the fact that Count Karl Dönhoff served the Foreign Office was a reason in the eyes of my superiors for refusing to consent to my marriage then I should leave the service. I ended the discussion by telling Herbert, calmly but decisively: " *C'est à prendre ou à laisser.* If consent to my marriage is withheld—a marriage from which I hope not only my own life's happiness but that of the woman I love—I shall resign. I can live quite well as a private citizen. By the side of the woman I love and with a few good books I can manage anywhere." I should like here to say in anticipation that, long after my marriage, Count Karl Dönhoff continued in diplomacy, and did further good service at his Dresden post. Not long before his death, when, at the age of seventy-three, for reasons of health, he wrote to resign and had his resignation accepted in a form very flattering to himself, he wrote me that he considered it a matter of duty and honour to thank me for the kindness and tact I had displayed towards him as his superior for ten years. In life, as in politics, awkward situations may be smoothed over by cleverness and the exercise of that quality which the old Greeks called Μεγαλοψυχία —breadth of spirit.

The summer of 1885 passed off quietly as regards politics. In Russian domestic affairs reaction triumphed on all sides. The Catholic bishop of Vilna was exiled to Iaroslav on the Volga, because he had carried on a direct correspondence with Rome instead of through the officially prescribed channels. The church dignitary appointed to his diocese after his banishment was deported for a similar reason to Koli, on the Arctic Sea. I was on friendly terms with Prince Cantakuzene, president of the department for non-orthodox religions. He was a cultured and charming man, married to a delightful Frenchwoman. When I visited him in his official quarters a number of Catholic priests were waiting in an ante-room, who had been summoned *ad audiendum verbum* and were tremblingly awaiting his verdict. The evangelical pastors in the Baltic states did not have a much better time.

In contrast to these bad and sad internal conditions Russian foreign politics were under the favourable influence of the meeting at Skierniewice, and the agreements concluded there between the three Imperial Powers. At the end of August, 1885, a meeting between the Austrian Emperor and the Tsar, who were accompanied by their ministers, Kálnoky and Giers, took place in Kremsier, the Moravian provincial city, where the first Austrian parliament had been convened, from November 1848 to March 1849. The meeting passed off well. The criticism of the Hungarian press, which saw in it a strengthening of the Slavs within the Hapsburg monarchy, and so a danger to Dualism and the Magyar race, was rightly disregarded. At the beginning of September Herr von Giers paid a visit to Prince Bismarck in Friedrichsruh, where, according to confidential information which reached us at the Embassy, everything went off very well. Then, on 18th September, 1885, an event occurred which my chief, the Ambassador von Schweinitz, declared at once to be the most important since 1879.

In eastern Rumelia which, by the Berlin Congress, had been constituted an autonomous Turkish province under a Turkish Governor-General, a revolution broke out. The rebellious Bulgarians took the Turkish Governor-General prisoner, and formed a provisional government which turned for protection to Prince Alexander of Bulgaria. The Prince went to Philippopolis, gave orders for mobilization of the army, convoked the Chambers, and issued a proclamation in which he declared himself Prince of North and South Bulgaria by the will of All-Mighty God and the noble Bulgarian people. He recognized the sovereignty of the Sultan, but Eastern Rumelia had ceased to exist, the union of both Bulgarian countries was an established fact and the desires of all Bulgarians thereby fulfilled. I have related how, during the Berlin Congress, the Russian delegates supported Bulgarian aspirations with tireless zeal. This zeal, on the one hand, was due to the fact that both Gortchakov and Peter Shuvalov, as once Ignatiev, saw the Bulgarians as the particular protégés and most faithful friends of Russia. In addition to this were the personal wishes and feelings of Alexander II. The Indian summer of the exalted gentleman, manifest in his penchant for the pretty Catherine Dolgoruki, had caused pain to his Imperial consort. Noble gentleman that he was he wished to compensate her for her domestic troubles. He knew how much she loved her brother, Prince Alexander of Hesse, and his children by the morganatic marriage with Fräulein Julie Hauke, the Battenberg princess. Therefore he supported and furthered the appointment of Prince Alexander Battenberg to the throne of Bulgaria and remained a benevolent patron to him till his death. Alexander III was different. He had never liked the Battenberg " cousins." In particular he disliked Alexander Battenberg.

As soon as he had heard of the entry of Prince Alexander into Philippopolis he commanded the Bulgarian Minister of Defence, the Russian General Cantakuzene, and all Russian officers in Bulgarian service, to send in their papers. To a Bulgarian deputation which tried to win over the Tsar during his customary autumn vacation in Castle Bernstorff in Copenhagen, Alexander III declared that he sympathized with the Bulgarians but disapproved of the revolution in Eastern Rumelia. At the beginning of November, 1885, Prince Alexander of Bulgaria was excluded from the Russian army. Tsar Nicholas I had degraded the prince's father, Prince Alexander of Hesse, to the rank of sergeant, because of his *mésalliance* with the court lady, Julie Hauke, and now the Tsar Alexander III gave his unceremonious discharge to the son of the Hessian prince.

In the middle of November, 1885, Serbia declared war on the Bulgarians. The Battenberg gave the Serbs a good hiding at Slivnitsa and forced them to retire behind the Serbian frontiers. They were saved from complete annihilation by Austria, which was to be ruined by them thirty years later. Just as in the 'seventies, Russian policy was deceived in regard to the future behaviour of the Bulgars, so was Austria deceived in the 'eighties by that of the Serbs. Prince Bismarck had said more than once that it was never possible to see more than four or five years ahead at the most. In the year 1885, by command of the Emperor Francis Joseph, the Austrian Ambassador in Belgrade, Count Rudolf Khevenhüller, went through the front lines of both armies to the headquarters of the victorious Bulgarian prince, and threatened him, in the case of a new advance, with Austrian military intervention. Whereupon Prince Alexander ceased his advance. Through the negotiations of an international military commission, consisting of the military attachés of the Viennese embassies, an armistice, founded upon purely strategic considerations, was declared. Both this East-Rumelian *pronunciamento* and the Serbian-Bulgarian War, confirm, for the thoughtful observer, the old adage that politics is the art of adapting oneself to changing and changeable conditions. In the Balkans especially the relationship between the various nations, Serbs, Bulgars, Greeks, Rumanians, and Turks, and those of the Great Powers in rivalry in the Near East, changed more often and rapidly than figures in a kaleidoscope.

Russia, in summer, possesses a charm not far behind that of its winters. What the sleigh drives are to the winter, boating on the Neva is to the summer. These St. Petersburg summer nights are mild and wonderfully light. Missy Durnov possessed a fine steam yacht and invited her friends to join her there. Among her guests her half-brother, Prince Beloselski, was nearly always to be found. He was general *à la suite* to the Tsar and married to Nadine Dmitrievna Skobelev, the eldest sister of the famous general. The younger sister, Zeneide, was morganatically married to Duke Eugen von Leuchtenberg, grandson of the Emperor Napoleon's step-son. She had first been made a Countess Beauharnais and then advanced to Duchess with the title "Highness." Zeneide, always called "Zina," was radiantly beautiful. The Grand Duke Alexei Alexandrovitch, third son of the Tsar Alexander II, paid court to her without any attempt at concealment. He thought in terms of the French proverb: "*Où il y a de la gêne il n'y a pas de plaisir.*" When he walked through the *salons* of the Winter Palace with "Zina" on his arm Schweinitz used to say smiling: "This *sans-gêne* rejoices my reactionary heart since it recalls the glorious days of Louis XIV and Augustus the Strong." Alexei and Eugen were constant visitors to the yacht club, where I often played a game of écarté myself. It sometimes happened that the communal views on property prevailing between them would cause Eugen to appear at the club, wearing the admiral's cap of Alexei, and Alexei in the infantry cap of Eugen. "Zina" sighed whenever a woman friend commiserated her on her pallor: "*Que voulez-vous, ma chère? Je suis aimeé par deux hercules.*" Grand Duke Alexei and his cousin Eugen Leuchtenberg were both men of uncommonly handsome proportions.

We used to embark for our nocturnal excursions on the Neva at midnight. The yacht glided on the majestic, clear, and gently flowing stream, past islands, large and small. At about three in the morning we would land on one of them. The provender brought with us, all delicacies of the Russian ' Sakuska " (*hors d'œuvres*), was spread out. If the dawn was cool a fire was lighted of twigs, quickly gathered, and we warmed ourselves. Sometimes we took singers with us, whose folk songs floated out, melodious and melancholy, over the water.   I was rarely home before six o'clock, but I always appeared punctually at eleven at the Embassy Chancellery, though my Russian friends, both men and women, all stayed on in bed till the afternoon. " One of the greatest charms of life consists in turning night into day and day into night," Missy Durnov used to say, " *Tout plutôt, que la monotonie, l'affreuse règle.*"

And so summer passed and autumn came. My thoughts were in Rome with Countess Marie. Her mother had written me that Minghetti was hopeful about the attempt to annul the marriage. A discrepancy in form had been discovered which was contained in the first marriage certificate, and this provided the basis for an annulment. Donna Laura, accompanied by her daughter, had paid a visit to all the cardinals, in whose hands the decision lay, and had been received by the " *Porporati* " with kindness and amiability. One little ecclesiastic had said, with a smile, to the ladies: " *Ma, Signore mie, perchè avere paura di me? Mi chiamano Nano* (the dwarf). *Questo non è il nome di un Nerone.* Many hazy views exist as to the annulments which the Holy See dispenses in certain cases. In particular the opinion is rife that, in the long run, it is a matter of money. This is incorrect. The annulment which is in question here only cost a few thousand lire for chancery charges, not more than is paid for any trifling case that comes before the Berlin law courts. With wisdom and goodness the Catholic Church has so arranged it that, through annulment, the status of the children of a marriage is in no wise affected. Through a so-called " *Sanatoria* " they enjoy all the rights of legitimate children.

At the beginning of December 1885 a telegram was brought me late one afternoon. Are there premonitions? I felt this to be an important, decisive telegram. But was it the decision in the annulment case? A life's verdict therefore? I could not manage to open it at once. My father had taught me as a boy to approach important decisions with calm. I therefore put it in my pocket and went for a walk towards the Neva. Frozen for weeks past, its irregular surface was like an ice-desert. Nowhere a living thing to be seen, neither human being nor animal. Utter loneliness surrounded me; it was dark. Only far away in the distance glimmered the lights of the St. Petersburg houses. When I got to a street-lamp, which shed a dim light from a high standard, I opened the telegram. I read four words: " Annulment granted. Blissful Marie." I thanked the good God from my innermost heart.

Next day I asked for a fortnight's leave for Christmas, which I obtained, and which began as soon as I had handed in my official request to the Chancellor for my marriage to Countess Marie Dönhoff. I went to Vienna via Warsaw. There I met Countess Marie, who was visiting our friend, Countess Salm-Liechtenstein. I told her that, in Berlin, I would submit to no shilly-shally or excuses, but should give the Office the choice between consent and my resignation. Then I asked the Countess if she would be content to lead an outwardly modest life by my side in the case of my leaving the diplomatic service. She said: "With you, wherever you will and as you will."

In Berlin I wrote to ask Herbert for an interview. He received me next day in his official study where, eleven years later, promoted Secretary of State, I was to read many a report and dictate many an order—Herbert did not get up from his office chair as I entered. I saw at once how agitated he was. When Holstein was excited he used to make spasmodic clenching movements with the fingers of his right hand. Herbert betrayed inner emotion by wrinkling the skin of his forehead up and down. Beside him stood the head of the personal department, Privy Councillor Humbert, who had initiated me, twelve years earlier, as a young attaché, into the secret workings of the Chancellory. He looked at me with an expression of mingled fear and commiseration, much as the chaplain might look who is called upon to be present at the execution of a criminal. Obviously he knew no more than I did what decision the Chancellor had taken. Herbert rose and shook my hand with the words: "My father will ask His Majesty's consent in person. As soon as this is granted the Empress will receive your wife in a special audience." With genuine pleasure and a warmth that was almost unofficial, Privy Councillor Humbert hurried to wish me joy. He spoke from the bottom of his heart. Later, when I became a Minister, I found in him a very valued colleague. Arrived home I telegraphed Countess Marie: "Wotan consents."

That evening I was asked to dine at the Bismarck's. The Prince held out his hand to me with a kind smile. "You have got your way. Good luck!" Bill told me that he said to him, not long afterwards: "The skill and decision with which Bülow manœuvred in the whole affair does him credit. Let us hope his passion for his wife, who is certainly charming, does not clip this young eagle's wings." I have more than once heard Bismarck say that, in his opinion, celibacy is just as desirable for diplomats as the Catholic Church considers it for its priests. To the day of his death he was full of kindness to my wife.

On 9th January our marriage was solemnized in Vienna, first

COUNTESS MARIE DÖNHOFF, THE LATER PRINCESS BÜLOW

After Lenbach

according to Catholic and then with Evangelical rites. The Cathedral dean, Prälat Ignaz Estl, said to my wife, laying his hand on her head after the service: "This time there can be no annulment. All formalities have been fulfilled. This marriage is irrevocable." That was true indeed, not only of the form of our marriage, but also of our feelings before God and man. At the evangelical service Pastor Zimmermann spoke from his heart. At the quiet breakfast, held in the Hotel Meissl and Schadn, in the Neuen Markt, my best man, the German Ambassador in Vienna, Prince Heinrich Reuss VII, in toasting the newly married couple, ended his speech as he turned to me: "*Per aspera ad astra!*" On this same day I announced my marriage to my chief, von Schweinitz. My dear friend, Fritz Vitzthum, then Second Secretary of our St. Petersburg embassy, wrote to tell me how, on receiving the information, General von Schweinitz had come running, full of astonishment, into the Embassy Chancellery. " I should never have thought," he said, " that such a clever fellow as Bülow would have made a love match. I imagined he would choose an heiress to some entailed estate or a dollar princess." Vitzthum, who did not mince his words with Schweinitz in St. Petersburg any more than he had in London with Münster, replied: " Your Excellency is quite wrong if you took Bülow for a cold-blooded climber." Of my wife Schweinitz had said: " She is gifted to the point of genius yet as unsophisticated as my twelve-year-old daughter. She is natural, sincere, and candid. Not a trace of affectation, posing, or snobbery, in her. She is a lady and fit to take any position."

CHAPTER XLII

Salzburg—Visit to Marco Minghetti in Rome—In Berlin—An evening at the Bismarck's—Dinner with the Crown Princess—Visit of the Crown Prince to Frau von Bülow—Her reception by the Empress Augusta—Conversation with Emperor Wilhelm I—Reception in St. Petersburg—Court, society, and diplomacy—The Russian Foreign Ministry: Vlangaly, Lambsdorff—Revolution in Sofia—Bismarck's attitude towards the Bulgarian question and " Battenbergeries "—Berlin in spring 1887—Luncheon with the Crown Princes—Engagement of Princess Victoria to Alexander von Battenberg; Bismarck's opposition.

WE spent the first weeks of our young marriage in Salzburg. The charming town was veiled in snow but the sun shone brightly in the sky and sun was in our hearts. I do not remember ever having been so gay and happy. And now, after forty years, I can still thank God and say to myself, as an old man, that my marriage brought me only happiness and blessings.

From Salzburg we went to Rome: the health of my wife's stepfather was more and more unsatisfactory. We found Minghetti extremely weak physically, but mentally clear and very composed. Seated in his armchair between his wife and his stepdaughter he talked to us freely on all the greatest topics which can occupy the human mind. Goethe says somewhere that, in the old age of privileged souls, thoughts arise which, like blessed daimons, haunt the highest reaches of the mind (or something to this effect—I am quoting from memory). In spite of the terrible pain of his cruel disease (a cancer of the bladder), Minghetti, during this summer (1886) had been to Turin. Turin had taken it bitterly amiss when he transferred the Italian capital to Florence by the Franco-Italian convention of 15th September 1864. It was his last pleasure, this reconciliation before death, with the city which had first inspired the ideals of a united Italy, and with the Piedmontese whom, as he often said, he considered the Prussians of Italy, and highly respected. The dying man, accompanied only by his wife, Donna Laura, was received by all Turin with the greatest ovations. When, with the last of his strength, he had delivered his speech, as polished a speech as he ever made, in the City Hall, he said to his wife: " Now I can die happily. Turin and I have found each other again."

The visit of his beloved stepdaughter gave him great pleasure. He told me he could die in peace since he believed that I would make her happy. On looking back this confidence which he showed in me means more to me now than any political future he might have prophesied. Of that he never spoke. Minghetti had not consented to our marriage because he believed his stepdaughter would have an important career. In the last conversation I had with him he said: "Happiness in life does not depend upon externals. I think that after your Embassy-post in St. Petersburg, you may become consul-general perhaps, in Warsaw, and then perhaps diplomatic agent in Egypt and in time Minister at Athens. That would be a pleasant ending." Nor did my wife expect that I was going to have what one calls a career. Soon after our marriage she received a letter from her friend, Malvida von Meysenbug (who later became my friend also, and a very close and admired one), in which stood the following: " You write me that you loved your husband passionately, although you were well aware that he was not particularly gifted. I believe you underrate him mentally. Frenchmen, whom I met last autumn in Paris, at the house of my adopted daughter Olga and her husband, the historian, Gabriel Monod, Professor at the Collège de France and Director of the École des Hautes Etudes, spoke of Bülow to me with great admiration, and told me that Gambetta had prophesied for him a brilliant future." My wife, with the simplicity which is one of her good qualities, showed me this letter, saying that she still maintained that the chief thing was that we should love each other. Of course she was right.

On 10th December, 1886, Minghetti died. Before his death King Humbert and Queen Margherita visited him. As they entered the room, the dying man took off the little black cap he wore and exclaimed, in a feeble voice: " *Viva la casa di Savoia!* " Then, as a practising Catholic, and with the greatest solemnity, he received the Sacraments for the Dying, and his pure and noble soul followed in the wake of St. Francis, Dante, and Thomas à Kempis. In Italy two fine monuments have been erected to him; in Rome, before the Palazzo Braschi and, in Bologna, outside the university.

In Rome my old chief, von Keudell, gave a dinner in my honour at which there occurred a comic incident. When Keudell, who, as I have said was no Cicero, had welcomed my wife and myself in a halting speech, the Austrian Ambassador, Count Ludolf, famous for his simplicity, rose to his feet, and expressed in the floweriest terms the hope that such a charming couple as Herr and Frau von Bülow might soon be installed in the Palazzo Caffarelli. General silence, intense embarrassment. Keudell turned pale. It was difficult to begin to talk again. When we rose from table Keudell took me aside. " I was your chief, and as I hope, a good chief. Tell me now, honestly, has the great Otto promised you my Roman job ? " I was able to assure Keudell with a good conscience that Prince Bismarck had promised me neither the Roman nor any other Embassy. I did not even think of competing for an embassy yet. I was only thirty-six years old, and before fifty people are not made ambassadors. After a while the worthy Keudell calmed down. Eight years later I moved into the Palazzo Caffarelli as Ambassador. *Fata viam inveniunt.*

From Rome, after a moving good-bye to Minghetti, and my dear mother-in-law, we went to Berlin. We were invited to the Imperial Chancellor's palace on the very first day. My wife was placed on the Prince's right hand. The " big bow-wow," as young and disrespectful attachés called him, was amiability itself. I have met few elderly men who could be so attentive and charming to ladies, as Prince Bismarck. In this he resembled his courtly master, the Emperor William I. The Prince told me " to make myself as useful as before " in St. Petersburg. Next day my wife was received by the Empress Augusta, whose daughter, Louise, Grand Duchess of Baden, was sitting beside her. Not only were they both extremely kind to her but gave her, out of the fullness of their life's experience and wisdom, excellent advice for the tasks awaiting her in St. Petersburg. The Empress Augusta and her daughter were genuine representatives of the " Weimar spirit." During my wife's audience with the Empress, the Emperor entered. " I must have a look at this charming lady," he said smilingly to the Empress, " who has turned the head of one of my best diplomats." He sat down and enquired after a number of beautiful Italians whom he had met in his youth and still remembered with enthusiasm. These erstwhile beauties, in so far as they were still alive, were all between seventy and eighty.

We dined *en famille* with the Crown Prince and Princess who received my wife like a daughter. The Crown Princess, true to her English education and turn of mind, spoke with horror of the Russian form of government, of autocracy and orthodoxy, but with lively sympathy of the Grand Duchess Elizabeth Feodorovna, her Hessian niece, the second daughter of the Grand Duchess Alice of Hesse. Who would have foreseen that this entrancingly beautiful young woman would have, first to see the murder of her husband, the Grand Duke Sergei Alexandrovitch, and then herself be choked to death by the unslaked lime poured down over her shattered, half-dead body, after having been thrown into a deep ravine and left to lie. What are hopes, what are plans? The kind Crown Prince paid my wife a personal visit in the Hotel Continental, where we were staying, and talked with her long and very well on Russian conditions and our relations towards our eastern neighbours. Prince and Princess William, who had wired to Vienna, their hearty good wishes on our marriage, asked us to dine in Berlin. Both were enthusiastic about my wife, whom they had often met in the New Palace when she stayed with the Crown Princess there. We saw many of our old Berlin friends, Prince and Princess Otto Stolberg, the Bavarian Minister, Hugo Lerchenfeld, my dear war-comrades, Franz Arenberg and Bodo Knesebeck. But what made me happiest of all was that my mother, not only embraced my wife with sincere love, but grew fonder of her every day, and said to me, with real conviction: " She is just the right wife for you. With God's help and blessing you will be very happy with her."

After ten days' stay in Berlin we set out for St. Petersburg. Now that I was married, and happily married, I saw St. Petersburg with other eyes than ten years ago when I first landed there, careless and full of foolish ideas. I was soon aware that my official duties were considerably lightened by my wife. And this not only because she could create the right home atmosphere, in which whatever ability I possessed was able to express itself freely—but because, through her, I established relations with families and circles whom I had never before approached. The Princess Helena Kotchubei, chief Lady-in-Waiting to the Empress, mother of Marie Durnow, I had only known slightly until then. As an old friend of my mother-in-law she visited my wife as soon as she had heard of her arrival. The old Princess herself drove with my wife to Gatchina to present her to the Empress, though, as a rule, she only did this for ambassadors' wives. Princess Helena Kotchubei was one of the last of the very great ladies Europe once possessed. A Bibikov, one of the oldest Moscow Boyar families, she had married, first a Prince Beloselski and later become Princess Kotchubei. She was etiquette personified, and full of prejudice, but a character, and entirely herself. Her son-in-law, General Durnov, husband of Missy, was president of the Slavophil Benevolent Committee, and as such, of course, an ardent Pan-Slavist. Once at a dinner-party a lively discussion on Bulgarian affairs cropped up and Princess Helena had the last word: " *Je ne comprends pas comment on peut tant s'occuper des Bulgares qui sont des gens si peu comme il faut.*" She liked my wife, and, best of all, her political simplicity. When, during the winter of 1886-7, my wife once asked me who were the two generals who were so much spoken of, Boulanger and Kaulbars, I told her, for a joke, that Boulanger was a Russian general who had been sent to Bulgaria, and Kaulbars the French Minister of Defence. Everybody with a scrap of political knowledge is, of course, aware that it was really the other way round, Boulanger was French Minister of Defence and Kaulbars a Russian general, and diplomatic representative in Sofia. In her innocence my wife asked, at a soirée of Princess Helena's, how it ever happened that the Russian representative in Bulgaria, had a French name and the French war minister a German. Everybody laughed. But Princess Kotchubei said: " *Je vous ai dit que cette petite femme était dé-li-cieuse. Elle a mille fois raison de ne pas s'occuper de politique.*" Prince Bismarck agreed. A year later, when I told him of what Princess Helena had said, he answered: " I congratulate you on your wife's political innocence. All the better for her and you. Women have music and the theatre, and all the poets; they even have the kitchen. Let them keep out of politics." Princess Helena had been pretty in her youth. She is said to have been very much in love with her second husband. Original and extremely Russian is the following: She had a superstitious fear of robbers and evil spirits, and so always had one of the house porters to sleep in her bedroom, perfectly oblivious of the fact that, *malgré lui*, he witnessed her conjugal joys. The *dvornik* disturbed her just as little as a faithful St. Bernard would have done.

I should like once again to advise every young German who gets sent abroad as diplomat to cultivate friendly relations with his colleagues of the other embassies. In this way he can control and test news which he receives from the natives. He will also have an opportunity of hearing news. Above all he will make acquaintances who will be of use for his further diplomatic career. The diplomats of all countries form to a great extent a big coterie, where everyone knows or has at least heard of everyone else. I myself, as I mentioned when reviewing my activities in Athens, always preferred to associate with my English colleagues. I look back with pleasure on Dering, Herbert, Harding, Grosvenor, Welby, Townley, Rodd, Wyndham, Lascelles, Browne, Vansittart and many others. When I first went to St. Petersburg, in 1875, Sir Edward Thornton was English Ambassador there. Very different from this worthy Scotsman was the English Ambassador I found on the Neva in 1884, Sir Robert Morier. Bismarck is said to have expressed his opinion that the Russian is only trustworthy so long as he wears his shirt over his trousers and the Englishman so long as he doesn't speak French. Morier not only spoke French but was the son of a tutor from Neuchâtel, who had emigrated to England. Intelligent, cultured, and insinuating, Sir Robert, as a young man, had attracted the attention of Prince Albert of Coburg. Like every friend of the Prince Consort he was protected after Albert's death by Queen Victoria. As minister at petty German courts, in Coburg, Darmstadt, and in Munich, he had penetrated into all the weaknesses and foolishnesses of German particularism. He was one of the few Englishmen who, even before Sedan, long before the days when German progress in industry and commerce were beginning to arouse English jealousy, long before we began to build our navy, held the view that a weak and therefore a humble Germany was best suited to English interests. Still it would have been possible to live very amicably with Morier if he had not felt grossly insulted by the rash procedure of Herbert Bismarck. My old war comrade, Deines, had made the acquaintance of Bazaine as military attaché in Madrid and found him living there in the depths of poverty, after his flight from the isle of Sainte-Marguerite. The ex-Marshal told Deines that, during the Franco-German War, as commander-in-chief of the Metz army, he had been kept well-informed of German military conditions and plans by Morier, who was then British Minister in Darmstadt. In August 1870 he had received from Morier the first news of the advance of the German army across the Mosel. Was that really so? Did Morier really play such an ugly part? Or did Bazaine invent it all? In any case Herbert would have done better not to let the questionable insinuation into the newspapers. We had no proofs of the insinuation: Bazaine, in the eyes of the world, was not a reliable witness. The English press, according to English custom, unanimously and vehemently upheld the innocence of their countryman, Morier, who since then had done all in his power to injure us in Russian eyes and fan Russian suspicion of us. He was one of the first of the serious and dangerous upholders of that English attitude which saw in neither Russia nor France but in Germany—ever stronger economically and politically—the rival, and therefore enemy, of the British Empire. Morier was well accredited with the Prince of Wales. Unfortunately he also possessed the confidence of the Crown Princess Victoria. When it was necessary to find a tutor for Prince William, the future king and emperor, the Crown Princess asked Morier's advice, and he recommended Hinzpeter, who was then tutor in the house of Count Görtz at Castle Schlitz in Upper Hesse.

Quite unlike Sir Robert Morier was the Italian Ambassador Greppi, a pleasant man of the world, a perfect *galantuomo*, though certainly no Cavour or Talleyrand. He was destined to outlive all his contemporaries, after seeing the Great War as the last of a number of others. He died at the age of one hundred and three.

More important to me than diplomatic colleagues and the St. Petersburg *salons* were Giers and his staff. Vlangali was adjutant in the Foreign Ministry (a post which is equivalent to the Under-Secretary of State in the Berlin Foreign Office). He was by birth a Greek, like Zographos, Katakazy, Basily, Persiany, and many other Russian diplomats. Very different from Vlangaly, the refined amiable and careful almost to the point of anxiety, was Privy Councillor Zinoviev, the Chief of the Asiatic Department. A Russian of the deepest dye, not always very choice in his manners or his speech, he was a man of sound common-sense. More than once he said to me: " Our misfortune is the Balkan people. We shed our blood for them without really gaining any advantage; we throw away money for them which would be better spent in the heart of Russia, where there is much to improve and to create. May God grant that these little brothers, the *bratushkas*, as our simple Russians call them, do not drag us into another bad war."

Chief confidant of Giers was Count Vladimir Nikholaievitch Lambsdorff. He was the official whom Giers first informed of the Re-Insurance Treaty. Lambsdorff only became our adversary much later when, as I shall relate in due season, Kaiser William II, under the evil influence of Prince Max Fürstenberg, had offended him deeply by tactless and unfriendly treatment. In these days Alexander Petrovitch Isvolski was an ambitious but somewhat pushing Secretary of Legation, at the Russian Foreign Office. I often played cards with him at the Club. As he knew of my friendly relations with Zinoviev, who was his immediate superior, he asked me to put in a word for him. When I praised Isvolski's brilliant qualities to Zinoviev, he replied in the rough manner peculiar to him: " Isvolski gets himself up like a monkey. Whoever wears bright plaid trousers and a blue tie is no use to me as an official."

On 20th August, 1886, I met Vlangali at a dinner given by Sir Robert Morier. As we left Vlangali proposed a drive together to the islands. That would refresh us both after the great heat of the day. The *troika*, drawn by three smart-stepping horses, took us past fine country houses and charmingly laid out parks, but Vlangali was full of brooding misgivings and complained of the of the cast-iron weight of responsibility which, at certain moments, lies so heavy on the shoulders of those who direct the foreign policy of a great Empire. Next day I saw what it was that had so visibly preoccupied him during our nocturnal drive. The news was wired that a revolution had broken out in Sofia. A mutinous Bulgarian cavalry regiment had surrounded the *Konak* of Prince Alexander. Officers of the cadet-school had forced their way into his bedroom, informed him of his deposition, and taken him, at the point of a loaded revolver, to Rahova, on the Danube, where they placed him on his own yacht, and had him sent to Reni, a little town in the Russian department of Bessarabia. Here the Prince was released and had betaken himself to Galicia. By order of Alexander III the news of this *coup d'état* was told to the regiments assembled in the barracks of Krasnoie Selo for summer manœuvres. The troops received the glad tidings with loud cheers and started the Russian national hymn: "*Bozhe Tsaria Khrani!*" (God save the Tsar!)

The joy on the Neva did not last. Scarcely had a provisional government been formed in Sofia, consisting of the Bishop Klemens, the venerable Metropolitan of Trnovo, Major Gruev, one of the military conspirators, and the leader of the pro-Russian party in the Chamber, Tsankov, than a reaction set in in Bulgaria. In all big towns the garrisons declared in favour of the Prince. In Sofia the pro-Russian provisional government was overthrown, after three days of office, and a new government formed, at whose head was the most important politician of the country, Stefan Stambulov.

Meanwhile, Prince Alexander had been received in Lvov by the Poles with enthusiasm. This soon spread over the whole of German Austria. In Germany too, the democratic and Catholic press, in particular, passionately championed the Battenberger. Prince Bismarck, with the same indifference to public opinion, as impervious to sentiment and even to international ethics as he had been twenty-five years before, when he had refused to support the Poles against Russia, took the Russian side with absolute decision. The *Norddeutsche Anzeiger* stated officially that German interests would not be affected by Bulgarian events. When the opposition press in Germany continued to glorify Prince Alexander, demanding at least, as a moral duty, a diplomatic action, to help him, the official organ, in an article inspired by Bismarck himself, declared with a violent attack on Eugen Richter and Windthorst, that these parliamentarians and their followers did not seem to possess enough acuteness of vision even to forsee the immediate future. No educated German citizen, trained by the study of history, or practically concerned with politics, could be in an instant's doubt as to the grave dangers which lay along the path suggested by the Clericals and Democrats. This Bismarckian exposé contained the following: " Centre and Democracy are preaching war, a more terrible war than any hitherto."

This adamant opposition of Prince Bismarck to the " Battenbergery," as he scornfully termed this movement which had arisen more by reasons of sentiment than those of political acumen, was strengthened by a suspicion that possibly this was an English intrigue, to embroil us with Russia. Just as *per omnia discrimina rerum* Bismarck saw, in a good understanding with Russia, the safest support for Germany, so was he always persuaded that English policy wished to estrange Germany from Russia, or in any case prevent an alliance. He considered this quite natural from the English point of view. But he did not want us to fall into the trap.

The Bulgarian question was complicated by a love affair behind which, with a certain amount of reason, Bismarck suspected an English intrigue. The third daughter of the German Crown Prince, the twenty-year-old Princess Victoria, had fallen in love with the hero of Slivnitsa. Their first meeting had been arranged by the Princess' uncle, the Prince of Wales. Under his paternal eyes Alexander and Victoria had exchanged engagement rings. It had not been hard for the Prince of Wales to make his sister, the German Crown Princess, upon whom he had great influence, very enthusiastic for this match. But Bismarck's suspicion of " Battenbergery " was only increased by the danger of a marriage between the daughter of the future German Emperor and Alexander Battenberg.

Meanwhile, Prince Alexander, to the continued ovations of the Galician Poles, had begun his return journey to Bulgaria. In Bucharest he was met by the Rumanian Premier, Bratianu, in the Rumanian frontier town, Giurgevo, by Stambulov, and greeted, on Bulgarian territory in Rustchuk, by popular acclamations. All foreign consuls except the Russian appeared at his reception. The German Consul, Herr von Saldern, had been so worked up by the general enthusiasm for Prince Alexander that he kissed his hand in tears. Saldern, with whom I had worked fourteen years earlier as a law student in Metz, was what is generally called a " good sort "; that is to say he suffered from a certain sentimentality, rather widespread in Germany, which at times can lead to complete misapprehension of political realities. His kiss, unfortunately, " got into the newspapers," and he received a severe reprimand from his great chief for such " idiotic sentimentality." From Rustchuk Prince Alexander sent the Tsar a humble and pathetic telegram which was answered in lofty and negative tone. On the entry of the Battenberger into Sofia, both the Russian and—by direct orders from Berlin—the German representatives were absent. Prince Alexander lost his nerve. He summoned a ministerial council and informed it that he had decided to relinquish his position for good. He commanded the release of the leader of the pro-Russian party, Dragan Tsankov, who had been arrested after the

attack of 21st August, arranged for a regency under Stambulov, and
set out for Vienna.   The Battenberg episode in Bulgaria was over.
     Whence came these Battenbergers whose ambitions not only
gave such trouble to Bismarck but even, for a time, really threatened
the peace of Europe?   In the eighteenth century, which was so rich
in favourites, one of the most impertinent of them all was the Saxon
Minister, Count Heinrich Brühl, who was, moreover, a danger to
public welfare.   He had been the favourite page-boy of Augustus
the Strong.   Under Augustus III he advanced to the all-powerful
post of Prime Minister.   He strengthened his position by becoming
a convert like his sovereign.   He was soon the real master of Saxony,
whose army he neglected, whose existence during the Seven Years'
War, he endangered, through his careless policy, but from whose
ruler he could always manage to get the money to satisfy his luxurious tastes.   He was for ever at the Prince-Elector's side, without
uttering a word.   Only when his master, who smoked like a chim-
ney, asked, from time to time, out of a smoke-cloud: " Brühl, have
I any money? " did the favourite open his mouth: " Yes, Sire."
Brühl's personal display was on a level with his sovereign's love of
magnificence.   When Frederick the Great marched into Dresden
he found in Brühl's palace eight hundred dressing-gowns, fifteen
hundred wigs, and two thousand pairs of shoes.   Count Heinrich
Brühl had thirty cooks and two hundred servants.   Among the
latter he particularly valued a Saxon named Haucke.   In Warsaw
whither Brühl followed his royal master, when the latter assumed the
crown in 1783, the faithful Haucke married the daughter of a
worthy German baker and confectioner.   Count Brühl was gracious
enough to place the son of this marriage in the Polish cadet corps,
from which he entered the Polish army, independent till 1830, and
rose as high as General.   When, in 1830, the great Polish rebellion
broke out the majority of Polish officers joined the insurgents.
Only a few remained true to the Tsar, among them Haucke, who,
for his pains, was assassinated by the rebels.   That was disagreeable
for him, but opened up the way for his descendants to rise to great
heights.   After the overthrow of the Polish rebellion the Tsar
Nicholas appeared in Warsaw.   He held a grim parade of the rebels,
but the loyal were rewarded.   Two children had been born of the
marriage of the murdered General.   The son became a Russian
officer, the daughter a maid-of-honour to the Tsarevna, the future
Tsaritsa, Marie Alexandrovna.   In attendance upon her Fräulein
Haucke often met the brother of Her Royal Highness, Prince
Alexander of Hesse-Darmstadt, who commanded a crack St.
Petersburg regiment, the Horse Guards.   Between these two a

tender romance developed. Once when the maid-of-honour, Julie Haucke followed her royal mistress into the ball-room, the Master of the Horse, Meyendorff expressed his opinion of the lady's condition in the veterinary terms to which he was accustomed. A few days later Fräulein Haucke threw herself at the Tsarevna's feet and confessed to her that she was an expectant mother. Prince Alexander stood by his mistress gallantly. The severe Tsar Nicholas exiled the pair from his country. Prince Alexander married Fräulein Haucke in 1851 and went to Austria, where he was reinstated as a general. His wife first became a Countess in Hesse and was later raised to the rank of a Princess Battenberg.

The eldest son, who entered the English navy and became completely English, I have already mentioned. The second, Alexander, was the Bulgarian prince. The only daughter married a Count Erbach of the distinguished Frankish dynasty, whose family tree runs back to Eginhard and Imma, daughter of Charlemagne. The third son, Henry, entered the service of Saxony. I met him in 1879 in Ems, where I also made the acquaintance of his parents. Prince Alexander of Hesse was a fine gentleman, through and through, and kindly as well; Princess Julie a very clever, very ambitious woman. I persuaded the son, aided by my friend, Prince Heinrich XVIII of Reuss, to exchange the Saxon service for that of Prussia. I myself composed the request to the King of Saxony in which he asked to be allowed to resign. He first entered the King's Hussar regiment in Bonn, whose charms I had depicted to him in glowing colours. From there he was transferred to the *Garde du Corps* and, as captain in this fine regiment, chosen by Queen Victoria as husband for her youngest daughter, Beatrice. He advanced in this capacity to a Royal Highness, received the Order of the Garter, and became Governor and Captain of the Isle of Wight and Governor of Carisbrooke Castle. He died in 1896 on an expedition in West Africa. Twelve years later his daughter married King Alfonso XIII and became the Queen of Spain. If the worthy lackey Haucke could have seen that!

In Sofia, after the departure of the Battenberg, General Kaulbars arrived as representative of the Tsar. Kaulbars was one of those German-Russians who aggravated all those evils peculiar to the Tsarist system, brutality, arrogance, and arbitrariness, by German " thoroughness," to the point where they became unbearable. In Bulgaria he adopted the style of Paskevitch, Berg, Muraviev, and other Pro-Consuls sent to Poland. His first address to the Bulgarian government ended with the words: " The conditions which I am authorized to transmit to the Bulgarians are very categorical.

The Tsar demands completest confidence and absolute obedience."
The round trip which Kaulbars made in Bulgaria was a pitiful
failure. The populace everywhere displayed a cool and negative
attitude. St. Petersburg now suggested Prince Nicholas Dadian of
Mingrelia as candidate for the throne. Giers, Vlangaly, and Zinoviev, did not disguise from me the fact that they considered the
Mingrelian a "*pauvre Sire*," who, save for the fact that he was a
son-in-law of the Russian aide-de-camp, Adlerberg, had few trumps
in his hand. The Bulgarian regency answered immediately that
the Bulgarian people would never permit a Caucasian to rule them,
who had sold his own Fatherland to Russia for money.

Six months later, in the spring of 1887 when I was staying with
my wife in Berlin, the Battenberg affair was still the general topic of
conversation there. People were less interested in whether Prince
Alexander would return to Bulgaria than in the question whether
Victoria and Alexander would " get each other " or not. My wife
and I were invited to lunch at the New Palace. After luncheon was
over we went into the beautiful garden, where Princess Victoria
was playing lawn tennis with some of the gentlemen of the Crown
Prince's court. While the Princess played tennis with all the grace
or at least with all the energy with which Princess Nausicaa played
ball, the Crown Princess poured out her sorrows to me. Her poor
little daughter was so miserable she could neither eat nor sleep. She
wept day and night at being prevented by the cruel policy of Prince
Bismarck, from marrying her beloved Prince Alexander. She would
either die of grief or commit suicide. At just the moment I heard
these complaints Princess Victoria was winning her game with a
masterly stroke of her racket, amid acclamations, so I could assure
the Crown Princess, with a good conscience, that her daughter did
not appear to be quite as unhappy as Ophelia or Juliet. The love
affair between Alexander and Victoria soon came to an end after
this. Both quickly consoled themselves. Princess Victoria was
married, in 1890, to the worthy Prince Adolf of Schaumburg Lippe.
Prince Alexander, who had hoped to become the German Emperor's son-in-law, had married, before this, a pretty soubrette of
the Darmstadt Court Theatre, Fräulein Johanna Loisinger. His
ambitious dreams were unfulfilled. But nobody could rob him of
the reputation of a brave man, which he won for himself at Slivnitsa,
sword in hand.

Next to her daughter's unhappy love the Crown Princess
seemed most to be occupied with the forthcoming diamond jubilee
of her mother, Queen Victoria. The Crown Princess wished the
Crown Prince to attend this jubilee, which, in her English eyes,

appeared the most important festival of any age or country. Bu
the Crown Prince had been ailing for some time past: an obstinat
affection of the throat, which had not been improved by a difficul
cure in Ems. The exalted gentleman did not look well. He wa
pale, very hoarse, and speaking was obviously painful to him
Kindly as ever, he did not wish his guests or family to be worried by
his physical discomfort. But I could not rid myself of the feeling
that this heroic man was in continual pain.

As we said good-bye the Crown Prince offered to come with us
to the station. We drove in an open brake, as the weather was very
mild. Arrived at the station the Crown Prince warmly shook hands
with us. It was the last time I saw this Siegfried or looked into his
dear kind face.

Next day we attended a large dinner-party at the Bismarck's
house. The Prince spoke of little else than the Battenberg affair.
The widespread enthusiasm in German circles for the Battenberger
did not surprise him. It was a German peculiarity to get excited
over foreign events, even when German interests were endangered
by them. Whoever reigned in Bulgaria, Tom, Dick, or Harry, it
mattered nothing to us, but our relationship to Russia certainly did.
The plan of marrying off the Princess Victoria to the Battenberger
was an English intrigue. Neither the Emperor nor the Crown
Prince had approved of this project, which they considered to be a
mésalliance. He, Bismarck, had been especially against it because
it endangered our relationship with Russia. Bismarck drew an
interesting parallel between the situation of 1887, and the state of
things when he took office. Democrats and Clericals now accused
him of not taking the part of the " noble " Battenberger against
" wicked " Russia. In 1863 he had been abused by the progressive
party in the Prussian House of Deputies, because he had not taken
the part of the " noble " Poles against this same " wicked " Russia.
If, in 1863, he had followed the advice of Schulze-Delitzsch,
Duncker, Grabow, Hoverbeck, Waldeck, and such pot-house
politicians and tub-thumpers, we should never have known 1864,
nor 1866, nor, in particular, 1870-71. The Prince concluded with
a very bitter, very violent dissertation upon the " stupidity " of
German " district judges " and " Professors." The Professor
wanted to judge political events on their " scientific basis," and
discover political solutions to problems subjected to " scientific
investigation." But politics are not a science but an art. The dis-
trict-judge looks at politics from the legal standpoint: " Who is
right, who is wrong? " That was equally foolish.

No objective critic to-day will deny that Prince Bismarck was

ight in his criticism.   It is another question whether the evils he
deplored could not have been improved and, in the long run, overcome by educating the "district judges" and "professors"
politically, and giving them some share in affairs of state, just as
Cavour had done in Italy, and as a number of great statesmen had
done in England, and so, passing on by degrees to a sensible parliamentary system.   This would have been just as compatible with a
strong monarchy as with the upkeep of the full status of our army,
so necessary in the interest of the country.

In the circles in close touch with Prince Bismarck opinions
were divided as to the Battenberg affair, just as they were towards
Russia.   Herbert, as usual, repeated the views of his father, several
degrees more pronounced and several degrees more one-sided.
Holstein criticized and opposed the pro-Russian course.   Holstein,
for as long as I knew him, that is to say, for thirty years, was anti-
Russian and pro-English.   This attitude, like all sympathies and
antipathies of this strange man, could be traced back to personal
feeling.   His first post had been at St. Petersburg.   He had been
met with a bad social reception there.   The *élite* of St. Petersburg
had not liked the youthful, awkward, vain and sensitive Holstein,
who had neither passed through the school of a students' corps, nor
the discipline of a regiment, and who seemed a queer type.   Later
conflicts with Russian colleagues in Paris, and the Russian embassy
in Berlin, added fuel to flame.   On the other hand Holstein had
pleasant memories of several visits in England, and a long stay in
America.   Several English publicists were among his best friends.
Bill Bismarck and Rantzau thought, like Holstein, that Prince
Bismarck considered Russian sensibilities too much.   It was a
proof of the exceptional position that Holstein enjoyed with Bismarck till his fall that the suspicious Chancellor who, in general,
could brook no contradiction nor criticism, should not have taken
this opposition in the Battenberg and Russian question amiss.
He was even silent when Holstein's intimate, the Berlin correspondent of the *Kölnische Zeitung*, the Lawyer, Fischer, wrote in his
paper of "a crawling-match to Russia's feet."   When I asked
Herbert what he felt about Holstein's anti-Russian attitude, he
smiled: "Holstein has once and for all a jester's privilege."   He
forgot that there can be dangerous jesters.

CHAPTER XLIII

Visit to my mother in Seelisberg—With General Loë and General Count Waldersee in Axenstein—Reichstag dissolution and Septennat—Grave danger of war (1887)—The domestic situation and Russia—The Grand Duke Vladimir—The Re-Insurance Treaty.

IN January, 1887, I spent some weeks with my mother in Seelisberg on Lake Constance. Soon after my arrival I received a letter from my old commander Loë who had, meanwhile, been promoted cavalry general, and commander of the army corps of his Rhenish home, the eighth army. He asked if he could visit my mother and stay a few days with us, a suggestion which we gladly and gratefully accepted. When we had been together to visit the old pilgrim chapel, Maria Sonnenberg, and rejoiced in the beautiful view over the Reuss valley, the Myths and the lake of Urn, Loë told me the real reason of his visit. He wished me to make the acquaintance of Count Alfred Waldersee who, with his wife, was staying opposite us in Axenstein.

Next morning, a Sunday, we started out early to visit him. It was a lovely day. As we walked down to the lake and then again as we climbed up the hill on the opposite side, the General explained to me why he wished to introduce me to Waldersee. His Majesty the Emperor had celebrated his ninetieth birthday not long since, in the midst of the love and gratitude of all good Germans and the confidence of every judicious foreigner. We ought to thank God for every day our old gentleman still lived. But he could not be expected to reign much longer. The General went on, very gravely, to say that the illness of the Crown Prince, whom he loved just as truly, was serious. Loë did not mention the word "cancer," but he left no doubt about the fact that it was a serious affection of the throat. Prince William was not yet thirty, quite gifted but still quite immature. " I am convinced," said the General, " that Prince William, although just now, to annoy his mother, he pretends to a boundless admiration for Bismarck, will not keep friends with him for long. His inexperience is a matter of youth. But he is vain and thoughtless. He wants to know everything better than other people and decide it all without possessing the qualities needed for such independence. He craves for spectacular triumphs. Appearances are, unfortunately, more important to Prince William than realities. And the great Chancellor has become more irritable and more inflexible with age. He is very spoilt by his gigantic successes, as well as by the goodness and tact of our old gentleman. The only person who has influence on the twenty-eight-year-old Prince William is Waldersee, and no doubt the Prince will make him Chancellor one day."

Loë in his lucid manner then gave me a character sketch of Waldersee. " As a military man he is an ace. A strong will, a clear eye, smartness, decisiveness, initiative. He is of the same stuff as were Frederick the Great's soldiers, and Napoleon's marshals. But I see two rocks ahead. He is excessively ambitious, both on the military and political sides, and inclined to intrigues. I believe that if ever he is Chancellor he will take a very drastic line against the two parties he hates so much, the Centre and the Social-Democrats. In Germany, with our strong sense of justice, and the federative construction of the Empire, a *coup d'état* is a very serious matter and a ' prophylactic ' war has its reverse side. Waldersee believes that Prince Bismarck's love of peace can be traced to the fact that the old Chancellor is personally satisfied with past successes, and could not bear anybody else to gain fresh laurels. But there are very important practical reasons against a ' prophylactic ' war, which Bismarck has defined as ' suicide for fear of death.' " Loë closed his exposé as follows: " I should like to see you Secretary of State for Foreign Affairs if ever Waldersee becomes Chancellor." I answered at once that, in view of my old and close connection with the Bismarck family, whom I had known since my earliest childhood, I could not become the direct successor of Herbert Bismarck, if the Prince were unwilling to resign. The General, like the gentleman he was, understood my standpoint, but insisted that Waldersee, without a skilful and experienced diplomat at his side, would only inspire misgivings.

In the meantime we had arrived in Axenstein. Before us stood Count and Countess Waldersee. They came straight from service at the English Church. In his long black frock-coat and white tie the Count, at this first meeting, reminded me of a methodist pastor, in spite of his military moustache. This first impression was, of course, not the lasting one. In uniform—I often met Waldersee afterwards—he was a striking military figure. The Countess, an American, resembled both outwardly and inwardly those excellent English and American ladies I often met at my mother's house, who liked their religious outlook. After dinner, at which both generals made inroads into some bottles of a good Moselle, we all lay down

on the grass. Waldersee examined me on Russian conditions. His
questions were cleverly chosen. It struck me that, in contrast to
many highly placed personages, he listened attentively and that
the Quartermaster-General did not resent the contradictions of
the embassy attaché, seventeen years his junior. He doubted both
the personal love of peace of the Tsar as well as the sincerity of
Giers, in which he believed only so far as one can ever believe
foreign sovereigns and ministers. He held the view that war with
Russia could only be avoided for the next two or three years and
thought that, to-day, our political and military chances were more
favourable than they would be in a few years time. He spoke of
Bismarck with barely concealed hate, as a man who, after serving his
purpose in life, had become an avowed opportunist without principles, and so gravely endangered our future. He thought the
Crown Prince to be at death's door, though this did not appear to
upset him much, and soon he began a hymn of praise to his eldest
son, Prince William. It was so easy to deal with this open-hearted,
honest, good young man. He was a real Hohenzollern like his
grandfather! " If Bismarck should not be able to get on with him,
it will be Bismarck's fault not Prince William's. With Prince
William every good Prussian, every soldier, and every Christian
ought to be able to agree." Before us as we discussed such serious
and far-reaching questions, the Lake of Constance lay glittering in
the sunshine. Mountains on either side of it, with peaceful, sunny
green, slopes and white-capped summits raised their heads in the
perfumed air. In the grass the crickets chirped. The scene of our
conference was an idyll worthy of Theocritus the Bucolic.

When we parted in Axenstein, von Waldersee asked me to call
on him in Berlin, where he would always be pleased to see me. On
the way back to Seelisberg Loë returned, confidentially, to the
question whether, in view of the ever-growing seriousness of the
international situation, we should do better to anticipate our enemies
preparations and proceed to war with either Russia or France, beat
the one decisively and then do the same to the other. " We are
literally surrounded," said the General, " France, since the Peace of
Frankfort is absolutely inimical to us and in Russia the anti-German
Pan-Slavists seem to be gaining more and more ground. Italy
will sit on the fence and then go over to the victor as she did in 1870.
England is egotistical and begins to be jealous of our economic successes and progress. Shall we do like Frederick the Great in 1756,
when he broke the net which his enemies meant to throw over his
head?" When I repeated the reasons which made me believe
Bismarck's policy of waiting to be the best, Loë told me that the

chief of general staff, our great Moltke, had said to him a short while before: " From the purely military point of view there is much to be said in favour of a war against Russia, or even against France, before either grows any stronger. That is what the great King did in 1756. But one can also bleed to death on victories, as Napoleon showed, who made one prophylactic war after another. And then, with a ninety-year-old Emperor, a Crown Prince at death's door, and a future King and Emperor who has the political and military maturity of a lieutenant, no one should wage offensive warfare."

The years 1887 and '88 were both the most eventful and critical which Europe had known since the Franco-German War. It was seventeen years before a similar crisis arose again, in February, 1905. In both cases the danger to peace came from France. It was embodied in 1887 in Boulanger, in 1905 in Delcassé. Both were inspired by that boundless ambition which has urged the French to brilliant actions but also to terrible misdeeds. Both were full of resolute confidence in the patriotism, the pride, efficiency, and elasticity of the French people. Both aspired to the laurels to be gained by that Frenchman who should restore Alsace-Lorraine, and give back to France with her " revanche " her pre-eminent position on the continent.

The increase of Chauvinism in France was not without its reaction on Russia. In March, 1887, Petersburg Chauvinists sent General Boulanger a splendid Cossack sword with the Russian inscription: " Dare, God helps the Bold! " In Moscow, at the jubilee of the popular national poet, Slavianski, a congratulatory telegram, from this same Boulanger, was read out amid frantic applause. Not long before this some prominent Moscow personages had sent the French general, Saussier, a silver soup tureen, in gratitude for a speech glorifying Russia, as " the old symbol of Russian brotherhood." The Czechs were scenting the dawn. Their leader, Ladislaus Rieger, declared, in a manifesto sent to a great Russian newspaper, that the Czechs were the powerful dyke in the heart of Europe which restrained, within its natural banks, the German sea that flowed towards the east and protected the flanks of the Slav. In the autumn the poet of " revanche," Paul Déroulède, appeared in Russia, was fêted in St. Petersburg and Moscow, and made the object of pro-French demonstrations in other Russian towns. The Bulgarian events depicted in my last chapter helped to inflame Russian public opinion in the Pan-Slav interests. They were discussed in the entire Russian press with violent attacks on Austrian intrigue and sometimes with quite unjust criticism of German policy. In particular the choice of Prince Ferdinand of Coburg as reigning Prince in Bulgaria was attributed, most unjustly in Russia, to German machinations, as well as Austrian.

The Russian government was not entirely passive in the matter of this eruption of Chauvinist feeling. General Bogdanovitch, who had gone to Paris to get into touch with the *Ligue des Patriotes*, was " sent away " to a spot in the Urals and a number of newspapers " warned." But when, in August, 1887, Katkov, the prophet of the nationalist, autocratic, and orthodox party died, Alexander III sent his widow a telegram, written by himself, in which he said: " In unison with all true Russians I heartily deplore your and our loss. The Tsaritsa and I unite in prayer for the peace of the patriot Mikhail Nikeforovitch's soul."

While Russian Nationalists were acting in this nonsensical fashion, the symptoms of the Nihilist disease had been forcibly repressed, but the evil itself had not been healed. The Imperial family lived in constant dread of bombs. I myself remember one such affair, which was later to gain particular significance on account of the personality in question. I was lunching, as I often did, in the palace of the Grand Duke Vladimir. He was not present, having been summoned to his brother, the Tsar. When he appeared after lunch he told the Grand Duchess and myself, with great agitation, that a dreadful plot against the Tsar had been discovered. On the Nevski Prospect some students had been arrested who, provided with dynamite bombs, were awaiting the Tsar's sleigh. Their leader, whom the Grand Duke called by every name he could lay his tongue to, was a certain Iulianov, who was to be hanged the following night. Lenin, the brother of this Iulianov who was hanged, overthrew the Romanovs and created the U.S.S.R., the *Soyúz Sovyétskikh Sotsialisticheskikh Respúblik*, union of Soviets. Like Hannibal he had sworn revenge and kept his oath.

When I became First Secretary of the St. Petersburg Embassy, I got into closer contact with Grand Duke and Duchess Vladimir. The Grand Duke was the most gifted of Alexander II's sons. A cultured spirit dwelt in a rather rough exterior. His knowledge of art was greater than that of the average dilettante. He had more than common historical knowledge and extended it by constant reading. He loved Paris and Parisian pleasures but was too clever not to see that a war between the three Empires would probably mean an overthrow of them all, and that the Tsar's throne would go first. The Grand Duchess Maria Pavlovna was a handsome woman. She was aware of her beauty, and not averse to being paid court to. She was a daughter of the Grand Duke Frederick Francis II of Mecklenburg-Schwerin, and his pious spouse, Princess Augusta of Reuss-Schleiz-Köstritz. Brought up in the strictest religious principles she was the first German princess who refused to renounce her Protestant faith when she married a Russian Grand Duke. Only shortly before the outbreak of the Great War did she enter the Orthodox church. A great granddaughter of Queen Louise of Prussia, she had long been loyal to Prussia and Germany until the Great War forced her to change her mind, like many another German princess. She was not only beautiful but ambitious in the grand manner. I told her once that she had the stuff of a Catherine the Great in her, a compliment she did not disdain. I had received permission from her to appear at her afternoon teas. In her *salon* I met all the Russian Grand Dukes. There were many anti-Germans among them, particularly among the younger ones. When one of these gentlemen had seen me frequently in her *salon* he asked me: " Since when have you been so intimate with Maria Pavlovna?" He said nothing more when I replied: " *Il y'a plus de sept siècles que ma famille a l'honneur de servir la sienne.*"

When next I took tea with the beautiful Princess the Grand Duke appeared and took me aside. Stressing the strictly confidential character of his information, he told me that he had had a long talk on the previous evening with the Tsar, who had declared that, after the latest events in Bulgaria, where Austria had been so openly anti-Russian, formerly with the Battenberger, and now with the Coburger, he would not be able to renew the agreement of Skiernie-wice. On the other hand he would be willing to enter into a new agreement with Germany. When I informed Prince Bismarck of this I received a direct reply from him which he, as rarely happened, had signed personally. He had been very glad to receive Prince Vladimir's news and advised me to go on spinning such useful threads. Von Schweinitz, who had been on leave for some weeks past, would soon be back at his post in Friedrichsruhe, and before his return, should be provided with full instructions for the further handling of this satisfactory suggestion of a new treaty. I must anticipate to add that these treaty negotiations were prepared, first in St. Petersburg between Schweinitz and Giers, and then in Berlin by the Bismarck's, father and son on the one hand, and Paul Shuvalov, the Russian Ambassador in Berlin, on the other. Count Paul Shuvalov was the brother of the Count Peter I often mentioned at the time of the Berlin Congress, and like him and most aristo-

cratic old Russians, Conservative and pro-German. These negotiations led to the conclusion of the much discussed so-called Re-
Insurance Treaty, denounced so foolishly by William II, Caprivi,
Marschall, and Holstein, at the time of Prince Bismarck's dismissal.

CHAPTER XLIV

Operation on the Crown Prince—Death of Emperor Wilhelm— *(9.3.1888)—Mourning in St. Petersburg—Frau von Bülow in* *Berlin with the Empress Frederick and Queen Victoria of England—* *The Queen on Bismarck—The evening at Bismarck's—Minister in* *Bucharest—King Carol—Rumanian politicians, Peter Carp and* *Bratianu—Death of the Emperor Frederick (15.6.1888)—The* *Mission of the Imperial Minister in Bucharest.*

ON 9th February, 1888, three days after Prince Bismarck had made his great speech on the European situation and the German-Russian relations, the sad news arrived from San Remo that the doctors who were treating the Crown Prince saw themselves forced to undertake a tracheotomy as breathing difficulties had reached alarming proportions.

The eldest son of the Crown Prince, Prince William, went to San Remo. Here there were violent and regrettable quarrels between William and his mother. The Prince demanded that his father be immediately and ruthlessly informed of the true nature of his illness.

The Crown Princess always said, and she has often repeated it to me, that Prince William declared he came at Bismarck's behest to tell his father to waive his rights of succession, since he had become incapable of ruling. Bismarck very rightly denied ever having given Prince William such a commission. Both his sons afterwards assured me that their father had never sent the Prince on any such errand to his father's death-bed. At this time my wife received some very sad, even desperate letters from the Crown Princess, in which she complained of the " heartlessness," [1] the " rudeness," [1] even " cruelty " [1] of her eldest son.

Prince William's standpoint was upheld in embassy circles at St. Petersburg with zeal, by the very gifted and efficient Major Count Maximilian Yorck, who, however, inclined to narrowness and rudeness. When Yorck had been perorating in this manner, *ad nauseam*, the old Ambassador, von Schweinitz, replied: " My dear Yorck, a father's blessing builds up houses for his children but a mother's curse pulls them down again. Have you forgotten

[1] English in text.

615

the fifth commandment?" When Yorck repeated his opinion Schweinitz asked: "And would you treat your mother the same way as Prince William is treating his?" Yorck was silent.

On 7th March, 1888, von Schweinitz showed me a telegram just arrived from Berlin with the words: "Lord abide with us for the evening draws nigh." This added that the health of the Emperor who, for several days, had had a cold and intestinal trouble, gave rise to anxiety. We awaited further news with anxiety and more telegrams and letters from the Emperor's entourage informed us of the course of the old gentleman's illness. On 8th March came news that the Emperor had passed a restless night. On 9th March, at half-past eight in the morning, the old Emperor William passed peacefully out without a struggle—into eternal peace. A few hours later Prince Bismarck made the most beautiful obituary speech ever delivered by mortal man.

Three days after the death of our old Master a memorial service was held in the Protestant Church, St. Anne's, in St. Petersburg, which was attended by the Tsar and Tsaritsa and all the Grand Dukes and Duchesses. Alexander III, who sat opposite me, looked very grave, an expression which well became this massive, broad-shouldered man. Von Schweinitz, in a letter to Bismarck, had once characterized, not at all badly, the feelings of the Tsar towards Germany: "The Tsar venerates our most gracious Master; for His Royal and Imperial Highness the Crown Prince, he feels hearty friendship; and for Your Excellency fear and admiration." When, at the close of the religious service, the mightiest German hymn, the powerful choral, " *Ein feste Burg*," rang out, I noticed my chief. He was weeping, and tears filled my eyes too. Our sorrows and hopes, feelings and prayers, were the same. I had not always agreed with Schweinitz. He was not a pleasant superior, and was on bad terms with nearly all his secretaries. But rough, self-willed, angular and difficult as he was, taken for all in all, he was a splendid old Prussian type. He had served in the First Grenadiers. When I once praised the qualities of my dear friend, Count Adolf Keller, whose career had lain in the Second Kaiser-Franz-Grenadier Guards, Schweinitz growled: "That's all very fine, but Keller lacks the guts of the First Guard regiment." The Prussian army and the Jesuit order were considered by Schweinitz to be the two finest organizations in the world. He was born in Silesia and often said how much he would have given to have been born in the Altmark. He was a rigid Tory, and Bismarck stood too far Left to please him. His sentiments were those of Kleist-Retzow, of aide-de-camp Leopold Gerlach, of Thadden-Triglaff, and Moritz

Blanckenburg, and, at the bottom, those of the great Minister of Defence, Roon. But like all these he was a character. He had not only a good education but what was, even then, becoming ever rarer, deep culture. As military attaché in St. Petersburg in 1866, Ambassador in Vienna (1870), and later as Ambassador in St. Petersburg, he did splendid service to his country.

Even before the death of our old Emperor, Herbert Bismarck (who became Secretary of State in 1886) had written to tell me that I should soon be appointed to a Legation. His father had been against it since he considered me indispensable in St. Petersburg. When his son pointed out that it would be wrong to hamper my advancement because of good qualities, His Excellency replied that, in a few years, I might become ambassador direct in St. Petersburg. Herbert had replied, quite rightly, that such promotion in the same capital would be neither in my personal interest nor consonant with the principles of the diplomatic service. I had, therefore, been considered for Washington and Herbert asked me, in his letter, if I would care to be Minister in Washington. I had answered at once that I would go wherever I could be useful. In spite of the tears of my dear wife, who feared the long sea trip and the separation from her mother and children, I added that I should particularly like Washington, since it would be interesting for me to see the world from the other side of the globe. In the end the critical state of affairs in Rumania made the Chancellor decide to send me to Bucharest. I was instructed, at the same time, to prepare, in all haste, for my new post, where there was *periculum in mora*.

I did not like leaving St. Petersburg where I had spent four interesting and, since my marriage, two particularly happy years. Before our departure I and my wife were invited to dine with Their Russian Majesties. Alexander III, who sat next to her, spoke to my wife of his friendship for the Emperor Frederick: " *Je donnerais beaucoup, mais beaucoup, pour que Dieu nous le conserve. J'ai foi dans sa loyauté et confiance dans son bon sens. Il est un des meilleurs hommes qui existent.*" The Grand Duke and Duchess Vladimir had asked us to dine on the evening of the day of our old Emperor's funeral, so that we spent the end of this sad day with those who, as we knew, loved their great-uncle truly and faithfully. Not a few Russian ladies gave me letters before I left, begging me to post them across the frontier. They were all addressed to Geneva and Berne. I imagine that many of these letters were intended for the forerunners of those exiles who themselves, thirty years later, seized the power in Russia.

In Berlin my wife's first visit was to the Empress Frederick.

She found the poor Empress in tears, in desperation. She understood at last that her husband was dying. Her unpopularity, which she was made to feel on all sides, in some cases in a brutal and ugly fashion, intensified the pain caused by his tragic fate. Few women, I think, can have suffered like the Empress Frederick during those ninety-nine days. She led my wife to the Emperor's bed-side. My wife knelt down beside the bed and kissed the Emperor's hand. He pointed upwards with an indescribably touching look, to the place where there is no pain, and all tears are dried. In a barely audible voice he whispered something which the Empress interpreted to my wife as her husband's pleasure at having signed my appointment to Bucharest. When my wife took her leave His Majesty laid his hand on her head in blessing and again pointed to the sky. When the Empress left the bedroom with my wife she broke into convulsive sobs in the next room. Strong as she was, she wished to hide her tears from her husband, so as to avoid depressing him still more. The Empress herself presented my wife to her mother, Queen Victoria, who had just arrived in Charlottenburg. The Queen spoke with real feeling of her eldest daughter's sorrow and of her beloved son-in-law, simply and quite humanly. My wife spoke of this hour in the death-chamber as the most moving in all her life, as indelibly graven in her memory.

Though Queen Victoria, in view of the purely family character of her Berlin visit, refrained from all official receptions, she did not let slip the opportunity of meeting Prince Bismarck. She had always been interested in him, and often asked her representative in Berlin: " What does Prince Bismarck think about me? " [1] The great fisher of souls, Bismarck, treated this queen of a world-wide empire just as Disraeli, that fine psychologist, had treated her—as a woman, whose exalted virtues and talents, whose mind and charm, must be respected by all who approached her. After the audience of the Chancellor, the Queen said to her Ambassador, Sir Edward Malet: " I don't understand why my daughter could not get on with Prince Bismarck. I think him a very amiable man and we had a most charming conversation." [1]

On the evening of that day on which my wife had her last sight of the Emperor Frederick, we were invited to dinner with Prince Bismarck. She sat next the Chancellor, who asked whether she had seen the Emperor, and how she had found him. As my wife told him of her visit to the bedroom, she burst into tears. With a kind and sad look I shall never forget, Prince Bismarck laid his big hand on her little one and said: " Don't be ashamed of your tears. The

[1] English in text.

poor Emperor is worthy of tears not only from the human point of view but from that of politics as well. His death will be a misfortune. It is always bad when a link is missing in the dynastic chain." On this point Herbert Bismarck differed from his father. Herbert was enthusiastic about Prince William, and said to me after dinner: " I understand that you and your wife are overcome by the dreadful fate of the Emperor, which also touches my father so nearly. But I disagree with my father. I think the Emperor's political departure a good thing. Considering the influence his wife has on him and her very English attitude of mind, a long reign of the Emperor Frederick would make us dependent on England, and that would be our greatest misfortune. It could affect us politically at home as well as abroad."

When I said good-bye to my ex-chief, von Schweinitz, he had said: " It's ticklish ground in Rumania for you to make your début as Minister." I did, indeed, owe my appointment to Rumania, to the fact that the Three Power Pact appeared to be endangered, and with it the Hohenzollern dynasty. The leader, for many years past, of Rumanian politics, Joan Bratianu, had seen himself forced to resign in March owing to the bitter and unbridled attacks directed against him from all sides, and the increasing revolutionary movement in the country. In the capital, Bucharest, and in other big cities, there had been riotous tumults. A few days before my arrival in Bucharest a policeman had fired two shots at a window of the royal palace, where the writing-table of the King was placed. The panes had been shattered, but the King remained uninjured. With the calm peculiar to himself, King Carol declared that this could only be an act of a madman and had no political significance, and that the matter should be treated in this light. King Carol was one of the best men and wisest regents I have ever met, and I have had much to do with princes during my lifetime. When I handed the King my credentials, in the spring of 1888, he said that he approached me with confidence. I am proud of the fact that he retained this confidence till his death. His strength lay in his patience, his attention to the details of his duty, the high ideal he had of his princely calling, for all his outwardly modest bearing. He paid no attention to the attacks, suspicions, and libels with which he was overwhelmed, particularly during the first half of his reign. He treated all Rumanian politicians alike, without either sympathy or antipathy, but solely according to their political usefulness. He would even accept as ministers such politicians as had opposed and insulted him personally. Yet, without hesitation, he dismissed Bratianu, to whom he owed his crown, as soon as it seemed to him politically advisable to do so. He governed in strictly parliamentary fashion and yet he wielded the greatest influence, not only on foreign affairs, but on domestic policy.

At my very first audience, with the objectivity peculiar to him, he drew me a picture of foreign affairs. It was not difficult for Rumania to keep on good, even intimate terms, with Germany. Certainly there existed in Rumania which, in contrast to its Slav neighbours, was proud of being a Latin nation, lively sympathies with France. Most Rumanians of the upper classes had been given a French education. But that the French displayed their enthusiasm for Russia so patently and so passionately acted like a cold douche on Rumanians. Rumanians had not forgotten how Russia, in gratitude for the aid given in a dark hour in the Russo-Turkish War, had seized the fruitful Bessarabia peopled by Rumanians. "The relationship with Russia," said the King, "is a difficult problem of our foreign policy. We do not want to irritate Russia. We even want to do everything possible to avoid war with Russia. But in view of the powerful Russian menace we need the support of the Central Powers."

I had many a similar talk with the wise King Carol during my six year stay in Rumania. He repeated constantly that Rumanian co-operation with the Three Power Pact was only possible for so long as the leadership of the Three Powers remained openly and convincingly in German hands. Germany and Rumania had no widely diverging interests. There existed scarcely two other countries between whom real friendship was more natural and possible. Things were quite different in regard to Austria-Hungary. The way in which millions of Rumanians were oppressed and, now and then, mishandled in the realm under the Crown of St. Stephen, was bound to cause bad feeling in Rumania. But for the power of Russia and Germany a clash between Rumanians and Magyars would be inevitable. Yet, since the dangers threatening Rumania from Russia were more serious than any hostility to the Hapsburg monarchy, or than anger and pain at the ill-treatment of Rumanians domiciled in Hungarian territory, Rumania sought protection and safety at the hands of the Triple Alliance. But the condition for this was that Germany should lead Austria, not Austria Germany. Many years later it was to be King Carol's greatest sorrow that, at the end of his reign and of his life, the clumsiness with which Berlin allowed us to be manœuvred into war by Vienna, made it impossible for him to lead his country to war on the side of the Central Powers, as he had hoped to do for nearly half a century. On the resignation of Bratianu in March, 1888, King Carol had called upon the Young-

Conservatives, the so-called Junimists, to form a government. Doubtless, politically and morally, they were the most distinguished politicians of Rumania. But their good qualities, their culture, their polished manners, and their moral unimpeachability, made the political struggle harder in a country only recently freed from the Turkish yoke and not, as yet, of any very high cultural standing. My French colleague, M. Coutouly who, like many of his countrymen, enjoyed telling funny tales, related the following little anecdote with gusto, and many variations of it, which he laid in the time of Prince Alexander Cusa who, in 1859, united Moldavia with Wallachia and, in 1861, became the first Prince of Rumania. A new French minister came to Bucharest. He was invited to dinner on the same evening by the Foreign Secretary. During the soirée, which was brilliant and animated, he noticed that his watch and chain were missing. The loss was a painful one since both were handsome pieces of jewellery. Then he observed that his splendid chain was adorning the waistcoat of a gentleman who had been introduced to him as the brave General X, Minister of Defence in the Principality. After some hesitation he decided to inform the host, the Foreign Secretary, of the situation. The latter said calmly: " *Laissez moi faire, j'arrangerai cette petite affaire.*" After a short time the Foreign Secretary came back with the watch. The victim of the theft thanked him profusely, but asked whether the return had not been preceded by painful explanations. " *Oh, non!* " replied the excellent man, " *mon collègue ne s'en est pas aperçu.*" Things were not quite the same under the noble King Carol as in Cusa's day. But many a Rumanian politician cultivated the morality of a bygone age.

The leader of the Junimists, Peter Carp, a man of honour to the bone, had had an entirely German education. He had studied in Germany and been a member of the Bonn Borussians' student corps. His was a noble nature, absolutely dependable, courageous, and sincere. But he was not really liked by King Carol because he was sometimes a little tempestuous in matters of inner politics, which the monarch would have preferred to see materialize slowly. Carp had a deadly enemy. This was his brother-in-law, Sturdza. Sturdza was just as pro-German as Carp but the intimate friend of Bratianu, who had always violently opposed him. *Hinc illae irae.* A fortunate stroke of destiny had, finally, so arranged it that the excellent son of Sturdza, who had received his military training with a Guards regiment in Berlin, married the charming daughter of Carp. But the fathers, at least politically, were as inimical to one another as before.

A deep and wide chasm separated Peter Carp and Demeter Sturdza, his inimical brother-in-law, who were both good patriots and honourable men, from Take Jonescu. In contrast to Sturdza and Carp, who were both descended from old Boyar families, Jonescu was of the humblest origin but, with the great natural gifts of the Rumanian, had managed to secure a glittering, even if superficial culture, *à la française*. He spoke French like his native tongue, had married an English governess, and so spoke English as well. He was not a witty and still less a profound speaker but, like the French demagogue, depicted in so masterly a manner by Alphonse Daudet, he was never at a loss for a phrase, a sophistic prevarication, or a lie. He was corruptible. Take Jonescu was not above bribery. He was very instrumental in getting Rumania on to the side of the Entente in the Great War.

One of my first visits in Bucharest was paid to Bratianu. It has always been my principle to frequent Ministers who have been overthrown because it is from them that one hears the most. Two remarks of Bratianu have remained in my memory. He asked me, at our first conversation, whether I was of Russian or of French origin. When I denied both categorically, and told him I was pure German he said: " Strange! You have an easy pleasant manner which one rarely finds in Germans." As his summing up of his experience of the struggles of domestic politics, he remarked: " Every new government is like a man who goes into the water without having learnt how to swim. As long as the water only comes up to his knees one must leave him alone. If it rises to his belly keep a sharp eye on him. If the water rises to his chin leap on his shoulder and drown him." This was the standpoint from which Rumania viewed her domestic politics. Another Rumanian party-leader gave me a lesson I never forgot. His name was Vernescu. He had given me, while in opposition, many seemingly heart-felt promises for the moment when he should come into power. When he became Minister and kept none of them I reminded him discreetly of his assurances. He answered: " *Vous ne sauriez croire mon cher Monsieur, à quel point le gouvernement change les idées d'un homme.*"

My predecessor in Rumania was the Minister, Dr. Klemens Busch. A clever philologist, he had been the dragoman of our embassy at Constantinople, where not only did he study Homer, but rendered very good diplomatic services. My father, who was fond of cultured people, appointed him to the Foreign Office, where he rose to Under-Secretary of State and was efficient in that capacity. In a few years, at his own wish, he was given a Legation to direct. When I called on him, on arrival in Bucharest, he told me of a strange remark of Prince Bismarck's. When Busch went to his farewell visit before his departure for Rumania, the Prince had asked, what had made him so eager to leave the Foreign Office. " You seem not to have been able to get on with my son Herbert, the new Secretary of State? Yes, yes, my son is not yet forty, and more obstinate and self-assertive than I am even to-day, after successes which not even my enemies belittle." Busch had replied that his dealings with Count Herbert had always been satisfactory. It was Privy-Councillor Holstein with whom he had had such difficulty. Very seriously the great Prince had replied: " I see—then I cannot help you. I must have one man on whom I can depend entirely, and that is Holstein." Busch added when he told me this: " May Bismarck never be disappointed in Holstein as the great Wallenstein was disappointed in Octavio Piccolomini." And the highly cultured Dr. Busch quoted from Schiller's tragedy, *The Death of Wallenstein*, the famous monologue in which the Friedländer first speaks of the moments when we seem most at one with the universe, and, so in the end, calls Octavio Piccolomini his good angel! Busch went from Bucharest to Stockholm, a change he desired, since his family could not stand the Rumanian climate.

During my second audience with King Carol on 15th July, he received a telegram which he opened in my presence. It was the news of the death of the Emperor Frederick. Deeply moved and with tears in his eyes the King handed me the telegram. " I lose a beloved cousin," he said, " and Germany one of the best and noblest princes that ever was." After a short pause, he added:

Our new Kaiser has many brilliant qualities. He is very gifted. He is what is called a dazzler, or if you like the word better, a charmer. But he has qualities that arouse misgivings. In any case he needs a skilful adviser and this is what we must all wish him. Above all, he must keep Prince Bismarck! There is a rumour that he would like to replace him by Waldersee. Alfred Waldersee is an old regimental comrade and friend of my young days. Prince Bismarck has often dealt with me harshly, sometimes ruthlessly. But, as the good Prussian and good German I have remained, I pray God that our new king and emperor will not part with the great adviser of his grandfather.

The task set me in Bucharest was to convert the very indeterminate " understanding "—it could scarcely be termed an alliance—concluded five years previously between the Central Powers and

Rumania, into a formal agreement. At the outset I was persuaded that such a union between Rumania and the two Empires must be an open one, but in this King Carol opposed me. He thought that such a public alliance would not only increase Russian intrigues with France to a point where they became intolerable, but provoke far too violent and startling protests from those Rumanian politicians enthusiastic for France, or bribed by Russia. I received instructions from Berlin not to insist on the publication of the agreement, since our first and necessary objective was to get anything done at all. And so an agreement was concluded between Austria-Hungary and Rumania, to which Germany and Italy subscribed, and in which the Rumanian kingdom and Hapsburg Monarch promised one another support if either should be attacked by Russia. The King most skilfully initiated all the politicians in the country, one after another, into the treaty, and pledged them to it—Carp and Bratianu, Rosetti, Marghiloman, Florescu, Katargi, Majorescu, Stirbey, the Liberals, the Conservatives and the Junimists. When this was done I had the task of bringing about a commercial treaty between ourselves and Rumania. In this I had the intrigues of the Austrians to contend with, who did not like to see us penetrate the Rumanian market, hitherto controlled by themselves. For these negotiations I had an excellent assistant in Mumm, the Secretary of the Legation, who afterwards became Minister in Pekin, and Ambassador in Tokio.

Monsieur Coutouly, my French colleague already mentioned, used to say: "*Bucarest est le tremplin des ambassadeurs*" (the spring-board for ambassadors). As a matter of fact my English colleague, Lascelles, the Italian minister, Curtopassi, and my humble self, all became ambassadors after Bucharest, while Goluchowski, the Austrian Minister, was even made Foreign Secretary. Lascelles has been my friend ever since. I met him again in Berlin when I became Secretary of State in the Foreign Office. In Bucharest I often went for walks with his daughter Florence, along the " *Chauseé*," the Avenue du Bois de Boulogne of the Rumanian capital. Later, when this charming girl married that clever English diplomat, Spring Rice, I toasted the newly married pair at the wedding breakfast. My connections with Goluchowski were just as friendly. Count Agenor Goluchowski was, at the time, a convinced and very zealous partisan of the Triple Alliance, particularly of the friendship with Germany, since he saw in Russia Poland's chief enemy. Later he made no secret of his Polish sympathies. When Bethmann Hollweg, in an hour of almost insane delusion, restored Poland, Count Goluchowski remembering, like all Poles, that there are beautiful and fruitful German provinces which once were theirs, went to Warsaw and gave anti-German advice to his countrymen. " Russia is done for," he preached to them, " now we have only one enemy—Germany."

The Russian Minister in Bucharest, Hitrowo, was one of those Russian Balkan diplomats who used, in the Near East, the same terrorist methods as did the Nihilists in Russia. From Bucharest he organized conspiracies and attacks on Bulgaria, and even tried to stir up dissension in Rumania. His wife, a charming and cultured lady, was the niece of the poet, Alexei Constantinovitch Tolstoi, who, besides a creditable novel, *Prince Serebrianiv*, had written a dramatic trilogy which, much admired in Russia in those days, was indeed full of vivid action: *Ivan the Terrible*, *Tsar Feodor*, and *Tsar Boris*.

CHAPTER XLV

Nieuport in the summer season 1889—Franz Arenberg—First signs of Bismarck's approaching fall—In Berlin—Conversation with the chief of the Imperial Chancellery, Rottenburg—Dinner with Count Wilhelm Pourtalès, Herbert Bismarck, and Hugo Lerchenfeld— Return to Bucharest—King Carol on Bismarck—My letter to Philip Eulenburg of 2nd March 1890—Bismarck's dismissal (20th March, 1890)—Denunciation of the Re-Insurance Treaty with Russia—The Franco-Russian Alliance—German public opinion after Bismarck's resignation.

IN the summer of 1889 I spent some weeks with my wife at the Belgian seaside resort Nieuport. There, as I bathed and fished, I did not dream that this peaceful landscape would one day be the scene of the worst battles, nor that on these fruitful fields by the banks of the Yser, the *Ver sacrum* of the German people, our students, would go to their death with " *Deutschland über alles* " on their lips.

During our stay in Nieuport my dear old friend, Franz Arenberg, came to visit us. He was spending the summer with his parents in Marche-les-Dames, near Namur. He expressed his conviction that William II would let Bismarck go sooner or later. Waldersee, who exercised the greatest influence on our young Emperor, wanted to become Chancellor himself, in order, as the General put it, to pursue again a " robust " policy, both at home and abroad. Bismarck underrated the danger threatening him. Since I knew that Herbert Bismarck was staying at Ostende, not far from Nieuport, I wrote and asked him to meet me as I had interesting things and, perhaps important ones, to tell him. He answered in his usual friendly way that he would like to see me soon, but that at present he had no time.

In the autumn I came to Berlin for four or five days. My political impressions there were unfavourable. At a dinner of younger diplomats the impending resignation of Prince Bismarck was openly discussed. The Councillor of the Legation, Count Monts, whom I had known for years to be a climber and an opportunist, pleaded for Waldersee, who had, he said, more " push " than Bismarck, and was also " more artful." Next day I went for a walk with Holstein in the Tiergarten. I found him preoccupied.

He sharply criticized the pro-Russian policy of the " chief," telling me how he himself had quarrelled with Rantzau, and in consequence no longer visited the Countess Marie Rantzau and her mother, Princess Johanna Bismarck. This seemed to me to bode no good, since I remembered how, in Paris, the enmity between Holstein and his then chief, Count Harry Arnim, had begun by Holstein's ceasing to appear at Countess Arnim's receptions. We walked together to the Foreign Office. As they opened the door to us Holstein suddenly asked, in that lightning-flash with which he always asked insidious questions: " Your brother Adolf, the aide-de-camp and friend of our young Kaiser, is on Bismarck's side isn't he? " I answered at once and quite naturally: " Of course. He is very devoted to the Prince and would regard his dismissal as a grave misfortune." Holstein's face took on a look of almost diabolical disappointment. Without replying he turned and went on up the stairs which lead, between the two sphinxes, to the first floor of the Foreign Office. I felt that in his innermost heart Holstein had turned against Prince Bismarck.

Next day I dined with Herbert, who had also invited Kiderlen. Whenever Herbert spoke to me Kiderlen watched us suspiciously. I could sense that Kiderlen, who had always been a tool of Holstein, was among those who desired the fall of the Prince, and were working for it. Kiderlen too enjoyed Bismarck's confidence, and was very good friends with Herbert, whom he had pleased when they were together at the St. Petersburg embassy, by his intelligence, and even more by his capacity for holding his liquor. Two traitors, therefore, in his own house into which, from outside, Waldersee and his followers, ambitious climbers, honest but stupid die-hard conservatives and pietists were trying to penetrate! A few days later I met Herbert again at the house of Count Wilhelm Pourtalès, the father of the future ambassador to St. Petersburg. He was a *bon vivant* but a man of tact, a good observer, and possessed intelligence. He, too, seemed not to consider that the great Prince would stay in office much longer. Among the guests was the Bavarian Ambassador, Count Hugo Lerchenfeld. At table, conversation turned on Holstein and his peculiarities. Lerchenfeld permitted himself a few ironic remarks about Holstein. Herbert rebuked him with a violence which surprised me, since they were intimate friends and had been students in the same corps. " Holstein is true as steel! " roared Herbert, warmed by the good claret of Count Pourtalès. " Whoever says a word against Holstein will have to answer for it to me."

Before leaving Berlin I had a long talk with Privy Councillor

Rottenburg, Chief of the Imperial Chancellery. I gave him my
Berlin impressions, frankly, fully, and very seriously. He replied:

> I too think the situation very critical. There are intrigues
> against the Prince on all sides. I do not believe in the depend-
> ability of the Kaiser. I consider the Kaiser as very immature,
> and have no confidence in his character either. But the Prince
> feels quite safe. When I returned, about ten days ago to Fried-
> richsruhe, after a short stay in Berlin, I did not want to begin
> about my bad impressions on the first evening. But next morn-
> ing I spoke my mind and told His Excellency everything. He
> laughed and said to me: " Franz, you must have eaten too much
> of that indigestible game soup last night, and that's the reason
> for these bad dreams! " When he is in a good temper the Prince
> calls me by my Christian name, and the game soup really was
> indigestible.

As Bismarck said all this to his chief subordinate, he had gone
to his desk and drawn out a telegram, received some short while
before, from His Majesty. It ran: " As I say my prayers, both
morning and evening, I always remember Your Excellency, with
the earnest request that Almighty God may long preserve you, my
dear Prince, as my teacher and guide, and the pilot of the ship of
State." I felt that Rottenburg had not let himself be blinded by
this somewhat overpowering token of imperial esteem, and so
returned, with a heavy heart, to Bucharest. Only too soon my
fears were to be justified.

In my second year of office at Bucharest, King Carol informed
me that he would like to receive me more often. But he did not
want our meetings to be formal, since this would awaken unnecessary and, moreover, injurious suspicion. We could talk in summer
when the court removed to Sinaia, on the shady paths of the beautiful
woods there, and in winter in Bucharest, in the Cismegiu Garden,
and be unobserved. One day, in Cismegiu, in the middle of
February, 1890, the King, who seemed upset, told me that he had
had bad news from Berlin. One of his relatives there, not his
ambassador, had written to say that relations between Kaiser and
Chancellor were growing visibly strained. Their differences
chiefly turned on questions concerning the workers. Under the
influence of his tutor, Hinzpeter, and " some other dilettantes,"
the Kaiser wanted to go further along this line than the Chancellor
deemed advisable. That was why Bismarck had resigned his
presidency of the ministry for trade and commerce, which he had
held for some time, to the Oberpräsident of the Rhine provinces,

Herr von Berlepsch, who aired progressive views in matters of working-men's protection, and so enjoyed the confidence of his Majesty. The trouble, King Carol added, was that these differences between Emperor and Chancellor were only slightly concerned with technical points, and did not merely affect the direction which social policy was to take, but far more, the civil status of the Chancellor, the whole relationship between Chancellor and Crown, and that between a premier and his colleagues. King Carol also said that, beside the Secretary of State for internal affairs, von Bötticher had wormed his way well into the Kaiser's favour. He was, perhaps, more in favour even than Berlepsch. When, not long after this Herr von Bötticher received the Black Eagle, the King said: "A storm signal! Now that Bötticher has become His Majesty's confidential favourite, Bismarck does not trust him any more. Such a distinction bestowed on Bötticher, without Bismarck's having been consulted, will be felt by the Prince as a breach of tact—even as an act of open unfriendliness." The social proclamations published in the *Reichsanzeiger* in February increased King Carol's misgivings. "These edicts have probably been drawn up by Berlepsch or Hinzpeter or Bötticher, or by all three together. They have not been countersigned by Bismarck. The thoughts and intentions they reflect are all very fine, but in carrying them out, practical difficulties are sure to arise." The King quoted Wallenstein the elder to the young Max Piccolomini: "Ideas may live at peace, side by side, but facts clash eternally in space."

Soon afterwards, on 2nd March, 1890, I received a letter from Phili Eulenburg, in which he wrote that the relation of His Majesty the Kaiser to Bismarck had become an "untenable" one. The Chancellor did not understand our new master. In the interests of both parties a separation seemed the lesser evil. Probably Herbert would resign along with his father. I should be the best successor for Herbert and the Kaiser was counting on me. Phili's letter was short, very hasty, and rather confused. Since the courier who brought it had to continue his journey a few hours after his arrival, I was obliged to reply straight away *au courant de la plume*, after putting down a few headings, without making a draft. But I possess a copy of my letter, written out from my notes soon after I sent it, and which, in any case, gives its spirit. In *The Memoirs of Prince Eulenburg*, by Professor Haller, this letter is not included. I began by saying how delighted I was to learn from the latest Bucharest newspapers that the phase which Eulenburg had described to me seemed to have reached at least a temporary conclusion, in a long and satisfactory conversation between His Majesty and the Chancellor, leading to a compromise after mutual concession. " Their reasons for differing, which have gradually become public, will doubtless remain a chronic evil and this, from time to time may become acute." I continued:

As far as I can judge the situation from a distance I maintain that, in spite of all difficulties, everything should be done to retain both the Chancellor and Herbert. It would cast a heavy shadow over the long and happy reign which we all desire for our most gracious master if, at the very outset, our great Chancellor, the servant for so many years of the Emperor William I, should resign. Since nature herself will scarcely permit the seventy-five-year-old Chancellor a much longer life, it is doubly desirable that this great career should end without a clash with the Crown. His Excellency's temperament is scarcely such as to make it likely that he will retire in an amicable fashion. He will write no farewell letter à la Moltke. But though I do not think he would purposely create difficulties on resigning, he is sure to choose his own time and conditions. He will take care that he has what the French call " une belle sortie." Such a resignation would cause great pain to many good and worthy people in Germany. The dismissed Chancellor would appear to them in the light of a Belisarius, a victim of princely caprice who, though indeed he need not beg his bread, is yet condemned to spend his last days in lonely idleness in Varzin. Ill-disposed people might compare our Kaiser to the young lord of Edenhall, who tempts fortune in spite of the warnings of old Schenk, his house's eldest vassal. Moreover, the Chancellor, unless he is very old and tired—and I see no signs of it—would depart cum animo revertendi. That would make every government without Bismarck a government against Bismarck! It would paralyse all rulership and would also influence, most unfavourably, the temper and behaviour of His Excellency. His return, after such a ruffled departure, to settle any future foreign difficulty, would seem like a capitulation of Emperor to subject, and the Prussian Crown should be spared that. No Imperial Chancellor must return, as did Wallenstein after the Battle of Breitenfeld, at a moment of need, with carte blanche. To guard against any such unprecedented contingency in our history nothing should be left undone to avert Bismarck's unwilling resignation.

It is another question whether the inevitable return to the former system of a ministry, presided over by the monarch, after this twenty-eight-year-long Bismarckian dictatorship, should not, slowly and gradually, be inaugurated. It would be more dramatic if the Chancellor remained, to his last day, in possession of complete power, the sole pillar of government, and so left this earth with tremendous effect. But for our house it is better that the main support should not give way suddenly, bringing the building down along with it, but rather that other pillars be placed around it in time, to share the burden and lessen the effect of its collapse. It is vital for us to relieve the Imperial Chancellor, bit by bit, of his burdens, to get the nation gradually accustomed to the thought that, whether we will or no, we shall, in the end, be obliged to dispense with this phenomenon. And even if we cannot keep the Chancellor everything must be done to keep Herbert. If Herbert stays the eventual retirement of the Chancellor will lose some of its terrors and will, in any case, seem less painful. It would be balm as well as a fetter for the Chancellor and form the only certain bridge between himself and the Kaiser. But there must be no simultaneous resignation of the Imperial Chancellor, Herbert, and possibly other specifically Bismarckian ministers. To keep Herbert will not, in my opinion, be too difficult. An active and enthusiastic nature, which enjoys power, and is used to wielding it, he would be like a fish out of water if he found himself no longer in the Foreign Office. Both father and son are " fond of power." [1] To the father age may have brought resignation and philosophic calm; the son, if I know him rightly, will resign very much à contre cœur, especially if his only choice is to be that between the Ministry and idleness, and he is not allowed to choose say a Secretaryship of State or the London Embassy. To apply these general truths to the individual case is certainly difficult, even with all the patience, skill, and self-denial which our All-Highest Master has exercised up to now. May he be strengthened in applying them, by the thought that their reward, in the case of Bismarck, will most certainly be a blessing on the rest of his reign. The Chancellor is not only responsive to personal, even purely formal amiabilities, but is sure to respond to an appeal to his dynastic sentiments. At heart he feels himself still a vassal of the Margrave of Brandenburg, and his King, to him, is no mere abstraction, but the feudal lord, whom every true Teuton judges by a special standard. Hagen von Trojne was no sentimentalist, and yet his Burgundian masters meant a great deal to him. Herbert is very different, a man of moods—dependent on the state of his nerves at the moment. He is more responsive to attentions than one would

---

[1] English in text.

expect in a man who has been so spoilt. Quiet treatment soothes him. He is far too intelligent to run his head against a wall, once he knows it to be solid and permanent. We, who love Herbert so much, can only deplore many of his failings, the worst of which is, I think, his contempt for humanity. This feeling alone makes him a bad judge of human nature. Though human beings are unfortunately rarely angels they are certainly not all villains. I have met many people who were unselfishly kind to me, and have even sometimes been so with others. The coldest realism in politics, whose *suprema lex* is the *salus publica*, should not prevent one's kindness to one's own, or the desire to develop people's higher instincts. Herbert thinks all other people *canaille*, attributes every possible bad motive to them, and so discourages and demoralizes just the best in them. Therefore he soon mistrusts where he ought to trust, and puts his faith in many a swindler. We would gladly see Herbert less cynical, better balanced, and more considerate. He could do so much good and make himself so many friends! But even with this dark side Herbert is still the best Secretary of State so long as his father is still alive. I do not say this only for reasons of sentiment. My personal feeling for Herbert precludes my ever opposing or becoming his rival. But I am too fanatical a patriot not to set the welfare and good name of Kaiser and Empire above all other feelings and considerations. From the most objective, cool, and common-sense standpoint, I still think that Herbert has better qualifications than any other candidate for the Secretary-ship of State. He is a hard worker. He has learnt much from his father. His name has great prestige. It would be most risky to take an outsider. Diplomacy is like learning whist: everybody thinks he can do it if only he has watched a rubber or played a rubber, perhaps with a little luck. Gradually he is made aware how much practice and special skill are necessary, quite apart from diplomatic gift.

As regard the result of the Reichstag elections I should only be nervous if our people were liable to lose their heads which, thank goodness, need not enter into the question. There are many reasons for victory of the opposition parties. The fact that peace-talk has been made so much of recently may have had something to do with it. The German still lacks the sensitive national pride of other nations, just as he lacks their schooled political sense of his own advantage. He therefore indulges all too readily in self-assertive obstinacy and naïve dogmatism, so long as the sky appears to him cloudless. Our home and foreign policy should both, in spite of every prospect of peace, be so laid down that the end of the century may bring us the decisive struggle for the Monarchist national State. The Socialist movement may lead to absolutism, it has seldom led to parliamentary government. History teaches us that it is often in periods of highly developed civilization that socialistic-communistic tendencies are shown by the masses. Society and State have, however, always been strong enough to crush such movements. Rome controlled its slaves and proletarians, the middle ages their peasants and baptists, modern France her Jacobins and her Commune. Horses may kick and bite as much as they please; in the end they are harnessed to the cart again, and get a driver again who directs them with whip and bit. But in the meantime care must be taken that nothing serious happens to the cart and its occupants. It is necessary to prevent the State being hampered, both internally and externally, by an eventual repression, and better to defeat such tendencies without it. There is no other way than that we have been pursuing, namely, on the one hand measures of reform on a large scale, and on the other the repression of violent rebellion. The one need not exclude the other. But even if armed force is necessary, social reform must by no means be given up. The All-Highest's edicts and suggestions on the workers' question are the most significant measures we have witnessed since the Stein-Hardenberg reforms. Why should not the monarchy succeed in roping in the fourth estate and making it a part of its organism since it managed, at the beginning of the century, to placate the third, under even more difficult circumstances. Let us hope that a sympathetic and careful treatment of the workers and a continuation of the social welfare movement will steadily proceed, in a practical and progressive fashion along the lines already laid down. Consistency is the next important quality of German domestic policy. Anything sudden and unforseen upsets the phlegmatic German temperament; capers and contradictions seem frivolous to our serious-minded and thorough German people.

There is certainly no chance of a permanent alliance with the genuine " Ultramontanes," but I am firmly opposed to a second instalment of the *Kulturkampf*. The first was probably the only real great political mistake Prince Bismarck made, since opinions may differ as to the introduction of universal suffrage. The *Kulturkampf* weakened our Protestant church during its enforcement, and humiliated it when peace was made. It strengthened and gave prestige to the Catholic Church, it really developed the

Centre Party, and in so doing has confused and complicated our whole parliamentary structure for some time to come. And worst of all, that most perilous wound in the body of our noble Mother, Germania, made religious differences to which already we owe the Thirty Years' War; and all the evils it brought along with it were all embittered and intensified. Of course it is no use complaining because, unlike France and Russia, we have not the great political advantage of a united and firmly knit religious faith. We must reckon with things as they are, and carefully avoid any measure likely to intensify the conflict. The results of these last religious struggles, as of former disorders of the kind, are plain enough. They are much the same as those of the religious war in the sixteenth and seventeenth century, as the consequences of the Ecclesiastical policy of the Hohenstaufen and the Saliers. Though I consider perfect calm in our dealings with Rome and great forbearance towards German Catholics in all questions of domestic religious policy, the only right course, I am far from trustful of " Ultramontanism." With this we may arrange a *modus vivendi* but never eternal peace. Our foreign policy must certainly never be inspired by the Papal See or even influenced by it. The policy of the Triple Alliance, especially, can only be pursued to our advantage by men who are Prussian to the core, men who have sucked at their mother's breast the policy of Frederick the Great. Convinced ultramontanes, working for the firm " Triple Alliance," would really be getting business for other people.

There is no need to attack the National-Liberals. Would to God this inwardly tame and outwardly patriotic political variety were even more numerous than it is. And at present, in South Germany, National-Liberals are the only really steadfast representatives of the Imperial idea. Much water will have to flow down the Main, the Rhine, and the Danube, before, on the banks of these three rivers, the Catholic magnates and populations, have undergone a change of heart without any possible recrudesence of opinions, which were in turn particularistic, Pan-German, ultramontane, and even Rhine-federalist—but never pro-Hohenzollen! Skill, tolerance, and patience must be used. But we must not sacrifice great interests or genuinely faithful adherents.

Much as it interests me to hear of happenings in Berlin I feel no wish to be there myself at present. Not out of laziness or cowardice, but because I feel that, as things are in the Foreign Office, I could not be of the slightest use, even with the best will in the world. The post of Under-Secretary of State is the one

I would refuse most energetically, in spite of my otherwise docile spirit. It is my dream to remain on here until I can have an embassy. For the rest the ambitious restlessness of my youth has long since given place to a mental attitude which places its trust in leadership from on high: my ambitions and wishes are confined to the hope that my father would have approved of whatever work I may do where the government sends me.

Phili did not answer this letter at once but spoke of it several times in later years. He reminded me, as I well remember, both after the death of the great Prince and that of Herbert Bismarck, how earnestly, in March 1890, I had warned him of the consequences of any unfriendly removal of the great Chancellor. Sighing, and with the melancholy air peculiar to him whenever he felt inclined to fear and repentance, he said: " Who would have thought that the elimination of the Bismarcks could have such lasting and far-reaching consequences! Neither Waldersee, Bötticher, His Majesty, nor I myself, anticipated this! "

On 20th March the news reached Bucharest of Bismarck's dismissal by William I. This was not believed at once in Rumania, and later it caused the greatest astonishment. The pro-French circles could not hide their joy. Our Rumanian friends hung their heads. A few days later King Carol said to me: " My Minister in Berlin telegraphs me that public opinion there has taken Prince Bismarck's dismissal quietly, almost indifferently, and in some cases with satisfaction. Later we shall see what it has meant to the young Kaiser and Germany—perhaps to the whole world."

To use the words of the Persian poet, Firdusi, more books have since been written on Bismarck's dismissal by William II, than a camel could carry through the desert. Unfortunately it can be said of most of them, as indeed of not a few political essays of the post-war period, that they conceal more than they illuminate. Most are written without real knowledge of the events and persons they describe, and so they do not touch the core of the matter. Not one fulfils the demand of the brilliant Ferdinand Lassalle, of telling what happened, *as* it happened. I was not in Berlin in those eventful days, but could form a complete picture of what occurred from all the letters I received, both from Herbert and his intimates on the one hand, and the enemies of the Bismarcks on the other.

The separation between Kaiser and Chancellor was brought about by the Kaiser. The Prince would gladly have remained in office not only because, accustomed to power for twenty-eight years he loved it, but also because of his patriotism. He saw, in contrast to the Kaiser, what his removal from the Chancellorship of the Empire he had been chiefly instrumental in creating, would mean. It was the Kaiser who engineered the break, because he did not realize its implications—did not even realize them in the first years that followed. He was like the young Lord of Edenhall who, as he filled and refilled his high crystal goblet, also failed to foresee the results of his bravado. I believe that William II ten, or even only five years later, would not have dismissed Prince Bismarck so thoughtlessly. The not yet thirty-year-old monarch lacked experience, maturity, and seriousness. His callow shortsightedness combined with a mystic over-estimation of the attributes of high office which filled his mind at the time, and from which he never managed to free himself, impelled him to break with Bismarck. An old German proverb says that " to whomsoever God gives a task He gives him also the understanding necessary for its fulfilment." This thought has comforted many an official and civil servant and even a cabinet minister. Now, since we live in a Republic, many neophytes in office also cling to it. But the Kaiser, by a kind of auto-suggestion, had persuaded himself, as Bismarck once expressed it, that a special wire connected him with the Throne, and that, confident of special protection from Above, he could occasionally disregard the laws of common-sense down here. He became imbued with this unhealthy mysticism at an age when he had no bitter experiences to make him, if not wiser, at least more careful.

It is a mistake to believe that William II quarrelled with Bismarck solely on account of social questions, the laws for the protection of workers, and the attitude towards Socialism bound up with them. He only used this difference of opinion to rid himself of his uncomfortable " tutor," as he called Bismarck at that time, in conversation with Phili Eulenburg. Bismarck had not long been dismissed before he was demanding of Caprivi a more severe treatment of Social democracy. He repeated this, again and again, to old Prince Hohenlohe. And, during my period of office, not a year passed without the Kaiser now amiably, now excitedly and stormily, demanding drastic measures against the " Reds." I told him that if he thought the Social-Democrats should be crushed by force, he should not have parted from Prince Bismarck. I do not know whether Prince Bismarck would have succeeded in suppressing Social-Democracy, but in any case he was the only person who could have undertaken to attempt it.

A difference of opinion on the policy to be adopted towards Russia had, to a certain extent, helped to bring about Bismarck's fall. The Kaiser wanted to influence the Russo-German relations favourably by personal intervention, frequent visits to Russia, occasional presents, grandiloquent speeches, and friendly demonstrations of all descriptions. The Chancellor depended more upon a cleverly directed policy and the Re-Insurance Treaty, which he had concluded, the renewal of which was shortly due and desired by the Tsar Alexander and the Minister Giers. The Kaiser was persuaded by the enemies of his great Minister that Bismarck was too confident of Russia. He even, under the influence of Waldersee, went so far as to insult Bismarck, whom he roughly accused of " blindness " to the " dreadful " danger threatening from Russia. Holstein, at the time in Waldersee's intimate confidence, had so contrived matters that an agitated report of the Consul Raffauf, in Kiev, had been used to stir the Emperor.

The real, deep, and authentic reason for Bismarck's dismissal, lay in the fact that William II desired to play " Bismarck " himself; he wanted, both at home and abroad, to occupy the position which Bismarck had held for decades. This Bismarck perceived when he said that the Kaiser wanted to be his own Chancellor, and certainly that is what William II meant when, a few days after Bismarck's removal, he telegraphed to his old tutor Hinzpeter: " I am as sad as though I had lost my grandfather over again, but God's will be done even if one collapses under the blow. The duties of officer on the bridge of the ship of state devolve on me. Her course remains the same. Full steam ahead! " The Chief of the Civil Cabinet, Herr von Lucanus, feared it might make a bad impression if the monarch sent such a plainly political announcement to his old tutor. It was therefore pretended that the Grand Duke Charles Alexander of Weimar, the brother-in-law of the Emperor Wilhelm I, was the recipient.

The manner of this separation of Chancellor and Kaiser was most unfortunate for Germany. It should have been done with dignity, with due regard for the deference to which Bismarck was entitled, and in the careful avoidance of all harmful and unnecessary recriminations. And, above all, Bismarck should only have been dismissed if the Kaiser, after his retirement, had been determined to pursue a liberal policy—i.e., to take some definite steps in the direction of western parliamentary methods at once. A dictatorship of William II should not have followed that of Bismarck, since Bismarck was a genius and William was not.

A direct consequence of this dismissal was the denunciation of the Re-Insurance Treaty—the severing of the bond that connected Germany with Russia—as Bismarck himself expressed it. The impression which this made was all the worse because, shortly before his dismissal of the Prince had become an established fact, the Kaiser had assured the Russian Ambassador, Count Paul Shuvalov, personally and categorically, that he guaranteed a renewal of the Treaty, with or without the present Chancellor. Herr von Giers insisted in vain, declaring that if we refused to prolong the agreement Alexander III, against his own inner convictions, would be forced to ally himself with the French Republic. In vain did Shuvalov point out that the non-prolongation of the treaty, after the German Emperor had promised it, must of necessity arouse consternation, and the deepest suspicions in St. Petersburg, and in any case make deplorable impression on the Tsar and literally drive Russia into the arms of France. Caprivi did not understand the situation. With a modesty, almost touching from a moral standpoint, but unbecoming in the leader of a great Empire, he said, after hearing the reports of Marschall and Holstein: " Bismarck was able to juggle with three balls but I can only juggle with two." The difference between soldier and statesman showed itself here. The soldier forges straight ahead to his goal. The statesman can often only attain it by roundabout ways, temporising and patience. He must play the waiting game, like the hunter in ambush for his prey. He works in nuances. The mentality of the worthy Caprivi was too simple, almost naïve. Marschall, at the time, was entirely the "*Ministre étrangeraux affaires*" Bismarck had described him as, in cruel mockery, after his appointment to the Secretaryship of State for Foreign Affairs. He was completely under the influence of Holstein who, with the grim zeal peculiar to him, sometimes almost verging on monomania, took the bit between his teeth after the fall of the great Chief, let his old hatred of our easterly neighbour run away with him, and wanted to do everything " differently " to Bismarck, whom he hated because he had betrayed him.

The Kaiser was persuaded that the Re-Insurance Treaty was an act of " disloyalty " to the venerable Emperor Francis Joseph, and unworthy of so knightly a monarch as William II. It was also suggested to him that, if anything contained in the Treaty with Russia leaked out, we should not only lose for ever the confidence and respect of the Austrians but also be scorned in England. The Kaiser, not long after he came to the throne, had been appointed an English admiral, Rear-Admiral of the Fleet, a distinction doubly intoxicating to him because he believed it to imply that his strained relations with his mother, and ill-behaviour towards his father, had not really injured him in England. The continuance of the Russo-German Re-Insurance Treaty was as compatible with our Austrian alliance, as with good relations towards England. The Austro-

Hungarian Ambassador for many years in Berlin, Count Szögyényi, told me more than once, in after years, that the denunciation of the Re-Insurance Treaty had even been a misfortune for Austria. " This treaty," said Szögyényi, " was not only an important guarantee for the world's peace, but it was also a benefit to the Hapsburg monarchy, since it prevented our doing silly things." As for England the better our relations towards Russia the more consideration she would have had for us.

The immediate, automatic result of our withdrawal from the treaty, was just what Bismarck had predicted: the conclusion of the Franco-Russian Alliance. Even in May, 1890, the leader of the Pan-Slav party, Tchernaiev, who had formerly been punished, was reinstated and nominated à la suite of the General Staff and member of the Council of War. In May, 1890, the Tsar and his family visited in a demonstrative fashion an exhibition in Moscow, arranged by the French. On 23rd July a French squadron appeared in Kronstadt, commanded by Admiral Gervais, where it was received by the populace and the sailors of the Russian ships with enthusiasm. Grand Duke Alexei Alexandrovitch, supreme Admiral of the Fleet, gave Admiral Gervais, his staff, and the commanders of the French ships, a gala dinner. The Tsar and Tsaritsa went on board the flagship " Marengo." At a dinner given in honour of the French squadron, in Peterhof, the Tsar toasted the President of the French Republic. As the band played the " Marseillaise" the Tsar stood bareheaded and listened. William II, who only too often tried to make mountains out of molehills, more than once magnified insignificant events into " historic milestones," while failing to appreciate the important ones. This moment, when the Tsar took off his helmet to the rallying-cry of the French revolution, was a really historic one. It meant the end of a Russo-German friendship which had been based, not only on politics, but on real emotion, and which had lasted eighty years. With care and skill rupture and war with Russia were still avoidable, but everybody felt that relations between the northern empires were not as they had been. In a telegram to President Carnot the Tsar spoke of the " deep sympathies " which united France and Russia. In Moscow Admiral Gervais and his officers were received officially and enthusiastically. The Admiral concluded his toast, at the banquet given in his honour, with the words: " The attention of the whole world is now directed towards you and ourselves. I drink to holy Moscow, the great Russian nation and its noble Tsar." The once retired but now reinstated General Tchernaiev replied with a reference to the refrain of the " Marseillaise": " If the call sounds in France

' *Aux armes, citoyens*! ' that call will find its echo here also. *Formez vos bataillons*! We Russians will form our battalions from the Vistula to Kamtchatka. I drink to the noble French people and to Paris, capital of the civilized world! " Gervais replied that, " strengthened in the friendship of a great and powerful monarch," France regarded the future with confidence. Nobody in Europe doubted that a Franco-Russian alliance and corresponding military convention, had been concluded. The erstwhile French Ambassador in St. Petersburg, Laboulaye, an inoffensive and phlegmatic old gentleman, was recalled. In his place came one of the most brilliant French diplomats, Count Montebello, with his charming and elegant wife. Within a few months the world had changed. Nor could William II fail any longer to perceive the consequences of having denounced the Treaty. He tried in every way to make good his mistake. This did not succeed with Alexander III, who disliked him, and continued to do so. All the more zealously therefore did he pay his respects to Nicholas II, urging him to make some formal agreement, and so at last there came into being the grotesque Convention of Björkö.

It would be a mistake to suppose that Bismarck's dismissal had evoked the majority of Germans, especially of German politicians, either to protest, indignation, or even regrets. At first there was no sign of anything like it. Soon after Bismarck's resignation Dr. Kropatschek, the editor-in-chief of the *Kreuz-Zeitung*, a patriot and an excellent man, entered the Conservative Club in Rathenow with the words: " Glad tidings, gentlemen! From now on we shall no longer be governed by the Bismarck family but by the House of Hohenzollern! " The leader of the *bourgeois* democracy, Eugen Richter, a sound enough man in many respects, published an article on the greatest German statesman which, for pettiness and meanness, would be hard to beat. Neither the president of the Reichstag —which, without Bismarck, would never have existed—of that very House of Deputies where, during the period of conflict, he had made some of his finest speeches, nor of the Austrian Diet, whose estimable and certainly most famous member he was, took any notice of his dismissal. If I am not mistaken, all three Presidents were Conservatives, that is to say, members of the party which, at the time when Bismarck began to govern, would all have found seats in the one cab, to use a well-known parliamentary expression, but which now, both in the Reichstag and Upper House, had swelled to imposing numbers.

CHAPTER XLVI

King Carol on Prince Bismarck's dismissal—Betrothal festivities in the Rumanian Royal House—My appointment to the Ambassadorship in Rome—Farewell audience with King Carol—Last meeting with my mother in Berlin.

WHEN, not long after the resignation of Prince Bismarck, I came for a few days to Berlin, I found the atmosphere there filled with that spirit the French express as " *Ouf!* " Democrats and Clericals were jubilant. The Conservatives drew a long breath of relief. The very intelligent and thoroughly sincere embassy-councillor of the Bucharest Legation, Baron von Dörnberg, to whom, before sending it, I had shown my letter of warning to Philip Eulenburg and who, at the time, had called the letter an " action, and a good action," said, when I met him again at my brother Alfred's in Stuttgart that, in South Germany also, the deepest emotion aroused by Prince Bismarck's dismissal was satisfaction : " Things will go better now and life be more comfortable," was the consensus of opinion on all sides.

Herbert Bismarck, who had just visited me in Wildbad, where we were spending a few weeks, spoke very differently. He told me that he had come to thank me for having been so loyal to his father. He was sure I would continue in my loyalty. Herbert had heard from an official in the central bureau of the Foreign Office that, I alone, of all Imperial diplomats, had made the dismissal of Prince Bismarck the subject of an official letter, pointing out its possible serious consequences. All our other representatives had either held their tongues or affirmed that our youthful, vigorous Kaiser, was our best augury for the future. Herbert gave me astonishing details of the ruthlessness with which his father had been personally treated by William II. The Kaiser had been too impatient to await the request for resignation of this faithful servant of his grandfather, demanding, again and again, through the chief of his Civil Cabinet, Herr von Lucanus, the aide-de-camp Hahnke, or other intermediaries, that his formal request to resign should be presented. " My poor old father was dismissed like a dishonest or troublesome servant." Of the last conversation between His Majesty and the Chancellor Bismarck, Herbert related the following: His father, at seventy-five years of age, after his hard-working life, needed a certain amount of consideration. The doctors insisted upon his taking care of himself in the early morning. They wished him to take an early cup of tea in bed, and then be massaged after a warm bath, and not go out until about midday, particularly in the raw March weather. But on that morning of dismissal the Kaiser had arrived quite early in his, the Secretary of State, Herbert's villa and, in a very ungracious, impatient tone, commanded the Prince to appear at once in his presence.

And so my father, scantily dressed and shivering, had to go in the rain and the cold, through the garden of the Chancellor's palace to the villa of the Secretary of State. When he arrived the Kaiser asked him roughly: " When am I going to get your request for resignation? " The Prince replied, with complete self-control and perfect courtesy: " I beg your Majesty most humbly to have a few hours patience with an old man. After thirty years' activity as Premier and Chancellor, I not only have the right, but, as I imagine, the duty to put down in writing for the benefit of Your Majesty, the country, and for history, in all veneration, the reasons for my resignation." The Kaiser answered curtly and dryly: " There can be no question of publishing your request for resignation."

Herbert and Bill Bismarck both assured me, in later years, that their father, when openly insulted by William II, had never been upset or out of temper even. When the speeches were laid before him in which William II had proclaimed, plainly in reference to him, that he intended to crush his enemies, that he alone was master in the country, that his grandfather, Emperor William I, had had many good ministers but that, compared with the Emperor, they had been only pygmies and servants of the All-Highest's will, Prince Bismarck contented himself with writing under the cutting in question: " *Sunt pueri pueri! Pueri puerilia tractant.*" (Boys are but boys and behave like boys.)

Herbert Bismarck did not conceal from me in Wildbad that his father regarded the future of the Reich with anxiety. " Kaiser William II is riding for a fall with a hurra," Bismarck said, shortly after his dismissal to Herbert. " Let us hope that in the crisis the Kaiser will be brave and risk his own life like Frederick the Great at Zorndorf, Hochkirch, and Kunersdorf. And, if ever it comes to the worst, to rebellion and revolution, may he fight, and if it needs be, fall fighting on the steps of the throne, fighting for the Crown, and the rights and the honour of the Crown."

When the news of Prince Bismarck's dismissal reached Bucharest I had written twice to Herbert, to express my deep regret at the turn things had taken in Berlin. I begged him at the same time to give his great father the assurance of my unshakeable homage, admiration, and loyalty. He replied on 7th April, 1890, from Berlin:

Many thanks for both your kind letters. I feel I must let you know how much pleasure your words have given. I cannot say much more than that, since who knows the destiny of this letter before it comes into your hands? My health has been worse than ever this winter. I have not yet recovered from a heavy influenza attack in December, when I could not lie up owing to pressure of work. If my father had stayed in office the doctors tell me I should have needed a long leave of four months. But now that my father has been forced to resign against his will, in so brusque a manner, it has become impossible for me to take over the increased duties and responsibilities which my name causes to be thrust upon me. Even if I were in the best of health this step would give me the gravest misgivings, since my position under a new Chancellor, quite inexperienced in diplomacy, would have been a very difficult one. Of the two new people—Caprivi and Marschall—nobody expects anything in regard to foreign policy because everybody knows that, not only have they not had anything to do with it, but do not understand it in the least. That Alvensleben refused to be my successor I regret, for the sake of the service which will go to pieces, since more is needed for that most difficult of all branches, the foreign, than can be learned as a public prosecutor and parliamentarian in Baden. Marschall, I hear, had counted on the post for a long time, and certainly has a bad conscience where I am concerned, for he has completely ignored me since his nomination. I should have left Berlin already if the Kaiser had not invited himself to dinner with me to-morrow. As it is I leave the day after for Friedrichsruh, and shall probably not see Berlin again. Good-bye, dear Bülow, and do good business under the new management.

Always yours,
HERBERT.

On 18th April, 1890, the day on which, twenty-six years earlier, the storming of the Düppel trenches had given us the first striking proof of the rightness of the Bismarck policy, I wrote again to Herbert.

Dear Herbert,—Your kind lines of the 7th instant reached me safely. Thanks most heartily for finding time to write me at a moment when so many demands are being made on your time. Your letter gave me, even if only by hints, the first real explanation, both of the development and origin of the most fateful crisis in the life of our State since 1848. Meanwhile I have received other information from Berlin and Vienna which enables me to form at last a fairly correct idea of the latest events. My regrets over what has happened are not lessened by further insight. On the other hand I need not tell you that the boundless admiration and homage I began to feel for your great father as soon as ever I started to think in political terms at all, can be touched by no external change. I now understand the reasons why you do not wish to stay in office. My regret at your decision is certainly not diminished by knowing them. At this moment any suggestion of your return will be disagreeable to you. But *dans mon for intérieur* I cling to the hope that, sooner or later, you will again consent to be the head of the foreign department. I am still of the opinion that we have nobody better than you for this important and responsible position, and my conviction of this is not merely based on unchanged friendship and affection. I hope that your health, so taxed by over-work—your industry has indeed been incredible—will now swiftly improve. It would be a great pleasure to me if I could meet you somewhere this summer when, I think of taking a leave, *more solito*, if only for a few hours, to tell you in person what fills my heart. That I shall do " good business " under the new management seems not very probable *a priori*. I am as far removed from Caprivi as from Marschall, and I have many enemies among those who now call the tune in the Foreign Office—but you know all that. Be assured though that whatever *Invidia* may say of me, the cause means more to me than personal ambitions. My wishes are centered upon the maintenance of that which your father created, by uniting all men of goodwill, and on wise and unselfish service of our young Master and the nation. I have reported officially that your father's departure has aroused here the deepest regrets of all supporters of the present order, and co-operation with Germany. I must tell you now that King Carol, Carp, and Sturdza expressed these sentiments to me in a warm and seemly manner. With the request that you give your parents my devoted compliments, and in the hope that God will grant you all the happiness which I pray He may with my whole soul, I am, in old friendship,

Always your B.

Herbert replied on 3rd May from Friedrichsruh:

Heartiest thanks for your kind letter of the 18th instant which I received a few days ago. I was very pleased to hear from you, and the warm words in which you express your feelings for us went to my heart. We have known one another from childhood and there is no need for more assurances. I, too, should be glad to talk to you, and I hope very much to meet you this summer. The day after to-morrow I am going to England for three weeks. I shall spend the greater part of June here in Friedrichsruh and July in Königstein. In August and September I shall, perhaps, go to the seaside or eventually with my father to Kissingen—should he go there, that is: he has, of course, little inclination for this spa and would prefer the sea. Schweninger will have to decide. My address remains in the meantime Friedrichsruh. I do not think I shall come back to the service although one should never say, *source je ne boirai pas de ton eau*; and probably I shall not be asked to. I have no faith in the talent of the public prosecutor from Baden who now directs our foreign policy, and have been much against his appointment. Besides he intrigued so basely against my father and behaved so rudely towards myself, that I would not serve under him if I were as healthy as a fish in water. Unfortunately I am not. I have overdone it during the long and hard years, and shall need much time to patch myself up again. I do not think you can have many friends among the new heads of the Foreign Office and their amanuensis. This applies still more to our good friend Vitzthum, and it was one of my last acts in office to secure him a new post. As he was not yet far enough advanced for embassy-councillor, I thought he would prefer to come to you; otherwise he would have been dumped down in Lisbon or Rio. Many greetings to him, please, from me. My parents are, thank God, fairly well. King Carol answered a long letter my father sent him with a very warm telegram. Farewell until we meet again in summer!

Always your faithful,
HERBERT BISMARCK.

The " public prosecutor from Baden " is, of course Marschall, the " amanuensis " of the Secretary of State is Holstein, in whom poor Herbert had been so bitterly disappointed.

After his fall Herbert never spoke of Holstein with other than boundless hatred. It was that hate which the French call " *l'amour tourné à l'aigre,*" the reaction from his many years of enthusiasm for Holstein—the blind confidence he had reposed in him from childhood. He felt that Holstein had deceived and betrayed him. He felt " taken-in," to use a slang expression. Kiderlen was for him only the mercenary, who fights for anybody who pays him well, ready at any moment to change shirt, and even skin if necessary. He spoke of Phili Eulenburg with scorn. The Bavarian Ambassador, Count Hugo Lerchenfeld, told him that Eulenburg boasted of possessing the political confidence of Prince Bismarck, and of having been used politically by him. " My father," said Herbert, in an almost contemptuous tone, " never took Eulenburg *au sérieux* politically. He only wanted to use the courtier's talents of " Phili " to work upon Prince William through his favourite, since Phili had soon wormed his way in there, as he did wherever anything was to be gained." I went for many walks with Herbert in the beautiful woods that surround this charming Black Forest spa. It touched him greatly that everybody greeted him kindly, and that here and there a pretty Swabian girl would hand him a bunch of flowers, with a curtsey.

On my return to my Bucharest post I found King Carol most upset at Prince Bismarck's dismissal. " I saw this misfortune coming," he said. " You remember everything I told you about confidential information from Germany. Bismarck's resignation is a great historical event, towards which, as towards most historical events, one may adopt any attitude one likes. But this inconsiderate and tactless form of dismissal will confuse and embitter many in Germany as the real facts begin to be known. The way in which one of the greatest statesmen of all countries, or ages, the greatest Prussian since Frederick the Great, has been 'sent packing,' is, between you and me, crude and puerile." In this connection the King repeated some letters from German relatives, written him when the young Kaiser came to the throne. The Crown Prince William, when his poor father lay in the last agony, had ordered the Hussars of the Guard, a regiment which he had formerly commanded and therefore especially favoured, to surround the Neues Palais. Whenever the Empress Frederick came for a moment from the bed in which her husband lay dying, to snatch a breath of air at the window, she would see the red uniforms of Hussars, set there to prevent anyone leaving the Palace without permission. They had particular orders to prevent any correspondence of the unhappy Empress with foreign countries. The Empress, when she left the Palace, was only to take such letters and documents as her son had examined beforehand. Dr. Mackenzie was also to be detained. King Carol declared that William II had originally wanted to

arrest and imprison the English doctor. That had been prevented by Bismarck, since any such action would not merely have
made a bad impression in England, but might have caused diplomatic difficulties. Several times had Bismarck urged the young
Kaiser not to be so inconsiderate to his mother. King Carol could
never sufficiently praise the truly Christian patience and heroism
which the Emperor Frederick had displayed to the last. " A hero
and a saint," was the King's verdict on this noble Emperor. The
behaviour of this son who, immediately after the father's death, with
his sword girded at his side and the fur busby of the Guards' Hussars
in his hand, had come to make a scene with his mother, would
scarcely bring him good fortune. As formerly, the Ambassador von
Schweinitz, so did King Carol quote the fifth commandment,
which makes our earthly welfare depend on the honour we pay our
parents. The King, with fine psychological acumen, remarked that
the Kaiser's brutality towards his parents, his inconsiderate rudeness
to Bismarck, were not due to any hardness of heart, but rather to
such a lack of self-control and reflection as is often found in
neurasthenics.

On June, 1892, came the betrothal of the heir to the Rumanian
throne, Prince Ferdinand of Hohenzollern, with the eldest daughter
of the Duke of Edinburgh. Prior to this alliance with an equal the
future King of Rumania had been the tragi-comic hero of an absurd
love affair, which revealed him as the vacillating creature he showed
himself to be, as king, in the Great War. Among the ladies of
Queen Elizabeth's court was a Mlle. Vacarescu, who looked like
a fat cook and had the manners of one, but had been cunning enough
to ensnare the simple-minded Prince Ferdinand. He entered into
a secret engagement with her. Queen Elizabeth of Rumania was
a broad-minded woman, very gifted, with a warm heart, and if her
poems, under the pseudonym of Carmen Sylva, did not quite equal
those of Sappho, they showed at least the imagination and the
temperament of a poetess. She adored Helen Vacarescu who wrote
verses even worse than her own. Helen succeeded in winning over
the Queen to the idea of a marriage with the Rumanian Crown
Prince, and even inspired her with enthusiasm. Supported by Her
Majesty's Cabinet-Secretary, a pro-French Alsatian, she managed
to interest the Queen in spiritualist experiments. The exalted lady
not only hoped to gain poetic inspiration from spiritualism, but
also a few prophetic hints. The spirit of the Queen's father, Prince
Hermann of Wied was summoned up. Asked what he would
advise the Queen to do he replied in hollow tones that she should
rank the laurels of a poetess higher than any earthly crown. Asked

what was in store for Helen Vacarescu the answer rang out—
"*Hélène-Reine!*" The spirit spoke fluent French. The Queen
saw in this a sign from Heaven, which had destined her beloved
Helen to succeed her. The Vacarescu family and her Cabinet-
Secretary persuaded her that this alliance of the future King of
Rumania would be acclaimed with jubilation throughout the
country. Her Majesty urged King Carol to give his consent.
The King, as always, manœuvred with cleverness and kindness.
He told his wife that in so delicate a matter he must act on the advice
of his ministers, and party leaders. These all, without exception,
declared that the marriage of the future King of Rumania to a
Rumanian would arouse a storm of indignant protest. The Rumanians had chosen a foreign king because no Rumanian could bear to
be ruled by a compatriot. No Rumanian woman would permit one
of her countrywomen, and not a handsome one at that, to be queen
instead of herself. Prince Ferdinand was then summoned to His
Majesty and asked to decide between his love and his claim to the
crown. Carmen Sylva, with divine afflatus, exclaimed that Romeo
would not have relinquished Juliet for a crown. King Carol refrained from anything more than the quiet but firm indication that
it was an ultimatum: either the Crown or Mlle. Vacarescu. In a
tearful voice Prince Ferdinand declared for the Crown. He was
sent for some time to Sigmaringen, where his parents wrote to tell
him what they thought of him. When the whole affair had been
forgotten he was permitted to return to Rumania and so, at the end
of the World War, unfortunately had his opportunity as a Hohenzollern and a Prussian officer, to betray his German Fatherland.

In the late autumn of 1893 I was with my wife at the German
Embassy in Vienna, on a visit to Prince Henry VII of Reuss and
the Princess. Here, in the previous year, at Herbert's wedding
with Countess Hoyos, Prince Bismarck had not been received by
the Emperor Francis Joseph. (William II's spiteful letter to the
Emperor was published after the revolution by the Republican
Government.) Prince Henry, who had been warned by Caprivi to
refuse any invitation to the wedding, informed me that I was
destined to be Ambassador in Rome. Except my advancement from
private to corporal in the King's Hussars no promotion ever pleased
me more than this one. I hoped I might be able to do good work
in Rome. I loved Italy with the old love of so many Germans, from
Goethe and Winckelmann to Gregorovius and Anton Dohrn, for
that country which Mignon yearned for. My wife was happy in the
thought of being reunited to her mother whom she loved tenderly.
Although not vain I felt equal to the position of Ambassador. I had

1ot done badly seventeen years before, as chargé d'affaires in 1thens, during the Balkan War. More than once, for six years in ?aris and four in St. Petersburg, I had taken over these difficult and mportant Embassies as chargé d'affaires, created a good position 'or myself on the Seine and on the Neva, and managed to accom-)lish one or two things. So I faced my approaching task with the 'esolute trust in God which beseems young men.

In Vienna, as soon as my appointment was finally settled, Phili Eulenburg called. His pleasure at my promotion was great and, I magine, quite sincere. He charmed my wife by his cordial expres-ions of delight. She compared him to a good angel who rejoices vith the glad, comforts the unhappy, and wants to help everyone. My appointment to Rome was mainly due to Holstein. He had urged it with the fiery zeal he put into everything he attempted. Not out of any particular love for me but because he considered the ituation in Rome to be more dangerous than in Rumania six years)reviously, and I seemed to him now to be as suited to the Roman)ost as I had been then to Bucharest. Caprivi was not interested in .iplomatic personalities. Marschall was against my appointment s Ambassador since, long before I had ever imagined such a con-ingency, he saw in me a rival for the Chancellorship which he iimself so coveted.

When I bade farewell to King Carol he told me that Rome ught only to be a temporary position. I would, he hoped and)elieved, be Imperial Chancellor in five years time. I parted un-villingly from the good and wise King to whom I had become as ttached as formerly to the good and wise Prince Chlodwig Hohen->he. I left Rumania unwillingly, where I had spent six quiet and .appy years with my wife. We really regretted having to leave the)eautiful forest round Sinaia. I had often climbed up to Stina from vhence one has a magnificent view of the valley of the Prahova. More than once I had ascended the Wurfucudor which gives a iew of Rumania and Transylvania. Once, on a fairly cool Septem-)er day, I climbed the Wurfucudor twice, for a bet. At six o'clock 1 the morning I left Sinaia and got to the top at nine, when I rested n hour. At ten I started downwards, got to Sinaia by twelve, unched, and started off again at two. At six o'clock I again enjoyed he lovely view and at nine was again in the " Hotel Joseph " at)inaia, a little inn kept by a worthy Austrian, which, like the Inn f St. Wolfgang, thirteen years earlier, recalled the " White Horse " f the famous musical comedy.

In Berlin, where I paid my official visits to the Chancellor and)ecretary of State before taking up my new office, I saw my dear good mother for the last time. She had had two strokes in close succession which, at the age of seventy-two, had affected her badly. As I said good-bye she took my hand and pleaded with a touching glance: " Bernhard, do not forsake our Lord Jesus." She died on 29th January 1894 without a struggle, murmuring the words: " Come, Lord Jesus." We buried her in the Church of the Twelve Apostles in Berlin between my father and their only daughter.

CHAPTER XLVII

Taking over the Embassy in Rome—Situation in Italy—Crispi, Blanc—The German Colony—Kaiser's birthday, 1894—William II visits King Humbert in Venice.

IN Berlin I had been told on many sides, in the Foreign Office and by leading personalities in Economics and Political Economy that, in Italy, everything was at sixes and sevens. In fact, for the moment, things did not look rosy. The Prime Minister, Giolitti, was being criticized and insulted in the Chamber, in the Senate, in the cafés, and in *salons*. To calm those who are apt to let themselves be bluffed by unfair criticism I add that when this same Giolitti, after the Great War and under difficult conditions, seized the reins again and presented himself to the Senate, all the members of this exalted body rose from their seats and bowed silently to the aged statesman. More serious than the criticism of the *salons* and cafés was the fact that in the autumn of 1893, in Sicily, in Calabria, and the Romagna, revolutionary disorders had occurred. There had been heavy tumults in Milan and Naples as well. Painful bank scandals, involving journalists and deputies, had forced government and Chamber to appoint a commission of investigation. At the government's request the Chamber approved judicial proceedings against the deputy Zerbi for corruption by the Banca Romana. A fortnight later Zerbi died under mysterious circumstances. His fate is reminiscent of the scandal caused by the Minister of Posts and Telegraphs, Höfle, in the German Republic, which exposed German officialdom, surpassed by none in the world, under the Monarchy, for its conscientiousness and uprightness. The Italian funds had sunk lower than they had been since 1866, after the defeats of Custozza and Lissa.

Three influential party-leaders, Rudini, Zanardelli, and Sonnino, all three later Presidents of Council, had turned against Giolitti, whom they had hitherto supported, and who was also challenged by Crispi and Nicotera. Baron Giovanni Nicotera, a Calabrian, had been condemned to life-long slavery at the galleys under the Bourbons, for participation in a revolt. Liberated by Garibaldi, he had been elected deputy and not long afterwards became Minister of the Interior. His martyrdom, borne with dignity, had made him popular. Attacked on all sides the Giolitti Cabinet had resigned at the end of November, 1893. Only after a fortnight's wearisome negotiations and an unsuccessful attempt by Zanardelli to form a government, was Crispi entrusted with the formation of the new ministry.

I had told those in Berlin who despaired of the political, and perhaps still more of the economic future of Italy, that I was unable to share their pessimism. I had confidence in the passionate patriotism and the political flexibility of the Italian people which, in the course of the nineteenth century, the century of its *Risorgimento*, had overcome far worse difficulties. Further developments proved me to be right. Crispi was a statesman of parts: clear, energetic, steady in pursuit of his aim, and absolutely fearless. By birth a Sicilian, he had taken part as a youth in the revolt of the patriots against the Bourbons. Condemned to death he had lived as an exile in great poverty in Malta and in Paris, and plotted further. Placed at the head of his country's government he turned against the revolutionary movement, which had to be crushed with all the resolution which he once, as a conspirator, had shown in fighting Bourbon corruption. He read out a courageous declaration in the Chamber of Deputies and the Senate, in which he appealed to the memories of Garibaldi and Mazzini, " our two great ones," and stated the situation of the country to be serious " as never before." The power of the law must be strengthened, finances reorganized, and great sacrifices demanded of the country to this end. The material unity of the Fatherland must be assured, its moral unity consolidated. The task before the new government would be the most important since the proclamation of the national Constitution of 1859. Next day Crispi proclaimed martial law, strengthened the garrisons in the revolutionary areas, and caused numerous agitators to be arrested. The efficient General Morra was nominated Supreme Commander in Sicily. He had been tutor to King Victor Emanuel III and afterwards Ambassador in St. Petersburg. In the revolutionary districts all weapons had to be delivered up to the police stations. The import of arms was universally prohibited. In skirmishes between the military and the rebels the former fired without hesitation. Not only in Sicily but everywhere where riots had taken place, in Massa and Carrara, in Bari, Ancona and Mantua, law and order were restored with severity. The deputy, De Felice, the intellectual author of the Sicilian rebellion, was arrested and deported. When his wife threw herself at the feet of Prime Minister Crispi and pleaded for the liberation of her husband, he turned his back on her with the words that he knew no other motive for action than the *raison d'état*, and that this demanded firmness on the part of a Prime Minister. The lawyer, Molinari, who had organized the revolt of the workers in the marble quarries of Massa-Carrara, was sentenced to twenty-three years hard labour. The statesmen of Latin countries differ from their German colleagues, more doctrinaire and more " sickled o'er by the pale cast of thought," in that they do not shrink in case of necessity either from inconsistency or ruthlessness. The ex-revolutionary, Crispi, overthrew the revolutionary movement in Italy in the winter of 1893-4 along the whole line, just as, twenty-three years earlier, in France, a Liberal *par excellence*, Thiers, one of the pioneers of the July revolution of 1830, drenched the Paris Commune in streams of blood, and as during the Great War, Clemenceau Viviani, Briand, Painlevé, and other French Radicals and Socialists fought defeatism which, in Germany, was handled with kid gloves on, by Bethmann, Michaelis, Hertling, and Prince Max of Baden.

I got on well with Crispi. He had a strong sense of self-assertiveness. In personal contact he was natural, amiable, and tranquil, and this in the energetic man with the finely cut features, glittering eyes, and the bushy, snow-white moustache was pleasant. Crispi was authoritative to the bone—a realist in politics. The high-falutin' phrases, illusions, and delusions into which we Germans lapse so easily, were far removed from his temperament. His admiration for Prince Bismarck was boundless. To-day, in Italy, Crispi is remembered with blessings. In the present Foreign Office in Rome—the old Palazzo Chigi—a marble tablet was set up in his honour after the war, in commemoration of his patriotism and resolution. The windows of the Villa Malta look out on to one of the main streets of Rome which bears his name.

The Foreign Secretary, Baron Blanc, was by birth a Savoyard like Menabrea, Pelloux, Barral, Launay, and many other personalities of modern Italy. When he was created Baron he chose as motto the charming " *Savoye indique la voie.*" In Berlin Blanc was considered too busy and restless, and Holstein, himself far more excitable, complained of Blanc's excitability. Alberto Blanc had, it is true, a passionate nature, but his passions were centred, not on his own personal spites and vanities, but only on the glory and the greatness of his Fatherland. In his youth he had been secretary to the founder of modern Italy, Count Cavour. Cavour had two secretaries, Artom for the Italian, Blanc for the French language and correspondence. Cavour himself had an equal mastery of both tongues. Blanc sometimes described his chief's methods, who rose very late but was accustomed to work from midnight to morning.

Cavour demanded acute attention from his subordinates, untiring industry, and complete discretion, and was himself always equably polite and never moody or violent. Blanc did not believe that Cavour had taken office with the fixed idea of creating a united Italy from Monte Rosa to Cape Passaro at the earliest possible moment. His first aim had been only the freeing of North Italy from the foreign yoke of Austria. When the premature armistice concluded by Napoleon III, who had lost his nerve after Solferino, impeded this, Cavour organized revolts in Tuscany, Parma, Modena, and in the Papal Legations, and used them to unite these territories with the Kingdom of Sardinia, after the Piedmontese General, Cialdini, had defeated the Papal troops, led by the French General, Lamoricière, in September, 1860.

Blanc often told me that Cavour had not expected the annexation of the kingdom of the two Sicilies, and the patrimony of St. Peter, to take place as soon as they did. Cavour had said to Blanc, in the late autumn of 1860, that the Papal States and Southern Italy were so backward, economically and morally, in consequence of centuries of Papal and Bourbon misgovernment, that it was still too early to unite them with the better governed North and Central Italy, which were on a far higher plane. If they were united too soon with the rest of Italy they would infect the whole country with their own demoralization. The fiery impatience and boldness of Garibaldi forced Cavour to go further than he intended. And so the greatest Italian statesman, one of the greatest statesmen of all time saw, barely three months before his death, the whole peninsular, save Venice and the district around Rome, united under the sceptre of his King. On 17th March, 1861, King Victor Emanuel II was proclaimed King of Italy. On 6th June, 1861, Cavour died. More fortunate than Moses, he had beheld with his bodily eyes the Promised Land his soul yearned for. To the friends gathered at his death-bed he said: " *La cosa va, e l'Italia.*" I can still well remember the impression made by the death of Cavour on the Frankfort diplomats. We were standing, on 7th June, at the entrance to the Zoological Gardens. An extra edition, shouted by newspaper boys, announced the death of the Premier of the new Italy. The very clerical Austrian Minister to the Diet said, with a mixture of malicious delight, and moral indignation: " I should not like to stand now in the place of this wicked man at the gate of Hell." Some other representatives of German kingdoms and Grand Duchies, although Protestants, agreed to this, not without hypocrisy. The Italian Minister, Count Barral, a Savoyard and loyal servant of the house of Savoy but strictly Catholic, was silent

with embarrassment. The French Minister shrugged his shoulders.
Like nearly all French diplomats he was against the pro-Italian
policy of the Emperor Napoleon III. Only my father, an objective
critic, holding the hand of his barely twelve-year-old boy replied:
"*Comme légitimiste je ne puis louer la politique du Comte Cavour, mais
son nom restera dans l'histoire.*"

The most intelligent of Baron Blanc's fellow workers was
M. Malvano, an official of untiring industry and rich experience,
meticulous and of penetrating insight. He too had served under
Cavour. Malvano, like Artom, was an Israelite. So was the Minister of Finances, Sidney Sonnino, whom I met here for the first time.
He was at that moment completely pro-German. He knew Germany, its language and literature. One of his sisters was married
to a Bavarian diplomat, Baron von Tautphoeus. He was considered
what the French call a "*mauvais coucheur*," irritable and disputatious.
He was eccentric and seldom went out into society. But, together
with the deputy Franchetti, another Jew, he had written a good
book on economic conditions in Sicily. He had read a lot, and
thought a lot, and he had a firm will.

M. Ratazzi, minister of the royal house, impressed me with his
cleverness. He was a nephew of the radical Parliamentarian who
had been in such sharp opposition to Cavour. Political differences
in Italy rarely lead to personal, almost never to unbridgable personal
enmities. Italy was built up by men who were very different from
one another by birth and aims, by Piedmontese and Sicilians, by
high-born aristocrats and by men whose cradles had stood in
poverty-stricken homes, by orthodox, fiery Catholics, by Free-
masons and Atheists. But on the main object, that Italy was to be
made strong, the whole placed before the parts, the national idea
above all regional and particularist tendencies, all intellectuals were
agreed. On this point the cultured section of the Italian people has
never wavered, neither during the whole course of the *Risorgimento*
nor later, up to present times.

The Kaiser's birthday, 27th January, 1894, gave me the desired
opportunity of getting to know the German colony in Rome. This
colony had a long and proud history. When Charlemagne entered
Rome, on 29th November, 799, all the *Scholæ Peregrinorum*, those
of the Franks, Frisians, Saxons, and Longobards, went to meet him
with banners and song as far as the Ponte Molle. Every German
traveller to Rome knows the Campo Santo of the Germans near St.
Peters, inscribed with the simple and beautiful words, "*Teutones in
Pace.*" Everybody, too, knows the church *Santa Maria dell'Anima*,
with the tomb of Pope Hadrian VI, the last German to sit on the

throne of St. Peter.   Its melancholy inscription: " *Proh dolor. Quantum refert, in quae tempora vel optimi cujusque virtus incidat!* " could be taken as motto by many a military commander, many a statesman, and many a public man.   The correspondent in Rome, for many years, of the *Cologne Gazette*, Frederick Noack, wrote a fine history of the Germans in Rome called *German Rome*, which he kindly dedicated to myself.   What a long road—and how many great and dear memories there are from the Campo Santo of the German Catholics in the shadow of St. Peter's, a swallow's nest nestled against the mighty cathedral, where lies the painter, Joseph Anton Koch and Johann Martin Wagner, the historian; Pater Teiner and Ernst Plattner, Pope Gregory XVI, Dr. Alerto—where many worthy German craftsmen and Swiss guards rest under mighty cypresses and eucalyptus wreathed with roses; where, in my presence, Cardinal Prince Gustav Hohenlohe was laid to rest—to the churchyard of the non-Catholics, near the pyramid of Cestius, where Jacob Asmus Carstens and two children of Wilhelm von Humboldt, the painters, August Riedel and Hans von Marées, the architect Gottfried Semper, the archæologist, Wilhelm Henzen and Goethe *filius patri antevertens*, repose, and where the ashes of my dear friend, Malvida von Meysenbug, fill an urn on which are engraved only the words: " *Amore e pace.*"

The German colony were present to a man on 27th January, 1894, since news had arrived from Berlin a few days earlier which touched all German hearts.   On 22nd January the aide-de-camp of the Kaiser, Count Kuno Moltke, handed Prince Bismarck an imperial letter in which William II conveyed his good wishes for the Prince's recovery from an attack of influenza, along with a bottle of old Rhine wine.   Moltke added to these an invitation to a fête on the Kaiser's birthday.   Prince Bismarck begged, in his reply, to be permitted to express his thanks in person, before the birthday of the All-Highest, on account of his weak state of health, a request which was acceded to by telegram.   The *Reichs Gazette* stated that the despatch of aide-de-camp Moltke was due to the entirely independent initiative of His Majesty, and that nobody in government circles had had any knowledge of this intention.   This was correct. As I was informed from Berlin, the Imperial Chancellor Caprivi was completely surprised by His Majesty's action.   Secretary of State Marschall could scarcely conceal his annoyance.   Holstein raged out loud, and Phili Eulenburg sighed discreetly.   Both these, at the time still my close personal friends and political allies, wired to me at once that this " gesture " of the Kaiser's had no political significance, and that the Bismarck's, father and son, were still politically eclipsed. This was meant as a warning. The Conservative and the National-Liberal press warmly welcomed the imperial step towards reconciliation, the Liberals declared that there could be no question of political consequences resulting from this turn of events. The Socialists and Clericals used the occasion to deliver new, and in part extremely base, attacks upon the great architect of the German Empire.

On 26th January Prince Bismarck arrived at midday at the Lehrter Banhof, from which he had entrained for Friedrichsruh, after his dismissal. He was met at the station by Prince Henry, the Kaiser's brother, who embraced and kissed him, and by the venerable and famous Lieutenant-Colonel von Pape, the hero of St. Privat. Escorted by a squadron of Cuirassier Guards and hailed jubilantly by enormous crowds, he drove to the imperial palace. Here the Kaiser received him—he was greeted by the Empress and the elder princes. Always correct in matters of formal etiquette, Bismarck paid a visit of half an hour to the Empress Frederick. How much had those two experienced together during nearly three decades, how they had worked against one another! Bismarck received the Premier, Count Botho Eulenburg, and after him his faithful friend of the great days, the aide-de-camp, Count Heinrich Lehndorf and his ever-loyal colleague, the Minister of Public Works, Albert von Maybach who, under him, had carried out the great task of nationalizing the private railways. Caprivi and Marschall had to content themselves with sending in their cards. Holstein never left his room, next to the bureau of the Secretary of State, during the whole day, where he walked up and down, clenching and unclenching his fingers as his habit was when agitated. When I began my speech in Rome with the words that this year we could celebrate the birthday of His Majesty with particular pleasure, since our Kaiser had stretched out the hand of reconciliation to the great servant of his grandfather, the greatest of Germans, such applause interrupted me that I was forced to pause before continuing. This hour laid the foundation of the cordial relations which bound me in Rome to my German countrymen as they had done before in Bucharest.

At the end of March, 1894, His Majesty the Kaiser telegraphed me that it would give him uncommon pleasure to see King Humbert again. As meeting-place the Kaiser suggested Venice, a spot specially beloved by him, whither he thought of proceeding from Abbazia, where he proposed to spend some time beforehand. It was that happy time in William II's life when he could indulge his passion for travelling to the full. Berlin humour had christened him the "*Reise-Kaiser*" (Travel Emperor), in contrast to his invalid father the "*leise Kaiser*" (quiet Emperor), and his grandfather, the "*weise Kaiser*" (wise Emperor). I was able to send immediate acceptance on the part of the King of Italy. The sovereigns spent three days in Venice, 7th, 8th, and 9th April. The Kaiser reached the city of lagoons on an English yacht. German naval men were annoyed that he was so fond of English boats. He justified himself by saying that, as Rear-Admiral of the British navy, he had the right and even the duty to sail in British vessels. His Majesty was accompanied only by the three aides-de-camps on duty and by Philip Eulenburg who, shortly before, had achieved the summit of his ambitions at the time, the Ambassadorship in Vienna, where Prince Reuss had to make way for him. The meeting in Venice went off well. William II behaved naturally and simply, and whenever he did that he was fascinating. On the evening of his arrival a great crowd gave him an enthusiastic ovation on the Piazza San Marco. Next day, after an hour's conference with King Humbert, the Kaiser suggested that he would like a gondola ride with me to the romantic churchyard San Michele. The following dialogue took place between us. I noted it down since it was the first official conversation between William II and myself.

The Kaiser: "I am overwhelmed by this splendid reception. I have never had such a reception nor seen such enthusiasm. Now Italians are often said to be politically untrustworthy. What is your opinion?"

Myself: "In politics there is no hard and fast, no positive confidence. The Italians are to be trusted just as much—or as little—as the Russians, English, French, or any other nation. Relations between Great Powers are not as those of regimental comrades in a casino. Italy's relations towards us will depend on our politics."

The Kaiser: "The Italians in 1870 left the French in the lurch after they had concluded an agreement with them beforehand. Would they act so towards us?"

Myself: "When the French, misled by Gramont and Ollivier, stumbled blindly into war, the Italians used the fact to break off their alliance with them. If we were equally foolish they would do the same by us. Francesco Guicciardini, the Italian historian, who won himself a great reputation in his native city Florence, in his youth, and later did good service, as a diplomat, for Popes Clement VII, Leo X, and Paul III, writes in his *History of Italy*: '*Pregate Dio di trovarvi sempre dove si vince.*' (Pray God that you may always be found on the victorious side.) The father of modern Italy, Count Camillo Cavour, called this *Istoria d'Italia* his political bible. I may also remind your Majesty of what Prince Bismarck said in his last great speech on 6th February, 1888, as to the nature and value of alliances."

The Kaiser (who did not like to be reminded of Bismarck, with a frown): " Is that intended as an *Avis au lecteur* for me? Well, I don't take it amiss, but rest assured that I shall do nothing stupid. What do you think of King Humbert? I like him very much indeed. And of Queen Margherita? I am enthusiastic about her."

Myself: " King Humbert is a man of distinction to the core. Every inch a great gentleman; fearless, generous, and large-minded. The Queen has no other interests save the glory and the honour of her country and her house. She embodies, so to speak, the Italian state, and that with *esprit* and grace."

The Kaiser: " Do you think the Queen likes Germany? "

Myself: " As long as the friendship is compatible with Italian interests—yes."

The Kaiser went with me to see Countess Annina Morosini whom, a year ago when he made her acquaintance in Rome, he had called the most beautiful woman in Italy. She lived in an historical palace in Venice, the Cà Doro, the most graceful Gothic palace of Venice. The Kaiser's admiration for this Countess was well known. But nothing would be more false than to suppose that William II had paid court to her in the sense understood by the censorious world. The Countess has told me herself that whenever she was alone with the Kaiser the conversation turned chiefly on the majestic appearance of the Empress, and the virtues of his seven children. And I have no doubt that this was true. The Kaiser had presented this fair Venetian with a New Testament, in Italian translation, and urged her, with touching zeal, to read it every night before going to bed. William II was anything but frivolous. To me he was very gracious in those days. It was a pleasure to him to invest me personally with the Star of the Order of the Red Eagle, saying jokingly: " That is only a small beginning. There'll be more to come."

A fortnight after the meeting in Venice I learned from a reliable source that, while the two sovereigns were together, Crispi and Blanc had sent the Minister of Finances, Boselli (called Bosellino because of his smallness), to the French Ambassador, to assure him that the meeting with the German Kaiser was not directed against France. Italy's love for France, her Latin sister, the ally of Magenta and Solferino was, and remained, the same as ever. Almost four hundred years earlier Pope Clement VII, a son of the clever house of Medici, wrote to his legate in Vienna, that a statesman must, like a sailor, always have more than one anchor in readiness. If Austria won the victory the Pope wanted to cast anchor in Vienna " but never too firmly." If France gained the upper hand His Holiness would go with the French. Boselli is still alive. He has experienced many changes in Italian politics and always done it with dignity. He has been head of several departments, always conscientiously and skilfully. On every state occasion he was chosen to deliver the addresses to the King and draw up public manifestos. He acquitted himself with particular tact.

The Italian Court was well kept up. The King disposed of palaces in Rome and Turin, Florence, Naples, Venice, Milan and Palermo, which are among the finest in the world. The household was brilliant and distinguished. The courtiers were polite, not in the least stiff or pompous. They had no political influence. Since Cavour's time it had been strictly understood that they should confine themselves to their courtly functions. The sovereign was allowed no favourites, no irresponsible advisers. A Phili Eulenburg, a Max Fürstenberg, who exercised considerable influence as personal friends of the monarch, without being called upon to justify themselves before the representatives of the people, with neither the knowledge, industry, nor scruples necessary to guide a ministerial department, would have been unthinkable in Italy. Cavour, when a court lady complained to him of the many disadvantages of the parliamentary system, replied: " *La plus mauvaise chambre vaut mieux que l'antichambre.*" The chief aide-de-camp of King Humbert, General Ponzio Vaglia, was a simple and efficient soldier, absolutely devoted to his master, with no political ambition. He told me on one occasion that he had once accompanied King Humbert on a journey through the Romagna, where radical tendencies, socialistic as well as republican, had always been strong. When they arrived in Forli the King asked General Ponzio Vaglia to move into another carriage, since he desired to take the Sindaco of Forli, Signor Fortis, into his own. Fortis was at the time leader of the Radicals in the Romagna; he called himself a Republican. After this conversation with his sovereign he became Under-Secretary of State. Later Alessandro Fortis was made a minister, and in 1906 Premier. If I am not mistaken he once visited me in that capacity, in Berlin. As Ambassador in Rome I often conversed with him. He was a skilful and alert politician, in no wise a rigid upholder of die-hard principles. He was pleasant to talk to. He died in Rome soon after my retirement in 1909. All Italian politicians praised the sensitive and broad-minded spirit with which the house of Savoy adapted itself to circumstances, from the outset, trimming its sails to the wind, making the best of every situation, and so winning adherents to dynasty and monarchy and gaining in strength. It was thus that Victor Emanuel II won over Garibaldi, Depretis, Nicotera, Crispi and Zanardelli to the Monarchy, and even kept up a certain connection with Mazzini. King Humbert held fast to these traditions and tactics.

The position of Prefect of the Palace was equivalent to that of Lord Marshal at the Berlin court. The Chief Master of the Horse, Corsini, was a member of the great family which had produced Pope Clement III, who did not succeed in reuniting the Greek Church with the Roman, but who built the Palazzo Corsini, and laid out its magnificent gardens. When I was first in Rome in the winter 1874-75, this garden was not yet open to the public. On my return as ambassador in 1894, my first drive with my mother-in-law was through the Passegiata Margherita, in the former Corsini Garden which now, for the last ten years, had been incorporated with, and extended to, the Gianicolo, by handsome ornamental grounds, leading past the splendid equestrian statue of General Garibaldi, unveiled in 1895, past the Villa Lante, Tasso's oak, and St. Onofrio, as far as St. Peter's square and the church. In the Villa Lante lived the clever archæologist, Helbig, who was married to a Russian, a Princess Shakhovskoi, distinguished as much for her mind as for her heart, and her ample proportions. She was enormously fat. The witty Russian Embassy Secretary Shevitch said once to her husband: "*Vous avez écrit tant et tant sur l'archéologie. Ecrivez nous un petit livre que vous intitulerez: 'Voyage autour de ma femme.'*" As is well known Xavier de Maistre wrote a delightful *Voyage autour de ma chambre* as well as the moving *Lépreux de la cité d'Aoste*.

CHAPTER XLVIII

Journey to Sicily—Prince Paolo Camporeale—Altavilla—Donna Laura Minghetti—Malvida von Meysenbug—The Abyssinian adventure—Crispi's fall—Marchese Rudini.

IN the autumn of 1894 I spent several weeks with my brother-in-law, Paolo Camporeale, in Palermo, a city I love if only because two great German Emperors are buried in its Cathedral, the Hohenstaufen Henry VI and Frederick II. They are lying on sarcophagi of reddish-brown porphyry—the great genius among the Hohenstaufen Emperors, Frederick II, next his violent but mighty father, Henry VI. He lies in the cathedral of his favourite city, wrapped in Saracen garments, beside him the narrow German sword and the Imperial apple, denoting the world. The inscription on his tomb runs: " *Hic situs est ille magni nominis Imperator et Rex Siciliae Fridericus II. Obiit Fiorentini in Apulia idibus decembris anno MCCL.*" Frederick II died in Fiorentino, in Apulia, on 13th December, 1250, not yet fifty-six years of age.

Prince Paolo Camporeale of the house of Beccadelli di Bologna was a gentleman, though an eccentric one. He was distinguished from most politicians not only in Italy by the fact that, first as Deputy, then as Senator, he liked to oppose the ministers in office, but champion the overthrown. He was thus the opposite of an opportunist. He was to prove his strength of character in 1915, when, as the only member of the Italian parliament, he voted against the War. In his life he had had disappointments. Fortune was unkind to him as to many another good man. But, before his death during the Great War, he had the joy of seeing his good and charming only daughter betrothed to the excellent Prince Filiberto Castelcicala, eldest son of the Duke of Calvello, with whom she now lives in the most harmonious wedlock in the fine villa in Palermo, which she inherited from her father. My brother-in-law took me to the cathedral dedicated to St. Rosalia, patron saint of Palermo, on whose cupola the arms of the Camporeali are suspended. He took me to Zisa. Originally a Saracen summer palace it later served King William I of Sicily as a residence. After him the Zisa was for a time in possession of the Casa Camporeale. From its roof there is, in my opinion, the most romantic view in all Palermo.

I admired the garden of the Villa Serra di Falco. We went to Monreale. Of all Italian churches St. Mark's in Venice and the cathedral of Monreale seem to me those in which the seriousness and the sublimity of the Catholic cult is best expressed. I could not have found a better guide for Palermo than my brother-in-law. He felt himself a real Sicilian and citizen of Palermo where, in his younger days, he had been *Sindaco*. The Beccadellis come from Bologna to whose *Consiglio generale* they belonged as long ago as the beginning of the thirteenth century. Even before that they had possessed the Castello Beccadilli not far from Bologna. Colaccio Beccadelli was lord of Imola, and is said to have ruled wildly indeed. Once from Bologna I paid a visit to his tomb in Imola. On the stone under which he reposes is his effigy, on horseback. His breast-plate and his horse's cloth are covered with eagle's claws, which the family of Beccadelli still carry in their arms. The inscription on his tomb runs:

" *Clauditur sub ista presenti Colacius Archa*
Qui mira tanta fecit quod sibi multa subjecit
Dum tenuit Bononiam dans Beccadelli nomina.
Qui obiit anno Domini MCCCXLI Indicione VIII Die XIII Marcii
Bitinus de Bononia me fecit."

With Vanino Beccadelli a branch of the family moved from Bologna to Sicily in 1304 where, in 1470, they became Marchesi of Sambuca, in 1620 Marchesi of Altavilla, 1664 Princes of Camporeale, 1707 Dukes of Aldragna and Grandees of Spain of the First Class, and acquired considerable estates. For more than five hundred years they supplied the kings of Spain and Naples of the house of Aragon, and later the kings of Naples of the house of Bourbon with a large number of generals, admirals and statesmen. After the Battle of Lepanto, in which several sons of the old house distinguished themselves, the privilege was granted them that every Camporeale should automatically become a knight of the Maltese Order by right of birth. A Beccadelli, who turned to the Church, acted at the Council of Trent as Papal representative, and upheld her claims with skill and penetration. Titian painted the portrait of this intellectual prelate. It hangs in the Palazzo degli Uffizzi in Florence.

From Palermo I visited Altavilla, about twenty kilometres distant which my wife had inherited from her father, Prince Domenico Camporeale. The estate lies on a promontory jutting out to sea. The church of Altavilla, the so-called Chiesazza, was built in 1077 by Robert Guiscard, the son of Tancred of Hauteville. In honour of his father he gave the place he had created the name of Altavilla. In the further course of his career Robert Guiscard became Count of Apulia, conquered Sicily and Calabria, undertook a victorious crusade against the Greek Empire, and liberated Gregory VII from the Castle St. Angelo, where he was besieged by the German Emperor, Henry IV. He died on his second crusade to Constantinople, in 1085 at Cephallonia, the largest of the Ionian isles opposite the opening of the Gulf of Patras. A kind welcome was prepared me by the worthy parish priest of Altavilla. When I handed him a small sum of money for his poor he said, with charming courtesy: " *Io sono certo che Dio vuole molto bene alla nostra Signora. Ma io domandero a la santissima Madonna di Altavilla, chi ha fatto tanti miracoli, di pregare Dio di fare ancora più e sempre più per la nostra cara Signora, vostra moglie.*"

The non-renewal of the Re-Insurance Treaty with Russia had been justified by both Holstein and Marschall on the grounds that, freed from all obligation towards Russia, we should be better able to cultivate our relations with England. The telegram which William II sent on 3rd January, 1896, to President Krüger was not in accordance with such a policy. The Italians who, for obvious reasons, desired good connections between their Ally, the German Empire, and their traditional friends, the English, were such good friends with us in those days, that, although they were saddened by the Krüger telegram, they did not say much about it. But my English colleague Sir Clare Ford, said to me: " England will not forget this box on the ear your Kaiser has given her." When I pointed out the illegality of the invasion of the Transvaal and the far graver insults that England had sustained from Russia and France, Sir Clare said: " But they were spoken by ministers, parliamentarians, and publicists, not by an Emperor." When I spoke of our European love and veneration for England to whom ties, not only of relationship but also habits and inclination bound him, my English colleague replied: " It is just because of these many and intimate ties that the English people will not forgive your Kaiser this affront. The Englishman feels as a gentleman at a club might feel if another member—say, his cousin, with whom he played whist and drunk brandy and soda for many years, suddenly slapped his face." A few weeks later, in the House of Commons, the First Lord of the Admiralty, Lord Goschen, made a sharp attack on the German Emperor, and laid a naval programme before the House by which England was to be placed in the position to build as many ships as all other European nations put together. His suggestions were accepted almost unanimously. Many years later, a year before my retirement, the English Ambassador in Berlin, Sir Edward Goschen, said to his Italian colleague, who congratulated him on recent improved relations between England and Germany which would, it was hoped, lead to a close and real friendship: " There can be no question of any such thing since the Krüger telegram. Germany has forgotten it, or would like to forget it, but England thinks of it."

In another volume of my memoirs I have fully discussed this Krüger telegram, which Prince Bismarck described at once and condemned as " tempestuous." Later, at every opportunity, the Prince of Wales would refer me to the Krüger telegram, which, in one spontaneous outburst, had revealed his nephew's true feelings. He had also heard from various quarters, from English diplomats, neutrals, and even from his sister, the Empress Frederick, that Hohenlohe, Marschall, and Holstein had only passed this crude and vehement telegram because the Imperial author had, originally, far more eccentric intentions. He had wanted to send one of his aides-de-camp to Africa to place him, as chief of general staff, at the service of the Boers. The Princess of Wales said to her confidante, Miss Charlotte Knollys, who repeated it to me in Sandringham: " In his telegram to Krüger my nephew Willy has shown us that he is inwardly our enemy, even if he surpasses himself every time he meets us, in flatteries, compliments, and assurances of his love and affection. His heartless treatment of his dying father and his behaviour to his mother show that he has as little heart as he has political common-sense."

I did not need much leave, but as I could only take two months in the year I have spent July three times in Rome. My wife who, although an Italian born, stood the heat worse that I did, always left at the end of June for the Semmering where, on the stretch of land that lies between the mountains of lower Austria and green Styria, we had found comfortable quarters at the Hotel Panhans. Two women helped me over my time as grass-widower in Rome. These ladies were very dissimilar, but both distinguished in heart and mind—my mother-in-law, Donna Laura Minghetti, and Malvida von Meysenbug. Donna Laura was a member of the Acton family, who apart from the Howards, were the only English aristocratic family that remained consistently loyal to Catholicism. Her great-uncle the baronet John Francis Acton, had come, in his youth, to Naples where he won the favours of Queen Maria Carolina, the sister of poor Queen Marie Antoinette. He advanced to Prime Minister and prince. As a deadly enemy of the French revolution and its ideas, he ruled the two Sicilies in a very reactionary spirit, arbitrarily and cruelly. The good political reputation of the Acton family was restored in our own times by Lord John Acton, the distinguished man of letters and Liberal statesman. He was married to a German, a Countess Arco, and he had had a German mother, a daughter of the historic house of Dalberg. Already, before Lord John Acton, Cardinal Acton had endeavoured by his devout life to obliterate the impious memory of his uncle the Prince. Donna Laura had a French mother, Countess Zoë d'Albon, daughter of a great house, of which the famous Julie de l'Espinasse was a member, albeit an illegitimate one, the friend of Madame du Deffand, of d'Alembert, and many other Encyclopædists. Her *Lettres*, published in 1809, are among the most sparkling and graceful in the French literature, so rich in this branch of letters. They have been translated into German several times. Both grandmothers of my mother-in-law were Germans, from the Rhine, one a Countess Hompesch, the other a Countess Berghe von Trips. She had, therefore, English, French, and German blood. Her only sister had married a German, Count Kurt zur Lippe-Biesterfeld. At the same time Donna Laura's outward appearance was that of an Italian of the purest type, *Italianissima*. Whoever studies the picture Lenbach painted of her, a wonderful reproduction of her classic beauty, and probably the best female portrait of this great Munich artist, will certainly think he sees the perfect type of Italian before him. A new proof of the contestability of the racial theory, and certainly an argument against its exaggeration. Donna Laura had married Prince Domenico Camporeale when she was very young and after his death the distinguished Italian statesman, Marco Minghetti. She died at the age of eighty-six in her Villa Mezzaratta, near Bologna, on 12th September, 1915, during the Great War, which brought her into painful conflict between her glowing Italian patriotism and deep sympathy for Germany, without being able to see her tenderly loved daughter once again. She was buried in the Certosa of Bologna one of the oldest and most romantic churchyards in the world, " *al fianco del mio Marco*," as she had decreed in her will, next to Marco Minghetti.

Seldom was so much heart united to so much mind as in Donna Laura. From her mother she had inherited the French gift of repartee. When once a well known blue stocking described herself as having only intellectual interests and despising the woman who cared for house, kitchen, and cellar, Donna Laura retorted, quick as lightning: " *C'est très bien, mais de grâce ne m'invitez jamais à diner.*" When I was once dining with her at Herbert Bismarck's, who loved good wine, he pressed her to drink a third and a fourth

glass of Château Lafitte. " *Buvez encore de ce vin, Donna Laura,* "
he encouraged her. " *Ce vin serait capable de ressusciter un mort.* "
Whereupon Donna Laura: " *Et d'enterrer un vivant!* " Everything about Donna Laura was natural, sincere, and distinguished.
She had been friends with all the statesmen of the Risorgimento,
the Italian movement for unity. Bismarck and Andrássy, Gladstone
and her cousin the Earl of Granville, the Bishop Strossmeyer and
Monseigneur Duchesne, the clerical historian and academician,
appreciated her wit and her charm. She displayed, with pleasure,
a photograph which Richard Wagner had sent her together with
his gratitude, when she took up cudgels on his behalf after the first
failure of *Tannhäuser* in Paris. She was the friend of the Empress
Eugénie and Princess Mathilde Bonaparte. She had been invited
to the dinner in Paris at which Napoleon III announced his betrothal
to the handsome Countess Eugénie Montijo, and on the eve of the
Great War she received a visit in Bologna from the dethroned and
aged Empress Eugénie. King Ludwig I of Bavaria had invested
the sixteen-year-old girl with the Order of St. Anne, which, in
1714, Prince Bishop Johann Philipp of Würzburg had inaugurated
for devout maidens of the ages of twelve to seventeen of aristocratic
Catholic families, with eight quarterings on either side. William II
conducted the nearly eighty-year-old Donna Laura personally
through his Berlin and Potsdam palaces. She was a Liberal to the
core and hated the memory of all that she had experienced in her
youth at Naples, fanaticism and ignorance. In those days her first
husband, Prince Camporeale, risked imprisonment because he
possessed a copy of Dante whom the Bourbons detested as an
Italian patriot.

In 1870, when the Franco-German War broke out, Donna
Laura was staying with Princess Mathilde in Paris. Napoleon III
came to see his cousin before his departure to French headquarters,
to take leave from her. She received the Emperor in the presence
of her friend Donna Laura. The Emperor gave the impression of
a sick, even a very sick, quite broken man. His cousin, Mathilde,
said to him à propos of two well known French songs, the official
national anthem of the Second Empire, composed by Queen
Hortense, and an old street song, dating from the wars of the
Spanish Succession: " *Mon cousin, vous ne me rappellez guère
Dunois jeune et beau qui avant de partir pour la Syrie allait prier Marie
de bénir ses exploits. Vous me rappellez plutôt ce pauvre Marlborough
qui s'en allait en guerre.* " The Emperor did not seem to be annoyed
at these somewhat brutal words of his cousin. He gazed out sadly
into space. Donna Laura felt that the Napoleon III had lost the

old belief in his star. In describing this little scene to me she added: " *L'Empereur sentait qu'il allait au devant d'une catastrophe.*"

Malvida von Meysenbug had trodden quite different paths to Donna Laura. The daughter of a Hessian Minister who, before 1848, was considered too reactionary, and that is saying a great deal, she had joined the revolutionary movement in that famous year and was forced, after its overthrow, to flee to London, where she spent many years in exile with such friends as Mazzini, Gottfried, and Johanna Kinkel, Louis Blanc, Ledru-Rollin, and other revolutionary stars. Lothar Bucher taught her the rudiments of national economy. When the Russian revolutionary, Alexander Herzen, lost his wife in a shipping accident, she devoted herself to the education of his daughters of whom the one, Olga, married the distinguished French scholar, Gabriel Monod. Malvida openly proclaimed the most advanced political and religious views. She declared the assassin, Felice Orsini, whom she had known well in exile, to be a noble youth, comparable to Harmodios and Aristogeiton, who were hymned in Athens for their murder of the tyrants. She gave me the little book, since become rare, in which Orsini describes his uncommonly daring flight from Austrian captivity, in the dungeons of Mantua. The book, which was published in 1858, in Mastricht, bears the title, " *Les Prisons Autrichiennes en Italie. Quinze mois de captivité. Évasion du Fort St. Georges à Mantoue.*" Felice Orsini begins the description of his escape with the words: " *Douze ans se sont écoulés depuis que pour la première fois, j'ai encouru la vengeance des oppresseurs de ma patrie, en leur montrant par mes discours et par mes actes que le désir de soustraire l'Italie à leur joug était le grand mobile de mon existence. Le peu de succès de mes efforts dans l'accomplissment de cette tâche ne fait que m'exciter davantage à la poursuivre avec tout ce qui me reste d'énergie et de ressources.*" That was no mere *façon de parler*. Not long afterwards, on 14th January, 1858, Felice Orsini, in Paris, threw his bomb at Napoleon III, which killed a number of passers-by, but from which however the Emperor miraculously escaped. Condemned to death Orsini wrote a letter to the Emperor before his execution, urging him to liberate Italy from the Austrian yoke. If Napoleon, in memory of the oath he had once taken as a Carbonari, would liberate Italy, he, Orsini, would gladly die, and die with blessings for the French Emperor on his lips. Orsini appears to have had this letter in his pocket at the time of his execution for it shows traces of blood. This strange epistle is preserved in the museum at Turin, where I saw it. Perhaps these splotches of blood are renewed from time to time like the ink spot at the Wartburg.

If her memories of Orsini were touching ones, Malvida von Meysenbug spoke with scorn of Georg Herwegh who had behaved "shabbily" to Alexander Herzen and his wife. I am inclined to believe this verdict the correct one. Not long after the Franco-German War, a French lady, an ardent patriot, showed me an inscription Herwegh had written in her album, in 1873, at Baden-Baden. It was in verse, and I have forgotten its exact text but the purport was as follows: "Heat of the summer and the dog-days! And yet Bismarck is not yet dead of sunstroke. Diarrhoea and dysentery everywhere and yet old William is still alive." Treitschke was right when he said that there is a depth of baseness of which only certain Germans are capable. Herwegh was married to a Berlin Jewess, the daughter of the banker Siegmund. The son of this marriage became a naturalized Frenchman and, during the Great War, attacked and libelled his German home in newspaper articles and pamphlets, with all the zeal and the bitterness of the renegade. Heinrich Heine sinned greviously politically. But the verses in which, in his *Last Poems* under the title of "Simplicissimus," he lampoons Georg Herwegh, his wife, and his cowardice at the Dossenbach fight in Baden during the Republican revolt must be reckoned to his credit:

> "*Die Schüsse knallen-der Held erblasst,*
> *Er stottert manche unsinnige Phrase,*
> *Er phantasierte gelb-die Gattin*
> *Hält sich das Tuch vor der langen Nase.*" [1]

Whereas my mother-in-law dined regularly with me on the terrace of the Palazzo Caffarelli, Malvida von Meysenbug, nearly eighty years old at the time, was my guest during the summer of 1896. We were together nearly the whole day. We held different views on many, many matters. But that did not impair my deep veneration for her nor our mutual love. In our heavenly Father's home are many mansions. I shall never forget the summer I spent with my dear Malvida.

Crispi had interested himself as Prime Minister particularly for the colony of Eritrea, which lies on the Red Sea, between Abyssinia, the French Somali coast, and the Egyptian Sudan. As leader of the troops there General Baratieri had been appointed on his suggestion. Baratieri was an irredentist of Trentino, who was more distinguished

---

[1] Shots are falling—the hero pales
He stammers nonsensical phrases.
He lost his head, but his wife
Holds the handkerchief to her own long nose.

by noisy chauvinism than by military qualities. At first Fortune
appeared to favour him. In the summer of 1894 he had captured
Cassala, the chief point of vantage of the enemy Dervishes and, in
May, 1895, he proclaimed the sovereignty of Italy over Tigré.
But in the autumn of 1895 Menelik II, Emperor of Abyssinia,
took up arms to shake off the mandatory supervision of Italy which
had grown irksome to him. After preliminary failures he succeeded
in surprising an exposed Italian battalion and wiping it out by sheer
force of numbers. Crispi was determined to make this good immediately. Public opinion was still on his side and Parliament voted,
by a large majority, the war credits he demanded. In February,
1896, however the position of the Italians changed for the worse.
They were in the midst of an inimical populace. They faced the
numerically far superior army of the Abyssinians, on their right
flank the Dervishes menaced them. The Italian commanders
planned a concentrated attack against Harrar by marching through
Zeila, to strike at the heart of the Abyssinian forces. But England,
with the cool egotism which everywhere and at all times distin-
guishes her policy, hesitated to give the Italians, whose presence
in Africa did not altogether please her, permission for the necessary
march through English territory. Rome began to be uneasy.
Crispi recognized the inefficiency of his protégé Baratieri, and laid
a decree before the King, nominating the well-qualified General
Baldissera supreme commander of the Italian troops. At the same
time further reinforcements were sent to Africa. In contrast to the
irredentist and chauvinist Baratieri, Baldissera, who had been born
an Austrian subject in Venice, served in the Austrian army, and
distinguished himself by bravery in the Battle of Custozza on the
Austrian side, gave proof that, in a General, military qualifications are
worth more than political views. Unfortunately, Baratieri, through
an indiscretion, heard the news of his approaching recall. He wished
to win a victory beforehand and, on 1st March, 1896, near Adoua,
attacked, with barely fifteen thousand men, the far superior army
of the Negus Menelik. Personally, he acted bravely, was in the
front firing line, and retreated among the last. But his army was
completely decimated. Two generals, Dabormida and Arimondi,
died a hero's death. Italian casualties amounted to four thousand
men. Among the dead was the young Prince Agostino Chigi, who
belonged to an ultra-clerical family, of which Pope Alexander VII
had been a member, and which, for two hundred years, has held the
hereditary office of Marshal of the Holy Church and Protector of
the Conclave. He had volunteered for the expedition against
Menelik to show that the so-called Blacks, the papally-minded,

were not inferior in Italian patriotism to the Whites, the supporters
of the Monarchy.

On 2nd March, 1896, the Foreign Secretary, Baron Blanc,
received, early in the morning, a telegram beginning with the
words, " *Immane disastro!* " (Horrible catastrophe!) Crispi's
African policy had been criticized with increasing severity ever
since bad news began to come in from Africa. Now the storm
broke, and the Prime Minister suffered the fate of most unsuccessful
statesmen. Parliament and press threw all the blame upon him, or
at least turned away from him. Crispi sent in his resignation. I
was in the diplomatic box at the session in which Crispi informed
the Chamber that he had resigned and that the King had granted
his request. Erect and proud the seventy-seven year old Prime
Minister faced the Parliament. No hint of emotion in his clear-cut
manly face. When in the court box, a court lady, not in favour with
the Prime Minister, received the news with a cry of " Bravo! " He
gave this female such a glance as proved that this old fighter felt
himself as superior to ordinary praise and blame as he did to all
the moods of the *Mobilium turba Quiritium*.

A few days later a new cabinet was formed under the Marchese
Rudini. Rudini was another Sicilian, but whereas Crispi had been
a son of the people the Marchese Rudini belonged to one of the
oldest families in the country. He too was a man of energy. But
Crispi had given open expression to his superabundant vitality by
speeches and gestures in every direction and in every manner.
Rudini, on the other hand, showed his more by firmness, patience,
and tenacity. He terminated the Abyssinian adventure without
any loss of Italian prestige, by the peace concluded with Abyssinia,
on 26th October, 1896, two days after the marriage of the present
King of Italy.

When it was announced that the Crown Prince of Italy was
betrothed to Princess Helena of Montenegro, whom he had met
and grown to love during the coronation festivities in Moscow, the
foreign diplomats in Rome shook their heads. Where and how
would this marriage be solemnized? The King, in view of Italian
public opinion, must insist upon the wedding being celebrated in
Rome, the capital of *Italia unita*. But this the Pope would never
allow. The Italians on this occasion showed their gift for finding a
practical solution to two conflicting principles. The Prime Minister,
Rudini, and the Cardinal-Secretary of State, Rampolla, both
Sicilians, arrived at a compromise in the course of a quiet walk which
they took together early one morning, in the secluded avenue of the
Villa Doria. St. Peter's, said the Secretary of the Holy See with a

smile, could scarcely be placed at the royal pair's disposal, but they could use the church of Santa Maria degli Angeli, whose vast interior lent itself admirably to spectacular ceremonies. An agreement was easily reached as to the ecclesiastic who could perform the service. In far off Norman times the Archbishop of Bari had enjoyed special privileges. King Umberto took advantage of these, as successor to the rights of the Norman princes. And so the young and beautiful Princess Helena was able to undertake the journey to Rome with an easy mind. She, too, like many other lovers, had had to surmount great difficulties. The Montenegrin people were somewhat fanatically loyal to the Orthodox Greek Church. To become Crown Princess of Italy, Princess Helena had to be converted to Catholicism. She left the paternal capital, Cetinje, still an orthodox believer. Thanks to the persuasive talents of an Italian cleric, sent to meet her, her conversion took place at sea, on the way to Bari, where the future Queen of Italy received Holy Communion from the hands of the archbishop in the famous old church of the holy miracle-worker, Nicola, according to Roman Catholic rite. The archbishop conducted the service in the church, Santa Maria degli Angeli. His sermon was reminiscent of the finest speeches of Cicero, father and model of all Latin rhetoricians. In sonorous yet harmonious periods the beloved Italian fatherland, the venerated Holy See, the skilful Pope Leo XIII, and the courtly King Umberto were celebrated.

As we left the church, Rudini asked me how I liked the sermon. "*Pas mal, n'est-ce pas?*" he inquired with a satisfied smile, and I could answer truthfully: "*Un chef d'oeuvre de tact et de finesse.*" I remained on the best of terms with Rudini, just as I had been with his predecessor, Crispi. His clever and charming wife had asked me to come often in the mornings and take him out for a walk, so that he might get enough exercise. Whenever I called I found his anteroom full of people. Once when he had escaped through a second door, Rudini said to me: "It is not the work which tires me most, but the streams of visitors who take up so much time and nearly kill me with their chatter." I never really appreciated this until I became a minister myself.

CHAPTER XLIX

William II's visit to Southern Italy—Ascent of Vesuvius—Meeting with Cardinal Sanfelice, Archbishop of Naples—The Papal diplomacy—Cardinals and prelates—The Russo-German Re-Insurance Treaty and Prince Bismarck—The Cretan question—Marschall's successor—Conferences with Phili Eulenburg in Meran and Venice—Correspondence with Berlin—Uncertainty and insecurity before the final decision.

DURING the visit that William II paid to Southern Italy soon after the resignation of Crispi, I came, for the first time, into closer contact with His Majesty. The Kaiser got to know me and I him. I can understand now, on looking back, what made my impressions so contradictory, for William II was the most unbalanced person I have ever met. It was difficult to form a definite and final opinion of him. When he visited, in Naples, the zoological collection of the distinguished scientist and charming person, Anton Dohrn, the Kaiser amazed us by his quick and easy perceptions and the lively interest in biology he displayed. In this, as in many other matters, he was the true son of his mother, who was interested in everything and gave dissertations upon everything, *de omnibus rebus et quibusdam aliis*. With this difference only that, whereas she displayed her knowledge of, for instance, biology or botany, or of any other branch of organic science in a modest tone, and with downcast eyes, the Kaiser was loud and triumphant. To the Empress Frederick her very cultured father, the Prince Consort, had said when she was still a child: " The days are past when kings and princes could pretend that by divine gifts they understood everything better than the rest of humanity. When the Emperor Sigismund had his attention called to a mistake in grammar, which he had made at the Council of Constance, he answered haughtily: ' *Cæsar supra grammaticam!* ' In our times a prince must have learnt so much from good teachers and by his own industry, that he can hold his own in all branches of knowledge." William II was convinced that his own undoubtedly great gifts, combined with the insight and help supplied from Above, would enable him to know everything and do everything.

Soon after the new Emperor had filled us all with admiration,

by a long exposé of the science of life, especially zoology, he shocked
the worthy Dohrn, and displeased me highly, by the brutality with
which he declared that he would decorate any sentinel, on principle,
who shot down the passer-by who had failed to halt when challenged.
Such *boutades*, of which later I heard a great many, did not express
a cruel nature. William II had nothing of a Nero or a Dionysius,
the Tyrant of Syracuse, to whom Damon crept with his dagger
hidden in his robes. He was, in fact, in every day matters rather
what one might call "a good sort." Such verbal excesses were no
sign of that brutality which, in Peter the Great, Tsar Nicholas I, or
the great Napoleon, expressed the eruptions of abnormal and overpowering energy. In William II they were the sign of a neuras-
thenic nature. He was as lacking in quiet courage as he was in
genuine strength. This made him strive to give an heroic impression
by words and gestures. Of course, he often chose the wrong
methods.

After he had inspected the Zoological Garden in Naples, the
Kaiser ascended Vesuvius, accompanied by myself and some of his
suite. Count Beugnot, in his delightful memoirs, relates how, in
the spring of 1813, at the time when he was Prime Minister of the
Grand Duchy of Berg, created by Napoleon, he went on a boating
trip near Biebrich with the Emperor and the Prefect of Mainz, a
former *Conventionnel*, named Jean-Bon Saint-André. During the
trip Napoleon, sunk in thought, stared at the water. The Prefect
and Beugnot were alone with the Emperor in the boat. The ex-
revolutionary, suddenly inspired by the spirit of 1793, the spirit of
the Terror, whispered to Beugnot: "*Quelle étrange position! Le
sort du monde dépend d'un coup de pied de plus ou de moins.*" When
the party landed again Beugnot reproached the Prefect with his
remark: "*Savez vous que vous m'avez furieusement effrayé! Vous
êtes un insensé!*" But the old Terrorist replied: "*Et vous un
imbécile. Tenez-vous pour dit que nous pleurerons des larmes de sang
que cette promenade de l'Empereur n'ait pas été la dernière.*" As we
stood with William II looking down into the crater of Vesuvius
from which hot steam and gases came pouring, I heard one of the
suite whisper to his neighbour: "If this pleasant and charming
man, but incoherent and highly dangerous ruler, suddenly grew
faint and fell into the crater would that really be a misfortune?"

William II was *novarum rerum cupidus* like any Gaul of Cæsar's
time. Especially in his youth did he long for ever-new impressions.
When told that the Archbishop of Naples, Cardinal Sanfelice, was
greatly beloved, he wished to meet him. I proposed a visit to the
Archbishop, but this he declared would be going too far. He ex-

FRANCESCO CRISPI, ITALIAN PREMIER

pressed the wish that their meeting should take place in the Camaldoli monastery, from which, he had read in Baedeker, there was a magnificent view. Not many views indeed are to be compared with that from the monastery gardens over the Bay of Naples and Pozzuoli, the Gulf of Gaëta, populous Naples, the smoking summit of Vesuvius, Posilipo, and Cape Miseno, Procida and Ischia, Baiae and Cumae, Capri, Sorrento, and Castellamare. The Kaiserin would gladly have stayed on board the " Hohenzollern," partly because she was tired, and partly because, though, very properly, she treated Roman prelates with great courtesy, these gentlemen rather frightened her. The Kaiser, however, permitted no denials from his Spouse. Her Majesty must come too! At the entrance to the monastery the Cardinal awaited us. We could not keep our eyes off the view and, in unison, praised the omnipotence of God, who has blessed this earth so abundantly. Then the Kaiser expressed the desire for a serious conversation with the Cardinal. Since His Majesty spoke no Italian and the Cardinal only his mother tongue, I had to act as interpreter. The Kaiser asked a number of questions which the Cardinal answered cleverly and tactfully. Suddenly, the Kaiser turned to me and cried: " Ask him if he thinks that Protestants go to Heaven." I replied that perhaps it would be better not to put such a question to the Archbishop of Naples. The Kaiser insisted. I still demurred. The Cardinal, who did not understand our conversation, but had noticed that I did not wish to pass on a question asked by His Majesty, smilingly announced that he was willing to satisfy the imperial curiosity on all points. So there remained nothing for me but to ask His Eminence whether, in his opinion, Protestants too would be allowed to partake in the glories of Paradise. The Cardinal thought a moment. Then he said: " *La misericordia divina è infinita.*" (Divine mercy knows no limits.) This satisfied both the Kaiser and Cardinal. The Cardinal gave me his portrait as a souvenir of the meeting at Camaldoli. It stands before me as I dictate. Its sight recalls to mind a good and wise and sensitive prince of the Church, a man of the world who, with the same tact that he used to parry the Kaiser's difficult question always understood how to keep the full confidence of the Holy See, while, at the same time, maintaining the best relations with the Italian Government and enjoying general popularity in Naples.

If England, for the last few centuries, has been the most wisely and successfully governed country, the diplomacy of the Holy See is nowhere surpassed for calm tact, and patience, penetration, knowledge of human nature, and the art of handling human beings. This is true of the Monsignori, of the bishops and prelates, legates and cardinals. I have already spoken of my relations with the charming and intellectual Nuncio Czacki in Paris. I should like to mention Cardinal Rampolla too, with whom I was already on a friendly footing, during my Chancellorship, and of whom I saw a great deal during the first years of my residence at the Villa Malta. He united a fiery spirit with a clear head and a steady hand. Unshakable on all questions of principle involving the Papal Chair and the Roman Church, he was tolerant in manner and conversation. His admiration for Bismarck was as great as that of his Sicilian compatriot, Crispi. In his study there hung only two pictures: a fine copy of the Murillo Madonna, whose original is in the Palazzo Corsini, and the picture depicting Prince Bismarck in audience with his royal master William I. Vincenzio Vanutelli, the dean for many years of the Sacro Collegio, is a magnificent type of dignified Cardinal. At nearly ninety he is as strong as a well preserved man of sixty, always with a kind smile on his lips, of lucid mind, and many interests. As a patriotic Italian he is proud of having persuaded Pius XI, after his election, to bless the crowd assembled on the Piazza San Pietro from the loggia of the church, in contrast to his three predecessors. "*L'ho spinto io*" ("I urged him!") he said, as he described this historic scene to me, not without pride. Vincenzo Vanutelli saw five Popes, and twice, as Archbishop of Santa Maria Maggiore, closed the Sacred Gate in an *Anno Santo*, in 1900 and 1925. A kind friend to my wife and myself is Cardinal Ragonesi, a prince of the Church who combines to a rare degree outstanding political gifts and experience with that quality which the French describe so charmingly as "*La politesse du cœur.*" I only know one German Cardinal to compare with the Italian prelates for spiritual sensitiveness and charm of manner—Cardinal Kopp.

Although my official interests and observations all centered on the home and foreign policy of Italy, I also kept an eye on events at home, where the central figure was still the mighty Bismarck. On 1st April, 1895, Prince Bismarck would have concluded his eightieth year. On 23rd March the President of the Reichstag, Herr von Levetzow, suggested that the House should congratulate the Prince on his birthday. Count Hompesch, in the name of the Clerical Centre, Eugen Richter for the two People's Parties, the Social-Democrat, Singer, the Pole, Prince Radziwill, and the Guelph, von Hodenberg, protested against this homage to Prince Bismarck. The Reichstag, by 163 Clerical, Democrat, and Socialist votes, against 146 of the Conservatives and National-Liberals, rejected the motion. Everybody knew that Herr von Marschall, Secretary of State, had used his influence on the Centre in favour of withholding these birthday honours. When William II heard of the result of the division, he forgot all he himself had done to Prince Bismarck and sent him a telegram expressing his " deep indignation " at the Reichstag's attitude. Bismarck answered frigidly, though correctly. When the French Ambassador in Berlin, M. Herbette, heard of this Reichstag decision of 23rd March, 1895, he said, in the presence of several other foreign diplomats: " *Les Allemands diront et feront ce qu'ils voudront, ils ne seront jamais un grand peuple.*"

In October, 1896, the *Hamburger Nachrichten* published details of the so-called Re-Insurance Treaty, the agreement of neutrality formerly concluded by Prince Bismarck. A Liberal organ had declared that relations between Germany and Russia had been strained during the last years of Bismarck's Chancellorship, even after the death of Prince Gortchakov. Bismarck's personality, therefore, had not been the only obstacle to good feeling between Germany and Russia. The great ex-Chancellor angrily contradicted this in his Hamburg-mouthpiece. The statement that Alexander III and Baron Giers had continued Gortchakov's policy after his death was " absolutely inaccurate." Even at Skierniewice, that is to say almost immediately after Gortchakov's retirement, good relations between Russia and Germany had been renewed and they had continued until Bismarck's resignation. Up to 1890 both Empires had been firmly agreed that, if one were attacked, the other would keep benevolent neutrality. If therefore, for example, Germany had been attacked by France, she could have reckoned on a friendly though neutral Russia, and had Russia suffered an unprovoked attack our attitude would have been the same. The article concluded: " This agreement has not been renewed since the retirement of Prince Bismarck and, if we are correctly informed as to events in Berlin, it was not Russia, but Germany, who refused to continue this mutual assurance. Russia would be quite willing to do so. If, at the same time, we consider from its political aspect the wave of Polonization characterized by the names of Stablewski and Koscielski, we see that the Russian Government must have asked itself: What is the object of this Prussian Polonization which seems in such flagrant opposition to the traditions of the Emperor William I ? "

This outburst of the *Hamburger Nachrichten*, which showed the lion's claw in every line, caused a very great stir in Germany and in Europe. Democratic, Clerical, and Social-Democratic newspapers, heaped outrageous insults on the old man in Sachsenwald. A Liberal organ declared that " Caprivi, who with perfect calm may appeal to the judgment of posterity rather than to the passions of to-day, stands head and shoulders above the 'ill-tempered policy of the old man from the Sachsenwald.'" The chief Clerical paper, *Germania*, declared that, apart from certain die-hard satellites of Prince Bismarck, the whole of Germany condemned his policy. William II was in a state of high indignation; on the occasion of his visit to the shooting-butts in Meppen and the Krupp Works at Essen, he boldly declared, before witnesses, that he intended to imprison Bismarck for high treason in Spandau. The press was prevented from spreading this, but it found its way to Friedrichsruh. Prince Bismarck thereupon declared, through the columns of the *Leipziger Neueste Nachrichten*, that he regretted, after the upward curve of the last thirty years to see Germany already in decline. He himself would not live to see the end, but was sorry for his son's sake. To the threat that legal action might be taken against him, the Prince had remarked, according to the *Leipziger Neueste Nachrichten*, that he had nothing against a dramatic end.

In the Reichstag an interpellation on the disclosures of the *Hamburger Nachrichten* was answered by Marschall with dialectic skill, but feebly, and without inspiration. The deputy, Eugen Richter, suggested that, by his Re-Insurance Treaty, Bismarck had been guilty of a breach of confidence against Austria and brought discredit on German politics. He had also betrayed state secrets, said Richter, and only by reason of his great age and certain services rendered in former years, did he merit mercy instead of justice. The Socialist, Liebknecht, declared that Prince Bismarck had " betrayed " Austria through his Re-Insurance Treaty. This wise Theban added: " This two-faced morality of diplomacy must cease." Old Prince Hohenlohe disuaded the Emperor from imprisoning Prince Bismarck, in Spandau, as he intended, by finesse, and a certain dash of humour. It was not impossible, he told the Kaiser, that rage and agitation under arrest might cause the eighty-year-old Bismarck to have a stroke. Then would come the question of the funeral. The Kaiser would naturally arrange this to be ceremonial and wish to attend it. Would it be worthy of so great a monarch to have the funeral *cortège*, of the first and most famous Imperial Chancellor, proceed from a second-rate fortress such as Spandau? William II gradually calmed down.

As European conditions had shaped themselves since the Berlin Congress, and conclusion, a year later, of the Austro-German agreement, the Balkan Peninsular was now the storm-centre most likely to dispel the peace of Europe. And for forty years past, ever since the middle of the 'seventies, real danger had threatened the world from this point. Its most dangerous area had once been Herzegovina, was to be Bulgaria, and later still, Bosnia and Serbia. For the moment Crete was the danger-zone where, in February, 1896, there had been revolts.

The task that fell to me in Rome during the Cretan crisis was to keep Italy from backsliding, and so, on the one hand, prevent the conflagration from spreading while, on the other, for the benefit of outsiders, I emphasized the inner consolidation of the Triple Alliance. William II was so delighted at the way in which I solved this problem that he sent me the ribbon of the Order of the Crown, my first Prussian ribbon, and with it wired: " The decoration which is sent you on my initiative you have earned in the highest degree. During the past few months your masterly manœuvres kept Italy and the Near East sensible. I owe you my heartiest thanks."

In January, 1897, I received a letter from Philip Eulenburg, who wrote that he must see me without fail. He was too ill to come to Rome or give me a *rendezvous* in Venice. I must, therefore, sacrifice myself and come to Meran where he was visiting his mother. I found him in Meran, less ailing than he had made himself out to be. He always had been a *malade imaginaire*. I hasten to add that, as my dear friend the distinguished doctor, Professor Renvers, once said, the " *malade imaginaire* " suffers subjectively as much as though he were really ill. Stretched on the sofa, two pillows under his head, placed there by his affectionate mother, assisted by an aunt who had come on a visit, his legs covered with thick rugs, he explained to me that he was very upset by an imperial letter, received a few days ago. The Kaiser, in jerky, agitated sentences, interspersed with countless exclamation marks, had written him that he could not longer abide Secretary of State Marschall. Marschall had " betrayed " him! He was in league with the Blacks and the Reds. Marschall must go! as soon as possible! if he, the Kaiser, was not to collapse, physically and morally! ! The Chancellor, Hohenlohe, was equally convinced that Marschall could no longer remain. " The proper successor to Marschall is Bernhard Bülow, who, as my uncle, Chlodwig Hohenlohe, has told me repeatedly, has the best head in our diplomatic service." Prince Chlodwig Hohenlohe became Prussian Prime Minister and Imperial Chancellor after the simultaneous resignation of the Chancellor Caprivi and the Prussian Premier, Botho Eulenburg, on 26th October, 1894.

For three days in Meran Philip Eulenburg, with all his persuasive talents and resource, kept saying that it was my duty, to

Kaiser and Fatherland, not to refuse this successorship to Marschall. But I told him that I preferred to stay in Rome, as far as I myself was concerned. I did not even speak of the wishes of my wife, who would find it hard to part from her mother. Of course such personal reasons counted for nothing against the interests of the Empire. But I really believed that my services were of more use in Rome than they would be in Berlin. The political difficulties of the post assigned to me did not deter me, although I was a novice in Parliamentary matters and, apart from a *plaidoyer* as a law student, in Metz, twenty-three years before, and occasional toasts on the Kaiser's birthday, had never spoken in public. "But shall I always see eye-to-eye with the Emperor? For instance: H.M. is at daggers drawn with Prince Bismarck, but nothing will prevent my expressing my veneration and admiration for Prince Bismarck, even in public. I should, if I were appointed minister, pay a call as soon as possible on Prince Bismarck. I should also continue to associate with Herbert with the same cordial friendship as ever." Phili, who since the crisis of 1890, had quite broken with Herbert and was also in the bad books of his great father, made a grimace. He took pains to prove to me that if I were made Minister, it would be my duty, to king and emperor, to see his friends and enemies as my own, and King William II had, at the moment, no more dangerous and ruthless enemy than Prince Bismarck, the "wicked old man," and his son, the "horrible" Herbert. The detestable and highly treasonable articles of the *Hamburger Nachrichten*, on the perfidious Re-Insurance Treaty, had naturally increased the just wrath of His Majesty. I stuck to my point and Eulenburg said, with a sigh: "The Kaiser is so determined to have you that he will swallow even your Bismarck cult, which I dislike just as much as he does."

These arguments, for and against, lasted from morning till evening, only broken by the reading aloud of some Northern ballads, which Phili had lately been composing. It is always my custom, when disturbed, to take up a good book to calm my mind and, as Homer says, "disperse the soul's disquiet." When, years before, in Florence, I had, with youthful impressionability, despaired of my diplomatic future on hearing my chief, Herr von Keudell, say that the Crown Princess disliked both my father and myself, I took up Balzac. Later, during the long and wearisome discussions on tariff-duties, I would bury myself, of an evening, in Lamartine's, somewhat too lyrical but very absorbing, *Histoire des Girondins*. The tragic greatness of the revolutionary figures, of Vergniaud, Danton, Saint-Just, helped me to forget the wooden pedantry of the Philistines, with whom I had to chaffer. Now, in Meran, I read *Jürg*

Jenatsch, by Conrad Ferdinand Meyer. This novel, by a great Swiss writer, with its masterly psychology, is one of the best novels in modern German, none too rich so far in good works, and it steeled me against the difficulties of the moment, increasing my resolution to dare the plunge into a new world, with all its varying fortunes, and helped me, too, to understand the motives impelling Phili. He had been genuinely glad when Holstein who, at the time, was his intimate friend, had had me transferred to Rome—partly because he really was my friend and partly because I should make his pace for Vienna. He was not so pleased when later I became Imperial Chancellor. Hohenlohe-Langenburg would have seemed a more acceptable appointment to him, because then Strassburg would have been vacant for Phili. Eulenburg had done all he possibly could to have me appointed Secretary of State. It was essential to him here to have a friend, or at least, not an enemy. Personally, he did not care much for Marschall, yet, like his ally Holstein, he would not have minded his keeping his post for the present. But this way was closed by the sudden and violent aversion of the Kaiser and, in matters relating to persons, Phili did not willingly oppose His Majesty. He disliked all those who might have been considered, besides myself. Alvensleben, Rotenhan, Richthofen, Monts, Kiderlen, Derenthall, were either unknown by Phili or antipathetic to him. He feared a return of Herbert Bismarck as the devil fears holy water. He did not feel equal to filling the post himself, since he possessed neither the industry nor the knowledge necessary for a Secretaryship of State, nor had he the nerves with which to face the Reichstag.

When I parted from Phili in Meran everything was still undecided. He still hoped to make me change my mind. I remained stubbornly recalcitrant. During the following weeks there was a rather unpleasant correspondence between Eulenburg, Holstein, and myself. I was by no means Holstein's ideal. He would rather have kept Marschall who, as a novice in foreign politics, without knowledge of foreign affairs or diplomatic experience, was easy to manage. But Holstein knew that William II wanted to be rid of Marschall and that His Majesty would brook no opposition. Holstein refused Kiderlen, although the latter, since their mutual betrayal of Bismarck, was accounted his most dependable pawn. He refused Monts still more energetically, because Monts was just as clumsy and tactless as Kiderlen and, in contrast to him, not even politically gifted. Kiderlen himself had no desire to be Secretary of State. He knew that the Kaiser no longer liked him, and he disliked His Majesty just as heartily. With Swabian humour he told

me that he was " completely fed up " with the duty of accompanying
His Majesty on journeys, in his capacity of representative of the
Foreign Office. He would much prefer a post abroad. Monts,
then Ambassador at Munich, was different. He sent me a letter
couched in the most humble, almost servile tone, in which he
insisted that, " of course," I was much the best successor to Marschall, who had succumbed " at last " to his own incapacity. But
if I preferred to stay in Rome, as he well understood that I might,
and would so far honour him with my confidence as to advise him,
he would not shrink, fortified by such trust and advice, from the
post of Secretary of State.

In Venice, in April, 1897, I had another meeting with Phili
Eulenburg. He was accompanied by his mother. Since Phili
hated walking we took a gondola *à trois* through the canals of the
enchanted and melancholy city. The mother joined her prayers to
his, telling me it was my duty as a good Prussian not to refuse the
summons of my king. With increasing emphasis I repeated my
reasons for not feeling certain that I should agree with His Majesty
in the long run. I pointed out again, still more clearly, our different
attitudes towards Bismarck. Apart from this I differed from our
Kaiser on many points, both of home and foreign policy. Abroad
we needed steadiness above everything. Having unfortunately cut
the Bismarckian wires, which had bound us to Russia, we must not
let England excite us against her. And just as little must we be
Russia's cat's-paw against England. For the present we had to
maintain our independent position and keep on good terms with
both countries. But the Kaiser favoured Russia one day and
England the next, always with exaggeration, mistaken ideas, and
" full steam ahead." In domestic politics I certainly stood for a
strong monarchy, as befitted the Prussian tradition and the welfare
of the German Empire. But I considered continual interference
on the part of the Kaiser to be an evil, if only for the reason that
H.M. really knew very little of politics. He occasionally had an
inspiration, but he had not the sobriety, quiet, and steadiness, indispensable for directing the politics of a great Empire. He did not
know foreign countries. He had no knowledge of human nature.
He was inclined to take his dreams for realities and see his wishes
as things already accomplished. I used an English expression and
said that, in my opinion, William II lived in a " fool's paradise." [1]
The too numerous Imperial speeches, generally good from the
oratorical standpoint, and often sparkling with wit, were not always
logical, sometimes tactless, sometimes actually eccentric and did us

---

[1] English in text.

harm, both at home and abroad.   Finally, in contrast to our monarch, inclined of late towards free trade, I regarded protection as indispensable for German agriculture.   Phili did not contradict me outright; he even declared that in many points he shared my views. But I felt that I had not entirely convinced him, and that he regarded my call to Berlin not only as desirable, but even as absolutely necessary.   He was convinced, as he said many times during our conversations, that I should get on very well with the Kaiser, but, of course, I must learn " how to treat him."

Phili said, again and again:

You owe it to the country to obey the Imperial summons. But if you can't make up your mind to take the Kaiser as he's got to be taken, you would certainly sacrifice yourself *pro nihilo*. Arguments make no impression on the Kaiser.   He is only sensitive to the personal standpoint or personal influences.   If you want to do anything of use to your country and help it, you must win the Kaiser's affection.   You are an angler of souls, a great *charmeur*.   You have charmed many people in your life. Now try and fascinate the Kaiser.   *Pro patria esto!* You can always contradict him when necessary, only do it when you are alone together and do not annoy him in little ways.   If the Kaiser does not get the impression that you love him, and admire him, you can do nothing with him.   You were an Hussar, you are a good rider.   H.M. is a horse who only goes well when the rider has a light hand—who will stand the pressure of the thighs but must never be tugged at the bit, and not feel the spurs too often; and, above all, must often be given a bit of sugar.   Never forget the sugar! Without sugar this mount will not clear a single obstacle, it bolts and is quite unrideable.

Eulenburg who, like his exalted master, saw everything from the personal angle, never ceased to explain that, if I wished to succeed in Berlin, the two factors to be reckoned with were the Kaiser and Holstein.   When I told him that Holstein, who had always mystified my father, inspired no confidence in me either, and warned him against the " great privy councillor," Eulenburg said: " I believe that at bottom Holstein has a soft, even a tender heart. And, in my time, I have met many odd and abnormal people and got on well with them.   I manage to get on with Holstein and feel quite happy in his company."

Back in Rome, I heard from Berlin that von Alvensleben was the most likely person to succeed von Marschall.   Rotenhan, Holleben, Richthofen, and Derenthall were also mentioned.   I will not conceal the fact that I received many letters, from sincere and disinterested patriots, all appealing to my sense of duty, and urging me to accept the Secretaryship of State. From circles in touch with Prince Bismarck I got warm and urgent pleas to this effect. Two German admirals visited me at Rome in May, on separate occasions, both of whom spoke of the question then to the forefront of our home politics; the naval question. These admirals differed widely from one another. The first to call at the Palazzo was the State Secretary of the Imperial Naval Office, Friedrich Hollmann, then fifty-five years old. The Kaiser called him " Hollmannikin " and, although he had distinguished himself on the " Grille " at the Battle of Hiddensee, in 1870, he had something undignified about him, something of the manners of those people who, in a regiment, a students' corporation, or a club, are universally popular, and yet are never taken quite seriously. The other, seven years younger, a man of about my own age, who soon replaced him, was a different kind of person altogether—Alfred Tirpitz. Everything about him was serious and thorough, resolute and weighty. A man of iron will! Hollmann made a friendly and pleasant impression; Tirpitz one of strong ambition, suppressed fire, the capacity to hate, and a love of fighting for fighting's sake.

In March, 1897, the Budget Commission of the Reichstag had curtailed all of the naval estimates. On 18th March, 1897, exactly forty-nine years after the Berlin revolutionary outburst of 1848, the second reading of the Navy Bill took place at the plenary session of the Reichstag. In vain did the Chancellor, Hohenlohe, in a short, sensible, speech read out, as his habit was, from scattered notes, and Marschall, the Secretary of State, in long and detailed explanations, both plead for the two cruisers demanded by the Imperial Naval office. In vain did Count Posadowsky, at the time Secretary of the Treasury, afterwards Secretary of State for the Interior, oppose the financial misgivings of Eugen Richter. These two cruisers were refused by two hundred and four of the Centre, Liberals, Social-Democrats, Guelphs and Alsatians, against a hundred and forty-three Conservative and National Liberal votes. Admiral Hollmann, before his departure from Rome, had left me in no doubt that he considered a strengthening of our navy not only desirable but, in view of the increasing development of our overseas trade, actually necessary. It was quite impossible to vote this increase in the Reichstag, in the face of the solid opposition of Centre, Liberals, and Socialists, particularly since even the Conservatives and, most of all, the extreme Agrarians in the Conservative party, were reserved in their attitude towards all naval programmes, if they did not actually oppose them. " Don't let yourself be inveigled to Berlin," said the " Hollmannikin " to me as we walked up and down on the terrace of the Palazzo Caffarelli, with the view of the Forum Romanum before us, " You're very comfortable here in Rome. In Berlin you would head for a fiasco. Nobody will be able to get the Kaiser's naval wishes through the Reichstag, not even you, Mr. Ambassador, whom our All-gracious Master is said to be considering as successor to the used-up Marschall. Don't walk into the trap. I am giving you sound advice! " Tirpitz spoke more optimistically. In cultured Germany, in the circles of industry and commerce, and those of professors and intellectuals, there was some understanding of our desire for a position in the naval world. Tirpitz seemed anxious to know if I thought I should be able to speak in the Reichstag. That would be eminently desirable, since the Chancellor, Hohenlohe, was no orator, and he himself on account of his weak voice and a certain nervousness, could not describe himself as such. I replied that I had never yet attempted it. But in my opinion, the chief difficulty of the naval question lay outside the Reichstag. I believed it to consist in the fear and envy which a stronger navy, a larger and more efficient German fleet, would be certain to arouse in England, who was already becoming daily more jealous of our rapid, perhaps all too rapid, progress in trade, industry, and shipping.

In the meantime Marschall's position as Secretary of State was becoming more and more untenable. The Conservative party, on whose benches he had once sat as a member, pursued him with special fury as a " renegade." The angry Titan in Friedrichsruh attacked him continuously in his newspapers, which ridiculed, more than they actively opposed, him. Marschall had not come quite cleanly out of the unsavoury Tausch case. His expression " Flight into publicity," to which he was forced by ceaseless attacks, was certainly incorporated in Buchmann's collection of " German Winged-Words " but, nevertheless, an aftermath of ridicule attached to it.

Not for seven years, since Bismarck's dismissal, had there been such confusion in Berlin. At last it gave place to certainty.

INDEX

Abatsa, Alexander Aggeievitch, 578.

Abd-ul-Aziz, 403.

Adhéma, M., 464, etc.

Adolphus Frederick IV, Grand Duke of Mecklenburg-Strelitz, 56.

Adolphus Frederick, Hereditary Grand Duke of Mecklenburg-Strelitz, 69.

Aegidi, Professor, 222, 512.

Aehrenthal, Baron Aloys Lexa von, 573.

Afghanistan, English-Russian conflict, 581, etc.

Albedyll, General von, 283.

Albert, Prince of Saxe-Coburg-Gotha (Prince-Consort), 462, 599, 673.

Albert, King of Saxony, 168.

Albrecht, Archduke, 94, 155, 158, 262.

Albrecht, Prince, 224.

Albrecht, President of the Court of Appeal, 281.

Alençon, Duchess Sophia d', 524.

Alexander I, Tsar, 388, etc., 484, 511, 569, 571.

Alexander II, Tsar, 161, etc., 217, 308; Peace is secured, 358, 359, 361, 374, etc.; Assassinated, 381; His character, 383, etc.; Marriage, 385; Princess Dolgoruki and, 385, etc., 389, 391; Visits Berlin, 394, 402; Meeting at Reichstadt, 404; On Constantinople, 419, etc.; Speech, 422; Headquarters at Plojesti, 428; Returns to St. Petersburg, 433; Bessarabia, 434; Tired of war, 435; Ungracious reception of Peter Shuvalov, 457; Meets William I at Alexandrovo, 508; Attitude towards Prussia, 511; Bismarck on, 557; Grand Duke Constantine Nikholaievitch and the assassination of, 578.

Alexander III, Tsar, 305, 375, etc., 425, 484, 557, 568, 569; At Skierniewice, 572; D. A. Tolstoi, 575; No war with England, 582; Heavy hand, 585; Two Emperors Meeting at Kremsier,

588; Against Alexander Battenberg, 589, 601; Telegram to Katkov's widow, 612; Discovery of an attempt on the life of, 612; Attends memorial service for William I, 616; On Frederick III, 617; Alliance with France, 638; Visits French exhibition, 639; Kronstadt, 639; Dislikes William II, 640; Bismarck on his attitude towards Germany, 677.

Alexander, King of Greece, 424.

Alexander (Battenberg), Prince of Bulgaria, 375; Proclamation, 588; Tsar punishes, 589; War with Serbia, 589; *Coup de main* against, 600, etc.; Abdication, 602; Princess Victoria and, 602, 605.

Alexandra, Queen of England, 17, 159, 426, 463, 531, 582, 665.

Alexei Alexandrovitch, Grand Duke, 590, 639.

Alexei Nikholaievitch, Tsarevitch, 195.

Alexis, Landgrave of Hesse-Philipsthal-Barchfeld, 52.

Alfonso XII, King of Spain, 533, etc.

Alfonso XIII, King of Spain, 604.

Alfred, Duke of Edinburgh, 426, 647.

Alice, Maud Mary, Grand Duchess o. Hesse, 596.

Alopæus, Russian Minister, 305, 306.

Alsace-Lorraine, 285.

Alvensleben, Count Johann, 371, 373, 375, 377, etc., 383, 643, 681, 683.

Amadeus, Duke of Aosta, 463.

Andrássy, Count Gyula, 155, 169, 357; Reform programme for Balkans, 377, 394; Bismarck invites, 394; Herbert Bismarck opposes, 400; Character, 401, etc.; Berlin meeting, 402; Speech, 403; *Entrevue* at Reichstadt, 404; Telegram to Beust, 404; 1849 condemned to death, 402, 407; Bismarck on, 423; Berlin Congress, 441; Reads

688

Andrássy, Count Guyla—*continued.*
out memorandum, 446; R le at Con-
gress, 453; On Werner's picture, 456;
At final banquet, 456; With Bismarck
at Gastein, 509, 571; Laura Minghetti
and, 667.
Andrássy, Countess Katinka, 407.
André, Herr, 78.
Annunzio, Gabriele d' (Rapagnetta), 415.
Antonelli, Giacomo, Cardinal, 102, 279,
etc., 284.
Arenberg, Prince Anton, 292.
Arenberg, Prince Francis zu, 178, 274,
etc., 280, etc., 284, 285, 291, 336,
492, 495, 597, 626.
Arenberg, Princess Franziska, 407.
Arenberg, Princess Maria Ghiselaine,
292, etc., 356.
Arenberg, Prince Philip zu, 285, etc.
Ariosto, 538.
Armansperg, Count Ludwig, 546.
Arndt, Ernst Moritz, 3, 44, 70, 271.
Arnim, Count Harry, Countess (Princess)
Bismarck against, 184, 309; Holstein's
intrigues, 395; For monarchistic
France, 486; Henckel-Donnersmarck
and, 498; Holstein's enmity, 627.
Arnim-Boitzenburg, Count Adolf, 294.
Astorg, Comte d', 167.
Athens (1877), 414, 418, etc.
Auber, Professor, 370.
Auerbach, Berthold, 123.
August, Prince of Württemberg, 90.
Augusta, German Empress, 2, 65, 96;
Countess (Princess) Bismarck against;
184, 252; Confidence in Loë, 261;
Against Bucher, favours Paul Hatzfeldt,
303; Against Bismarck, 308; Her
reader Gérard, 314, etc.; Schleinitz
her favourite, 316; On Heinrich von
Bülow, 322; Her receptions, 327,
353, etc.; At Ems, 504, etc.; On
universal franchise and *Kulturkampf,*
505; Her good influence, 554; Receives Bülow and his wife, 596.
Augusta, Grand Duchess of Mecklenburg-Strelitz, 62.
Augusta Victoria, German Empress, 18,
140, 229, 596, 659, 675.
Aumale, Duke Henry (Orléans), 245,
326, 524, etc.

Austria (Austria-Hungary), 51; Dualism,
158; Neutrality 1870, 167, etc.; Bismarck's policy after 1870 towards,
308; During the Orient crisis, 423;
Alliance of 1879, 509, etc.; Bismarck
on (1884), 557; At Kremsier, 588;
German-Russian Re-Insurance Treaty,
638.
Avarna di Galtieri, Duke of, 528.
Azeglio, Massimo, Marchese d', 538.

Babeuf (Baboeuf), 476.
Bach, Baron Alexander, 169.
Baldissera, Antonio, 670.
Balkans, Insurrection in Herzegovina,
377; Andrássy's reform programme,
377; Berlin Memorandum, 394, 403;
Meeting at Reichstadt, 404; Turkish
massacre in Bulgaria, 397 f., 405; Cir-
cular of Secretary of State Bülow
(6.10.1876), 418, etc.; Russia's ulti-
matum to the Porte, 419; Diet debate
on Orient crisis, 420; Russian-Turkish
War, 428, etc.; Greece neutral, 431;
Peace of San Stefano, 433; Greek in
Thessalia, 434; Berlin Congress on
Bulgarian question, 445; Austria-
Hungaria occupies Bosnia, 447; Greek
question, 447; Serbian, Montenegrin,
Rumanian question, 448; Berlin
Treaty, 456; East Rumelia, 588; Ser-
bian-Bulgarian War, 589; Revolution
in Bulgaria, 600, etc., 604, etc.; Crete
crisis, 679.
Ballin, Albert, 498.
Balzac, Honoré de, 123, 350, 410, 495,
502, 680.
Baratieri, Oreste, 669, etc.
Barberina (Barbara Campanini), 306.
Barnekow, Lieutenant-General von, 249,
264.
Barral, Count, 528, 653, 654.
Barrère, Camille, 471, 549.
Barth, Deputy, 165.
Barthélemy-Saint-Hilaire, Jules, 489.
Bassermann, Ernst, 116, 174, 327.
Battenberg, Prince Henry, 604.
Battenberg, Prince Louis (Mountbatten),
426, 604.
Baudissin, Count Hermann, 44.

Baudissin, Imperial Count Karl von, 41, 42, 50.

Baudissin, Count Karl, 44.

Baudissin, Imperial Countess Sophie Charlotte, 47.

Baudissin, Count Wolf, 42, etc., 46, 76, 107, 118.

Baudissin, Count Wolf, Professor, 45.

Bavaria, 163, etc.

Bazaine, François Achille, 599.

Beaumarchais, Caron de, 520.

Bebel, August, 476, 583.

Beck, Friedrich von, 13, 399.

Beckmann, Albert, 137.

Beethoven, Ludwig van, 531.

Beissel von Gymnich, Count, 198, 202, 231.

Bekker, Ernst Immanuel, 277, etc., 281.

Belgium, Napoleon III and neutrality of, Bismarck's revelations, 177, etc.

Bell, Deputy, 455.

Bellegarde, Count, 398.

Beloselski, Prince, 590.

Below, Otto von, 176.

Benedek, Ludwig Ritter von, 100.

Benedetti, Count Vincent, 92; At Ems, 133, 168; Secret draft of treaty, Bismarck's revelations, 179, etc., 300.

Benkendorf, Countess Luise, 318, etc.

Benkendorf, Baron Mitia, 325, etc.

Bennigsen, Rudolf von, 116.

Bentheim, General von, 264.

Béranger, Pierre Jean, 40, 138.

Bérard, Victor, 134.

Berchem, Count Max, 489.

Berchtold, Count Leopold, 397.

Beresford, Sir Charles, 553.

Beretsovsky, Makes an attempt on the life of Tsar Alexander II, 163.

Berger, Baron Alfred von, 492.

Berlepsch, Oberpräsident von, 629.

Berlin (1863), 64, 311; (1869), 128, etc.; (1870), 183, etc.; (1873), 298-329; (1875), 353, etc., 369, etc.; (1876), 393, etc.; (1878), 435, etc.; (1879), 507, etc.; (1885), 583, etc., 592, etc.; (1888), 617, etc.; (1889), 626, etc.; (1890), 641, etc.

Berlin Congress, 441, etc.

Bernhardt, Sarah, 454.

Bernstorff, Count Albrecht, 97, 304.

Bernstorff, Count Christian Günther, 49, 304, etc.

Bernuth, Herr von, 86.

Bert, Paul, 506, etc., 530.

Bethmann, Hugo, 24.

Bethmann-Hollweg, Theobald von, 91, 134, 135, 154, 160, 162, 176, 183, 481, 584, 624, 653.

Beust, Count Friedrich Ferdinand, 10, 155, 158, 168, 169; Circular dispatch (20.7.1870), 169; Dispatch to Richard Metternich, 169; Andrássy substitutes, 404; Andrássy's telegram on Reichstadt, 404; Ambassador to Paris, 527, etc.

Beyens, Baron, 530.

Beyer, Gustav Friedrich von, 99.

Biegeleben, Ludwig Maximilian von, 168, 402.

Bille, H. von, 14.

Bismarck, Count Herbert, 23; Introduces Bülow to Holstein, 183; Favourite song of, 184; Attitude towards Elisabeth Carolath, 261; Incited by Holstein against Bucher, 304; Tactless, 348; Character, 360, 370; Congratulates Bülow, 370; Prince Bismarck on Andrássy to, 423; Kind to Bülow, 444; At the final banquet of the Berlin Congress, 457; Holstein impresses him strongly, 459; Bad influence on his father, 461; Bülow's friend, 492; Philip Eulenburg, 493; Meets Jérôme Napoleon, 523; On Holstein, 548; Paris visit, 548, etc.; Invites Bülow to London, 549; On Count Münster, 551; Letter to Bülow, 558; etc.; At Skierniewice, 573; Careless remarks on England and Russia, 580, 581; At torch-light procession in honour of his father, 584; Conversation with Bülow, 585, etc.; Marries Countess Hoyos, 587; Conference with Bülow, 592; More difficult than his father, 607; On Holstein, 607; Russian Re-Insurance Treaty, 613; Asks Bülow whether he would like to become Minister to Washington, 617; Enthusiastic about Prince William, 619; His father on, 623; Dinner parties, 627; Defends Holstein, 627; Bülow to Eulenburg

Bismarck, Count Herbert—*continued*.
on, 631, etc.; After resigning, 641, etc.; Writes to Bülow, 643, 645; Hates Holstein, 645; Marriage, 648; Loves good wine, 666; On bad terms with Eulenburg, 680.

Bismarck, Johanna von, Piety of, 6; Keudell in the drawing-room of, 99; Consoled by Moravian hymn, 161; Homely, 183; Our great steersman, 296; Good hostess, 307; Keudell and, 333, etc.; Otto's patent boots, 390; Against Radowitz, for Holstein, 459; Cries at engagement of her daughter, 461; Delicacies, 555; On Berlin society, 555; Holstein no longer visits, 627.

Bismarck, Countess Marie von, 188, 183, 184; Engaged to Count Wendt Eulenburg, his death, 370, etc.; Marries Rantzau, 371, 461; Friend of Adda Eulenburg, 493; Holstein's quarrel with Rantzau, 627.

Bismarck, Otto von, Minister to Frankfort, 5, etc.; On the seven-year-old Bülow, 5; Gortchakov on, 6; Walks with Bülow's father, 8; On annexations, 8; Goes to St. Petersburg, 11; His Frankfort secretary on, 14; In the Frankfort wood, 19; On a knowledge of languages, 19; Names Herbert after Tsar Nicholas, 23; Germany's unification, 43; Against Lasker, 47; Schleswig-Holstein question, 50; On the Oertzens, 57; On Mecklenburg, 60; Junker, 63; Bülow's father visits (1863), 64; Underrated, 81; Speeches, 81; Does not give up his game, 82; On youngest heir to the throne (William II), 82; Edict to Prussian representatives (14.3.66), 85; Attempt on the life of, 86; Spirit of 1813, 88; Writes General von Manteuffel, 89; Wanted war 1866, 91; *Vive le roi!*, 92; Negotiations before outbreak of war, 95; Countess Oriola and, 96; Count Robert Goltz and, 97; Dispatch to Ysenburg, 99; Hohenfriedberg March, 99; Threatens to annex Mecklenburg-Strelitz, 104; After Königgrätz, 105; Corps-student, 116; Lassalle and, 124; Policy, 130; Ems Dispatch, 133, etc.; Wires Bülow's father, 152; Assists army, 154; Usedom's memorandum, 158; Russia and, 155 *ff*., 159, etc.; Anti-Polish, 160; Forced William I (1866) to desist from annexing South Germany, 163; His genius in framing constitution, 166; Sends Holstein to Florence, 170; William I toasts, 172, 173; On Hereditary Prince Leopold, 173; Imponderables, 176; Reveals secret negotiations with Napoleon III, 179, etc.; On cowardice, 205; Suspicious, 261; Praises Loë, 262; At Greifswald, 277; Prof. Bekker on, 278; Antonelli on in *Kulturkampf*, 279; Princess Arenberg on, 293; Creation of Alsace-Lorraine, 295, etc.; Appoints Bülow attaché to Foreign office, 298; On diplomacy, 299; Hatzfeldt's recipe, 302; Wilhelmstrasse, 305, etc.; Character, 307, etc.; Russia after 1870 and, 308; Adversaries, 308, etc.; Schleinitz *bête noire* of, 315, etc., 318; Bleichröder on, 318; Confirmation, 320; Perglas, 326; Threatens Italy, 339; Crown Prince on, 351; Angry, 354; "Cold douche" on Paris, 358; Bülow visits, 360, etc.; At funeral of Wendt Eulenburg, 370; Dislikes Werder, 375; Balkan conflicts, 377; Patent shoes, 390; His ideal, 393; No friend of alliances, 393, etc.; On Holstein, 394; Austrian autumn crocus, 399, etc.; Coriolanus, 400, etc.; Chevalier-Perspective, 401; Berlin memorandum, 403; On Orient crisis, 422, etc.; On Andrássy, 423; "Pomeranian musketeer," 435; Ignores Gortchakov, 435; Dissolves Diet, 440; Overestimates force, 441; At Berlin Congress, 441, etc.; Prestige policy, 442, etc.; On "young Bülow," 444; Sneers at Gortchakov's speech, 445; Rude to Turkish delegate, 447; In favour of a Russian Bessarabia, 448; Skilful whip, 450; Werner's picture, 456; Final Banquet, 456; Against Radowitz, for Holstein, 458; Herbert and, 461; His physician at Biarritz, 464, etc.; Appetite, 474; Gambetta on, 479; On France, 479; Welcomes Grévy's presidency, 483; On German-Semitic marriages, 489; Against Henckel-Donnersmarck, 498; Outbursts of temper, 508; Audience with Francis Joseph, 509; Organizes press campaign, 512; Bülow hands over his father's resignation, 513; Visits the latter, 514; Condoles with Bülow, 516; Friendship with Nikholai Orlov, 527; Alfonso XII insulted by French, 534; On Dr. Nachtigal, 542; Censures Count Münster, 551; Münster on, 551; At Varzin, 554, etc.; On "prophylactic" wars, 556, etc.; On domestic enemies, 558; Arranges Three Emperors meeting, 569; Bülow's report, 570; At Skierniewice, 572; On Stock Exchange and Afghan conflict, 582, etc.; seventieth birthday, 584, etc.; Giers at Friedrichsruh, 588; Sanctions Bülow's marriage, 592; Receives the newly married couple, 596; On Bülow's wife, 598; For Russia, 601; Against Battenberg, 601, etc.; Against the latter's followers, 606; Prince William and, 608, etc.; Waldersee hates, 610; Waldersee on Prince William and, 610; Re-Insurance Treaty with Russia, 613, etc.; Speech (6.2.1888), 615; Obituary on William I, 616; Sends Bülow to Bucharest, 617, Audience with Queen Victoria, 618; Bülow dines with, 618; On Frederick III, 618, etc.; On Herbert and Holstein, 623; Crisis, 626, etc.; Dismissal, 635, etc.; Effect of resignation, 640, etc.; Herbert on dismissal, 641, etc.; Bismarck on William II, 642; Not received at Vienna, 648; Admired by Crispi, 653; Received by William II, 657; Condemns Krüger telegram, 665; Admired by Rampolla, 676; eightieth birthday, 676; Disclosures, 677, etc.; William II threatens, 678; Against Marschall, 685; ill. 206.

Bismarck, Count Wilhelm (Bill), 184, 360, etc., 401; Against Holstein, 459; At Varzin, 555, etc.; Writes Bülow, 569, 592; Father too Russophile,

607; On his father and William II, 642.

Bismarck-Bohlen, Count Friedrich Alexander, 492.

Bismarck-Bohlen, Count Karl, 278, 334.

Blanc, Baron Alberto, 528, 653, etc., 659, 671.

Blanc, François, 117.

Blanc, Louis, 668.

Blaserna, Pietro, 536, etc., 539.

Bleichröder, Gerson, On Bismarck, 318; French war compensation, 499.

Blome, Count Gustav, 402.

Blücher, Prince, 58, 60, 63, 261.

Blum, Hans, 558, etc.

Blum, Robert, 8, 546, 558.

Blumenthal, Leonhard von, 151, 293.

Bock, Colonel von, 192, 205, 237, 239.

Bockum-Dolffs, Florens Heinrich von, 81.

Börne, Ludwig, 536.

Böselager, Herr von, 265.

Bötticher, Karl Heinrich von, 629.

Bogdanovitch, General, 612.

Bollati, Ambassador, 528.

Bonin, Adolf von, 100.

Bonn (1870), 137, 140, etc., 269, etc., 284, etc.

Bonnechose, de, Archbishop of Rouen, 201.

Bonnemain, Madame de, 503.

Borcke, Richard von, 230.

Borsig, Albert, 319.

Boselli, Paolo, 659, etc.

Bouillé, Vicomte de, 324.

Boulanger, Georges, 503, 597, etc., 611.

Bourbaki, Charles Denis, 191, 198, 199, 202.

Bourgoing, Baron Otto, 168.

Brahms, Johannes, 108.

Brailas-Armeni, M., 529.

Brandenburg, Count Friedrich Wilhelm, 152.

Brandenburg, Count Wilhelm, 152.

Brandis, Herr von, 283.

Bratianu, Joan, 448, 602, 619, 620, 621, 622, 624.

Braun, Karl, 421.

Braun, Baron von, 13.

Bray, Count Camillus Hugo, 164.

Breysig, Kurt, 413.

Briand, Aristide, 294, 484, 653.

Bright, John, 180.
Brillat-Savarin, 520.
Brincken, Baron von, 298, 314.
Brisson, Henri, 519.
Brockdorff, Countess Therese, 322.
Broglie, Albert Victor, 338, 479.
Brohan, Madelaine, 114.
Brühl, Countess Hedwig, 348.
Bucharest (1888-1893), 617-625, 628-629, 646-649.
Bucher, Lothar, 80, 300, etc.; Follows Bismarck to Friedrichsruh, 304, 334, 365, 369; Against Holstein, 460; Malvida von Meysenbug and, 668.
Büchsel, Preacher, 444, 514, 516.
Buckle, Henry Thomas, 411, 412.
Budde, Hermann, 272.
Bulgaria, Principality through treaty of San Stefano, 433; Berlin Congress, 446; Insurrection in East Roumelia, 588; Serbian-Bulgarian War, 589; Coup de main against Prince Alexander, 600, etc.; His abdication, 602; Ferdinand of Coburg elected, 612.
Bülow, Adolf von, 42, 47, etc.
Bülow, Adolf von, aide-de-camp, 22, 24, 34, 51, 59, 62, 68, 72, 105, 114, 116, 123, 128, 131, 136, 152, 189, 213, 216, 253, etc., 333, 507, 516, 517, 554, 570, 627.
Bülow, Alfred von, 22, 69, 443, 641.
Bülow, Adolf von, General, 468, 489.
Bülow, Bernhard von; ill. Frontispiece, 336.
Bülow, Bernhard von, 48.
Bülow, Bernhard Ernst, Danish Minister, 5; Frankfort days, 5, etc.; Death of Tsar Nicholas, 23; Trip to Heligoland, 39; Childhood at Plön, 45; Leaving Danish services, 47, 51, etc.; Goes over to Mecklenburg, 53; Trip to Berlin and Baden-Baden, 64, etc.; On religion, 83; On German Confederation, 103; Mecklenburg Minister to Berlin, 103; Letter to his son, 111, 112; Death of his daughter Bertha, 128; Against Bernhardt's volunteering, 136; Domestic cares, 188; Inscription in Bible on return of his son, 270; Assigns him to the diplomatic service, 283; Becomes Foreign Secretary, 285, 298; Prince Bismarck on, 285; Advises his son, 299, etc.; Empress Augusta on, 328; Sends his son abroad, 330; Conference with Minghetti at Milan, 340, etc.; On war danger, 358, etc.; On the situation of 1876, 392, etc.; Circular to Prussian representatives, 418, etc.; Declaration in Imperial Diet, 420, etc.; Influence on his son's development, 438; On Bismarck's prestige policy, 442, etc.; Werner's Congress picture, 456; At final banquet, 456; On Holstein, 460; Sufferings, 507; Audience with William I, 509, etc.; Resignation, 512, etc.; Bismarck visits, 514; Death, 515; Condolatory messages of William I and Bismarck, 515, etc.; Memorial service, 516; ill. 22.
Bülow, Bernhard Joachim von, 47, 59.
Bülow, Bernhard Vollrath von, 12.
Bülow, Bertha von, 128, 221, 235.
Bülow, Charlotte von, 47.
Bülow, Christian von, 130, 136, 558.
Bülow, Christoph Karl von, 282.
Bülow, Friedrich von, 47.
Bülow, Friedrich von, Youngest brother of Bernhardt, 131, 514.
Bülow, Friedrich Wilhelm von, 149.
Bülow, Gabriele von, 48, 319, etc.
Bülow, Hans von, 63.
Bülow, Heinrich von, 48, 319, etc.
Bülow, Karl von, 47.
Bülow, Karl Ulrich von, 128.
Bülow, Luise von, Piety, 6; Familiar with English, 20; Trip to Italy, 35; Against Countess Danner, 53; Death of her daughter, 128; New Testament, 186; Inquiries after church attendance, 247; Faith in prayer, 440; Bismarck talks with, 514; Death of her husband, 515; At memorial service, 516; On Bülow's wife, 597; At Seelisberg, 608; Death, 650; ill. 52.
Bülow, Marie von, 185, 320, 333, 349, etc., 406, etc., 436, etc., 531, etc., 536, etc., 538, etc., 560, etc., 586, etc., 591, etc., 594, etc., 605, 617, etc., 626, 649, 663, 665, 666.
Bülow, Paula von, 12.
Bülow, Susanne von, 41, 45, etc.

Bülow, Vollrath von, 12.
Bülow, Waldemar von, 22, 128.
Bülow-Wendhausen, Marie von, 103.
Bürger, Gottfried August, 73, 380.
Bulwer, Edward (Lytton), 123.
Bunsen, Josias von, 344.
Buol-Schauenstein, Count Karl Ferdinand, 404.
Busch, Klemens, 460, 622, etc.
Bylandt-Rheidt, Count, 398.
Byron, Lord, 272, 345, etc., 427, etc., 526.

Cambon, Jules, 471, 485, 549.
Cambon, Paul, 471, 541, 549.
Cambridge, Duke of, 62.
Campenon, Edouard, 520.
Camporeale, Prince Domenico, 539, 663, 666.
Camporeale, Prince Paolo, 662, etc.
Canova, Antonio, 319.
Cantù, Cesare, 538.
Caprivi, Leo von, 222, 327, 484, 614, 636, 638, 643, 644, 648, 649, 656, 657, 677; Resignation, 679.
Carayon-Latour, M. de, 482.
Carlyle, Thomas, 81, 525.
Carneri, Philosoph, 13.
Carnot, Sadi, 639.
Caro, Elme Marie, 525.
Carol (Karl) von Hohenzollern, Prince, then King of Rumania, 132, 173; Plevna, 428, 448; Character, 619, etc.; On William II and Bismarck, 628, etc., 635, 646, 647; Bülow takes leave, 649.
Carolath, Prince Karl, 241.
Carp, Peter, 621, 624, 644.
Carrel, Armand, 500.
Castelar, Emilio, 473.
Castelnau, Vicomte de, 477.
Catherine Mikhailovna, Grand Duchess, 61, 216, 387.
Cavaignac, Louis Eugène, 477.
Cavour, Count Camillo, 297, 341, 414, 472, 479, 538, 607, 653, etc., 659, 660.
Challemel-Lacour, Paul Armand, 331.
Chambord, Count de, 533.
Chamisso, Adelbert von, 16, 251.

Charles, Emperor of Austria, King of Hungary, 94.
Charles, Prince of Prussia, 516.
Charlotte, Tsaritsa, wife of Nicholas I, 386, 512, 571.
Charlotte, Princess, 323.
Charmes, Francis, 549.
Charmes, Xavier, 175, 466.
Chartres, Duke Robert de, 524.
Chateaubriand, François René de, 430.
Cherbuliez, Victor, 583.
Chigi, Prince Agostino, 670.
Christian VIII, King of Denmark, 52.
Christian IX, King of Denmark, 17, 18, 305, 423.
Cialdini, Enrico, Duke of Gaeta, 528, 654.
Cissey, de, General, 338.
Clam-Gallas, Count Eduard, 168.
Classen-Kappelmann, Herr, 87.
Clausewitz, Karl von, 263.
Clemenceau, Georges, 93, 138, 294, 475, 477, 485, etc., 488; Overthrows Gambetta, 521, 553, 653.
Cobden, Richard, 180.
Cohn, Dr., 130, 137, 138, 464.
Cohn-Blind, Ferdinand, 86.
Combes, Emile, 294.
Consalvi, Marchese Ercole, 319.
Constantine Nikholaievitch, Grand Duke, 423, 578.
Constantine Pavlovitch Grand Duke, 246, 571.
Constantine, Crown Prince of Greece, 424.
Coppée, François, 44.
Corcelle, Baron de, 324, 355.
Corsini, Chief Master of the Horse, 661.
Corti, Count, 447, 454, 456.
Courier, Paul-Louis, 520.
Cousin, Victor, 412.
Coutouly, M., 621, 624.
Creizenach, Theodor, 26.
Crispi, Francesco, 473, 538, 651, 652, 653, 659, 661; War with Abyssinia, 669, etc.; Resigns, 671, 672, 673; ill. 674.
Curtius, Ernst, 34, 429.
Curtopassi, Signor, 624.
Cusa, Prince Alexander, 621.
Custine, Marquis Adolphe, 567.
Czacki, Monsignore, 529, etc., 676.

Dadian, Nikholai, Prince of Mingrelia, 605.

Dagmar, Maria Fedorovna, Wife of Tsar Alexander III, 17, 196, 376, 582, 597.

Dalwigk, Reinhard Baron von, 10, 167, 182.

Danckelmann, Countess, 315.

Daniel, Hermann Adalbert, 74, etc., 80, 84, 105, 106, 108, 109, 110, 111, 113, 438.

Danish-German War (1864), 66, etc.

Danner, Countess, 53.

Dante, 538, 595.

Danton, 473, 484, 680.

Darboy, Georges, Archbishop of Paris, 471.

Daudet, Alphonse, 473, 533, 622.

Deák, Franz, 401.

Decazes, Duke of, 324, 338, 357, 482, 508.

De Felice, Signor, 652.

Degoutte, General, 138, 201.

Deines, Adolf von, 238, 250, 599.

Delaunay, M., 114.

Delbrück, Hans, 162, 295, 413.

Delcassé, Théophile, 611.

Deligeorges, M., 432.

Democrats, Social, 439, etc., 633, 636.

Depretis, Agostino, 538, 661.

Derby, Lord, 404, 435.

Derenthall, Herr von, 681, 683.

Déroulède, Paul, 522, 612.

Desprez, M., 454, 456.

Dilke, Sir Charles, 553.

Dillmann, Professor, 45.

Dincklage, Major von, 200, 246, 263.

Disraeli, Benjamin, 123; On war and peace, 421; Salisbury appointed Foreign Secretary, 434; At Berlin Congress, 441; Replies Gortchakov, 445; Sarcastic, 447; Character, 452, etc.; Werner's picture, 456; At final banquet, 456; Eye-glass, 473; Jew, 474; On religion, 552; Subtle psychologist, 618; ill. 456.

Dohm, Ernst, 152.

Dohna, Count Adalbert, 76, 77.

Dohna, Count Ludwig, 76, 77.

Dohna-Schlodien, Count Nikolaus, 176.

Dohrn, Anton, 648, 673, etc.

Dolgoruki, Princess Catherine Mik-

hailovna, mistress of Tsar Alexander II (Iurevskaia), 385, etc., 433, 579.

Döllinger, Ignaz von, 468, 552.

Dönhoff-Friedrichstein, Count August, 380.

Dönhoff, Count Fritz, 257.

Dönhoff, Count Karl, 406, 532, 539, 587.

Dönhoff, Countess Marie von, later Princess von Bülow (see also Bülow); ill. 592.

Dörnberg, Baron Karl von, 492, 641.

Dostoievski, Fedor Mikhailovitch, 379.

Dove, Alfred, 133.

Dreyfus, Alfred, 478.

Dryander, Herr, 73, etc., 108.

Dryander, Ernst von, 73.

Duchesne, Louis, 667.

Dumas, Alexandre, fils, 531, 535.

Dumreicher, Armand, 13.

Duncker, Franz, 81, 606.

Dupanloup, Philippe, 156.

Durnov, Missy, 196, 423, 579, 581, 590, 591, 597.

Ebner-Eschenbach, Marie von, 107, 123.

Echtermeyer, Theodor, 79.

Edel, Deputy, 165.

Edward VII (Albert Edward, Prince of Wales), 17, 34, 159, 272, 424; At Paris, 462, etc., 484, 529, 531; Against Germany, 551, 582; Appreciates Morier, 599; Match-maker, 602; On Krüger dispatch, 665.

Eichhorn, Hermann von, 176.

Eichstedt, Herr von, 306.

Eickstedt, Countess Christa, 10.

Eisendecher, Herr von, 5, 10.

Eisendecher, Karl von, 10.

Eisner, Kurt, 439, etc.

Elizabeth, Empress of Austria, 407, 415, 524, 528.

Elizabeth, Queen of Rumania (Carmen Sylva), 647, etc.

Elizabeth Feodorovna, Princess of Hesse, wife of Grand Duke Sergei, 596.

Elliot, Sir Henry George, 428.

Emil Prince of Hesse-Darmstadt, 15.

Ems Dispatch, 133, etc., 162, 305.

Encke, Johann Franz, 311.

Engels, Friedrich, 302.

England, Relations with Prussia and France (1870), 154 f., 159; Russian negotiations at London (1878), 434, etc.; Krüger dispatch, 664, etc.

Eötvös, Baron, 399.

Erckert, General von, 390.

Erffa, Lieutenant von, 205, 233.

Erlanger, Baron Emil, 26, 483.

Erzberger, Matthias, 20, 196, 315, 439, etc., 453.

Esterházy, Count Moritz, 94.

Esterneaux, Secretary of Legation, 222.

Estournelles de Constant, Baron d', 541, 542.

Eu, Count (Gaston d'Orléans), 524.

Eugénie (Countess Montijo), Empress of France, 23, 97, 139, 156, 173, 397, 501, 523, 667.

Eulenburg, Count August, 370.

Eulenburg, Count Botho zu, 116, 294, 370, 657, 679.

Eulenburg, Count Frederick, 325.

Eulenburg, Count Karl, 370.

Eulenburg, Count (Prince) Philip zu, Herbert Bismarck to, 261; Against Count Kuno Rantzau, 283; Deserts Bismarck, 326; Replaces Henry VII of Reuss in Vienna, 382; Character, 490, etc.; Memoirs, 586; On Bismarck, 629, etc.; The Bismarcks on, 646; Visits Bülow in Vienna, 649; Sighs, 656; Accompanies William II to Venice, 658; Friend of the Kaiser, 660; At Meran, with Bülow, 679, etc.; Afraid of Herbert Bismarck's return, 681; Meets Bülow at Venice, 682.

Eulenburg, Count Wendt zu, Engaged to Marie von Bismarck, and death, 370, etc.

Faidherbe, César, 204, 214, 232, 233, 236, 239, 244.

Failly, Achille de, 157.

Faltin, Herr, 110.

Fels, Consul, 416.

Ferdinand, Emperor of Austria, 398.

Ferdinand, King of Rumania, 173, 647, etc.

Ferdinand, Prince of Coburg, King of Bulgaria, 612.

Fériol, Vicomte de, 324.

Ferry, Jules, 294, 473, 486, 487, etc., 505, etc., 519, 520, 530.

Fersen, Count Nicholas, 574, etc.

Festetics, Countess Marie, 407.

Fichte, Johann Gottlieb, 43.

Figner, Vera, 575, etc.

Fischer, Deputy, 165.

Flaischlen, Cäsar, 13.

Flaubert, Gustave, 123, 541.

Fleury, Count Félix de, 501.

Floquet, Charles Thomas, 163.

Florescu, Joan Emanuel, 624.

Flotow, Johannes von, 183.

Foch, Marshal, 93, 196, 201.

Folliot de Crenneville, Lord High Chamberlain, 398.

Fontane, Theodor, 123.

Ford, Sir Clare, 664.

Forkel, Johann Nikolaus, 43.

Fortis, Alessandro, 660.

Fouché, Joseph, 288, 332.

Fourton, Bardy de, 338.

France, Anatole, 157, 332, 335, 529.

France, Bismarck's secret negotiations with Napoleon III, 176, etc.; Alarming articles, 357; Gambetta on alliance with Germany, 475, etc.; Bismarck for consolidation of republicanism, 483; Tongking expedition, 487; Education Bill, 505, etc.; Boulanger, 611; Alliance with Russia, 639, etc.

Francis I, Emperor of Austria, 407, etc.

Francis Ferdinand, Archduke, 181.

Francis Joseph, Emperor of Austria, 5, 13, 23; War of 1866, 94, 105; Before 1870, 153, 155; Three Emperors meet at Berlin (1872), 308; Accession to the throne, 398; For acquisition of Bosnia and Herzegovina, 400; Meeting at Reichstadt, 404; Orient crisis, 423; Bismarck's audience (1879), 509; Removes Beust, 528; Frankfort Convention of Princes, 546; At Skierniewice, 570, 572, etc.; At Kremsier, 588; Threatens Alexander of Bulgaria, 589; Re-Insurance Treaty, 638; Letter of William II on Bismarck, 648.

François, Bruno von, 151.

Frankfort (Childhood), 2-27.

Frederick I, King of Württemberg, 48.

696

Frederick II (the Great), King of Prussia, 8, 62, 151, 380.

Frederick III (Crown Prince Frederick William of Prussia), 35, 141; Weissenburg and Wörth, 150, etc., 223, 230, 248, etc., 260, 261, 262, 293, 329, 344; Trip to Italy (1875), 348, etc.; On Bismarck, 351, etc.; War rumours, 356, etc., 375; San Remo, 413, 424; Curtius, 429; Berlin Congress, 441, etc.; Toast, 456; Herbert Bismarck unjust towards, 461; Bülow visits, 596; Illness, 606; Waldersee on, 610; Operation at San Remo, 615; At Charlottenburg, 618; Death, 623; Behaviour of William II, 646, etc.

Frederick VI, King of Denmark, 305.

Frederick VII, King of Denmark, 51, etc., 62, 64, 66, 438.

Frederick Charles, Prince of Prussia, 100, 151, 188, 261, 354, 516.

Frederick William III, King of Prussia, 40, 65, 304, etc., 322, 568.

Frederick William IV, King of Prussia, 5, 11, 23, 52, 96, 230, 237, 263, 312, 322, etc., 344, 390, 513, 550.

Freiligrath, Ferdinand, 153.

Freycinet, de Saulces, 473, 488, etc., 520, 521, 530.

Freytag, Gustav, 42, 44, 123, 133.

Friedjung, Dr. Heinrich, 407.

Friedrich I, Grand Duke of Baden, 10, 167, 177, 229.

Friedrich II, Grand Duke of Baden, 177.

Friedrich, Duke of Augustenburg, 47.

Friedrich, Prince of Hohenzollern, 314.

Friedrich Franz II, Grand Duke of Mecklenburg-Schwerin, 103, 613.

Friedrich Franz III, Grand Duke of Mecklenburg-Schwerin, 40.

Friedrich Wilhelm, Grand Duke of Mecklenburg-Strelitz, 53, 60, etc., 103.

Friedrich Wilhelm, last Elector of Hesse-Kassel, 95.

Friedrich Wilhelm, Landgrave of Hesse-Kassel, 95.

Friesen, Baron Richard von, 168.

Fröbel, Dr. Julius, 545, etc.

Fürstenberg, Prince Max Egon, 600, 660.

Gablenz, Baron Ludwig von, 90, 95.

Gablenz, Baron Wilhelm von, 89, 95, 100.

Gagern, Heinrich von, 8, 167.

Gagern, Max von, 168, 402.

Galen, Count Wilderich, 269, 273, 284.

Galliffet, Gaston Alexandre Auguste Marquis de, 476, etc., 481.

Gallmeyer, Josefine, 406.

Gambetta, Léon, 79, 175, 236, 245, 293, 294, 315, 466, etc.; Character, 472, etc.; Against MacMahon, 483, 484; Wilson's attacks, 487; Ferry, 488; Against the Germans in Paris (1870), 497; Against the Church, 505; Speech, 518; Government, 519, etc.; Resigns, 520; Death, 521; ill. 176.

Garibaldi, Giuseppe, 156, 293, 335, 651, 652, 654, 661.

Gay, Professor, 117, 129.

Geibel, Emanuel, 44.

George V, King of Hanover, 29, 61, 527.

George, Grand Duke of Mecklenburg-Strelitz, 59, 62.

George, Duke of Mecklenburg-Strelitz, 61, 216, 387, etc., 390.

George, King of Greece, 18; Audience with Bülow, 423; Murdered, 424; Neutral in Russian-Turkish War, 431; Greeks march in Thessaly, 434; Bülow takes leave of, 438, 531.

Gérard, M., 314, etc.

Gerlach, Leopold von, 32.

German-French War (1870), 131, etc.; Bülow's reports, 186, etc.

Gervais, Alfred Albert, 639.

Giers, Nikholai Karlovitch, 425, 557, 568, etc.; At Skierniewice, 573; On Alexander III, 580; Afghan conflict, 582; At Kremsier, 588; At Friedrichsruh, 588; Bülow and, 600; Bulgarian question, 605; Waldersee on, 610; Re-Insurance Treaty, 613; Treaty not renewed, 638, 677.

Gioberti, Vincenzo, 538.

Giolitti, Giovanni, 651.

Giordano Bruno, 540.

Girardin, Emile de, 500, etc.

Gladstone, William Ewart, 180; Against Turkish atrocities, 405; Representations to Prince of Wales, 463; Franchise reform bill, 550; Character, 552, etc.; Afghanistan, 582; Overthrown, 582; Laura Minghetti and, 667.

Gneist, Rudolf von, 129, 319, 369, 370, 505.

Gobineau, Count Arthur, 360.

Goblet, René, 519.

Goeben, August von, 63, 189, 196, etc., 203, 208, 210, 214, 220, 224; Character, 224, etc., 231, 232, 240, 243, 244, 257, 264, 293.

Goethe, 1, 2, 19, 21, 40, 43, 58, 59, 67, 74, 105, 106, 110, 120, 124, 125, 126, 130, 184, 293, 327, 328, 330, 338, 343, 356, 364, 377, 380, 401, 406, 414, 436, etc., 450, 478, 490, etc., 522, 531, 535, 536, 554, 585, 594, 648, 656.

Gogol, Nikholai Vasilivitch, 379.

Goltz, Count Robert, 97, 334.

Goltz, Lieutenant von der, 265.

Goluchowski, Count Agenor, 528, 573, 624.

Gontaut-Biron, Vicomte de, 252, 309, 324, 360.

Gontcharov, Ivan Alexandrovitch, 379.

Gorce, Pierre de la, 196.

Gortchakov, Prince Alexander Mikhailovitch, On Bismarck, 6; Bülow's father and, 23; Bismarck's scorn, 319; Tension between Bismarck and, 358, 359, 383, 393, 396, 403; Receives Bülow, 391, etc.; On Bismarck, 392; At Berlin, 394, 402, etc.; At Reichstadt, 404; At Moscow, 422; Offended by Bismarck, 443, 450; Speech, 445; Agrees to occupation of Bosnia and Herzegovina, 447; Oppert-Blowitz on, 452; Ridiculed, 452; Werner's picture, 456; Malicious, 458; Interview, 508; Death, 566; For Bulgarians, 589; His rôle, 677; ill. 320.

Goschen, Sir Edward, 183, 665.

Goschen, G. J. Lord, 664.

Govone, Giuseppe, 158.

Grabow, Wilhelm, 81, 606.

Gramont, Duke of, 132, 164, 166, 168, 173, 176, 182, 344, 472, 658.

Granville, Earl of, 463, 667.

Gregorovius, Ferdinand, 337, etc., 648.

Griefswald (University), 275, etc.

Greppi, Count Giuseppe, 599.

Grévy, Jules, 473, 483; Wilson affair, 486, etc., 519, 520, 534.

Grey, Sir Edward, 183.

Grigorovitch, Dmitri Vasilivitch, 379

Grillenberger, Karl, 308.

Grillparzer, Franz, 376.

Grimm, Gisela, 338.

Grimm, Herman, 338.

Grote, Count Otto, 34.

Gruev, Major, 601.

Grünne, Count Karl Ludwig, 397.

Gurko, General, 428.

Gutzkow, Karl, 123.

Haase, Hugo, 439, etc.

Häckel, Ernst, 13.

Hänel, Albert, 47.

Hagedorn, Friedrich von, 31.

Hahnemann, Samuel Christian Friedrich, 145.

Hahnke, Wilhelm von, 641.

Halle (*Pädagogium*), 72-115.

Haller, Johannes, 413, 629.

Hamburg (and Klein-Flottbek), 28, etc., 269, etc., 271, etc., 285, etc.; ill. 284.

Hammann, Otto, 222.

Hammerstein, Baron, 104.

Hammerstein-Loxten, Ernst Baron von, 61.

Hansemann, Adolf von, 319.

Harcourt, Marquis d', 324.

Hardenberg, Prince, 41, 63, 304, 322.

Harding, Mr., 553, 598.

Hardinge, Sir Charles, 553.

Hartington, Marquis of, 553.

Hartmann, Chaplain, 275, etc., 279.

Hasperg, Herr von, 354.

Hasse, Ernst, 42.

Hassenpflug, Hans Daniel, 15.

Hatzfeldt, Prince Albert, 122.

Hatzfeldt, Countess Elisabeth, 241, 261, 316, 492, 548, 586.

Hatzfeldt-Trachenberg, Prince Hermann, 316, etc.

Hatzfeldt, Count Paul, 124, 301, etc., 334; Bismarck against, 513, etc.

Hatzfeldt, Countess Sofie, 123, 124, 301.

Haucke, Julie (Countess), 426, 589, 603, etc.

Haussmann, Friedrich and Konrad, 166.

Haussmann, George Eugène Baron, 487.

Haymerle, Baron Heinrich Karl, 573.

Hebbel, Friedrich, 399.

Hegel, Georg Wilhelm Friedrich, 84, 307, 577.

Hegel, Immanuel, 577.

Hehn, Viktor, 465.

Heilbron, Secretary of Legation, 222.

Heine, Heinrich, 106, 162, 258, 296, 415, 536, 669.

Helena, Princess of Montenegro, married to Crown Prince Victor Emmanuel (III) of Italy, 671, etc.

Helena Pavlovna, Grand Duchess, 390, 527.

Helfft, Banker, 61.

Hellwig, Secretary of Legation, 301.

Helmholtz, Hermann von, 537.

Helmholtz, Frau von, 587.

Hemmer, Herr, 315.

Henckel-Donnersmarck, Countess Blanche (see Païva).

Henckel-Donnersmarck, Count Guido, 148; Character, 497, etc.

Henckel, Count Karl Lazarus, 148, 498.

Hendrikov, Countess, 386.

Hengemüller, Baron, 573.

Henning, Lieutenant-Colonel von, 235.

Henry, Prince of Prussia, 657.

Henry VII, Prince of Reuss, 334, 359, 371, 377, 382, etc., 593, 648, 658, ill. 156.

Henry IX, Prince of Reuss, 307, 308.

Henry XIII, Prince of Reuss, 196, 273, 283, 284.

Henry XIV, Prince of Reuss, 502.

Henry XVIII, Prince of Reuss, 314, 327, 502, 604.

Herbette, Jules, 677.

Herbst, Dr. Eduard, 399, etc.

Herder, Johann Gottfried, 107.

Hertling, Baron Georg von, 178, 273, etc., 653.

Hertsen, Alexander (Iakovlev), 379, 390, 669.

Hertz, Henriette, 40.

Hervé, Gustave, 484.

Herwarth von Bittenfeld, General, 99.

Herwegh, Georg, 669.

Herzogenberg, Heinrich Baron von, 108.

Heyse, Paul, 44.

Hildebrand, Adolf, 108.

Hillebrand, Karl, 39, 355, etc.

Hillern, Wilhelmine von, 123.

Hindenburg, Paul von, 63, 176.

Hinzpeter, Georg, 599, 629, 637.

Hirsch, Moritz, 10.

Hirschfeld, General von, 141.

Hirschfeld, Secretary of Legation, 414.

Hitrovo, Russian Minister to Bucharest, 625.

Hodenberg, Deputy von, 676.

Hödel, Max, 438, etc.

Hoensbroech, Count Paul, 13.

Hoffmann, E. T. A., 487.

Hofmann, Leopold Friedrich Baron von, 402.

Hohenlohe - Langenburg, Prince Hermann, 295, 681.

Hohenlohe - Langenburg, Hereditary Prince Ernst, 528.

Hohenlohe-Schillingsfürst, Prince Chlodwig zu, 163, 165, 202, 222, 295, 397, 451, 456; Bülow's chief, 467; Character, 467, etc., 481; MacMahon incident, 482; On marriage of his son, 489; Bülow guest of, 517; Goes to Aussee, 533; Bülow's memorandum on North Africa, 547; Should take steps against Social Democrats, 636; Bülow cordially attached to, 649; Krüger Dispatch, 665; Appeases Kaiser, 678; Against Marschall, 679; For Navy Bill, 684, etc.

Hohenlohe-Schillingsfürst, Prince Gustav, Cardinal, 397, 656.

Hohenlohe-Schillingsfürst, Prince Konstantin, 397, 468.

Hohenlohe - Schillingsfürst, Princess Marie, 469, etc.

Hohenthal, Count Wilhelm, 213.

Hölderlin, Friedrich, 436, 531.

Holleben, Theodor von, 683.

Hollmann, Friedrich, 684, etc.

Holstein, Friedrich von, Sent to Florence, 170; Unter den Linden, 183; Against Bismarck's son-in-law, 283; Bucher's enemy, 304; Launay and, 325; Intrigues against Keudell, 334; Bismarck and, 394, etc.; Quarrel with Radowitz, 458; Visits Bülow, 460; Notice of Re-Insurance Treaty, 484; Hates Henckel-Donnersmarck, 498; Increasing interest in Bülow, 548, 586; Excited, 592; For England, against Russia, 607; Against Re-Insurance Treaty, 614; Bismarck on, 623; Leaves Bismarck, 627; Consul Raffauf's report, 637; Re-Insurance Treaty not renewed, 638, 664; Herbert Bismarck hates, 645; Bülow's appointment to Rome and, 649, 681; Rages, 656; Krüger dispatch, 665; Philip Eulenburg's ally, 681; Correspondence with Bülow, 681; Philip Eulenburg on, 683.

Hölz, Max, 494.
Hompesch, Count, 676.
Hopf, Tutor, 15, 16, 72.
Houssaye, Henry, 500.
Hoverbeck, Leopold Baron von, 81, 606.
Hübner, Baron Alexander von, 397, etc., 401.
Hugo, Victor, 247, 475, 521, 535.
Humbert, King of Italy, 156, 352, 595, 657, etc., 672.
Humbert, Privy Councillor, 592.
Humbert, Gustave Amédée, 519, 521.
Humboldt, Alexander von, 319, 321, 322.
Humboldt, Wilhelm von, 48, 319, 321, 411, 438, 656.

Iadovski, M., 431.
Ignatiev, Nikholai Pavlovitch, Ultimatum to Porte, 419; Character, 428, etc.; At San Stefano, 433; Aplomb, 568; For Bulgaria, 589.
Isabella II, Queen of Spain, 524.
Isvolski, Alexander Petrovitch, 183, 433, 600.
Itajuba, Vicomte, 529.
Italy, Relations to Prussia (1866), 158; Bismarck threatens, 339, etc.; Tunis, 454; Crispi, Premier, 652, etc.; Abyssinian war, 669, etc.; Crispi in disgrace, 671.
Ittenbach, Max, 287, 290.

Jacoby, Johann, 293, 484.
Jagow, Gottlieb, 162, 176, 183.
Janssen, Johannes, 25.
Jaurès, Jean, 473.
Jean Paul (Richter), 126.
Jenisch, Gottlieb, 33.

Jenisch, Martin, 32, 118.
Jenisch, Martin Johann, 32; ill. 32.
Jérôme Napoléon, Imperial Prince, 98, 155, 174, 175, 181, 523.
Johann, Archduke of Austria, 396.
John, King of Saxony (Philalethes), 168.
John, Franz Baron von, 168.
Joinville, Prince François (Orléans), 524.
Jomini, Baron, 403, 422.
Jonas, Herr, 290.
Jonescu, Take, 622.
Jörg, Josef Edmund, 163, etc., 182, 420.

Kainz, Josef, 13.
Kaisenberg, Major von, 150, 152.
Kalbeck, Max, 108.
Kálnoky, Count Gustav, 94; At Skierniewice, 573, etc.; At Kremsier, 588.
Kanitz, Count, 344.
Kanitz, Count Konrad, 314.
Kant, Immanuel, 206, 303, 438, 531.
Kantakuzen, Prince, 588.
Kapnist, Count Peter Alexeievitch, 527.
Karatheodory, Alexander, 455, 456.
Karl Alexander, Grand Duke of Sachsen-Weimar, 637.
Karl Anton, Prince of Hohenzollern-Sigmaringen, 132.
Karoline Amalie, Queen of Denmark, 18.
Károlyi, Count Aloys, 324, 456.
Károlyi, Countess Franziska, 314.
Katargi, M., 624.
Katkov, Mikhail Nikoforovitch, 567, 612.
Kaulbars, Baron Nikholai, 597, etc., 604, etc.
Kautsky, Karl, 450.
Kelchner, Herr, 14.
Kempis, Thomas à, 538, 595.
Kern, Johann Konrad, 506.
Kessler (Count), Adolf, 502, etc.
Kessler, Count Harry, 503.
Ketteler, Wilhelm Emanuel Baron von, 269.
Keudell, Robert von, 98, 99, 333, etc., 339, etc., 342, 348, 352, 353, 356, 539, 595, etc., 680.
Khevenhüller, Count Rudolf, 573, 589.
Kiderlen-Wächter, Alfred von, 627, 646, 681, etc.
Kinkel, Gottfried, 668.
Kinsky, Princess Marie, 407

Klaczko, Julian, 402.
Kleinmichl, Count, 373.
Kleinmichl, Countess Marie, 386, 578, etc., 581.
Kleist, Heinrich von, 63, 380, 461, 531.
Kleist-Retzow, Hans Hugo von, 616.
Klemens, Bulgarian bishop, Metropolitan of Trnovo, 601.
Klitzing, Georg von, 76.
Klopp, Onno, 402.
Klüber, Major von, 78, 79.
Knesebeck, Bodo von dem, 140, 147, 205, etc., 220, 328, 504, 597.
Knollys, Miss Charlotte, 426, 665.
Köhler, Ulrich, 437.
Kommunduros, Greek Premier, 432, 434.
Kopp, Dr. Georg, Prince Bishop of Breslau, Cardinal, 676.
Koppelow, Major von, 257.
Körner, Theodor, 34, 136, 320, 493.
Koscielski, Josef Theodor Stanislaus von, 677.
Kossuth, Ludwig, 402.
Kotchubei, Princess Helena, 97, 196, 597, etc.
Kotze, Leberecht von, 213.
Krafft von Dellmensingen, General, 176.
Kramer, Director, 73, 80, 101, 108, etc.
Kräuter, Secretary, 14.
Kropatschek, Dr., 640.
Krüger, Paul, President of the South African Republic, 664, etc.
Krüger, Dr., 327.
Kügelgen, Wilhelm von, 571.
Kühlmann, Richard von, 176.
Kuhn, Franz Baron von, 168.
Kullmann, Eduard, 457.
Kulturkampf, 278, etc., 338, etc., 441, 505, etc., 633.
Kummer, Ferdinand von, 216, 224, 243.

Laboulaye, Antoine de, 640.
Labruyère, Jean de, 465.
Ladewig, Professor, 63, 540.
Lafontaine, Jean de, 465.
Lamarmora, Alfonso, 158.
Lamartine, Alphonse Marie Louis de, 484, 680.
Lamber, Juliette (Madame Adam), 314, 527.

Lambsdorff, Count Vladimir Nikholaie- vitch, 600.
Lamennais, Félicité Robert de, 412.
Lamoricière, Juchault de, 528, 654.
Landsberg, Moritz, 536.
Langenbeck, Bernhard von, 439, 443, etc.
Larochefoucauld, François Duke of, 413.
Larochefoucauld-Bisaccia, Sosthène Duke of, 324.
Lascelles, Sir Frank Cavendish, 598, 624.
Lasker, Eduard, 47, 293, 514.
Lassalle, Ferdinand, 82, 124, 302, 474, 547, 635.
Lasson, Adolf, 413.
Latapie, Baron de, 256.
Launay, Count, 325, 451, 653.
Lausanne (University), 116, etc.
Leboeuf, Marshall, 155.
Lederer, Hugo, 584.
Ledru-Rollin, Alexandre Auguste, 80, 302, 668.
Leflô, Adolphe Charles Emmanuel, 324.
Lehmann, Orla, 51.
Lehndorff, Count Georg, 254.
Lehndorff, Count Heinrich, 254, 502, 512, 516.
Lehndorff, Count Karl, 254, 257.
Leibnitz, Gottfried Wilhelm, 146.
Leipzig (University), 120, etc.
Lenbach, Franz von, 406, 552, 666.
Lenin (Iulianov), Vladimir Ilyitch, 373, 612.
Lentze, August, 192.
Leo XIII, Pope, 286, 348, 530, 540, 672.
Leo, Heinrich, 79, 80.
Léon, Léonie, 521.
Leonrod, Baron von, Bishop, 286.
Leopardi, Count Giacomo, 560, etc.
Leopold, Prince of Bavaria, 176.
Leopold, Hereditary Prince of Hohen- zollern, 132, 133, 173.
Lerchenfeld, Count Hugo, 467, 597, 627.
Lermontov, Mikhail Iurievitch, 379.
Leuchtenberg, Duke Eugen, 590.
Leuchtenberg, Duke Georg, 388.
Levetzow, Albert von, 676.
Lewald, Fanny, 330.
Leyden, Ernst von, 443, 461.
Lichnowsky, Prince Felix, 65.
Lichnowsky, Prince Karl Max, 183.
Lichnowsky, Princess Mechtild, 107.

Lichtenberg, Georg Christoph, 39.
Liebermann von Sonnenberg, Deputy, 42.
Liebknecht, Karl, 439.
Liebknecht, Wilhelm, 476, 678.
Ligne, Prince Karl Josef, 126.
Liliencron, Detlev von, 63.
Lindau, Paul, 13.
Lindau, Rudolf, 512.
Linsingen, Colonel-General von, 223.
Liszt, Franz, 107.
Litzmann, Karl, General, 176.
Lobanov, Prince Alexei Borisovitch, 568.
Loë, Deginhard von, 191.
Loë, Dietrich von, 229, 231.
Loë, Walter von, 97, 124, 140, 190, etc.,
    193, 197, 199, 207, 208, 209, 211,
    214, etc., 221, 239, 241, 242, 243,
    244, 246, 248, 249, 250, 256, 257,
    259; Character, 260, etc.; 282, 313,
    316, 383, 444, 608, etc.
Loeper, Gustav von, 461.
Loftus, Lord, Augustus William Frederik
    Spencer, 419, etc.
Lohr, Tutor, 3, 4, 15, 26.
Loisinger, Johanna, 605.
London (1884), 549, etc.
Lopatin, Russian conspirator, 581.
Loris-Melikov, Count, 575, 578, 579.
Louis XVI, King of France, 195, 332,
    524.
Louis XVIII, King of France, 470.
Louis Ferdinand, Prince of Prussia, 41,
    148.
Louis-Josèphe-Philippe, Duke of Orleans
    (Philippe Egalité), 524, etc.
Louis (Loulou) Napoléon (IV), 23, 24,
    195, 501, 523.
Louis-Philippe, King of France, 159, 245,
    485, 500, 536.
Löwenstein, Rudolf, 149.
Lübke, Wilhelm, 141.
Lucanus, Friedrich von, 637, 641.
Ludendorff, Erich, 79, 176.
Ludolf, Count, 595.
Ludwig I, King of Bavaria, 65, 667.
Ludwig II, King of Bavaria, 163, 298.
Ludwig III, Grand Duke of Hesse-
    Darmstadt, 167.
Luise, Queen of Prussia, 41, 59, 62, 111,
    216, 217, 571, 613.
Luise, Queen of Denmark, 305, 423, 582.

Luise, Grand Duchess of Baden, 230, 261,
    353, etc., 438, 456, 509, 596.
Lüttichau, Count Konrad, 309.
Luxemburg, Rosa, 439.
Luzzatti, Luigi, 341, 474.
Lynar, Prince Alexander, 97, 353.
Lyons, Lord Richard Bickerton Pemell,
    451, 528.

Macaulay, Thomas Babington, 81.
Mackensen, August von, 176.
Mackenzie, Sir Morell, 646, etc.
MacMahon, Duke of Magenta, 79, 338,
    462; Character, 481, etc.; Resigna-
    tion, 483.
Maffei, Count, 426.
Magdeburg, Herr, 287, 290.
Majorescu, Titus, 624.
Makart, Hans, 406.
Malaret, Baron de, 174.
Malet, Sir Edward Balwin, 618.
Malvano, Signor, 655.
Mangin, General, 138.
Manin, Daniele, 474.
Manteuffel, Edwin von, Bismarck writes,
    89, etc.; Entry in Hanover, 99; Com-
    piègne, 196; Rouen, 201; Character,
    202, 293, 295; Sent to Warsaw, 508;
    Bismarck suspicious, 508, 511.
Manteuffel, Otto von, 5, 287.
Manzoni, Alessandro, 538.
Marat, Jean Paul, 471.
Marées, Captain von, 144, 147.
Marées, Hans von, 147, 656.
Mareuil, Vicomte de, 335.
Margherita, Queen of Italy, 337, 595,
    659.
Marghiloman, M., 624.
Maria Alexandrovna, Princess of Hesse,
    Tsaritsa, 384, etc., 534, 603.
Maria Feodorovna, Princess of Württem-
    berg, Tsaritsa, 385, 388, etc.
Maria Feodorovna, Tsaritsa (see Dagmar).
Maria Pavlovna, Princess of Mecklenburg-
    Schwerin, Wife of Grand Duke
    Vladimir, 385, 388, 389, 612, etc., 617.
Maria, Queen of Hanover, Wife of
    George V, 107, 431.
Maria, Princess of Prussia, 308, etc.
Marie Antoinette, Queen of France, 43,
    195.

Marlitt (Eugenie John), 123.
Marschall von Bieberstein, Baron Adolf von, 213, 484, 614, 638, 643, 644, 645, 649, 657, 665, 676, 678; Traitor, 679; For Navy Bill, 684; Lawsuit, 685.
Marwitz, General von, 176.
Marx, Karl, 80, 124, 302, 365, 474, 476, 576.
Mary, Queen of England, Wife of George V, 62.
Mathilde, Archduchess of Austria, 156.
Mathilde, Princess Bonaparte, 181, 667.
Mathy, Karl, 327.
Maupassant, Guy de, 123.
Max, Prince of Baden, 223, 653.
Maximilian, Archduke of Austria, Emperor of Mexico, 12.
Maybach, Albert von, 657.
Mayer, Karl, 166.
Mayweg, Dr., 142.
Mazarin, Cardinal, 474, 479.
Mazzini, Giuseppe, 80, 170, 171, 302, etc., 414, 652, 661, 668.
Mecklenburg (Neu-Strelitz, Malchin, Sternberg, Schwerin, Rostock, Wismar, Neu-Brandenburg, etc.), 55, etc.
Meding, Oskar, 137.
Mehemed-Ali (Karl Detroit from Magdeburg), 455, 456.
Meinecke, Friedrich, 413.
Menabrea, Count Luigi Federigo, 157, 528, 653.
Menelik, King of Abyssinia, 670, etc.
Mensdorff-Pouilly, Count Alexander, 94.
Merck, Syndic, 38.
Mérode, Count Friedrich Xavier, 294, 336.
Mérode, Count Werner, 294.
Messmer-Saldern, de, Bülow's uncle, 50.
Metternich, Prince Klemens, 132, 158, 304, 323, 397, 401.
Metternich, Prince Richard, 155, 170, 396, etc., 501; ill. 156.
Metz (1872-1873), 285, etc.
Metz, General de, 138, 201.
Meyendorff, Baron Ernst, 392.
Meyer, Conrad Ferdinand, 127, 681.
Meyerbeer, Giacomo, 324.
Meysenbug, Malvida von, 168, 595, 656, 665, 668, etc.

Meysenbug, Wilhelm von, 168, 402.
Michael Pavlovitch, Grand Duke of Russia, 387.
Michaelis, Dr. Georg, 176, 653.
Milan (Obrenovitch) Prince, then King of Serbia, 431.
Millerand, Alexandre, 484.
Minghetti, Donna Laura, 27, 349, 523, 531, etc., 536, etc., 559, 591, 594, 661, 665, etc.; ill. 532.
Minghetti, Marco, 335, 340, 347, 536, etc., 591; Death, 595, 666.
Miquel, Johannes, Dr., 2, 129, 538.
Mirabeau, Count Honoré Gabriel Victor Riquetti, 470, 473.
Miribel, Marie François Joseph de, 477.
Mischke, General, 348, etc.
Molière, 42, 129, 293, 535.
Molinari, Signor, 653.
Möller, Privy Councillor von, 202, 295.
Moltke, Count Hellmuth von, 60, 63, 78; For immediate attack (1866), 91; Steinmetz recalled, 100; Strategic leader (1870), 154, 157, 168, 173, 198; William I toasts, 173; Peace preliminaries, 247; Princess Arenberg on, 293, 555; On war question, 611; On Prince William, 611; Letter, 630.
Moltke, Count Hellmuth, 154.
Moltke, Count Kuno, 656.
Moltke-Hvitfeld, Count, 529.
Mommsen, Theodor, 25, 277, 293, 308, 338.
Mommsen, Tycho, 25.
Monod, Gabriel, 595, 668.
Monod, Dr., 503.
Montebello, Count Adrien, 549, 640.
Montesquieu, 413.
Montpensier, Duke Antoine (Orléans), 524.
Monts, Count Anton, 626, 681, 682.
Morgan, Pierpont, 33, 498.
Morier, Sir Robert, 598, etc., 600.
Morny, Charles Auguste Louis Josèphe, Duke of, 500, 501.
Morosini, Countess Annina, 659.
Morra, General, 652.
Mossner, Walter, 239, 241, etc., 249.
Motley, John Lothrop, 81.
Mouy, Count, 458.
Mozart, 406.

Mudra, General von, 176.
Mühler, Heinrich von, 279.
Müller, Hermann, 455.
Müller, Otfried, 436.
Müller, Wilhelm, 71.
Mumm von Schwarzenstein, Secretary of Legation, 624.
Mun, Count Albert, 294, 477.
Münch-Bellinghausen, Baron Joachim von, 131, 314, 361, 426, etc., 437.
Münster - Derneburg, Count (Prince) Georg Herbert, 550, etc., 593.
Muraviev, Count Mikhail Nikholaievitch, 527, 569.
Musset, Alfred de, 114, 118.

Nachtigal, Dr. Gustav, 174, 541, etc.
Napoleon I, 11, 15, 52, 93, 112, 180, 184, 201, 203, 216, 295, 307, 331, 332, 441, 465, 474, 479, 505, 509, 556, 557, 674.
Napoleon III, 11, 23, 52, 79, 92, 93, 97, 102, 124; Rôle before and during war (1870), 131, 132, 139, 155, etc., 167, 169, 170, 173, 174, 179, etc., 472; Wilhelmshöhe, 184; Government, 255; Remark, 398; At Biarritz, 465; Coup d'état, 501; Fantastic and weak, 524; Heine and, 536; Piedmont convention, 538; Engagement, 667; At Mathilde Bonaparte, 667, etc.; Orsini's attempt on life of, 668.
Naumann, Friedrich, 56, 162.
Nelidov, Alexander Ivanovitch, 228, 433.
Nelson, Admiral, 45.
Nemours, Duke Louis of (Orléans), 524.
Nesselrode, Count Karl Robert, 420, 568.
Nesselrode-Ehreshofen, Count Maximilian, 124.
Neuville, M. de, 256.
Nicholas Nikholaievitch, Russian Grand Duke, 433.
Nicholas I, Tsar, 11; Death, 23, 323, 373, 376, etc., 386, 387, 388, 389, 390, 391, 398, 420, 469, 484, 505, 511, 512, 569, 589, 603, 604.
Nicholas II, Tsar, 372, 586, 640.
Nicholas, Prince, then King of Montenegro, 431.
Nicolai, Christoph Friedrich, 414.
Nicotera, Baron Giovanni, 538, 651, 661.

Niebuhr, Barthold, 110, 343.
Niesewand, Franz Maria von, 189, etc., 207, 221, 232, 239.
Nimptsch, Guido von, 227, etc., 296, 316, 317.
Nimptsch, Paul von, 227, 316.
Noack, Friedrich, 35, 656.
Noailles, Marquis de, 324.
Nobiling, Dr. Karl, 439.
Nollet, General, 201.
Nord, Graf Roger du, 471, etc., 474, 476, 477, etc.
Nostitz, Count, 228.
Nothomb, Baron, 325.
Nunes, Fernan, 528, 529.

Oberg, Dr. Emil, 130.
Obolenski, Princess, 360.
Oertzen, Friedrich von, 76.
Oertzen, Jaspar von, 57, 103.
Olga, Queen of Greece, 423, etc., 431.
Olga, Queen of Württemberg, 359.
Ollivier, Emile, 131; Au coeur léger, 134, 173, 472, 481, 658.
Oppeln-Bronikowski, Major von, 208, 209, 240.
Oppert-Blowitz, Herr, 450, etc.; ill. 452.
Oriola, Count, 237.
Oriola, Countess Luise, 95.
Orlov, Prince Nikholai Alexeievitch, 526, etc., 568, 569.
Orsini, Felice, 668, etc.
Osman Nuri Pasha, Ghasi, 428.
Ouida (Louisa de la Ramée), 364.

Paget, Lady Walburga, 354, 355.
Pahlen, Count Peter Ludwig, 388, etc.
Pailleron, Edouard, 525.
Painlevé, Paul, 653.
Païva, Marquess Blanche de (Countess Henckel-Donnersmarck), 498, etc., 502.
Paléologue, Maurice, 183.
Pallain, Georges, 470.
Pallavicini, Margrave Johann, 573.
Palmerston, Lord, 50, 552.
Pansa, Alberto, 337.
Pape, Colonel-General von, 584, 657.
Paris (1878-1884), 462, etc., 466-508, 517-536.

Paris, Count of (Louis-Philippe d'Orléans), 524.
Pascal, Blaise, 175.
Pastor, Ludwig von, 25.
Paul I, Tsar, 387, etc.; Assassinated, 388, etc., 424.
Paul Alexandrovitch, Grand Duke, 385.
Paul Friedrich, Grand Duke of Mecklenburg-Schwerin, 65.
Payer, Friedrich, 166.
Pedro II, Emperor of Brazil, 524.
Peel, Sir Robert, 552.
Pélissier, General, 11.
Pelloux, Luigi, 528, 653.
Pemberton-Ground, Mr., 230, etc.
Perglas, Herr von, 326.
Perovskaia, Countess Sofia, 380, etc.
Perponcher, Countess Wanda, 314, etc.
Peters, Karl, 116.
Petery, General, 263.
Pfizer, Gustav, 3.
Pfordten, Ludwig Karl Heinrich Baron von der, Family, 9, 10.
Philipsborn, Director von, 362.
Photiades, M., 425.
Pietri, M., 288.
Pistor, Herr, 288.
Pitt, William (Lord Chatham), 445.
Pius VII, Pope, 319.
Pius IX, Pope, 335, 336, 338, 339, 355, 537, etc.
Planitz, Colonel von der, 262.
Platen, Count Adolf, 10, 49, 528.
Platen-Hallermund, August von, 29, 49.
Platen-Hallermund, Count Georg von, 49.
Plener, Ernst von, 399.
Plener, Ignaz von, 399.
Pobiedonostsev, Konstantin Petrovitch, 577, etc., 581.
Poincaré, Raymond, 93, 138, 183.
Poland, Prussia and Russia united against Polish insurrection, 160, etc., 510; Debate on (1863), 161, etc.
Polignac, Auguste Jules, Count de, 501.
Polovtsov, Russian State Secretary, 567, etc.
Posadowsky, Count Arthur, 684.
Pourtalès, Count Max, 215, etc., 237.
Pourtalès, Count Wilhelm, 627.
Pranckh, Baron von, 164.

Prévost, Marcel, 412.
Prillwitz, Frau von, 314, etc.
Prokesch-Osten, Count Anton, 9.
Protasov, Countess, 376, etc.
Prussian-Austrian War (1866), 85, etc.
Pückler-Muskau, Prince Hermann Ludwig Heinrich, 545.
Pushkin, Alexander Sergeievitch, 379, 535.
Putbus, Prince, 70.

Raabe, Wilhelm, 583.
Radetzky, Count, 5, 13.
Radowitz, Josef Maria von, 97, 360, 383, 414; Quarrel with Holstein, 458, etc., 512; Bismarck against, 513.
Radziwill, Prince Anton, 572, etc.
Radziwill, Prince Ferdinand, 676.
Radziwill, Princess Marie, 152.
Raffauf, Consul, 637.
Ragonesi, Cardinal, 676.
Rahel (Varnhagen), 41, 567.
Rainer, Archduke, 397.
Rampolla, Cardinal, 671, etc., 676.
Rancis y Villanuova, Spanish Minister, 11.
Rantzau, Count Kuno, 282, 283, 371, 461, 607, 627.
Ratazzi, Signor, 655.
Rathenau, Walter, 87, 439, etc.
Ratibor, Duke Viktor, 397.
Rauch, General von, 575.
Rechberg-Rothenlöwen, Count Bernhard, 9.
Rechenberg, Julius von, 574, etc.
Redern, Count Heinrich, 48, 96, 297, 323.
Redern, Count Wilhelm, 322, etc., 517.
Reichardt, Herr, 301.
Reichenberg, Suzanne, 114.
Reinach, Joseph, 519.
Renan, Ernest, 412.
Renvers, Herr von, 117, 464, 679.
Retz, de, Cardinal, 474.
Reuter, Fritz, 56, 69.
Rhodes, Cecil, 498.
Richelieu, Cardinal, 471, 474, 479.
Richter, Eugen, 279, 293, 308, 361, 435, 583, 601, 640, 676, 678, 684.
Richter, Gustav and Cornelia, 318, 323.
Richthofen, Oswald Baron von, 681, 683.
Rieger, Ladislaus, 611.

Ring, Baron de, 166.
Robespierre, Maximilien, 244.
Rochefort, Count Henry, 519, etc.
Rodbertus, Johann Karl, 547.
Rodd, Sir Rennell, 337, etc., 598.
Roggenbach, Baron Franz von, 229, etc.
Rome (1874-1875), 333, etc.; (1884), 536, etc.; (1886), 594, etc.; (1893-1897), 651-685; ill. 336.
Ronsard, Pierre de, 291.
Roon, Albrecht von, 162, 173, 235, 293.
Roosevelt, Theodore, 337.
Roscher, Wilhelm, 121, etc., 129.
Rosenberg, Major von, 131, 132, 133.
Rosenzweig, Colonel von, 225, 257.
Rosetti, Konstantin, 624.
Rosmini-Serbatti, Count, 538.
Rotenhan, Baron von, 681, 683.
Rothan, Gustave, 11.
Rothschild, Baron Anselm Mayer, 26.
Rothschild, Baron Mayer Carl, 26, 483.
Rothschild, Baron Willy, 27.
Rothschild, Baroness Mathilde, 27.
Rottenburg, Franz von, 628.
Rouher, Eugène, 93, 156, etc., 170.
Rousseau, Jean-Jacques, 2, 113, 118, 289, 465, 495, etc.
Rouvier, Maurice, 519.
Rudini, Antonio Starraba, Marchese di, 651, 671, etc.
Rudolf, Crown Prince of Austria-Hungary, 23, 195.
Rudolphi, Ferdinand, 237, etc.
Rücker, Alfred, 32, 33, 34.
Rücker, Emilie, 28, 35, 36.
Rücker, Oskar, 35.
Rücker, Wilhelm, 35.
Rücker-Jenisch, Martin Baron von, 35.
Rückert, Friedrich, 37.
Ruge, Arnold, 79.
Ruhland, Dr., 165.
Rumania, Peace Treaty of San Stefano, 433; Bessarabia ceded to Russia, 448; Sympathies towards Triple Alliance, 449; Bülow sent to, 617, etc.; Secret agreement, 624.
Ruprecht, Prince, 176.
Russell, Odo, Lord Ampthill, 324, 452, 456.
Russia, Relations with Prussia under Bismarck, 159, etc.; His policy after 1870 towards, 308; Three Emperors meet at Berlin (1872), 308; Peace is assured, 358; Bismarck for alliance, 393, etc.; Alexander II on Constantinople, 420; Russian-Turkish War, 428, etc.; Negotiations at London (1878), 434, etc.; William I and Alexander II at Alexandrovo, 508; Bismarck on Berlin and St. Petersburg, 556, etc.; Skierniewice, 570, etc.; Kremsier, 588; Policy towards Bulgaria, 600, etc.; Turns towards France, 611; Re-Insurance Treaty, 613; William II on, 638; Re-Insurance Treaty not renewed, 639; Alliance with France, 639, etc.; Bismarck's revelations, 677, etc.
Ruville, General von, 251, etc., 264, etc.

Saburov, Ambassador, 424, etc.
Sacy, Silvestre de, 412.
Sadullah Bey, Ambassador, 455, 456.
Saint-Just, 680.
St. Petersburg (1875-1876), 372-392; (1884-1888), 566-583, 590-591, 597-601, 612-617.
Saint-Vallier, Count, 454, 456.
Salamanca, Count, 262.
Saldern, Consul von, 602.
Salisbury, Lord, 423, 434; At Berlin Congress, 446, 452, 456; Gladstone and, 550; On Russia, 582; Prime Minister, 582.
Salm, Princess Elise, 407, 573, 592.
Salm-Horstmar, Prince Karl, 468.
Sand, George, 266, 364.
Sandeau, Jules, 364.
Sanden-Tussainen, Herr von, 221, 222, 237.
Sanfelice, Cardinal, 674, etc.
Saracco, Signor, 538.
Sardou, Victorien, 525.
Sasonov, Sergei Dmitrivitch, 183.
Saussier, General, 611.
Savigny, Karl Friedrich von, 88, 334, 505.
Say, Léon, 519, 521.
Sayn-Wittgenstein, Prince Emil, 378.
Sayn-Wittgenstein, Prince Ferdinand, 378.
Schack, General von, 390.

Schadow, Gottfried, 58.
Scharffenberg, Karl Xavier, 226, 229, etc.
Scheel-Plessen, Count Karl, 46.
Scheel-Plessen, Count Magnus, 46.
Scheel-Plessen, Count Otto, 46.
Scheel-Plessen, Count Wulf, 46.
Scheer, Admiral Reinhard, 176.
Schenkendorf, Max von, 268.
Scherff, Herr von, 12.
Scheurer-Kestner, Senator, 478.
Schill, Ferdinand von, 70.
Schiller, 1, 2, 19, 22, 34, 40, 64, 90, 125, 127, 143, 184, 202, 203, 235, 295, 321, 332, 386, 401, 411, 467, 519, 531, 535, 577, 585, 623.
Schlegel, August Wilhelm, 42.
Schlegel, Friedrich, 38.
Schleiermacher, Friedrich Ernst Daniel, 320.
Schleinitz, Alexander von, 314, etc.; Bismarck's enmity, 315, 555.
Schleinitz, Countess Marie, 314, 317; Intercedes for Wagner, 318; Her drawing-room, 319, 356; Princess Bismarck against, 555, 587.
Schleswig-Holstein, Question, 51, etc.
Schlichting, Max von, 187, 195, 196, 198, 200.
Schlieffen, Count Alfred, 154, 516.
Schliemann, Heinrich, 429.
Schlözer, Kurd von, 280, 347, 539.
Schmerling, Anton Ritter von, 396, 401.
Schmettow, Count, 153.
Schmidt, Julius, 437, etc.
Schmidt, Professor, 63.
Schmoller, Gustav, 121, etc., 559.
Schön, Wilhelm von, 183.
Scholz, General, 176.
Schopenhauer, Dr. Arthur, 8, 15, 25, 39, 46, 78, 129, 281, 291, 331, 380, 406, 496, 525, 531.
Schopenhauer, Johanna, 46.
Schrader, Karl von, 211, etc., 229, 265, 267, 284.
Schreckenstein, Baron Max von, 20, 140, 141, 186, etc.
Schreckenstein, Baron von, 140.
Schubert, Franz, 408.
Schulenburg, Herr von der, 131, 132, 137.

Schulze-Delitzsch, Franz Hermann, 81, 293, 484, 505, 606.
Schuselka, Franz, 107.
Schwarzenberg, Prince Felix, 5, 169, 401.
Schweinitz, Lothar von, 97, 167, 169, 334, 371, 382, 554, 567, etc., 569, 570, 572, 578, 590, 593, 613, 615, etc., 619, 647.
Schweitzer, Baron Allesina von, 174, 353, etc.
Schweitzer, Jean Baptiste von, 378.
Schweninger, Professor Ernst, 307, 645.
Scott, Walter, 571.
Seckendorff, Baron Götz von, 349.
Seckendorff, Baron Rudolf von, 287, 290.
Seiler, Pastor, 83, 102.
Semper, Gottfried, 406, 656.
Senden, Otto von, 333.
Sepp, Johann Nepomuk, 165.
Sermoneta, Duke Onorato, 336, 337.
Shakespeare, William, 22, 42, 380, 535, 536.
Shuvalov, Count Paul, 613, 638.
Shuvalov, Count Peter, 386, 435, 445, etc., 448, 456, 457, etc.; Misfortune, 457, etc.; Aplomb, 568; For Bulgarians, 589.
Sierstorpff, Karl von, 40, 199, 227, 243.
Simon, Jules, 486.
Simrock, Karl Josef, 273.
Simson, Eduard von, 160.
Singer, Paul, 676.
Skobelev, Mikail Dmitrivitch, General, 567, 590.
Slavianski, 611.
Solms, Count Eberhard, 97, 371.
Solms-Laubach, Count Hermann, 429.
Soloviev, Vladimir Sergeievitch, 577.
Sombart, Werner, 413.
Sonnino, Sidney, 651, 655.
Sophia, Wife of Archduke Francis Charles of Austria, Mother of Emperor Francis Joseph, 13.
Sophia, Crown Princess, then Queen of Greece, 424.
Spee, Count Maximilian, Admiral, 176.
Spielhagen, Friedrich, 123.
Spitzemberg, Baron von, 326.
Spitzemberg, Hildegard von, 326; Princess Bismarck on, 555.
Spuller, Eugène, 519, 530.

Stablewski, Florian von, Archbishop, 677.
Staël, Madame de, 118.
Stahl, Friedrich Julius, 16.
Stahr, Adolf, 330.
Stambulov, Stefan, 601, 602, 603.
Stauffenberg, Imperial Baron von, 163, etc.
Stein, Baron von, 261, 384.
Stein, Charlotte von, 504.
Steinberg, Ernst von, 211, 215, 217, 225.
Steinmetz, Karl Friedrich von, 100.
Stendhal (Henry Beyle), 59, 123, 330.
Stiebel, Dr. 15, 78.
Stieber, Wilhelm, 137.
Stiehle, Gustav von, 151.
Stinnes, Hugo, 498.
Stirbey (Bibescu), M., 624.
Stock, Aulic Councillor, 356.
Stockhausen, Bodo von, 107, 140.
Stockhausen, Elisabeth von, 107, 108, 140.
Stolberg, Count Friedrich Leopold, 106, 395.
Stolberg, Count (then Prince) Otto, Goes to Vienna, 395; Reception, 396; Andrássy's visit, 404; Alliance with Austria-Hungary, 511, etc.; At Prince William's, 597.
Stolzenberg, Herr von, 187, 195.
Strossmayer, Josef Georg, Bishop, 667.
Strubberg, Major-General von, 189, 192, 225, 243, 257.
Stuart, Mr., 424, etc.
Studemund, Wilhelm, 277.
Stumm, Ferdinand von, 96.
Stumm, Baron Wilhelm von, 183.
Sturdza, Demeter, 621, 644.
Subov, Count, Murderer of Tsar Paul, 389.
Sybel, Heinrich von, 81, 160, 161, 274.
Szögyényi-Marich, Count, 639.

Taaffe, Count Edward, 400.
Taine, Hippolyte, 312, 330, 412, 465, 475.
Tallenay, "le Marquis de," 11, 13.
Talleyrand, Prince, 47, 65, 139, 178, 181, 303, 470, 471.
Talleyrand and Dino, Duchess Dorothea of, 65.

Talleyrand-Périgord, Count Archambault, 251, etc., 253, 256.
Tasso, Torquato, 538.
Tcherevin, Adjutant-General to Tsar Alexander III, 579, etc., 581.
Tchernaiev, General, 639, etc.
Thackeray, William Makepeace, 123.
Thielmann, Max von, 483, 489, etc., 492.
Thierry, Augustin, 412, 447.
Thiers, Adolphe, Speech against Napoleon III, 93; Debate on Roman question, 157; President of the Republic, 202; Suppression of the Commune, 254, 472, 653; Princess Arenberg, 293; Appoints diplomats of the old regime, 324; Speech at Bordeaux, 331; Richard Metternich and, 397; Saviour of France, 471; Weeps, 484; Specialists and, 490; Gortchakov to, 508.
Thile, Under-Secretary of State von, 131, 282, 283.
Thiron, M., 114.
Tholuck, Professor August, 80.
Thomas, Albert, 484.
Thomas Aquinas, 540.
Thornton, Sir Edward, 598.
Thorwaldsen, Bertel, 319.
Thun-Hohenstein, Count Friedrich, 20.
Thurn und Taxis, Hereditary Prince von, 546.
Tieck, Ludwig, 42.
Tirard, M., 519.
Tirpitz, Alfred, Grand Admiral, 684, etc.
Tissot, M., 426.
Tisza, Count Stefan, 95.
Tocqueville, Alexis de, 534.
Tolstoi, Count Alexei Konstantinovitch, 625.
Tolstoi, Count Dmitri Alexandrovitch, 575, etc., 581.
Tolstoi, Count Leo Nikholaievitch, 123, 379, 534.
Tosti, Luigi, 538.
Traube, Ludwig, Professor, 130, 136, 183.
Trauttmansdorff, Princess Anna, 407.
Treitschke, Heinrich von, 149, 465, 669.
Trikupis, Charilaos, 432.
Troeltsch, Ernst, 413.
Trompette, Gambetta's cook, 520.

Tsankov, Dragan, 601, 602.
Türckheim, Baron von, 327.
Turgeniev, Ivan Sergeievitch, 123, 379, 381, 535, etc., 585.
Twesten, Karl, 505.

Ubril, Ambassador, 325, 384, 445, etc., 456.
Uexküll, Baroness, 354.
Uhland, Ludwig, 9, 192, 289, 458.
Ungern, Sternberg, Baron, 457, etc.
Urusov, Princess Monia, 525, 534, etc.
Usedom, Count Guido, 158, 297.
Ushakov, General, 389.

Vacarescu, Helene, 647, etc.
Vaglia, Ponzio, 660.
Vaillant, Edouard, 477.
Valuiev, Count Peter Alexandrovitch, 578, etc.
Vanutelli, Vincenzo, Cardinal, 676.
Varnbüler, Axel von, 326.
Varnbüler, Karl von, 326.
Varnhagen von Ense, 567.
Vauvenargues, M., 413.
Vernescu, M., 622.
Vernon-Harcourt, Sir W., 553.
Veuillot, Louis, 156.
Viardot-Garcia, Pauline, 490, 536.
Victor, Prince Bonaparte, 523.
Victor Emmanuel II, King of Italy, 157, 174, 175, 335, 336, 340, 347, 348, 351, 463, 484, 654, 661.
Victor Emmanuel III, King of Italy, 652.
Victoria, Queen of England, 34, 159, 321, 453; Censures Prince of Wales, 463; For Disraeli, against Gladstone, 552; Chooses Heinrich Battenberg for son-in-law, 604; Jubilee, 605, etc.; At Charlottenburg, 618.
Victoria (Empress Frederick), 27, 223, 228, 230, 261; Against Bismarck, 308; Trip to Italy (1875), 348, etc.; Against the Bülow's, father and son, 349, etc.; Cannot forget England, 441, 463; Berlin Congress, 456; Herbert Bismarck complains about, 462; Bülow guest of, 596; Confidence in Morier, 599; Battenberg, 602, 605; Complains about Bismarck, 605; Scenes with her son William at San Remo, 615; At

Charlottenburg, 618; Behaviour of her son towards, 646, etc.; Bismarck visits, 657; On Krüger telegram, 665; Scientific education, 673.
Victoria, Princess of Prussia, The Battenberg affair, 602, 605.
Vienna (1876), 396, etc.; (1893), 648, etc.
Vilatte, César, 63.
Villaume Major von, 525, etc.
Villers, Herr von, 354, 407.
Vilmar, Herr, 15, 16.
Vincke, Ludwig Baron von, 73.
Virchow, Rudolf, 81, 279, 293, 308, 484.
Visconti-Venosta, Marchese Emilio, 157, 171, 174, 339, etc., 347.
Vitzthum von Eckstadt, Imperial Count Friedrich, 492, 493, etc., 549, 551, 593, 645.
Vitzthum, Count, 34.
Vitzthum, Count Karl, 155.
Viviani, René, 183, 484, 653.
Vladimir, Russian Grand Duke, 326, 385, 388, 568, 612, 617.
Vlangaly, M., 600, 605.
Vogel von Falckenstein, General, 98.
Voigt, Professor, 108.
Völderndorff, Baron von, 517, etc.
Völk, Deputy, 165.
Voltaire, 130, 138, 369, 379, 465, 472, 506, 520, 525.
Voss, Johann Heinrich, 51, 60.

Wach, Adolf, Professor, 107.
Waddington, William Henry, At Berlin Congress, 447, 454, 456.
Wagner, Adolf, 121, 362, 370.
Wagner, Cosima, 587.
Wagner, Richard, 163, 309, 318, 360, 402, 406, 531, 667.
Waldeck, Benedikt Franz Leo, 81, 293, 484, 606.
Waldeck-Rousseau, Premier, 473, 477, etc., 519.
Waldemar, Prince of Prussia, 223.
Waldersee, Count Alfred, 148, 498, 608, etc.; On Bismarck and Prince William, 610; King Carol on, 623; Monts for, 626; In close touch with Holstein, 637.
Wallwitz, Count Nikolaus, 494, etc.

Walter, Mr. 451.
Wartensleben, Count Bernhard, 371.
Weber, Max, 413.
Weber, Reinhold, 413.
Weddigen, Otto, 176.
Wedel, Count (Prince) Karl, 295.
Weiss, Herr, 165.
Werder, August von, 63, 293.
Werder, Bernhard von, General, 373, etc.
Werner, Anton von, 456, 585.
Werther, Baron Karl von, 95, etc., 297.
Werthern, Commandant von, 283.
Westermayer, Dr., 165.
Wied, Prince Hermann von, 647.
Wilamowitz-Möllendorf, Ulrich von, 63.
Wilbrandt, Adolf, 58, 60, 328, 406.
William I, Likes Pauline Scherff, 12; His
    sister Alexandrine, 65; At a military
    inspection, 77; Reply to address of City
    of Breslau (1866), 88; "Call to my
    people," 88; Countess Oriola and, 96;
    Victorious, 105; At Ems 1870, 133,
    148; After Mars-la-Tour, 148, 153;
    Meets Francis Joseph (1867), 155;
    Conversation with General Govone,
    158; Forced by Bismarck to desist from
    annexations (1866), 163; Toast after
    Sedan, 172, 173; Mossner, 241; Peace
    preliminaries, 247; Confidence in Loë,
    261; Loë's duel, 262; Princess Aren-
    berg on, 293; Bucher not received,
    303; Three Emperors meet (1872),
    308; Economy, 311; The old Kaiser,
    312, etc.; Dance, 314; For Schleinitz,
    316; At Bayreuth, 318; Reply to
    Countess Benkendorf, 318; At recep-
    tions of Kaiserin, 327; At Milan, 340;
    Werder, 375; Countess Hendrikov,
    386; Hödel and Nobiling, 438, etc.;
    Sends strawberries to Bülow, 444; At
    Ems, 503, etc.; At Alexandrovo, 508;
    Resistance against Alliance with Aus-
    tria-Hungary, 510; Gives in, 512;
    Receives Bernhard Bülow in saloon
    carriage, 516; At memorial service,
    516; Sedan anniversary, 518, etc.; At
    Skierniewice, 570, etc.; Writes to Bis-
    marck, 585; To Kaiserin, 596; Death,
    616; Bismarck on his traditions, 677;
    ill. 504.
William II, 7, 10, 18, 27, 35, 44, 61, 70;
    Bismarck on (1863), 82; Attitude to-
    wards Bismarck, 105; His chancellors
    during World War, 154; On Bülow,
    192; Kotze, 213; Loë, 261; Against
    Arenberg, 275; Rome trip (1888),
    347, etc.; Against pessimists, 403; At
    Corfu, 415; King George of Greece,
    438; Russian Treaty, 484; Adolf von
    Bülow his personal adjutant, 517;
    Wrong view on French North Africa,
    545; At Bismarcks, 570; Receives
    Bülow, 597; Hinzpeter, 599; Offends
    Lambsdorff, 600; Loë on, 608, etc.;
    Waldersee on, 610; Re-Insurance
    Treaty with Russia, 614; Scenes at San
    Remo, 615; King Carol on, 623;
    Admiral of the Fleet, 638; Exaggerates,
    639; Alexander III dislikes, 640; Be-
    haviour at Bismarck's resignation, 641,
    etc.; Bismarck on, 642; Behaviour
    towards his parents, 646, etc.; Receives
    Bismarck, 657; Goes to Venice, 658;
    Conversation with Bülow, 658, etc.;
    Does not wish to be reminded of Bis-
    marck, 659; Krüger telegram, 664,
    etc.; Laura Minghetti and, 667;
    Visits Naples, 673, etc.; Telegram to
    Bismarck, 677; Threatens Bismarck,
    678; Betrayed by Marschall, 679;
    Bismarck the "wicked old man," 680;
    Philip Eulenburg on, 683.
William, Crown Prince, 176, 375.
William, Landgrave of Hesse, 17.
Willich, Captain von, 132.
Wilms, Professor, 507.
Wilson, Daniel, 486, etc.
Wimpffen, Count Felix, 324.
Winckelmann, Johann, 648.
Wind, Secretary von, 14, 376.
Windischgraetz, Prince Alfred, 546.
Windthorst, Ludwig, 308, 361, 505, 583,
    601.
Wirth, Josef, 315.
Wittgenstein, Prince Fritz, 253.
Wittgenstein, Princess Léonille, 517.
Witzendorf, Colonel von, 257.
Wohlfahrt, Burgomaster, 68.
Wolff-Metternich, Count Dietrich von,
    229, 231.
Wolzogen, Ernst von, 13.
Woyrsch, General von, 176.

710

Wrangel, Count Friedrich Heinrich Ernst, 222, etc.

Wrangel, Gustav von, 222, etc.

Wunderlich, Sergeant-major of the King's Hussars at Bonn, 141, 143, 185, 374.

Wyndham, Mr., 424, 427, etc., 598.

Yorck, Count Maximilian, 615, 616.

Ysenburg, Prince, 99.

Zanardelli, Giuseppe, 651, 652, 661.

Zelter, Karl Friedrich, 43.

Zerbi, Signor, 651.

Zglinicki, Colonel von, 225.

Zinoviev, 600, 605.

Zinzendorf, Count Nikolaus Ludwig, 41, 42, 73.

Zola, Emile, 451.

Zschokke, Heinrich, 577.

Zuylen, Baron, 529.

LONDON: CHARLES WHITTINGHAM AND GRIGGS (PRINTERS), LTD.
CHISWICK PRESS, BRUNSWICK PARK ROAD, N.11.